The Legal Environment of Business

The Legal Environment of Business

ROBERT N. CORLEY

*Professor of Business Law
and Business Administration
University of Illinois*

ROBERT L. BLACK

*Associate Professor of Business Law
and Business Administration
University of Illinois*

Third Edition

McGRAW-HILL BOOK COMPANY

*New York   St. Louis   San Francisco   Düsseldorf   Johannesburg
Kuala Lumpur   London   Mexico   Montreal   New Delhi
Panama   Rio de Janeiro   Singapore   Sydney   Toronto*

Library of Congress Cataloging in Publication Data

Corley, Robert Neil.
    The legal environment of business.

        1. Trade regulation—United States.   I. Black,
Robert L., joint author.   II. Title.
KF1600.C6   1973   346'.73'07   72-5523
ISBN 0-07-013180-5

The Legal Environment of Business

        67890   DODO   798765

*This book was set in Vega by Rocappi, Inc. The editors were
Richard F. Dojny and Joseph F. Murphy; the designer was Judith
Michael; and the production supervisor was Thomas J. Lo Pinto.
The printer and binder was R. R. Donnelley & Sons Company.*

Contents

CHAPTER NINE   Taxation of Business

CHAPTER TEN   Introduction to Antitrust Law—The Sherman Act

CONTEMPORARY PROBLEMS

CHAPTER ELEVEN   The Clayton Act and Its Amendments

CHAPTER TWELVE   Legal Aspects of Mergers, Consolidations, and Acquisitions

CHAPTER SEVENTEEN   Property

CHAPTER EIGHTEEN   The Law of Torts

CHAPTER NINETEEN   Protection of Consumers and Debtors

List of Cases

Preface

This third edition of *The Legal Environment of Business* extends the basic philosophy and approach of the former editions, refined by a decade of experience. During the sixties the merits of a "traditional" course in business law versus an "environmental" one were widely discussed and debated. There was much disagreement even about how these courses basically differ, and, indeed, no unanimity of viewpoint on that issue exists today. Our previous editions have reflected our position on the matter: that essentially a traditional course emphasizes private law, an environmental course public law and the regulation of business. In addition, we feel that macro law (the nature, formation, and application of law in general) should be stressed in the environmental approach, as contrasted with the traditional preoccupation with micro law (the detailed substantive rules in areas such as contracts, agency, and business organizations). At the same time, we believe that private law should not be ignored and that students should be given at least an overview of its major areas. This edition continues to reflect these views.

As we prepared these materials for an environmental course in law, several basic thoughts, in addition to those just noted, guided our approach. Among them was the conviction that we should seek to design a course in law for businessmen rather than a compact version of law courses related to business as they are taught in law schools. In our view, such a course would not only contribute to the general education of students in the social sciences but also play a vital role in the training of managers for the decision-making process, since the law is, in fact, a tool for generating policy. Believing law to be the most important of the social sciences, we concluded that our purpose should be not to educate lawyers or even clients but to familiarize citizens with the predominant system of our society—the legal system. We were influenced by the fact that law is a cultural subject and as such plays a significant role in education at all levels.

Among other ideas which materially influenced the preparation of this text was the belief that the law must be understood by all Americans as a means to social, political and economic change. We felt a deep obligation to make students aware of the importance of the "rule of law" in our society. We were concerned not with the legal equivalent of a first-aid course in medicine but with a course which emphasized jurisprudence and espoused justice as the ultimate goal of civilized society.

In short, rather than merely mimicking law school courses, we attempted to stress the legal system and to approach law from the standpoint of its sources and its philosophy, with special emphasis on business relations and the role of government in affecting them.

Besides having the usual aims in revising a text—to polish, reorganize, expand coverage, and generally update—we undertook the third edition because of the many major changes which have recently taken place in our legal system. Among these are the several new appointments to the Supreme Court, which have altered its complexion substantially from the activist Warren Court in office when the second edition was published. Also significant are the changed postures of the Federal Trade Commission and the National Labor Relations Board, and new legislation such as the trend toward no-fault statutes in the law of torts.

The more significant aspects of the third edition include (1) a separate chapter on constitutional law, (2) a separate chapter on the Federal Trade Commission, (3) a complete reorganization of the antitrust materials, (4) greatly expanded coverage of labor law, (5) a separate chapter on the law as it relates to consumers, and (6) review questions at the end of each chapter.

We feel that the third edition is suitable as the text for a complete course at either the graduate or undergraduate level. While our prime objective has been to provide a book for use in the business curriculum, we believe that this one is also geared to general education courses for liberal arts, engineering, or agriculture students. Some may want to build their law program by starting with an introductory course using this text, followed by one or more separate courses concentrating on the technical aspects of private law such as contracts or negotiable instruments. Those teachers of business law who still wish to place primary emphasis on the traditional private law approach may use this book as an introduction to law and business that will enrich and supplement the subject matter of their present courses.

The materials in this book include text discussions, summaries of important legislation, articles, speeches, and decided cases—both landmark decisions and very recent ones. The student will be exposed to the philosophies and works of many of the great legal scholars, such as Cardozo, Hughes, Brandeis, Pound, Stone, Corbin, Douglas, and Marshall. Many of the judicial decisions which have led to a regulated economy with government policy and control as a primary limitation on business activity are presented so that the student will know something of the boundary lines of legal forces in the environment of business. To conserve space, portions of the articles and cases presented have been omitted, along with most of their footnotes and citations of authority.

The authors are grateful for the fine work of Betty Hampel, who assisted in the final preparation of the manuscript.

The authors also express their gratitude to Professor Arthur L. Corbin and the *Yale Law Journal* for permission to reprint excerpts from Corbin, *Legal Analysis and Terminology;* the Yale University Press for permission to reprint excerpts from Cardozo, *The Nature of the Judicial Process;* Professor H. E. Willis for permission to reprint excerpts from Willis, *Introduction to Anglo-American Law;* Associate

Justice William O. Douglas for permission to reprint excerpts from Douglas, *Stare Decisis;* The University of Chicago Press for permission to reprint excerpts from Levi, *An Introduction to Legal Reasoning;* the New York County Lawyers' Association for permission to reprint excerpts from an address given by Associate Justice Benjamin N. Cardozo; Professor Philip B. Kurland for permission to reprint excerpts from Kurland, *Recent Trends in United States Supreme Court Decisions;* the Yale University Press for permission to reprint excerpts from Pound, *An Introduction to the Philosophy of Law;* the Marshall Jones Company for permission to reprint excerpts from Pound, *The Spirit of the Common Law;* the *Illinois Bar Journal* and Mr. Anthony Lewis for permission to reprint excerpts from Lewis, *The Changing Role of the Supreme Court of the U.S.A.;* and the American Bar Association and the *American Bar Association Journal* for permission to reprint excerpts from the following articles: Harlan, *The Bill of Rights and the Constitution;* Murphy, *The Constitution: Interpretation and Intent;* Cole, *Administrative Agencies and Judicial Powers;* Cooper, *Turning the Spotlight on State Administrative Procedure;* Bergan, *The Role of Law in Labor Relations;* and Marshall, *The Unreality of Accident Litigation: A Plea for a New Approach.*

Robert N. Corley
Robert L. Black

Chapter One

Law

1   INTRODUCTION

Perhaps no word of such common usage is so incapable of exact definition or expresses a variety of concepts so well as does the word "law." For example, "law" is used to describe specific statutory enactments and also to denote a general system of rules for governing conduct. Popular uses of the terms "law," "legal," and "illegal" are illimitable. The meaning of these words in any particular situation must be determined from the context in which they are used. This chapter is devoted to a discussion of some of the various definitions of law, as well as legal terminology and classifications of law.

In his commentaries on the law, Blackstone defined law generally as "that rule of action which is prescribed by some superior and which the inferior is bound to obey."[1] He defined civil law as a "rule of civil conduct prescribed by the supreme power in a state, commanding what is right and prohibiting what is wrong."[2] It can be seen that Blackstone viewed law as flowing from a superior to an inferior person by a command. These definitions and concepts have been generally rejected in the United States, where the constitutional system has established that law stems from the people and flows to the government and that there is no power superior to the people.

Blackstone's definition also fails to describe many areas of our law because such laws as those pertaining to contracts and torts do not "command compliance" in the technical sense but are so constructed that an aggrieved party is given a remedy against one who violates accepted legal principles in these areas. Civil courts, except in unusual situations, do not require compliance but instead impose liability for noncompliance.

However, Blackstone's theory was followed by Justice Stone when he said:

Law emanates from the sovereign not from its creatures. The sum total of all those rules of human conduct for which there is a state sanction . . . [is law]. Law in its essence is made up of those rules of human conduct which are made mandatory by the state upon all its citizens and without which social order and well-being could not exist.

The American Law Institute has defined law as "the body of principles, standards, and rules which the courts . . . apply in the decision of controversies

---

[1] Blackstone, *Commentaries* 38.
[2] Blackstone *Commentaries* 44.

brought before them."[3] It further pointed out that law is made up of three elements: (1) formulated legislation including constitutions, statutes, treaties, local ordinances, and bylaws, (2) rules of law adopted by the courts, and (3) "the system of legal concepts and the traditional legal technique which forms the basis of its judicial action."[4] Subsequent chapters will discuss laws created by legislation and judicial decision, and the court procedures and techniques established to enforce these laws. The Institute's analysis of the elements composing law actually designates those sources to which courts turn in search of the law.

Justice Oliver Wendell Holmes, in what is perhaps the most succinct definition of law, said "Law is a statement of the circumstances in which the public force will be brought to bear through courts."[5]

Other judges have stated that law is "a rule of reason applied to existing conditions,"[6] that "it is an expression of the public will,"[7] and that it is "that which must be obeyed and followed by citizens subject to sanctions or legal consequences."[8]

Professor H. E. Willis, in his *Introduction to Anglo-American Law,*[9] stated that law was "a scheme for controlling the conduct of people." He emphasized that law was concerned with social interests and that where social interests recognized a right in one person, courts would create machinery to assist the person with this right in obtaining redress against the person with the duty or obligation, in the event the duty were not performed or the obligation were not fulfilled. By his concept, the law has four characteristics:

1. It is a scheme of social control.
2. It is for the protection of social interests.
3. It accomplishes its purpose by the recognition of a capacity in persons to influence the conduct of others.
4. It affords the machinery of the courts and legal procedures to help the person with the capacity.

In rejecting Blackstone's definition, Willis concluded: "Order through generality, equality, and certainty, and not compulsion, is the fundamental characteristic of the law. . . . Law is a scheme of social control, for the protection of social interests, by means of capacities of influence, backed and sanctioned by the power of the state."[10]

In addition to many definitions of law, there are various schools of legal thought which provide insight into the meaning and development of the law.

---

[3] *Restatement, Conflict of Laws,* §3 (1934).
[4] *Ibid.*
[5] *American Banana Co. v. United Fruit Co.,* 213 U.S. 347, 356 (1909).
[6] *City of Milwaukee v. Milwaukee Ry. & Light Co.,* 173 Wis. 400, 180 N.W. 339 (1920).
[7] *Ware v. Hylton,* 3 U.S. (3 Dall.) 199, 212 (1796).
[8] *Koenig v. Flynn,* 258 N.Y. 292, 179 N.E. 705 (1932).
[9] By permission from Willis, *Introduction to Anglo-American Law* 10–11 (Indiana University Studies, Vol. XIII, No. 69, 1926).
[10] *Id.* at 11.

Among the more generally recognized schools of legal thought are the historical, the analytical, the natural, the sociological, and the realist.

The historical school gives great weight to custom and history as a source of law. Law comes from the habits and traditions of people. For example, conduct such as taking the life of another has traditionally been considered wrongful by all civilized peoples, and therefore we have laws relating to homicide. Similarly, the laws relating to business transactions developed out of the manner of doing business and customary business practices. By this school of legal thought, people's actions and beliefs formed the law and not vice versa.

The analytical school of legal thought is predicated upon a belief and reliance on logic as the basis of law. Under this philosophy, law is conceived as a "brooding omnipresence" of Reason, of which decisions are merely evidence and not themselves the controlling formulations. Law comes from the sovereign or government because of the need for order and a system of known rules which are to be followed. Social order logically requires definite rules for governing human conduct.

The natural school of legal thought gives great weight to the influence of religion and divine principles in developing the law. Law is based on right, reason, and the intelligence of man as derived from his Creator. Law distinguishes right from wrong. The natural law theorist uses justice as the applicable standard to govern conduct. The natural law philosophy gave us courts of equity and, indeed, much of our constitutional theory. Such concepts as due process of law and equal protection of the laws came from the natural law philosophy.

The sociological school of legal thought gives recognition to the law as a scheme of social control. It is consistent with the definition of law given by Professor Willis on page 2. This legal philosophy considers the law to be the result of competing social forces and values. Law emanates from its purposes and by what may be accomplished. The sociologist uses facts, economic and social theory in developing the law and views the law as the means of resolving disputes and conflicts between different groups and interests in society.

The realist school of legal thought is a development of this century. The realist takes a very pragmatic approach to law. Law comes from experience. Holmes's definition of law on page 2 is an example of the realist reasoning. Realists are impressed with the role of facts and are willing to recognize exceptions to almost every general rule of law. Realists recognize that law is constantly changing.

These schools of legal thought further demonstrate the difficulty of defining "law" and of understanding its sources, uses, and development. It will be helpful to keep the various philosophies in mind as the subject matter of this text is studied.

2 THE RULE OF LAW

Justice Frankfurter in his concurring opinion in *United States v. Mine Workers*, 330 U.S. 258 (1947), began with these words: "The historic phrase 'a government of laws and not of men' epitomizes the distinguishing character of our political society. When John Adams put that phrase into the Massachusetts Declaration of Rights he was not indulging a rhetorical flourish. He was expressing the aim of those who, with him, framed the Declaration of Independence and founded the Republic." Adams's statement, which recognizes the role of the rule of law in our society, had its origin in England prior to the Magna Charta. The Magna Charta used the term "per legem terrae"—the law of the land. English history is filled with numerous instances in which it has been proclaimed that even the royal power must be exercised subject to the law.

The concept of the rule of law has been the cornerstone of our society and government from the beginning, and it is simply accepted as part of our heritage. As Lincoln said, it is the political religion of the country.

In our society, it is the law which is used to decide disputes, not the wishes or ideas of any mere mortal, irrespective of his position. Moreover, the parties for the most part accept the fact that the dispute will be decided by a rule of law and that the winner and the loser alike accept the determination without resort to some other method of dispute resolution such as force.

The role of the rule of law as the basic ingredient in ordered liberty is obvious from even a cursory examination of the matters before the Supreme Court in any term. The issues presented involve due process of law, equal protection of the laws, and the power of the governors over the governed. To a substantial extent, the failures of our society can be directly attributed to the failure of people to accept and abide by application of rules of law. In a real sense, the subject matter of this text is the rule of law as it is applied to business.

President Nixon in his 1971 Law Day proclamation noted that the rule of law has the inherent capacity for change. He said in part:

Change is the immutable first law of nature, and governments reveal themselves most in the manner by which they provide for change. History is littered with the remains of governments that failed to meet this challenge: of those that gave too great a scope to unbridled impulse, and of those that gave too little scope to the human spirit.

Between these two extremes—between the tyranny of anarchy and the tyranny of totalitarianism—the law has its dominion. Our forefathers established government and founded a free nation on that high plane. They gave us laws that could be changed by orderly process so that the nation and its people might remain free.

This ability to change by orderly process is essential to democratic government, for the success of such a form of government depends upon a capacity constantly to resolve the basic paradox of a system of liberty under law; that the supremacy of the law rests on its recognition of the supremacy of the people.

The continuing success of America testifies to the wisdom with which the founders of this nation addressed this paradox, and to the legal skill with which they resolved it.

It is fitting that we honor not merely the law, but the law giver, and that ve honor above all those citizens who keep the law.

Perhaps the best argument for and illustration of the role of the rule of law lies in the observation that if we could apply the concept to nations, there would be no wars. The settlement of international disputes by the rule of law is the goal of the World Peace Through Law organizations.

3   LAW AND JUSTICE

"Law" and "justice" are not synonymous, just as legal justice and social justice are not synonymous. Justice has been defined as "that which is founded in equity, honesty, and right." [11] It is the attempt of honorable men to do that which is fair. Justice is the purpose and end of government and civil society. It is apparent that the achievement of justice is dependent upon the concept of right and wrong in the society involved. The purpose of justice in our society, as stated in the Declaration of Independence, is to secure for all men "life, liberty, and the pursuit of happiness."

Social justice recognizes more rights and duties than does legal justice, although the trend of the law is toward equating these concepts. Perfect justice would require that all persons discharge all their obligations and duties so that all other persons might enjoy all their rights and privileges. Our society through law determines which rights and duties will be protected and strives through its judicial system for perfect justice. Of course, the law is incapable of perfect justice because it is in the hands of imperfect men and operates with imperfect procedures. As law tends to achieve perfect justice, legal justice and social justice tend to merge.

Pound attempted to define law in terms of justice when he said that the science of law is "that organized body of knowledge that has to do with the administration of justice by public or regular tribunals in accordance with principles or rules of general character and more or less uniform application." [12]

As the judicial process and those forces which affect it are discussed in subsequent chapters, the student is exhorted to develop his own concept of law and justice and to test critically the judicial decisions studied to determine whether they meet his standard.

4   CLASSIFICATION OF SUBJECT MATTER

It is not possible to classify the many subject matters of the law into categories that will be completely acceptable. There have been numerous attempts at such a classification, but each has been vulnerable to the criticism of being either "too inclusive" or "too exclusive." The law has often been described as "a seamless web" in which principles of law are hopelessly and endlessly intertwined with each other. For this reason, any attempted classification or description of the many and

---

[11] *Spencer v. Terry's Estate*, 133 Mich. 39, 94 N.W. 372 (1903).
[12] 1 Pound, *Library American Law and Practice* 1.

varied legal subjects is necessarily inaccurate. The following classifications are, however, generally accepted by most legal scholars.

Law may be generally divided into matters of public law and matters of private law. Public law includes such subject areas as constitutional law, administrative law, and criminal law. In each of these areas, society or "the people" are directly involved and their interests are represented by some governmental agency, officer, or official whose obligation it is to see that justice is accomplished and the ends of society are fulfilled. The public law provides a major portion of the legal environment of business, and for this reason, much of the material in subsequent chapters is concerned with the constitutional and administrative areas of the public law and their application to business.

The criminal law is generally subdivided into felonies, misdemeanors, and treason. This classification is based on the punishment which may be imposed in the event of a conviction. Felonies are punishable by fine or imprisonment in a penitentiary for a period of one year or more, while misdemeanors are punishable by a fine or a jail sentence of less than one year. Treason fits neither definition since it is usually punishable by a mandatory death penalty. The criminal law includes many crimes which may be committed by a corporate enterprise as well as those which may be committed by individuals. Some of these, such as violating the antitrust laws, will be discussed later in this book.

Private law encompasses those legal problems and relationships which exist between individuals, as contrasted with those in which society is involved. Private law is traditionally separated into the law of contracts, the law of torts, and the law of property. The body of law known as contracts is concerned with the legal relationships created between individuals by their own agreement and contains several subbodies of law which are frequently treated as separate classifications. For example, the law of sales, the law of commercial paper, and the law of secured transactions are subjects concerned with special contractual situations. Each has its own body of legal principles and many of these principles conflict with traditional general contract law.

The law of torts is concerned with wrongs committed by one person against another or his property. It is predicated upon the fundamental concept that a member of a civilized society will not injure another member or his property either intentionally or by the lack of exercise of due care and caution in the conduct of his affairs. This body of law, which is designed to give damages to the victim of the tort, is the major source of litigation in this country since it includes suits for personal injuries based on a theory of negligence. Tens of thousands of tort cases are filed each year as a result of automobile accidents, and more tens of thousands of cases are settled without suit being filed. Many torts are labeled intentional as contrasted with negligent. An example of such a tort action is a suit for defamation of character, which is known as libel if the defamation is written and slander if it is oral. Trespass actions comprise still another area of intentional tort litigation. There are three types of trespass: trespass to the person, usually referred to as assault and battery; trespass to goods, frequently called conversion of goods; and trespass to land. It should be noted that frequently conduct which is tortious is also criminal—for example, assault and battery. In such cases, society brings suit for the wrong to society, but the victim must bring his own civil suit if he wishes to be compensated for the wrong done to him. Some activities are actually a hybrid between a tort and a crime. These are sometimes referred to as public torts and include such misconduct as violation of traffic laws. A criminal-type punishment is often imposed.

There is a growing body of tort law that is concerned with business torts. These include suits for damages because an individual or a corporate business has interfered with the employer-employee relationship or with some other contract of someone else. For instance, if A employs B, and C encourages A to discharge B, B may have a tort action against C for the damage caused by his discharge. Business may also have tort liability for violating statutes such as the antitrust laws.

Another growing area of litigation is difficult to classify as either *ex contractu* (arising from a contract) or *ex delicto* (arising from a tort). This area is concerned with the liability of manufacturers and sellers for injuries caused by their products. The theory of such a suit may be negligence, for example, a suit against a soft drink bottler by a person who swallowed a dead mouse with the contents. It also may be on a theory of breach of warranty (contract), as in a case where a purchaser of canned goods which contain ground glass sues the retailer who sold him the goods. In the latter case, there would be no negligence but liability for another reason. In many instances, the actual theory has become obscured and liability is imposed according to a theory known as "strict liability." Under the latter, liability is imposed if an injury occurs, regardless of fault. It is also commonly invoked against public carriers for injury to property being shipped.

The law of property is concerned with the rights and duties arising out of the ownership and possession of real estate and personal property. Property is considered to be a "bundle of rights." These rights are frequently created by contract and protected by the law of torts. Thus, some legal scholars do not consider property to be a separate classification. The concept of private property is of great importance and is dealt with in detail in Chapter 17.

Another important classification or distinction in the law is the one between substance and procedure. This is discussed in the next section.

5 DISTINCTION BETWEEN PROCEDURE AND SUBSTANCE

Substantive law defines the legal relationships of people with other people or as between them and the state. Thus, the rules of contract law are substantive in nature. Procedural law is concerned with the method and means by which substantive law is made and administered. In other words, substantive rules of law define rights and duties, while procedural rules of law provide the machinery for the enforcement of those rights and duties. Every organ of society has rules by which it conducts its affairs or "proceeds." There are rules of law relating to legislative procedure which govern the steps that must be taken for a statute to be valid. A typical rule of legislative procedure might require that all bills be read to the assembly twice before adoption. Failure to follow this rule of procedure might void the legislature's attempt to create rights or duties in the statute.

Administrative agencies also have rules of procedure which vary from agency to agency. For example, the National Labor Relations Board and the Internal Revenue Service each have procedures which must be followed in matters before these agencies.

Judicial procedures involve the method of conducting law suits, appeals, and the enforcement of judgments. The rules for conducting civil trials are different from those for criminal trials. For example, each party may call the other party to the witness stand for the purpose of cross-examination in a civil trial, but the defendant may not be required to testify in a criminal case. Procedural problems also arise concerning the papers which are filed in the lawsuit, the admission of evidence, and the various other techniques involved in trying the case. They are the rules of the game. It would appear that many rules which are classified as procedural in character might be just as easily classified as substantive because they actually affect rights and duties. Chapter 2 deals with the procedural aspects of law in greater depth.

6   LEGAL TERMINOLOGY

Prior to undertaking a study of law, it would be helpful to understand certain basic terminology. The study of law is essentially concerned with "rules of law." A rule of law, using Holmes's definition, is a statement that if certain facts exist, then the judicial branch of government will take certain action or refuse to take certain action at the request of someone involved. In other words, a rule of law is a prediction as to what a court will or will not do in a given factual situation. It is then obvious that facts create legal issues which are resolved by using rules of law. The student should therefore be aware of the tremendous importance of facts to the law. A majority of our legal procedures are designed to ascertain the facts.

Legal relations exist between two persons and usually are complex in that there may be a variety of rights and duties in each party with regard to the specific subject matter in question. For purposes of analyzing basic legal relationships, Professor Arthur L. Corbin, formerly professor of law at Yale University, suggests the following definitions:

From **Legal Analysis and Terminology** [13]
Arthur L. Corbin, Professor of Law, Yale University

Assuming that we wish to determine the legal relations of A and B, we may ask ourselves the following questions:

1   What may A (or B) do, without societal penalty assessed for the benefit of the other?

[13] By permission from Corbin, Legal Analysis and Terminology, *29 Yale L.J.* 163 (Dec. 1919).

2 What must A (or B) do, under threat of societal penalty assessed for the benefit of the other?
3 What can A (or B) do, so as to change the existing legal relations of the other? (This has no reference to mere physical power.)

If we determine that A may conduct himself in a certain way, he has a privilege with respect to B, and B has no-right that A shall not so conduct himself.

If we determine that A must conduct himself in a certain manner, he has a duty to B, and B has a right against A.

If we determine that by his own voluntary act A *can* change B's legal relations with A (or with X), A has a legal *power* and B has a *liability.*

If we determine that A *cannot* by his own voluntary act change the legal relations of B, then A has a *disability* and B has an *immunity.*

Having isolated these definite concepts and chosen these specific terms with which to express them—all being found in the actual decisions and usage of the courts—Professor Wesley N. Hohfeld then arranged them in the following pairs of *opposites* and *correlatives:*

Opposites {	right	privilege	power	immunity
	no-right	duty	disability	liability
Correlatives {	right	privilege	power	immunity
	duty	no-right	liability	disability

Each pair of correlatives must always exist together; when some person (A) has one of the pair, another person (B) necessarily has the other. One of the terms expresses the relation of A to B; the other term expresses the relation of B to A.

No pair of opposites can exist together. That is, when a person has a right, he cannot have a no-right with respect to the same subject matter and the same person. When he has a privilege, he cannot have a duty.

The following grouping of terms may be useful:

May	permission	privilege—no-right
Must (may not)	compulsion	right—duty
Can	danger or possibility	power—liability
	(of new relations)	
Cannot	safety (from new relations)	immunity—disability

Observe that when we assert that some fact or group of facts will operate to create a particular legal relation we are stating a *rule of law.* The mere statement that a certain legal relation exists is a statement of *fact.* Thus: (a) A owes B $100—statement of fact. (b) C owns Blackacre—statement of fact. (c) An offer creates a power in the offeree—rule of law. (d) The delivery of a deed conveys title to land—rule of law. (e) The delivery of a release under seal discharges a debtor (creates privilege in place of duty)—rule of law.

We may now proceed to the more formal definition of the eight named legal relations. . . .

1 Right: A legal relation between two persons. . . . It is the legal relation of A to B when society commands action or forbearance by B and will at the instance of A in some manner penalize disobedience.

A, knowing that he has a particular right, can answer the question, "What *must another do* for me?" (The court will aid me by using compulsion if he does not do it.) . . .

2 Duty: . . . It is the legal relation of a person, B, who is commanded by society to act or to forbear for the benefit of another person, A, either immediately or in the future, and who will be penalized by society for disobedience.

B, knowing that he has a particular duty, can answer this question, "What must I do for another?" (A court will use compulsion against me if I do not do it.)

3 Privilege: . . . The legal relation of A to B when A (with respect to B) is *free* or *at liberty* to conduct himself in a certain matter as he pleases; when his conduct is not regulated for the benefit of B by the command of society; and when he is not threatened with any penalty for disobedience, for the reason that society has made no command.

A, knowing that he has a particular privilege, can answer this question, "What *may* I do?" (A court will not prevent me or penalize me.)

Observe carefully that the concept *privilege* does not itself include a *right* to noninterference by another person, although such a privilege and such a right very commonly are found together. Being the opposite of duty, it is another name for *no duty*. If I am under no duty to A, I am with respect to A privileged. . . .

4 No-Right: . . . The legal relation of a person (A) in whose behalf society commands nothing of another (B). A has no control over B. A, knowing that he has no-right against B, can answer this question, "What *may* another person (B) do?" (A court will not prevent him or penalize him.)

5 Power: . . . The legal relation of A to B when A's own voluntary act will cause new legal relations either between B and A or between B and a third person.

A, knowing that he has a particular power, can answer this question, "What new legal relations can I create between B and myself or others?"

A sharp distinction must be drawn between *legal* power and *physical* power. Thus a person may have a legal power to make a will even though he is too weak physically to sign his name; i.e., he has the legal power but is physically unable to do the volitional act by which it is to be exercised.

6 Liability: . . . The relation of A to B when A may be brought into new legal relations by the voluntary act of B. A is *liable* to have new legal relations created for himself through the exercise by B of B's power. The new relations

may be with third persons, or with B, or with both; but the liability-power relation is between A and B only.

A, knowing that he has a certain liability, can answer this question, "What new legal relations can B create between me and himself or others?"

7 Immunity: .. The relation of A to B when B has no legal power (has disability) to affect some one or more of the existing legal relations of A. As to that particular existing relation A has an immunity with respect to B.

A, knowing that he has a certain immunity, can answer this question, "Which one of my existing relations is safe from alteration by B?"

8 Disability: . . . The relation of A to B when by no voluntary act of his own can A extinguish one (or more) of the existing legal relations of B.

A, knowing that he has a particular disability, can answer this question, "What existing legal relation of another person (B) is it impossible for me to extinguish?" . . .

7 RES JUDICATA AND STARE DECISIS

"Res judicata" and "stare decisis" are two additional terms which must be distinguished and understood. Res judicata comes from Latin and literally means that the thing has been decided. As a legal principle it means that a final decision in a lawsuit by a competent court is conclusive and final of the rights and duties of the parties on all points and matters decided. This prevents successive suits involving the same question between the same parties and brings disputes to a final conclusion. A matter once litigated and legally determined is conclusive between the parties in all subsequent proceedings. The case which follows illustrates this concept.

Cummings v. Dresher
218 N.E.2d 688 (N.Y. 1966)

DESMOND, CHIEF JUDGE: There was a collision between an automobile owned by Martin Cummings and driven by Mary Cummings and an automobile driven by Bernard Dresher. The car driven by Bernard Dresher was owned by Standard Electric Co., Inc., and in it Henry Dresher was a passenger. Driver Bernard Dresher and passenger Henry Dresher as coplaintiffs sued driver Mary Cummings and owner Martin Cummings in the Federal District Court for damages for personal injuries sustained by the two Dresher brothers. The issues up for determination in that *Dresher v. Cummings* suit included, therefore, questions as to the negligence of either or both the Dreshers and either or both of the defendants Cummings. Returning their verdict, the jury told the Federal Judge that it found in favor of the passenger Henry Dresher against defendants Cummings and found also that Mrs. Cummings was "guilty of negligence" and that "plaintiff" (apparently meaning driver Bernard Dresher) "was guilty" of contributory negligence to a very minor degree. The Judge, to "complete" the verdict, instructed the Clerk to ask the jury whether it intended a verdict of no cause of action in Bernard Dresher's suit. The jurors replied that such was their intention. Judgment was thereupon entered in favor of Mr. and Mrs. Cummings dismissing the complaint of Bernard Dresher and the judgment was affirmed by the Federal Court of Appeals 325 F.2d 156 (2d Cir.). At the close of these Federal court proceedings it was completely clear that the jury had found that driver Mary Cummings had been found guilty of negligence and that, therefore, she as driver and her husband as owner had to pay damages to passenger Henry Dresher. Equally clear was the Federal court jury's finding that driver Bernard Dresher had been guilty of contributory negligence and so, notwithstanding the found negligence of driver Mary Cummings, Bernard Dresher could not recover against the defendants Cummings.

Despite this definite and unmistakable Federal court jury finding as to both drivers being at fault, driver Mary Cummings and her husband brought the present suit against driver Dresher and the corporate owner of the Dresher car. The courts below, for inscrutable reasons, held that the Federal court judgment was not determinative here. We do not understand why in a reasonable, prompt and nonrepetitious judicial system the negligence or no of these two drivers must be decided all over again, after having once been settled after a jury trial in which all these same people were parties and all the same issues tried and decided. "One who has had his day in court should not be permitted to litigate the question anew. . . ." Under such circumstances the judgment is held to be conclusive upon those who were parties to the action in which the judgment was rendered. Where a full opportunity has been afforded to a party to the prior action and he has failed to prove his freedom from liability or to establish liability or culpability on the part of another, there is no reason for retrying these issues. . . . [REVERSED]

Stare decisis is the concept by which courts adhere to decided cases as precedent. When a court once determines that a certain rule of law is applicable to a certain set of facts, then it will follow that rule in all future cases involving essentially the same facts and thus the same issue. Under stare decisis the same rules of law are applicable between different sets of parties. This doctrine, which is the basis of our common law, is the subject matter of the major portion of Chapter 5.

In subsequent chapters, additional terms peculiar to the legal system will be discussed. Caution should be exercised to make sure that the meaning of each term is understood in the context in which it is used.

8   THE JUDICIAL PROCESS—IN GENERAL

The American Law Institute's definition of law, set forth on page 1, indicates that law comes from constitutions, treaties, statutes, ordinances, and decided cases. In the event of litigation, a determination of the law applicable to the facts involved is necessary to a final disposition of the case. In addition, law plays a major role in the determination of the facts by supplying the fact-finding procedures. How do courts or judges make the determination or find the law of the case? Is there a hierarchy or priority as between the many sources? What factors enter into the decision? How do courts resolve or reconcile conflicting laws? When may courts refuse to follow a law or precedent? What formulas do courts use in reaching their decisions? What processes are followed that enable a court to reach one result rather than another? The purpose of the chapters which follow is to attempt an answer to these questions in detail. However, it is noted at this point that the judicial system has established a general priority among the various sources of law. Constitutions prevail over statutes, and statutes prevail over common-law principles established in court decisions. Courts will not turn to case decisions for law if a statute is directly in point, but it should be remembered that statutes usually deal in generalities and require interpretation. Since cases deal with specific problems, interpretation is necessary to fill in the gaps of the legislation and to eliminate the ambiguities caused by the general language of statutes.

Decisions which provide precedent for future cases are those which are appealed to reviewing courts. These courts are generally concerned only with questions of law, and their decisions are printed so that judges and lawyers may study them and use them as a basis for research in finding the law. The decisions set forth later in the text are cases which have been decided by a court of review. All cases which have been decided are available to interested persons, for use in legal research, as are the statutory enactments of legislatures.

Case law as a basis for law and judicial decisions often provides only the point of departure from which the difficult labor of the reviewing court begins. Courts of review must examine and compare cases cited as authority to them, to determine whether the principles or rules of law therein contained should be followed or rejected on some ground, such as changing conditions. In reaching and preparing its decision, the court must consider whether the law as announced will provide justice in the case at bar and will establish sound precedent for future cases involving similar issues.

The chapters immediately following, about the court system, the various sources of law, and the nature of the judicial process, seek to develop some understanding of law prior to the examination of some of the more important legal principles that compose the environment in which business operates.

REVIEW QUESTIONS—CHAPTER 1

1 Give three definitions of law. Compare each with the other.
2 List four schools of legal thought. Give an example of an area of the law that has been influenced by each school.
3 Which school of legal thought is most dominant today? Why?
4 What is the importance of "the rule of law" to our society?

5 What is the distinction between law and justice?
6 Define the following: felony, misdemeanor, treason.
7 What is a tort?
8 Define the following: negligence, trespass, property.
9 What is the distinction between substance and procedure?
10 What is the opposite of: *(a)* right, *(b)* privilege, *(c)* power, *(d)* immunity?
11 Compare res judicata and stare decisis.

Chapter Two

The Court System and Litigation

1 INTRODUCTION

Liberty and justice are abstractions that can only be realized when individuals operate a system in such a manner as to achieve them. The law can only work through individuals; it is not self-enforcing. Among the individuals involved in operating our legal system are lawyers, trial judges, reviewing court justices, and juries. Countless words have been written about each of these, and no discussion about the court system would be complete without some discussion of the role each plays. This chapter will briefly examine these roles and then will discuss courts and litigation.

2 LAWYERS

The practice of law is a profession. It involves a dedication to mankind in which the character of the service performed is more important than any remuneration received for the service. The individual practitioner assumes duties and responsibilities which extend to the courts, to the public, and to the client.

A lawyer's first duty is to the administration of justice. As an officer of the court, it is his obligation to see that proceedings are conducted in a dignified and orderly manner and that issues are tried on their merits only. The practice of law is not a game or mere battle of wits, but rather a means to promote justice. The lawyer's duties to his client require the highest degree of fidelity, loyalty, and integrity.

To engage in the practice of law is not a natural or constitutional right but a privilege conferred upon one as a result of his knowledge of the law and possession of good moral character. The latter involves a proper conception of the nature and duties of the office of attorney and also of the ethics of the profession. It has sometimes been described as absolute obedience to the unenforceable. Absolute honesty and integrity are minimum standards for the profession.

A lawyer serves in essentially three capacities—counselor, advocate, and public servant. As a counselor, a lawyer is by the very nature of his profession privy to his client's most important secrets and affairs. A lawyer is often actively involved in the business and personal lives of his clients, ranging from their business affairs and family matters such as divorce to their alleged violations of the criminal law. These relationships dictate that a lawyer meet the highest standards of professional and ethical conduct.

As an advocate, a lawyer is not only a "fighter" in court but a negotiator of compromise. A lawyer spends most of his efforts in seeking solutions to the differences between adversaries. Advocacy is practiced not only before courts and juries but before opposing counsel and with one's own client as well.

As a public servant, a lawyer serves in all capacities at all levels of organized society. His formal education, training, and experience make him better equipped than most to render valuable public service.

It is obvious that if a lawyer is to give competent advice and adequate representation he must know to the extent possible all of the facts involved in any legal problem presented to him by his client. In attempting to ensure that a lawyer may be fully advised of his client's problems and all matters affecting them, the rules of evidence provide that certain confidential communications to a lawyer are privileged. The law does not permit a lawyer to reveal such facts and testify against his client, even if called to the stand to do so at a trial. This is called the attorney-client privilege, and may extend to communications made to employees of the lawyer in certain cases. The decision which follows discusses the rationale behind the attorney-client privilege, as well as its historical development and application to corporate clients.

Radiant Burners, Inc. v. American Gas Ass'n
320 F.2d 314 (1963)

The plaintiff, Radiant Burners, Inc., brought this antitrust action against the defendants, the American Gas Association, a trade association, its members and others, alleging that they were involved in a conspiracy and combination in restraint of trade in violation of Section 1 of the Sherman Act, which had the purpose of controlling the market and foreclosing the plaintiff from competition. For this violation, the plaintiff sought an injunction and treble damages. In the pretrial discovery proceedings, each of the parties made available to the others upon their request, the unprivileged documents it had on file relating to the case. However, a dispute arose concerning certain documents in the possession of the defendants. The defendants contended that these were not discoverable by the plaintiff, since they were within the scope of the attorney-client privilege. The trial court held that privilege was not available to corporations and ruled in favor of the plaintiff. The defendants appealed.

HASTINGS, CHIEF JUDGE: . . . The broad question for decision on this interlocutory appeal is whether the district court erred in holding that in a private antitrust action a corporation may not claim the attorney-client privilege to bar discovery of documents. . . .

The rationale of the district court's holding on the merits of the question was that the privilege is not available to corporations because it is historically personal in nature and may be claimed only by natural persons. Further, that since secrecy or confidentiality is essential to a claim of the privilege in any event, it is not possible to maintain this relationship because of the possibility of disclosure to persons who constitute or are necessarily related to the corporate entity. . . .

Dean Wigmore teaches that the history of the attorney-client privilege finds its origin in the reign of Elizabeth I, "where the privilege already appears as unquestioned.'' It arose from "a consideration for *oath and the honor* of the attorney rather than for the apprehensions of his client." The doctrine that the privilege was that of the attorney rather than the client began to give way to a new concept in the 1700's. The "new theory looked to the necessity of *providing subjectively for the client's freedom of apprehension* in consulting his legal adviser. It proposed to assure this by removing the risk of disclosure by the attorney even at the hands of the law." By the middle of the 1800's, the privilege became substantially recognized as that of the client "to include communications made, first, during any other litigation; next, in contemplation of litigation; next, during a controversy but not yet looking to litigation; and, lastly, in any consultation for legal advice, wholly irrespective of litigation or even of controversy." 8 Wigmore, Evidence § 2290 (McNaughton Rev. 1961).

The policy of the privilege has been grounded on subjective considerations since the latter part of the 1700's. "In order to promote freedom of consultation of legal advisers by clients, the apprehension of compelled disclosure by the legal advisers must be removed; hence the law must prohibit such disclosure except on the client's consent. Such is the modern theory." 8 Wigmore § 2291

There seems to be general acceptance of the four fundamental conditions recognized as necessary by Wigmore "to the establishment of a privilege against the disclosure of communications:''

1 *The communications must originate in a* confidence that they will not be disclosed.
2 *This element of* confidentiality must be essential *to the full and satisfactory maintenance of the relation between the parties.*
3 *The* relation *must be one which in the opinion of the community ought to be sedulously fostered.*
4 *The* injury *that would inure to the relation by the disclosure of the communications must be* greater than the benefit *thereby gained for the correct disposal of litigation.*

Only if these four conditions are present should a privilege be recognized.

That they are present in most of the recognized privileges is plain enough; and the absence of one or more of them serves to explain why certain privileges have failed to obtain the recognition sometimes demanded for them. In the privilege for communications between attorney and client, for example, all four are present, the only condition open to any dispute being the fourth. 8 Wigmore § 2285.

Finally, on the attorney-client privilege itself, Wigmore makes a summation "of the general principle so as to represent all its essentials" in the following sequence:

(1) Where legal advice of any kind is sought (2) from a professional legal adviser in his capacity as such, (3) the communications relating to that purpose, (4) made in confidence (5) by the client, (6) are at his instance permanently protected (7) from disclosure by himself or by the legal adviser, (8) except the protection be waived. 8 Wigmore § 2292.

We turn now to the application of this deep rooted privilege—recognized for more than a century as existing between attorney and client for the benefit of a natural person—to a corporate client. . . .

Plaintiff argues that the privilege developed before the utilization of the corporation as a business entity and that it finds its origin in terms of a personal immunity. We believe this is a misconception of the principles underlying the privilege. Our conclusion is that the privilege is that of a "client" without regard to the non-corporate or corporate character of the client, designed to facilitate the workings of justice.

It is argued that because corporations have been denied the protection of the constitutional privilege against self-incrimination, because of their impersonal character, that by analogy they are to be denied the protection of the attorney-client privilege. We shall not attempt to reconcile the scholarly divergence of views on this proposition. In *White,* the Supreme Court was moved to its conclusion because it found the constitutional privilege against self-incrimination to be essentially personal in character, "applying only to natural individuals." It is our view, as we have previously stated, that the attorney-client privilege derives from a regard for the rights of a client, personal or impersonal in character, fostering a social policy concerned with facilitating the workings of justice.

Plaintiff urges that the benefits to society through the application of the privilege are outweighed by the superior benefits of full disclosure. There is eminent authority in support of this view. . . . These are in essence forceful arguments urged against recognition of the attorney-client privilege in any form. Plaintiff argues: "It would seem a universally accepted proposition that the dubious value of the attorney-client privilege requires its contraction rather than expansion. Most of the commentators agree that the doctrine even as applied to individuals should be abolished and would be, but for the hue and cry that lawyers would raise about such denigration of their prime status symbol."

Plaintiff follows this thought to urge that the privilege be contracted rather than expanded to include corporations. We do not regard the resolution of the question before us as requiring an expansion of the privilege. We think it already is in existence and has been for more than a hundred years. We cannot agree that the proper remedy is annihilation. If, on the other hand, a change in social policy dictated by modern liberalization of discovery procedures is in order, the cure would seem to lie in the area of accommodation of the privilege to modern business practice.

It is our considered judgment that based on history, principle, precedent and public policy the attorney-client privilege in its broad sense is available to corporations, and we so hold.

Giving recognition to what we believe is already an established rule of law, requires the acknowledgment that it is an obstruction to full and free discovery. We have chosen to follow Wigmore, with whom several noted scholars have disagreed. We, therefore, quote his admonition:

Nevertheless, the privilege remains an exception to the general duty to disclose. Its benefits are all indirect and speculative; its obstruction is plain and concrete. Even the answers to Bentham's argument concede that the privilege is well founded in its application to a certain proportion of cases. It is worth preserving for the sake of a general policy, but it is nonetheless an obstacle to the investigation of the truth. It ought to be strictly confined within the narrowest possible limits consistent with the logic of its principle. 8 Wigmore § 2291, at 554, citing *Foster v. Hall*, 12 Pick. 89, 29 Mass. 89, 97 (1831), *("The rule of privilege, having a tendency to prevent the full disclosure of the truth, ought to be construed strictly").*

The district court has asked us to spell out the answers to questions relating to confidentiality in the corporate chain of command. We are asked "to apply the elements of simple common law personal privilege to complex corporate transactions." With due respect, we must decline the invitation to decide, in a vacuum, the limitations to be imposed in the application of the privilege by a corporation. If there be a place for a "guide-lines" opinion at our court's level, this is not it. . . .

Where a corporation is the client it must act through its officers and agents. The character of the corporate organization and management will vary from the small, family type, one-man variety to the giant with its thousands of employees. The problems concerning confidentiality will necessarily vary accordingly. . . .

There is no reason to believe that the required confidentiality cannot properly be maintained within the corporate family. It can just as readily be dissipated. These matters will all have to be resolved on a case-by-case basis. No one is wise enough to decide them in advance.

Certainly, the privilege would never be available to allow a corporation to funnel its papers and documents into the hands of its lawyers for custodial purposes and thereby avoid disclosure. Likewise, it seems well settled that the requisite professional relationship is not established when the client seeks business or personal advice, as opposed to legal assistance.

In balancing the competing goals of the free and unobstructed search for the truth with the right and absolute necessity for confidential disclosure of information by the client to its attorney to gain the legal advice sought thereby, the courts will realize that they are not dealing with a blanket privilege. . . .

A corporation is entitled to the same treatment as any other "client"—no more and no less. If it seeks legal advice from an attorney, and in that relationship confidentially communicates information relating to the advice sought, it may protect itself from disclosure, absent its waiver thereof. . . . [REVERSED]

3 JUDGES AND JUSTICES

Trial judges provide the main link between the law and the citizens it serves. The trial judge renders decisions which deal directly with people in conflict. He bears the burden of upholding the dignity of the courts and maintaining respect for the law. It is he who has the primary duty to observe and to apply constitutional limitations and guarantees. He should not be swayed by public clamor or consideration of personal popularity nor be apprehensive of unjust criticism. He should not improperly interfere in the conduct of a trial. He should be mindful of the general law and administer justice with due regard for the integrity of the legal system. He has the responsibility for conducting the "search for truth."

Persons serving on reviewing courts are sometimes called *justices* to distinguish them from trial court *judges*. The roles of the justice and the judge substantially differ. Where the trial judge has direct contact with the litigation and the litigants, the justice rarely has any contact with them.

Justices do more than simply decide an appeal—they give the reasons for their decisions in written form so that they will become precedent and a part of our body of law. Thus, the decisions of the justices may affect society as a whole in addition to their effect on the litigants. Justices, in deciding cases before them, must consider not only the result between the parties but the total effect of the decision on the law. In this sense, their role is similar to that of "legislators."

For the foregoing reasons, the personal characteristics required for a justice are somewhat different from those desirable for a trial judge. The manner of performing duties and the methodology also varies between trial and reviewing courts. The trial judge who has observed the witnesses is able to use knowledge gained from participation as an essential ingredient in his decision. The justice must spend most of his time in the library studying the briefs, the record of proceedings, and the law in reaching his decisions.

4 THE JURY

The function of the jury is to ascertain the facts, as contrasted with the function of the court to ascertain the law applicable to the case. Of course, in cases tried without a jury, the court also is the finder of the facts.

The jury system was adopted as a matter of right in the Constitution of the United States. The Sixth and Seventh Amendments to the United States Constitution guarantee the right of trial by jury in both criminal and civil cases. The Fifth Amendment provides for indictment by a grand jury for capital offenses and infamous crimes. In civil cases the right to trial by a jury is preserved in suits at common law when the amount in controversy exceeds $20. State constitutions have like provisions guaranteeing the right of trial by jury in state courts.

The jury system has been subject to much criticism. It has been contended that many jurors are not qualified to distinguish fact from fiction, that they vote their prejudices, and that their emotions are too easily swayed by skillful trial lawyers. However, the "right to be tried by a jury of his peers" in criminal cases is felt by most members of the bench and bar to be as fair and effective a method of ascertaining the truth and giving an accused "his day in court" as has been devised.

As Jeremiah Black, the attorney for the defendant in the famous case of *Ex Parte Milligan*, said:

I do not assert that the jury trial is an infallible mode of ascertaining truth. Like everything human, it has its imperfection. I only say, that it is the best protection for innocence and the surest mode of punishing guilt that has yet been discovered. It has borne the test of longer experience, and borne it better than any other legal institution that ever existed among men.

In most states the decision of the jury must be unanimous or a total assertion. It Is believed that the truth is more nearly to be found and justice rendered if the jury acts only on one common conscience. Statutes and constitutions provide the number of jurors who must concur for a verdict. In some states less than a unanimous verdict is constitutionally permissible.

Jurors do not take notes as a general rule and do not give reasons for their decision. Actually, it would be almost impossible for the jury to agree as to the reasons for its verdict. A jury may agree as to the result but disagree on some of the facts, and different jurors may have different ideas on the significance of various items of testimony.

5   THE STATE COURT SYSTEM

Government in the United States is based on a scheme of dual sovereignty, and the judicial branch is an essential element of government at both the state and Federal levels. Both the state and Federal court systems are created and their operations governed from three sources. First of all, constitutions provide the general framework for the court system. Second, the legislature, pursuant to constitutional authority, enacts statutes which add body to the framework. This legislation may provide for various courts, establish their jurisdiction, and deal with such problems as the tenure, selection, and duties of judges. Other legislation may establish the general rules of procedure to be used by these courts. Finally, each court promulgates its own rules of procedure within the statutory bounds set. These rules are detailed and may involve, for example, the form of a summons or the times at which various documents must be filed with the clerk of the court. Thus, a study of the court system for any particular state requires reference to its constitution, such legislation as Civil Practice Acts, and the rules of the various courts. Each state has its own terminology and arrangement for its courts, but the chart below is representative of the court organization of a state with a complex system.

The general jurisdiction trial court is frequently known as the "circuit court," deriving the name from times earlier in our history when the judge "rode the circuit," or in other words traveled from town to town in a certain territory over which his court had jurisdiction, hearing and deciding cases. Some states call the basic trial court the "superior court" while others call it the "district court" or "court of common pleas." In New York it is known as the "Supreme Court." The term "general jurisdiction" means that the court has the power to hear any type of case. The courts below this trial court on the chart are limited in the types of cases which they may hear and thus are referred to as "inferior courts" or courts of limited jurisdiction.

The basic trial courts at one time were divided into two branches, one known as a "court of law" and the other a "court of chancery or equity," but this is no longer the case in most states. The distinction between law and equity is discussed in section 7 of this chapter.

Many states do not have intermediate appellate courts between the trial court and the court of final resort; however, intermediate reviewing courts are usually found in the more heavily populated states. Some states call their court of last resort "Supreme Court of Appeals" or "Court of Appeals."

In states with two levels of reviewing courts, most appeals are taken to the lower of the two courts, and the highest court of the state reviews only very important cases. The lower appellate court will review the findings and rulings of

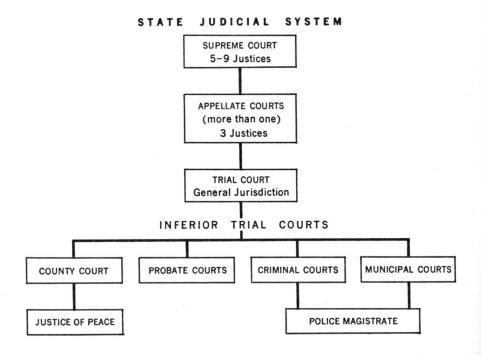

STATE JUDICIAL SYSTEM

SUPREME COURT
5–9 Justices

APPELLATE COURTS
(more than one)
3 Justices

TRIAL COURT
General Jurisdiction

INFERIOR TRIAL COURTS

COUNTY COURT PROBATE COURTS CRIMINAL COURTS MUNICIPAL COURTS

JUSTICE OF PEACE POLICE MAGISTRATE

the trial court on questions of fact as well as questions of law. While a party is entitled to one trial and one appeal, he may obtain a second review if the higher reviewing court, in the exercise of its discretion, agrees to such a review. The procedure for requesting a second review is to file what is called a "petition for leave to appeal" in some states and a "petition for a writ of certiorari" in others. In such a review, only questions of law are considered.

6 THE FEDERAL COURT SYSTEM

The United States Constitution, Article III, provides:

Section 1. The judicial Power of the United States, shall be vested in one supreme Court, and in such inferior Courts as the Congress may from time to time ordain and establish. . . .

Section 2. The judicial Power shall extend to all Cases, in Law and Equity, arising under this Constitution, the Laws of the United States, and Treaties made, or which shall be made, under their Authority;—to all Cases affecting Ambassadors, other public Ministers and Consuls;—to all Cases of admiralty and maritime Jurisdiction;—to Controversies to which the United States shall be a Party;—to Controversies between two or more States;— between a State and Citizens of another State; between Citizens of different States;—between Citizens of the same State claiming Lands under Grants of different States, and between a State or the Citizens thereof, and foreign States, Citizens or Subjects.

In all Cases affecting Ambassadors, other public Ministers and Consuls, and those in which a State shall be Party, the supreme Court shall have original Jurisdiction. In all the other Cases before mentioned, the supreme Court shall have appellate Jurisdiction, both as to Law and Fact, with such Exceptions, and under such Regulations as the Congress shall make . .

In the foregoing provision, the Constitution defines the original jurisdiction of the Supreme Court (cases which may be initiated in the Supreme Court) and authorizes Congress to establish inferior courts and to determine their jurisdiction. It also indicates the extent of the judicial power and establishes the Federal court system as one that shall have limited jurisdiction.

The fact that the Supreme Court is given original jurisdiction in any case involving a state and citizens of another state does not mean that the Court will always exercise its jurisdiction. The distinction between the power to hear a case and the willingness to exercise that power is illustrated in the air pollution case which follows.

Ohio v. Wyandotte Chemicals Corp.
91 S.Ct. 1005 (1971)

The State of Ohio asked the Supreme Court for permission to file an original lawsuit against certain businesses which were allegedly polluting Lake Erie. The suit asked the Supreme Court to abate the nuisance of the defendants in dumping mercury into streams which feed Lake Erie and for damages. The defendant corporations were citizens of states other than Ohio. The Court was asked to accept the case under its original jurisdiction as a case between a state and a citizen of another state.

HARLAN, JUSTICE: . . . While we consider that Ohio's complaint does state a cause of action that falls within the compass of our original jurisdiction, we have concluded that this Court should nevertheless decline to exercise that jurisdiction.

That we have jurisdiction seems clear enough. Beyond doubt, the complaint on its face reveals the existence of a genuine "case or controversy" between one State and citizens of another, as well as a foreign subject. Diversity of citizenship is absolute. Nor is the nature of the cause of action asserted a bar to the exercise of our jurisdiction. While we have refused to entertain, for example, original actions designed to exact compliance with a State's penal laws, or that seek to embroil this tribunal in "political questions," this Court has often adjudicated controversies between States and between a State and citizens of another State seeking to abate a nuisance that exists in one State yet produces noxious consequences in another. In short, precedent leads almost ineluctably to the conclusion that we are empowered to resolve this dispute in the first instance.

Ordinarily, the foregoing would suffice to settle the issue presently under consideration: whether Ohio should be granted leave to file its complaint. For it is a time-honored maxim of the Anglo-American common law tradition that a court possessed of jurisdiction generally must exercise it. Nevertheless, although it may initially have been contemplated that this Court would always exercise its original jurisdiction when properly called upon to do so, it seems evident to us that changes in the American legal system and the development of American society have rendered untenable, as a practical matter, the view that this Court must stand willing to adjudicate all or most legal disputes that may arise between one State and a citizen or citizens of another even though the dispute may be one over which this Court does have original jurisdiction.

As our social system has grown more complex, the States have increasingly become enmeshed in a multitude of disputes with persons living outside their borders. Consider, for example, the frequency with which States and non-residents clash over the application of state laws concerning taxes, motor vehicles, decedents' estates, business torts, government contracts and so forth. It would, indeed, be anomalous were this Court to be held out as a potential principal forum for settling such controversies. . . . And the evolution of this Court's responsibilities in the American legal system has brought matters to a point where much would be sacrificed, and little gained, by our exercising original jurisdiction over issues bottomed on local law. This Court's paramount responsibilities to the national system lie almost without exception in the domain of federal law. As the impact on the social structure of federal common, statutory, and constitutional law has expanded, our attention has necessarily been drawn more and more to such matters. We have no claim to special competence in dealing with the numerous conflicts between States and non-resident individuals that raise no serious issues of federal law.

This Court is, moreover, structured to perform as an appellate tribunal, ill-equipped for the task of fact-finding and so forced, in original cases, awkwardly to play the role of fact-finder without actually presiding over the introduction of evidence. Nor is the problem merely our lack of qualifications for many of these tasks potentially within the purview of our original jurisdiction; it is compounded by the fact that for every case in which we might be called upon to determine the facts and apply unfamiliar legal norms we would unavoidably be reducing the attention we could give to those matters of federal law and national import as to which we are the primary overseers.

Thus, we think it apparent that we must recognize "the need [for] the exercise of a sound discretion in order to protect this Court from an abuse of the opportunity to resort to its original jurisdiction in the enforcement by States of claims against citizens of other States." . . .

Our reasons for thinking that, as a practical matter, it would be inappropriate for this Court to attempt to adjudicate the issues Ohio seeks to present are several. History reveals that the course of this Court's prior efforts to settle disputes regarding interstate air and water pollution has been anything but smooth. . . .

The difficulties that ordinarily beset such cases are severely compounded by the particular setting in which this controversy has reached us. For example, the parties have informed us without contradiction, that a number of official bodies are already actively involved in regulating the conduct complained of here. . . .

We are in a quandary whereby we must opt either to pick and choose arbitrarily among similarly situated litigants or to devote truly enormous portions of our energies to such matters.

To sum up, this Court has found even the simplest sort of interstate pollution case an extremely awkward vehicle to manage. And this case is an extraordinarily complex one both because of the novel scientific issues of fact inherent in it and the multiplicity of governmental agencies already involved. Its successful resolution would require primarily skills of factfinding, conciliation, detailed coordination with—and perhaps not infrequent deference to—other adjudicatory bodies, and close supervision of the technical performance of local industries. We have no claim to such expertise nor reason to believe that, were we to adjudicate this case, and others like it, we would not have to reduce drastically our attention to those controversies for which this Court is a proper and necessary forum. Such a serious intrusion on society's interest in our most deliberate and considerate performance of our paramount role as the supreme federal appellate court could, in our view, be justified only by the strictest necessity, an element which is evidently totally lacking in this instance.

What has been said here cannot, of course, be taken as denigrating in the slightest the public importance of the underlying problem Ohio would have us tackle. Reversing the increasing contamination of our environment is manifestly a matter of fundamental import and utmost urgency. What is dealt with above are only considerations respecting the appropriate role this Court can assume in efforts to eradicate such environmental blights. We mean only to suggest that our competence is necessarily limited, not that our concern should be kept within narrow bounds. . . . [JURISDICTION DECLINED]

Pursuant to its constitutional authorization, Congress has enacted legislation which establishes various inferior Federal courts and defines their jurisdiction. The United States Code also contains provisions concerning such matters as appellate procedure and the review of actions by administrative agencies. The Federal Rules of Civil Procedure have been adopted to provide the details concerning the procedures to be followed in litigation in the Federal courts.

Observe that the jurisdiction of the Federal courts is *limited* to only certain types of cases. The two most important of these types by far are those in which a *Federal question* is involved or in which the parties on one side of the litigation are citizens of different states from *all* the parties on the other side of the case. The latter group of cases falls under what is commonly referred to as "diversity jurisdiction." It should be noted that a corporation is a citizen of the state of incorporation *and* of the state in which it has its principal place of business, for purposes of diversity jurisdiction. In addition, access to the Federal courts in both diversity and Federal question cases is limited to those in which a sum of money in excess of $10,000 is involved. There are certain exceptions to this jurisdictional amount requirement, such as civil rights cases and others not directly involving money, but the stated dollar limitation is generally required to obtain access to the Federal system.

It is possible to transfer from the state court system to the Federal court system under three circumstances. First of all, a defendant sued in a state court may have his case removed to the Federal system if it meets the requirements of those cases which could have been brought in the Federal system in the first instance. In other words, if the case involves a Federal question or if there is diversity of citizenship and the requisite amount is involved, the case may be removed by a defendant to the Federal district court. Second, a party may appeal as a matter of right from a decision of the highest court of a state to the Supreme Court of the United States if (1) the case involves the validity of a treaty or statute of the United States and the decision is against its validity, or (2) the case involves the validity of a state statute against the charge that it violates the United States Constitution and the decision is in favor of its validity. Third, a party may seek review of the decision of a highest court of a state by writ of certiorari where a Federal question is involved. In such cases, the Supreme Court has discretion as to whether or not it will review the case, as contrasted with those situations listed above in which the appeal, if properly perfected, is a matter of right. Writs of certiorari are granted only in cases of substantial Federal importance or where there is an obvious conflict between decisions of two or more Circuit Courts of Appeal in an area of the law which needs clarification. Certiorari may be granted before or after the decision of the Circuit Court of Appeals.

A case which is filed in the Federal court system may be held in abeyance and the litigants directed to try their case in the state court. This is true even if a

Federal question is involved under a doctrine known as "abstention." This doctrine is invoked to allow the state to decide state issues prior to the Federal court's deciding Federal issues, especially where the state decision may end the litigation. The doctrine allows Federal courts to eliminate guesswork on the meaning of local laws and is designed to further harmonious relations between state and Federal courts. The state court may decide the Federal question if the parties so desire or it may leave the Federal question to the Federal courts. In the event the state court decides the Federal question, the losing party may appeal to the United States Supreme Court.

Many cases, such as those involving injunctions, are heard by three judges at the district court (trial) level. When a case is heard by three judges, appeal is taken directly to the Supreme Court. However, as is true in those states which have appellate courts, most decisions do not come from three judge courts and are reviewed by a Court of Appeals and not by the Supreme Court. Since litigants are entitled to one review as a matter of right, parties may obtain additional review of decisions only if the Court of Appeals holds a state statute to be unconstitutional or contrary to Federal law or upon the granting of a writ of certiorari by the Supreme Court. In addition, the Supreme Court will review questions of law certified to it for decision by the Court of Appeals. The Federal court system is thus limited in types of cases it will entertain originally and in the types of cases which it will review either by appeal or certiorari. As will be explained in Chapter 5, there is no Federal common law.

The chart which follows illustrates the Federal judicial system, including the administrative agencies.

FEDERAL JUDICIAL SYSTEM

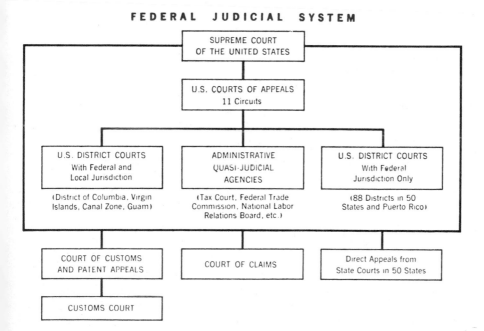

7   LAW AND EQUITY

Courts having general jurisdiction in the United States have traditionally been divided into courts of law and courts of equity. Some states historically had two separate courts and others simply had one court with one side known as law and the other side known as equity or chancery.

Courts of law were developed early in English jurisprudence to handle cases such as the various forms of trespass, other torts, and breach of contract. These courts were concerned with legal disputes wherein one party was seeking dollar damages from another. Courts of law were not equipped to give remedies such as requiring a person to do or not to do something.

In those situations where courts of law were inadequate to furnish the desired relief, a practice developed of petitioning the King of England for such relief. As the number of such petitions grew, the King delegated his authority in granting or denying the petitions to his Chancellor. The name chancery is derived from this situation. Since the action taken was originally taken by the King, the results were not a matter of right but in each case rested in the grace and favor of the King; or, by modern terminology, the decisions were strictly discretionary.

The concept of equity did not originate in England, however. Aristotle had defined equity to be the "correction of the law, where, by reason of its universality, it is deficient." The purpose of equity has always been to remedy defects in the law. When courts of chancery were growing and developing in England, the courts of law strenuously objected, but the need for supplemental legal procedures where courts of law were inadequate assisted the steady growth of equity.

Courts of chancery or equity were firmly entrenched in English jurisprudence by the time the American court system was developed. Those who established our courts recognized the need for resort to natural principles to define and interpret positive law and to remedy its defects and they therefore provided for equity jurisprudence.

In recent years, Federal law and many state laws have attempted to abolish the distinctions between law and equity. These attempts have affected the procedural aspects of the distinction but have not changed its substantive aspects. These attempts have combined the procedures of law and equity into one action known as a "civil action," and in doing so, they have generally used the equitable concepts and adopted them for actions at law. The influence of equity has predominated over law where the procedures have been combined.

Notwithstanding statements that the distinctions between law and equity have been abolished, since the historical substantive distinctions are still important, it is usually necessary to decide whether an action would have been "at law" or "in chancery," and many states require that the pleading so indicate.

Many matters are dependent on whether the action is legal or equitable in nature. For example, cases in chancery, with a few exceptions such as will contests, are not tried before a jury; the court, or in a few states a person appointed by it, known as a "master in chancery," serves as the trier and finder of the facts. Thus, the nature of the action will decide whether a party has a right to a trial by jury.

Equity jurisdiction is used in those cases where the remedy at law is deemed inadequate; that is, where dollar damages are not an adequate remedy, a court of chancery will entertain the case. Such cases as suits for an accounting; cancellation, rescission, or reformation of a contract; injunctions; partition suits; suits to quiet title; and suits for specific performance are litigated in chancery. It should be noted that, as a general rule, equitable jurisdiction cannot be used to prevent the commission of a crime even though the criminal conduct may result in irreparable damage.

Courts of equity use maxims instead of rules of law. Strictly speaking, there are no legal rights in equity, for the decision is to be based on moral rights and natural justice. A court of equity is a court of conscience in which precedent is secondary to natural justice.

Some of the typical maxims of equity are:

1 "Equity will not suffer a right to exist without a remedy."
2 "Equity regards as done that which ought to be done."
3 "Where there is equal equity, the law must prevail."
4 "He who comes into equity must do so with clean hands."
5 "He who seeks equity must do equity."
6 "Equity aids the vigilant."
7 "Equality is equity."

These maxims serve as guides for the chancellor to use in exercising his discretion. For example, the clean hands doctrine (no. 4) prohibits a party who is guilty of misconduct in the matter in litigation from receiving the aid of a court of conscience. Maxim 6 is the equity version of the statute of limitations establishing a concept known as "laches." Thus if, by lapse of time, it would be inequitable to grant relief, this maxim will govern. Maxim 2 is the basis of the remedy of specific performance.

Equity jurisprudence has played a significant role in our system of jurisprudence, and it will continue to do so. The movement toward social justice will require more reliance on the equitable maxims and less reliance on rigid rules of law. This will also contribute to the further decay of the doctrine of stare decisis.

8 JURISDICTION OF COURTS

Jurisdiction refers to the power of a court to hear a case. To have the power to hear a case, the court must have jurisdiction over the subject matter of the case and jurisdiction over the parties to the case. Jurisdiction over the subject matter is present if the case is of the type which the court is authorized to hear. This is not a problem with state courts of general jurisdiction but is involved in cases before the inferior state courts and can be an issue in all Federal cases because, as previously noted, all Federal courts are courts of limited jurisdiction. For example, a Federal court would not have jurisdiction over the subject matter of a breach of contract suit for $5,000 damages between citizens of different states because of lack of the jurisdictional amount. If the amount were $15,000 and the parties were citizens of the same state, the Federal court would still have no power to hear the case because of lack of diversity of citizenship. Similarly, a state probate court would lack the power to hear a murder case.

Jurisdiction over the person of the plaintiff is obtained by his filing the suit. Such action is the voluntary submission to the power of the court. Jurisdiction over the person of the defendant is usually obtained by the service of a summons on him, although in some cases it is obtained by publication of notice and mailing a summons to his last known address. Service of summons on the defendant usually is valid if it is served upon any member of his household above a specified age and another copy addressed to him is mailed to the home. This procedure recognizes the practical difficulties which may exist in finding the defendant and at the same time accomplishes the goal of the summons which is simply to give the defendant fair notice of the suit. For many years, it was felt that a summons could not be properly served beyond the borders of the state in which it was issued. However, this concept has changed and most states now have "long-arm" statutes which provide for the service of process beyond their boundaries.

The following case developed the legal theory which made long-arm statutes possible.

International Shoe Co. v. Washington
326 U.S. 310 (1945)

The State of Washington filed suit against International Shoe Company to collect unemployment compensation taxes it claimed were due because of certain commissions paid to employees of the shoe company who worked in Washington. The suit was initiated by serving a copy of the process on an employee of the company in the state. A notice of suit was also sent to the company by registered mail at its home office.

At the time of this action, International Shoe Company was a Delaware corporation with its principal place of business in Missouri. It had no office in Washington and made no contracts either for sale or purchase of merchandise there. It maintained no stock of merchandise in that state and made no deliveries of goods in intrastate commerce there. During the years from 1937 to 1940, it employed eleven to thirteen salesmen under direct supervision and control of sales managers located in St. Louis. These salesmen resided in Washington; their principal activities were confined to that state; and they were compensated by commissions which totaled over $31,000 per year based upon the amount of their sales. The salesmen only had authority to solicit orders which were accepted or rejected in Missouri and filled by shipment of goods in interstate commerce from places other than Washington. Occasionally they rented rooms for exhibiting samples and these costs were reimbursed by the company. International Shoe contended that the method attempted by Washington to obtain jurisdiction over the person of the company did not meet the procedural requirement of due process of law as set by the Fourteenth Amendment, and hence Washington had no power to sue for the tax. In other words, the shoe company argued that a salesman was not a proper agent of the company to receive personal service of process, since his authority had no connection with its legal activities; that the company itself was not in the state of Washington; and that the notice sent by registered mail was not personally served and had no force or effect outside the borders of the state of Washington. The Supreme Court of Washington held that the activities of International Shoe were sufficient to constitute doing business in that state and to subject the company to suit there. The defendant company appealed to the Supreme Court of the United States, since the application of the Federal Constitution was in issue.

STONE, CHIEF JUSTICE: Historically the jurisdiction of courts to render judgment in personam is grounded on their de facto power over the defendant's person. Hence his presence within the territorial jurisdiction of a court was prerequisite to its rendition of a judgment personally binding him. But now that the capias ad respondendum[1] has given way to personal service of summons or other form of notice, due process requires only that in order to subject a defendant to a judgment in personam, if he be not present within the territory of the forum, he have certain minimum contacts with it such that the maintenance of the suit does not offend "traditional notions of fair play and substantial justice. . . ."

Since the corporate personality is a fiction, although a fiction intended to be acted upon as though it were a fact, it is clear that unlike an individual its "presence" without, as well as within, the state of its origin can be manifested only by activities carried on in its behalf by those who are authorized to act for it. . . . The terms "present" or "presence" are used merely to symbolize those activities of the corporation's agent within the state which courts will deem to be sufficient to satisfy the demands of due process. Those demands may be met by such contacts of the corporation with the state of the forum as make it reasonable, in the context of our federal system of government, to require the corporation to defend the particular suit which is brought there. An "estimate of the inconveniences" which would result to the corporation from a trial away from its "home" or principal place of business is relevant in this connection.

"Presence" in the state in this sense has never been doubted when the activities of the corporation there have not only been continuous and systematic, but also give rise to the liabilities sued on, even though no consent to be sued or authorization to an agent to accept service of process has been given. . . . Conversely it has been generally recognized that the casual presence of the corporate agent or even his conduct of single or isolated items of activities in a state in the corporation's behalf are not enough to subject it to suit on causes of

---

[1] A *capias ad respondendum* is "a judicial writ (usually simply termed a 'capias' . . .) by which actions at law were frequently commenced; and which commands the sheriff to *take* the defendant, and him safely keep, so that he may have his body before the court on a certain day to *answer* the plaintiff in the action. . . ." *Black's Law Dictionary* 262 (4th ed., 1951).

action unconnected with the activities there. . . . To require the corporation in such circumstances to defend the suit away from its home or other jurisdiction where it carries on more substantial activities has been thought to lay too great and unreasonable a burden on the corporation to comport with due process. . . .

It is evident that the criteria by which we mark the boundary line between those activities which justify the subjection of a corporation to suit, and those which do not, cannot be simply mechanical or quantitative. The test is not merely, as has sometimes been suggested, whether the activity, which the corporation has seen fit to procure through its agents in another state, is a little more or a little less. Whether due process is satisfied must depend rather upon the quality and nature of the activity in relation to the fair and orderly administration of the laws which it was the purpose of the due process clause to insure. That clause does not contemplate that a state may make binding a judgment in personam against an individual or corporate defendant with which the state has no contacts, ties, or relations.

But to the extent that a corporation exercises the privilege of conducting activities within a state, it enjoys the benefits and protection of the laws of that state. The exercise of that privilege may give rise to obligations; and, so far as those obligations arise out of or are connected with the activities within the state, a procedure which requires the corporation to respond to a suit brought to enforce them can, in most instances, hardly be said to be undue. . . .

Applying these standards, the activities carried on in behalf of appellant in the State of Washington were neither irregular nor casual. They were systematic and continuous throughout the years in question. They resulted in a large volume of interstate business, in the course of which appellant received the benefits and protection of the laws of the state, including the right to resort to the courts for the enforcement of its rights. The obligation which is here sued upon arose out of those very activities. It is evident that those operations establish sufficient contacts or ties with the state of the forum to make it reasonable and just according to our traditional conception of fair play and substantial justice to permit the state to enforce the obligations which appellant has incurred there. Hence we cannot say that the maintenance of the present suit in the State of Washington involves an unreasonable or undue procedure. [AFFIRMED]

Subsequent to this decision, most states have adopted statutes giving extraterritorial effect to process in specified cases. The typical statute allows a court to obtain jurisdiction over a defendant even though the process is served beyond its borders if the defendant has (1) committed a tort within the state, (2) owns property within the state which property is the subject matter of the lawsuit, or (3) entered into a contract within the state or has transacted the business within the state which is the subject matter of the lawsuit.

"Long-arm" statutes do not authorize extraterritorial service of process in all cases. It is only where the requiring of a defendant to appear and defend does not violate our traditional notions of justice and fair play (due process) that jurisdiction is obtained under them. The case which follows discusses the extent to which modern long-arm statutes allow the extraterritorial service of process to obtain jurisdiction.

Foye v. Consolidated Baling Machine Company
229 A.2d 196 (Me.) 1967

WEBBER, JUSTICE: This case requires an interpretation of . . . our so-called "long-arm" statute. . . . [T]he statute subjects a nonresident "to the jurisdiction of the courts of this State as to any cause of action arising from . . . [t]he commission of a tortious act within the State *resulting in physical injury to person or property.*" . . . In *Nelson v. Miller,* (1957) 11 Ill., 2d 378, the Illinois Supreme Court said that the Illinois long-arm statute upon which the Maine act was based reflected "a conscious purpose to assert jurisdiction over nonresident defendants to the extent permitted by the due process clause." . . . We are satisfied . . . that the Legislature intended to fashion a "long-arm" statute of maximum permissible reach "to the extent permitted by the due process clause."

In the case before us the complaint charged the nonresident defendant as manufacturer and vendor of a dangerous and defective paper press. It charged defendant with knowledge of defects and failure to warn. Plaintiff was alleged to have been injured as a result of these defects while operating the machine in Maine. Service was made on defendant in New York. Defendant appeared specially and filed motion to dismiss on jurisdictional grounds. An affidavit filed in support of the motion showed that defendant was vendor but not manufacturer of the paper press, that it purchased the machine from the manufacturer and sold it to a Massachusetts company and that upon the order and request of the purchaser the defendant shipped the machine directly to the plaintiff's employer in Maine. . . . It is not disputed that defendant maintained no office or employees within this State, transacted no other business here, and jurisdiction must rest if at all, on this single transaction.

In our view a vendor who by direct shipment places a dangerous instrumentality in the hands of a citizen of this State where it can and subsequently does cause injury thereby commits a "tortious act" within this State, at least within the broad interpretation which we have said should be given to the "long-arm" statute. In discussing the New Hampshire "long-arm" statute which has also been interpreted as "exerting jurisdiction over foreign corporations up to the constitutional limit," Kenison, C. J. said . . . :

If a defendant, whether an individual or foreign corporation, negligently shoots a bullet from state X into state Y, or while engaged in blasting operations in state S causes a stone to be hurled into state Y causing damage, we do not seriously question the right of the injured person to seek redress in state Y and exercise judicial jurisdiction over the defendant in state Y. . . . "While no one recently seems to have stood in one state and fired a gun at a human target across the state line, currently we do find jurisdiction over nonresidents in civil damage cases based on such out-of-state activities as sending dangerous or defective products into the state and broadcasting defamatory statements received within the state." . . .

This dictum suggests to us the concept of what we may term the continuing act. For jurisdictional purposes from the time the dangerous instrumentality set in motion by the defendant enters the State and while it proceeds within the State to the point of injurious contact with the plaintiff, the defendant may properly be deemed to be "acting within the State." . . .

We go no farther than the facts of this case. We treat the defendant who makes the intentional direct shipment of the dangerous and injury producing product to the consumer as "acting" within the forum state. We conclude that the papers in this case sufficiently allege that the defendant committed a "tortious act within this State." . . .

The defendant here contends that if the statute be so construed, the subjection of the defendant to the jurisdiction of the Maine courts under the circumstances of this case would constitute a deprivation of due process of law. We cannot agree. . . . In *McGee v. International Life Insurance Co.,* (1957) 355 U.S. 220, the court held that a *single transaction* could under appropriate circumstances satisfy the "minimum contacts" requirement. . . . Mr. Justice Black, speaking for a unanimous court in *McGee,* said:

Looking back over this long history of litigation a trend is clearly discernible toward expanding the permissible scope of state jurisdiction over foreign corporations and other nonresidents. In part this is attributable to the fundamental transformation of our national economy over the years. Today many commercial transactions touch two or more States and may involve parties separated by the full continent. With this increasing nationalization of commerce has come a great increase in the amount of business conducted by mail across state lines. At the same time modern transportation and communication have made it much less burdensome for a party sued to defend himself in a State where he engages in economic activity.

We are satisfied that, giving consideration to the nature of defendant's alleged activity in this State and the relative convenience and protection of the parties if Maine be the forum for trial, maintenance of the suit in this State will not offend "traditional notions of fair play and substantial justice." [REMANDED TO SUPERIOR COURT FOR FURTHER PROCEEDINGS NOT INCONSISTENT WITH THIS OPINION]

The foregoing discussion of jurisdiction was in relation to civil suits. In criminal suits, the crime must have been committed within the state for the court to have jurisdiction of the subject matter of the case. Jurisdiction of the person of the defendant is obtained by arrest. In the event of arrest in a state other than that in which the crime was committed, extradition is necessary. This is obtained by the voluntary act of the governor of the state of arrest in turning the prisoner over to the governor of the requesting state. Extradition is thus discretionary with the executive branch of government. However, in those states which have adopted the Uniform Extradition Act, which details extradition proceedings, it is the stated statutory duty of the governor to have arrested and deliver up to the executive authority of any other state of the United States, any person charged in that state with treason, felony, or other crime who has fled from justice and is found in the former state.

9   VENUE

A question similar to jurisdiction refers to the place or court in which the lawsuit should be brought or what is the proper *venue*. While jurisdiction determines if a court has the *power* to hear a case, venue determines whether a court *should* hear the case when any one of several courts might technically have jurisdiction. A typical venue statute provides that suit must be commenced in the county of residence of any defendant who is joined in good faith and with probable cause for the purpose of obtaining a judgment against him and not solely for the purpose of fixing venue in that county, or in the county in which the transaction or some part thereof occurred out of which the cause of action arose. Actions against nonresidents can usually be commenced in any county which has jurisdiction, with jurisdiction being obtained under a long-arm statute. Domestic corporations and foreign corporations authorized to do business in a state are usually considered to be residents of any county in which they have a registered office or are doing business. Foreign corporations not authorized to do business are usually treated as nonresidents. Similar rules usually exist for partnerships, and they are generally considered to be residents of any county in which a partner resides, in which there is a partnership office, or in which the partnership does business. Thus venue statutes provide, as one of two possibilities for the proper forum for a lawsuit, the place of residence of the defendant, and define where this is.

Most venue statutes have special provisions relating to suits involving real estate which require the suit to be brought in the county in which the real estate is located. Special provisions frequently allow suits against insurance companies in the county in which the plaintiff resides.

A defendant may object to the venue for several reasons. First of all, he may complain that the requirements of the venue statute as discussed above are not met. This will not usually be the case because as noted, the statutes are specific and relatively clear. Venue may also be objected to on the ground of prejudice of either the judge or in some cases the probable jury to be selected. The latter objection is frequently made in a criminal trial which has been the subject of substantial publicity. For example, the conviction of Jack Ruby for killing Lee Harvey Oswald was reversed in part because the defendant Ruby could not have a fair trial in Dallas County, Texas, and the court erred in denying his motion for a change of venue. Motions for a change of venue based on the prejudice of the trial judge must usually be supported by affidavit but are granted as a matter of right if in proper form. It must be noted that failure to object to the venue is a waiver, and the trial may proceed if the court where the suit was brought has jurisdiction, in spite of the provisions of the venue statute, or constitutional requirements of due process.

Another ground for a change of venue is the doctrine of *forum non conveniens.* The defendant may attempt to involve this principle, which literally means that the place of trial is not convenient, in cases in which the plaintiff has attempted to have the suit tried in a county which produces juries known for large verdicts.

10 QUESTIONS OF LAW

Most lawsuits are commenced by the plaintiff's filing a pleading called a "complaint" with the clerk of the court. The complaint contains allegations by the plaintiff and a statement of the relief sought. The clerk issues a summons which, together with a copy of the complaint, is served on the defendant by leaving it either with him personally or with some member of his family, if the law so provides. The summons notifies the defendant of the date he is required to file his pleading, usually called an "answer," or his appearance in the suit. Failure to file an appearance is a default which may result in the court's awarding the plaintiff the relief sought. The defendant's answer will either admit or deny each allegation of the plaintiff's complaint and may contain affirmative defenses such as payment of the obligation which will defeat the plaintiff's claim. The answer may also contain causes of action the defendant has against the plaintiff, called "counterclaims." Upon receipt of the defendant's answer, the plaintiff will, unless the applicable rules of procedure do not so require, file a reply which specifically admits or denies each allegation of the defendant's answer. The factual issues of a lawsuit are thus formed by one party's making an allegation and the other party's either admitting it or denying it. Pleadings give notice of each party's contentions and serve to set the boundary lines of the litigation.

Not all lawsuits involve questions of fact. In many cases the parties may be in complete agreement as to the facts, in which case the issue to be decided is the legal effect of these facts. Such cases involve only questions of law. Questions of law may be raised at several stages of the lawsuit.

First of all, the defendant may, instead of filing an answer, file a pleading, which at common law was called a "general demurrer" but which today is usually called a "motion to dismiss for failure to state a cause of action or a claim for relief." By this pleading the defendant in effect says to the court: "Even if everything the plaintiff says in his complaint is true, he is not entitled to the relief he seeks." For example, in a state where mental cruelty is not a ground for divorce, a divorce complaint which seeks a divorce on the grounds of mental cruelty would be dismissed on the filing of such a motion, and the litigation would end unless the plaintiff would thereafter file an amended complaint properly alleging a ground on which a divorce might be granted.

In addition to a motion to dismiss for failure to state a cause of action, a defendant may also move to dismiss the suit for reasons which as a matter of law prevent the plaintiff from winning his suit. Such matters as a release in bankruptcy, lack of jurisdiction of the court to hear the suit, or expiration of the time limit during which the defendant is subject to suit may be raised by such a motion. These are matters of a technical nature which raise questions of law for the court's decision.

Most states and the Federal courts have procedures where either party may submit the case for final decision by procedures known as "motions for summary judgment" or "motions for judgment on the pleadings." In these hearings, the court examines all papers on file in the case, including affidavits that may have been filed with the motion or in opposition to it, to see if a genuine material issue of fact remains. If there is no such question of fact, the court will then decide the legal question raised by the facts and find for one party or the other.

It should be kept in mind that all the above discussion refers to matters which occur prior to any trial of the case. As the trial itself proceeds, the questions of fact raised by the pleadings may be resolved, leaving only questions of law. If the case is being tried by a jury, a party moves to take the case from the jury by asking the judge to direct a verdict. The court can only direct a verdict if the evidence taken in the light most favorable to the party resisting the motion establishes as a matter of law that the moving party is entitled to a verdict. Either party may make such a motion, although it is usually used by defendants to argue that the plaintiff has failed to prove each allegation of his complaint. Just as a plaintiff must *allege* certain facts or have his complaint dismissed by motion to dismiss, he must have some *proof* of each essential allegation, or lose his case on a motion for a directed verdict.

In cases tried without a jury, either party may move for a finding in his favor. Such a motion will be allowed during the course of the trial if the result is not in doubt. While the judge on such motions weighs the evidence, he may end the trial only if there is no room for a fair difference of opinion as to the result.

Finally, questions of law may be raised after the trial proper is completed by motions seeking such relief as a new trial or a judgment notwithstanding the verdict of the jury. A motion seeking a new trial may be granted if the judge feels that the verdict of the jury is contrary to the manifest weight of the evidence. The court may enter a judgment opposite to that of the verdict of the jury if the judge finds that the verdict is, as a matter of law, erroneous. To reach such a conclusion, the court must find that reasonable men viewing the evidence could not reach the verdict returned. For example, a verdict for the plaintiff may be based on sympathy instead of evidence. Thus, the results of lawsuits may turn on procedural questions of law such as those raised by the pleadings or evidence. These issues of law are the sole province of the court to resolve.

11 DISCOVERY PROCEDURES

During the period that the parties are filing their pleadings and before the trial itself, modern law has provided for procedures commonly referred to as "discovery procedures." These discovery procedures have been designed to take the "sporting aspect" out of litigation and to ensure that the results of lawsuits are based on the merits of the controversy and not on the ability, skill, or cunning of counsel. Historically, an attorney who had no case on the facts or law could win a lawsuit through surprise by keeping silent about a fact or by concealing his true case until the trial. Lawsuits should not be based on the skill or lack thereof of counsel, but on the relative merits of the controversy. Discovery practice is designed to ensure that each side is fully aware of all the facts involved in the case and of the intentions of the parties, prior to trial. One of its avowed purposes is to encourage settlement of suits and to avoid actual trial.

Discovery practices include the taking of the deposition of other parties and witnesses, the serving of written questions to be answered under oath by the opposite party, compulsory physical examinations by doctors chosen by the other party, orders requiring the production of exhibits, documents, maps, photographs, etc., and the serving by one party on another of demands to admit facts under oath. (Some courts, those of Illinois for example, have gone as far as to allow the discovery of the amount of insurance coverage possessed by the defendant in a personal injury case.) The following Federal rule on the scope of inquiry at depositions and the case which follows are illustrative of the modern thinking about discovery procedures.

1954 Federal Rules of Civil Procedure—26 (b)

Scope of Examination . . . the deponent may be examined regarding any matter, not privileged, which is relevant to the subject matter involved in the pending action, whether it relates to the claim or defense of the examining party or to the claim or defense of any other party, including the existence, description, nature, custody, condition and location of any books, documents, or other tangible things and the identity and location of persons having knowledge of relevant facts. It is not ground for objection that the testimony will be inadmissible at the trial if the testimony sought appears reasonably calculated to lead to the discovery of admissible evidence. . . .

West Pico Furniture Company v. Superior Court
364 P.2d 295 (Cal.) 1961

Petitioner in this cause sued Pacific Finance Loans, hereafter referred to as Pacific, to have certain transactions declared to be usurious (illegal rate of interest). Petitioner served written interrogatories on Pacific. Pacific answered some of the interrogatories and filed objections to others. The court sustained the objections to some of the interrogatories, and this action was commenced by the petitioner against the court to force the court to set aside its decision sustaining the objections.

PETERS, JUSTICE: . . . Interrogatory No. 4 requests the names and addresses of all employees who participated in the various transactions between the parties, together with the duties performed by each, and the period of time during which each such employee participated. . . .

It is apparent that the information requested in this interrogatory is "reasonably calculated to lead to the discovery of admissible evidence." From a list of the names of Pacific's employees who handled the transactions, together with some indication of dates and duties, petitioner will be placed in a position so that it can select one or more such employees for the purpose of taking depositions. . . .

Pacific's contention that the interrogatory calls for its opinions and conclusions is unsound. Obviously the names and duties of one's own employees, and the dates on which they performed specific duties, is not a matter of opinion. . . . Moreover, even if it be conceded that the question does call for an opinion and conclusion, that fact, *of itself*, is not a proper objection to an interrogatory. . . .

The last objection of Pacific to interrogatory No. 4 is that it is burdensome and oppressive. In support of that objection Pacific filed, in the trial court, the declaration of the manager of its commercial operations and administration department, alleging that the information requested could only be obtained by a search of the records of 78 of its branch offices. Other specific requirements were also set forth, but no estimate was made of the total man hours required to accomplish the task. Certainly that declaration indicated some burden would be imposed on Pacific to answer the interrogatory, but the extent thereof was not specifically set forth. But the declaration did not indicate any evidence of oppression. Oppression must not be equated with burden. The objection based upon burden must be sustained by evidence showing the quantum of work required, while to support an objection of oppression there must be some showing either of an intent to create an unreasonable burden or that the ultimate effect of the burden is incommensurate with the result sought. Certainly, in the instant case, . . . the trial court, in its discretion, could properly hold that interrogatory No. 4 was burdensome. . . . But, under the pertinent code sections burden, alone, is not a ground for objection. . . .

The objection of burden is valid only when that burden is demonstrated to result in injustice. Hence, the trial court is not empowered to sustain an objection in toto, when the same is predicated upon burden, unless such is the only method of rendering substantial justice. From the facts presented here, it is clear that total rejection of the interrogatory indicates a failure by the trial court to recognize the discretionary power to grant in part and deny in part, and to balance the equities, including costs, that is to balance the purpose and need for the information as against the burden which production entails. . . .

The order of the respondent court, insofar as it applies to interrogatory No. 4, should be set aside to permit a review at the trial level for the purpose of determining whether or not justice requires that the objection be sustained in toto or in part, or be denied in toto, or be denied with limitations as to the manner of bearing the burden and the party who should bear it.

Interrogatories Nos. 6a to 6g, inclusive, . . . are what, for the lack of a better phrase, can be described as "shotgun" questions. The form is such that requires the reader to spend extra unnecessary time and effort in order to ascertain that he has not overlooked the impact of references back to preceding subinterrogatories. This type of interrogatory should be avoided, and the trial court possesses the power to regulate them. But, such form alone cannot be made the sole basis for sustaining an objection in toto to the requested interrogatory. Rather, it is a fact to be considered by the trial court in arriving at the exercise of its discretion. Rather than deny the interrogatory in toto, the trial court, in a proper case, of which this may be one, should require it to be rephrased. . . .

There is another reason why the objection now under consideration may not be sustained. The objection overlooks the provisions of subdivision (c) of section 2030. That section provides, in part:

Where the answer to any interrogatory may be derived or ascertained from the business records of the party to whom such interrogatory is addressed or from an examination, audit or inspection of such business records . . . it shall be a sufficient answer to such interrogatory to specify the records from which the answer may be derived or ascertained and to afford to the party by whom the interrogatory was proposed reasonable opportunity to examine. . . .

Under this section, if Pacific did not desire to answer interrogatory No. 6, and each of its subdivisions, in full, it had the opportunity to place the burden of obtaining that information on the petitioner by simply specifying the documents in which the information is contained, and affording petitioner an opportunity to examine them. It failed to avail itself of this procedure. It is, therefore, in no position to object to the interrogatories on the ground that they call for the inspection of documents.

Let a peremptory writ of mandate issue requiring respondent court to vacate its order sustaining the objections to the specified interrogatories, and directing it to reconsider those objections, and to make its order in reference thereto in accordance with the views expressed herein. [SO ORDERED]

12 CONDUCT OF A TRIAL

In addition to questions of law, most lawsuits involve questions of fact. Such cases as automobile negligence actions and criminal proceedings are essentially questions of fact. Suits at law and criminal actions have traditionally been tried before a jury, while suits in equity have been considered too complicated for juries and as a general rule the questions of fact have been found by the master in chancery. It should be noted that juries are sometimes used in chancery cases to serve as the trier of the facts.

For purposes of examining a trial, we shall assume a typical suit for dollar damages either in tort or contract being tried before a jury. As the case is called, the first order of business is to select a jury. Prior to the calling of the case, the clerk of the court will have summoned prospective jurors. Their names will be drawn at random from lists of eligible citizens and twelve of them will be selected or called into the jury box for the conduct of *voir dire* examination. *Voir dire* examination is simply a method by which the court and the attorneys for each party examine the jurors as to their qualifications and ability to hear the case. Each side in the lawsuit may challenge or excuse a juror for cause. In addition, each side will be given a certain number of challenges known as "peremptory challenges" for which no cause need be given. Each side is given an opportunity to examine the jurors and either to accept them or to reject them until his challenges are exhausted. The prospective jurors are sworn to give truthful answers to the questions on *voir dire*. The processes continue until the full jury is selected.

After selecting the jurors to hear the case, the attorneys then make their opening statements. An opening statement is not evidence but is only used to familiarize the jury with the essential facts in the case which each side expects to prove. It is similar to the prologue of a book. In order that the jury may understand the overall picture of the case and the relevancy of each bit of evidence as presented, each side informs the jury of the facts he expects to prove and the witnesses he expects to call to make such proof. After the opening statements are made, the party with the burden of proof, which is usually the plaintiff, presents his evidence. The term "burden of proof" may be used to designate the party who has the burden of coming forward with the evidence in the first instance or it may designate the party with the burden of persuasion. These are usually the same party, typically the plaintiff for the case in chief and the defendant for affirmative defenses.

One special aspect of the burden of proof (persuasion) must be noted. In criminal cases, the state must meet the burden by proving guilt beyond a reasonable doubt. In other words, the scales of justice must be *completely* "out of balance" toward guilt. In most civil cases, the party with the burden of persuasion must prove his contentions by the preponderance or greater weight of the evidence. In terms of the scales of justice, they must be *just* "out of balance" in favor of the plaintiff for him to succeed. In a few civil cases, courts have said that the party with the burden of proof must prove his case by clear and convincing evidence. This is greater than the mere preponderance but less than beyond a reasonable doubt. It is evident that these definitions of burden of proof require very subjective judgment on the part of the jury.

Evidence is normally presented in open court by means of the examination of witnesses and the production of documents and other exhibits. Testimony at a trial is privileged and cannot result in defamation suits. The party calling a witness has a right to examine that witness and ask him questions to establish the facts with which he is familiar about the case. As a general rule, a party calling a witness is not permitted to ask "leading questions." After the party calling the witness has completed his direct examination, the other party is given the opportunity to cross-examine the witness. Matters inquired into on cross-examination are limited to those matters which were raised on direct examination. Cross-examination is an art, and the well-prepared lawyer will usually not ask a question on cross-examination to which he does not already know the answer. After the cross-examination, the party calling the witness again has the opportunity of examining the witness and this examination is called "redirect examination." It is limited to the scope of those matters gone into on cross-examination and is used to clarify matters raised on cross-examination. After redirect examination, the opposing party is allowed re-cross-examination, with the corresponding limitation as to scope of the questions. Witnesses may be asked to identify exhibits. Expert witnesses may be asked to give their opinion, within certain limitations, about the case, and sometimes experts are allowed to answer hypothetical questions. For example, a doctor in a personal injury case may be given all the evidence surrounding the accident and then be asked hypothetically whether such an occurrence might have or could have caused the injury which the plaintiff suffers.

After the party with the burden of proof has presented his evidence, the opposing party usually makes the motion for a directed verdict, as heretofore mentioned. If the motion for directed verdict is overruled, the defendant then presents his evidence. The order of examination of these witnesses is the same as those for the plaintiff. The party calling a witness vouches for his credibility. He is not allowed to impeach witnesses which he has called. After the defendant has presented all his evidence, the original party may bring in rebuttal evidence. When neither party has any additional evidence, the attorneys and the judge retire for a conference to consider the instructions to be given the jury.

Jury instructions serve to acquaint the jury with the law applicable to the case. As previously stated, the function of the jury is to find the facts and the function of the court is to determine the applicable law. The purpose of the jury instructions is to bring these two together in an orderly manner that will result in a decision. At the conference, each attorney submits to the court instructions which he feels should be given to the jury. The court examines these instructions and confers with the attorneys. He then decides which instructions will be given to the jury. A typical jury instruction follows:

The plaintiff in his complaint has alleged that he was injured as the proximate cause of the negligence of the defendant and that the plaintiff was in exercise of due care and caution for his own safety at the time of the occurrence. If you find from the evidence that the plaintiff was guilty of negligence, which proximately caused his injuries, then your verdict will be for the defendant.

In this instruction, the court is in effect saying that the plaintiff must prove that he was not at fault and if you find that he was at fault your verdict must be for the defendant. Thus the concept of contributory negligence is applied to the facts and the jury is instructed as to the result to be returned if they find certain facts.

After the conference on jury instructions, the attorneys argue the case to the jury. The party with the burden of proof, usually the plaintiff, is given an opportunity to open the argument and to close it. The defendant's attorney is only allowed to argue after the plaintiff's argument and is only allowed to argue once. After the arguments are completed, the court reads the instructions to the jury and the jury retires to deliberate. Upon reaching a verdict the jury returns from the jury room, announces its verdict, and judgment is entered. Thereafter the losing party starts the procedure of posttrial motions and appeals. Any final decision of the court, whether on a motion made before trial, during the trial, or after the trial, or on the court's judgment or decree, may be appealed within certain prescribed time limits. If the appeal is perfected according to law, the right of review is absolute.

13 RULES OF EVIDENCE

In the conduct of a trial, the rules of evidence govern the admissibility of testimony and exhibits, and establish which facts may be presented to the jury and which facts may not. It is a lawyer's problem to be concerned with the specific rules of evidence but an understanding of the areas in which these rules operate will give some insight into the workings of our judicial system.

One of the major rules for excluding evidence is based on what the law calls "privileged communications" or "privilege." Nearly everyone is aware that the Fifth Amendment contains a privilege against compulsory self-incrimination. In addition, communications between husband and wife, doctor and patient, clergy and penitent, and attorney and client are considered privileged by the law in order that these communications can be made without fear of their subsequent use against the parties involved. Fair play requires that an attorney not be required to testify as to matters told him in confidence by his client. The preservation of the home requires that a spouse not be required to testify against the other spouse regarding confidential communications. Some matters are privileged, such as the existence of insurance coverage of a party, because of the great effect that knowledge of the existence of insurance would have on a jury. Matters which are privileged are matters which by the rules of fair play should not be admitted into evidence.

Another basic concept of our judicial system is the right of confrontation, or the right to be confronted by the witnesses against you and to cross-examine them about their allegations or contentions. Cross-examination in open court, as a fundamental right, provides the background for the rule of evidence known as the "hearsay rule." Hearsay is an out-of-court statement which is being offered to prove the truth of the matter contained in the statement. For example, if the issue of the case were whether certain stock had been purchased, the testimony of a witness that his broker had *told* him the stock had been purchased would be hearsay. The statement is offered to prove the purchase of the stock and the *broker* is not available for cross-examination. The lack of cross-examination establishes that hearsay evidence should not be admitted. There are many exceptions to the hearsay rule. For example, if the party *himself* had made the statement, he could hardly object to the fact that he was not able to cross-examine himself and thus we have the exception for admissions against interest by a party to the suit. Testimony at a former trial at which the party was able to cross-examine and subsequent unavailability of the witness create another exception to the hearsay rule. Business entries made in the ordinary course of business constitute still another exception, and may be introduced as evidence of the facts they represent. In a criminal case a dying declaration by the victim of murder is an exception, because the effect of impending death is considered by the courts to give sufficient credibility to the truthfulness of the testimony to eliminate the need for cross-examination. There are many other exceptions to the hearsay rule, but each of them is based on the fact that cross-examination has either been had at a former time or is not required to give a fair trial in the instant case.

There are other rules of evidence, such as the rule requiring that all evidence be relevant to the matter involved in the litigation. If a person is involved in a suit for breach of contract for the sale of goods, wares, or merchandise, the fact that he has been divorced five times should have no effect on the litigation and would not be admissible evidence. It might, if presented, influence some member of the jury who had a particular dislike of divorced persons. In cases where direct testimony as to what happened is not available, evidence of habit or practice is sometimes admitted to show what probably happened, and is considered relevant.

Another rule of evidence concerns the requirement of producing the best evidence available as proof in a lawsuit. The "best evidence rule," as it is commonly referred to, pertains only to written documents. There are many other rules of evidence concerning written documents such as the "parol evidence rule," which prevents the proof of modification or change of a written document by the use of oral evidence. It can be seen from this short examination of these very elementary rules of evidence that they provide the rules of the game, so to speak, to ensure that there is a fair trial and that each party is given ample opportunity to present his contentions and his case without unduly taking advantage of the other party. They were not created to serve as a stumbling block to meritorious litigants or to create unwarranted roadblocks to justice. On the contrary, the rules of evidence were created and should be applied to ensure fair play and to aid in the goal of having controversies determined on their merits.

14 APPELLATE PROCEDURE

Sections 5 and 6 of this chapter discussed the structure of the court system including courts of review. Each state prescribes its own appellate procedure and determines the jurisdiction of its various reviewing courts. While the procedure to be followed in an appeal is essentially a problem for the lawyer, certain aspects of this procedure assist in understanding our judicial system.

Courts of review are concerned with the record of the proceedings below. All the pleadings, testimony, and motions are reduced to a written record, which is filed with the court of review to enable it to study the issues, testimony, and proceedings in order to determine whether prejudicial errors occurred or whether the lower court reached an erroneous result. In addition to the record, each party files a brief (the appellant may file a reply brief on receipt of the appellee's brief) which contains a short description of the nature of the case, the factual situation involved, the points and authorities on which the party relies, and his argument for reversing or affirming the decision of the court below, depending on whether he is an appellant or appellee. The points and authorities contain the statutes and judicial decisions relied upon as precedent in the argument.

In addition to the brief, the reviewing court is often given the benefit of oral argument in deciding the case. The attorneys are allotted a specified amount of time to explain orally to the court their position in the case. This also affords the court of review an opportunity to question the attorneys about the various aspects of the case.

After oral argument, an impression vote is usually taken and the case is assigned to one justice to prepare an opinion. Each justice has a staff of clerks to assist him in the preparation of opinions. The intellectual backgrounds of these clerks have some influence on the decisions. The opinion as prepared by the clerks and the justice may not follow the impression vote. After the opinion is prepared, it will be circulated among the other members of the court. If a majority approve the opinion it is adopted. Those who disagree may prepare a dissenting opinion. Thereafter the opinion is announced and the losing party may ask for a rehearing on points stated in the opinion which he believes to be erroneous. Such rehearings are rarely granted. If the rehearing is denied or none is requested, the decision then becomes final and the mandate of the reviewing court is forwarded to the trial court for appropriate proceedings either by way of enforcement of the decision or new proceedings, if required.

Courts of review are essentially concerned with questions of law. However, a reviewing court may be asked to grant a new trial on the ground that the decision below is contrary to the manifest weight of the evidence found in the record. Thus questions of fact may be examined.

15 ENFORCEMENT OF JUDGMENTS AND DECREES

After a judgment in a court of law or a decree in a court of equity has become final, either because of the decision on appeal or because the losing party failed to perfect his appeal within the proper time, it may become necessary for the successful party to obtain judicial assistance in enforcing the decision of the court. For example, the judgment debtor may not voluntarily pay the amount of the judgment to the judgment creditor.

In such a case the judgment creditor may levy execution on the property of the judgment debtor and cause any property which is not exempt from execution by statute to be sold at public sale and to have the proceeds applied on the judgment. The judgment creditor may also garnishee the wages of the judgment debtor, subject to the amount that is exempt, or attach any property which may be due him. Modern statutes authorize the judgment creditor to question the judgment debtor in open court in order to discover assets that might be applied to the debt. It must be noted that all states provide that a debtor shall be allowed to keep certain items of property and a certain amount of his wages free from his debts. For example, in one state the debtor is allowed to keep the first $5,000 from the sale of his homestead, the first $400 of his personal property and such personal effects as the family Bible and wearing apparel. The same state exempts the first $45 or 85 percent of a judgment debtor's weekly wages from garnishment, whichever is greater. Not only do the exemption laws protect debtors, but the law of bankruptcy may be used to have a judgment discharged.

Court orders in equity may require assistance of court officers to ensure compliance. Noncompliance with such orders may be punished by arrest and fine, or by jail sentence for contempt of court. The Federal government was compelled to resort to the use of United States Marshals and even the United States Army to enforce some of the decrees in the cases which involved school integration. Fortunately, force is usually unnecessary. The respect for and voluntary or automatic compliance with court orders by our citizens is one of the hallmarks of our "rule-of-law" society which distinguishes it from one in which there is "rule by man."

It should be kept in mind that there is a statute of limitations on the enforcement of a judgment or decree. This statute limits the time (which may vary from state to state) during which the judgment or decree may be enforced by further judicial proceedings.

REVIEW QUESTIONS—CHAPTER 2

1 Define the following terms introduced in this chapter: jurisdiction; equity; long-arm statute; venue; summary judgment; deposition; interrogatory; *voir dire;* the doctrine of abstention.
2 Discuss the three roles or capacities in which lawyers serve.
3 What is the purpose of the lawyer-client privilege? Is it available to corporations?
4 Chart the court system of your state.
5 Over what type of cases do Federal courts have jurisdiction?
6 What is the jurisdictional amount in the Federal courts?
7 Compare the types of cases tried in courts of law with those tried in courts of equity.
8 What are equitable maxims? Illustrate them with five examples.
9 Under what circumstances may a court obtain jurisdiction over the person of a nonresident defendant?
10 What is the function of the pleading stage of the lawsuit? Explain how this function is accomplished.
11 What is the function of discovery procedures? Illustrate three such procedures.
12 What is a motion for a directed verdict? When will it be allowed?
13 List three methods for collecting a judgment and illustrate each.

Chapter Three

Constitutional Law

1 INTRODUCTION

"Written law" in the narrow sense includes constitutions drafted and adopted by the people, treaties entered into by the executive branch of the Federal government and ratified by the Senate, and statutes and ordinances enacted by legislative bodies such as Congress, state general assemblies, and city councils. In this chapter some of the more important aspects of constitutional law will be examined with special emphasis on the Bill of Rights.

Under a constitutional system such as ours, the constitution of the governmental unit is its basic and supreme law. All other laws, written or unwritten, must be in harmony with it or they are void. By and large, state constitutions are modeled after the Federal Constitution and, as such, provide the same general organization for government, dividing it into executive, legislative, and judicial branches, giving each branch checks and balances on the others. This doctrine of separation of powers is testimony to the strong fear the founders of this country felt that too much power might be concentrated in any branch of government. The doctrine will be further explored in subsequent chapters. It plays a major role in law created by judicial decisions as well as in administrative law.

In addition to providing a government's organization, constitutions define the powers and functions of the various branches. Historically there was a distinction in this respect between the Federal and state constitutions. The Federal Constitution when ratified was a delegation of authority from the states, which were the basic sovereigns, to the Federal government. All powers not contained therein were retained by the states. In other words, the Federal Constitution contains grants of power to the Federal government, which was established by the states. On the other hand, state governments have all powers not denied them by the Federal or their own constitution. State constitutions, therefore, generally contain limitations on the power of state government.

Early Court interpretation of the Constitution strictly limited the Federal government to those grants of authority enumerated, and "states' rights" were held to be supreme in all other areas. As the need for a strong central government developed, this distinction was eroded by legislation as well as judicial decision, which placed more and more power in the hands of Congress and the President. The distinction, however, still exists in part, and many legal problems arise in connection with the location of the boundary between Federal and state power.

2   THE UNITED STATES CONSTITUTION: BASIC DOCUMENT

The Constitution as originally enacted contained seven articles and a preamble. The Preamble sets forth the purposes of the Constitution, which include such general goals as the establishment of justice and the promotion of general welfare.

Article I establishes the legislative branch of government and defines its functions, powers, method of conducting business, and limitations on its powers as well as the manner of election and removal of its members. Section 8 of Article I grants Congress the following powers:

To lay and collect Taxes, Duties, Imposts and Excises, to pay the Debts and provide for the common Defence and general Welfare of the United States; but all Duties, Imposts and Excises shall be uniform throughout the United States;

To borrow Money on the credit of the United States;

To regulate Commerce with foreign Nations, and among the several States and with the Indian Tribes;

To establish an uniform Rule of Naturalization, and uniform Laws on the subject of Bankruptcies throughout the United States;

To coin Money, regulate the Value thereof, and of foreign Coin, and fix the Standard of Weights and Measures;

To provide for the Punishment of counterfeiting the Securities and current Coin of the United States;

To establish Post Offices and Post Roads;

To promote the Progress of Science and useful Arts, by securing for limited Times to Authors and Inventors the exclusive Right to their respective Writings and Discoveries;

To constitute Tribunals inferior to the supreme Court;

To define and punish Piracies and Felonies committed on the high Seas, and Offences against the Law of Nations;

To declare War, grant Letters of Marque and Reprisal, and make Rules concerning Captures on Land and Water;

To raise and support Armies, but no Appropriation of Money to that Use shall be for a longer Term than two Years;

To provide and Maintain a Navy;

To make Rules for the Government and Regulation of the land and naval Forces;

To provide for calling forth the Militia to execute the Laws of the Union, suppress Insurrections and repel Invasions;

To provide for organizing, arming, and disciplining, the Militia, and for governing such Part of them as may be employed in the Service of the United States, reserving to the States respectively, the Appointment of the Officers, and the Authority of training the Militia according to the discipline prescribed by Congress;

To exercise exclusive Legislation in all Cases whatsoever, over such District (not exceeding ten Miles square) as may, by Cession of particular States, and the

Acceptance of Congress, become the Seat of the Government of the United States, and to exercise like Authority over all Places purchased by the Consent of the Legislature of the State in which the Same shall be, for the Erection of Forts, Magazines, Arsenals, dock-Yards, and other needful Buildings;—And

To make all Laws which shall be necessary and proper for carrying into Execution the foregoing Powers, and all other Powers vested by this Constitution in the Government of the United States, or in any Department or Officer thereof.

Some of the foregoing powers such as the power to regulate commerce will be discussed in detail later in the text.

Article II vests the executive power in the President. It defines his term of office, the qualifications for office, and manner of election. This latter provision, together with Amendment XII concerning the electoral college, is currently the subject of much criticism, with many people advocating election by popular vote. Article II also makes the President the Commander in Chief of the Armed Forces and authorizes him to enter into treaties with the advice and consent of the Senate. It is this article that requires the annual State of the Union message by the President.

Article III creates the judicial branch of government. It defines the original jurisdiction of the Supreme Court and authorizes Congress to create other Federal courts. Article III also defines treason.

Article IV contains several miscellaneous provisions relating to the relationships between the states such as the "full faith and credit" clause, which requires each state to recognize the public acts and proceedings of other states, and the provisions relating to extradition of those accused of crimes in other states.

Article V sets forth the methods for amending the Constitution. To date, there have been twenty-six amendments approved by one of the authorized methods. Article VI contains the supremacy clause, which means that Federal laws and treaties are the supreme law of the land. It also requires all state officials to be bound by oath or affirmation to support the Constitution of the United States. Article VII is the clause providing for the original ratification.

Many of the foregoing powers and functions of the Federal government will be discussed throughout this text. Before the Bill of Rights and other amendments to the Constitution are taken up, some further comments relative to the conduct of external affairs of the nation will be helpful.

3 THE CONSTITUTION AND EXTERNAL AFFAIRS

The President is given the power to make treaties, with the advice and consent of the Senate, in Article II, Section 2 of the Constitution. This power has grown in its importance to the economic life and defense of the nation, as the United States has become a leader in world affairs.

The treaties of most countries affect only their external relations with other countries. The United States is unique in that its treaties are part of the "supreme Law of the Land," and thus have the internal force of the Constitution and laws enacted by Congress. Because of this, many persons have argued for a limitation on the treaty-making power, as well as the power of the President to make "executive agreements" with the heads of other governments. Article VI of the Constitution provides in part: "This Constitution, and the Laws of the United States which shall be made in Pursuance thereof; and all Treaties made, or which shall be made, under the Authority of the United States, shall be the supreme Law of the Land; and the Judges in every State shall be bound thereby, any Thing in the Constitution or Laws of any State to the Contrary notwithstanding."

Note that the language employed makes the laws enacted by Congress binding only if made within the limitations of the Constitution but apparently provides no such restriction on the effect of treaties made "under the Authority of the United States."

The development of the European Common Market has presented economic challenges which our Federal government may desire to meet by joining its activities, and it has reaffirmed the importance of the treaty-making power to the economic life of the United States.

In *United States v. Curtis-Wright Corp.*,[1] the Supreme Court had occasion to discuss the difference in the powers of the Federal government over foreign affairs and internal affairs. Justice Sutherland, speaking for the court, noted:

. . . It will contribute to the elucidation of the question if we first consider the differences between the powers of the federal government in respect of foreign or external affairs and those in respect of domestic or internal affairs. That there are differences between them, and that these differences are fundamental, may not be doubted.

The two classes of powers are different, both in respect of their origin and their nature. The broad statement that the federal government can exercise no powers except those specifically enumerated in the Constitution and such implied powers as are necessary and proper to carry into effect the enumerated powers, is categorically true only in respect of our internal affairs. In that field, the primary purpose of the Constitution was to carve from the general mass of legislative powers then possessed by the states such portions as it was thought desirable to vest in the federal government, leaving those not included in the enumeration still in the states. Carter v. Carter Coal Co., 298 U.S. 238, 294. That this doctrine applied only to powers which the states had, is self evident. And since the states severally never possessed international powers, such powers could not have been carved from the mass of state powers but obviously were transmitted to the United States from some other source. . . .

Rulers come and go; governments end and forms of government change; but sovereignty survives. A political society cannot endure without a supreme will

---

[1] 299 U.S. 304 (1936).

somewhere. Sovereignty is never held in suspense. When, therefore, the external sovereignty of Great Britain in respect of the colonies ceased, it immediately passed to the Union. . . .

The Amendments

4   INTRODUCTION

Perhaps no part of the United States Constitution is so well known or held as sacred as the so-called Bill of Rights, the first ten amendments to the Constitution. Most of us are acquainted to some degree with the freedoms of speech, press, religion, and assembly. Usually we do not think of these matters in a business context but more as dealing with personal rights of individuals in a free society. There are, however, very important aspects of these freedoms which relate to economic opportunity and business activity.

The Bill of Rights is probably thought by many people to contain more protection and rights than are actually guaranteed. It has a certain connotation which gives it significance far beyond its actual content. Justice Harlan in the excerpt which follows discusses the significance of these first ten amendments.

The Bill of Rights and the Constitution[2]
John M. Harlan, Associate Justice of the Supreme Court of the United States

(After reviewing the language of each amendment, Justice Harlan continued:)

While these amendments symbolize the respect for the individual that is the cornerstone of American political concepts, it would be a grave mistake to regard them as the full measure of the bulwarks of our free society. Except for the first three amendments, they are largely procedural protections against particular kinds of arbitrary governmental action and touch the activities of relatively few people; standing alone they do not account for the broad spectrum of freedoms which the people of this country enjoy. They were indeed not a part of the original handiwork of the framers of the Constitution.

The men who wrote the Constitution recognized, with unmatched political wisdom, that true liberty can rise no higher or be made more secure than the spirit of a people to achieve and maintain it. Their prime concern was to devise a form of government for the new nation under which such a spirit might thrive and find the fullest opportunity for expression. The amendments comprising the Bill of Rights followed only after the structure of government had been established by the Constitution proper. They resulted not so much from what the framers considered to be new ideological imperatives as from fears among the states that the national government might seek to tamper with individual rights already largely

[2] 50 *A.B.A.J.* 918 (Oct., 1964). Used by permission from the American Bar Association and the *American Bar Association Journal*.

assured under the laws of the various states. The movement for a Bill of Rights was given added impetus by the passage of the Northwest Ordinance, under which the Federal Government was to administer the western territories, all claims to sovereignty over which had been relinquished by the states. That instrument, passed by the Continental Congress sitting at Federal Hall in New York at the same time as the Constitutional Convention was meeting in Philadelphia, contained what amounted to a formal Bill of Rights of its own.

For the most part the rights assured by these first ten amendments against federal invasion were simply those enjoyed by Englishmen under the institutions of the mother country, having their origins in the provisions of Magna Charta, that famed fountainhead of individual liberty. There were, however, two notable extensions of those rights: freedom of religion and freedom of speech and press, the former stemming from what had been growing colonial practice, and the latter being spurred by the prosecution and acquittal of John Peter Zenger for seditious libel, which had taken place in New York in 1735.

In short, as the debates at the Constitutional Convention and the terms of the Constitution itself both reveal, the framers proceeded on a premise which many years later Judge Learned Hand was to state in the following words: "Liberty lies in the hearts of men and women; when it dies there, no constitution, no law, no court can save it; no constitution, no law, no court even can do much to help it." They staked their faith that liberty would prosper in the new nation not primarily upon declarations of individual rights but upon the kind of government the Union was to have. And they determined that in a government of divided powers lay the best promise for realizing the free society it was their object to achieve.

The matter had a double aspect: *first,* the division of governmental authority between the states and the central government; *second,* the distribution of power within the federal establishment itself. The former, doubtless born not so much of political principle as of the necessity for achieving a more perfect union than had proved possible under the Articles of Confederation, was solved by making the authority of the Federal Government supreme within the sphere of powers expressly or impliedly delegated to it and reserving to the states all other powers—a reservation which subsequently found express protection in the Bill of Rights through the provisions of the Tenth Amendment. The second aspect of the governmental structure was solved, purely as a matter of political theory, by distributing the totality of federal power among the legislative, executive and judicial branches of the government, each having defined functions. Thus eventuated the two great constitutional doctrines of federalism—often inaccurately referred to as the doctrine of states' rights—and separation of powers.

These doctrines lie at the root of our constitutional system. It is manifest that no view of the Bill of Rights or interpretation of any of its provisions which fails to take due account of them can be considered constitutionally sound.

In the sections which follow, each of the first ten amendments will be discussed in detail. Many of the cases involve the criminal law, which is significant to the study of the legal environment of business. In recent years, the crime wave which has swept the country has imposed substantial losses on business and has drastically increased the cost of doing business through increased insurance costs and losses of inventory. Crimes of violence have made many areas unsafe and have greatly boosted the cost of government, with a resulting rise in taxes. The criminal law in many ways typifies the moral climate of business activity and serves as a focal point for comparing the interests of society with the interests of individuals. Therefore, a look at some aspects of criminal laws and trends in criminal decisions is important to the student of the law of business.

5   FIRST AMENDMENT

Congress shall make no law respecting an establishment of religion, or prohibiting the free exercise thereof; or abridging the freedom of speech, or of the press; or the rights of the people peaceably to assemble, and to petition the Government for a redress of grievances.

A   FREEDOM OF RELIGION

Freedom of religion becomes a business issue frequently as a result of the enactment of Sunday closing legislation.

Since the time of the Roman Empire, Christians have considered Sunday to be a day of rest. Those of the Jewish faith worship from sundown Friday to sundown Saturday. Atheists and agnostics presumably have no day of worship. It is, therefore, not surprising that controversy and litigation result when legislative bodies at either the state or local level attempt to prohibit activities, such as conducting a business at designated times, for religious purposes.

Many states and some municipalities by statute prohibit business activity on Sunday with certain specified exceptions. These statutes, usually referred to as "blue laws," may limit an activity to a specified time or may prohibit it altogether. The motives behind such laws are at least in part religious but many have economic justification. For example, car dealers may want to close at least one day a week to reduce overhead, etc., but will not dare do so if their competitors are open for business. A "blue law" prohibiting the sale of autos on Sundays at least has some economic justification. In addition, these laws have been justified as improving the state of health and well-being of citizens by giving a day of rest.

Sunday closing laws are attacked for a variety of reasons including the constitutional ones that they violate the guarantee of freedom of religion, the prohibition against taking property without due process of law, and the prohibition against denying people equal protection under the laws. The current attitude of the Supreme Court is that there may be valid reasons for Sunday closing laws. Justice Frankfurter in *Brownfield v. Brown*, 366 U.S. 599 (1961), noted the nonreligious reasons for Sunday closing when he stated:

It cannot be fairly denied that the institution of Sunday as a time whose occupations and atmosphere differ from those of other days of the week has now been a portion of the American cultural scene since well before the Constitution;

that for many millions of people life has a hebdomadal rhythm in which this day, with all its particular associations, is the recurrent note of repose. Cultural history establishes not a few practices and prohibitions religious in origin which are retained as secular institutions and ways long after their religious sanctions and justifications are gone. In light of these considerations, can it reasonably be said that no substantial nonecclesiastical purpose relevant to a well-ordered social life exists for Sunday restrictions?

It is urged, however, that if a day of rest were the legislative purpose, statutes to secure it would take some other form than the prohibition of activity on Sunday. Such statutes, it is argued, would provide for one day's labor stoppage in seven, leaving the choice of the day to the individual; or, alternatively, would fix a common day of rest on some other day—Monday or Tuesday. But, in all fairness, certainly, it would be impossible to call unreasonable a legislative finding that these suggested alternatives were unsatisfactory. A provision for one day's closing per week, at the option of every particular enterpriser, might be disruptive of families whose members are employed by different enterprises. Enforcement might be more difficult, both because violation would be less easily discovered and because such a law would not be seconded, as is Sunday legislation, by the community's moral temper. More important, one-day-a-week laws do not accomplish all that is accomplished by Sunday laws. They provide only a periodic physical rest, not that atmosphere of entire community repose which Sunday has traditionally brought and which, a legislature might reasonably believe, is necessary to the welfare of those who for many generations have been accustomed to its recuperative effects.

The same considerations might also be deemed to justify the choice of Sunday as the single common day when labor ceases. For to many who do not regard it sacramentally, Sunday is nevertheless a day of special, long-established associations, whose particular temper makes it a haven that no other day could provide. The will of a majority of the community, reflected in the legislative process during scores of years, presumably prefers to take its leisure on Sunday. The spirit of any people expresses in goodly measure the heritage which links it to its past. Disruption of this heritage by a regulation which, like the unnatural labors of Claudius's shipwrights, does not divide the Sunday from the week, might prove a measure ill-designed to secure the desirable community repose for which Sunday legislation is designed. At all events, Maryland, Massachusetts and Pennsylvania, like thirty-one other States with similar regulations, could reasonably so find. Certainly, from failure to make a substitution for Sunday in securing a socially desirable day of surcease from subjection to labor and routine a purpose cannot be derived to establish or promote religion.

Freedom of religion issues are also present in numerous other cases, for example, those concerning school prayer, the support of parochial schools with tax funds, and even the possession and use of drugs. In the latter case, it was held that freedom of religion was not violated by laws prohibiting the possession and use of hallucinatory drugs even though they were claimed to be used as a part of a religious ceremony.

B FREEDOM OF SPEECH AND THE PRESS

In our early legal history and into the early portion of this century, the freedoms of speech and the press were an issue in cases involving picketing, especially by unions. The right to picket peacefully for a lawful purpose is well recognized today. Courts may limit the number of pickets in order to preserve order and promote safety but the right to express opinions in a picket line cannot be denied. Currently, the issues involving these freedoms are illustrated by the cases dealing with obscenity, libel, and various forms of dissent.

Our laws dealing with obscenity may be traced to an 1857 English Statute known as "Lord Campbell's Act." This act gave magistrates the power to order the destruction of books and prints if, in their opinion, publication of them would amount to a misdemeanor. In 1868, the Lord Chief Justice Cochbum in the case of *The Queen v. Hicklin* stated: "I think the test of obscenity is this, whether the tendency of the matter charged as obscene is to deprave and corrupt those whose minds are open to such immoral influences, and into whose hands publications of this sort may fall." Note that this rule did not examine the whole manuscript and used the persons who were susceptible to influence as the criterion.

In 1873, Congress passed a statute relating to the sending of obscene literature through the mails. This statute, known as the Comstock Act, provided: ". . . no obscene, lewd, or lascivious book, pamphlet, picture, print, or other publication of indecent character shall be carried in the mails." Prosecutions under this statute were successful if the publication would have a tendency to suggest impure and libidinous thoughts depraving and corrupting morals. Freedom of the press and speech were not violated, as the protection of the First Amendment did not extend to obscene literature.

The twentieth century has seen drastic changes in the legal attitude toward obscenity. In 1913, Judge Learned Hand noted that "contemporary society should not 'be required to' reduce its treatment of sex to the standard of a child's library in the supposed interest of a salacious few." In 1930, Judge Augustus N. Hand in reviewing a book entitled *The Sex Side of Life,* stated: ". . . the pamphlet is intended to be given to parents and then to their children, and thus is not distributed to children indiscriminately. . . . [A]rticles dealing with sex may arouse lust under some circumstances, but the law did not prohibit everything that might arouse sex impulses." In 1934, Judge Hand expanded the possible publication of materials when he announced the "dominant effect" test in a case involving the book *Ulysses.* In recent years, many cases arose involving obscenity and the extent to which pornographic literature should be permitted to be available. These cases established that some publications or other items may properly be sold to adults but not to children. In discussing the protection of the First Amendment, the court in *Roth v. United States*[3] said: "All ideas having even the slightest redeeming social importance . . . have the full protection of the guarantees. . . . But implicit in the history of the First Amendment is the rejection of obscenity as utterly without redeeming social importance. . . . We hold that obscenity is not within the area of constitutionally protected speech or press." The court then stated the test of obscenity to be: ". . . whether to the average person, applying contemporary community standards the dominant theme of the material taken as a whole appeals to prurient interest."

Courts in reviewing material alleged to be obscene have been unable to announce any very satisfactory standards, but, among others, the courts have used the following tests:

1 The dominant theme of the material *considered as a whole* must be obscene; it is not enough if it is obscene in parts.
2 Its obscenity must be judged by its prurient appeal to the *average normal adult*, and not by its prurient appeal to the susceptible or immature.
3 The obscenity of the material must be judged in light of *contemporary community standards.*
4 To be obscene it must *appeal to prurient interests.*

The application of the foregoing rules has resulted in constitutional protection of books and movies that many people find morally objectionable. These persons often believe that court decisions protecting such publications and communications are contributing to the general moral decay of the country. Others feel that such decisions contribute to the free expression of ideas and the advancement of society.

Obscenity is not the only area in which freedom of speech and press play a role in business decisions or the political process. For example, the State of Alabama had a statute which made it a crime to publish an editorial on election day urging people to vote a certain way. This statute was challenged in *Mills v. State of Alabama*,[4] on ground that it violated the first amendment. Justice Black in addressing himself to this issue stated:

The First Amendment, which applies to the States through the Fourteenth, prohibits laws "abridging the freedom of speech, or of the press. . . ."

Whatever differences may exist about interpretations of the First Amendment, there is practically universal agreement that a major purpose of that Amendment was to protect the free discussion of governmental affairs. This of course includes discussions of candidates, structures and forms of government, the manner in which government is operated or should be operated, and all such matters relating to political processes. The Constitution specifically selected the press, which includes not only newspapers, books, and magazines, but also

[3] 354 U.S. 476 (1957).
[4] 384 U.S. 214 (1966).

humble leaflets and circulars, to play an important role in the discussion of public affairs. Thus the press serves and was designed to serve as a powerful antidote to any abuses of power by governmental officials and as a constitutionally chosen means for keeping officials elected by the people responsible to all the people whom they were selected to serve. Suppression of the right of the press to praise or criticize governmental agents and to clamor and contend for or against change, which is all that this editorial did, muzzles one of the very agencies the Framers of our Constitution thoughtfully and deliberately selected to improve our society and keep it free. The Alabama Corrupt Practices Act by providing criminal penalties for publishing editorials such as the one here silences the press at a time when it can be most effective. It is difficult to conceive of a more obvious and flagrant abridgment of the constitutionally guaranteed freedom of the press.

Admitting that the state law restricted a newspaper editor's freedom to publish editorials on election day, the Alabama Supreme Court nevertheless sustained the constitutionality of the law on the ground that the restrictions on the press were only "reasonable restrictions" or at least "within the field of reasonableness." The Court reached this conclusion because it thought the law imposed only a minor limitation on the press—restricting it only on election days—and because the court thought the law served a good purpose. It said:

"It is a salutary legislative enactment that protects the public from confusive last-minute charges and countercharges and the distribution of propaganda in an effort to influence voters on an election day; when as a practical matter, because of lack of time, such matters cannot be answered or their truth determined until after the election is over." This argument, even if it were relevant to the constitutionality of the law, has a fatal flaw. The state statute leaves people free to hurl their campaign charges up to the last minute of the day before election. The law held valid by the Alabama Supreme Court then goes on to make it a crime to answer those "last-minute" charges on election day, the only time they can be effectively answered. Because the law prevents any adequate reply to these charges, it is wholly ineffective in protecting the electorate "from confusive last-minute charges and countercharges." We hold that no test of reasonableness can save a state law from invalidation as a violation of the First Amendment when that law makes it a crime for a newspaper editor to do no more than urge people to vote one way or another in a publicly held election.

Many cases involve symbolic speech issues. Among such are the so-called "sit-in cases," which were part of the civil rights movement of the sixties, and protest cases such as those involving the wearing of black arm bands by school children to protest the war in southeast Asia. In these cases, conduct has been equated to speech, and it has been given broad and almost unlimited protection.

It must be kept in mind that all the First Amendment freedoms are limited to some degree. None are absolute. Mr. Justice Black, dissenting in *Tinker v. Des*

Moines Independent Community School Dist., 89 S.Ct. 733 (1969), discussed these limitations:

> *The truth is that a teacher of kindergarten, grammar school, or high school pupils no more carries into a school with him a complete right to freedom of speech and expression than an anti-Catholic or anti-Semitic carries with him a complete freedom of speech and religion into a Catholic church or Jewish synagogue. Nor does a person carry with him into the United States Senate or House, or to the Supreme Court, or any other court, a complete constitutional right to go into those places contrary to their rules and speak his mind on any subject he pleases. It is a myth to say that any person has a constitutional right to say what he pleases, where he pleases, and when he pleases.*

C FREEDOM OF ASSEMBLY AND ASSOCIATION

The freedom of assembly and association protection has been relevant to many cases involving Communists. Some have concerned the issuance of passports to Communists, others laws prohibiting Communists from holding certain positions, such as officers in labor unions or jobs in defense plants. The latter issue is involved in the case which follows.

United States v. Robel
88 S.Ct. 419 (1967)

The Subversive Activities Control Act, Section 5(a) (1) (D), made it unlawful for a member of a Communist-action organization to engage in any employment in any defense facility. It was challenged by a shipyard worker who was indicted under it as a violation of the First Amendment right of association. The lower court held the law to be unconstitutional.

WARREN, JUSTICE: . . . The Government seeks to defend the statute on the ground that it was passed pursuant to Congress' war power. The Government argues that this Court has given broad deference to the exercise of that constitutional power by the national legislature. That argument finds support in a number of decisions of this Court. However, the phrase "war power" cannot be invoked as a talismanic incantation to support any exercise of congressional power which can be brought within its ambit. "[E]ven the war power does not remove constitutional limitations safeguarding essential liberties." More specifically in this case, the Government asserts that § 5(a) (1) (D) is an "expression of the growing concern shown by the executive and legislative branches of government over the risks of internal subversion in plants on which the national defense depend[s]." Yet, this concept of "national defense" cannot be deemed an end in itself, justifying any exercise of legislative power designed to promote such a goal. Implicit in the term "national defense" is the notion of defending those values and ideals which set this Nation apart. For almost two centuries, our country has taken singular pride in the democratic ideals enshrined in its Constitution, and the most cherished of those ideals have found expression in the First Amendment. It would indeed be ironic if, in the name of national defense, we would sanction the subversion of one of those liberties—the freedom of association—which makes the defense of the Nation worthwhile.

When Congress' exercise of one of its enumerated powers clashes with those individual liberties protected by the Bill of Rights, it is our "delicate and difficult task" to determine whether the resulting restriction on freedom can be tolerated. The Government emphasizes that the purpose of § 5(a) (1) (D) is to reduce the threat of sabotage and espionage in the Nation's defense plants. The Government's interest in such a prophylactic measure is not insubstantial. But it cannot be doubted that the means chosen to implement that governmental purpose in this instance cuts deeply into the right of association. Section 5(a) (1) (D) put appellee to the choice of surrendering his organizational affiliation, regardless of whether his membership threatened the security of a defense facility, or giving up his job. When appellee refused to make that choice, he became subject to a possible criminal penalty of five years' imprisonment and a $10,000 fine. The statute quite literally establishes guilt by association alone, without any need to establish that an individual's association poses the threat feared by the Government in proscribing it. The inhibiting effect on the exercise of First Amendment rights is clear.

It has become axiomatic that "[p]recision of regulation must be the touchstone in an area so closely touching our most precious freedoms." Such precision is notably lacking in § 5(a) (1) (D). That statute casts its net across a broad range of associational activities, indiscriminately trapping membership which can be constitutionally punished and membership which cannot be so proscribed. It is made irrelevant to the statute's operation that an individual may be a passive or inactive member of a designated organization, that he may be unaware of the organization's unlawful aims, or that he may disagree with those unlawful aims. It is also made irrelevant that an individual who is subject to the penalties of § 5(a) (1) (D) may occupy a nonsensitive position in a defense facility. Thus, § 5(a) (1) (D) contains the fatal defect of overbreadth because it seeks to bar employment both for association which may be proscribed and for association which may not be proscribed consistently with First Amendment rights. This the Constitution will not tolerate.

We are not unmindful of the congressional concern over the danger of sabotage and espionage in national defense industries, and nothing we hold today should be read to deny Congress the power under narrowly drawn legislation to keep from sensitive positions in defense facilities those who would use their positions to disrupt the Nation's production facilities. We have recognized that, while the Constitution protects against invasions of individual rights, it does not withdraw from the Government the power to safeguard its vital interests. Spies and saboteurs do exist, and Congress can, of course, prescribe criminal penalties for those who engage in espionage and sabotage. The government can deny access to its secrets to those who would use such information to harm the Nation.

And Congress can declare sensitive positions in national defense industries off limits to those who would use such positions to disrupt the production of defense materials. The Government has told us that Congress, in passing § 5(a) (1) (D), made a considered judgment that one possible alternative to that statute—an industrial security screening program—would be inadequate and ineffective to protect against sabotage in defense facilities. It is not our function to examine the validity of that congressional judgment. Neither is it our function to determine whether an industrial security screening program exhausts the possible alternatives to the statute under review. We are concerned solely with determining whether the statute before us has exceeded the bounds imposed by the Constitution when First Amendment rights are at stake. The task of writing legislation which will stay within those bounds has been committed to Congress. Our decision today simply recognizes that, when legitimate legislative concerns are expressed in a statute which imposes a substantial burden on protected First Amendment activities, Congress mush achieve its goal by means which have a "less drastic" impact on the continued vitality of First Amendment freedoms. The Constitution and the basic position of First Amendment rights in our democratic fabric demand nothing less. [AFFIRMED]

D   OTHER FIRST AMENDMENT PROTECTIONS

The First Amendment also contains provisions relating to the right to petition. In addition to these clear-cut protections, the First Amendment has been interpreted to include the right of privacy and the right to knowledge. These rights were derived from the others actually specified. For example, the right of freedom of speech and press has been held to include not only the right to utter or to print but the right to distribute, the right to receive, the right to read, and the freedom of inquiry, the freedom of thought, and the freedom to teach. Moreover, the right of association is more than the right to attend a meeting. It includes the right to express an attitude or philosophy by group membership. Thus the specifics of the Bill of Rights have penumbra such as the right of privacy, as the birth control case which follows illustrates.

Griswold v. State of Connecticut
85 S.Ct. 1678 (1965)

The defendants were charged and convicted with violating the Connecticut birth control law. This law made it a crime to use birth control devices or to assist anyone else to do so. Defendants gave information, instruction, and medical advice on birth control.

DOUGLAS, JUSTICE: . . . The association of people is not mentioned in the Constitution nor in the Bill of Rights. The right to educate a child in a school of the parents' choice—whether public or private or parochial—is also not mentioned. Nor is the right to study any particular subject or any foreign language. Yet the First Amendment has been construed to include certain of those rights. . . .

The State may not, consistently with the spirit of the First Amendment, contract the spectrum of available knowledge. The right of freedom of speech and press includes not only the right to utter or to print, but the right to distribute, the right to receive, the right to read and freedom of inquiry, freedom of thought, and freedom to teach—indeed the freedom of the entire university community. Without those peripheral rights the specific rights would be less secure. And so we reaffirm the principle of the *Pierce* and the *Meyer* cases.

In *NAACP v. State of Alabama*, 357 U.S. 449, 462, 78 S.Ct. 1163, 1172, we protected the "freedom to associate and privacy in one's associations," noting that freedom of association was a peripheral First Amendment right. Disclosure of membership lists of a constitutionally valid association, we held, was invalid "as entailing the likelihood of a substantial restraint upon the exercise by petitioner's members of their right to freedom of association." In other words, the First Amendment has a penumbra where privacy is protected from governmental intrusion. In like context we have protected forms of "association" that are not political in the customary sense but pertain to the social, legal, and economic benefit of the members. In *Schware v. Board of Bar Examiners*, 353 U.S. 232, 77 S.Ct. 752, 1 L.Ed.2d 796, we held it not permissible to bar a lawyer from practice, because he had once been a member of the Communist Party. The man's "association with that Party" was not shown to be "anything more than a political faith in a political party" and not action of a kind providing bad moral character.

Those cases involved more than the "right of assembly"—a right that extends to all irrespective of their race or ideology. The right of "association," like the right of belief, is more than the right to attend a meeting; it includes the right to express one's attitudes or philosophies by membership in a group or by affiliation with it or by other lawful means. Association in that context is a form of expression of opinion; and while it is not expressly included in the First Amendment its existence is necessary in making the express guarantees fully meaningful.

The foregoing cases suggest that specific guarantees in the Bill of Rights have penumbras, formed by emanations from those guarantees that help give them life and substance. Various guarantees create zones of privacy. The right of association contained in the penumbra of the First Amendment is one, as we have seen. The Third Amendment in its prohibition against the quartering of soldiers "in any house" in time of peace without the consent of the owner is another facet of that privacy. The Fourth Amendment explicitly affirms the "right of the people to be secure in their persons, houses, papers, and effects, against unreasonable searches and seizures." The Fifth Amendment in its Self-Incrimination Clause enables the citizen to create a zone of privacy which government may not force him to surrender to his detriment. The Ninth Amendment provides: "The enumeration in the Constitution, of certain rights, shall not be construed to deny or disparage others retained by the people."

The Fourth and Fifth Amendments were described in *Boyd v. United States*, 116 U.S. 616, 630, as protection against all governmental invasions "of the sanctity of a man's home and the privacies of life." We recently referred in *Mapp v. Ohio*, 367 U.S. 643, 656, to the Fourth Amendment as creating a "right to privacy, no less important than any other right carefully and particularly reserved to the people." . . .

The present case, then, concerns a relationship lying within the zone of privacy created by several fundamental constitutional guarantees. And it concerns a law which, in forbidding the *use* of contraceptives rather than regulating their manufacture or sale, seeks to achieve its goals by means having a maximum destructive impact upon that relationship. Such a law cannot stand in light of the familiar principle, so often applied by this Court, that a "governmental purpose to control or prevent activities constitutionally subject to state regulation may not be achieved by means which sweep unnecessarily broadly and thereby invade the area of protected freedoms." Would we allow the police to search the sacred precincts of marital bedrooms for telltale signs of the use of contraceptives? The very idea is repulsive to the notions of privacy surrounding the marriage relationship.

We deal with a right of privacy older than the Bill of Rights—older than our political parties, older than our school system. Marriage is a coming together for better or for worse, hopefully enduring, and intimate to the degree of being sacred. It is an association that promotes a way of life, not causes; a harmony in living, not political faiths; a bilateral loyalty, not commercial or social projects. Yet it is an association for as noble a purpose as any involved in our prior decisions. [REVERSED]

6   AMENDMENTS II AND III

II

A well regulated Militia, being necessary to the security of a free State, the right of the people to keep and bear Arms, shall not be infringed.

III

No Soldier shall, in time of peace be quartered in any house, without the consent of the Owner, nor in time of war, but in a manner to be prescribed by law.

These two amendments are of relatively little significance today. They arose out of the experiences of people at the time of the Revolutionary War. However, the second amendment has been recently invoked by persons who cbject to gun-control legislation.

7   AMENDMENT IV

The right of the people to be secure in their persons, houses, papers, and effects, against unreasonable searches and seizures, shall not be violated, and no Warrants shall issue, but upon probable cause, supported by Oath or affirmation, and particularly describing the place to be searched, and the persons or things to be seized.

This amendment is the basis of the multitude of cases involving illegal search and seizure. There are several issues which are raised under this amendment. Among the more common are: (1) the validity of searches incident to an arrest, (2) the validity of search warrants—the presence of probable cause, (3) the validity of consents to searches, and (4) whether such action as taking blood samples and electronic surveillance are within the protection of the amendment. One recent case involved the right of a caseworker to visit the homes of welfare recipients. In this case it was held that such home visits did not violate the Fourth Amendment. The following is a typical case under the Fourth Amendment. Note the rather strong language of the dissent and the fact that while the majority found lack of probable cause for the arrest, the police did arrest the individuals who had in fact committed the crime.

Whiteley v. Warden, Wyoming State Penitentiary
91 S.Ct. 1031 (1971)

Petitioner Whiteley was convicted in 1965 of breaking and entering. At all times during his trial and appeal, he challenged the admissibility of evidence seized at the time of his arrest which he claimed was illegal. This is an appeal from a denial of a Writ of Habeas Corpus.

HARLAN, JUSTICE: . . . The circumstances surrounding petitioner's arrest and the incidental search and seizure, as stated by the Wyoming Supreme Court, 418 P.2d 164, 165–166, are as follows:

On November 23, 1964, certain business establishments in Saratoga were broken into, including the Rustic Bar and Shively's Hardware, the offenses being investigated by the Carbon County Sheriff, [Sheriff Ogburn] who, acting on a tip, the next day signed a complaint charging defendant and another with breaking and entering the building identified as the Rustic Bar. This complaint was made before a justice of the peace at approximately 11:30 a. m. on the 24th, and a warrant issued. After the investigation, the sheriff put out a state item on the radio to pick up two suspects of the breaking and entering, defendant and another. The message went to the network at Casper and was transmitted over the State, received by the Albany County Sheriff's Office and communicated to the Laramie Police Department, the message giving names and descriptions of the two persons and advising the type of car probably being driven and the amount of money taken, including certain old coins with the dates. Late at night on November 24, a Laramie patrolman, in reliance on the information in the radio item, arrested the defendant and his companion. At the time, the patrolman had no warrant for defendant's arrest nor search warrant. The officer together with a deputy sheriff, who had come up in the meantime, searched the car and removed a number of items introduced in evidence, including tools and old coins, identified at the trial as taken from Shively's Hardware. . . .

Sheriff Ogburn's complaint, which provided the basis for the arrest warrant issued by the justice of the peace, is as follows:

I, C. W. Ogburn, do solemnly swear that on or about the 23 day of November, A. D. 1964, in the County of Carbon and State of Wyoming, the said Harold Whiteley and Jack Daley, defendants, did then and there unlawfully break and enter a locked and sealed building [describing the location and ownership of the building].

[The state introduced the A.P.B. put on the radio by the Sheriff which led to the arrest and search.]

The decisions of this Court concerning Fourth Amendment probable cause requirements before a warrant for either arrest or search can issue require that the judicial officer issuing such a warrant be supplied with sufficient information to support an independent judgment that probable cause exists for the warrant.

The State, however, contends that regardless of the sufficiency of the complaint to support the arrest warrant, the Laramie police officer who actually made the arrest possessed sufficient factual information to support a finding of probable cause for arrest without a warrant. In support of this proposition, the State argues that a reviewing court should employ less stringent standards for reviewing a police officer's assessment of probable cause as a prelude to a warrantless arrest than the court would employ in reviewing a magistrate's assessment as a prelude to issuing an arrest or search warrant. That proposition has been consistently rejected by this Court. And the reason for its rejection is both fundamental and obvious: less stringent standards for reviewing the officer's discretion in effecting a warrantless arrest and search would discourage resort to the procedures for obtaining a warrant. Thus the standards applicable to the factual basis supporting the officer's probable cause assessment at the time of the challenged arrest and search are at least as stringent as the standards applied with respect to the magistrate's assessment.

Applying those standards to the instant case, the information possessed by the Laramie police officer at the time of arrest and search consisted of: (1) the data contained in state bulletin 881, reproduced, *supra;* (2) the knowledge, obtained by personal observation, that two men were driving a car matching the car described in the radio bulletin; (3) the knowledge, possessed by one of the arresting officers, that one of the people in the car was Jack Daley; (4) the knowledge, acquired by personal observation, that the other individual in the car fitted the description of Whiteley contained in state bulletin 881, and (5) the knowledge, acquired by the officer after stopping Whiteley, that he had given a false name.

This Court has held that where the initial impetus for an arrest is an informer's tip, information gathered by the arresting officers can be used to sustain a finding of probable cause for an arrest that could not adequately be supported by the tip alone. But the additional information acquired by the arresting officers must in some sense be corroborative of the informer's tip that the arrestees committed the felony or, . . . were in the process of committing the felony. In the present case, the very most the additional information tended to establish is that either Sheriff Ogburn, or his informant, or both of them, knew Daley and Whiteley and the kind of car they drove; the record is devoid of any information at any stage of the proceeding from the time of the robbery to the event of the arrest and search that would support either the reliability of the informant or the informant's conclusion that these men were connected with the crime.

The State, however, offers one further argument in support of the legality of the arrest and search: the Laramie police relied on the radio bulletin in making the arrest, and not on Sheriff Ogburn's unnamed informant. Clearly, it is said, they had probable cause for believing that the passengers in the car were the men described in the bulletin, and, in acting on the bulletin, they reasonably assumed that whoever authorized the bulletin had probable cause to direct Whiteley's and Daley's arrest. To prevent arresting officers from acting on the assumption that fellow officers who call upon them to make an arrest have probable cause for believing the arrestees are perpetrators of a crime would, it is argued, unduly hamper law enforcement.

We do not of course question that the Laramie police were entitled to act on the strength of the radio bulletin. Certainly police officers called upon to aid other officers in executing arrest warrants are entitled to assume that the officers requesting aid offered the magistrate the information requisite to support an independent judicial assessment of probable cause. Where, however, the contrary turns out to be true, an otherwise illegal arrest cannot be insulated from challenge by the decision of the instigating officer to rely on fellow officers to make the arrest.

In sum, the complaint on which the warrant issued here clearly could not support a finding of probable cause by the issuing magistrate. The arresting officer was not himself possessed of any factual data tending to corroborate the informer's tip that Daley and Whiteley committed the crime. Therefore, petitioner's arrest violated his constitutional rights under the Fourth and Fourteenth Amendments; the evidence secured as an incident thereto should have been excluded from his trial. . . . [REVERSED AND REMANDED]

BLACK, JUSTICE, with whom THE CHIEF JUSTICE joins, dissenting: With all respect to my Brethren who agree to the judgment and opinion of the Court, I am constrained to say that I believe the decision here is a gross and wholly indefensible miscarriage of justice. For this reason it may well be classified as one of those calculated to make many good people believe our Court actually enjoys frustrating justice by unnecessarily turning professional criminals loose to prey upon society with impunity. . . .

I think it is a distortion of the Fourth Amendment's meaning to hold that this petitioner's arrest and the seizure of the goods he had stolen were an "unreasonable arrest" and an "unreasonable seizure." In deciding this question it should always be remembered that the Fourth Amendment itself does not expressly command that evidence obtained by its infraction should always be excluded from proof.

There was certainly probable cause to arrest this man. The store was burglarized. The county was a sparsely settled one in which people knew one another. Petitioner, whose previous life would appear to have earned for him the title of professional in the stealing vocation, was seen around the store with his car the very night of the burglary. Undoubtedly this longtime county sheriff (who appears still to be sheriff) was bound to know petitioner. The tip he received was so persuasive to him that in the performance of his official duty he was willing to assume all the risk incident to having petitioner arrested. It surely cannot be said that when a sheriff, with his prestige and standing, and bond against civil suit, communicates an emergency message to arrest men in cars as burglars, a policeman must stand supinely by while two people denounced as burglars go along their way. Of course these policemen had enough information from the sheriff to have probable cause to arrest petitioner.

My disagreement with the majority concerning the wisdom and constitutional necessity of a "little trial" before a magistrate or justice of the peace prior to the issuance of a search or arrest warrant is a matter of record. But even accepting those decisions arguendo, they do not control the disposition of this case which involves the apprehension of criminals in an automobile moving away from the scene of the crime less than 24 hours after its commission. The sheriff's belief that Whiteley and Daley were guilty, even if it was only a "suspicion" as the majority seems to label it, gave police officers proper grounds to stop petitioner's car and inquire about its passengers. And once the officers stopped the car and positively identified Jack Daley, they had every reason to believe that Whiteley was lying and attempting to escape detection when he reported a false name. At least at that point, if not before, the Laramie police had probable cause to arrest petitioner and Daley. With probable cause to arrest the men, they also had authority to search the car. Such a search could be justified under either of two theories. Even under *Chimel v. California*, 395 U.S. 752, 89 S.Ct. 2034, 23 L.Ed.2d 685 (1969), the search of an automobile incident to the arrest of the occupants is permissible. And in this very case, the officers found a fully loaded handgun in the glove compartment. The search was also permissible under the "moveable vehicle" exception to the usual requirement for a search warrant. I consider it a travesty of justice to turn this man out of jail or give him a new trial six years after he was convicted.

. . . After the United States District Court and the Court of Appeals rejected his unlawful search claim bringing to 10 the number of state and federal judges who have consistently and unanimously rejected petitioner's claim, this Court reverses his judgment of conviction, although petitioner does not, of course, now allege his innocence. . . . [C]onvictions should remain final unless a petitioner seeking habeas corpus alleges that he can currently show he was innocent. There is not even a suspicion here that this hardened criminal is innocent and I would let him stay in confinement to serve his sentence.

8 AMENDMENT V

No person shall be held to answer for a capital, or otherwise infamous crime, unless on a presentment or indictment of a Grand Jury, except in cases arising in the land or naval forces, or in the Militia, when in actual service in time of War or public danger; nor shall any person be subject for the same offense to be twice put in jeopardy of life or limb; nor shall be compelled in any criminal case to be a witness against himself, nor be deprived of life, liberty, or property, without due process of law; nor shall private property be taken for public use, without just compensation.

The Fifth Amendment is best known for its protection against compulsory self-incrimination. People frequently plead "the Fifth," and everyone knows that they are exercising their right to its protection. The Fifth Amendment goes much further, however. It contains other protections, and, more specifically, it (1) requires indictment by a grand jury for a capital offense or infamous crime, (2) prohibits double jeopardy, (3) requires just compensation in eminent domain proceedings, and (4) contains the due process clause.

A grand jury has the function of deciding if there is sufficient evidence of guilt to justify the accused's standing trial. Grand juries are usually made up of twenty-three persons, and it takes a majority vote to indict a defendant. It takes less proof to indict a person and to require him to stand trial than it does to convict. The grand jury provision contains an exception for court martial proceedings.

"Double jeopardy" is a greatly misunderstood term. It means that a person cannot be tried twice by the same governmental body for the same offense. It does not mean that a person may not be tried twice or punished twice for the same conduct. For example, a person may be guilty of drunken driving within the limits of a city. He may be tried by the city and also by the state in which the violation occurred. He may also lose his job. There is no double jeopardy involved because the three punishments were meted out by different entities—two governmental bodies and a private party, the employer.

"Eminent domain" is used by governmental bodies to acquire real property for public purposes. The Fifth Amendment requires just compensation, and this is question of fact for a jury if the property owner and the condemning governmental unit cannot agree on the fair value of the property taken.

The Fifth Amendment protects life, liberty, and property from deprivation by the Federal government without due process of law. The Fourteenth Amendment contains an identical provision which is applicable to the states. Due process affects both substantive rights and procedures used by government to enforce and take away rights. While due process is difficult to define, it basically amounts to "fundamental fairness." Since the interpretations of the due process clauses of the Fifth and Fourteenth Amendments are for all practical purposes identical, the discussion of due process under the Fourteenth Amendment and the case included there also illustrate due process under the Fifth Amendment.

The *Byers* case which follows illustrates the protection against compulsory self-incrimination.

California v. Byers
91 S.Ct. 1535 (1971)

BURGER, CHIEF JUSTICE: This case presents the narrow but important question of whether the constitutional privilege against compulsory self-incrimination is infringed by California's so-called "hit and run" statute which requires the driver of a motor vehicle involved in an accident to stop at the scene and give his name and address. Similar "hit and run" or "stop and report" statutes are in effect in all 50 States and the District of Columbia. . . .

Whenever the Court is confronted with the question of a compelled disclosure that has an incriminating potential, the judicial scrutiny is invariably a close one. Tension between the State's demand for disclosures and the protection of the right against self-incrimination are likely to give rise to serious questions. Inevitably these must be resolved in terms of balancing the public need on the one hand, and the individual claim to constitutional protections on the other; neither interest can be treated lightly.

An organized society imposes many burdens on its constituents. It commands the filing of tax returns for income; it requires producers and distributors of consumer goods to file informational reports on the manufacturing process and the content of products, on the wages, hours, and working conditions of employees. Those who borrow money on the public market or issue securities for sale to the public must file various information reports; industries must report periodically the volume and content of pollutants discharged into our waters and atmosphere. Comparable examples are legion.

In each of these situations there is some possibility of prosecution—often a very real one—for criminal offenses disclosed by or deriving from the information which the law compels a person to supply. Information revealed by these reports could well be "a link in a chain" of evidence leading to prosecution and conviction. But under our holdings the mere possibility of incrimination is insufficient to defeat the strong policies in favor of a disclosure called for by statutes like the one challenged here.

United States v. Sullivan, 274 U.S. 259 (1927), shows that an application of the privilege to the California statute is not warranted. There a bootlegger was prosecuted for failure to file an income tax return. He claimed that the privilege against compulsory self-incrimination afforded him a complete defense because filing a return would have tended to incriminate him by revealing the unlawful source of his income. Speaking for the Court, Mr. Justice Holmes rejected this claim on the ground that it amounted to "an extreme if not an extravagant application of the Fifth Amendment." Sullivan's tax return, of course, increased his risk of prosecution and conviction for violation of the National Prohibition Act. But the Court had no difficulty in concluding that an extension of the privilege to cover that kind of mandatory report would have been unjustified. In order to invoke the privilege it is necessary to show that the compelled disclosures will themselves confront the claimant with "substantial hazards of self-incrimination."

[The court then reviewed three cases in which a law had been held to violate the privilege against self-incrimination, noting that in all three cases the law was directed at a highly selective group inherently suspect of criminal activities. It also noted that the privilege was applied only in "an area permeated with criminal statutes"—not in "an essentially noncriminal and regulatory area of inquiry."]

Although the California Vehicle Code defines some criminal offenses, the statute is essentially regulatory, not criminal. The California Supreme Court noted that § 20002(a) (1) was not intended to facilitate criminal convictions but to promote the satisfaction of civil liabilities arising from automobile accidents. . . .

§ 20002(a) (1), like income tax laws, is directed at all persons—here all persons who drive automobiles in California. This group, numbering as it does in the millions, is so large as to render § 20002(a) (1) a statute "directed at the public at large." It is difficult to consider this group as either "highly selective" or "inherently suspect of criminal activities." Driving an automobile, unlike gambling, is a lawful activity. Moreover, it is not a criminal offense under California law to be a driver "involved in an accident." An accident may be the fault of others; it may occur without any driver having been at fault. No empirical data is suggested in support of the conclusion that there is a relevant correlation between being a driver and criminal prosecution of drivers. So far as any available information instructs us, most accidents occur without creating criminal liability even if one or both of the drivers are guilty of negligence as a matter of tort law.

The disclosure of inherently illegal activity is inherently risky. . . . But disclosures with respect to automobile accidents simply do not entail . . . substantial risk of self-incrimination. . . . Furthermore, the statutory purpose is noncriminal and self-reporting is indispensable to its fulfillment.

Even if we were to view the statutory reporting requirement as incriminating in the traditional sense, in our view it would be the "extravagant" extension of the privilege Justice Holmes warned against to hold that it is testimonial in the Fifth Amendment sense. Compliance with § 20002(a) (1) requires two things: first, a driver involved in an accident is required to stop at the scene; second, he is required to give his name and address. The act of stopping is no more testimonial—indeed less so in some respects—than requiring a person in custody to stand or walk in a police lineup, to speak prescribed words, to give samples of handwriting, fingerprints or blood. Disclosure of name and address is an essentially neutral act. Whatever the collateral consequences of disclosing name and address, the statutory purpose is to implement the state police power to regulate use of motor vehicles.

Section 20002(a) (1) first requires that a driver involved in an accident "shall immediately stop the vehicle at the scene of the accident. . . ." It is of course possible that compliance with this requirement might ultimately lead to prosecution for some contemporaneous criminal violation of the motor vehicle code if one occurred, or an unrelated offense, always provided such offense could be established by independent evidence. In that sense it might furnish the authorities with what might be called "a link in the chain of evidence needed to prosecute. . . ." In *Schmerber v. California,* 384 U.S. at 764, 86 S.Ct. at 1832, the Court held that "the privilege is a bar against compelling 'communications' or 'testimony,' but . . . compulsion which makes a suspect or accused the source of 'real or physical evidence' does not violate it." There the petitioner had been compelled to undergo the forcible withdrawal of blood samples for alcohol content analysis, and the Court sustained this procedure over petitioner's claim that he had been compelled to furnish evidence against himself. . . .

Stopping in compliance with § 20002(a) (1) therefore does not provide the State with "evidence of a testimonial or communicative nature" within the meaning of the Constitution. It merely provides the State and private parties with the driver's identity for, among other valid state needs, the study of causes of vehicle accidents and related purposes, always subject to the driver's right to assert a Fifth Amendment privilege concerning specific inquiries. . . .

After having stopped, a driver involved in an accident is required by § 20002(a) (1) to notify the driver of the other vehicle of his name and address. A name, linked with a motor vehicle, is no more incriminating than the tax return, linked with the disclosure of income, in *United States v. Sullivan, supra.* It identifies but does not by itself implicate anyone in criminal conduct.

Although identity, when made known, may lead to inquiry that in turn leads to arrest and charge, those developments depend on different factors and independent evidence. Here the compelled disclosure of identity could have led to a charge that might not have been made had the driver fled the scene; but this is true only in the same sense that a taxpayer can be charged on the basis of the contents of a tax return or failure to file an income tax form. There is no constitutional right to refuse to file an income tax return or to flee the scene of an accident in order to avoid the possibility of legal involvement.

The judgment of the California Supreme Court is vacated and the case is remanded for further proceedings not inconsistent with this opinion. [REMANDED]

The application of the Fifth Amendment privilege against self-incrimination to corporations creates difficult legal problems. Assuming that a corporation cannot plead the Fifth Amendment, the question often arises of whether or not a corporate official may plead it when he himself might be incriminated by giving testimony relating to activities of the corporation in which he was involved. To allow him to do so might effectively extend the privilege to the corporation; but failure to do so would deny him the constitutional privilege. Insofar as corporate business records are concerned, it seems that the official may be required to produce them but may not be required to testify concerning them if the privilege against self-incrimination is asserted by him. Thus, the protection of the Fifth Amendment does not extend to corporations but does to their officers. It should be kept in mind that corporations have been held to be "citizens" for most purposes, including the rights to due process and equal protection of the laws, and that the situations in which constitutional guarantees are not extended to corporations are relatively few.

9 AMENDMENT VI

In all criminal prosecutions, the accused shall enjoy the right to a speedy and public trial, by an impartial jury of the State and district wherein the crime shall have been committed, which district shall have been previously ascertained by law, and to be informed of the nature and cause of the accusation; to be confronted with the witnesses against him; to have compulsory process for obtaining witnesses in his favor, and to have the Assistance of Counsel for his defense.

The Sixth Amendment, like the Fifth, provides multiple protection in criminal cases. Essentially its protections give one the right: (1) to a speedy and public trial, (2) to a trial by jury, (3) to be informed of the charge against him, (4) to confront his accuser, (5) to subpoena witnesses in his favor, and (6) to have the assistance of an attorney.

The right to a jury trial does not extend to state juvenile court delinquency proceedings because they are not criminal prosecutions. However, juveniles do have the right to counsel, to confront the witnesses against them, and to cross-examine them. Thus it can be seen that there are many technical aspects to the Sixth Amendment, and numerous cases still arise concerning it.

Perhaps no provision of the Sixth Amendment has been the subject of more controversy than the right to counsel. Does the right begin at the trial, at preliminary hearings, at the time of arrest, or at the time of questioning? Is it applicable to misdemeanors?

In the 1960s a sharply divided Supreme Court handed down a series of decisions which greatly expanded the application of the Sixth Amendment protection of the right to counsel. Several justices vigorously dissented from these decisions, and their soundness was the subject of political debate. President Nixon's appointment of Justices Burger, Blackmun, Powell, and Rehnquist changed, at least to some degree, the attitude of the Court in regard to the time at which the right to counsel attaches. The middle 1970s will see developments in the difficult search for answers to the many questions raised by the Sixth Amendment. The first case expanding the right to counsel is set forth below.

Escobedo v. Illinois
378 U.S. 478 (1964)

GOLDBERG, JUSTICE: The critical question in this case is whether, under the circumstances, the refusal by the police to honor petitioner's request to consult with his lawyer during the course of an interrogation constitutes a denial of "the Assistance of Counsel" in violation of the Sixth Amendment to the Constitution as "made obligatory upon the States by the Fourteenth Amendment," . . . and thereby renders inadmissible in a state criminal trial any incriminating statement elicited by the police during the interrogation.

On the night of January 19, 1960, petitioner's brother-in-law was fatally shot. At 2:30 a.m. that morning, petitioner was arrested without a warrant and interrogated. Petitioner made no statement to the police and was released at 5 p.m. that afternoon pursuant to a state court writ of habeas corpus obtained by Mr. Warren Wolfson, a lawyer who had been retained by petitioner.

On January 30, Benedict DiGerlando, who was then in police custody and who was later indicted for the murder along with petitioner, told the police that petitioner had fired the fatal shots. Between 8 and 9 p.m. that evening, petitioner and his sister, the widow of the deceased, were arrested and taken to police headquarters. En route to the police station, the police "had handcuffed the defendant behind his back," and "one of the arresting officers told defendant that DiGerlando had named him as the one who shot" the deceased. Petitioner testified, without contradiction, that the "detectives said they had us pretty well, up pretty tight, and we might as well admit to this crime," and that he replied, "I am sorry but I would like to have advice from my lawyer." A police officer testified that although petitioner was not formally charged "he was in custody" and "couldn't walk out the door."

Shortly after petitioner reached police headquarters, his retained lawyer arrived. The lawyer described the ensuing events in the following terms:

On that day I received a phone call (from "the mother of another defendant") and pursuant to that phone call I went to the Detective Bureau at 11th and State. The first person I talked to was the Sergeant on duty at the Bureau Desk, Sergeant Pidgeon. I asked Sergeant Pidgeon for permission to speak to my client, Danny Escobedo. . . . Sergeant Pidgeon made a call to the Bureau lockup and informed me that the boy had been taken from the lockup to the Homicide Bureau. This was between 9:30 and 10:00 in the evening. Before I went anywhere, he called the Homicide Bureau and told them there was an attorney waiting to see Escobedo. He told me I could not see him. Then I went upstairs to the Homicide Bureau. There were several Homicide Detectives around and I talked to them. I identified myself as Escobedo's attorney and asked permission to see him. They said I could not. . . . The police officer told me to see Chief Flynn who was on duty. I identified myself to Chief Flynn and asked permission to see my client. He said I could not. . . . I think it was approximately 11:00 o'clock. He said I couldn't see him because they hadn't completed questioning. . . . [F]or a second or two I spotted him in an office in the Homicide Bureau. The door was open and I could see through the office. . . . I waved to him and he waved back and then the door was closed, by one of the officers at Homicide. There were four or five officers milling around the Homicide Detail that night. As to whether I talked to Captain Flynn any later that day, I waited around for another hour or two and went back again and renewed by [sic] request to see my client. He again told me I could not. . . . I filed an official complaint with Commissioner Phelan of the Chicago Police Department. I had a conversation with every police officer I could find. I was told at Homicide that I couldn't see him and I would have to get a writ of habeas corpus. I left the Homicide Bureau and from the Detective Bureau at 11th and State at approximately 1:00 A.M. (Sunday morning). I had no opportunity to talk to my client that night. I quoted to Captain Flynn the Section of the Criminal Code which allows an attorney the right to see his client.

Petitioner testified that during the course of the interrogation he repeatedly asked to speak to his lawyer and that the police said that his lawyer "didn't want to see" him. The testimony of the police officers confirmed these accounts in substantial detail.

Notwithstanding repeated requests by each, petitioner and his retained lawyer were afforded no opportunity to consult during the course of the entire interrogation. At one point, as previously noted, petitioner and his attorney came into each other's view for a few moments but the attorney was quickly ushered away. Petitioner testified "that he heard a detective telling the attorney that the latter would not be allowed to talk to [him] 'until they were done'" and that he heard the attorney being refused permission to remain in the adjoining room. A police officer testified that he had told the lawyer that he could not see petitioner until "we were through interrogating" him.

There is testimony by the police that during the interrogation, petitioner, a 22-year-old of Mexican extraction with no record of previous experience with the police, "was handcuffed" in a standing position and that he "was nervous, he had circles under his eyes and he was upset" and was "agitated because he had not slept well in over a week."

It is undisputed that during the course of the interrogation Officer Montejano, who "grew up" in petitioner's neighborhood, who knew the family, and who uses "Spanish language in [his] police work," conferred alone with petitioner "for about a quarter of an hour. . . ." Petitioner testified that the officer said to him "in Spanish that my sister and I could go home if I pinned it on Benedict DiGerlando," that "he would see to it that we would go home and be held only as witnesses, if anything, if we had made a statement against DiGerlando . . . , that we would be able to go home that night." Petitioner testified that he made the statement in issue because of this assurance. Officer Montejano denied offering any such assurance.

A police officer testified that during the interrogation the following occurred:

I informed him of what DiGerlando told me and when I did, he told me that DiGerlando was [lying] and I said, "Would you care to tell DiGerlando that?" And he said, "yes, I will." So, I brought . . . Escobedo in and he confronted DiGerlando and he told him that he was lying and said, "I didn't shoot Manuel, you did it."

In this way, petitioner, for the first time admitted to some knowledge of the crime. After that he made additional statements further implicating himself in the murder plot. At this point an Assistant State's Attorney, Theodore J. Cooper, was summoned "to take" a statement. Mr. Cooper, an experienced lawyer who was assigned to the Homicide Division to take "statements from some defendants and some prisoners that they had in custody," "took" petitioner's statement by asking carefully framed questions apparently designed to assure the admissibility into evidence of the resulting answers. Mr. Cooper testified that he did not advise petitioner of his constitutional rights, and it is undisputed that no one during the course of the interrogation so advised him.

Petitioner moved both before and during trial to suppress the incriminating statement, but the motions were denied. Petitioner was convicted of murder and he appealed the conviction.

. . . We granted a writ of certiorari. . . . We . . . reverse the judgment of conviction.

In *Massiah v. United States*, 377 U.S. 201, this Court observed that "a Constitution which guarantees a defendant the aid of counsel at . . . trial could surely vouchsafe no less to an indicted defendant under interrogation by the police in a completely extrajudicial proceeding. Anything less . . . might deny a defendant 'effective representation by counsel at the only stage when legal aid and advice would help him.'"

The interrogation here was conducted before petitioner was formally indicted. But in the context of this case, that fact should make no difference. When petitioner requested, and was denied, an opportunity to consult with his lawyer, the investigation had ceased to be a general investigation of "an unsolved crime." Petitioner had become the accused, and the purpose of the interrogation was to "get him" to confess his guilt despite his constitutional right not to do so. At the time of his arrest and throughout the course of the interrogation, the police told petitioner that they had convincing evidence that he had fired the fatal shots. Without informing him of his absolute right to remain silent in the face of this accusation, the police urged him to make a statement. As this Court observed many years ago:

It cannot be doubted that, placed in the position in which the accused was when the statement was made to him that the other suspected person had charged him with a crime, the result was to produce upon his mind the fear that, if he remained silent, it would be considered an admission of guilt, and therefore render certain his being committed for trial as the guilty person, and it cannot be conceived that the converse impression would not also have naturally arisen that, by denying, there was hope of removing the suspicion from himself. Bram v. United States, *168 U.S. 532.*

Petitioner, a layman, was undoubtedly unaware that under Illinois law an admission of "mere" complicity in the murder plot was legally as damaging as an admission of firing of the fatal shots. The "guiding hand of counsel" was essential to advise petitioner of his rights in this delicate situation. This was the "stage when legal aid and advice" were most critical to petitioner. It was a stage surely as critical as was the arraignment in *Hamilton v. Alabama*, 368 U.S. 52, and the preliminary hearing in *White v. Maryland*, 373 U.S. 59. What happened at this interrogation could certainly "affect the whole trial," since rights "may be as irretrievably lost, if not then and there asserted, as they are when an accused represented by counsel waives a right for strategic purposes." Ibid. It would exalt form over substance to make the right to counsel, under these circumstances, depend on whether at the time of the interrogation, the authorities had secured a formal indictment. Petitioner had, for all practical purposes, already been charged with murder. . . .

In *Gideon v. Wainwright*, 372 U.S. 335, we held that every person accused of a crime, whether state or federal, is entitled to a lawyer at trial. The rule sought by the State here, however, would make the trial no more than an appeal from the interrogation; and the "right to use counsel at the formal trial [would be] a very hollow thing [if], for all practical purposes, the conviction is already assured by pretrial examination." "One can imagine a cynical prosecutor saying: 'Let them have the most illustrious counsel, now. They can't escape the noose. There is nothing that counsel can do for them at trial.'"

It is argued that if the right to counsel is afforded prior to indictment, the number of confessions obtained by the police will diminish significantly, because most confessions are obtained during the period between arrest and indictment, and "any lawyer worth his salt will tell the suspect in no uncertain terms to make no statement to police under any circumstances." This argument, of course, cuts two ways. The fact that many confessions are obtained during this period points up its critical nature as a "stage when legal aid and advice" are surely needed. The right to counsel would indeed be hollow if it began at a period when few confessions were obtained. There is necessarily a direct relationship between the importance of a stage to the police in their quest for a confession and the criticalness of that stage to the accused in his need for legal advice. Our Constitution, unlike some others, strikes the balance in favor of the right of the accused to be advised by his lawyer of his privilege against self-incrimination.

We have learned the lesson of history, ancient and modern, that a system of criminal law enforcement which comes to depend on the "confession" will, in the long run, be less reliable and more subject to abuses than a system which depends on extrinsic evidence independently secured through skillful investigation. As Dean Wigmore so wisely said:

[A]ny system of administration which permits the prosecution to trust habitually to compulsory self-disclosure as a source of proof must itself suffer morally thereby. *The inclination develops to rely mainly upon such evidence, and to be satisfied with an incomplete investigation of the other sources. The exercise of the power to extract answers begets a forgetfulness of the just limitations of that power. The simple and peaceful process of questioning breeds a readiness to resort to bullying and to physical force and torture. If there is a right to an answer, there soon seems to be a right to the expected answer,—that is, to a confession of guilt. Thus the legitimate use grows into the unjust abuse; ultimately, the innocent are jeopardized by the encroachments of a bad system. Such seems to have been the course of experience in those legal systems where the privilege was not recognized.*

This Court also has recognized that "history amply shows that confessions have often been extorted to save law enforcement officials the trouble and effort of obtaining valid and independent evidence. . . ."

We have also learned the companion lesson of history that no system of criminal justice can, or should, survive if it comes to depend for its continued effectiveness on the citizens' abdication through unawareness of their constitutional rights. No system worth preserving should have to *fear* that if an accused is permitted to consult with a lawyer, he will become aware of, and exercise, these rights. If the exercise of constitutional rights will thwart the effectiveness of a system of law enforcement, then there is something very wrong with that system.

We hold, therefore, that where, as here, the investigation is no longer a general inquiry into an unsolved crime but has begun to focus on a particular suspect, the suspect has been taken into police custody, the police carry out a process of interrogations that lends itself to eliciting incriminating statements, the suspect has requested and been denied an opportunity to consult with his lawyer, and the police have not effectively warned him of his absolute constitutional right to remain silent, the accused has been denied "the Assistance of Counsel" in violation of the Sixth Amendment to the Constitution as "made obligatory upon the States by the Fourteenth Amendment," and that no statement elicited by the police during the interrogation may be used against him at a criminal trial. . . .

Nothing we have said today affects the powers of the police to investigate "an unsolved crime," by gathering information from witnesses and by other "proper investigative efforts." We hold only that when the process shifts from investigatory to accusatory—when its focus is on the accused and its purpose is to elicit a confession—our adversary system begins to operate, and, under the circumstances here, the accused must be permitted to consult with his lawyer.

The judgment of the Illinois Supreme Court is reversed and the case remanded for proceedings not inconsistent with this opinion. [REVERSED AND REMANDED]

STEWART, JUSTICE, dissenting: Under our system of criminal justice the institution of formal, meaningful judicial proceedings, by way of indictment, information, or arraignment, marks the point at which a criminal investigation has ended and adversary litigative proceedings have commenced. It is at this point that the constitutional guarantees attach which pertain to a criminal trial. Among those guarantees are the right to a speedy trial, the right of confrontation, and the right to trial by jury. Another is the guarantee of the assistance of counsel.

The confession which the Court today holds inadmissible was a voluntary one. It was given during the course of a perfectly legitimate police investigation of an unsolved murder. The Court says that what happened during this investigation "affected" the trial. I had always supposed that the whole purpose of a police investigation of a murder was to "affect" the trial of the murderer, and that it would be only an incompetent, unsuccessful, or corrupt investigation which would not do so. The Court further says that the Illinois police officers did not advise the petitioner of his "constitutional rights" before he confessed to the murder. This Court has never held that the Constitution requires the police to give any "advice" under circumstances such as these.

Supported by no stronger authority than its own rhetoric, the Court today converts a routine police investigation of an unsolved murder into a distorted analogue of a judicial trial. It imports into this investigation constitutional concepts historically applicable only after the onset of formal prosecutorial proceedings. By doing so, I think the Court perverts those precious constitutional guarantees, and frustrates the vital interests of society in preserving the legitimate and proper function of honest and purposeful police investigation.

Like my Brother CLARK, I cannot escape the logic of my Brother WHITE'S conclusions as to the extraordinary implications which emanate from the Court's opinion in this case, and I share their views as to the untold and highly unfortunate impact today's decision may have upon the fair administration of criminal justice. I can only hope we have completely misunderstood what the Court has said.

WHITE, JUSTICE, dissenting (joined by JUSTICE CLARK and JUSTICE STEWART): In *Massiah v. United States*, 377 U.S. 201, the Court held that as of the date of the indictment the prosecution is disentitled to secure admissions from the accused. The Court now moves that date back to the time when the prosecution begins to "focus" on the accused. Although the opinion purports to be limited to the facts of this case, it would be naive to think that the new constitutional right announced will depend upon whether the accused has retained his own counsel, or has asked to consult with counsel in the course of interrogation. At the very least the Court holds that once the accused becomes a suspect and, presumably, is arrested, any admission made to the police thereafter is inadmissible in evidence unless the accused has waived his right to counsel. The decision is thus another major step in the direction of the goal which the Court seemingly has in mind—to bar from evidence all admissions obtained from an individual suspected of crime, whether involuntarily made or not. It does of course put us one step "ahead" of the English judges who have had the good sense to leave the matter a discretionary one with the trial court. I reject this step and the invitation to go farther which the Court has now issued.

By abandoning the voluntary-involuntary test for admissibility of confessions, the Court seems driven by the notion that it is uncivilized law enforcement to use an accused's own admissions against him at his trial. It attempts to find a home for this new and nebulous rule of due process by attaching it to the right to counsel guaranteed in the federal system by the Sixth Amendment and binding upon the States by virtue of the due process guarantee of the Fourteenth Amendment. . . . The right to counsel now not only entitles the accused to counsel's advice and aid in preparing for trial but stands as an impenetrable barrier to any interrogation once the accused has become a suspect. From that very moment apparently his right to counsel attaches, a rule wholly unworkable and impossible to administer unless police cars are equipped with public defenders and undercover agents and police informants have defense counsel at their side. I would not abandon the Court's prior cases defining with some care and analyses the circumstances requiring the presence or aid of counsel and substitute the amorphous and wholly unworkable principle that counsel is constitutionally required whenever he would or could be helpful. . . . These cases dealt with the requirement of counsel at proceedings in which definable rights could be won or lost, not with stages where probative evidence might be obtained. Under this new approach one might just as well argue that a potential defendant is constitutionally entitled to a lawyer before, not after, he commits a crime, since it is then that crucial incriminating evidence is put within the reach of the government by the would be accused. Until now there simply has been no right guaranteed by the Federal Constitution to be free from the use at trial of a voluntary admission made prior to indictment.

It is incongruous to assume that the provision for counsel in the Sixth Amendment was meant to amend or supersede the self-incrimination provision of the Fifth Amendment, which is now applicable to the States. That amendment addresses itself to the very issue of incriminating admissions of an accused and resolves it by proscribing only compelled statements. Neither the Framers, the constitutional language, a century of decisions of this Court nor Professor Wigmore provide an iota of support for the idea that an accused has an absolute constitutional right not to answer even in the absence of compulsion—the constitutional right not to incriminate himself by making voluntary disclosures.

Today's decision cannot be squared with other provisions of the Constitution which, in my view, define the system of criminal justice this Court is empowered to administer. The Fourth Amendment permits upon probable cause even compulsory searches of the suspect and his possessions and the use of the fruits of the search at trial, all in the absence of counsel. The Fifth Amendment and state constitutional provisions authorize, indeed require, inquisitorial grand jury proceedings at which, a potential defendant in the absence of counsel, is shielded against no more than compulsory incrimination. A grand jury witness, who may be a suspect, is interrogated and his answers, at least until today, are admissible in evidence at trial. And these provisions have been thought of as constitutional safeguards to persons suspected of an offense. Furthermore, until now, the Constitution has permitted the accused to be fingerprinted and to be identified in a line-up or in the courtroom itself.

The Court chooses to ignore these matters and to rely on the virtues and morality of a system of criminal law enforcement which does not depend on the "confession." No such judgment is to be found in the Constitution. It might be appropriate for a legislature to provide that a suspect should not be consulted during a criminal investigation; that an accused never be called before a grand jury to answer, even if he wants to, what may well be incriminating questions; and that no person, whether he be a suspect, guilty criminal or innocent bystander should be put to the ordeal of responding to orderly noncompulsory inquiry by the State. But this is not the system our Constitution requires. The only "inquisitions" the Constitution forbids are those which compel incrimination. Escobedo's statements were not compelled and the Court does not hold that they were.

This new American judge's rule, which is to be applied in both federal and state courts, is perhaps thought to be a necessary safeguard against the possibility of extorted confessions. To this extent it reflects a deep seated distrust of law enforcement officers everywhere, unsupported by relevant data or current material based upon our own experience. Obviously law enforcement officers can make mistakes and exceed their authority, as today's decision shows that even judges can do, but I have somewhat more faith than the Court evidently has in the ability and desire of prosecutors and of the power of the appellate courts to discern and correct such violations of the law.

The Court may be concerned with a narrower matter; the unknowing defendant who responds to police questioning because he mistakenly believes that he must and that his admissions will not be used against him. But this worry hardly calls for the broadside the Court has now fired. The failure to inform an accused that he need not answer and that his answers may be used against him is very relevant indeed to whether the disclosures are compelled. Cases in this Court, to say the least, have never placed a premium on ignorance of constitutional rights. If an accused is told he must answer and did not know better, it would be very doubtful that the resulting admissions could be used against him. When the accused has not been informed of his rights at all the Court characteristically and properly looks very closely at the surrounding circumstances. I would continue to do so. But, in this case Danny Escobedo knew full well that he need not answer and knew full well that his lawyer had advised him not to answer.

I do not suggest for a moment that law enforcement will be destroyed by the rule announced today. The need for peace and order is too insistent for that. But it will be crippled and its task made a great deal more difficult, all in my opinion, for unsound, unstated reasons, which can find no home in any of the provisions of the Constitution.

Subsequent to *Escobedo*, many decisions were forthcoming which expanded the Sixth Amendment protection. Perhaps the best known of these cases is *Miranda v. State of Arizona*, 86 S.Ct. 1602 (1966), which resulted in the development of what is known as the "*Miranda*-type warning." This warning, which is now literally on the walls of every police station in the country, tells the accused that he has the right to remain silent, that anything he says can be used against him in court, and that he has the right to the presence of an attorney and to have an attorney appointed before questioning if he cannot afford one. The *Miranda* decision also held that a defendant may waive the right to counsel and to remain silent, provided that the waiver is made voluntarily, knowingly, and intelligently. The *Miranda* case extended the right to counsel to in-custody interrogation. Subsequent cases extended the *Miranda*-type warnings to situations in which the accused was not in custody at a police station but the investigation was centering on the accused and he was being deprived of his freedom of action in any significant way. It has also been extended to lineups, and today a person in a lineup usually has a right to have his attorney present. The protection was held not to be retroactive, but it has been extended to Internal Revenue investigations and to juveniles. However, in one case the Burger Court held that a statement which could not be used because the *Miranda*-type warning had not been given could nevertheless be used for impeachment purposes if the defendant took the witness stand. The Supreme Court has indicated some concern with the law relative to the *Miranda* warning, and new developments in its application are anticipated in the months and years ahead.

10 AMENDMENTS VII, VIII, IX, AND X

VII

In Suits at common law, where the value in controversy shall exceed twenty dollars, the right of trial by jury shall be preserved, and no fact tried by a jury, shall be otherwise reexamined in any Court of the United States, than according to the rules of the common law.

VIII

Excessive bail shall not be required, nor excessive fines imposed, nor cruel and unusual punishments inflicted.

IX

The enumeration in the Constitution of certain rights, shall not be construed to deny or disparage others retained by the people.

X

The powers not delegated to the United States by the Constitution, nor prohibited by it to the States, are reserved to the States respectively, or to the people.

Amendment Seven incorporates the English common law and provides for a trial by jury in civil cases involving more than $20. With the inflation of the last 200 years, this dollar amount should probably be changed, since jury trials in civil controversies cost far more than $20.

The Eighth Amendment also provides protection in the criminal law field. Bail is excessive if greater than necessary to guarantee the presence of the accused in court at the appointed time. The function of bail is not to prohibit freedom prior to trial since the accused is presumed to be innocent. Many states only require a small percentage of the actual bail, such as 10 percent, to be deposited with the court. In 1972, the Eighth Amendment provision on cruel and unusual punishments was used as the basis for declaring the death penalty to be unconstitutional.

The Ninth and Tenth Amendments, which are the last of the so-called Bill of Rights, state simple truisms. They recognize the concept of the Federal government as one of limited powers created by the states and the people. The case which follows discusses the status of a treaty in our legal system as well as the significance of the Tenth Amendment.

State of Missouri v. Holland
252 U.S. 416 (1920)

HOLMES, JUSTICE: This is a bill in equity brought by the State of Missouri to prevent a game warden of the United States from attempting to enforce the Migratory Bird Treaty Act of July 3, 1918, . . . and the regulations made by the Secretary of Agriculture in pursuance of the same. The ground of the bill is that the statute is an unconstitutional interference with the rights reserved to the States by the Tenth Amendment, and that the acts of the defendant done and threatened under that authority invade the sovereign right of the State and contravene its will manifested in statutes. The State also alleges a pecuniary interest, as owner of the wild birds within its borders and otherwise admitted by the Government to be sufficient, but it is enough that the bill is a reasonable and proper means to assert the alleged quasi sovereign rights, of a State. . . . A motion to dismiss was sustained by the District Court on the ground that the act of Congress is constitutional. . . . The State appeals.

On December 8, 1916, a treaty between the United States and Great Britain was proclaimed by the President. It recited that many species of birds in their annual migrations traversed certain parts of the United States and of Canada, that they were of great value as a source of food and in destroying insects injurious to vegetation, but were in danger of extermination through lack of adequate protection. It therefore provided for specified closed seasons and protection in other forms, and agreed that the two powers would take or propose to their law-making bodies the necessary measures for carrying the treaty out. . . . The above mentioned Act of July 3, 1918, entitled an act to give effect to the convention, prohibited the killing, capturing or selling any of the migratory birds included in the terms of the treaty except as permitted by regulations compatible with those terms, to be made by the Secretary of Agriculture. Regulations were proclaimed on July 31, and October 25, 1918. . . . It is unnecessary to go into any details, because, as we have said, the question raised is the general one whether the treaty and statute are void as an interference with the rights reserved to the States.

To answer this question it is not enough to refer to the Tenth Amendment, reserving the powers not delegated to the United States, because by Article II, § 2, the power to make treaties is delegated expressly, and by Article VI treaties made under the authority of the United States, along with the Constitution and laws of the United States made in pursuance thereof, are declared the supreme law of the land. If the treaty is valid there can be no dispute about the validity of the Statute under Article I, § 8, as a necessary and proper means to execute the powers of the Government. The language of the Constitution as to the supremacy of treaties being general, the question before us is narrowed to an inquiry into the ground upon which the present supposed exception is placed.

It is said that a treaty cannot be valid if it infringes the Constitution, that there are limits, therefore, to the treaty-making power, and that one such limit is that what an act of Congress could not do unaided, in derogation of the powers reserved to the States, a treaty cannot do. An earlier act of Congress that attempted by itself and not in pursuance of a treaty to regulate the killing of migratory birds within the States had been held bad in the District Court. . . . Those decisions were supported by arguments that migratory birds were owned by the States in their sovereign capacity for the benefit of their people, and that under cases like *Geer v. Connecticut*, 161 U.S. 519, this control was one that Congress had no power to displace. The same argument is supposed to apply now with equal force.

Whether the two cases cited were decided rightly or not they cannot be accepted as a test of the treaty power. Acts of Congress are the supreme law of the land only when made in pursuance of the Constitution, while treaties are declared to be so when made under the authority of the United States. It is open to question whether the authority of the United States means more than the formal acts prescribed to make the convention. We do not mean to imply that there are no qualifications to the treaty-making power; but they must be ascertained in a different way. It is obvious that there may be matters of the sharpest exigency for the national well being that an act of Congress could not deal with but that a treaty followed by such an act could, and it is not lightly to be assumed that, in matters requiring national action, "a power which must belong to and somewhere reside in every civilized government" is not to be found. *Andrews v. Andrews,* 188 U.S. 14, 33. What was said in that case with regard to the powers of the States applies with equal force to the powers of the nation in cases where the States individually are incompetent to act. We are not yet discussing the particular case before us but only are considering the validity of the test proposed. With regard to that we may add that when we are dealing with words that also are a constituent act, like the Constitution of the United States, we must realize that they have called into life a being the development of which could not have been foreseen completely by the most gifted of its begetters. It was enough for them to realize or to hope that they had created an organism; it has taken a century and has cost their successors much sweat and blood to prove that they created a nation. The case before us must be considered in the light of our whole experience and not merely in that of what was said a hundred years ago. The treaty in question does not contravene any prohibitory words to be found in the Constitution. The only question is whether it is forbidden by some invisible radiation from the general terms of the Tenth Amendment. We must consider what this country has become in deciding what the Amendment has reserved.

The State as we have intimated founds its claim of exclusive authority upon an assertion of title to migratory birds, an assertion that is embodied in statute. No doubt it is true that as between a State and its inhabitants the State may regulate the killing and sale of such birds, but it does not follow that its authority is exclusive of permanent powers. To put the claim of the State upon title is to lean upon a slender reed. Wild birds are not in the possession of anyone; and possession is the beginning of ownership. The whole foundation of the State's rights is the presence within their jurisdiction of birds that yesterday had not arrived, tomorrow may be in another State and in a week a thousand miles away. If we are to be accurate we cannot put the case of the State upon higher ground than that the treaty deals with creatures that for the moment are within the state borders, that it must be carried out by officers of the United States within the same territory, and that but for the treaty the State would be free to regulate this subject itself.

As most of the laws of the United States are carried out within the States and as many of them deal with matters which in the silence of such laws the State might regulate, such general grounds are not enough to support Missouri's claim. Valid treaties of course "are as binding within the territorial limits of the States as they are elsewhere throughout the dominion of the United States." *Baldwin v.*

Franks, 120 U.S. 678, 683. No doubt the great body of private relations usually fall within the control of the State, but a treaty may override its power. We do not have to invoke the later developments of constitutional law for this proposition; it was recognized as early as *Hopkirk v. Bell,* 3 Cranch 454, with regard to statutes of limitation, and even earlier, as to confiscation, in *Ware v. Hylton,* 3 Dall. 199. It was assumed by Chief Justice Marshall with regard to the escheat of land to the State in *Chirac v. Chirac,* 2 Wheat. 259, 275. . . . So as to a limited jurisdiction of foreign consuls within a State. *Wildenhus's* case, 120 U.S. 1. . . . Further illustration seems unnecessary, and it only remains to consider the application of established rules to the present case.

Here a national interest of very nearly the first magnitude is involved. It can be protected only by national action in concert with that of another power. The subject-matter is only transitorily within the State and has no permanent habitat therein. But for the treaty and the statute there soon might be no birds for any powers to deal with. We see nothing in the Constitution that compels the Government to sit by while a food supply is cut off and the protectors of our forests and our crops are destroyed. It is not sufficient to rely upon the States. The reliance is vain, and were it otherwise, the question is whether the United States is forbidden to act. We are of opinion that the treaty and statute must be upheld. *Carey v. South Dakota,* 250 U.S. 118. [DECREE AFFIRMED]

11 AMENDMENTS XI, XII, and XIII

The Eleventh Amendment prohibits suits against states by citizens of other states or of foreign countries. The aforementioned Twelfth Amendment further clarifies the method of operating the electoral college to select the President and Vice President. The Thirteenth Amendment abolished slavery.

12 FOURTEENTH AMENDMENT

The Fourteenth Amendment is quite important since it is generally considered to make all the constitutional guarantees of the Bill of Rights applicable to the states. The Fourteenth Amendment is quite general in its language and to the extent relevant here provides: "No State shall make or enforce any law which shall abridge the privileges or immunities of citizens of the United States; nor shall any State deprive any person of life, liberty or property, without due process of law, nor deny to any person within its jurisdiction the equal protection of the laws."

A   DUE PROCESS

Many of the cases naming Fourteenth Amendment issues do so alleging that state action is a denial of due process. Due process has been used to strike down such varied state action as: (1) school regulations relating to the length of male students' hair and sideburns, (2) forced pleas of guilty in criminal cases, (3) garnishment statutes which held up a defendant's wages without a hearing, and (4) trials held with excessive publicity.

Due process is both procedural and substantive. In due process cases, the issue is whether the law is a fair, reasonable, and appropriate exercise of the police power of the state or an unreasonable, unnecessary, and arbitrary interference with the right of the individual. Procedural due process is frequently an issue in criminal cases but may also be involved in civil matters, as the following case illustrates.

Bell v. Burson
91 S.Ct. 1586 (1971)

BRENNAN, JUSTICE: Georgia's Motor Vehicle Safety Responsibility Act provides that the motor vehicle registration and driver's license of an uninsured motorist involved in an accident shall be suspended unless he posts security to cover the amount of damages claimed by aggrieved parties in reports of the accident. The administrative hearing conducted prior to the suspension excludes consideration of the motorist's fault or liability for the accident. The Georgia Court of Appeals rejected petitioner's contention that the State's statutory scheme, in failing before suspending the licenses to afford him a hearing on the question of his fault or liability, denied him due process in violation of the Fourteenth Amendment: the court held that " 'Fault' or 'innocence' are completely irrelevant factors." . . . We reverse.

Petitioner is a clergyman whose ministry requires him to travel by car to cover three rural Georgian communities. On Sunday afternoon, November 24, 1968, petitioner was involved in an accident when five-year-old Sherry Capes rode her bicycle into the side of his automobile. The child's parents filed an accident report with the Director of the Georgia Department of Public Safety indicating that their daughter had suffered substantial injuries for which they claimed damages of $5,000. Petitioner was thereafter informed by the Director that unless he was covered by a liability insurance policy in effect at the time of the accident he must file a bond or cash security deposit of $5,000 or present a notorized release from liability, plus proof of future financial responsibility, or suffer the suspension of his driver's license and vehicle registration. App., at 9. Petitioner requested an administrative hearing before the Director asserting that he was not liable as the accident was unavoidable, and stating also that he would be severely handicapped in the performance of his ministerial duties by a suspension of his licenses. A hearing was scheduled but the Director informed petitioner that "[t]he only evidence that the Department can accept and consider is: (a) was the petitioner or his vehicle involved in the accident; (b) has petitioner complied with the provisions of the Law as provided; or (c) does petitioner come within any of the exceptions of the Law." At the administrative hearing the Director rejected petitioner's proffer of evidence on liability, ascertained that petitioner was not within any of the statutory exceptions, and gave petitioner 30 days to comply with the security requirements or suffer suspension. Petitioner then exercised his statutory right to an appeal *de novo* in the Superior Court. At that hearing, the court permitted petitioner to present his evidence on liability, and, although the claimants were neither parties nor witnesses, found petitioner free from fault. As a result, the Superior Court ordered "that the petitioner's driver's license not be suspended . . . [until] suit is filed against petitioner for the purpose of recovering damages for the injuries sustained by the child. . . ." This order was reversed by the Georgia Court of Appeals in overruling petitioner's constitutional contention.

If the statute barred the issuance of licenses to all motorists who did not carry liability insurance or who did not post security, the statute would not, under our cases, violate the Fourteenth Amendment. It does not follow, however, that the Amendment also permits the Georgia statutory scheme merely because not all motorists, but rather only motorists involved in accidents, are required to post security under penalty of loss of the licenses. Once licenses are issued, as in petitioner's case, their continued possession may become essential in the pursuit of a livelihood. Suspension of issued licenses thus involves state action that adjudicates important interests of the licensees. In such cases the licenses are not to be taken away without that procedural due process required by the Fourteenth Amendment. This is but an application of the general proposition that relevant constitutional restraints limit state power to terminate an entitlement whether the entitlement is denominated a "right" or a "privilege."

We turn then to the nature of the procedural due process which must be afforded the licensee on the question of his fault or liability for the accident. A procedural rule that may satisfy due process in one context may not necessarily satisfy procedural due process in every case. Thus, procedures adequate to determine a welfare claim may not suffice to try a felony charge. Clearly, however, the inquiry into fault or liability requisite to afford the licensee due process need not take the form of a full adjudication of the question of liability. That adjudication can only be made in litigation between the parties involved in the accident. Since the only purpose of the provisions before us is to obtain security from which to pay any judgments against the licensee resulting from the accident, we hold that procedural due process will be satisfied by an inquiry limited to the determination whether there is a reasonable possibility of judgments in the amounts claimed being rendered against the licensee.

The State argues that the licensee's interest in avoiding the suspension of his licenses is outweighed by countervailing governmental interests and therefore that this procedural due process need not be afforded him. We disagree. In cases where there is no reasonable possibility of a judgment being rendered against a licensee, Georgia's interest in protecting a claimant from the possibility of an unrecoverable judgment is not, within the context of the State's fault-oriented scheme, a justification for denying the process due its citizens. Nor is additional expense occasioned by the expanded hearing sufficient to withstand the constitutional requirement. "'While the problem of additional expense must be kept in mind, it does not justify denying a hearing meeting the ordinary standards of due process.'"

The main thrust of Georgia's argument is that it need not provide a hearing on liability because fault and liability are irrelevant to the statutory scheme. We may assume that were this so, the prior administrative hearing presently provided by the State would be "appropriate to the nature of the case." But "[i]n reviewing state action in this area . . . we look to substance, not to bare form, to determine whether constitutional minimums have been honored." And looking to the operation of the State's statutory scheme, it is clear that liability, in the sense of an ultimate judicial determination of responsibility, plays a crucial role in the Safety Responsibility Act. If prior to suspension there is a release from liability executed by the injured party, no suspension is worked by the Act. The same is true if prior to suspension there is an adjudication of nonliability. Even after suspension has been declared, a release from liability or an adjudication of nonliability will lift the suspension. Moreover, other of the Act's exceptions are developed around liability related concepts. Thus, we are not dealing here with a no-fault scheme. Since the statutory scheme makes liability an important factor in the State's determination to deprive an individual of his licenses, the State may not, consistently with due process, eliminate consideration of that factor in its prior hearing.

The hearing required by the Due Process Clause must be "meaningful," and "appropriate to the nature of the case." It is a proposition which hardly seems to need explication that a hearing which excludes consideration of an element essential to the decision whether licenses of the nature here involved shall be suspended does not meet this standard.

Finally, we reject Georgia's argument that if it must afford the licensee an inquiry into the question of liability that determination, unlike the determination of the matters presently considered at the administrative hearing, need not be made prior to the suspension of the licenses. While "many controversies have raged about . . . the Due Process Clause," it is fundamental that except in emergency situations (and this is not one) due process requires that when a State seeks to terminate an interest such as that here involved, it must afford "notice and opportunity for hearing appropriate to the nature of the case" *before* the termination becomes effective.

We hold, then, that under Georgia's present statutory scheme, before the State may deprive petitioner of his driver's license and vehicle registration it must provide a forum for the determination of the question whether there is a reasonable possibility of a judgment being rendered against him as a result of the accident. We deem it inappropriate in this case to do more than lay down this requirement. The alternative methods of compliance are several. Georgia may decide merely to include consideration of the question at the administrative hearing now provided, or it may elect to postpone such a consideration to the *de novo* judicial proceedings in the Superior Court. Georgia may decide to withhold suspension until adjudication of an action for damages brought by the injured party. Indeed, Georgia may elect to abandon its present scheme completely and pursue one of the various alternatives in force in other States. Finally, Georgia may reject all of the above and devise an entirely new regulatory scheme. The area of choice is wide: we hold only that the failure of the present Georgia scheme to afford the petitioner a prior hearing on liability of the nature we have defined denied him procedural due process in violation of the Fourteenth Amendment.

The judgment is reversed and the case is remanded for further proceedings not inconsistent with this opinion. [REVERSED AND REMANDED]

B   EQUAL PROTECTION OF THE LAWS

A major use of the equal protection clause has been to require the integration of public schools. (See the discussion on page 171 of Chapter 6.) In recent years, the equal protection clause has been widely used in several other areas of the law to bring about substantial change. As a matter of comparison, the equal protection clause in recent years has played a more significant role as an instrument of social change than the due process clause.

The broad range of subjects which come under the purview of the equal protection clause, in addition to segregation cases of all kinds involving schools and public facilities, includes: (1) questions as to the apportionment of legislative bodies, (2) racial segregation in the sale and rental of real estate and in the performance of the function of broker, (3) laws barring interracial marriages, (4) the makeup of juries, (5) voting requirements, (6) welfare residency requirements, (7) citizenship of aliens, and (8) the use of property taxes as the means of financing public schools. The equal protection clause is the means to the end, or goal, of equality of opportunity. As such, it may be utilized by anyone claiming unequal treatment in any case. The following case illustrates the application of the equal protection clause.

Evans v. Newton
382 U.S. 296 (1966)

DOUGLAS, JUSTICE: In 1911 United States Senator Augustus O. Bacon executed a will that devised to the Mayor and Council of the City of Macon, Georgia, a tract of land which, after the death of the Senator's wife and daughters, was to be used as "a park and pleasure ground" for white people only, the Senator stating in the will that while he had only the kindest feeling for the Negroes he was of the opinion that "in their social relations the two races (white and negro) should be forever separate." The will provided that the park should be under the control of a Board of Managers of seven persons, all of whom were to be white. The city kept the park segregated for some years but in time let Negroes use it, taking the position that the park was a public facility which it could not constitutionally manage and maintain on a segregated basis.

Thereupon, individual members of the Board of Managers of the park brought this suit in the state court against the City of Macon and the trustees of certain residuary beneficiaries of Senator Bacon's estate, asking that the city be removed as trustee and that the court appoint new trustees, to whom title to the park would be transferred. The city answered, alleging it could not legally enforce racial segregation in the park. The other defendants admitted the allegation and requested that the city be removed as trustee.

Several Negro citizens of Macon intervened, alleging that the racial limitation was contrary to the laws and public policy of the United States, and asking that the court refuse to appoint private trustees. Thereafter the city resigned as trustee and amended its answer accordingly. Moreover, other heirs of Senator Bacon intervened and they and the defendants other than the city asked for reversion of the trust property to the Bacon estate in the event that the prayer of the petition were denied.

The Georgia court accepted the resignation of the city as trustee and appointed three individuals as new trustees, finding it unnecessary to pass on the other claims of the heirs. On appeal by the Negro intervenors, the Supreme Court of Georgia affirmed, holding that Senator Bacon had the right to give and bequeath his property to a limited class, that charitable trusts are subject to supervision of a court of equity, and that the power to appoint new trustees so that the purpose of the trust would not fail was clear. The case is here on a writ of certiorari.

There are two complementary principles to be reconciled in this case. One is the right of the individual to pick his own associates so as to express his preferences and dislikes, and to fashion his private life by joining such clubs and groups as he chooses. The other is the constitutional ban in the Equal Protection Clause of the Fourteenth Amendment against state-sponsored racial inequality, which of course bars a city from acting as trustee under a private will that serves the racial segregation cause. A private golf club, however, restricted to either Negro or white membership is one expression of freedom of association. But a municipal golf course that serves only one race is state activity indicating a preference on a matter as to which the State must be neutral. What is "private" action and what is "state" action is not always easy to determine. Conduct that is formally "private" may become so entwined with governmental policies or so impregnated with a governmental character as to become subject to the constitutional limitations placed upon state action. The action of a city in serving as trustee of property under a private will serving the segregated cause is an obvious example. A town may be privately owned and managed, but that does not necessarily allow the company to treat it as if it were wholly in the private sector. Thus we held in *Marsh v. Alabama*, 326 U.S. 501, that the exercise of constitutionally protected rights on the public streets of a company town could not be denied by the owner. A State is not justified, we said, in "permitting a corporation to govern a community of citizens so as to restrict their fundamental liberties. . . ." We have also held that where a State delegates an aspect of the elective process to private groups, they become subject to the same restraints as the State. That is to say, when private individuals or groups are endowed by the State with powers or functions governmental in nature, they become agencies or instrumentalities of the State and subject to its constitutional limitations.

Yet generalizations do not decide concrete cases. Only by sifting can we determine whether the reach of the Fourteenth Amendment extends to a particular case. The range of government activities is broad and varied, and the fact that government has engaged in a particular activity does not necessarily mean that an individual entrepreneur or manager of the same kind of undertaking suffers the same constitutional inhibitions. While a State may not segregate public schools so as to exclude one or more religious groups, those sects may maintain their own parochial educational systems.

If a testator wanted to leave a school or center for the use of one race only and in no way implicated the State in the supervision, control, or management of that facility, we assume *arguendo* that no constitutional difficulty would be encountered.

This park, however, is in a different posture. For years it was an integral part of the City of Macon's activities. From the pleadings we assume it was swept, manicured, watered, patrolled, and maintained by the city as a public facility for whites only, as well as granted tax exemption under Ga. Code Ann. § 92-201. The momentum it acquired as a public facility is certainly not dissipated *ipso facto* by the appointment of "private" trustees. So far as this record shows, there has been no change in municipal maintenance and concern over this facility. Whether these public characteristics will in time be dissipated is wholly conjectural. If the municipality remains entwined in the management or control of the park, it remains subject to the restraints of the Fourteenth Amendment just as the private utility in *Public Utils. Comm'n v. Pollak*, 343 U.S. 451, remained subject to the Fifth Amendment because of the surveillance which federal agencies had over its affairs. We only hold that where the tradition of municipal control had become firmly established, we cannot take judicial notice that the mere substitution of trustees instantly transferred this park from the public to the private sector.

This conclusion is buttressed by the nature of the service rendered the community by a park. The service rendered even by a private park of this character is municipal in nature. It is open to every white person, there being no selective element other than race. Golf clubs, social centers, luncheon clubs, schools such as Tuskegee was at least in origin, and other like organizations in the private sector are often racially oriented. A park on the other hand, is more like a fire department or police department that traditionally serves the community. Mass recreation through the use of parks is plainly in the public domain; . . . and state courts that aid private parties to perform that public function on a segregated basis implicate the State in conduct proscribed by the Fourteenth Amendment. Like the streets of the company town in *Marsh v. Alabama, supra,* the elective process of *Terry v. Adams, supra,* and the transit system of *Public Utils. Comm'n v. Pollak, supra,* the predominant character and purpose of this park is municipal.

Under the circumstances of this case, we cannot but conclude that the public character of this park requires that it be treated as a public institution subject to the command of the Fourteenth Amendment, regardless of who now has title under state law. We may fairly assume that had the Georgia courts been of the view that even in private hands the park may not be operated for the public on a segregated basis, the resignation would not have been approved and private trustees appointed. We put the matter that way because on this record we cannot say that the transfer of title *per se* disentangled the park from segregation under the municipal regime that long controlled it.

Since the judgment below gives effect to that purpose, it must be and is Reversed. [REVERSED]

C   THE APPLICATION OF THE BILL OF RIGHTS TO STATES

The two cases which follow illustrate the pick-up aspect of the Fourteenth Amendment.

NAACP v. Button
371 U.S. 415 (1963)

The National Association for the Advancement of Colored People brought suit against the Attorney General of Virginia and others for a declaration that a Virginia statute calling for the licensing and regulating of attorneys was unconstitutional. The statute prohibited any arrangement by which prospective litigants were advised to seek assistance of particular attorneys and made it a crime for a person to advise another that his legal rights have been infringed upon. It was also a crime to refer a person to a particular attorney or group of attorneys such as the legal staff of the Virginia conference of NAACP for assistance. The statute allegedly violated freedoms of the First Amendment protected against state action by the Fourteenth Amendment.

The lower courts held for the State, affirming its right to regulate the legal profession and to prevent solicitation of legal business.

BRENNAN, JUSTICE: We reverse the judgment of the Virginia Supreme Court of Appeals. We hold that the activities of the NAACP, its affiliates and legal staff shown on this record are modes of expression and association protected by the First and Fourteenth Amendments which Virginia may not prohibit, under its power to regulate the legal profession, as improper solicitation of legal business violative of Chapter 33 and the Canons of Professional Ethics.

We meet at the outset the contention that "solicitation" is wholly outside the area of freedoms protected by the First Amendment. To this contention there are two answers. The first is that a State cannot foreclose the exercise of constitutional rights by mere labels. The second is that abstract discussion is not the only species of communication which the Constitution protects; the First Amendment also protects vigorous advocacy, certainly of lawful ends, against governmental intrusion. In the context of NAACP objectives, litigation is not a technique of resolving private differences; it is a means for achieving the lawful objectives of equality of treatment by all government, federal, state and local, for the members of the Negro community in this country. It is thus a form of political expression. Groups which find themselves unable to achieve their objectives through the ballot frequently turn to the courts. Just as it was true of the opponents of New

Deal legislation during the 1930's, for example, no less is it true of the Negro minority today. And under the conditions of modern government, litigation may well be the sole practicable avenue open to a minority to petition for redress of grievances.

We need not, in order to find constitutional protection for the kind of cooperative, organizational activity disclosed by this record, whereby Negroes seek through lawful means to achieve legitimate political ends, subsume such activity under a narrow, literal conception of freedom of speech, petition or assembly. For there is no longer any doubt that the First and Fourteenth Amendments protect certain forms of orderly group activity. Thus we have affirmed the right "to engage in association for the advancement of beliefs and ideas." We have deemed privileged, under certain circumstances, the efforts of a union official to organize workers. We have said that the Sherman Act does not apply to certain concerted activities of railroads "at least insofar as those activities comprised mere solicitation of governmental action with respect to the passage and enforcement of laws" because "such a construction of the Sherman Act would raise important constitutional questions," specifically, First Amendment questions. And we have refused to countenance compelled disclosure of a person's political associations in language closely applicable to the instant case:

Our form of government is built on the premise that every citizen shall have the right to engage in political expression and association. This right was enshrined in the First Amendment of the Bill of Rights. Exercise of these basic freedoms in America has traditionally been through the media of political associations. Any interference with the freedom of a party is simultaneously an interference with the freedom of its adherents. All political ideas cannot and should not be channeled into the programs of our two major parties. History has amply proved the virtue of political activity by minority, dissident groups. . . .

The NAACP is not a conventional political party; but the litigation it assists, while serving to vindicate the legal rights of members of the American Negro community, at the same time and perhaps more importantly, makes possible the distinctive contribution of a minority group to the ideas and beliefs of our society. For such a group, association for litigation may be the most effective form of political association. . . .

We conclude that under Chapter 33, as authoritatively construed by the Supreme Court of Appeals, a person who advises another that his legal rights have been infringed and refers him to a particular attorney or group of attorneys (for example, to the Virginia Conference's legal staff) for the assistance has committed a crime, as has the attorney who knowingly renders assistance under such circumstances. There thus inheres in the statute the gravest danger of smothering all discussion looking to the eventual institution of litigation on behalf of the rights of members of an unpopular minority.

It is apparent, therefore, that Chapter 33 as construed limits First Amendment freedoms. As this Court said in *Thomas v. Collins*, 323 U.S. 516, 537, " 'Free trade in ideas' means free trade in the opportunity to persuade to action, not merely to describe facts." Thomas was convicted for delivering a speech in connection with an impending union election under National Labor Relations Board auspices, without having first registered as a "labor organizer." He urged workers to exercise their rights under the National Labor Relations Act and join the union he represented. This Court held that the registration requirement as applied to his activities was constitutionally invalid. In the instant case, members of the NAACP urged Negroes aggrieved by the allegedly unconstitutional segregation of public schools in Virginia to exercise their legal rights and to retain members of the Association's legal staff. Like Thomas, the Association and its members were advocating lawful means of vindicating legal rights.

We hold that Chapter 33 as construed violates the Fourteenth Amendment by unduly inhibiting protected freedoms of expression and association. . . . However, the State's attempt to equate the activities of the NAACP and its lawyers with common-law barratry, maintenance and champerty, and to outlaw them accordingly, cannot obscure the serious encroachment worked by Chapter 33 upon protected freedoms of expression. The decisions of this Court have consistently held that only a compelling state interest in the regulation of a subject within the State's constitutional power to regulate can justify limiting First Amendment freedoms. Thus it is no answer to the constitutional claims asserted by petitioners to say, as the Virginia Supreme Court of Appeals has said, that the purpose of these regulations was merely to insure high professional standards and not to curtail free expression. For a State may not, under the guise of prohibiting professional misconduct, ignore constitutional rights.

However valid may be Virginia's interest in regulating the traditionally illegal practices of barratry, maintenance and champerty, that interest does not justify the prohibition of the NAACP activities disclosed by this record. Malicious intent was of the essence of the common-law offenses of fomenting or stirring up litigation. And whatever may be or may have been true of suits against government in other countries, the exercise in our own, as in this case, of First Amendment rights to enforce constitutional rights through litigation, as a matter of law, cannot be deemed malicious. Even more modern, subtler regulations of unprofessional conduct or interference with professional relations, not involving malice, would not touch the activities at bar; regulations which reflect hostility to stirring up litigation have been aimed chiefly at those who urge recourse to the courts for private gain, serving no public interest. Hostility still exists to stirring up private litigation where it promotes the use of legal machinery to oppress: as, for example, to sow discord in a family; to expose infirmities in land titles, as by hunting up claims of adverse possession; to harass large companies through a multiplicity of small claims; or to oppress debtors as by seeking out unsatisfied judgments. For a member of the bar to participate, directly or through intermediaries, in such misuses of the legal process is conduct traditionally condemned as injurious to the public. And beyond this, for a lawyer to attempt to reap gain by urging another to engage in private litigation has also been condemned; that seems to be the import of Canon 28, which the Virginia Supreme Court of Appeals had adopted as one of its Rules.

Objection to the intervention of a lay intermediary, who may control litigation or otherwise interfere with the rendering of legal services in a confidential relationship, also derives from the element of pecuniary gain. Fearful of dangers thought to arise from that element, the courts of several States have sustained regulations aimed at these activities. We intimate no view one way or the other as to the merits of those decisions with respect to the particular arrangements against which they are directed. It is enough that the superficial resemblance in form between those arrangements and that at bar cannot obscure the vital fact that here the entire arrangement employs constitutionally privileged means of expression to secure constitutionally guaranteed civil rights. There has been no showing of a serious danger here of professionally reprehensible conflicts of interest which rules against solicitation frequently seek to prevent. This is so partly because no monetary stakes are involved, and so there is no danger that the attorney will desert or subvert the paramount interests of his client to enrich himself or an outside sponsor. And the aims and interests of NAACP have not been shown to conflict with those of its members and nonmember Negro Litigants; compare *NAACP v. Alabama ex rel. Patterson*, 357 U.S. 449, 459, where we said:

[The NAACP] and its members are in every practical sense identical. The Association, which provides in its constitution that "[a]ny person who is in accordance with (its) principles and policies . . ." may become a member, is but the medium through which its individual members seek to make more effective the expression of their own views.

Resort to the courts to seek vindication of constitutional rights is a different matter from the oppressive, malicious, or avaricious use of the legal process for purely private gain. Lawsuits attacking racial discrimination, at least in Virginia, are neither very profitable nor very popular. They are not an object of general competition among Virginia lawyers; the problem is rather one of an apparent dearth of lawyers who are willing to undertake such litigation. There has been neither claim nor proof that any assisted Negro litigants have desired, but have been prevented from retaining, the services of other counsel. We realize that an NAACP lawyer must derive personal satisfaction from participation in litigation on behalf of Negro rights, else he would hardly be inclined to participate at the risk of financial sacrifice. But this would not seem to be the kind of interest or motive which induces criminal conduct.

We conclude that although the petitioner has amply shown that its activities fall within the First Amendment's protections, the State has failed to advance any substantial regulatory interest, in the form of substantive evils flowing from petitioner's activities, which can justify the broad prohibitions which it has imposed. Nothing that this record shows as to the nature and purpose of NAACP activities permits an inference of any injurious intervention in or control of litigation which would constitutionally authorize the application of Chapter 33 to those activities. . . . [REVERSED]

Malloy v. Hogan
378 U.S. 1 (1964)

BRENNAN, JUSTICE: In this case we are asked to reconsider prior decisions holding that the privilege against self-incrimination is not safeguarded against state action by the Fourteenth Amendment.

The petitioner was arrested during a gambling raid in 1959 by Hartford, Connecticut, police. He pleaded guilty to the crime of pool selling, a misdemeanor, and was sentenced to one year in jail and fined $500. The sentence was ordered to be suspended after 90 days, at which time he was to be placed on probation for two years. About 16 months after his guilty plea, petitioner was ordered to testify before a referee appointed by the Superior Court of Hartford County to conduct an inquiry into alleged gambling and other criminal activities in the county. The petitioner was asked a number of questions related to events surrounding his arrest and conviction. He refused to answer any question "on the grounds it may tend to incriminate me." The Superior Court adjudged him in contempt, and committed him to prison until he was willing to answer the questions. Petitioner's application for a writ of habeas corpus was denied by the Superior Court, and the Connecticut Supreme Court of Errors affirmed. The latter court held that the Fifth Amendment's privilege against self-incrimination was not available to a witness in a state proceeding, that the Fourteenth Amendment extended no privilege to him, and that the petitioner had not properly invoked the privilege available under the Connecticut Constitution. We granted certiorari. We reverse. We hold that the Fourteenth Amendment guaranteed the petitioner the protection of the Fifth Amendment's privilege against self-incrimination, and that under the applicable federal standard, the Connecticut Supreme Court of Errors erred in holding that the privilege was not properly invoked.

The extent to which the Fourteenth Amendment prevents state invasion of rights enumerated in the first eight Amendments has been considered in numerous cases in this Court since the Amendment's adoption in 1868. . . .

Gitlow v. New York, 268 U.S. 652, initiated a series of decisions which today hold immune from state invasion every First Amendment protection for the cherished rights of mind and spirit—the freedoms of speech, press, religion, assembly, association, and petition for redress of grievances. . . .

In 1961, . . . it was taken as settled that ". . . the Fourth Amendment's right of privacy has been declared enforceable against the States through the Due Process Clause of the Fourteenth. . . . [O]nly last Term . . . it was held that provision of counsel in all criminal cases was "a fundamental right, essential to a fair trial," and thus was made obligatory on the States by the Fourteenth Amendment.

We hold today that the Fifth Amendment's exception from compulsory self-incrimination is also protected by the Fourteenth Amendment against abridgment by the States. We discuss first the decisions which forbid the use of coerced confessions in state criminal prosecutions.

Brown v. Mississippi, 297 U.S. 278, was the first case in which the Court held that the Due Process Clause prohibited the States from using the accused's coerced confessions against him. . . . The admissibility of a confession in a state criminal prosecution is tested by the same standard applied in federal prosecutions. . . .

The marked shift to the federal standard in state cases began with *Lisenba v. California,* 314 U.S. 219, where the Court spoke of the accused's "free choice to admit, to deny, or to refuse to answer." The shift reflects recognition that the American system of criminal prosecution is accusatorial, not inquisitorial, and that the Fifth Amendment privilege is its essential mainstay. Governments, state and federal, are thus constitutionally compelled to establish guilt by evidence independently and freely secured, and may not by coercion prove a charge against an accused out of his own mouth. Since the Fourteenth Amendment prohibits the States from inducing a person to confess through "sympathy falsely aroused," or other like inducement far short of "compulsion by torture," it follows *a fortiori* that it also forbids the States to resort to imprisonment, as here, to compel him to answer questions that might incriminate him. The Fourteenth Amendment secures against state invasion the same privilege that the Fifth Amendment guarantees against federal infringement—the right of a person to remain silent unless he chooses to speak in the unfettered exercise of his own will, and to suffer no penalty for such silence. . . .

This conclusion is fortified by our recent decision in *Mapp v. Ohio.* . . . We said in Mapp:

We find that, as to the Federal Government the Fourth and Fifth Amendments and, as to the States, the freedom from unconscionable invasions of privacy and the freedom from convictions based upon coerced confessions do enjoy an "intimate relation" in their perpetuation of "principles of humanity and civil liberty [secured] . . . only after years of struggle." . . . The philosophy of each Amendment and of each freedom is complementary to, although not dependent upon, that of the other in its sphere of influence—the very least that together they assure in either sphere is that no man is to be convicted on unconstitutional evidence. . . .

[REVERSED]

13 AMENDMENTS XV THROUGH XXVI

The remaining amendments deal with a variety of subjects. The Fifteenth Amendment guarantees the right to vote to all citizens. The Sixteenth Amendment authorized the income tax. The Seventeenth is concerned with the election and selection of United States Senators.

The Eighteenth Amendment, on prohibition, was repealed by the Twenty-first Amendment. The Nineteenth Amendment gave women the right to vote, while the Twentieth Amendment moved the inauguration of the President to January 20 and specified the time for beginning the terms of members of Congress. Amendment Twenty-two limits a President to two terms. Amendment Twenty-three provides for the method of governing the District of Columbia. Amendment Twenty-four prohibits the poll tax as a condition for voting. The Twenty-fifth governs the succession to the Presidency, and the Twenty-sixth gave eighteen-year-olds the right to vote. It is apparent that most of the amendments since the Bill of Rights (with the exception of the Thirteenth and Fourteenth, which followed the Civil War) have been concerned with the election of governmental officials and with the right to vote.

There are several proposed constitutional amendments pending. Among those given a substantial chance of adoption is the amendment that would guarantee equal rights for women. A constitutional amendment on the issue of school busing is also a realistic possibility.

REVIEW QUESTIONS—CHAPTER 3

1 Define the following terms introduced in this chapter: separation of powers; full faith and credit; symbolic speech; illegal search and seizure; self-incrimination; grand jury; double jeopardy; eminent domain; due process of law; subpoena; *Miranda*-type warning; equal protection of the laws.
2 What is the role of constitutions in our judicial system?
3 What is the status of a treaty in our judicial system?
4 List the five freedoms protected by the First Amendment. To what extent have these been expanded? Explain.
5 Explain dual federalism.
6 Discuss the problems faced by courts in obscenity cases.
7 To what extent are the First Amendment freedoms limited? Explain.
8 What function is served by the grand jury?
9 If a student is disciplined by his college for committing a felony for which he has been punished by civil authority, is this a violation of the Fifth Amendment? Explain.
10 Name three acts that may be required of an individual without violating his rights against compulsory self-incrimination.
11 When does the Sixth Amendment's right to have the assistance of counsel begin?
12 What must be contained in the *Miranda*-type warning?
13 Name five types of cases in which the equal protection clause has been used to protect an individual or to change the effect of a law.

Chapter Four

Legislation

1   INTRODUCTION

Legislation, in the technical sense, is a process by which general rules for the course of human conduct are consciously enacted for the general population by government. Legislation differs from law arising from an adjudicated case in that the latter is specific in application, is retroactive in effect, and involves secondary rights while the former is general in application, is prospective in effect, and involves primary rights. The doctrine of separation of powers indicates that the function of making laws, or legislation, is the province of the legislature. This function must be distinguished from the administrative function of the executive branch and the judicial function, but, as we shall see, the borders of these branches of government are not capable of exact location and each branch performs some of the functions of the other. While some persons would deny that courts or the executive legislate, this denial is without merit. This chapter uses the word "legislate" in the technical sense and not in its broader aspect which would include the creation of all laws.

When a problem of society has been recognized to exist, the legislative process involves the answering of the following questions by the governmental body entrusted with the legislative function: (1) Does the problem in question exist because of defects or voids in the system of control of human conduct now in use? (2) Could and would the problem be solved by legislation? (3) Should the problem be solved by this legislative body, or should it be solved by some other social force or legislative body? (4) What law should be adopted, that is, what is the best solution to the problem? (5) How should the selected law or rule of conduct be enforced? Each of these questions has been answered whenever legislation is adopted, the answers being controlled in part by social forces operating within the legislative body, and in part by social forces operating upon it from without. In addition, the answers involve value judgments which are influenced to a great extent by the background, experience, and conscious or subconscious motivations of the legislator.

Issues which are basic to our political system are raised by the foregoing questions. In determining whether legislation should be adopted or not, the argument often is reduced to one of "individualism" versus "paternalism" in government, with one side arguing for less governmental activity and the other for an expanding role of government. Question 3 requires a decision whether the best solution to the problem exists at the local, state, or Federal level. The concept of Federal revenue sharing raises many arguments on the foregoing points. Question 5 involves a selection from the variety of sanctions available to a legislative body, such as declaring certain conduct to be criminal for which fine or imprisonment is imposed; allowing civil remedies such as injunctions or causes of action for dollar damages; or simply granting or denying licenses to applicants.

Each state in its constitution and by statute has prescribed the procedural steps to be followed in enacting legislation. These usually require a number of readings of the bill and its formal presentation to the governor after its passage. Occasionally, in a controversy concerning the validity of a statute, a party challenging the statute may do so on the basis of the procedures followed by the legislative body. For example, several state constitutions provide that statutes are effective July 1, *after* passage. Legislative bodies in those states frequently "stop the clock" at midnight on June 30, ignoring the actual date, with the purpose of having their closing actions take effect immediately instead of being delayed for one year. In recent years, courts in some states have tended to allow the effective date of such statutes to be challenged.

The case which follows involves several aspects of legislative procedure. While the exact procedural rules will vary from state to state, this case does illustrate the types of legal problems which might arise concerning such rules. Note that the requirement of approval by the governor is a part of the concept of separation of powers. Most constitutions require a two-thirds majority to pass a statute over a veto. In many states, a veto may be of the whole statute or of only a part, called an "item veto." Most states which allow item vetoes require only a majority to override the veto.

Richards Furniture Corp. v. Board of County Commissioners
196 A.2d 621 (Md. 1964)

The appellant, which operated a furniture business as a part of a shopping market, challenged the validity of a Sunday closing law. It raised numerous objections to the procedures followed by the state legislature in enacting the law.

PRESCOTT, JUSTICE: . . . [A]ppellant . . . asserts that the Maryland Constitution prohibits a special session of the General Assembly from enacting "a non-emergency local bill," citing Article II, Section 16, and Article III, Sections 14, 15, and 27, thereof. It admits finding no Maryland decision to this effect and that the Constitution does not explicitly state any such prohibition, but argues the above sections implicitly do so. We do not find it necessary to set forth the sections in detail. The Maryland Constitution is not a grant of powers to the General Assembly, but a statement of limitations on its otherwise plenary powers. . . .

A careful reading of the Constitution reveals that the only constitutional limitations on extraordinary, or special, sessions are: (1) that the session be convened by a proclamation of the Governor . . . ; (2) the session shall last no longer than thirty days; and (3) no additional compensation, except mileage and other allowances provided by law, shall be allowed members for such sessions. Section 15 provides that the General Assembly, once properly convened, shall be the sole judge of how long "the public interest may require" (within certain limitations) it to continue in session. There can be little doubt that, at a special session, the public interest requires the Legislature to remain in session, within the thirty-day limit, as long as any necessary and proper legislation is under consideration and before it. . . .

We find no express nor implied provision in the Constitution preventing the passage of a "non-emergency local bill" at a special session. It is generally held that in the absence of constitutional limitation, the legislative power of a Legislature, when convened in extraordinary session, is as broad as its powers in its regular sessions. . . .

We, therefore, hold that the General Assembly was not prohibited from passing the Act because it was a non-emergency local bill. . . .

The appellant next attacks the Act on the ground that it was not within the Governor's proclamation. The Constitution of Maryland grants no authority to the Governor to limit, by his proclamation, the powers of the Legislature. In the absence of such a restrictive provision, the authorities hold, . . . that the powers of the Legislature at a special session are as broad as at its general ones. . . .

Appellant also claims it "was denied its constitutional rights because of a lack of notice of the intended legislation." . . . Unless the Constitution so provides, due process does not require that notice and hearing be provided in order to validate legislation. There is no provision for such notice in the Maryland Constitution. We may note, however, that "notice" is inherent in the legislative process in this State. Under our democratic form of government, the Senators and Delegates are elected as representatives of the people. Ample safeguards in the Constitution provide that these representatives shall have notice of proposed legislation: each bill must be read on three different days in each House (unless a two-thirds vote authorizes otherwise), Article III, Section 27; no bill shall be read a third time unless actually engrossed or printed, *Ibid.;* and a journal of the proceedings in both Houses must be made and published, Article III, Section 22. We find no merit in this contention. . . .

[A]ppellant contends that "the Governor vetoed (the Act) by reason of his failure to sign it within six days after presentation to him," and "a litigant . . . may inquire behind the forms of authentication (of a bill) and the General Assembly actions. . . ." The special session ended on March 9, 1962. On the same day, the Chief Clerk of the House of Delegates delivered the Bill to the Secretary of State, who, on March 12, 1962, handed it, together with other bills, to the Governor. The Governor acknowledged their receipt by letter, and, in accordance with normal procedure, forwarded them to the Attorney General for review as to form and legal sufficiency. The authenticated copy of the Bill states in a memorandum signed by the Chief Clerk of the House that it was sealed and presented to the Governor on March 23, 1962; and it was signed by him on the same day.

Appellant argues that the authentication on the Bill is not conclusive, it has a right to go behind the same, and the Governor's letter and the testimony of the Chief Clerk "imply" that the Bill was "presented" on March 12, 1962. It is true that in a proper case the courts may inquire beyond the forms of authentication on a bill to determine whether it has been constitutionally enacted. However, an act which has been duly authenticated and published as law, as the Bill in the instant case has, bears a strong presumption that all constitutional provisions have been complied with, and it has been validly enacted into law; and this presumption continues to exist until the contrary is clearly made to appear. And a statute which has been duly authenticated is not to be impeached by parol evidence alone.

The appellant's effort to impeach the certification by the Chief Clerk that the Bill was presented to the Governor on March 23, 1962, falls far short of what is necessary to accomplish such an impeachment; and demonstrates, we think, a failure to comprehend the true meaning of the "presentation" of a bill to the Governor as provided for by Article 2, Section 17, of the Constitution and Code (1957), Article 41, Section 45. Such a presentation to the Governor for his signature is a formal act and anticipates that the bill will be sealed with the great seal and actually and formally "presented" to the Governor for his signature by the Secretary of the Senate or Chief Clerk of the House, who in the presence of the Governor, shall make a memorandum thereon in writing of the day and hour of its presentation, and sign the same. The mere informal receipt by the Governor's office of a bill for other purposes is not a requirement of law, and carries with it no legal significance such as to require action by the Governor in any specified time. If this were not true, many practical difficulties would be encountered on such occasions as when several hundred bills passed by the General Assembly are delivered to the Governor before he has had time carefully to consider them and to have the Attorney General pass upon their validity. We hold that the Bill was actually presented to the Governor on March 23, 1962, and that this was a reasonable and legal time after passage of the Bill for its presentation. . . .

The Act was constitutionally enacted. . . . [AFFIRMED]

2   INTERPRETATION OF LEGISLATION

While there would be no need for interpretation of a statute which was direct, clear, and precise, most legislation is by its very nature general, being stated to cover a multitude of fact situations. Thus, courts constantly are faced with the problem of finding the meaning of general statutes as applied to the specific facts of the cases before them. They must fill in the "gaps" of the legislation or eliminate an ambiguity by construing the legislative intent. The application of a general principle to a particular situation makes honest differences of opinion inevitable. Since language is an imperfect method of communication between human beings, a determination that no ambiguity exists is itself an act of interpretation.

One technique of statutory interpretation is to examine the legislative history of an act to determine the purpose of the legislation, or the evil it was designed to correct. Courts try to find the legislature's answers to the five questions previously referred to by examining committee reports, amendments which were rejected, and other matters which transpired prior to the adoption of the statute. While this technique frequently is followed, the truth often is that the individual members of the legislature voted for the statute for many different reasons, and the legislative history does not give a clear meaning to the language used in the statute. History *may* supply the legislative intent, but many of the questions of interpretation which confront courts were never even visualized by the legislature. The real problem often is to determine what the legislature *would have* intended, had it considered the question.

The legislative intent is, therefore, either nonexistent or undiscoverable in many cases; in many others, a resort to legislative history affords an accurate and compelling guide to legislative meaning.

Judges frequently differ on the meaning of legislative history and some judges will choose to ignore it when resort to it will indicate that their opinion on the meaning of the statute was not intended. In the case which follows, the dissent relied on legislative history but the majority chose to ignore it. Notice that a person's liberty was taken by interpreting a statute but that the Justices themselves could not agree on its meaning. How, then, could the defendant, Caminetti, have been expected to know "the law" and govern his conduct accordingly? There are several rules of statutory construction used by both the majority and dissenting judges in the Caminetti case, besides its legislative history, to ascertain the meaning of the language of the statute in issue.

Caminetti v. United States
242 U.S. 470 (1916)

Petitioner was convicted for violation of the so-called White Slave Traffic Act for transporting in interstate commerce a certain woman with the intention and purpose that she should become his mistress and concubine. He appealed, contending that the statute was intended to reach only "commercialized vice" or the traffic in women for gain, and in support of his position relied on the legislative history of the act.

DAY, JUSTICE: It is elementary that the meaning of a statute must, in the first instance, be sought in the language in which the act is framed, and if that is plain, and if the law is within the constitutional authority of the law-making body which passed it, the sole function of the courts is to enforce it according to its terms. . . .

Where the language is plain and admits of no more than one meaning, the duty of interpretation does not arise, and the rules which are to aid doubtful meanings need no discussion. . . . There is no ambiguity in the terms of this act. It is specifically made an offense to knowingly transport or cause to be transported, etc., in interstate commerce, any woman or girl for the purpose of prostitution or debauchery, or for "any other immoral purpose," or with the intent and purpose to induce any such woman or girl to become a prostitute or to give herself up to debauchery, or to engage in any other immoral practice.

Statutory words are uniformly presumed, unless the contrary appears, to be used in their ordinary and usual sense, and with the meaning commonly attributed to them. To cause a woman or girl to be transported for the purposes of debauchery, and for an immoral purpose, to wit, becoming a concubine or mistress, for which Caminetti and Diggs were convicted; or to transport an unmarried woman, under eighteen years of age, with the intent to induce her to engage in prostitution, debauchery, and other immoral practices, for which Hays was convicted, would seem by the very statement of the facts to embrace transportation for purposes denounced by the act, and therefore fairly within its meaning.

While such immoral purpose would be more culpable in morals and attributed to baser motives if accompanied with the expectation of pecuniary gain, such considerations do not prevent the lesser offense against morals of furnishing transportation in order that a woman may be debauched, or become a mistress or a concubine, from being the execution of purposes within the meaning of this law. To say the contrary would shock the common understanding of what constitutes an immoral purpose when those terms are applied, as here, to sexual relations.

In *United States v. Bitty*, 208 U.S. 393, . . . it was held that the act of Congress against the importation of alien women and girls for the purpose of prostitution "and any other immoral purpose" included the importation of an alien woman to live in concubinage with the person importing her. In that case this court said:

There can be no doubt as to what class was aimed at by the clause forbidding the importation of alien women for purposes of "prostitution." It refers to women who, for hire or without hire offer their bodies to indiscriminate intercourse with men. . . . Now the addition in the last statute of the words, "or for any other immoral purpose," after the word "prostitution," must have been made for some practical object. Those added words show beyond question that Congress had in view the protection of society against another class of alien women other than those who might be brought here merely for purposes of "prostitution." In forbidding the importation of alien women "for any other immoral purpose," Congress evidently thought that there were purposes in connection with the importations of alien women which, as in the case of importations for prostitution, were to be deemed immoral. It may be admitted that, in accordance with the familiar rule of ejusdem generis, the immoral purpose referred to by the words "any other immoral purpose" must be one of the same general class or kind as the particular purpose of "prostitution" specified in the same clause of the statute. . . . But that rule cannot avail the accused in this case; for the immoral purpose charged in the indictment is of the same general class or kind as the one that controls in the importation of an alien woman for the purpose strictly of prostitution. The prostitute may, in the popular sense, be more degraded in character than the concubine, but the latter none the less must be held to lead an immoral life, if any regard whatever be had to the views that are almost universally held in this country as to the relations which may rightfully, from the standpoint of morality, exist between man and woman in the matter of sexual intercourse.

This definition of an immoral purpose was given prior to the enactment of the act now under consideration, and must be presumed to have been known to Congress when it enacted the law here involved.

But it is contended that though the words are so plain that they cannot be misapprehended when given their usual and ordinary interpretation, and although the sections in which they appear do not in terms limit the offense defined and punished to acts of "commercialized vice," or the furnishing or procuring of transportation of women for debauchery, prostitution, or immoral practices for hire, such limited purpose is to be attributed to Congress and engrafted upon the act in view of the language of § 8 and the report which accompanied the law upon its introduction into and subsequent passage by the House of Representatives.

In this connection, it may be observed that while the title of an act cannot overcome the meaning of plain and unambiguous words used in its body . . . the title of this act embraces the regulation of interstate commerce "by prohibiting the transportation therein for immoral purposes of women and girls, and for other purposes." It is true that § 8 of the act provides that it shall be known and referred to as the "White Slave Traffic Act," and the report accompanying the introduction of the same into the House of Representatives set forth the fact that a material portion of the legislation suggested was to meet conditions which had arisen in the past few years, and that the legislation was needed to put a stop to a villainous interstate and international traffic in women and girls. Still, the name given to an act by way of designation or description, or the report which accompanies it, cannot change the plain import of its words. If the words are plain, they give meaning to the act, and it is neither the duty nor the privilege of the courts to enter speculative fields in search of a different meaning.

Reports to Congress accompanying the introduction of proposed laws may aid the courts in reaching the true meaning of the legislature in cases of doubtful interpretation. . . . But, as we have already said, and it has been so often affirmed as to become a recognized rule, when words are free from doubt they must be taken as the final expression of the legislative intent, and are not to be added to or subtracted from by considerations drawn from titles or designating names or reports accompanying their introduction, or from any extraneous source. In other words, the language being plain, and not leading to absurd or wholly impracticable consequences, it is the sole evidence of the ultimate legislative intent. . . .

The fact, if it be so, that the act as it is written opens the door to blackmailing operations upon a large scale, is no reason why the courts should refuse to enforce it according to its terms, if within the constitutional authority of Congress. Such considerations are more appropriately addressed to the legislative branch of the government, which alone has authority to enact and may, if it sees fit, amend the law. *Lake County v. Rollins,* 130 U.S. 673. [JUDGMENT AFFIRMED]

[A total of five justices shared the viewpoint expressed by the foregoing opinion. However, three of the justices joined in the reasoning expressed by the following dissenting opinion, taking the stand that Caminetti ought not have been convicted under the language of the statute.]

MC KENNA, JUSTICE, dissenting: Undoubtedly, in the investigation of the meaning of a statute we resort first to its words, and, when clear, they are decisive. The principle has attractive and seemingly disposing simplicity, but that it is not easy of application, or, at least, encounters other principles, many cases demonstrate. The words of a statute may be uncertain in their signification or in their application. If the words be ambiguous, the problem they present is to be resolved by their definition; the subject matter and the lexicons become our guides. But here, even, we are not exempt from putting ourselves in the place of the legislators. If the words be clear in meaning, but the objects to which they are addressed be uncertain, the problem then is to determine the uncertainty. And for this a realization of conditions that provoked the statute must inform our judgment. Let us apply these observations to the present case.

The transportation which is made unlawful is of a woman or girl "to become a prostitute or go give herself up to debauchery, or to engage in any other immoral practice." Our present concern is with the words "any other immoral practice," which, it is asserted, have a special office. The words are clear enough as general descriptions; they fail in particular designation; they are class words, not specifications. Are they controlled by those which precede them? If not, they are broader in generalization and include those that precede them, making them unnecessary and confusing. To what conclusion would this lead us? "Immoral" is a very comprehensive word. It means a dereliction of morals. In such sense it covers every form of vice, every form of conduct that is contrary to good order. It will hardly be contended that in this sweeping sense it is used in the statute. But, if not used in such sense, to what is it limited and by what limited? If it be admitted that it is limited at all, that ends the imperative effect assigned to it in the opinion of the court. But not insisting quite on that, we ask again, By what is it limited? By its context, necessarily, and the purpose of the statute.

For the context I must refer to the statute; of the purpose of the statute Congress itself has given us illumination. It devotes a section to the declaration that the "act shall be known and referred to as the 'White Slave Traffic Act.'" And its prominence gives it prevalence in the construction of the statute. It cannot be pushed aside or subordinated by indefinite words in other sentences, limited even there by the context. It is a peremptory rule of construction that all parts of a statute must be taken into account in ascertaining its meaning, and it cannot be said that § 8 has no object. Even if it gives only a title to the act, it has especial weight. . . . But it gives more than a title; it makes distinctive the purpose of the statute. The designation "white slave traffic" has the sufficiency of an axiom. If apprehended, there is no uncertainty as to the conduct it describes. It is commercialized vice, immoralities having a mercenary purpose, and this is confirmed by other circumstances. . . .

[I]t is vice as a business at which the law is directed, using inter-state commerce as a facility to procure or distribute its victims. . . .

This being the purpose, the words of the statute should be construed to execute it, and they may be so construed even if their literal meaning be otherwise. . . . "[I]t is a familiar rule that a thing may be within the letter of the statute and yet not within the statute, because not within its spirit, nor within the intention of its makers." . . .

It is hardly necessary to say that the application of the rule does not depend upon the objects of the legislation, to be applied or not applied as it may exclude or include good things or bad things. Its principle is the simple one that the words of a statute will be extended or restricted to execute its purpose. . . .

The rule . . . not only rescues legislation from absurdity (so far the opinion of the courts admits its application), but it often rescues it from invalidity,—a useful result in our dual form of governments and conflicting jurisdictions. It is the dictate of common sense. Language, even when most masterfully used, may miss sufficiency and give room for dispute. Is it a wonder, therefore, that when used in the haste of legislation, in view of conditions perhaps only partly seen or not seen at all, the consequences, it may be, beyond present foresight, it often becomes necessary to apply the rule? And it is a rule of prudence and highest sense. It rescues from crudities, excesses, and deficiencies, making legislation adequate to its special purpose, rendering unnecessary repeated qualifications and leaving the simple and best exposition of a law the mischief it was intended to redress. Nor is this judicial legislation. It is seeking and enforcing the true sense of a law notwithstanding its imperfection or generality of expression.

There is much in the present case to tempt to a violation of the rule. Any measure that protects the purity of women from assault or enticement to degradation finds an instant advocate in our best emotions; but the judicial function cannot yield to emotion—it must, with poise of mind, consider and decide. It should not shut its eyes to the facts of the world and assume not to know what everybody else knows. And everybody knows that there is a difference between the occasional immoralities of men and women and that systematized and mercenary immorality epitomized in the statute's graphic phrase "white slave traffic." And it was such immorality that was in the legislative mind, and not the other. . . .

There is danger in extending a statute beyond its purpose, even if justified by a strict adherence to its words. The purpose is studied, all effects measured, not left at random,—one evil practice prevented, opportunity given to another. The present case warns against ascribing such improvidence to the statute under review. Blackmailers of both sexes have arisen, using the terrors of the construction now sanctioned by this court as a help—indeed, the means—for their brigandage. The result is grave and should give us pause. It certainly will not be denied that legal authority justifies the rejection of a construction which leads to mischievous consequences, if the statute be susceptible of another construction. . . . For these reasons I dissent. . . .

The foregoing opinions illustrate the use of several rules of statutory construction in addition to resort to the legislative history. Among these are:

1 Unless contrary intent appears, statutory words are uniformly presumed to be used in their ordinary and usual sense, and with the meaning commonly attributed to them.

2 Statutes which are consistent with one another, and which relate to the same subject matter, are *in pari materia* and should be construed together, and effect be given to them all, although they may contain no reference to one another and were passed at different times.

3 Where a general word in a statute follows particular and specific words of the same nature as itself, it takes its meaning from them, and is presumed to be restricted to the same genus as those words (e.g., a statute naming "ox, cow, heifer, steer, or other cattle" does not include a bull). This rule is called *ejusdem generis.*

4 The meaning of a doubtful word may be ascertained by reference to the meaning of words with which it is associated. (This rule is sometimes referred to as *noscitur a sociis;* it is similar to the rule of *in pari materia* but is applied to sentences and sections of a single statute.)

5 A thing may be within the letter of the statute and yet not within the statute because not within its spirit nor within the intention of the makers.

There are many rules of statutory construction in addition to those involved in the *Caminetti* case. Some of these are set forth in legislation usually known as the "statute on statutes"; other rules of statutory construction have developed as a part of the common law as an aid to courts in ascertaining legislative intent. These rules collectively will allow a court to support almost any view as to the meaning of the language of any statute. Among the more common rules in addition to the previously noted are:

1 Taxing laws should be strictly or narrowly construed.

2 Remedial statutes are to be liberally or broadly construed.

3 Statutes in derogation of the common law are to be strictly construed.

4 Exemptions from statutes will be construed strictly against the party claiming the exemption.

5 Every reasonable doubt must be resolved in favor of validity of a statute.

6 Repeal by implication is not favored.

7 The meaning of a statute may be established indirectly by the failure of the legislative body to act in an area in which the law has been based on judicial decision or on interpretation by the executive branch of government charged with its administration.

8 Criminal statutes should be strictly construed.

Rule 6 noted above means that courts have a duty to harmonize statutes, and they will not hold that one statute has been repealed by the enactment of another which is in apparent conflict with the former (repeal by implication) if they can avoid doing so. However, if two statutes are so clearly in conflict that they cannot stand together upon any reasonable construction of both, the legislature is presumed to have intended the repeal of the former by the latter. The difficulty of the task of statutory construction is further illustrated by examining two of the above rules.

1 Statutes in derogation of the common law are to be strictly construed.
2 Remedial statutes are to be liberally construed.

The problem presented by these two rules is simply stated: Every statute in derogation of the common law is remedial in some sense; and most remedial statutes are in derogation of the common law. How are statutes to be construed—strictly or liberally? Volumes have been written on the problems of statutory interpretation, but as Judge Learned Hand said, "They haven't advanced us very far."

One common complaint of lawyers in statutory construction cases is that judges, under the guise of liberally construing a statute, frequently construe the facts of the case. Another similar problem arises when the trial judge admits that he does not know the meaning of the statute but makes a decision stating words to the effect that "The appellate court can reverse me if I'm wrong." The appellate court often then affirms the trial judge, stating that great deference is owed to his decision, and the burden is on the appellant to show that it was clearly wrong.

The cases in the section which follows further illustrate some of the problems of statutory construction and the resulting difficulty that even a lawyer has in knowing what the law is. Notice that such other matters as the objectives of the legislation as stated in preambles and debates, statements by executives in requesting the particular legislation, prior judicial decisions involving the same subject matter, and the title of the act are used as extrinsic aids to judicial interpretations.

3 SOME ADDITIONAL INTERPRETATION PROBLEMS

The subsections which follow illustrate the application of some of the rules listed in the preceding section and in addition demonstrate some of the other problems facing courts as a result of the ambiguities of the English language. These cases also make it clear that if a court for some reason feels that the application of a particular rule of construction will not achieve the intention of the legislature, it will ignore the rule. The intention of the legislature encompasses not only what the legislature actually intended but what the court thinks it would have intended had it thought about the problem. In many cases, if the legislature had anticipated the issue, the statute in question would have eliminated the issue.

A ARE STATUTES RETROACTIVE?

Scheffler v. Ringhofer
214 N.E.2d 575 (Ill. 1966)

BRYANT, PRESIDING JUSTICE: This is an appeal from an order granting summary judgment and dismissing the appellant's complaint for failure to state a cause of action.

This action has been brought by Anne Marie Scheffler as administratrix of the estate of her deceased son, Ralph. The complaint alleged that on July 26, 1957 Ralph, then being three and one-half years old, fell through the screen in a window of a third floor apartment in a building owned by the appellees. It was also alleged that the screens were negligently allowed to fall into disrepair by the appellees. The appellees then filed an answer in which they denied that the fall was occasioned by any negligent act of theirs.

The appellees made a motion for summary judgment. They alleged that there was no agreement between them and the tenant of the apartment from which the deceased fell as to the furnishing of any protective devices on the windows. It was also alleged that the screens were in the windows for the purpose of keeping out insects and were not placed there for the purpose of keeping children from falling out. They also cited *Crawford v. Orner & Shayne Inc.*, 331 Ill. App. 568, 73 N.E.2d 615 (1947) for the proposition that "a landlord has no duty to furnish screens for the purpose of keeping persons from falling out of a window."

The appellant then added a Count II to her complaint alleging that the appellees had violated Chap. 75 of the Municipal Code of Chicago, which chapter required that there be guard rails on windows having a sill less than two feet from the floor. It was also alleged that the window from which the deceased fell was less than two feet from the floor. The appellees then filed a motion to strike Count II of the complaint alleging that Chap. 75 was passed after the erection of the building where the accident occurred and that this chapter was prospective in operation and had no retroactive operation. On February 26, 1964 the motion was granted and Count II of the complaint was ordered stricken. On November 30, 1964 a motion for summary judgment was granted. . . .

The appellant's theory of the case before this court has been that the appellees violated their statutory duty in not providing guard rails at the window from which the deceased fell in accordance with Chap. 75 of the Municipal Code of Chicago . . . the appellant's appeal must fail. Chap. 75 of the Municipal Code of Chicago operates prospectively only and has no application to buildings already in existence when the law was passed. This is the general rule in construing any statute and it has long been settled that a statute will operate retroactively only where that is the clear legislative intent. . . . [ORDER AFFIRMED]

B   WHAT DOES "OR" MEAN?

People v. Spencer
208 N.E.2d 192 (Ill. 1971)

DEMPSEY, JUSTICE: George Spencer, a Chicago school teacher, was assigned to Englewood High School. On May 6, 1969, the principal of the school presented him with a letter of dismissal and directed him to leave the school and report to the Bureau of Teacher Personnel, Board of Education. Spencer, who was seated at his desk, did not rise. After repeated warnings he was arrested, removed from his chair and escorted from the building. He was charged with criminal trespass to land, tried without a jury, found guilty and fined $25.00.

The statute under which Spencer was convicted recites:

Whoever enters upon the land or any part thereof of another, after receiving, immediately prior to such entry, notice from the owner or occupant that such entry is forbidden, or remains upon the land of another after receiving notice from the owner or occupant to depart, shall be fined not to exceed $100 or imprisoned in a penal institution other than the penitentiary not to exceed 10 days. Ill.Rev.Stat., 1967, ch. 38, para. 21-3(a).

The defendant's basic contention is that this statute refers only to one class of offenders—to interlopers who enter upon someone's premises after being notified not to do so or who, not having received notice before entering, stay there after being told to leave. He argues that the statute applies to those who intrude upon premises and not to those who enter lawfully. Specifically, he argues that the statute has no application to an employee whose work requires him to be on the premises and who is discharged while at work.

Although the statute could have been more precisely phrased, it is not ambiguous. The legislative intention seems clear. In construing a criminal statute the legislative intention must be ascertained by examining the language employed, the evil to be remedied and the objective sought to be accomplished. It is to be presumed that the legislature intended words to have their ordinary meaning unless a statutory definition indicates a contrary intention. The word "or" between the first part of the statute and the last: "Whoever enters upon the land . . . or remains upon the land . . . ," must be accorded significance. Whenever this disjunctive is used in a sentence the parts of the sentence are to be taken separately. The legislative intent becomes plain when the word "whoever," obviously understood but not used, is inserted after the "or." The statute, with the ellipsis supplied, would then read: "Whoever enters upon the land . . . or whoever remains upon the land. . . ." A word or words inadvertently omitted in a statute may be supplied to effectuate the legislative purpose.

The purpose of the legislature was to create two distinct offenses: the first, to enter upon the land of another despite a warning that entry is forbidden and, the second, to remain on the land of another after being notified to depart. The first offense is directed to interlopers, the second is not. The second makes any individual a trespasser who stays on the premises of another after receiving notice from the owner or occupant to leave.

Spencer was told to leave Englewood High School by the principal of the school who had legal authority to give such notice. By his noncompliance he falls within the purview of the statute. . . . [AFFIRMED]

C   HOW DEFINITE MUST A LAW BE?

The *Caminetti* case, page 101, illustrated the problems inherent in using language to declare an act to be criminal. The English language is not an adequate vehicle to define criminal conduct in a manner that will advise everyone as to what acts or conduct constitute crimes. Yet the criminal law must be applied in a workable manner. The case which follows typifies the inadequacy of language to regulate personal behavior.

People v. Byron
215 N.E.2d 345 (N.Y. 1966)

The defendant was convicted of violating a statute relating to mufflers. An intermediate or reviewing court reversed the conviction holding the statute unconstitutional for vagueness. The state appealed.

KEATING, JUSTICE: . . . On May 28, 1964, defendant was stopped by a State trooper and issued a uniform traffic ticket charging him with violating the Vehicle and Traffic Law which provides: "Mufflers. Prevention of noise. Every motor vehicle, operated or driven upon the highways of the state, shall at all times be equipped with an adequate muffler in constant operation and properly maintained to prevent any excessive or unusual noise and no such muffler or exhaust system shall be equipped with a cut-out, bypass, or similar device. . . ."

At the hearing, the trooper supplied a bill of particulars alleging that defendant operated his 1958 Studebaker without an adequate muffler, that the vehicle made a loud noise much in excess of the noise made by other vehicles which passed, that the muffler was in a bad state of repair and that defendant admitted it was in a bad state of repair and had been for some time. . . .

The prosecution in this case was for a "traffic infraction," not a crime, but such a prosecution is penal in nature and the rules of criminal law are generally applicable. As the County Judge stated, a criminal statute must be sufficiently definite, clear and positive to give unequivocal warning to citizens of the rule which is to be obeyed. It is also true, of course, that all presumptions and intendments favor the validity of a statute and mere doubt does not afford sufficient reason for a judicial declaration of invalidity.

It is our opinion that the statute in question states with sufficient clarity the rule which is to be obeyed. The test is whether a reasonable man subject to the statute would be informed of the nature of the offense prohibited and what is required of him. Such warning must be unequivocal but this requirement does not preclude the use of ordinary terms to express ideas which find adequate interpretation in common usage and understanding.

The evil sought to be prevented is "excessive or unusual noise." What is usual noise in the operation of a car has become common knowledge and anything in excess of that is excessive or unusual and any ordinary motorist should have no difficulty in ascertaining whether or not excessive or unusual noise accompanied the operation of his vehicle. The purpose of the statute, as made clear on its face, is not to *prohibit* noise but to *minimize* noise. We think the statute sufficiently describes the evil to be prevented and informs the motorist of his duty, not to eliminate all noise, but to have a properly maintained muffler to prevent unusual noise. When his muffler is in such a state of disrepair that the noise exceeds the usual level, the motorist has violated the statute.

The words of the Supreme Court upholding an ordinance prohibiting the use of instruments emitting "loud and raucous noises" are applicable here: "While these are abstract words, they have through daily use acquired a content that conveys to any interested person a sufficiently accurate concept of what is forbidden. . . ." [ORDER REVERSED AND MATTER REMITTED TO THE COUNTY COURT FOR FURTHER PROCEEDINGS NOT INCONSISTENT WITH THE OPINION HEREIN]

D WHEN CAN THE LITERAL INTERPRETATION BE IGNORED?

Eck v. United Arab Airlines, Inc.
203 N.E.2d 640 (N.Y. 1964)

The plaintiff, a resident of California, brought this action in the New York courts against the defendant, United Arab Airlines, an Egyptian corporation, for damages for injuries she sustained in a crash in Sudan. The trial court denied the defendant airline's motion to dismiss the complaint under Article 28 of the Warsaw Convention, which provides: "An action for damages *must* be brought, at the option of the plaintiff, *in the territory of one of the High Contracting Parties,* either *before the court of the domicile of the carrier or of his principal place of business, or where he has a place of business through which the contract has been made,* or *before the court at the place of destination."* [EMPHASIS ADDED] On review, the Appellate Division reversed, holding that New York was not one of the jurisdictions where suit may be brought under the Warsaw Convention, and dismissed the suit for lack of jurisdiction. The plaintiff then perfected this appeal to the Court of Appeals of New York.

BURKE, JUSTICE. . . . Plaintiff . . . contracted with Scandanavian Airlines System (SAS) on her behalf for passage in the early part of 1962 by air from Los Angeles to several countries in Europe, finally returning to Los Angeles. Plaintiff also arranged with the Oakland, California, office of SAS for the purchase of tickets for a side air trip while she was abroad between several cities in Europe and the Middle East. One of the flights listed in the ticket SAS obtained for the plaintiff was to be on defendant United Arab Airlines Flight No. 796 from Jerusalem to Cairo. Subsequently plaintiff was injured when Flight No. 796 crashed on March 16, 1962 in Wadi Halfa, Sudan, a place not scheduled as a stop on the flight, but where the pilot was diverted in an attempt to avoid bad weather at Cairo.

The defendant carrier maintains a place of business, a ticket office, in New York City. This office would have sold the plaintiff passage on the same United Arab Airlines flight that SAS ticketed her on. When the defendant opened its United States office in New York it anticipated that it would be amenable to suits there for claims arising out of any carriage sold by that office. If the plaintiff had purchased her ticket in that office the defendant would have to concede jurisdiction to our courts. But by happenstance the plaintiff made her purchase of a seat on Flight No. 796 in the SAS office which for our purposes could have been right next door. . . .

It is argued that Article 28 expressly provides that a place of business, other than a principal place of business, outside the domicile of the carrier, will support jurisdiction only if the contract of carriage was made through that office. Defendant quotes that part of the article that, it asserts, places jurisdiction in the court "in the territory of one of the High Contracting Parties . . . *where he* [the carrier] *has a place of business through which the contract has been made."* This is the basis for the result reached by the Appellate Division.

The crux of the problem is that the Appellate Division reached its conclusion by applying mechanically the *literal* translation of a phrase without an analysis of the treaty. The court overlooked the canon that, when a treaty is invoked, *what is to be applied are its principles if its purposes are to be observed presently as in the past.* . . . The reasoning which supports a strictly literal reading of the phrase might not have done violence to the overall scheme and design of the Convention under the conditions existing when the treaty was drafted. At that time it would have been in harmony with the methods under which the carriers were operating and with the objectives of the Convention. . . . Now, however, almost a half century later, when the carriers have radically changed their methods of booking passage, the whole scheme of the treaty in relation to international air travel makes it imperative to analyze this self-executing treaty in assigning meaning to any part of it. In doing this it must be recognized that the literal wording of one particularly applicable section of the entire treaty should not set the limits of our interpretive examination. . . . The proper procedure now is to examine the treaty as a whole, along with its history, and, in particular, to look into the problems which it was intended to solve. . . .

The overall principle of the Convention was one of allowing only a regulated burden to be the responsibility of the then struggling carriers. The purposes were to *provide uniform rules of limitation concerning the liability* of international air carriers to their passengers and to *provide a uniform remedy for these passengers* to the extent that this remedy would not burden the carrier more than the Convention provisions allowed. These principles were expected to be operative with respect to conditions developing after the enactment of the Convention. In this light, the particular wording of Article 28, with which we are here concerned, appears to have been intended to limit the bringing of suits to only those forums where the terms of the Convention were in force and would be applied. Moreover, the intent was to avoid suits in countries where the carrier had no office for the making of transportation contracts and where no passage on the carriers' aircraft had been purchased.

Allowing this suit does not run contrary to the Convention's provisions. Rather it gives a meaningful effect to the underlying principles by applying them to the realities of international air travel in these times. In 1926 these principles were put into a specific written formula which was meant to deal not only with the circumstances of an infant industry in that era but also accommodate itself consistently to changing conditions as the industry grew. The formula did not speak to the right to sue belonging to a traveler who purchased passage on one carrier from another carrier in a country where the first carrier itself maintained an office, because such a procedure was unknown. Travel agents and connecting carriers then cleared the bookings through the local officers. At the time of the enactment of the Convention, if a carrier had a ticket office in any particular country it would be a very exceptional case if the carriage was not booked through the airline's office there. Hence the phrase relied on by respondent then meant the office through which, *in the ordinary course of business*, the contract would be made. Today the volume of business done by the carriers requires a vast network of international communications and other ticket routing procedures— procedures not possible when this article was drafted in Paris in 1926, and ratified by this country in 1934.

. . . If the drafters of the treaty intended to discriminate against a passenger who purchased a ticket in a territory where the carrier had an office, but which the ultimate carrier decided should be cleared through an office outside that territory, such an intention should have been expressed. It cannot be implied, as such a change would take from the passengers, without notice, the very relief which the treaty gave them and intended that they continue to have. . . . A literal interpretation of the single clause in the convention, therefore, is at odds with the tenor of the document. . . . The interpretation given to the Convention by the Appellate Division would allow a passenger who purchased transportation through United Arab Airlines office in New York City to sue here, but compel a copassenger in the same accident who purchased transportation through another carrier in New York City in the same block to go abroad to bring suit. This construction rejects the fundamental rule set forth in the Convention. . . .

The preference of this court for being faithful to purpose rather than coldly literal is well established. In the case of *River Brand Rice Mills v. Latobe Brewing Co.*, 305 N.Y. 36, 110 N.E.2d 545 (1953) we said: " '[A] thing which is within the letter of the statute is not within the statute unless it be within the intention of the lawmakers, but a case within the intention of a statute is within the statute, though an exact literal construction would exclude it. . . .' " In the case of *New York Post Corp. v. Leibowitz*, 2 N.Y.2d 677 (1957) Judge FULD wrote: "In construing statutory provisions, the spirit and purpose of the statute and the objectives sought to be accomplished by the legislature must be borne in mind." . . .

The provisions can be read in an excessively literal manner, but it is unreasonable to think that the signatories intended such an unwarranted construction. We will not deny the plaintiff the right to sue here since the purposes of the Convention in respect to consistency of remedy must be heeded, and analogous cases should be dealt with in a similar fashion.

Accordingly, the order of the Appellate Division should be reversed and the motion to dismiss the complaint should be denied, and the action remanded to the Supreme Court for further proceedings. [REVERSED AND REMANDED]

4 TRENDS IN WRITTEN LAW

The American Law Institute has published *Restatements of the Law* in many fields such as contracts, torts, trusts, and conflicts of laws. These treatises have been drafted from the generally accepted principles of the common law found in numerous court decisions and have been prepared in reference form similar to a statute to assist in promoting certainty and clarity in the law. The statements of the law found in these compilations are prima facie correct. In the broadest sense, "written law" includes those references, which, although they do not have the force of legislation, are relied upon heavily by the courts and cited frequently with favor. The *Restatements of the Law* are under continual review and are revised as required.

The need for certainty and uniformity in the laws as between the states provided the impetus for several uniform statutes in areas previously controlled by court decisions, such as in the law of commercial paper, the law of sales, and the law of partnerships. The National Conference of Commissioners on Uniform State Laws, appointed by the governors of the various states, worked with the American Law Institute to draft these laws and has attempted to secure their passage in as many states as possible. For example, the desire for modernization, uniformity throughout the country, and consistency in all aspects of commercial law resulted in the preparation of a statute known as the Uniform Commercial Code. In one internally consistent body of laws, the Code deals with all the aspects of a commercial transaction, or sale of personal property, from the contract of sale itself, to the security device which may be used to ensure the seller payment, the instrument given the seller by the buyer (such as a check or note), and the document of title to goods being sold. The Code also concerns itself with other commercial matters such as bulk sales, investment securities, and the bank collection process. The Code had few adoptions until 1961; forty-nine states have now enacted it.

The field of commercial law is not the only area of new codification. Many states are adopting revised criminal codes which contain modern procedures and concepts. In addition, the past few years have seen dynamic changes in both state and Federal statutes setting forth civil procedures and revising court systems. The future will undoubtedly bring many further developments to improve the administration of justice. The trend, despite some objection, is to cover more areas of the law with statutes and to rely less on precedent in judicial decisions, or common law, as a source of law.

REVIEW QUESTIONS—CHAPTER 4

1 Define the following terms introduced in this chapter: legislative history; *ejusdem generis; in pari materia; noscitur a sociis;* Restatements of the Law.
2 Indicate the role of each branch of government in the legislative process.
3 List five rules of statutory construction and give an example of each.
4 What is the basic purpose of legislative interpretation? Explain.
5 Are all criminal statutes strictly construed? Explain.
6 Why are most statutes not retroactive?
7 Under what circumstances will the literal interpretation of a statute be ignored?
8 What is the function of the various Restatements of the Law?

Chapter Five

Law by Judicial Decision

1 STARE DECISIS

In addition to the written law of constitutions, treaties, and statutes, there is a body of judge-made law, created by judicial decisions, known as the "common law." The common law is based on the doctrine of "stare decisis," the principle that prior decisions provide precedents which should be followed in subsequent cases involving the same question of law. In other words, where a rule of law has been announced and followed by courts so that the rule has become settled by judicial decision, a precedent is established for future cases. Judicial decisions create precedent where there is no legislation as well as by interpreting legislation. The common law originated in England and was used by the colonies as the basis of their judicial systems. Most of the other states have also followed English precedent when establishing their laws. Many state constitutions specifically adopt the common law except where changed by statute.

Not all common-law rules require several decisions for acceptance as precedent, but a decision standing alone will not necessarily invoke the doctrine of stare decisis where the decision has not been cited by the courts for many years, or is lacking in reason. The doctrine is generally only applicable to rules of law announced by courts of review, and it is these decisions that are available for legal research.

Stare decisis arose from the desire of courts as well as society for certainty and predictability in the law. In addition, following precedent was expedient. The common law, through precedent, settled many legal issues and brought stability into many areas of the law, such as contracts, enabling individuals to act in reliance upon prior decisions, with reasonable certainty as to the results of their conduct.

Notwithstanding the fact that the common law arose out of a desire for certainty, and is designed to create it, the common law creates a great deal of uncertainty in the minds of laymen about the law. The sheer volume of judicial decisions, each possibly creating precedent, makes "the law" beyond the comprehension of lawyers let alone laymen. Large law firms employ lawyers whose sole task is to search the case reports for "the law" to be used in lawsuits and in advising their clients. Each lawyer must have access to literally hundreds of volumes so that he can find "the law." Since the total body of ruling case law is beyond the grasp of lawyers, it is obvious that laymen who are supposed to know the law and govern their conduct accordingly do not know the law and are somewhat bewildered by it. One legal scholar in discussing this anomaly, observed:

It is the judges that make the common law. Do you know how they make it? Just as a man makes laws for his dog. When your dog does anything you want to break him of, you wait till he does it, and then beat him for it. This is the way you make laws for your dog: and this is the way the judges make laws for you and me. They won't tell a man beforehand what it is he should not do— they won't so much as allow of his being told: they lie by till he has done something which they say he should not have done, and then they hang him for it. What way, then, has any man of coming at this dog-law? Only by watching their proceedings: by observing in what cases they have hanged a man, in what cases they have sent him to jail, in what cases they have seized his goods, and so forth.[1]

There are other problems inherent in a legal system based in part on precedent. These are compounded in a country which consists of fifty sovereign states because each of these creates its own body of common law and the rules are frequently in conflict. Moreover, the Federal legal system is superimposed on the state systems, thus creating additional bodies of judge-made laws. The methods of determining the applicable precedent where conflicts exist between the laws of different jurisdictions are discussed later in this chapter.

One significant problem involving case law arises because conflicting precedents in cases decided in the state where the action was brought are frequently cited to a court by the parties to an action. One of the major tasks of the courts in such cases is to determine which precedent is applicable to the case at bar, and which is correct, if the cited authorities are in actual conflict. In addition, even today, many questions of law arise on which there has been no prior decision, or in areas where the only authority is by implication. In such situations, the judicial process is "legislative" in character and involves the creation of law, not merely its discovery. It should also be noted that there is a distinction between precedent and mere dicta. A judicial decision, as authority for future cases, is coextensive only with the facts upon which it is founded and the rules of law upon which the decision actually is predicated. Frequently courts make comments on matters not necessary to the decision reached. Such expressions, called "dicta," lack the force of an adjudication and, strictly speaking, are not precedent which the court will be required to follow within the rule of stare decisis. However, dicta or implication in prior cases may be followed if sound and just, and dicta which have been repeated frequently are often given the force of precedent.

2 REJECTION OF STARE DECISIS

Courts usually hesitate to reject precedent. The assumption is made that a principle or rule of law announced in a former judicial decision, if unfair or contrary

---

[1] 5 Bentham, *Works* 235, quoted in 1 Steffen & Levi, *Cases and Materials on the Elements of the Law* 207 (3d ed. 1946).

to public policy, will be changed by legislation. Precedent has more force on trial courts than on courts of review, which have the power to make precedent in the first instance. However, stare decisis does not mean that former decisions *always* will be followed, even by trial courts. A former ruling may have been erroneous or the conditions upon which it was based may have changed or may no longer exist. The doctrine does not require courts to multiply their errors by using former mistakes as authority and support for new errors. Thus, just as legislatures change the law by new legislation, so also do courts change the law, from time to time, by reversing former precedents. Judges are subject to social forces and changing circumstances just as are legislatures. (The forces affecting decisions are discussed in Chapter 6.) The personnel of courts change, and each new generation of judges deems it a responsibility to reexamine precedents and to adapt them to the world of the times.

Some quotes from justices indicate their attitude toward stare decisis. For example, Justice Wanamaker in the case of *Adams Express Co. v. Beckwith,* 100 Ohio St. 348, said that "A decided case is worth as much as it weighs in reason and righteousness, and no more. It is not enough to say 'thus saith the court.' It must prove its right to control in any given situation by the degree in which it supports the rights of a party violated and serves the cause of justice as to all parties concerned." Or as Justice Musmanno stated in the case of *Bosley v. Andrews,* 393 Pa. 161 (1958),

Stare decisis is the viaduct over which the law travels in transporting the precious cargo of justice. Prudence and a sense of safety dictate that the piers of that viaduct should be examined and tested from time to time to make certain that they are sound, strong and capable of supporting the weight above. . . . A precedent, in law, in order to be binding, should appeal to logic and a genuine sense of justice. What lends dignity to the law founded on precedent is that, if analyzed, the particularly cited case wields authority by the sheer force of its self-integrated honesty, integrity, and rationale. A precedent cannot, and should not, control, if its strength depends alone on the fact that it is old, but may crumble at the slightest probing touch of instinctive reason and natural justice.

The changing of precedent is a strange phenomenon indeed. A party to a case who would lose under an established rule argues against stagnation and in favor of ignoring the rule of stare decisis. If he successfully convinces the court to change its view, he is armed with a new precedent, and he becomes the advocate of the status quo for the new rule. Those who attacked stare decisis may become champions of its cause.

Justices who desire a change in a particular area of the law argue that precedent should not be followed and that judges of today should not be bound by the limited vision of prior courts. They contend that judicial restraint should not be used to prevent progress and the elimination of wrongs in society. If these judges are successful in changing precedent, they then become aligned on the side of stare decisis and contend that the new precedent and judicial restraint toward change must be followed in all subsequent cases. This phenomenon has been graphically illustrated by the Supreme Court in recent years.

During the late 1960s the Warren Court was an activist court. It changed many precedents in the criminal law and other areas and exercised little judicial restraint. Many of these decisions were decided 5–4. The justices arguing for change contended that prior precedents should not be followed, using among other reasons the doctrine of constitutional relativity. These justices were accused of rewriting the Constitution to meet their own notions of what should be constitutional, and they were criticized for the activist approach. Chief Justice Warren and Justice Fortas were then replaced by Chief Justice Burger and Justice Blackmun. Later Justices Powell and Rehnquist replaced Justices Black and Harlan. The new "Burger Court," which was assumed to be more "judicial restraint"–oriented than "activist" in its outlook moved in new directions in some areas and modified or changed some of the precedents of the 1960s. Some of the activist justices who had argued that courts should not be bound by precedent openly complained that the new court was not following precedent but was rewriting the Constitution to suit its new majority viewpoint of what should be constitutional or unconstitutional. The activists complained that the new majority was not exercising judicial restraint.

Those justices who do not want to change precedent usually argue that it is the responsibility of courts to construe and enforce the Constitution and statutes as they are and that it is not the function of the courts to legislate social policy on the basis of personal inclinations. They argue that courts should use restraint in changing the law and should leave change to other branches of government and to the political process. Those tending toward the activist philosophy, on the other hand, believe that the political process is unable to bring about all necessary changes in society as expeditiously as desired and so the courts should correct any social wrongs they find. The next chapter will explore in more detail the reasons for following or changing precedent.

In the article which follows, Justice William O. Douglas discusses some of the reasons for rejecting stare decisis. Justice Douglas is generally regarded as following the activist philosophy. He was usually with the majority in the 5–4 decisions of the Warren Court but is most frequently with the minority in the close decisions of the Burger Court. The case which follows the article contains two dissents, each joined in by Justice Douglas, in which he noted with disdain the new justices' failure to follow precedent. In this case he seems to join in the argument for judicial restraint.

Stare Decisis[2]
William O. Douglas, Associate Justice of the Supreme Court of the United States

Most lawyers, by training and practice, are all too apt to turn their interests and their talents toward the finding not the creating of precedents. This lawyerly

[2] The Eighth Annual Benjamin N. Cardozo Lecture delivered before the Association of the Bar of the City of New York on Apr. 12, 1949. By permission from Justice William O. Douglas.

search is for moorings where clients can be safely anchored. But the search has, as well, a deeper, more personal impetus. For the lawyer himself shares the yearning for security that is common to all people everywhere. And this yearning grows as the world seems to grow more *insecure*.

We live in an age of doubt and confusion. Rules that once seemed fixed and certain today seem beclouded. Principles of law have been challenged and judges asked to refashion them. Many raised their voices in protest. Some were special pleaders with a stake in existing law. Others had a sincere belief that the foremost function of law in these days of stress and strain is to remain steady and stable so as to promote security. Thus judges have been admonished to hold steadfast to ancient precedents lest the courts themselves add fresh doubt, confusion, and concern over the strength of our institutions.

This search for a static security—in the law or elsewhere—is misguided. The fact is that security can only be achieved through constant change, through the wise discarding of old ideas that have outlived their usefulness, and through the adapting of others to current facts. There is only an illusion of safety in a Maginot Line. Social forces like armies can sweep around a fixed position and make it untenable. A position that can be shifted to meet such forces and at least partly absorb them alone gives hope of security.

I speak here of long-term swings in the law. I do not suggest that *stare decisis* is so fragile a thing as to bow before every wind. The law is not properly susceptible to whim or caprice. It must have the sturdy qualities required of every framework that is designed for substantial structures. Moreover, it must have uniformity when applied to the daily affairs of men.

Uniformity and continuity in law are necessary to many activities. If they are not present, the integrity of contracts, wills, conveyances, and securities is impaired. (See *United States v. Title Ins. Co.,* 265 U.S. 472, 486–487.) And there will be no equal justice under law if a negligence rule is applied in the morning but not in the afternoon. *Stare decisis* serves to take the capricious element out of law and to give stability to a society. It is a strong tie which the future has to the past.

It is easy, however, to overemphasize *stare decisis* as a principle in the lives of men. Even for the experts law is only a prediction of what judges will do under a given set of facts—a prediction that makes rules of law and decisions not logical deductions but functions of human behavior. There are usually plenty of precedents to go around; and with the accumulation of decisions, it is no great problem for the lawyer to find legal authority for most propositions. The difficulty is to estimate what effect a slightly different shade of facts will have and to predict the speed of the current in a changing stream of the law. The predictions and prophecies that lawyers make are indeed appraisals of a host of imponderables. The decisions of yesterday or of the last century are only the starting points.

As for laymen, their conception of the rules of law that govern their conduct is so nebulous that in one sense, as Gray said, the law in its application to their normal affairs is to a very considerable extent *ex post facto*.

The place of *stare decisis* in constitutional law is even more tenuous. A judge looking at a constitutional decision may have compulsions to revere past history and accept what was once written. But he remembers above all else that it is the Constitution which he swore to support and defend, not the gloss which his predecessors may have put on it. So he comes to formulate his own views, rejecting some earlier ones as false and embracing others. He cannot do otherwise unless he lets men long dead and unaware of the problems of the age in which he lives do his thinking for him.

This reexamination of precedent in constitutional law is a personal matter for each judge who comes along. When only one new judge is appointed during a short period, the unsettling effect in constitutional law may not be great. But when a majority of a Court is suddenly reconstituted, there is likely to be substantial unsettlement. There will be unsettlement until the new judges have taken their positions on constitutional doctrine. During that time—which may extend a decade or more—constitutional law will be in flux. That is the necessary consequence of our system and to my mind a healthy one. The alternative is to let the Constitution freeze in the pattern which one generation gave it. But the Constitution was designed for the vicissitudes of time. It must never become a code which carries the overtones of one period that may be hostile to another.

So far as constitutional law is concerned *stare decisis* must give way before the dynamic component of history. Once it does, the cycle starts again. Today's new and startling decision quickly becomes a coveted anchorage for new vested interests. The former proponents of change acquire an acute conservatism in their new *status quo*. It will then take an oncoming group from a new generation to catch the broader vision which may require an undoing of the work of our present and their past. . . .

Much of what courts do is little understood by laymen. Very few portions of the press undertake to show the social, economic, or political significance of the work of the judiciary or to educate the public on long-term trends. Lawyers often do not see the broader view which is exposed by the narrow and intensely personal efforts of a client to vindicate a position or gain an advantage. Yet the work of a court may send a whole economy in one direction or help shape the manifest destiny of an era. Two illustrations from different periods of our history will indicate what I mean.

For at least a decade or more it was commonly assumed that the Fourteenth Amendment was adopted to protect Negroes in their newly won rights. Other interests had sought to creep under its wing. Thus corporations claimed they were persons within the meaning of the equal protection clause. Woods (then circuit judge) thought the language of the Amendment and its history too clear to admit of doubt on the point. In 1870 he rejected the contention in *Insurance Co. v. New Orleans,* 1 Woods 85. Sixteen years passed. Woods was now a member of the Court on which Waite was Chief Justice. A railroad company pressed its claim that California's tax assessment against it violated the Equal Protection Clause of the Fourteenth Amendment. Before the point was even argued, Waite announced from the bench that the Court did not care to hear argument on the question whether the clause applied to corporations. "We are all of opinion that it does," he said. (*Santa Clara Co. v. Southern Pac. R.R.,* 118 U.S. 394, 396.) Thus without argument or opinion on the point the *Santa Clara* case became one of the most momentous of all our decisions. It was not long before the same constitutional doctrine was extended to the Due Process Clause. Again the decision was cryptic and oracular, without exposition or explanation.

These decisions, whether right or wrong, sound or unsound, may have changed the course of our industrial history. Corporations were now armed with constitutional prerogatives. And so armed, they proceeded to the development and exploitation of a continent in a manner never equaled before or since. Some think these decisions helped give corporations what Parrington has called "the freedom of buccaneers." They doubtless did release some of the dynamic quality of the drive that built industrial America in a brilliant (albeit ruthless) way.

These unexplained (and certainly not obvious) decisions are now so implicit in the financial and industrial undertaking of the nation that a recent challenge of them had a resounding effect. Such is the hold of *stare decisis* on the profession.

A half century passed and the Court made another decision whose impact on industrial America was almost as profound.

In 1918 the Court in the *Dagenhart* case (*Hammer v. Dagenhart*, 247 U.S. 251) had decided that Congress had no power to regulate the production of goods for commerce where the goods themselves were harmless. It thus struck down a child labor law. A process of erosion soon set in. Distinctions and qualifications were made in a long line of decisions. Finally in 1941 in a case involving the constitutionality of the Fair Labor Standards Act (*United States v. Darby*, 312 U.S. 100) a unanimous Court overruled the earlier five-to-four decision. Stone's exposition of the Commerce Clause in the *Darby* case was undoubtedly more faithful to Marshall's conception of it than that espoused by a bare majority of the Court in the *Dagenhart* case. However that may be, the *Darby* case gave sanction to a new centralized force in American industrial and social life.

Some have thought that but for the philosophy which it represents and the power of the Federal Government which it sanctions, the nation would not have been able to marshall all the strength and to develop all the ingenuity and resourcefulness necessary to deal with the increasingly national problems of the age.

The decision of the Court in the *Santa Clara* case protected the forces of free enterprise that were building America. We can never know how much the spectre of socialism and the fear of assaults on capitalism contributed to the decision. But the end result is plain: the Court itself became part of the dynamic component of history. It did not live aloof from the turbulence of the times. It was part of the life of the community, absorbed from it the dominant attitudes and feelings of the day, and moved with the impetus of the era.

The Court in the *Darby* case was likewise extremely sensitive to the critical problems of another day. The whole of the democratic world had long been reexamining the conditions that had produced the misery of depressions. It is a soul-searching decision when one is asked to deny the existence of the power of government to correct a social evil. The unanimity of the Court in the *Darby* case indicated how high experience had piled since *Dagenhart* was decided.

Neither the Court in the *Santa Clara* case nor the Court in the *Darby* case was insensitive to the implications of the decisions. Precedents are made or unmade not on logic and history alone. The choices left by the generality of a constitution relate to policy. That is why laymen and lawyers alike must look widely and diversely for understanding. The problem of the judge is to keep personal predilections from dictating the choice and to be as faithful as possible to the architectural scheme. We can get from those who preceded a sense of the continuity of a society. We can draw from their learning a feel for the durability of a doctrine and a sense of the rights of principles. But we have experience that they never knew. Our vision may be shorter or longer. But it is ours. It is better that we make our own history than be governed by the dead. We too must be dynamic components of history if our institutions are to be vital, directive forces in the life of our age.

One can respect the policy decision both in the *Santa Clara* case and in the *Darby* case. But whatever the view on the merits all will agree, I think, that the recent Court was more faithful to the democratic tradition. It wrote in words that all could understand why it did what it did. That is vital to the integrity of the judicial process. . . .

The study of changes in judicial precedents gives, of course, a distorted view. It is like the study of pathological cases in social or medical sciences. The norm is robust and enduring. The case that gets into the books often has an unsettling effect. Yet we are apt to forget that "the fact that a case is in the reports at all is in itself uncertain." The great body of law is unperturbed by events that may rock a nation.

When the changing stream of public law is studied there are three considerations to keep in mind.

First. We have had only one major dispute that struck at the vitals of our federalism. That was the Civil War. Our controversies and quarrels even at the level of constitutional law have been of a lesser kind. They have been disputes calling for adjustment within the framework of our Charter not for repudiation of it. As one of my Brethren recently stated, they have not involved reconsideration of our basic constitutional tenets which have been accepted since the days of Marshall. They have entailed arguments over the application of established doctrine. The problem has been to free the system for growth unhampered by the crippling restraints which men of cramped and narrow vision placed on it. In considering the charges leveled against those of any period who are responsible for giving new or broader interpretations to the Constitution or discarding precedents it is well to remember these words of Thayer.

And so it happens, as one looks back over our history and the field of political discussions in the past, that he seems to see the whole region strewn with the wrecks of the Constitution,—of what people have been imagining and putting forward as the Constitution. That it was unconstitutional to buy Louisiana and Florida; that it was unconstitutional to add new states to the Union from territory not belonging originally to it; that it was unconstitutional to govern the territories at all; that it was unconstitutional to charter a bank, to issue paper money, to make it a legal tender, to enact a protective tariff,—that these and a hundred other things were a violation of the Constitution has been solemnly and passionately asserted by statesmen and lawyers. Nothing that is now going forward can exceed the vehemence of denunciation, and the pathetic and conscientious resistance of those who lifted up their voices against many of these supposed violations of the Constitution. The trouble has been, then as now, that men imputed to our fundamental law their own too narrow construction of it, their own theory of its purposes and its spirit, and sought thus, when the question was one of mere power, to restrict its great liberty.

Second. It is sometimes thought to be astute political management of a shift in position to proclaim that no change is under way. That is designed as a sedative to instill confidence and allay doubts. It has been a tool of judges as well as other officials. Precedents, though distinguished and qualified out of existence, apparently have been kept alive. The theory is that the outward appearance of stability is what is important.

The idea that any body of law, particularly public law, should appear to stay put and not be in flux is an interesting phenomenon that Frank has explored in *Law and the Modern Mind*. He points out how it is—in law and in other fields too—that men continue to chant of the immutability of a rule in order to "cover up the transformation, to deny the reality of change, to conceal the truth of adaption behind a verbal disguise of fixity and universality." But the more blunt, open, and direct course is truer to democratic traditions. It reflects the candor of Cardozo. The principle of full disclosure has as much place in government as it does in the market place. A judiciary that discloses what it is doing and why it does it will breed understanding. And confidence based on understanding is more enduring than confidence based on awe.

Third. From age to age the problem of constitutional adjudication is the same. It is to keep the power of government unrestrained by the social or economic theories that one set of judges may entertain. It is to keep one age unfettered by the fears or limited vision of another. There is in that connection one tenet of faith which has crystallized more and more as a result of our long experience as a nation. It is this: If the social and economic problems of state and nation can be kept under political management of the people, there is likely to be long-run stability. It is when a judiciary with life tenure seeks to write its social and economic creed into the Charter that instability is created. For then the nation lacks the adaptability to master the sudden storms of an era. It must be remembered that the process of constitutional amendment is a long and slow one.

That philosophy is reflected in what Thomas Jefferson wrote about the Constitution,

Some men look at constitutions with sanctimonious reverence, and deem them like the ark of the covenant, too sacred to be touched. They ascribe to the men of the preceding age a wisdom more than human, and suppose what they did to be beyond amendment. I knew that age well; I belonged to it, and labored with it. It deserved well of its country. It was very like the present, but without the experience of the present; and forty years of experience in government is worth a century of book-reading; and this they would say themselves, were they to rise from the dead.

Jefferson's words are *a fortiori* germane to the fashioning of constitutional law and to the lesser lawmaking in which the judiciary necessarily indulges.

Rogers v. Bellei
91 S.Ct. 1060 (1971)

This was a suit to enjoin the Secretary of State from enforcing a provision of the Immigration and Nationality Act of 1952 which provides that a person born abroad who acquired United States citizenship by reason that one of his parents was an American citizen shall lose his citizenship unless he resides in the United States continuously for five years between the ages of fourteen and twenty-eight. The Court in a 5–4 opinion held that the law was constitutional. The majority of the Court found that Congress has the power to impose the condition subsequent of residence in this country on persons who do not come within the protection of the Fourteenth Amendment because they are not "born or naturalized in the United States." . . .

BLACK, JUSTICE, with whom JUSTICE DOUGLAS and JUSTICE MARSHALL join, dissenting: Less than four years ago this Court held that

the Fourteenth Amendment was designed to, and does, protect every citizen of this Nation against a congressional forcible destruction of his citizenship, whatever his creed, color, or race. Our holding does no more than to give to this citizen that which is his own, a constitutional right to remain a citizen in a free country unless he voluntarily relinquishes that citizenship.

The holding was clear. Congress could not, until today, consistently with the Fourteenth Amendment enact a law stripping an American of his citizenship which he has never voluntarily renounced or given up. Now this Court, by a vote of five to four through a simple change in its composition, overrules that decision.

The Court today holds that Congress can indeed rob a citizen of his citizenship just so long as five members of this Court can satisfy themselves that the congressional action was not "unreasonable, arbitrary," "misplaced or arbitrary," or "irrational or arbitrary or unfair." . . .

The Constitution, written for the ages, cannot rise and fall with this Court's passing notions of what is "fair," or "reasonable," or "arbitrary." The Fourteenth Amendment commands:

All persons born or naturalized in the United States, and subject to the jurisdiction thereof, are citizens of the United States and of the State wherein they reside.

Speaking of this very language, the Court held in *Afroyim* that no American can be deprived of his citizenship without his assent. Today, the Court overrules that holding. This precious Fourteenth Amendment American citizenship should not be blown around by every passing political wind that changes the composition of this Court. I dissent.

The Court today puts aside the Fourteenth Amendment as a standard by which to measure congressional action with respect to citizenship, and substitutes in its place the majority's own vague notions of "fairness." The majority takes a new step with the recurring theme that the test of constitutionality is the Court's own view of what is "fair, reasonable, and right." Despite the concession that Bellei was admittedly an American citizen, and despite the holding in *Afroyim* that the Fourteenth Amendment has put citizenship, once conferred, beyond the power of Congress to revoke, the majority today upholds the revocation of Bellei's citizenship on the ground that the congressional action was not "irrational or arbitrary or unfair." The majority applies the "shock-the-conscience" test to uphold, rather than strike, a federal statute. It is a dangerous concept of constitutional law that allows the majority to conclude that, because it cannot say the statute is "irrational or arbitrary or unfair," the statute must be constitutional.

Of course the Court's construction of the Constitution is not a "strict" one. On the contrary, it proceeds on the premise that a majority of this Court can change the Constitution day by day, month by month, and year by year, according to its shifting notions of what is fair, reasonable, and right. There was little need for the founders to draft a written constitution if this Court can say it is only binding when a majority finds it fair, reasonable, and right to make it so. That is the loosest construction that could be employed. It is true that England has moved along very well in the world without a written constitution. But with complete familiarity with the English experience, our ancestors determined to draft a written constitution which the members of this Court are sworn to obey. While I remain on the Court I shall continue to oppose the power of judges, appointed by changing administrations, to change the Constitution from time to time according to their notions of what is "fair" and "reasonable." I would decide this case not by my views of what is "arbitrary," or what is "fair," but rather by what the Constitution commands.

I dissent.

BRENNAN, JUSTICE, with whom JUSTICE DOUGLAS joins, dissenting: Since the Court this Term has already downgraded citizens receiving public welfare, and citizens having the misfortune to be illegitimate, I suppose today's decision downgrading citizens born outside the United States should have been expected. Once again, . . . the Court's opinion makes evident that its holding is contrary to earlier decisions. Concededly petitioner was a citizen at birth not by constitutional right, but only through operation of a federal statute. In the light of the complete lack of rational basis for distinguishing among citizens whose naturalization was carried out within the physical bounds of the United States, and those, like Bellei, who may be naturalized overseas, the conclusion is compelled that the reference in the Fourteenth Amendment to persons "born or naturalized in the United

States" includes those naturalized through operation of an Act of Congress, wherever they may be at the time. Congress was therefore powerless to strip Bellei of his citizenship; he could lose it only if he voluntarily renounced or relinquished it.

I dissent.

Those who do not desire to follow precedent take the position that a stagnant Constitution with rigid application will not meet the needs of our changing times. They argue that the words of justices of the Supreme Court of days gone by—justices who could not foresee the social and economic problems of our country today—should not hamstring today's court, which has the responsibility of deciding today's cases in light of changing conditions. Agreeing with the stand that the court should alter Constitutional construction to meet new conditions, Walter F. Murphy, assistant professor of politics at Princeton University, wrote: "The sociological approach is old and it is necessary." [3] Rejecting the notion that the court should be bound by the "intent" of the original framers as to the meaning of the Constitution, Professor Murphy states:

Not only is there grave danger of an unacceptable (and unworkable) system coming from an "intent" search, but such an investigation is really incomplete unless it takes into account the intent of the ratifiers as well as of the drafters. Just how such a research project would be undertaken would stagger the collective imagination of the historical profession. And it is highly improbable that, even if such a compilation could be made, it would reflect a clear, consistent purpose in many instances. It is difficult to "imagine how any known method of psychoanalysis, or plain crystal-ball gazing applied to such records or to the people who left them could give thoroughly reliable and irrefutable answers concerning the intention of these later framers."

Professor Murphy further states: "The sociological method is at least as old as the Court itself. . . ." He continues:

No scholar today would seriously argue that John Marshall's opinions were not heavily colored by his social views—his concept of the order and scaling of society and also his concept of proper social arrangements. His whole line of decisions reflects a deep concern for protection of vested interests and a supporting desire for strong national government. Pure logic and the wording of constitutional clauses were Marshall's instruments, not his masters. What the Framers had intended was seldom as important to him as what they should— as good Federalists—have intended.

[3] Murphy, The Constitution: Interpretation and Intent, 45 *A.B.A.J.* 592, 594 (June, 1959). Used by permission from the American Bar Association and the *American Bar Association Journal.*

Failure to follow precedent is not limited to issues of public law. The fact that precedent is to be given great weight in the areas of the private law does not mean that courts will continue to follow a rule of private law where the reasoning behind the rule no longer exists. The case which follows illustrates the rejection of such a rule of law.

Myers v. Drozda ✕
141 N.W.2d 852 (Nebr. 1966)

SMITH, JUSTICE: An infant girl and her father urge us to repudiate the court-made rule which has exempted nonprofit charitable hospitals from liability for negligent injuries to patients. In the district court the rule of exemption produced a summary judgment for the hospital on the personal injury claim of the girl and the derivative claim of her father. These appeals followed.

For purposes of review we assume the truth of the following statements. Defendant Lutheran Medical Center is a charitable corporation operating a nonprofit hospital. While the baby girl was a patient in the surgical quarters of the hospital, an employee of defendant hospital negligently anesthetized her. As a result she suffered a cardiac arrest. Defendant hospital carried hospital professional liability insurance with limits of $10,000 per claim and $30,000 aggregate.

In 1912 we adopted a policy of partial immunity which protected parties like defendant hospital. In 1955 we affirmed that policy. Today we reexamine it.

The rationale of exemption has these four labels: "Trust fund," "respondeat superior," "implied waiver," and "public policy." Under the trust fund theory the diversion of assets to satisfy tort judgments would breach the trust. Respondeat superior is said to govern a business for profit but not a charity. An implied waiver by a patient of his tort claim is defended as a fair conclusion from the patient-hospital relationship. The public policy contains the assumption that liability would dissipate the assets of charities.

Although the law of trusts and agency has exempted the hospital from tort liability to its patients, the law has not been applied to the claim of the invitee; a physician may recover, a patient may not.

Implied waiver is a fiction. Of many illustrations we choose one—plaintiff's allegations. At the same time of the "waiver" the age of the girl was 1 year. ". . . Waiver . . . amounts merely to imposing immunity as a rule of law in the guise of assumed contract or renunciation of right, when all other reasons are found insufficient to support the distinction."

The foreboding that tort liability would dissipate assets was dispelled years ago by the following language in *President & Directors of Georgetown College v. Hughes:* . . .

No statistical evidence has been presented to show that the mortality or crippling of charities has been greater in states which impose full or partial liability than where complete or substantially full immunity is given. Nor is there evidence that deference of donation has been greater in the former.

Charities seem to survive and increase in both, with little apparent heed to whether they are liable for torts or difference in survival capacity. . . .

What is at stake, so far as the charity is concerned, is the cost of reasonable protection, the amount of the insurance premium as an added burden on its finances, not the awarding over in damages of its entire assets. . . .

Whether immunity is founded on the "trust fund" theory, the rule of respondeat superior, so-called "public policy," or the more indefensible doctrine of "implied waiver," is not for us a controlling consideration. . . . They are merely different names for the same idea, cast according to the predilection of the user. . . . The differences in foundation do not affect even the extent of the departure.

If this exemption formerly met a need, it has had its day. In 1942 four states apparently imposed unqualified liability. In 1955 we named 22 states, exclusive of Nebraska, which had granted some degree of immunity, and we said that 10 of them had recently reaffirmed their position. Afterward courts in 8 of the 22 states abrogated the immunity, and 5 of the 10 "recent" decisions were overruled. Two legislatures intervened on one side or the other. It is doubtful that any court has overruled a decision declaring a charity to be nonexempt. Liability probably represents the majority view. The judicial trend is unmistakable.

Defendant hospital relies upon our prior announcement that any change ought to be made by the Legislature. If we endorsed legislation by silence, we erred. Stare decisis "was intended, not to effect a 'petrifying rigidity,' but to assure the justice that flows from certainty and stability. . . . We would be abdicating 'our own function, in a field peculiarly nonstatutory,' were we to insist on legislation and 'refuse to reconsider an old and unsatisfactory court-made rule.'"

. . . [J]udges of an earlier generation declared the immunity simply because they believed it to be a sound instrument of judicial policy which would further the moral, social and economic welfare of the people of the State. When judges of a later generation firmly reach a contrary conclusion they must be ready to discharge their own judicial responsibilities in conformance with modern concepts and needs. . . .

The old rule being clearly wrong, we hold that nonprofit charitable hospitals are not exempt from tort liability to their patients. Contrary decisions are overruled to the extent of their inconsistency.

The point of departure from precedent remains to be determined. Loss of exemption may be retrospective, partially retrospective, or prospective. The choice is influenced by these broad considerations: The reasons for overruling the prior decisions; the public interest in institutional stability; justifiable reliance upon the exemption; and uniformity of application to parties similarly situated.

Other courts have considered some of those policy factors. Several decisions removed the exemption prospectively except for the cases being decided. Three reasons were given. First, the charitable corporation may have relied on the old rule whether or not insurance coverage existed. Second, announcement of prospective operation would be dictum. Third, if the effort and expense of challenge were to go unrewarded, appellant would have no incentive to contest the old rule.

We too think that the new rule should be partially retrospective; however, insurance is insignificant. A differentiating factor between a charity and its insurer is reliance. An insured charity does not rely justifiably on the exemption within the limits of the insurer's liability. The impact of liability upon an insurer should be relatively light because of its ability to spread the loss. ". . . [O]rdinarily it is impossible to trace the impact of particular legal doctrine upon liability insurance rates." Factors concerning dictum and reward carry some weight but not much.

In conclusion the new rule applies to all causes of action arising after April 22, 1966, the filing date of this opinion. In respect to other causes of action the new rule applies if, but only if, the nonprofit charitable hospital was insured against liability on the claim of the patient, and then only to the extent of the maximum applicable amount of its insurance coverage.

The judgment is reversed, and the causes are remanded for proceedings consistent with this opinion. [REVERSED AND REMANDED]

3 SCOPE OF PRECEDENT

Each state has its own statutory laws and its own body of judge-made precedent. These laws cover both matters of substance and matters of procedure. Generally, the decisions of one state are considered to be applicable precedent only in that state. The decisions of other states, however, may be considered by way of analogy when there are no previous decisions on the point in question in the state where a case is being heard. For example, precedent of other states is frequently referred to in cases involving the construction of statutes such as the Uniform Acts where each state has adopted the same statute. Where there is no precedent a case is one of "first impression," and in such cases, each state is free to decide for itself questions concerning its common law and interpretation of its own constitution and statutes.

In addition to this system of fifty distinct bodies of state precedent there is the Federal legal system. The Federal courts have their own body of procedural law and their own body of substantive law on questions arising under the Federal Constitution, codes, statutes, or treaties. Decisions of the United States Supreme Court on Federal questions involving the United States Constitution, treaties, Federal statutes, and matters of interstate commerce are binding on state courts, while decisions of lower Federal courts are generally held not to be binding. Federal courts also have jurisdiction of cases involving citizens of different states under the Constitution, even though no Federal question is in issue. In the case which follows, it is established that there is no body of Federal common law, and that in suits based on diversity of citizenship, the Federal courts use the substantive law of the states in which they are sitting to determine the rights and duties of the parties. In such cases, the Federal courts do use their own rules of procedure, however. Thus, just as state courts are bound by Federal precedent in certain situations, so also are Federal courts bound by state precedent in others.

✗ Erie Railroad v. Tompkins
304 U.S. 64 (1938)

BRANDEIS, JUSTICE: The question for decision is whether the oft-challenged doctrine of *Swift v. Tyson* shall now be disapproved.

Tompkins, a citizen of Pennsylvania, was injured on a dark night by a passing freight train of the Erie Railroad Company while walking along its right of way at Hughestown in that state. He claimed that the accident occurred through negligence in the operation, or maintenance, of the train; that he was rightfully on the premises as licensee because on a commonly used beaten footpath which ran for a short distance alongside the tracks; and that he was struck by something which looked like a door projecting from one of the moving cars. To enforce that claim he brought an action in the federal court for Southern New York, which has jurisdiction because the company is a corporation of that state. It denied liability; and the case was tried by a jury.

The Erie insisted that its duty to Tompkins was no greater than that owed to a trespasser. It contended, among other things, that its duty to Tompkins, and hence its liability, should be determined in accordance with the Pennsylvania law; that under the law of Pennsylvania, as declared by its highest court, persons who use pathways along the railroad right of way—that is, a longitudinal pathway as distinguished from a crossing—are to be deemed trespassers; and that the railroad is not liable for injuries to undiscovered trespassers resulting from its negligence, unless it be wanton or willful. Tompkins denied that any such rule had been established by the decisions of the Pennsylvania courts; and contended that, since there was no statute of the state on the subject, the railroad's duty and liability is to be determined in federal courts as a matter of general law.

The trial judge refused to rule that the applicable law precluded recovery. The jury brought in a verdict of $30,000; and the judgment entered thereon was affirmed by the Circuit Court of Appeals, which held (2 Cir., 90 F.2d 603, 604) that it was unnecessary to consider whether the law of Pennsylvania was as contended, because the question was one not of local but of general law, and that

. . . *upon questions of general law the federal courts are free, in absence of a local statute, to exercise their independent judgment as to what the law is; and it is well settled that the question of the responsibility of a railroad for injuries caused by its servants is one of general law. . . . Where the public has made open and notorious use of a railroad right of way for a long period of time and without objection, the company owes to persons on such permissive pathway a duty of care in the operation of its trains. . . . It is likewise generally recognized law that a jury may find that negligence exists toward a pedestrian using a permissive path on the railroad right of way if he is hit by some object projecting from the side of the train.*

The Erie had contended that application of the Pennsylvania rule was required, among other things, by section 34 of the Federal Judiciary Act of September 24, 1789, c. 20, 28 U.S.C. § 725, 28 U.S.C.A. § 725, which provides: "The laws of the several States, except where the Constitution, treaties, or statutes of the United States otherwise require or provide, shall be regarded as rules of decision in trials at common law, in the courts of the United States, in cases where they apply."

Because of the importance of the question whether the federal court was free to disregard the alleged rule of the Pennsylvania common law, we granted certiorari. . . .

First. *Swift v. Tyson*, 16 Pet. 1, 18, 10 L.Ed. 865, held that federal courts exercising jurisdiction on the ground of diversity of citizenship need not, in matters of general jurisprudence, apply the unwritten law of the state as declared by its highest court; that they are free to exercise an independent judgment as to what the common law of the state is—or should be; and that, as there stated by Mr. Justice Story,

The true interpretation of the 34th section limited its application to state laws, strictly local, that is to say, to the positive statutes of the state, and the construction thereof adopted by the local tribunals, and to rights and titles to things having a permanent locality, such as the rights and titles to real estate, and other matters immovable and intra-territorial in their nature and character. It never has been supposed by us, that the section did apply, or was designed to apply, to questions of a fixed and permanent operation, as, for example, to the construction of ordinary contracts or other written instruments, and especially to questions of general commercial law, where the state tribunals are called upon to perform the like functions as ourselves, that is, to ascertain, upon general reasoning and legal analogies, what is the true exposition of the contract or instrument, or what is the just rule furnished by the principles of commercial law to govern the case.

The Court in applying the rule of section 34 to equity cases, in *Mason v. United States*, 260 U.S. 545, 559, . . . said: "The statute, however, is merely declarative of the rule which would exist in the absence of the statute." The federal courts assumed, in the broad field of "general law," the power to declare rules of decision which Congress was confessedly without power to enact as statutes. Doubt was repeatedly expressed as to the correctness of the construction given section 34, and as to the soundness of the rule which it introduced. But it was the more recent research of a competent scholar, who examined the original document, which established that the construction given to it by the Court was erroneous; and that the purpose of the section was merely to make certain that, in all matters except those in which some federal law is controlling, the federal courts exercising jurisdiction in diversity of citizenship cases would apply as their rules of decision the law of the state, unwritten as well as written.

Criticism of the doctrine became widespread after the decision of *Black & White Taxicab & Transfer Co. v. Brown & Yellow Taxicab & Transfer Co.*, 276 U.S. 518. . . . There, Brown & Yellow, a Kentucky corporation owned by Kentuckians, and the Louisville & Nashville Railroad, also a Kentucky corporation, wished that the former should have the exclusive privilege of soliciting passenger and baggage transportation at the Bowling Green, Ky., railroad station; and that the Black & White, a competing Kentucky corporation, should be prevented from interfering with that privilege. Knowing that such a contract would be void under the common law of Kentucky, it was arranged that the Brown & Yellow reincorporate under the law of Tennessee, and that the contract with the railroad should be executed there. The suit was then brought by the Tennessee corporation in the federal court for Western Kentucky to enjoin competition by the Black & White; an injunction issued by the District Court was sustained by the Court of Appeals; and this Court, citing many decisions in which the doctrine of *Swift v. Tyson* had been applied, affirmed the decree.

Second. Experience in applying the doctrine of *Swift v. Tyson* had revealed its defects, political and social; and the benefits expected to flow from the rule did not accrue. Persistence of state courts in their own opinions on questions of common law prevented uniformity, and the impossibility of discovering a satisfactory line of demarcation between the province of general law and that of local law developed a new well of uncertainties.

On the other hand, the mischievous results of the doctrine had become apparent. Diversity of citizenship jurisdiction was conferred in order to prevent apprehended discrimination in state courts against those not citizens of the state. *Swift v. Tyson* introduced grave discrimination by noncitizens against citizens. It made rights enjoyed under the unwritten "general law" vary according to whether enforcement was sought in the state or in the federal court; and the privilege of selecting the court in which the right should be determined was conferred upon the noncitizen. Thus, the doctrine rendered impossible equal protection of the law. In attempting to promote uniformity of law throughout the United States, the doctrine had prevented uniformity in the administration of the law of the state.

The discrimination resulting became in practice far-reaching. This resulted in part from the broad province accorded to the so-called "general law" as to which federal courts exercised an independent judgment. In addition to questions of purely commercial law, "general law" was held to include the obligations under contracts entered into and to be performed within the state, the extent to which a carrier operating within a state may stipulate for exemption from liability for his own negligence or that of his employee; the liability for torts committed within the state upon persons resident or property located there, even where the question of liability depended upon the scope of a property right conferred by the state, and the right to exemplary or punitive damages. Furthermore, state decisions construing local deeds, mineral conveyances, and even devices of real estate, were disregarded.

In part the discrimination resulted from the wide range of persons held entitled to avail themselves of the federal rule by resort to the diversity of citizenship jurisdiction. Through this jurisdiction individual citizens willing to remove from their own state and become citizens of another might avail themselves of the federal rule. And, without even change of residence, a corporate citizen of the state could avail itself of the federal rule by reincorporating under the provisions of the laws of another state, as was done in the *Taxicab* case.

The injustice and confusion incident to the doctrine of *Swift v. Tyson* have been repeatedly urged as reasons for abolishing or limiting diversity of citizenship jurisdiction. Other legislative relief has been proposed. If only a question of statutory construction were involved, we should not be prepared to abandon a doctrine so widely applied throughout nearly a century. But the unconstitutionality of the course pursued has now been made clear, and compels us to do so.

Third. Except in matters governed by the Federal Constitution or by acts of Congress, the law to be applied in any case is the law of the state. And whether the law of the state shall be declared by its Legislature in a statute or by its highest court in a decision is not a matter of federal concern. There is no federal general common law. Congress has no power to declare substantive rules of common law applicable in a state whether they be local in their nature or "general," whether they be commercial law or a part of the law of torts. And there is no clause in the Constitution that purports to confer such a power upon the federal courts. As stated by Mr. Justice Field when protesting in *Baltimore & Ohio R.R. v. Baugh,* 149 U.S. 368, 401, . . . against ignoring the Ohio common law of fellow-servant liability:

I am aware that what has been termed the general law of the country—which is often little less than what the judge advancing the doctrine thinks at the time should be the general law on a particular subject—has been often advanced in judicial opinions of this court to control a conflicting law of a state. I admit that learned judges have fallen into the habit of repeating this doctrine as a convenient mode of brushing aside the law of a state in conflict with their views. And I confess that, moved and governed by the authority of the great names of those judges, I have, myself, in many instances, unhesitatingly and confidently, but I think now erroneously, repeated the same doctrine. But, notwithstanding the great names which may be cited in favor of the doctrine, and notwithstanding the frequency with which the doctrine has been reiterated, there stands, as a perpetual protest against its repetition, the constitution of the United States, which recognizes and preserves the autonomy and independence of the states,—independence in their legislative and independence in their judicial departments. Supervision over either the legislative or the judicial action of the states is in no case permissible except as to matters by the constitution specifically authorized or delegated to the United States. Any interference with either, except as thus permitted, is an invasion of the authority of the state, and, to that extent, a denial of its independence.

The fallacy underlying the rule declared in *Swift v. Tyson* is made clear by Mr. Justice Holmes. The doctrine rests upon the assumption that there is "a transcendental body of law outside of any particular State but obligatory within it unless and until changed by statute," that federal courts have the power to use their judgment as to what the rules of common law are; and that in the federal courts "the parties are entitled to an independent judgment on matters of general law":

. . . But law in the sense in which courts speak of it today does not exist without some definite authority behind it. The common law so far as it is enforced in a State, whether called common law or not, is not the common law generally but the law of that State existing by the authority of that State without regard to what it may have been in England or anywhere else. . . .

The authority and only authority is the State, and if that be so, the voice adopted by the State as its own (whether it be of its Legislature or of its Supreme Court) should utter the last word.

Thus the doctrine of *Swift v. Tyson* is, as Mr. Justice Holmes said, "an unconstitutional assumption of powers by the Courts of the United States which no lapse of time or respectable array of opinion should make us hesitate to correct." In disapproving that doctrine we do not hold unconstitutional section 34 of the Federal Judiciary Act of 1789 or any other act of Congress. We merely declare that in applying the doctrine this Court and the lower courts have invaded rights which in our opinion are reserved by the Constitution to the several states.

Fourth. The defendant contended that by common law of Pennsylvania as declared by its highest court in *Falchetti v. Pennsylvania R.R.*, 307 Pa. 203, 160 Atl. 859, the only duty owed to the plaintiff was to refrain from willful or wanton injury. The plaintiff denied that such is the Pennsylvania law. In support of their respective contentions the parties discussed and cited many decisions of the Supreme Court of the state. The Circuit Court of Appeals ruled that the question of liability is one of general law; and on that ground declined to decide the issue of state law. As we hold this was error, the judgment is reversed and the case remanded to it for further proceedings in conformity with our opinion. [REVERSED]

Subsequent to the *Erie* case, in diversity of citizenship cases, many Federal decisions have been concerned with whether a given issue is one of substantive law, in which case the applicable state law will be followed, or one of procedure, in which case the Federal practice will be followed. If the state rule of law, whether created by statute or case decision, will affect the *result* of the controversy, the rule is treated as substantive and will be followed by the Federal court.

One further aspect of the scope of precedent must be noted. Article IV, Section 1, of the United States Constitution provides: "Full Faith and Credit shall be given in each State to the public Acts, Records, and judicial proceedings of every other State. . . ." This does not mean that the precedent in one state is binding in other states, but only that the final decisions or judgments rendered in any given state shall be enforced as between the original parties in other states. Full faith and credit is applicable to the result of a specific decision as it affects the rights of the parties, and not to the reasons or principles upon which it was based.

4   CONFLICTS OF LAW

In litigation involving a transaction or occurrence in only one state, the court may have the problem of selecting the applicable precedent from the conflicting citations of authority from previous decisions of that state made by the attorneys on each side of the case. Obviously, the problem is magnified many times when the transaction or occurrence is interstate in character. For example, suppose that a resident of Illinois boards an airline in St. Louis, Missouri, for a flight to California, and the plane crashes in Nebraska. Assuming that the ticket was purchased in Illinois, the liability of the airline could be based on the statutes and decisions of any one of these four different states. Illinois law might provide a $30,000 maximum liability for wrongful death, Missouri $25,000, Nebraska unlimited, and California still a different amount. The law of torts, though a part of the private law, does vary from state to state in such important matters as the burden of proof and the measure of damages. The law of contracts also is not uniform throughout the country. In such cases, what is the applicable precedent?

The problem of selecting the applicable law frequently arises in other areas of the law, such as marriage and divorce, and the passing of property on death. In the latter situation, for example, the retired person who is planning his estate and has a winter home in Florida, a summer home in Maine, and who was formerly a resident of New York may face a complex state inheritance tax question. It is possible that each of the states mentioned may claim him as a resident and attempt to tax the estate.

As a direct result of the multistate transaction or occurrence, there has developed a body of law, primarily through judicial decisions, which is generally referred to as "conflicts of law." The decisions which comprise this body of law simply determine which state's law is applicable to any given question when more than one state is involved. This usually arises where all or some of the facts occur in one state and the trial is held in another. For example, the conflicts-of-law rule for tort actions is, in most states, that the law of the place of injury is applicable. Thus, if a car accident occurred in Missouri but suit was brought in an Illinois state court, the judge would apply the law of Missouri in determining the rights of the parties. There are several different views held by courts about which law to select in resolving issues involving contracts. Some favor the law of the state where the contract was made, others the law of the place of performance, and still others have adopted the "grouping of contacts" theory which uses the law of the state with the most substantial contact with the contract.

In a multistate situation, the first problem confronting the court is, therefore, the selection of the appropriate state to turn to for legal precedent. Once a determination has been made of which state is appropriate, the court's business then is to review the citations of authority advanced by the opposing attorneys to determine which of that state's case decisions to apply in following the doctrine of stare decisis.

One further complicating factor should be noted in the process of a *Federal* court in selecting the law of the state's precedent it has decided to follow. The Federal court will look at the total body of law of the state in which it is sitting, *including the state's conflicts of law principles.* Thus, in using the law of state X it may in turn look to the law of some other state for the actual precedent. For example, assume that a citizen of the state of Illinois sues a citizen of the state of Indiana in the Federal district court in Indiana for personal injuries received in an automobile accident which occurred in the state of Kentucky. The Federal district court sitting in Indiana will use Federal procedure and the substantive law of the state of *Indiana.* The substantive law of the state of Indiana includes the conflicts-of-law principle that the applicable tort law is the law of the place of injury. The Federal court in Indiana will use the Kentucky tort law since that is the law which would be used by an Indiana state court.

Therefore, it must be recognized that there is a body of law used to decide the conflicts between the precedent of the various states, which is especially significant in our modern society with its ease of communication and transportation. The trend toward uniform statutes and codes has tended to decrease these conflicts, but many of them still exist. So long as we have a Federal system and fifty separate state bodies of substantive law, the area of conflicts of law will continue to be of substantial importance in the application of the doctrine of stare decisis.

5   SEPARATION OF POWERS AND JUDICIAL REVIEW

There are two doctrines which play a major role in our legal system as a result of the use of precedent as a source of law. First of all, there is the doctrine of separation of powers which simply affords to each branch of government its respective duties with the implication that they should not be performed by the others. The doctrine is also the basis of our so-called checks and balances system by which each branch serves in some way as a restricting power in the activities of the other. Separation of powers on the surface would seem to be violated when judges make law. This doctrine, if narrowly followed, would limit the law-making function to the legislature. However, as a practical matter, each branch has certain law-making functions—the Congress by legislation, the courts by judicial decision, and the executive by administrative action, decision, or regulation. (Administrative law making is discussed in Chapter 7.) Since each branch of government in its activities creates laws, it is not surprising that occasionally the action of one is inconsistent with the position of another. We have already seen that legislatures may change judicial decisions by enacting specific statutes. Of course, a court may "change a law" by giving a statute an interpretation which may or may not have been intended. The court may allow a statute to stand as interpreted and thus in one sense is exercising control over the legislative body. The second doctrine is that of judicial review, which empowers courts to review laws passed by the legislative body and to declare them to be unconstitutional and thus void. It also allows the courts to review actions taken by the executive branch and to declare them to be unconstitutional. While the Constitution does not expressly provide that the judiciary shall be the overseer of the government, the net effect of this doctrine is to make it so. Chief Justice Marshall in *Marbury v. Madison* announced the doctrine of judicial review and recognized the concept of separation of powers, using the following language and reasoning:

Marbury v. Madison ✕
5 U.S. (1 Cranch) 137 (1803)

MARSHALL, CHIEF JUSTICE: . . . . The question, whether an act, repugnant to the constitution, can become the law of the land, is a question deeply interesting to the United States; but, happily, not of an intricacy proportioned to its interest. It seems only necessary to recognise certain principles, supposed to have been long and well established, to decide it. That the people have an original right to establish, for their future government, such principles as, in their opinion, shall most conduce to their own happiness, is the basis on which the whole American fabric has been erected. The exercise of this original right is a very great exertion; nor can it, nor ought it, to be frequently repeated. The principles, therefore, so established, are deemed fundamental; and as the authority from which they proceed is supreme, and can seldom act, they are designed to be permanent.

This original and supreme will organizes the government, and assigns to different departments their respective powers. It may either stop here, or establish certain limits not to be transcended by those departments. The government of the United States is of the latter description. The powers of the legislature are defined and limited; and that those limits may not be mistaken or forgotten, the constitution is written. To what purpose are powers limited, and to what purpose is that limitation committed to writing, if these limits may, at any time, be passed by those intended to be restrained? The distinction between a government with limited and unlimited powers is abolished, if those limits do not confine the persons on whom they are imposed, and if acts prohibited and acts allowed, are of equal obligation. It is a proposition too plain to be contested, that the constitution controls any legislative act repugnant to it; or that the legislature may not alter the constitution by an ordinary act.

Between these alternatives, there is no middle ground. The constitution is either a superior paramount law, unchangeable by ordinary means, or it is on a level with ordinary legislative acts, and, like other acts, is alterable when the legislature shall please to alter it. If the former part of the alternative be true, then a legislative act, contrary to the constitution, is not law: if the latter part be true, then written constitutions are absurd attempts on the part of the people, to limit a power, in its own nature, illimitable.

Certainly, all those who have framed written constitutions contemplate them as forming the fundamental and paramount law of the nation, and consequently, the theory of every such government must be, that an act of the legislature, repugnant to the constitution, is void. This theory is essentially attached to a written constitution, and is, consequently, to be considered, by this court, as one of the fundamental principles of our society. It is not, therefore, to be lost sight of, in the further consideration of this subject.

If an act of the legislature, repugnant to the constitution, is void, does it, notwithstanding its invalidity, bind the courts, and oblige them to give it effect? Or, in other words, though it be not law, does it constitute a rule as operative as if it was a law? This would be to overthrow, in fact, what was established in theory; and would seem, at first view, an absurdity too gross to be insisted on. It shall, however, receive a more attentive consideration.

It is, emphatically, the province and duty of the judicial department, to say what the law is. Those who apply the rule to particular cases, must of necessity expound and interpret that rule. If two laws conflict with each other, the courts must decide on the operation of each. So, if a law be in opposition to the constitution; if both the law and the constitution apply to a particular case, so that the court must either decide that case, conformable to the law, disregarding the constitution; or conformable to the constitution, disregarding the law; the court must determine which of these conflicting rules governs the case: this is of the very essence of judicial duty. If then, the courts are to regard the constitution, and the constitution is superior to any ordinary act of the legislature, the constitution, and not such ordinary act, must govern the case to which they both apply.

Those, then, who controvert the principle, that the constitution is to be considered, in court, as a paramount law, are reduced to the necessity of maintaining that courts must close their eyes on the constitution, and see only the law. This doctrine would subvert the very foundation of all written constitutions. It would declare that an act which, according to the principles and theory of our government, is entirely void, is yet, in practice, completely obligatory. It would declare that if the legislature shall do what is expressly forbidden, such act, notwithstanding the express prohibition, is in reality effectual. It would be giving to the legislature a practical and real omnipotence, with the same breath which professes to restrict their powers within narrow limits. It is prescribing limits, and declaring that those limits may be passed at pleasure. That it thus reduces to nothing, what we have deemed the greatest improvement on political institutions, a written constitution, would, of itself, be sufficient, in America, where written constitutions have been viewed with so much reverence, for rejecting the construction. But the peculiar expressions of the constitution of the United States furnish additional arguments in favor of its rejection. The judicial power of the United States is extended to all cases arising under the constitution. Could it be the intention of those who gave this power, to say, that in using it, the constitution should not be looked into? That a case arising under the constitution should be decided, without examining the instrument under which it arises? This is too extravagant to be maintained. In some cases, then, the constitution must be looked into by the judges. And if they can open it at all, what part of it are they forbidden to read or to obey?

There are many other parts of the constitution which serve to illustrate this subject. It is declared, that "no tax or duty shall be laid on articles exported from any state." Suppose, a duty on the export of cotton, of tobacco or of flour; and a suit instituted to recover it. Ought judgment to be rendered in such a case? Ought the judges to close their eyes on the constitution, and only see the law?

The constitution declares "that no bill of attainder or *ex post facto* law shall be passed." If, however, such a bill should be prosecuted under it; must the court condemn to death those victims whom the constitution endeavors to preserve?

"No person," says the constitution, "shall be convicted of treason, unless on the testimony of two witnesses to the same *overt* act, or on confession in open court." Here, the language of the constitution is addressed especially to the courts. It prescribes, directly for them, a rule of evidence not to be departed from. If the legislature should change that rule, and declare one witness, or a confession out of court, sufficient for conviction, must the constitutional principle yield to the legislative act?

From these, and many other selections which might be made, it is apparent, that the framers of the constitution contemplated that instrument as a rule for the government of courts, as well as of the legislature. Why otherwise does it direct the judges to take an oath to support it? This oath certainly applies in an especial manner, to their conduct in their official character. How immoral to impose it on them, if they were to be used as the instruments, and the knowing instruments, for violating what they swear to support!

The oath of office, too, imposed by the legislature, is completely demonstrative of the legislative opinion on this subject. It is these words: "I do solemnly swear, that I will administer justice, without respect to persons, and do equal right to the poor and to the rich; and that I will faithfully and impartially discharge all the duties incumbent on me as _____, according to the best of my abilities and understanding, agreeably to the constitution and laws of the United States." Why does a judge swear to discharge his duties agreeably to the constitution of the United States, if that constitution forms no rule for his government? If it is closed upon him, and cannot be inspected by him? If such be the real state of things, this is worse than solemn mockery. To prescribe, or to take this oath, becomes equally a crime.

It is also not entirely unworthy of observation, that in declaring what shall be the supreme law of the land, the constitution itself is first mentioned; and not the laws of the United States, generally, but those only which shall be made in pursuance of the constitution, have that rank.

Thus, the particular phraseology of the constitution of the United States confirms and strengthens the principle, supposed to be essential to all written constitutions, that a law repugnant to the constitution is void; and that courts, as well as other departments, are bound by that instrument. . . .

The power of courts to declare void actions of the executive or legislature has played an important role in our history and in the law as it is related to business. The following case is a more recent example of the application of the doctrine of judicial review and contains significant discussions of the separation of powers concept, of which judicial review is a part.

Youngstown Sheet & Tube Co. v. Sawyer
343 U.S. 579 (1952)

During the Korean War, a dispute arose between certain steel companies and their employees over the terms and conditions which should be included in new collective-bargaining agreements. The dispute was not settled despite governmental attempts at a settlement, and a nationwide strike was called. Steel was used in the weapons of war and was in short supply. Just prior to the strike, the President, without specific congressional authority, issued an order directing the Secretary of Commerce to take possession of and operate most of the nation's steel mills. This action challenged the validity of that order.

BLACK, JUSTICE: The President's power, if any, to issue the order must stem either from an act of Congress or from the Constitution itself. There is no statute that expressly authorizes the President to take possession of property as he did here. Nor is there any act of Congress to which our attention has been directed from which such a power can fairly be implied. Indeed, we do not understand the Government to rely on statutory authorization for this seizure. . . .

Moreover, the use of the seizure technique to solve labor disputes in order to prevent work stoppages was not only unauthorized by any congressional enactment; prior to this controversy, Congress had refused to adopt that method of settling labor disputes. . . .

It is clear that if the President had authority to issue the order he did, it must be found in some provision of the Constitution. And it is not claimed that express constitutional language grants this power to the President. The contention is that presidential power should be implied from the aggregate of his powers under the Constitution. Particular reliance is placed on provisions in Article II which say that "The executive Power shall be vested in a President . . ."; and that he "shall be Commander in Chief of the Army and Navy of the United States."

The order cannot properly be sustained as an exercise of the President's military power as Commander in Chief of the Armed Forces. The Government attempts to do so by citing a number of cases upholding broad powers in military commanders engaged in day-to-day fighting in a theater of war. Such cases need not concern us here. Even though "theater of war" be an expanding concept, we cannot with faithfulness to our constitutional system hold that the Commander in Chief of the Armed Forces has the ultimate power as such to take possession of private property in order to keep labor disputes from stopping production. This is a job for the Nation's lawmakers, not for its military authorities.

Nor can the seizure order be sustained because of the several constitutional provisions that grant executive power to the President. In the framework of our

Constitution, the President's power to see that the laws are faithfully executed refutes the idea that he is to be a lawmaker. The Constitution limits his functions in the lawmaking process to the recommending of laws he thinks wise and the vetoing of laws he thinks bad. And the Constitution is neither silent nor equivocal about who shall make laws which the President is to execute. The first section of the first article says that "All legislative Powers herein granted shall be vested in a Congress of the United States. . . ." After granting many powers to the Congress, Article I goes on to provide that Congress may "make all Laws which shall be necessary and proper for carrying into Execution the foregoing Powers, and all other Powers vested by this Constitution in the Government of the United States, or in any Department or Officer thereof."

The President's order does not direct that a congressional policy be executed in a manner prescribed by Congress—it directs that a presidential policy be executed in a manner prescribed by the President. The preamble of the order itself, like that of many statutes, sets out reasons why the President believes certain policies should be adopted, proclaims these policies as rules of conduct to be followed, and again, like a statute, authorizes a government official to promulgate additional rules and regulations consistent with the policy proclaimed and needed to carry that policy into execution. The power of Congress to adopt such public policies as those proclaimed by the order is beyond question. It can authorize the taking of private property for public use. It can make laws regulating the relationships between employers and employees, prescribing rules designed to settle labor disputes, and fixing wages and working conditions in certain fields of our economy. The Constitution does not subject this lawmaking power of Congress to presidential or military supervision or control.

It is said that other Presidents without congressional authority have taken possession of private business enterprises in order to settle labor disputes. But even if this be true, Congress has not thereby lost its exclusive constitutional authority to make laws necessary and proper to carry out the powers vested by the Constitution "in the Government of the United States, or any Department or Officer thereof."

The Founders of this Nation entrusted the lawmaking power to the Congress alone in both good and bad times. It would do no good to recall the historical events, the fears of power and the hopes for freedom that lay behind their choice. Such a review would but confirm our holding that this seizure cannot stand. . . .

The *Youngstown Sheet & Tube* case contained concurring opinions and a dissent in which three of the nine justices joined. While six members of the Court agreed on the result, there were five separate methods of stating the result. Many of the principles and much of the philosophy underlying the doctrine of judicial review were set forth in Mr. Justice Frankfurter's concurring opinion, which follows in part.

FRANKFURTER, JUSTICE, concurring: . . . A constitutional democracy like ours is perhaps the most difficult of man's social arrangements to manage successfully.

Our scheme of society is more dependent than any other form of government on knowledge and wisdom and self-discipline for the achievement of its aims. For our democracy implies the reign of reason on the most extensive scale. The Founders of this Nation were not imbued with the modern cynicism that the only thing that history teaches is that it teaches nothing. They acted on the conviction that the experience of man sheds a good deal of light on his nature. It sheds a good deal of light not merely on the need for effective power, if a society is to be at once cohesive and civilized, but also on the need for limitations on the power of governors over the governed.

To that end they rested the structure of our central government on the system of checks and balances. For them the doctrine of separation of powers was not mere theory; it was a felt necessity. Not so long ago it was fashionable to find our system of checks and balances obstructive to effective government. It was easy to ridicule that system as outmoded—too easy. The experience through which the world has passed in our own day has made vivid the realization that the Framers of our Constitution were not inexperienced doctrinaires. These long-headed statesmen had no illusion that our people enjoyed biological or psychological or sociological immunities from the hazards of concentrated power. It is absurd to see a dictator in a representative product of the sturdy democratic traditions of the Mississippi Valley. The accretion of dangerous power does not come in a day. It does come, however slowly, from the generative force of unchecked disregard of the restrictions that fence in even the most disinterested assertion of authority.

The Framers, however, did not make the judiciary the overseer of our government. They were familiar with the revisory functions entrusted to judges in a few of the states and refused to lodge such powers in this Court. Judicial power can be exercised only as to matters that were the traditional concern of the courts at Westminster, and only if they arise in ways that to the expert feel of lawyers constitute "Cases" or "Controversies." Even as to questions that were the staple of judicial business, it is not for the courts to pass upon them unless they are indispensably involved in a conventional litigation—and then, only to the extent that they are so involved. Rigorous adherence to the narrow scope of the judicial function is especially demanded in controversies that arouse appeals to the Constitution. The attitude with which this Court must approach its duty when confronted with such issues is precisely the opposite of that normally manifested by the general public. So-called constitutional questions seem to exercise a mesmeric influence over the popular mind. This eagerness to settle—preferably forever—a specific problem on the basis of the broadest possible constitutional pronouncements may not unfairly be called one of our minor national traits. . . .

The pole-star for constitutional adjudications is John Marshall's greatest judicial utterance that "it is a *constitution* we are expounding." *McCullough v. Maryland,* 4 Wheat. 316, 407. That requires both a spacious view in applying an instrument of government "made for an undefined and expanding future," *Hurtado v. California,* 110 U.S. 516, 530, and as narrow a delimitation of the constitutional issues as the circumstances permit. Not the least characteristic of great statesmanship which the Framers manifested was the extent to which they did not attempt to bind the future. It is no less incumbent upon this Court to avoid putting fetters upon the future by needless pronouncements today.

Marshall's admonition that "it is a *constitution* we are expounding" is especially relevant when the Court is required to give legal sanctions to an underlying principle of the Constitution—that of separation of powers. "The great ordinances of the Constitution do not establish and divide fields of black and white." Holmes, J., dissenting in *Springer v. Philippine Islands*, 277 U.S. 189, 209.

The issue before us can be met, and therefore should be, without attempting to define the President's powers comprehensively. I shall not attempt to delineate what belongs to him by virtue of his office beyond the power even of Congress to contract; what authority belongs to him until Congress acts; what kind of problems may be dealt with either by the Congress or by the President or by both, cf. *La Abra Silver Mng. Co. v. United States*, 175 U.S. 423; what power must be exercised by the Congress and cannot be delegated to the President. It is unprofitable to lump together in an undiscriminating hotch-potch past presidential actions claimed to be derived from occupancy of the office, as it is to conjure up hypothetical future cases. The judiciary may, as this case proves, have to intervene in determining where authority lies as between the democratic forces in our scheme of government. But in doing so we should be wary and humble. Such is the teaching of this Court's role in the history of the country. . . .

A scheme of government like ours no doubt at times feels the lack of power to act with complete, all-embracing, swiftly moving authority. No doubt a government with distributed authority subject to be challenged in the courts of law, at least long enough to consider and adjudicate the challenge, labors under restrictions from which other governments are free. It has not been our tradition to envy such governments. In any event our government was designed to have such restrictions. The price was deemed not too high in view of the safeguards which these restrictions afford. I know no more impressive words on this subject than those of Mr. Justice Brandeis:

The doctrine of the separation of powers was adopted by the Convention of 1787, not to promote efficiency but to preclude the exercise of arbitrary power. The purpose was, not to avoid friction, but, by means of the inevitable friction incident to the distribution of the governmental powers among three departments, to save the people from autocracy. Myers v. United States, 272 U.S. 52, 240, 293.

It is not a pleasant judicial duty to find that the President has exceeded his powers and still less so when his purposes were dictated by concern for the Nation's well-being, in the assured conviction that he acted to avert danger. But it would stultify one's faith in our people to entertain even a momentary fear that the patriotism and the wisdom of the President and the Congress, as well as the long view of the immediate parties in interest, will not find ready accommodation for differences on matters which, however close to their concern and however intrinsically important, are overshadowed by the awesome issues which confront the world. . . .

REVIEW QUESTIONS—CHAPTER 5

1   Define the following terms introduced in this chapter: stare decisis; dicta; activist philosophy; judicial restraint; charitable immunity; conflicts of law; judicial review.

2   What rules of substantive law are used by Federal courts in diversity of citizenship cases?

3   To what extent is there a Federal common law? Explain.

4   Discuss two different meanings of the term "common law."

5   What are the advantages of a precedent-oriented legal system?

6   What are the disadvantages of a precedent-oriented legal system?

7   Compare the application of the doctrine of stare decisis in the public-law areas with its application in the private-law areas.

8   Illustrate how social progress may be achieved by a court's refusing to follow precedent.

9   Why are conflicts of law principles essential to our legal system? Explain.

10   Why was the doctrine of *Swift v. Tyson* overruled?

11   Is the judiciary the overseer of the government? Explain.

Chapter Six

Formulation of Judicial Decisions

1 INTRODUCTION

Previous chapters have been concerned with written law and the unwritten law announced in judicial decisions. We have seen that courts on occasion strike down legislation by finding it to be unconstitutional and former precedent by a simple process of overruling it. In addition, courts fill the gaps in legislation by interpretation and create legal principles where legislation is nonexistent. But what formula is used by courts in reaching these decisions? What process is followed that enables a court to reach one result rather than another? What forces tend to bear the heaviest influence in decisions concerned with the public interest?

There is, obviously, no simple answer to these questions. Many persons assume that logic affords the basic tool of the judicial decision. But Justice Holmes stated "the life of the law has not been logic; it has been experience."[1] Other persons argue that courts merely reflect the predominant attitude of the times and that they simply follow the more popular course in decisions where the public is involved.

Justice Benjamin Cardozo, in his lectures on the judicial process,[2] discussed the sources of information to which judges resort in deciding cases. He stated that if the answer were not clearly established by statute or by unquestioned precedent, the problem was twofold: "He [the judge] must first extract from the precedents the underlying principle, the *ratio decidendi*; he must then determine the path or direction along which the principle is to work and develop, if it is not to wither and die."[3] The first part of the problem is to separate legal principles from dicta so that the actual precedent is clear. Commenting on the second aspect of the problem, Cardozo said: "The directive force of a principle may be exerted along the line of logical progression; this I will call the rule of analogy or the method of philosophy; along the line of historical development; this I will call the method of evolution; along the lines of the customs of the community; this I will call the method of tradition; along the lines of justice, morals and social welfare, the *mores* of the day; and this I will call the method of sociology."[4]

[1] Holmes, *The Common Law*, 1 (1938).
[2] Cardozo, *The Nature of the Judicial Process* (1921). Excerpts are used by permission from the Yale University Press.
[3] *Id.* at 28.
[4] *Id.* at 30–31.

In Cardozo's judgment, the rule of analogy was entitled to certain presumptions and should be followed if possible. He believed that the judge who molds the law by the method of philosophy is satisfying the deep-seated desire of mankind for certainty. History, in indicating the direction of precedent, often makes the path of logic clear and plays an important part in decisions in areas such as real property. Custom or trade practice has supplied much of the direction of the law in the area of business. All judicial decisions are at least in part directed by the judge's viewpoint on the welfare of society. The end served by law must dictate the administration of justice, and ethical considerations, if ignored, will ultimately overturn a principle of law.

Noting the psychological aspects of judges' decisions, Cardozo observed that it is the subconscious forces which keep judges consistent with one another. In so recognizing that all persons, including judges, have a philosophy which gives coherence and direction to their thought and actions whether they admit it or not, he stated:

All their lives, forces which they do not recognize and cannot name, have been tugging at them—inherited instincts, traditional beliefs, acquired conviction; and the resultant is an outlook on life, a conception of social needs, . . . which when reasons are nicely balanced, must determine where choice shall fall. In this mental background every problem finds its setting. We may try to see things as objectively as we please. None the less, we can never see them with any eyes except our own. To that test they are all brought—a form of pleading or an act of parliament, the wrongs of paupers or the rights of princes, a village ordinance or a nation's charter.[5]

In the following comments, Cardozo summarized his view of the judicial process.

From **The Nature of the Judicial Process**[6]
Benjamin N. Cardozo

. . . My analysis of the judicial process comes then to this, and little more: logic, and history, and custom, and utility, and the accepted standards of right conduct, are the forces which singly or in combination shape the progress of the law. Which of these forces shall dominate in any case, must depend largely upon the comparative importance or value of the social interests that will be thereby promoted or impaired. One of the most fundamental social interests is that law shall be uniform and impartial. There must be nothing in its action that savors of prejudice or favor or even arbitrary whim or fitfulness. Therefore in the main there shall be adherence to precedent. There shall be symmetrical development, consistently with history or custom when history or custom has been the motive force, or the chief one, in giving shape to existing rules, and with logic or philosophy when the motive power has been theirs. But symmetrical development may be bought at too high a price. Uniformity ceases to be a good when it

[5] *Id.* at 12–13.
[6] *Id.* at 112–115.

becomes uniformity of oppression. The social interest served by symmetry or certainty must then be balanced against the social interest served by equity and fairness or other elements of social welfare. These may enjoin upon the judge the duty of drawing the line at another angle, or staking the path along new courses, of marking a new point of departure from which others who come after him will set out upon their journey.

If you ask how he is to know when one interest outweighs another, I can only answer that he must get his knowledge just as the legislator gets it, from experience and study and reflection; in brief, from life itself. Here, indeed, is the point of contact between the legislator's work and his. The choice of methods, the appraisement of values, must in the end be guided by like considerations for the one as for the other. Each indeed is legislating within the limits of his competence. No doubt the limits for the judge are narrower. He legislates only between gaps. He fills the open spaces in the law. How far he can go without traveling beyond the walls of the interstices cannot be staked out for him upon a chart. He must learn it for himself as he gains the sense of fitness and proportion that comes with years of habitude in the practice of an art. Even within the gaps, restrictions not easy to define, but felt, however impalpable they may be, by every judge and lawyer, hedge and circumscribe his action. They are established by the traditions of the centuries, by the example of other judges, his predecessors and his colleagues, by the collective judgment of the profession, and by the duty of adherence to the pervading spirit of the law. . . . None the less, within the confines of these open spaces and those of precedent and tradition, choice moves with a freedom which stamps its action as creative. The law which is the resulting product is not found, but made. The process, being legislative, demands the legislator's wisdom. . . .

This chapter will attempt to point out some of the more important of the infinite number of factors which play a part in the formulation of judicial decisions. The weight to be given any of these in a particular case cannot be predicted with any degree of certainty. The number of factors involved in any one case is likewise indeterminable. The product of these unknowns applied to a set of facts results in a judicial decision.

While these forces which shape the course of the law are discussed here in terms of their effect on court decisions specifically, it should be recognized that many or all of these same forces also have a profound effect on the type of legislation requested by the executive and his enforcement of existing law; the rule making, enforcement policies, and quasi-judicial decisions of administrative bodies; and the enactment of law by legislatures.

2   LOGIC

The first directive force in the formulation of judicial decisions that Cardozo listed was logic, which he also called the rule of analogy and the method of philosophy.

Cardozo considered judicial logic, or the following of prior decisions which are analogous to the case at bar as precedents, to be of prime importance to the judicial process because of the need for certainty in the law. Logic may involve deductive reasoning or inductive reasoning. Deductive reasoning takes the form of a syllogism in which a conclusion concerning a particular circumstance (minor premise) is drawn from a general principle (major premise). Inductive reasoning involves the process of using specific cases to reach a general conclusion. It is often said that application of the doctrine of stare decisis by basing a decision on precedents announced in prior cases is inductive in nature, while applying a statute to a given set of facts is an example of deductive reasoning, but these examples are open to some criticism.

Reasoning is a basic requisite to stability in the law. However, legal reasoning, as the discussion which follows indicates, has certain peculiarities all its own.

From An Introduction to Legal Reasoning[7]
Edward H. Levi

This is an attempt to describe generally the process of legal reasoning in the field of case law and in the interpretation of statutes and of the Constitution. It is important that the mechanism of legal reasoning should not be concealed by its pretense. The pretense is that the law is a system of known rules applied by a judge; the pretense has long been under attack. In an important sense legal rules are never clear, and if a rule had to be clear before it could be imposed, society would be impossible. The mechanism accepts the differences of view and ambiguities of words. It provides for the participation of the community in resolving the ambiguity by providing a forum for the discussion of policy in the gap of ambiguity. On serious controversial questions, it makes it possible to take the first step in the direction of what otherwise would be forbidden ends. The mechanism is indispensable to peace in a community.

The basic pattern of legal reasoning is reasoning by example.[a] It is reasoning from case to case. It is a three-step process described by the doctrine of precedent in which a proposition descriptive of the first case is made into a rule of law and then applied to a next similar situation. The steps are these: similarity is seen between cases; next the rule of law inherent in the first case is announced; then the rule of law is made applicable to the second case. This is a method of reasoning necessary for the law, but it has characteristics which under other circumstances might be considered imperfections.

---

[7] Reprinted from *An Introduction to Legal Reasoning,* by Edward H. Levi, pp. 1–3, by permission of the University of Chicago Press. Copyright 1948 by the University of Chicago.

[a] [footnote by Levi] "Clearly then to argue by example is neither like reasoning from part to whole, nor like reasoning from whole to part, but rather reasoning from part to part, when both particulars are subordinate to the same term and one of them is known. It differs from induction, because induction starting from all the particular cases proves . . . that the major term belongs to the middle and does not apply the syllogistic conclusion to the minor term, whereas argument by example does make this application and does not draw its proof from all the particular cases." Aristotle, *Analytica Priora* 69a (McKeon ed., 1941).

These characteristics become evident if the legal process is approached as though it were a method of applying general rules of law to diverse facts—in short, as though the doctrine of precedent meant that general rules, once properly determined, remained unchanged, and then were applied, albeit imperfectly, in later cases. If this were the doctrine, it would be disturbing to find that the rules change from case to case and are remade with each case. Yet this change in the rules is the indispensable dynamic quality of law. It occurs because the scope of a rule of law, and therefore its meaning, depends upon a determination of what facts will be considered similar to those present when the rule was first announced. The finding of similarity or difference is the key step in the legal process.

The determination of similarity or difference is the function of each judge. Where case law is considered, and there is no statute, he is not bound by the statement of the rule of law made by the prior judge even in the controlling case. The statement is mere dictum, and this means that the judge in the present case may find irrelevant the existence or absence of facts which prior judges thought important. It is not what the prior judge intended that is of any importance; rather it is what the present judge, attempting to see the law as a fairly consistent whole, thinks should be the determining classification. In arriving at his result he will ignore what the past thought important; he will emphasize facts which prior judges would have thought made no difference. It is not alone that he could not see the law through the eyes of another, for he could at least try to do so. It is rather that the doctrine of dictum forces him to make his own decision.

Thus it cannot be said that the legal process is the application of known rules to diverse facts. Yet it is a system of rules; the rules are discovered in the process of determining similarity or difference. But if attention is directed toward the finding of similarity or difference, other peculiarities appear. The problem for the law is: When will it be just to treat different cases as though they were the same? A working legal system must therefore be willing to pick out key similarities and to reason from them to the justice of applying a common classification. The existence of some facts in common brings into play the general rule. If this is really reasoning, then by common standards, thought of in terms of closed systems, it is imperfect unless some overall rule has announced that this common and ascertainable similarity is to be decisive. But no such fixed prior rule exists. It could be suggested that reasoning is not involved at all; that is, that no new insight is arrived at through a comparison of cases. But reasoning appears to be involved; the conclusion is arrived at through a process and was not immediately apparent. It seems better to say there is reasoning, but it is imperfect.[b]

Therefore it appears that the kind of reasoning involved in the legal process is one in which the classification changes as the classification is made. The rules change as the rules are applied. More important, the rules arise out of a process which, while comparing fact situations, creates the rules and then applies them.

[b] [footnote by Levi] The logical fallacy is the fallacy of the undistributed middle or the fallacy of assuming the antecedent is true because the consequent has been affirmed.

But this kind of reasoning is open to the charge that it is classifying things as equals when they are somewhat different, justifying the classification by rules made up as the reasoning or classification proceeds. In a sense all reasoning is of this type, but there is an additional requirement which compels the legal process to be this way. Not only do new situations arise, but in addition peoples want change. The categories used in the legal process must be left ambiguous in order to permit the infusion of new ideas. And this is true even where legislation or a constitution is involved. The words used by the legislature or the constitutional convention must come to have new meanings. Furthermore, agreement on any other basis would be impossible. In this manner the laws come to express the ideas of the community and even when written in general terms, in statute or constitution, are molded for the specific case.

But attention must be paid to the process. A controversy as to whether the law is certain, unchanging, and expressed in rules, or uncertain, changing, and only a technique for deciding specific cases misses the point. It is both. Nor is it helpful to dispose of the process as a wonderful mystery possibly reflecting a higher law, by which the law can remain the same and yet change. The law forum is the most explicit demonstration of the mechanism required for a moving classification system. The folklore of law may choose to ignore the imperfections in legal reasoning,[c] but the law forum itself has taken care of them. . . .

3　HISTORY

Cardozo stated that the second directive force which influences judicial decisions is exerted along the lines of historical development. He also called this force of history the method of evolution. Its importance is clear. There is an interaction between law and history; each shapes the other. Historical events have shaped the law and provided direction for society. Changes in social conduct and attitudes have given direction to the law. For example, the constitutional amendment calling for prohibition greatly affected the history of our country; and the historical events which followed prohibition led to its repeal.

We have seen the importance of the legislative history of an act as a factor in the interpretation of statutes in Chapter 2. Other historical events also are used by courts in determining the meaning and even the constitutionality of statutes, as the case which follows illustrates.

United States v. Brown
381 U.S. 437 (1965)

WARREN, CHIEF JUSTICE: In this case we review for the first time a conviction under § 504 of the Labor-Management Reporting and Disclosure Act of 1959, which

---

[c][footnote by Levi] "That the law can be obeyed even when it grows is often more than the legal profession itself can grasp." Cohen & Nagel, *An Introduction to Logic and Scientific Method* 371 (1934); see Stone, *The Province and Function of Law* 140–206 (1946).

makes it a crime for a member of the Communist Party to serve as an officer or (except in clerical or custodial positions) as an employee of a labor union. . . .

Respondent has been a working longshoreman on the San Francisco docks, and an open and avowed Communist, for more than a quarter of a century. He was elected to the Executive Board of Local 10 of the International Longshoremen's and Warehousemen's Union for consecutive one-year terms in 1959, 1960, and 1961. On May 24, 1961, respondent was charged in a one-count indictment returned in the Northern District of California with "knowingly and wilfully serv(ing) as a member of an executive board of a labor organization . . . while a member of the Communist Party, in wilful violation of Title 29, United States Code, Section 504." It was neither charged nor proven that respondent at any time advocated or suggested illegal activity by the union, or proposed a political strike. The jury found respondent guilty, and he was sentenced to six months' imprisonment. The Court of Appeals for the Ninth Circuit, sitting *en banc,* reversed and remanded with instructions to set aside the conviction and dismiss the indictment, holding that § 504 violates the First and Fifth Amendments to the Constitution. We granted certiorari.

Respondent urges—in addition to the grounds relied on by the court below— that the statute under which he was convicted is a bill of attainder, and therefore violates Art. 1, § 9, of the Constitution. We agree that § 504 is void as a bill of attainder and affirm the decision of the Court of Appeals on that basis. We therefore find it unnecessary to consider the First and Fifth Amendment arguments.

I

The provisions outlawing bills of attainder were adopted by the Constitutional Convention unanimously, and without debate.

No Bill of Attainder or ex post facto Law shall be passed [by the Congress]. Art. I, § 9, cl. 3.

No State shall . . . pass any Bill of Attainder, ex post facto Law, or Law impairing the Obligation of Contracts. . . . Art. 1, § 10.

A logical starting place for an inquiry into the meaning of the prohibition is its historical background. The bill of attainder, a parliamentary act sentencing to death one or more specific persons was a device often resorted to in sixteenth, seventeenth and eighteenth century England for dealing with persons who had attempted, or threatened to attempt, to overthrow the government. In addition to the death sentence, attainder generally carried with it a "corruption of blood," which meant that the attainted party's heirs could not inherit his property. The "bill of pains and penalties" was identical to the bill of attainder, except that it prescribed a penalty short of death, e.g., banishment, deprivation of the right to vote, or exclusion of the designated party's sons from Parliament. Most bills of attainder and bills of pains and penalties named the parties to whom they were to apply; a few, however, simply described them. While some left the designated parties a way of escaping the penalty, others did not. The use of bills of attainder and bills of pains and penalties was not limited to England. During the American Revolution, the legislatures of all thirteen States passed statutes directed against the Tories; among these statutes were a large number of bills of attainder and bills of pains and penalties.

While history thus provides some guidelines, the wide variation in form, purpose and effect of ante-constitutional bills of attainder indicates that the proper scope of the Bill of Attainder Clause, and its relevance to contemporary problems, must ultimately be sought by attempting to discern the reasons for its inclusion in the Constitution, and the evils it was designed to eliminate. The best available evidence, the writings of the architects of our constitutional system, indicates that the Bill of Attainder Clause was intended not as a narrow, technical (and therefore soon to be outmoded) prohibition, but rather as an implementation of the separation of powers, a general safeguard against legislative exercise of the judicial function, or more simply trial by legislature. . . .

Thus the Bill of Attainder Clause not only was intended as one implementation of the general principle of fractionalized power, but also reflected the Framers' belief that the Legislative Branch is not so well suited as politically independent judges and juries to the task of ruling upon the blameworthiness of, and levying appropriate punishment upon, specific persons.

Every one must concede that a legislative body, from its numbers and organization, and from the very intimate dependence of its members upon the people, which renders them liable to be peculiarly susceptible to popular clamor, is not properly constituted to try with coolness, caution, and impartiality a criminal charge, especially in those cases in which the popular feeling is strongly excited,—the very class of cases most likely to be prosecuted by this mode.

By banning bills of attainder, the Framers of the Constitution sought to guard against such dangers by limiting legislatures to the task of rule-making. "It is the peculiar province of the legislature, to prescribe general rules for the government of society; the application of those rules to individuals in society would seem to be the duty of other departments." . . . [The Court then discussed several previous bill of attainder cases.]

III

Under the line of cases just outlined § 504 plainly constitutes a bill of attainder. . . . The statute does not set forth a generally applicable rule decreeing that any person who commits certain acts or possesses certain characteristics (acts and characteristics which, in Congress' view make them likely to initiate political strikes) shall not hold union office, and leave to courts and juries the job of deciding what persons have committed the specified acts or possess the specified characteristics. Instead, it designates in no uncertain terms the persons who possess the feared characteristics and therefore cannot hold union office without incurring criminal liability—members of the Communist Party. . . .

The Solicitor General argues that § 504 is not a bill of attainder because the prohibition it imposes does not constitute "punishment." In support of this conclusion, he urges that the statute was enacted for preventive rather than retributive reasons—that its aim is not to punish Communists for what they have done in the past, but rather to keep them from positions where they will in the future be able to bring about undesirable events. . . .

Historical considerations by no means compel restriction of the bill of attainder ban to instances of retribution. A number of English bills of attainder were enacted for preventive purposes—that is, the legislature made a judgment undoubtedly based largely on past acts and associations (as § 504 is) that a given person or group was likely to cause trouble (usually, overthrow the government) and therefore inflicted deprivations upon that person or group in order to keep them from bringing about the feared event. It is also clear that many of the early American bills attainting the Tories were passed in order to impede their effectively resisting the Revolution.

In the progress of the conflict, and particularly in its earliest periods, attainder and confiscation had been resorted to generally, throughout the continent, as a means of war. But it is a fact important to the history of the revolting colonies, that the acts prescribing penalties, usually offered to the persons against whom they were directed the option of avoiding them, by acknowledging their allegiance to the existing governments.

It was a preventative, not a vindictive policy. In the same humane spirit, as the contest approached its close, and the necessity of these severities diminished, many of the states passed laws offering pardons to those who had been disenfranchised, and restoring them to the enjoyment of their property. . . .

Thus Justice Iredell was on solid historical ground when he observed, in *Calder v. Bull,* 3 Dall. 386, 399–400, 1 L.Ed. 648, that "attainders, *on the principle of retaliation and proscription,* have marked all the vicissitudes of party triumph." [EMPHASIS SUPPLIED]

We do not hold today that Congress cannot weed dangerous persons out of the labor movement. . . . Rather, we make again the point . . . that Congress must accomplish such results by rules of general applicability. It cannot specify the people upon whom the sanction it prescribes is to be levied. Under our Constitution, Congress possesses full legislative authority, but the task of adjudication must be left to other tribunals.

This Court is always reluctant to declare that an Act of Congress violates the Constitution, but in this case we have no alternative. As Alexander Hamilton observed:

By a limited constitution, I understand one which contains certain specified exceptions to the legislative authority; such, for instance, as that it shall pass no bills of attainder, no ex post facto laws, and the like. Limitations of this kind can be preserved in practice no other way than through the medium of the courts of justice; whose duty it must be to declare all acts contrary to the manifest tenor of the Constitution void. Without this, all the reservations of particular rights or privileges would amount to nothing.

The judgment of the Court of Appeals is affirmed. [JUDGMENT AFFIRMED]

Further aspects of the influence of history on judicial decisions should be noted. First of all, cases decided by the judiciary are historical events; thus, the following of precedent is an application of history to current controversies. Second, to evaluate the force of history properly, we cannot view past events in the abstract alone but must look beyond these occurrences themselves for the traditions which have grown up around them. The tradition resulting from an event compounds its effect on the law. Justice Cardozo noted that the tradition or myth surrounding an historical event frequently becomes the major force when he stated:[8]

Take Magna Charta for example. Today it is not what is written in the Charter—if the words are read in the sense in which they were understood by those who wrote them—that has any commanding interest, any throbbing and vital meaning, for those who walk the earth. What lives in the Charter today is the myth that has gathered around it—the things that it has come to stand for in the thought of successive generations—not the pristine core within, but the incrustations that have formed without.

The thought is tellingly expressed by Plucknett in his short history of the common law. "The Charter gradually grew bigger than the mere feudal details which it contained and came to be a symbol of successful opposition to the Crown which resulted in a negotiated peace representing a reasonable compromise. As time goes on, therefore, the Charter becomes more and more a myth, but nevertheless a very powerful one, and in the Seventeenth Century all the forces of liberalism rallied around it. . . . To explode the 'myth' of the great Charter is indeed to get back to its original historical meaning, but for all that, the myth has been much more important than the reality, and there is still something to be said for the statement that 'the whole of English constitutional history is a commentary upon the great Charter.' "

Now, what is true of Magna Charta is true, I think of our own constitution in many of its provisions; true, for example, of the bill of rights, which is much more important for the spirit it enshrines than for this or the other privilege or immunity which it professes to secure. Some of them have a vital meaning even

---

[8] From *An Address to the New York County Lawyers' Association*, given at its annual dinner Dec. 17, 1931, and published in the *New York County Lawyers' Yearbook* 369 (1932). Used by permission from the New York County Lawyers' Association.

to this day, others are reminiscent of battles long ago. The myth that has enveloped them has become greater than the reality, or rather in a sense the genuine reality.

4   CUSTOM

Cardozo's third directive force which shapes judicial decisions was along the lines of customs of the community, which he also called the method of tradition. The influence of custom and usage is of special importance in the field of business law. For example, a term not stated may be added to a contract, because of well-established custom and usage in the trade or business. The amount of a broker's commission, although not expressly agreed upon, has been determined by reference to usage.[9] Likewise, the questions of whether the buyer or seller of goods is bound to pay the freight for their transportation,[10] or who must bear the expenses of the sales tax,[11] when these matters were not settled by the contract of sale, have been determined by proof of custom.

Although the language employed in contracts by the parties is usually interpreted to have its normal, ordinary meaning, a custom and usage can be shown which changes meaning and therefore the performance required by the contract. Accepted scientific tables of weights and measures define a British barrel as 36 gallons and a United States barrel as 31.5 gallons. However, in the oil industry, a barrel is understood to amount to 42 gallons. In *Harvard Brewing Co. v. Killian*,[12] the court held that in the beer industry, by custom and usage, a barrel could be shown to mean only 31 gallons.

Most commercial law has its roots in the customs and trade practices of merchants. Early common-law courts provided no legal sanctions for the enforcement of commercial transactions. However, merchants, in activities such as buying and selling goods and in employing negotiable instruments as substitutes for money, developed customs and traditions which defined the rights and duties of the parties to these agreements. Usually a "judge" was appointed at fairs by the merchants to hear and render a summary decision on the basis of generally accepted usage, in any disputes which arose. His "judgments" were enforced by the ostracism of any merchant who refused to abide by them. Eventually the common law opened its doors to merchants, recognizing their agreements as creating legal rights and duties. Common-law court decisions in commercial matters gave the force of law to the custom and usage of merchants by following their practice. In modern times, these decisions in many areas have been codified into the uniform acts, such as the Uniform Sales Act, the Uniform Negotiable Instruments Law and more recently, the Uniform Commercial Code. Of course, as the customs involving commercial matters have varied, the law has varied, but it finds its basis in early usage and traditions, or the "law merchant."

[9] *Vanemburg v. Duffey*, 177 Ark. 663, 7 S.W.2d 336 (1928).
[10] *Carlsten-William Co. v. Marshall Oil Co.*, 187 Iowa 80, 173 N.W. 903 (1919).
[11] *Trueba Bros. v. Early-Foster Co.*, 256 S.W. 909 (Tex. Com. App. 1923).
[12] 222 Mass. 13, 109 N.E. 649 (1915).

5 THE MORES OF THE DAY OR THE METHOD OF SOCIOLOGY

Cardozo indicated that the fourth major force which gives direction to the formulation of judicial decisions is along the lines of justice, morals, and social welfare, or the mores of the day, which he also called the method of sociology. This method, he indicated, places the highest value on arriving at judicial decisions which have the greatest social utility or usefulness under current conditions and which are in accord with the presently accepted standards of right conduct. The method of sociology has steadily grown in importance in recent years and in the opinion of many observers is the dominant force which shapes the judicial opinions of our Supreme Court. It is used by all the justices to a varying degree and most often by those who are "activists."

It is clearly possible to have a system of law which fails to achieve justice. Rigid or strict application of "rules of law" may reach an unjust result. The converse is also possible—a system may achieve a just result without using "rules of law." Historically, our courts have felt that the need for certainty and predictability requires a system using "rules of law," and injustice has sometimes resulted. On occasion, however, they have refused to follow precedent and instead have striven toward a "right" solution, or one which would have greater social utility, in their view, than a mechanical application of previous decisions could provide. The method of sociology has played a significant role in all cases where precedent has been reversed. (See the discussion of rejection of stare decisis in section 2 of Chapter 5.)

A judge who is influenced by the force of the method of sociology might say to an attorney arguing a case words to this effect: "I'm not concerned with your precedent and authorities; tell me why your client is right and the other party is wrong as a matter both of justice and of social policy." Such a judge is result-conscious and does not want to apply a rigid rule of law which may achieve an unjust result.

The method of sociology is perhaps the most complex of all the forces which shape the law. It includes such elements as the judge's desire to achieve the "correct" result, the judge's own philosophy, political considerations, society's attitudes, and even the effect of emergencies. Each of these influences and the part it can play in shaping a judicial decision is discussed in more detail in the subsections which follow.

A RESULT DESIRED

It is perhaps shocking to the layman to realize that, in many cases, the result which a court desires to reach controls the statements of legal principles upon which its decision is based. Many people blindly assume that the law always controls the result, but the plain fact of the matter is that often the desired result controls the law applicable to a case at hand. A court frequently decides the outcome of a case and then searches precedent for some basis for its opinion. Similar cases with a different result are distinguished, statutes are construed or even declared to be unconstitutional, exceptions are made, or precedent is overruled simply to reach what the court believes to be the correct decision.

It is often said that "hard cases make bad law." Probably one of the most perplexing aspects of the law to laymen and law students comes from a study of those judicial decisions which are a product of ambivalence—a desire by the court to follow precedent, yet a feeling that to do so strictly will be unjust in the case at hand. Under these circumstances, the court *may* attempt to serve both the ends of logic and fairness by *stating* and laboriously reasoning that a case falls within a rule (when by ordinary logic it does not), as a pretext for arriving at a just result. If it follows this path, the court reaches an equitable conclusion without expressly overruling precedent, thereby keeping up the appearance of stability.

As an example of the foregoing, compare the following decisions. *International Paper Co. v. Rockefeller*[13] involved an action for damages for breach of a contract to cut and deliver 56,000 cords of wood from spruce growing on a designated tract of land, for $5.50 a cord. The defendant argued that he should be excused from the agreement, since a forest fire had destroyed all the tract but about 550 cords remaining on top of a high mountain, which would cost him $20 a cord to cut and deliver. The court excused the defendant as to the wood which had been destroyed, but said: "The defendant is not excused from delivering the live spruce . . . which survived the fire by the mere fact that its location upon the tract is such that it would be very expensive for him to deliver it. . . ."[14] This holding represents the strict, logical, and long-established view that a person who has made a contractual promise will not be excused simply because he suffers additional hardship and a financial loss. Only in cases where the act has become *absolutely impossible* may he ignore his contract. However, in *Mineral Park Land Co. v. Howard*,[15] the defendants had contracted to buy at an agreed price and remove from the plaintiff's land all the gravel needed to build a certain bridge. After the defendants had removed about one-half of the gravel needed, they began purchasing elsewhere, since the rest of plaintiff's gravel was under water and it would cost about 10 to 12 times as much as dry gravel to remove and ready for use. In its opinion, the court referred to cases where performance of similar contracts had been excused after the supply at an agreed source was *totally depleted*, then said:

The defendants were not binding themselves to take what was not there. And in determining whether the earth and gravel were "available" we must view the conditions in a practical and reasonable way. Although there was gravel on the land, it was so situated that the defendants could not take it by ordinary means, nor except at a prohibitive cost. To all fair intents then, it was impossible in legal contemplation for defendants to take it. . . . We do not mean to intimate that the defendants could excuse themselves by showing the existence of conditions

[13] 161 App. Div. 180, 146 N.Y.S. 371 (1914).
[14] *Id.*
[15] 172 Cal. 289, 156 Pac. 458 (1916).

which would make the performance of their obligations more expensive than they had anticipated, or which would entail a great loss upon them. But where the difference in cost is so great as here, and has the effect, as found, of making performance impracticable, the situation is not different from that of a total absence of earth and gravel. . . .[16] [The court disallowed recovery of damages for breach of contract.]

The Uniform Commercial Code—Sales, 2-615, permits a court to reach what it considers to be a fair result in certain cases without encountering the logical difficulty in defining "impossibility," by providing that a seller of tangible personal property is excused from his contract, if a change in assumed conditions makes performance "impracticable." The Code reflects a trend in court decisions away from predictability and toward liberality and "fairness" in defining what makes a contract "impossible" to perform.

Many of the factors affecting judicial decisions discussed in this chapter simply influence the court in determining the result it will reach rather than in finding "correct" principles of law. The importance of the doctrine of stare decisis varies in inverse proportion to the intensity of the desire of the judge for a certain result of a controversy, in controlling the principles of law to be announced.

B   BACKGROUND AND PHILOSOPHY OF JUDGES

Justice William O. Douglas in his lecture on stare decisis (Chapter 5) discussed the importance of each judge's philosophy on his decisions, particularly in the area of constitutional law. Judges are human beings subject to the same forces, pressures, and prejudices as are other human beings. The sum total of their experiences in life will necessarily affect their judicial decisions. However, this fact need not be viewed as an evil of our system of law. As Charles P. Curtis noted in *A Commonplace Book,* "There are only two ways to be quite unprejudiced and impartial. One is to be completely ignorant. The other is to be completely indifferent."

While the philosophy of each judge or justice has some effect on the law, the philosophy of members of the Supreme Court of the United States has a very dramatic effect. As previously noted, individual justices view differently the responsibility of the Court to serve as an instrument of social, political, and economic change. Those justices tending toward a belief that the Court should provide leadership in bringing about such change are sometimes described as "activist" judges, and those tending toward a belief that courts should decide only those issues which they must decide and should leave changes in society to other branches of government and the political process are described as adherents to the "judicial restraint" philosophy. It must be recognized that labels, whether "liberal," "conservative," "activist," or "judicial restraint-oriented," are never wholly accurate in describing any one justice or Court. They only illustrate trends

[16] *Id.*

or tendencies, and there are many cases and examples which both prove and disprove any label as applied to any one justice. In the 1960s, the Supreme Court tended toward the activist philosophy. In the 1970s the Burger Court is tending toward more judicial restraint, but the Court is continuing to play a significant role in the formulation of governmental policy, and its actions will continue to be the subject of major debate. Following are portions of an article and a speech of two prominent authorities on the Supreme Court which focus on the role it has played in shaping our political and social institutions.

The Changing Role of the Supreme Court of the U.S.A.[17]
Anthony Lewis[18]

Introduction
The subject of this article concerns that most curious institution in the American system of government—the Supreme Court of the United States. I say curious, first of all, because of some surface distinctions between the Court and other agencies of Government that are obvious to any newspaper man in Washington.

In a city thick with publicists, the Supreme Court is a last holdout from Madison Avenue. It is the only news beat in Washington where officials do not cultivate the press, and spoon-feed it. Reporters may be pals of Senators, and even of Presidents, but not of Supreme Court justices. . . .

Alone among Government agencies, the Supreme Court seems to have escaped Parkinson's law. The reader may remember Professor Parkinson's thesis—that the number of employees in any office continuously expands, and the amount of work automatically increases to keep the new hands busy. The work at the Supreme Court is still done by nine men, assisted by eighteen young law clerks. Nothing is delegated to committees of ghost writers or task forces.

The Court is at the same time the most aloof of Washington agencies and the most approachable. The great marble palace which houses it seems cold and inflated, and there is a formal, ceremonial air to the Court's public sessions. But during an oral argument in the courtroom, for all the austerity of the pillars and the pseudo-classical friezes, the atmosphere is remarkably intimate as court and counsel converse. It really is conversation—as direct, searching, focused discussion as can be found anywhere in Washington.

Power of the Supreme Court
But beyond those surface distinctions there is the deeper curiosity about the Supreme Court. That is the grant of power—in a society that proudly calls itself a democracy—to nine men appointed for life. For the power given to Supreme Court justices is great indeed, undoubtedly greater than that given to any other judges anywhere.

---

[17] *Ill. B.J.* 8 (1962). Used by permission from Mr. Anthony Lewis and the *Illinois Bar Journal.*
[18] Mr. Anthony Lewis is a New York newspaperman who has covered the Supreme Court.

De Tocqueville wrote a century ago, "Scarcely any political question arises in the United States that is not resolved, sooner or later, into a judicial question." And so issues that would be decided in most countries by parliament or prime ministers come to the Supreme Court of the United States.

One question before the Court this term was whether the public schools of New York State may constitutionally open each day with a prayer. As I heard counsel argue that case, ranging over all the policy reasons for and against strict secularism in our schools, it occurred to me that here was the kind of question committed to political decision in most countries—the kind it would be unthinkable to take to a court. (I may add that the unhappy history of political controversy in Europe over the religion in schools does not argue the wisdom of political resolution of such problems.) . . .

Grist of Supreme Court's Role

Of course, the Supreme Court does not spend all its time deciding great constitutional questions. The grist of its docket is statutory construction—deciding what Congress meant in some statute. But even that routine-sounding job can pose large and delicate problems in a governmental system as complex as ours.

In construing a statute the Court may be resolving a contest of power between the Federal Government and the States, as it does, for example, when it says whether the Taft-Hartley law permits a state court to entertain a case arising from a labor dispute or whether, instead, it commits the problem to the National Labor Relations Board.

One of the most important pieces of statutory construction in recent years took one sentence in the Taft-Hartley Act—a sentence that on its face simply gave the Federal courts jurisdiction over suits for violation of collective bargaining agreements—and made that sentence a charter for the Federal courts to fashion a whole new structure of law for labor contracts. Sometimes, under the heading of statutory construction, the Court has to resolve a head-on clash between two agencies of the same Federal Government. It did that this term when it held that the Federal Power Commission had no right to approve a merger of two natural gas companies, while a Justice Department suit attacking the merger as an antitrust violation was before the courts.

Congress Often Vague

The basic difficulty for the Supreme Court in saying what Congress meant is that so often Congress meant nothing at all. It simply never envisaged the problem before the Court. The Congress that wrote the Sherman Act back in 1890, prohibiting "every contract or combination in restraint of trade," simply gave the Court a blank check to fill in with contemporary legal and economic theory. It is hardly surprising that the Court has had some difficulty deciding what is an antitrust violation, or that the justices have disagreed.

The increasing demands on Congress have aggravated the problem. The fact is that Congress does not have time these days to legislate in detail. When it comes to a difficult problem, its tendency is to fuzz things over and let the Court resolve the difficulty under the guise of discovering what Congress "intended." I remember the offshore oil legislation, when Congress could have stated right in the statute how far out into the Gulf of Mexico state mineral rights should run. But it was too difficult politically to make that decision, and so Congress asked the Court to do it on the basis of some ambiguous history. At the argument Justice Frankfurter said something about Congress passing the buck. . . .

I turn to an area of judicial decision so new that one must read about it in the newspapers rather than the law reports—legislative apportionment.

In a 1946 decision, *Colegrove v. Green*—the Supreme Court seemed to close the doors of the Federal courts to complaints by urban and suburban voters that legislative districts were so unequal in population as to violate their constitutional rights. Justice Frankfurter's opinion said that trying to deal with unfair apportionments would lead the courts into a "political thicket," and he advised the city voters to work for reform through the political process. In a dozen cases after 1946 the Court followed the *Colegrove* doctrine of keeping hands off apportionment issues.

Then, last March 26, the Court suddenly told us that the doors were not closed after all. In *Baker v. Carr* it held that a suit challenging the apportionment of Tennessee's legislature stated a constitutional claim triable in the Federal courts. The opinion explained away all the earlier cases, starting with *Colegrove v. Green*, but for at least one reader the explanation did not explain. In fact, if not in theory, *Colegrove v. Green* and the other cases were overruled. Their spirit of abstention was rejected . . . and . . . Justice Frankfurter's advice to work for political change was useless; the political system provided no way of escape. The Supreme Court opened the way for political as well as legal forces to work for orderly change.

That was the moral seen by Attorney General Robert F. Kennedy in *Baker v. Carr*. "When people criticize the courts for invading spheres of action which supposedly belong to other parts of our constitutional system," he said of the Tennessee case, "they often overlook the fact that the courts must act precisely because the other organs of government have failed to fulfill their responsibilities."

Perhaps in 1946, when *Colegrove v. Green* was decided, it still seemed possible that the rural oligarchies in control of state legislatures would listen to reason. But by 1962 that hope had passed. It was plain that only the Supreme Court could begin to cure the disease of malapportionment eating away at the vitals of American democracy.

Conclusion

There, in impressionistic summary, . . . [is an area] of the law in which the Supreme Court's construction of the Constitution is contributing to profound changes in American government and society. Just as clearly, . . . [this case] represent[s] a shift to the Court's conception of its own role. . . .

The Court has begun to enforce new restraints on state action. And how different are the interests involved in these restraints from those that concerned the Supreme Court only a generation ago.

Just recall the dominant mood of the Court before 1937. The issues then were the right of the states to set maximum hours and minimum wages, the right of the Federal Government to use its tax and commerce powers against the great Depression. The Court's concern seemed to be with property, not with what we today would call human liberty.

Which brings us again to the question why. Why has there been this dramatic change in Supreme Court doctrine during the last quarter-century? Surely the area of decision at which we have looked suggests some answers.

First, it is clear that there has been an ethical element in the Court's motivation. In intervening in behalf of . . . the citizen disenfranchised by malapportionment, the Court has been responding to what it deemed a moral demand—a demand of the national conscience.

Moreover, the national conscience had found no way to express itself except through the courts. The Supreme Court moved in only when the political system was stymied—when there was no other way out of the moral dilemma.

Supreme Court as Instrument of National Moral Values

The conclusion is that the Supreme Court has tended in recent years to act as the instrument of national moral values that have not been able to find other governmental expression. If the Court has changed, it is because we have changed.

The unhappy recent history of the world *has* changed the values of Americans, and so it should be no great surprise that the Supreme Court puts its emphasis on different interests. We are more concerned, now, about abuse of official authority, mistreatment of racial minorities and sabotage of democracy than we are about the sanctity of property or even about state powers in a Federal system.

And the Framers drew our Constitution in deliberately vague terms so that it could reflect the values of each generation. The courts have inevitably drawn on the moral consensus of their own time to give content to such phrases as "due process" and "equal protection."

Of course, not everyone agrees on moral goals, much less ones that are judicially attainable. The nine justices cannot be expected to march in happy unanimity toward a legal heaven whose definition all applaud.

Only in the field of race relations—where, ironically, public reaction has been the most divisive—have the justices regularly been in agreement. They have apparently found the moral imperative here more obvious. But even in race relations it seems doubtful to me that unanimity can long be preserved as the Court reaches the difficult questions of how to distinguish "private" from "public" discrimination.

Court Deeply Divided

Outside the racial area the Court has been deeply divided. Justice Frankfurter has been the principal spokesman for the view that the Court should be hesitant to impose its moral ideals upon a complex political structure. He dissented not only from *Baker v. Carr* but, for example, from last year's decision outlawing illegally seized evidence in state criminal trials.

This does not mean that Justice Frankfurter likes unfair apportionments or illegal evidence—far from it. He is simply a believer in the independent power of the states, wisely or unwisely used; sometimes I think he is the last person in the country who holds that view as a matter of deep intellectual belief. And he is enough of a skeptic about the perfection of judges so that he hesitates to bind government to rigid judicial formulas.

Justice Frankfurter's fears can hardly be dismissed out of hand. The role now being played by the Supreme Court puts the justices—and the lower court judges who must carry out their decisions—on the frontiers of social change. And that may not always be a natural locale for a judge. Not every man trained to construe a contract will feel at home weighing great social problems. Judges will be strained to their intellectual and moral limits. Care in the selection of judges becomes even more crucially important.

But for all the difficulties, I myself see no satisfactory alternative to the role being taken up by the Court. I think it is better to take the risks of judicial intervention than to be satisfied with doing nothing. . . .

In this great country, so often riven by local interests with which Congress has neither the time nor the desire to deal, some agency has to bring local action into harmony with overriding national ideals. Its very remoteness, its freedom from sectional and political pressures have rightly made us choose as that instrument the Supreme Court of the United States.

Recent Trends in United States Supreme Court Decisions[19]
Philip B. Kurland[20]

Looking over the last decade of the Supreme Court's work—roughly the period between the school desegregation cases in 1954 and the reapportionment cases of 1964—one quickly discovers that the justices have wrought more fundamental changes in the political and legal structure of the United States than during any period in our history since Mr. Chief Justice Marshall first wrote meaning into the abstractions of the Constitution's language. And, to make my essential point at the outset, the problem is not primarily whether in your eyes or mine these changes are good or bad, but rather whether the Supreme Court, constituted as it is by nine lawyers with life tenure and politically irresponsible, is the proper organ of government to accomplish the goals it may decide to set for this country.

Three dominant movements are evident in the court's recent work. First, and foremost has been the emerging primacy of equality as a guide to constitutional decision. Perhaps an offshoot of the Negro revolution that the court helped to sponsor in *Brown v. Board of Education,* the equalitarian revolution in judicial

---

[19] Address delivered Jan. 7, 1965, before the Governmental Affairs Council of the Chicago Association of Commerce and Industry. Used by permission from Professor Philip B. Kurland and the *Chicago Tribune.*
[20] Professor Kurland is a member of the faculty of the Law School of the University of Chicago.

doctrine has made dominant the principles to be read into the equal protection clause of the 14th amendment rather than the due process clause, heretofore the polestar of Supreme Court action. . . . The decisions in the school segregation cases, the sit-in cases, and the reapportionment cases are merely the most prominent of a very large number of decisions pushing this egalitarian theme. Quite clearly the movement is at its inception; certainly it is nowhere near its conclusion.

Two fundamental difficulties face the court in this effort, or would face the court were it more conscious of its obligation to justify and explain its judgments. The first is the question whether the equal protection clause empowers the court to eliminate not only the inequalities imposed by law but the inequalities that derive from nongovernmental action or inaction, the social and economic inequalities as well as the political inequalities. . . . The second major problem . . . is the task of adequately reconciling the competing claims of equality on the one hand with liberty and other fundamental guarantees on the other. . . .

The second prominent theme of current Supreme Court adjudication, however important, is hardly novel. I am referring to the effective subordination, if not destruction, of the federal system. This movement is not entirely disparate from the egalitarian push. For each is a drive to uniformity and away from diversity. Equality demands uniformity of rules. Uniformity cannot exist if there are multiple rulemakers. It follows that the objective of equality cannot be achieved except by the elimination of authorities not subordinate to the central power. It, too, is an important part of our political and social and economic movement away from diversity toward conformity. . . . Perhaps the most amazing fact about the court's recent infringements on state authority is that, having taken so much power away from the states, it continues to find more to take away. . . .

The third of the major trends discernible from a study of the court's efforts over the last 10 years . . . [is] the enhancement of the judicial dominion at the expense of the power of other branches of government, national as well as state. . . . There was, at one time, a fairly substantial area of governmental action that the court had wisely declared off-limits for itself. The reapportionment cases seem to have dealt a fatal blow to the idea that there are certain functions of government beyond the competence of the court to perform. . . . It is only fair to note, however, that the court treats its own precedents with no less disdain than it accords congressional legislation. Indeed, a court that considers its pronouncements to be "the law of the land" might be expected to pay more respect to its own opinions. The fact of the matter is that the number of its own cases overruled by the court in the past decade, either openly or covertly, have accelerated at such a rate as almost to remove the hyperbole from Mr. Justice Roberts' charge that the court's judgments were coming to be like railroad excursion tickets, good for this day only. . . .

The solution of the problem of excessive judicial power . . . must be found in making the judicial branch of the government politically more responsible without impinging on its independence. It should be remembered . . . that the success of Anglo-American democracies has depended in no small part on the independence of the judiciary.

Such an answer, if it is to be found anywhere, is most likely to be found in the responsible utilization of the amending process, a prerequisite that will both justify the process and, in many instances, make it superfluous. That prerequisite is a real comprehension on the part of the electorate of the role and performance of the Supreme Court. And the obligation of this understanding falls particularly on the leaders of the community. For, I think I can say without fear of being proved wrong, that the press has failed in its obligation to educate the public about the decisions of the court. It is also unfortunately true that the bar has failed in this regard. . . .

Only an educated public can understand whether judicial decisions appropriately call for constitutional amendment. At the same time, an educated and aroused public may make the court politically more responsible than it has been.

C POLITICAL INFLUENCES

In many states judges are elected. In other states and in the Federal system, judges are appointed. Political considerations play some part in all such appointments and are controlling in others. An analysis of the party affiliation of the judges appointed by each President would make it appear that the party not in power is almost devoid of members with judicial qualifications. It should be noted, however, that many persons upon ascending the bench for life suddenly reject many of their former political philosophies and ideologies, so that attempts to control future judicial action by careful appointment have not and will not necessarily be successful.

The judges who must run for reelection must of necessity recognize and be influenced to some degree by the policies of the political party under whose banner and upon whose platform they must run. At the local level, judges often have substantial amounts of patronage and are sources of power within their party. Only the very naïve believe that political considerations can be divorced from judicial decisions entirely.

The judicial decisions involving the reapportionment of legislative districts at all levels of government changed the political climate of the entire country. They transferred the balance of political power from rural America to urban America. The reapportionment cases illustrate the effect of the law on our political system, and a brief look at them is helpful in understanding the interrelationship between politics and the law. The cases also illustrate the activist and judicial restraint philosophies.

Prior to 1962, the Supreme Court had held that questions of legislative district apportionment were political questions over which the courts had no jurisdiction. The precedent for this approach was a 1947 decision, *Colegrove v. Green,*[21] in which Justice Frankfurter, speaking for the majority of the Court, exercised judicial restraint and stated:

We are of the opinion that the appellants ask of this Court what it is beyond its competence to grant. This is one of those demands on judicial power which

[21] 328 U.S. 549 (1947).

cannot be met by fencing about "jurisdiction." It must be resolved by considerations on the basis of which this Court, from time to time, has refused to intervene in controversies. It has refused to do so because due regard for the effective working of our government revealed this issue to be of a peculiarly political nature and therefore not meant for judicial determination. . . . Nothing is clearer than that this controversy concerns matters that bring courts into immediate and active relations with party contests. From the determination of such issues this Court has traditionally held aloof. It is hostile to a democratic system to involve the judiciary in the politics of the people. . . . If Congress failed in exercising its powers, whereby standards of fairness are offended, the remedy ultimately lies with the people. . . . To sustain this action would cut very deep into the very being of Congress. Courts ought not to enter the political thicket. *The remedy for unfairness in districting is to secure state legislatures that will apportion properly or to invoke the ample powers of Congress.*

In 1962 the Court reversed *Colegrove v. Green*, with the majority showing an activist philosophy. In *Baker v. Carr*,[22] the Supreme Court held that legislative apportionment was a justiciable controversy. Justice Brennan, speaking for the majority of the Court, said:

An unbroken line of our precedents sustains the federal court's jurisdiction on the subject matter of federal constitutional claims of this nature. . . . The mere fact that the suit seeks protection of a political right does not mean it presents a political question. . . . Review reveals that in political question cases, it is the relationship between the judiciary and the coordinate branches of the Federal Government, and not the federal judiciary's relationship to the states, which gives rise to the "political question." . . . "Deciding whether a matter has in any measure been committed by the Constitution to another branch of government, or whether the action of that branch exceeds whatever authority has been committed, is itself a delicate exercise in constitutional interpretation, and is a responsibility of this Court as ultimate interpreter of the Constitution. . . ." When a state exercises power wholly within the domain of state interest, it is insulated from federal judicial review. But such insulation is not carried over when a state power is used as an instrument for circumventing a federally protected right. . . . We conclude that the complaint's allegations of a denial of equal protection present a justiciable constitutional cause of action upon which appellants are entitled to a trial and a decision. The right asserted is within reach of judicial protection under the Fourteenth Amendment.

Justice Frankfurter, as the leader of the judicial restraint minority seeking to maintain the doctrine of *Colegrove v. Green*, argued:

The Court today reverses a uniform course of decision established by a dozen cases, including one by which the very claim now sustained was unanimously rejected only five years ago. The impressive body of rulings thus cast aside

[22] 369 U.S. 186 (1962).

reflected the equally uniform course of our political history regarding the relationship between population and legislative representation—a wholly different matter from denial of the franchise to individuals because of race, color, religion or sex. Such a massive repudiation of the experience of our whole past in asserting a destructively novel judicial power demands a detailed analysis of this Court in our Constitutional scheme. Disregard of inherent limits in the effective exercise of the Court's judicial power not only presages the futility of judicial intervention in the essentially political conflict of forces by which the relation between population and representation has time out of mind been and now is determined. It may well impair the Court's position as the ultimate organ of the Supreme Law of the Land in that vast range of legal problems, often strongly entangled in popular feelings, on which this Court must pronounce. . . .

The notion that representation proportioned to the geographic spread of population is so universally accepted as a necessary element of equality between man and man that it must be taken to be the standard of political equality preserved by the Fourteenth Amendment—that it is, in appellant's words "the basic principle of representative government"—is, to put it bluntly, not true. However desirable and however desired by some among the great political thinkers and framers of our government, it has never been generally practiced, today or in the past. It was not the English system, it was not the colonial system, it was not the system chosen for the national government by the Constitution, it was not the system exclusively or even predominately practiced by the states at the time of the adoption of the Fourteenth Amendment, it is not predominately practiced by the states today. Unless judges, the judges of this Court, are to make their private views of political wisdom the measure of the Constitution—views which in all honesty cannot but give the appearance, if not reflect the reality, of involvement with the business of partisan politics so inescapably a part of apportionment controversies . . . [then] the case is of that class of political controversy which, by nature of its subject, is unfit for federal judicial action.

Once the court declared that the judiciary had jurisdiction over issues of legislative apportionment, a veritable flood of cases followed, challenging the composition of legislative bodies at all levels. Included were cases concerning the United States House of Representatives. In the case that involved Georgia's congressional representatives, the principle of "one man—one vote" was announced as the applicable doctrine in reapportionment cases. The Georgia case brought forth a strong dissent by Justice Harlan, who had assumed the role of spokesman for the judicial restraint group on the Court upon Justice Frankfurter's retirement. Justice Harlan, dissenting in *Wesberry v. Sanders*,[23] said:

I had not expected to witness the day when the Supreme Court of the United States would render a decision which casts grave doubt on the constitutionality of the composition of the House of Representatives. It is not an exaggeration to

[23] 376 U.S. 1 (1964).

say that such is the effect of today's decision. The court's holding that the Constitution requires States to select Representatives either by elections at large or by elections in districts composed "as nearly as is practicable" of equal population places in jeopardy the seats of almost all the members of the present House of Representatives.

In the last congressional election, in 1962, Representatives from 42 States were elected from congressional districts. In all but five of those States, the difference between the populations of the largest and smallest districts exceeded 100,000 persons. A difference of this magnitude in the size of districts the average population of which in each State is less than 500,000 is presumably not equality among districts "as nearly as is practicable," although the Court does not reveal its definition of that phrase. Thus, today's decision impugns the validity of the election of 398 Representatives from 37 States, leaving a "constitutional" House of 37 members now sitting.

Only a demonstration which could not be avoided would justify this Court in rendering a decision the effect of which, inescapably as I see it, is to declare constitutionally defective the very composition of a coordinate branch of the Federal Government. The Court's opinion not only fails to make such a demonstration. It is unsound logically on its face and demonstrably unsound historically. . . .

The Court holds that the provision in Art. I, § 2, for election of Representatives "by the People" means that congressional districts are to be "as nearly as is practicable" equal in population. Stripped of rhetoric and a "historical context," which bears little resemblance to the evidence found in the pages of history, the Court's opinion supports its holding only with the bland assertion that "the principle of a House of Representatives elected 'by the People'" would be "cast aside" if "a vote is worth more in one district than in another," i.e., if congressional districts within a State, each electing a single Representative, are not equal in population. The fact is, however, that Georgia's 10 Representatives are elected "by the People" of Georgia, just as Representatives from other States are elected "by the People of the several States." This is all that the Constitution requires.

Although the Court finds necessity for its artificial construction of Article I in the undoubted importance of the right to vote, that right is not involved in this case. All of the appellants do vote. The Court's talk about "debasement" and "dilution" of the vote is a model of circular reasoning, in which the premises of the argument feed on the conclusion. Moreover, by focusing exclusively on numbers in disregard of the area and shape of a congressional district as well as party affiliations within the district, the Court deals in abstractions which will be recognized even by the politically unsophisticated to have little relevance to the realities of political life. . . .

There is a further basis for demonstrating the hollowness of the Court's assertion that Article I requires "one man's vote in a congressional election . . . to be worth as much as another's." Nothing that the Court does today will disturb the fact that although in 1960 the population of an average congression-

al district was 410,481, the States of Alaska, Nevada, and Wyoming each have a Representative in Congress, although their respective populations are 226,167, 285,278, and 330,066. In entire disregard of population, Art. I, § 2, guarantees each of these States and every other State "at Least one Representative." It is whimsical to assert in the face of this guarantee that an absolute principle of "equal representation in the House of equal numbers of people" is "solemnly embodied" in Article I. All that there is is a provision which bases representation in the House, generally but not entirely, on the population of the States. The provision for representation of each State in the House of Representatives is not a mere exception to the principle framed by the majority; it shows that no such principle is to be found.

The upshot of all this is that the language of Art. I, §§ 2 and 4, the surrounding text, and the relevant history are all in strong and consistent direct contradiction of the Court's holding. The constitutional scheme vests in the States plenary power to regulate the conduct of elections for Representatives, and, in order to protect the Federal Government, provides for congressional supervision of the States' exercise of their power. Within this scheme, the appellants do not have the right which they assert, in the absence of provision for equal districts by the Georgia Legislature or the Congress. The constitutional right which the Court creates is manufactured out of whole cloth. . . .

Today's decision has portents for our society and the Court itself which should be recognized. This is not a case in which the Court vindicates the kind of individual rights that are assured by the Due Process Clause of the Fourteenth Amendment whose "vague contours," Rochin v. People of California, 342 U.S. 165, 170, 72 S.Ct. 205, 208, of course leave much room for constitutional developments necessitated by changing conditions in a dynamic society. Nor is this a case in which an emergent set of facts requires the Court to frame new principles to protect recognized constitutional rights. The claim for judicial relief in this case strikes at one of the fundamental doctrines of our system of government, the separation of powers. In upholding that claim, the Court attempts to effect reforms in a field which the Constitution, as plainly as can be, has committed exclusively to the political process.

This Court, no less than all other branches of the Government, is bound by the Constitution. The Constitution does not confer on the Court blanket authority to step into every situation where the political branch may be thought to have fallen short. The stability of this institution ultimately depends not only upon its being alert to keep the other branches of government within constitutional bounds but equally upon recognition of the limitations on the Court's own functions in the constitutional system.

What is done today saps the political process. The promise of judicial intervention in matters of this sort cannot but encourage popular inertia in efforts for political reform through the political process, with the inevitable result that the process is itself weakened. By yielding to the demand for a judicial remedy in this instance, the Court in my view does a disservice both to itself and to the broader values of our system of government.

The prevailing view of the cases following *Baker v. Carr* can be seen in *Reynolds v. Sims*,[24] in which Chief Justice Earl Warren said:

Legislators represent people, not trees or acres. Legislators are elected by voters, not farms or cities or economic interests. As long as ours is a representative form of government, and our legislatures are those instruments of government elected directly by and directly representative of the people, the right to elect legislators in a free and unimpaired fashion is a bedrock of our political system. . . . State legislatures are, historically, the fountainhead of representative government in this country. Full and effective participation by all citizens in a state government requires, therefore, that each citizen have an equally effective voice in the election of his state legislature. To sanction minority control of state legislative bodies would appear to deny majority rights in a way that far surpasses any possible denial of minority rights that otherwise might be thought to result. . . . Our constitutional system amply provides for the protection of minorities by means other than giving them majority control of state legislatures. We are told that the matter of apportioning representation in state legislatures is a complex and many-faceted one. We are advised that the states can rationally consider factors other than population in apportioning legislative representation. We are admonished not to restrict the power of the states to impose differing views as to political philosophy on their citizens. We are cautioned about the dangers of entering into political thickets and mathematical quagmires. Our answer is this: a denial of constitutionally protected rights demands judicial protection; our path and our office require no less of us. . . . We hold that, as a basic constitutional standard, the Equal Protection Clause requires that the seats in both houses of a bicameral state legislature must be apportioned on a population basis.

D SOCIETY'S ATTITUDE

The law is greatly influenced by the mood of the people or the attitude of society toward any particular problem. On many questions society's attitude will be divided, which makes it difficult to ascertain whether the court in a given case is reflecting the dominant attitude of the times or is providing leadership in bringing about social change by adopting the philosophy of an enlightened minority. The court usually does not have the benefit of a public opinion poll or an actual vote by the electorate on the great social questions before it. Most reviewing courts are not "politically responsible" in the sense that the voters can replace the judges if they hand down unpopular decisions. Nevertheless, a court of review generally has its ear to the feelings and attitudes of society, and its actions are frequently based on its own best judgment of what those attitudes and beliefs are, concerning the problem at hand. For example, the decisions on questions of obscenity in recent years have tended to hold that very few books or movies are

[24] 377 U.S. 533 (1964).

obscene. This has been a period of time during which society's attitude toward sex and morality has been changing. While it can not definitely be determined whether the courts have reflected society's ideas or society has been influenced by the judicial decisions, it is clear that the attitudes of both the court and society have moved away from the so-called "Victorian attitude" and toward a much more "liberal" view of the effects of pornography on society.

This view has come about by the Court's giving the maximum protection to freedom of speech and press as guaranteed by the First Amendment. However, it should be noted that the rising tide of hard-core pornography is causing some change in society's attitude and perhaps even in the Court's. A recent case which allowed censorship of a movie by a state was affirmed by the Supreme Court 4–4 (this was prior to Justice Blackmun's appointment). Another change in this area of the law may be forthcoming as a result of the changing attitude of society.

The doctrine of "constitutional relativity" stands for the proposition that the meaning of the language found in the Constitution is relative to the time in which it is being interpreted. The doctrine has been recently used rather frequently by the Supreme Court to give effect to society's attitudes. Under this concept great weight is attached to social forces and needs, as the court sees them, in formulating judicial decisions. As the attitudes and problems of society change, the law and the Constitution are changed also. The evolution in interpretation of law is accomplished by the courts' reflection of social evolution. Perhaps no single legal problem better illustrates the power of social pressure than that of school integration. As social forces demanded equality for blacks, the law, reflecting these demands, has gradually changed. Precedent was overturned and the dominant viewpoint of one portion of the country was dramatically rejected, at least by the Supreme Court in its unanimous holding. Judicial decree, brought about by social change, is accomplishing what was impracticable by legislation. The following is the landmark case on school integration.

Brown v. Board of Education X
347 U.S. 497 (1954)

WARREN, CHIEF JUSTICE: These cases come to us from the States of Kansas, South Carolina, Virginia, and Delaware. They are premised on different facts and different local conditions, but a common legal question justifies their consideration together in this consolidated opinion.

In each of the cases, minors of the Negro race, through their legal representatives, seek the aid of the courts in obtaining admission to the public schools of their community on a nonsegregated basis. In each instance, they had been denied admission to schools attended by white children under laws requiring or permitting segregation according to race. This segregation was alleged to deprive the plaintiffs of the equal protection of the laws under the Fourteenth Amendment. In each of the cases other than the Delaware case, a three-judge federal district court denied relief to the plaintiffs on the so-called "separate but equal" doctrine announced by this Court in *Plessy v. Ferguson,* 163 U.S. 537.

Under that doctrine, equality of treatment is accorded when the races are provided substantially equal facilities, even though these facilities be separate. In the Delaware case, the Supreme Court of Delaware adhered to that doctrine, but ordered that the plaintiffs be admitted to the white schools because of their superiority to the Negro schools.

The plaintiffs contend that segregated public schools are not "equal" and cannot be made "equal," and that hence they are deprived of the equal protection of the laws. Because of the obvious importance of the question presented, the Court took jurisdiction. Argument was heard in the 1952 Term, and reargument was heard this Term on certain questions propounded by the Court.

Reargument was largely devoted to the circumstances surrounding the adoption of the Fourteenth Amendment in 1868. It covered exhaustively consideration of the Amendment in Congress, ratification by the states, then existing practices in racial segregation, and the views of proponents and opponents of the Amendment. This discussion and our own investigation convince us that, although these sources cast some light, it is not enough to resolve the problem with which we are faced. At best, they are inconclusive. The most avid proponents of the post-War Amendments undoubtedly intended them to remove all legal distinctions among "all persons born or naturalized in the United States." Their opponents, just as certainly, were antagonistic to both the letter and the spirit of the Amendments and wished them to have the most limited effect. What others in Congress and the state legislatures had in mind cannot be determined with any degree of certainty.

An additional reason for the inconclusive nature of the Amendment's history, with respect to segregated schools, is the status of public education at that time. In the South, the movement toward free common schools, supported by general taxation, had not yet taken hold. Education of white children was largely in the hands of private groups. Education of Negroes was almost nonexistent, and practically all of the race were illiterate. In fact, any education of Negroes was forbidden by law in some states. Today, in contrast, many Negroes have achieved outstanding success in the arts and sciences as well as in the business and professional world. It is true that public school education at the time of the Amendment had advanced further in the North, but the effect of the Amendment on Northern States was generally ignored in the congressional debates. Even in the North, the conditions of public education did not approximate those existing today. The curriculum was usually rudimentary; ungraded schools were common in rural areas; the school term was but three months a year in many states; and compulsory school attendance was virtually unknown. As a consequence, it is not surprising that there should be so little in the history of the Fourteenth Amendment relating to its intended effect on public education.

In the first cases in this Court construing the Fourteenth Amendment, decided shortly after its adoption, the Court interpreted it as proscribing all state-imposed discriminations against the Negro race. The doctrine of "separate but equal" did not make its appearance in this Court until 1896 in the case of *Plessy v. Ferguson, supra,* involving not education but transportation. American courts have since labored with the doctrine for over half a century. In this Court, there have been six cases involving the "separate but equal" doctrine in the field of public education. In *Cumming v. County Board of Education,* 175 U.S. 528, and *Gong Lum v. Rice,* 275 U.S. 78, the validity of the doctrine itself was not challenged. In more recent cases, all on the graduate school level, inequality was found in that specific benefits enjoyed by white students were denied to Negro students of the same educational qualifications. *Missouri ex rel. Gaines v. Canada,* 305 U.S. 337; *Spiuel v. Oklahoma,* 332 U.S. 631; *Sweatt v. Painter,* 339 U.S. 629; *McLaurin v. Oklahoma State Regents,* 339 U.S. 637. In none of these cases was it necessary to re-examine the doctrine to grant relief to the Negro plaintiff. And in *Sweatt v. Painter, supra,* the Court expressly reserved decision on the question whether *Plessy v. Ferguson* should be held inapplicable to public education.

In the instant cases, that question is directly presented. Here, unlike *Sweatt v. Painter,* there are findings below that the Negro and white schools involved have been equalized, or are being equalized, with respect to buildings, curricula, qualifications and salaries of teachers, and other "tangible" factors. Our decision, therefore, cannot turn on merely a comparison of these tangible factors in the Negro and white schools involved in each of the cases. We must look instead to the effect of segregation itself on public education.

In approaching this problem, we cannot turn the clock back to 1868 when the Amendment was adopted, or even to 1896 when *Plessy v. Ferguson* was written. We must consider public education in the light of its full development and its present place in American life throughout the Nation. Only in this way can it be determined if segregation in public schools deprives these plaintiffs of the equal protection of the laws.

Today, education is perhaps the most important function of state and local governments. Compulsory school attendance laws and the great expenditures for education both demonstrate our recognition of the importance of education to our democratic society. It is required in the performance of our most basic public responsibilities, even service in the armed forces. It is the very foundation of good citizenship. Today it is a principal instrument in awakening the child to cultural values, in preparing him for later professional training, and in helping him to adjust normally to his environment. In these days, it is doubtful that any child may reasonably be expected to succeed in life if he is denied the opportunity of an education. Such an opportunity, where the state has undertaken to provide it, is a right which must be made available to all on equal terms.

We come then to the question presented: Does segregation of children in public schools solely on the basis of race, even though the physical facilities and other "tangible" factors may be equal, deprive the children of the minority group of equal educational opportunities? We believe that it does.

In *Sweatt v. Painter, supra,* in finding that a segregated law school for Negroes could not provide them equal educational opportunities, this Court relied in large part on "those qualities which are incapable of objective measurement but which make for greatness in a law school." In *McLaurin v. Oklahoma State Regents, supra,* the Court, in requiring that a Negro admitted to a white graduate school be treated like all other students, again resorted to intangible consider-ations: ". . . his ability to study, to engage in discussions and exchange views with other students, and, in general, to learn his profession." Such considerations apply with added force to children in grade and high schools. To separate them from others of similar age and qualifications solely because of their race generates a feeling of inferiority as to their status in the community that may affect their hearts and minds in a way unlikely ever to be undone. The effect of this separation on their educational opportunities was well stated by a finding in the Kansas case by a court which nevertheless felt compelled to rule against the Negro plaintiffs:

Segregation of white and colored children in public schools has a detrimental effect upon the colored children. The impact is greater when it has the sanction of the law; for the policy of separating the races is usually interpreted as denoting the inferiority of the negro group. A sense of inferiority affects the motivation of a child to learn. Segregation with the sanction of law, therefore, has a tendency to [retard] the educational and mental development of negro children and to deprive them of some of the benefits they would receive in a racial[ly] integrated school system.

Whatever may have been the extent of psychological knowledge at the time of *Plessy v. Ferguson,* this finding is amply supported by modern authority. Any language in *Plessy v. Ferguson* contrary to this finding is rejected.

We conclude that in the field of public education the doctrine of "separate but equal" has no place. Separate educational facilities are inherently unequal. Therefore, we hold that the plaintiffs and others similarly situated for whom the actions have been brought are, by reason of the segregation complained of, deprived of the equal protection of the laws guaranteed by the Fourteenth Amendment. This disposition makes unnecessary any discussion whether such segregation also violates the Due Process Clause of the Fourteenth Amendment.

Because these are class actions, because of the wide applicability of this decision, and because of the great variety of local conditions, the formulation of decrees in these cases presents problems of considerable complexity. On reargument, the consideration of appropriate relief was necessarily subordinated to the primary question—the constitutionality of segregation in public education. We have now announced that such segregation is a denial of the equal protection of the laws. In order that we may have the full assistance of the parties in formulating decrees, the cases will be restored to the docket, and the parties are requested to present further argument on Questions 4 and 5 previously pro-pounded by the Court for the reargument this Term.[25] [RESTORED TO DOCKET]

After *Brown v. Board of Education,* there were literally hundreds of cases relating to school integration. These cases involved the issues of how and when—

---

[25] The questions referred to concerned the nature of the decrees to be formulated by the court to enforce its decision.

not if—a given school district would be integrated. Following the approach of Justice Cardozo, the courts then determined how the principle of school integration was to work and develop, if it was not to wither and die. Courts were forced on a case-by-case basis to work out and apply the *ratio decidendi* of *Brown v. Board of Education.*

In 1971, the Supreme Court was still faced with several problems concerning school integration. Among the issues relative to student assignment confronting the Court were:

1 The extent to which racial balance or racial quotas may be used as an implement in a remedial order to correct a previously segregated system.
2 Whether every all-black and all-white school must be eliminated as an indispensable part of a remedial process of desegregation.
3 The limits, if any, on the rearrangement of school districts and attendance zones, as a remedial measure.
4 The limits, if any, on the use of transportation facilities to correct state-enforced racial school segregation.

The Court in *Swann v. Charlotte-Mecklenburg Board of Education,* 91 S.Ct. 1267 (1971), held (1) that the use of a mathematical ratio of white to black students, not as an inflexible requirement but as a starting point in the process of shaping a remedy, was within the equitable remedial discretion of the courts, (2) that the pairing and the grouping of noncontiguous school zones were permissible tools of integration to be considered in the light of the objectives of remedying past constitutional violations, and (3) that where it appeared that assignment of children to the school nearest their home serving their grade would not produce an effective dismantling of the dual segregated system, the ordering of a system of bus transportation was a constitutionally permissible tool of school desegregation.

Chief Justice Burger, speaking for a unanimous Court in that case, illustrated the development of a principle of law when he said in part:

Nearly 17 years ago this Court held, in explicit terms, that state-imposed segregation by race in public schools denies equal protection of the laws. At no time has the Court deviated in the slightest degree from that holding or its constitutional underpinnings. . . .

None of the parties before us questions the Court's 1955 holding in Brown II, *that*

"[s]chool authorities have the primary responsibility for elucidating, assessing, and solving these problems; courts will have to consider whether the action of school authorities constitutes good faith implementation of the governing constitutional principles. Because of their proximity to local conditions and the possible need for further hearings, the courts which originally heard these cases can best perform this judicial appraisal. Accordingly, we believe it appropriate to remand the cases to those courts.

"In fashioning and effectuating the decrees, the courts will be guided by equitable principles. Traditionally, equity has been characterized by a practical flexibility in shaping its remedies and by a facility for adjusting and reconciling public and private needs. These cases call for the exercise of these traditional attributes of equity power. At stake is the personal interest of the plaintiffs in admission to public schools as soon as practicable on a nondiscriminatory basis. To effectuate this interest may call for elimination of a variety of obstacles in making the transition to school systems operated in accordance with the constitutional principles set forth in our May 17, 1954, decision. Courts of equity may properly take into account the public interest in the elimination of such obstacles in a systematic and effective manner. But it should go without saying that the vitality of these constitutional principles cannot be allowed to yield simply because of disagreement with them."

Over the 15 years since Brown II, many difficulties were encountered in implementation of the basic constitutional requirement that the State not discriminate between public school children on the basis of their race. Nothing in our national experience prior to 1955 prepared anyone for dealing with changes and adjustments of the magnitude and complexity encountered since then. Deliberate resistance of some to the Court's mandates has impeded the good-faith efforts of others to bring school systems into compliance. The detail and nature of these dilatory tactics have been noted frequently by this Court and other courts.

By . . . 1968, very little progress had been made in many areas where dual school systems had historically been maintained by operation of state laws. In Green, the Court was confronted with a record of a freedom-of-choice program that the District Court had found to operate in fact to preserve a dual system more than a decade after Brown II. While acknowledging that a freedom-of-choice concept could be a valid remedial measure in some circumstances, its failure to be effective in Green required that

"The burden on a school board today is to come forward with a plan that promises realistically to work now . . . until it is clear that state-imposed segregation has been completely removed."

This was plain language, yet the 1969 Term of Court brought fresh evidence of the dilatory tactics of many school authorities. . . .

The problems encountered by the district courts and courts of appeals make plain that we should now try to amplify guidelines, however incomplete and imperfect, for the assistance of school authorities and courts. The failure of local authorities to meet their constitutional obligations aggravated the massive problem of converting from the state-enforced discrimination of racially separate school systems. This process has been rendered more difficult by changes since 1954 in the structure and patterns of communities, the growth of student population, movement of families, and other changes, some of which had marked impact on school planning, sometimes neutralizing or negating remedial action before it was fully implemented. Rural areas accustomed for *half a century to the consolidated school systems implemented by bus transportation could make adjustments more readily than metropolitan areas with dense and shifting population, numerous schools, congested and complex traffic patterns.*

The objective today remains to eliminate from the public schools all vestiges of state-imposed segregation. Segregation was the evil struck down by Brown I *as contrary to the equal protection guarantees of the Constitution. That was the violation sought to be corrected by the remedial measures of* Brown II. *That was the basis for the holding in* Green *that school authorities are "clearly charged with the affirmative duty to take whatever steps might be necessary to convert to a unitary system in which racial discrimination would be eliminated root and branch."*

We turn now to the problem of defining with more particularity the responsibilities of school authorities in desegregating a state-enforced dual school system in light of the Equal Protection Clause. . . . Independent of student assignment, where it is possible to identify a "white school" or a "Negro school" simply by reference to the racial composition of teachers and staff, the quality of school buildings and equipment, or the organization of sports activities, a prima facie *case of violation of substantive constitutional rights under the Equal Protection Clause is shown.*

When a system has been dual in these respects, the first remedial responsibility of school authorities is to eliminate invidious racial distinctions. . . .

In ascertaining the existence of legally imposed school segregation, the existence of a pattern of school construction and abandonment is . . . a factor of great weight. In devising remedies where legally imposed segregation has been established, it is the responsibility of local authorities and district courts to see to it that future school construction and abandonment is not used and does not serve to perpetuate or re-establish the dual system. . . .

The constant theme and thrust of every holding from Brown I *to date is that state-enforced separation of races in public schools is discrimination that violates the Equal Protection Clause. The remedy commanded was to dismantle dual school systems. . . .*

Our objective in dealing with the issues presented by those cases is to see that school authorities exclude no pupil of a racial minority from any school, directly or indirectly, on account of race; it does not and cannot embrace all the problems of racial prejudice, even when those problems contribute to disproportionate racial concentrations in some schools. . . .

An optional majority-to-minority transfer provision has long been recognized as a useful part of every desegregation plan. Provision for optional transfer of those in the majority racial group of a particular school to other schools where they will be in the minority is an indispensable remedy for those students willing to transfer to other schools in order to lessen the impact on them of the state-imposed stigma of segregation. In order to be effective, such a transfer arrangement must grant the transferring student free transportation and space must be made available in the school to which he desires to move.

The maps submitted in these cases graphically demonstrate that one of the principal tools employed by school planners and by courts to break up the dual school system has been a frank—and sometimes drastic—gerrymandering of school districts and attendance zones. An additional step was pairing, "clustering," or "grouping" of schools with attendance assignments made deliberately to accomplish the transfer of Negro students out of formerly segregated Negro schools and transfer of white students to formerly all-Negro schools. More often than not, these zones are neither compact nor contiguous; indeed they may be on opposite ends of the city. As an interim corrective measure, this cannot be said to be beyond the broad remedial powers of a court.

Absent a constitutional violation there would be no basis for judicially ordering assignment of students on a racial basis. All things being equal, with no history of discrimination, it might well be desirable to assign pupils to schools nearest their homes. But all things are not equal in a system that has been deliberately constructed and maintained to enforce racial segregation. The remedy for such segregation may be administratively awkward, inconvenient and even bizarre in some situations and may impose burdens on some; but all awkwardness and inconvenience cannot be avoided in the interim period when remedial adjustments are being made to eliminate the dual school systems.

The scope of permissible transportation of students as an implement of a remedial decree has never been defined by this Court and by the very nature of the problem it cannot be defined with precision. No rigid guidelines as to student transportation can be given for application to the infinite variety of problems presented in thousands of situations. Bus transportation has been an integral part of the public education system for years, and was perhaps the single most important factor in the transition from the one-room schoolhouse to the consolidated school. . . .

The decree provided that the buses used to implement the plan would operate on direct routes. Students would be picked up at schools near their homes and transported to the schools they were to attend. The trips for elementary school pupils average about seven miles and the district Court found that they would take "not over 35 minutes at the most." This system compares favorably with the transportation plan previously operated in Charlotte under which each day 23,600 students on all grade levels were transported an average of 15 miles one way for an average trip requiring over an hour. In these circumstances, we find no basis for holding that the local school authorities may not be required to employ bus transportation as one tool of school desegregation. Desegregation plans cannot be limited to the walk-in school. . . .

Thus it can be seen that the principle of a unitary school system is still in the process of being attained. Laws prohibiting busing are unconstitutional, and busing may be legally required if necessary to achieve the goal of an integrated school system. Boards of education have a duty to eliminate the dual school system, and if they fail to do so, the courts may do it for them. Faculty-staff and student ratios based on race may be used to achieve the purpose, for the law has the flexibility to fulfill the rationale of its principles. The law is capable of evolving to meet changing conditions and new challenges. While the issue of busing school children to achieve integration remains with us, the final decision on the matter will be made by the courts.

E EMERGENCIES

Emergency situations such as calamities caused by flood, fire or earthquake sometimes alter the application of a rule or require that a different rule be applied. In addition, an emergency may afford a reason for exercising a power of government otherwise dormant. National emergencies such as economic depressions have resulted even in court approval of statutes in partial impairment of the obligations of contracts, as is illustrated by the following case. Note that the emergency here was a force which operated both on the legislature in *adopting* a law, and on the Supreme Court in holding that law to be valid, in spite of Article I, Section 10 of the United States Constitution, which reads: "No State shall . . . pass any . . . Law impairing the Obligation of Contracts. . . ."

Home Building & Loan v. Blaisdell ✕
290 U.S. 398 (1934)

In 1933, Minnesota passed a Mortgage Moratorium law which declared that as a result of the economic emergency, mortgage foreclosure sales might be judicially postponed and periods of redemption of prior sales might be extended to May 1, 1935. Appellees applied to a court for an order extending the time during which they might redeem a lot which they owned but which had been sold at a foreclosure sale. Appellant had purchased the property at the foreclosure sale and contended that the statute was unconstitutional as being repugnant to the contract clause (Article 1, § 10) and the due process and equal protection clauses of the Fourteenth Amendment of the Federal Constitution. The statute was sustained by the Supreme Court of Minnesota as an emergency measure although the Minnesota Court admitted that the obligation of a contract had been impaired.

HUGHES, CHIEF JUSTICE: . . . In determining whether the provision for this temporary and conditional relief exceeds the power of the state by reason of the clause in the Federal Constitution prohibiting impairment of the obligations of contracts, we must consider the relation of emergency to constitutional power, the historical setting of the contract clause, the development of the jurisprudence of this Court in the construction of that clause, and the principles of construction which we may consider to be established.

Emergency does not create power. Emergency does not increase granted power or remove or diminish the restrictions imposed upon power granted or reserved. The Constitution was adopted in a period of grave emergency. Its grants of power to the federal government and its limitations of the power of the States were determined in the light of emergency, and they are not altered by emergency. What power was thus granted and what limitations were thus imposed are questions which have always been, and always will be, the subject of close examination under our constitutional system.

While emergency does not create power, emergency may furnish the occasion for the exercise of power. "Although an emergency may not call into life a power which has never lived, nevertheless emergency may afford a reason for the exertion of a living power already enjoyed" . . . [cases cited]. The constitutional question presented in the light of an emergency is whether the power possessed embraces the particular exercise of it in response to particular conditions. Thus, the war power of the federal government is not created by the emergency of war, but it is a power given to meet that emergency. It is a power to wage war successfully, and thus it permits the harnessing of the entire energies of the people in a supreme co-operative effort to preserve the nation. But even the war power does not remove constitutional limitations safeguarding essential liberties. When the provisions of the Constitution, in grant or restrictions, are specific, so particularized as not to admit of construction, no question is presented. Thus, emergency would not permit a state to have more than two Senators in the Congress, or permit the election of President by a general popular vote without regard to the number of electors to which the States are respectively entitled, or permit the States to "coin money" or to "make anything but gold and silver coin a tender in payment of debts." But, where constitutional grants and limitations of power are set forth in general clauses, which afford a broad outline, the process of construction is essential to fill in the details. That is true of the contract clause. The necessity of construction is not obviated by the fact that the contract clause is associated in the same section with other and more specific prohibitions. . . .

The occasion and general purpose of the contract clause are summed up in the terse statement of Chief Justice Marshall in *Ogden v. Saunders*, 12 Wheat. 213, 354, 355, 6 L.Ed. 606:

The power of changing the relative situation of debtor and creditor, of interfering with contracts, a power which comes home to every man, touches the interest of all, and controls the conduct of every individual in those things which he supposes to be proper for his own exclusive management, had been used to such an excess by the state legislatures, as to break in upon the ordinary intercourse of society, and destroy all confidence between man and man. This mischief had become so great, so alarming, as not only to impair commercial intercourse, and threaten the existence of credit, but to sap the morals of the people, and destroy the sanctity of private faith. To guard against the continuance of the evil, was an object of deep interest with all the truly wise, as well as the virtuous, of this great community, and was one of the important benefits expected from a reform of the government.

But full recognition of the occasion and general purpose of the clause does not suffice to fix its precise scope. . . . To ascertain the scope of the constitutional prohibition, we examine the course of judicial decisions in its application. These put it beyond question that the prohibition is not an absolute one and is not to be read with literal exactness like a mathematical formula. . . . Not only are existing laws read into contracts in order to fix obligations as between the parties, but the reservation of essential attributes of sovereign power is also read into contracts as a postulate of the legal order. The policy of protecting contracts against impairment presupposes the maintenance of a government by virtue of which contractual relations are worthwhile,—a government which retains adequate authority to secure the peace and good order of society. This principle of harmonizing the constitutional prohibition with the necessary residuum of state power has had progressive recognition in the decisions of this Court. . . .

Undoubtedly, whatever is reserved of state power must be consistent with the fair intent of the constitutional limitation of that power. The reserved power cannot be construed so as to destroy the limitation, nor is the limitation to be construed to destroy the reserved power in its essential aspects. They must be construed in harmony with each other. This principle precludes a construction which would permit the state to adopt as its policy the repudiation of debts or the destruction of contracts or the denial of means to enforce them. But it does not follow that conditions may not arise in which a temporary restraint of enforcement may be consistent with the spirit and purpose of the constitutional provision and thus be found to be within the range of the reserved power of the state to protect the vital interests of the community. It cannot be maintained that the constitutional prohibition should be so construed as to prevent limited and temporary interpositions with respect to the enforcement of contracts if made necessary by a great public calamity such as fire, flood, or earthquake. . . . The reservation of state power appropriate to such extraordinary conditions may be deemed to be as much a part of all contracts as is the reservation of state power to protect the public interest. . . . And, if state power exists to give temporary relief from the enforcement of contracts in the presence of disasters due to physical causes such as fire, flood, or earthquake, that power cannot be said to be nonexistent when the urgent public need demanding such relief is produced by other and economic causes.

Whatever doubt there may have been that the protective power of the state, its police power, may be exercised—without violating the true intent of the provision of the Federal Constitution—in directly preventing the immediate and literal enforcement of contractual obligations by a temporary and conditional restraint, where vital public interests would otherwise suffer, was removed by our decisions relating to the enforcement of provisions of leases during a period of scarcity of housing. . . .

It is manifest from this review of our decisions that there has been a growing appreciation of public needs and of the necessity of finding ground for a rational compromise between individual rights and public welfare. The settlement and consequent contraction of the public domain, the pressure of a constantly increasing density of population, the interrelation of the activities of our people and the complexity of our economic interests, have inevitably led to an increased use of the organization of society in order to protect the very bases of individual opportunity. Where, in earlier days, it was thought that only the concerns of individuals or of classes were involved, and that those of the state itself were touched only remotely, it has later been found that the fundamental interests of the state are directly affected; and that the question is no longer merely that of one party to a contract as against another, but of the use of reasonable means to safeguard the economic structure upon which the good of all depends.

It is no answer to say that this public need was not apprehended a century ago, or to insist that what the provision of the Constitution meant to the vision of that day it must mean to the vision of our time. If by the statement that what the Constitution meant at the time of its adoption it means to-day, it is intended to say that the great clauses of the Constitution must be confined to the interpretation which the framers, with the conditions and outlook of their time, would have placed upon them, the statement carries its own refutation. It was to guard against such a narrow conception that Chief Justice Marshall uttered the memorable warnings: "We must never forget, that it is *a constitution* we are expounding" (*McCulloch v. Maryland*, 4 Wheat. 316, 407, 4 L.Ed. 579); "a constitution intended to endure for ages to come, and, consequently, to be adapted to the various *crises* of human affairs." *Id.* page 415 of 4 Wheat. When we are dealing with the words of the Constitution, said this Court in *Missouri v. Holland*, 252 U.S. 416, 433, . . . "we must realize that they have called into life a being the development of which could not have been foreseen completely by the most gifted of its begetters. . . The case before us must be considered in the light of our whole experience and not merely in that of what was said a hundred years ago."

Nor is it helpful to attempt to draw a fine distinction between the intended meaning of the words of the Constitution and their intended application. When we consider the contract clause and the decisions which have expounded it in harmony with the essential reserved power of the states to protect the security of their peoples, we find no warrant for the conclusion that the clause has been warped by these decisions from its proper significance or that the founders of our government would have interpreted the clause differently had they had occasion to assume that responsibility in the conditions of the later day. The vast body of law which has been developed was unknown to the fathers, but it is believed to have preserved the essential content and the spirit of the Constitution. With a growing recognition of public needs and the relation of individual right to public security, the court has sought to prevent the perversion of the clause through its use as an instrument to throttle the capacity of the states to protect their fundamental interests. This development is a growth from the seeds which the fathers planted. . . . The principle of this development is, as we have seen, that the reservation of the reasonable exercise of the protective power of the state is read into all contracts. . . .

Applying the criteria established by our decisions, we conclude:

. . . The legislation was addressed to a legitimate end; that is, the legislation was not for the mere advantage of particular individuals but for the protection of a basic interest of society.

. . . We are of the opinion that the Minnesota statute as here applied does not violate the contract clause of the Federal Constitution. Whether the legislation is wise or unwise as a matter of policy is a question with which we are not concerned. . . .

The judgment of the Supreme Court of Minnesota is affirmed. [JUDGMENT AFFIRMED]

No emergency has a more direct impact on the nation as a whole than does war. The repercussions of war and the exercise of emergency war powers have directed the path of executive action, legislation, and judicial decisions even to the extent of denying to citizens their rights to liberty and property.

Toward the beginning of World War II, over 100,000 Japanese, approximately 70,000 of them citizens of the United States from birth, without being charged or indicted for any offense, without any investigation of their loyalty to the United States, were first subjected to a curfew and later removed from their homes in West Coast areas.[26] These people, aliens and citizens alike, were taken into custody by order of the Commanding General of the Western Defense Command and sent to "relocation camps" which were in reality concentration camps, and many of them were detained there for several years. The Japanese-Americans suffered great losses of property—furniture, homes, gardens, and businesses. *Aliens* from Italy and Germany, with whose countries we also were at war, and citizens of Japanese ancestry residing in Hawaii (over 30 percent of the population there) were not "relocated" in this manner. The military ordered and executed the relocation on the West Coast acting under the war powers and pursuant to an executive order of the President and supported by an act of Congress. The white populace of the West had been under great tension from fear of sabotage and an invasion or attack by Japan similar to Pearl Harbor. The military decision to remove the Japanese-Americans from coastal areas was no doubt greatly influenced by this public fear, since there was no known case of sabotage or spying by one of Japanese ancestry and since similar military measures were not undertaken any place else in the country. Several cases resulted challenging the validity of the military action as a discrimination between citizens of Japanese ancestry and those of other ancestry in violation of the Fifth Amendment to the Constitution which states: "No person shall . . . be deprived of life, liberty or property without due process of law. . . ." The decisions generally were in favor of the action of the government as a legitimate exercise of the war power and have been the subject of a great deal of criticism.

In *Hirabayashi v. United States*, 320 U.S. 81 (1943), the Court stated:

Whatever views we may entertain regarding the loyalty to this country of the citizens of Japanese ancestry, we cannot reject as unfounded the judgment of the military authorities and of Congress that there are disloyal members of that

[26] See Rostow, The Japanese American Cases—A Disaster, 54 *Yale L.J.* 489 (1945).

population, whose number and strength could not be precisely and quickly ascertained. We cannot say that the war-making branches of the government did not have ground for believing that in a critical hour such persons could not readily be isolated and separately dealt with, and constituted a menace to the national defense and safety, which demanded that prompt and adequate measure be taken to guard against it.

Justice Stone said in the *Hirabayashi* case:

The war power of the national government is "the power to wage war successfully." See Charles Evans Hughes, War Powers under the Constitution, 42 A.B.A. Rep. 232, 238. It extends to every matter and activity so related to war as substantially to affect its conduct and progress. The power is not restricted to the winning of victories in the field and the repulse of enemy forces. It embraces every phase of the national defense, including the protection of war materials and the members of the armed forces from injury and from the dangers which attend the rise, prosecution and progress of war. . . .

Since the Constitution commits to the Executive and to Congress the exercise of the war power in all the vicissitudes and conditions of warfare, it has necessarily given them wide scope for the exercise of judgment and discretion in determining the nature and extent of the threatened injury or danger and in the selection of the means for resisting it . . . [cases cited]. Where, as they did here, the conditions call for the exercise of judgment and discretion and for the choice of means by those branches of the Government on which the Constitution has placed the responsibility of warmaking, it is not for any court to sit in review of the wisdom of their action or substitute its judgment for theirs.

Justice Stone further indicated the effect of war on the courts when he held that it justified distinctions between citizens based on race, stating:

Distinctions between citizens solely because of their ancestry are by their very nature odious to a free people whose institutions are founded upon the doctrine of equality. For that reason, legislative classification or discrimination based on race alone has often been held to be a denial of equal protection . . . [cases cited]. We may assume that these considerations would be controlling here were it not for the fact that the danger of espionage and sabotage, in time of war and of threatened invasion, calls upon the military authorities to scrutinize every relevant fact bearing on the loyalty of populations in the danger areas. Because racial discriminations are in most circumstances irrelevant and therefore prohibited, it by no means follows that, in dealing with the perils of war, Congress and the Executive are wholly precluded from taking into account those facts and circumstances which are relevant to measures for our national defense and for the successful prosecution of the war, and which may in fact place citizens of one ancestry in a different category from others. "We must never forget, that it is a constitution we are expounding, . . . a constitution intended to endure for ages to come, and, consequently, to be adapted to the various crises of human affairs."

In *Korematsu v. United States,* 323 U.S. 214 (1944), Justice Jackson, while dissenting in another case involving the Japanese-Americans, indicated that courts should not interfere with the military in time of war when he said:

I should hold that a civil court cannot be made to enforce an order which violates constitutional limitations even if it is a reasonable exercise of military authority. The courts can exercise only the judicial power, can apply only law, and must abide by the Constitution, or they cease to be civil courts and become instruments of military policy.

Of course the existence of military power resting on force, so vagrant, so centralized, so necessarily heedless of the individual, is an inherent threat to liberty. But I would not lead people to rely on this court for a review that seems to me wholly delusive. The military reasonableness of these orders can only be determined by military superiors. If the people even let command of the war power fall into irresponsible and unscrupulous hands, the courts wield no power equal to its restraint. The chief restraint upon those who command the physical forces of the country, in the future as in the past, must be their responsibility to the political judgments of their contemporaries and to the moral judgments of history.

My duties as Justice as I see them do not require me to make a military judgment as to whether General DeWitt's evacuation and detention program was a reasonable military necessity. I do not suggest that the courts should have attempted to interfere with the Army in carrying out its task. But I do not think that they may be asked to execute a military expedient that has no place in law under the Constitution.

The emergency war power extends to activities of the government during so-called periods of peace. Technically, a state of war exists until a peace treaty becomes effective.

From the foregoing we have seen that economic and military emergencies may shape the law. Since we seem to live in almost a constant state of emergency, this factor adds uncertainty and instability to the law.

6   CONCLUSION

In this chapter, some of the forces and factors which influence judicial decisions have been discussed. It is not possible to predict with absolute certainty in any case the relative weight to be given them. Each case is peculiar in facts and circumstances and must be viewed in its own environment, and considered individually. Lawyers, in advising clients, must make an educated guess, many times, as to the outcome of a case. It should be readily apparent that in almost all legal disputes victory or defeat may depend on either the facts or the law. Each is variable to some extent. However, it must be recognized that "the authority to exercise judicial discretion is not an arbitrary power of the individual judge, to be exercised when, and as, his caprice, or passion, or partiality may dictate, or forsooth as his vindictiveness or his idiosyncrasies may inspire."[27] A judge may not say that he simply disagrees with a certain accepted rule of law and therefore it will not be used in his court. In many ways, the forces discussed in this chapter have a greater cumulative effect on the total process than on any particular judge in any particular case.

REVIEW QUESTIONS—CHAPTER 6

1 Define the following terms introduced in this chapter: *ratio decidendi;* bill of attainder; constitutional relativity; unitary school system.
2 Compare judicial reasoning with other forms of logic.
3 Explain Justice Holmes's statement: "The life of the law has not been logic; it has been experience."
4 What are the four directive forces on the law as discussed by Justice Cardozo? Explain the influence of each.
5 Illustrate deductive and inductive reasoning.
6 Discuss the accuracy of this statement: "The law is a system of known rules applied by a judge."
7 Why has custom had such a heavy influence on commercial law?
8 What are the problems inherent in a judicial system that places heavy emphasis on the *result* of a lawsuit?
9 Compare the activist philosophy with the philosophy of judicial restraint.
10 What are the three trends in Supreme Court decisions as discussed by Professor Kurland?
11 Does the Constitution require busing to achieve racial integration in schools? Is busing constitutional where it is ordered to achieve a unitary school system? Explain.
12 Why are segregated schools unconstitutional?
13 Explain how an emergency may affect the law applicable to a given case.

---

[27] *Smith v. Smith,* 17 N.J. Super. 131 (1951).

Chapter Seven

Law by Administrative Agencies

1   THE ADMINISTRATIVE PROCESS

As our industrial society has grown and become more and more complex, the social and economic problems which confront government have multiplied fantastically. Not only have these issues increased in number, but interrelationships and conflicting social goals have complicated their solution. Also, advances in technology have required special training and experience to make an intelligent attempt at the solution of problems in many areas. Having decided that regulation of one sort or another is desirable, governments of necessity have employed the device of the administrative agency to lighten the burdens imposed on the executive branch, legislative bodies, and courts by this growth and development. The multitude of administrative agencies performing governmental functions today has resulted from limitations due to the lack of time to devote to making, enforcing, and interpreting laws and the lack of expert familiarity with all aspects of all these problems to make informed and effectual decisions concerning them. The President, every governor, every legislator, and every judge cannot at once be equipped with an expert knowledge of all the problems in the fields of transportation, atomic energy, labor relations, television, and radio communications, to name a few. The fact that our society and economy are constantly changing requires that continuous attention be given to all areas in which the government is involved and that regulatory rules be flexible and some degree of discretion be given for their making and enforcement.

The direct day-to-day legal impact on business of the many local, state, and Federal administrative agencies is far greater than the impact of the courts and legislative bodies. Administrative agencies create and enforce the bulk of the laws which make up the legal environment of business. A brief examination of the functions of just a handful of the Federal agencies such as the NLRB, the FTC, the ICC, the FCC, and the FPC will illustrate this impact.

The National Labor Relations Board (NLRB) is involved in all aspects of labor-management relations. This agency annually conducts thousands of hearings involving labor disputes and engages in many other activities as well. The Federal Trade Commission (FTC) is concerned with the whole field of business competition and unfair trade practices including such fundamental aspects of business as advertising, pricing of products, and corporate growth by merger or acquisition.

The Interstate Commerce Commission (ICC) has the responsibility for licensing common carriers in interstate commerce and for approving their rates.

There are similar agencies at the state level which set rates and grant licenses for intrastate transportation and communication. The rates for services or products furnished by public utilities such as the telephone, water, gas, and electrical power companies, are set by these agencies.

The Federal Communications Commission (FCC) is responsible for supervising all aspects of television and radio broadcasting and the Federal Power Commission (FPC) is concerned with the production and distribution of natural gas and similar commodities. There are many other Federal agencies such as the Internal Revenue Service (IRS) which regulate and supervise activities which directly affect all our daily lives. Others like the Atomic Energy Commission (AEC) have a limited effect on us as individuals.

It is clear that, collectively, administrative agencies are directly or indirectly involved in practically every aspect of business as well as our private lives.

The functions of administrative bodies generally are described as (1) rule making, (2) adjudicating, (3) prosecuting, (4) advising, (5) supervising, and (6) investigating. These functions are not the concern of all administrative agencies to the same degree. Some agencies are primarily adjudicating bodies, such as the industrial commissions which rule on workmen's compensation claims. Others are primarily supervisory, such as the Securities and Exchange Commission (SEC) which oversees the issue and sale of investment securities. To be sure, most agencies perform all the foregoing functions to some degree in carrying out their responsibilities.

In addition to traditional executive functions, the administrative process involves performance of both quasi-legislative and quasi-judicial functions and therefore is by its very nature in a partial conflict with the doctrine of separation of powers. But, as we have seen, the utilization of administrative agencies is a product of necessity, and practicality demands that this doctrine, however good in theory, give way at least to some extent. It is unlikely today that a court would find that the exercise of executive, judicial, and legislative functions at once by an administrative agency is invalid because of the doctrine of separation of powers. The doctrine itself, however, is still very much alive. The original purpose for separating the functions of government was to create checks and balances on the exercise of governmental power and thereby prevent tyranny. Society views administrative agencies as desirable because they provide needed continuity and consistency in the formulation, application, and enforcing of rules and regulations. And, as we have seen, agencies can accomplish what the other branches cannot, because of limitations imposed on those branches by time, the volume of governmental activity, and the necessity of expert acquaintance with many problems and the factors to be considered in solving them. While in *form* administrative agencies appear to violate the doctrine of separation of powers, in *substance* they are compatible with its underlying purpose, as long as checks and safeguards prevent the abuse of administrative power.

The executive usually has a check on administrative actions, in that he normally is the one who appoints the top officials of an agency.

The legislature can review and control administrative activity by abolishing the agency, providing specific legislation contrary to rules adopted by the agency, more explicitly defining the limitations on the activities of an agency and its rule making, providing additional procedural requirements for the agency's adjudications, or limiting appropriations of funds to the agency.

The courts also provide a check on administrative bodies by judicial review of their actions. Just as the laws enacted by the legislature must be within its power as established by the Constitution or they are void, the rules and regulations promulgated by an administrative body must be within the confines of its grant of power from the legislature, or a court will find them void. However, once having determined that an act of the legislature is constitutional or a rule of an agency is authorized, the courts will not inquire into its wisdom or effectiveness. An unwise or ineffectual law may and should be corrected by political action at the polls; an unwise rule or regulation adopted by an agency may be corrected by the legislature which gave the agency power to make the rule in the first place. In this chapter, the bases for invasion of both the traditional legislative and judicial fields by administrative agencies will be discussed, along with the functions of courts in reviewing the activities of these agencies. Subsequent chapters also contain cases involving the exercise of power by administrative bodies.

2 THE QUASI-LEGISLATIVE POWER

The rule-making function in the administrative process is essentially legislative in character. Administrative agencies are usually created by enactments of the legislature in which the legislative branch is generally said to *delegate* certain responsibility to the agency. Some courts have taken the view that the legislature cannot delegate its lawmaking function at all, but have concluded that authorizing an administrative agency to "fill in the details" of legislation is valid as not being an exercise of the legislative power. Other courts have stated that the legislature *can* delegate part of its function to an agency as long as certain constitutional safeguards which will be discussed later in this chapter are met. The difference is largely a matter of semantics.

There are two basic issues in litigation challenging the validity of a rule made by an administrative agency. First of all, is the delegation valid, and secondly, has the agency exceeded its authority? The first involves questions of due process and questions regarding the standards included in the delegation which are to be used by courts in resolving the second issue. Some other issues concerning the quasi-judicial power of administrative agencies will be discussed in section 3 of this chapter.

A THE VALIDITY OF THE DELEGATION

Delegations of quasi-legislative authority to administrative agencies are subject to two constitutional limitations. First of all, a delegation must be definite, or it will violate due process. Definiteness means that the delegation must be set forth with sufficient clarity so that all concerned, and especially reviewing courts, will be able to ascertain the extent of the agency's authority. For many reasons, broad language has been held sufficiently definite to meet this test, as the case which follows illustrates.

Sears, Roebuck & Co. v. FTC
258 F. 307 (1919)

BAKER, CIRCUIT JUDGE: This is [a] petition to review an order entered by the respondent, the Federal Trade Commission, against the petitioner, Sears, Roebuck & Co., a corporation, commanding the petitioner to desist from certain unfair methods of competition in commerce.

. . . Respondent's authority over the subject matter of its order is derived from the following provision in [Section 5 of the Federal Trade Commission Act]: "Unfair methods of competition in commerce are hereby declared unlawful." Section 4 (Comp. St § 8836d) is a dictionary of terms used in the act. "Commerce" means interstate or foreign commerce; but the general term, "unfair methods of competition," is nowhere defined specifically, nor is there a schedule of methods that shall be deemed unfair.

In its complaint respondent averred that petitioner is engaged in interstate and foreign commerce, conducting a "mail-order" business; that petitioner for more than two years last past has practiced unfair methods of competition in commerce by false and misleading advertisements and acts, designed to injure and discredit its competitors and to deceive the general public, in the following ways:

1 By advertising that petitioner, because of large purchases of sugar and quick disposal of stock, is able to sell sugar at a price lower than others offering sugar for sale;

2 By advertising that petitioner is selling its sugar at a price much lower than that of its competitors and thereby imputing to its competitors the purpose of charging more than a fair price for their sugar;

3 By selling certain of its merchandise at less than cost on the condition that the customer simultaneously purchase other merchandise at prices which give petitioner a profit on the transaction, without letting the customer know the facts;

4 By advertising that the quality of merchandise sold by its competitors is inferior to that of similar merchandise sold by petitioner, and that petitioner buys certain of its merchandise in markets not accessible to its competitors, and is therefore able to give better advantages in quality and price than those offered by its competitors. . . .

Petitioner's sales of sugar during the second half of 1915 amounted to $780,000 on which it lost $196,000. Petitioner used sugar as a "leader" ("You save 2 to 4 cents on every pound"), offering a limited amount at the losing price in connection with a required purchase of other commodities at prices high enough to afford petitioner a satisfactory profit on the transaction as a whole, without letting the customer know that the sugar was being sold on any other basis than that of the other commodities. Petitioner obtained its sugar in the open market from refiners and wholesalers. Competitors got their sugar from the same sources, of the same quality and at the same price. Sugar is a staple in the market. Price concessions upon large purchases are unobtainable. From the facts respecting petitioner's methods of advertising and buying and selling sugar respondent found, and properly so, in our judgment, that petitioner intentionally injured and discredited its competitors by falsely leading the public to believe that the competitors were unfair dealers in sugar and the other commodities which petitioner was offering in connection with sugar. . . .

By the order issued on June 24, 1918, petitioner was commanded to desist from [the practices found to be unfair] . . .

Petitioner urges that the declaration of section 5 must be held void for indefiniteness. . . . But the phrase is no more indefinite than "due process of law." The general idea of that phrase as it appears in Constitutions and statutes is quite well known; but we have never encountered what purported to be an all-embracing schedule or found a specific definition that would bar the continuing processes of judicial inclusion and exclusion based upon accumulating experience. If the expression "unfair methods of competition" is too uncertain for use, then under the same condemnation would fall the innumerable statutes which predicated rights and prohibitions upon "unsound mind," "undue influence," "unfaithfulness," "unfair use," "unfit for cultivation," "unreasonable rate," "unjust discrimination," and the like. This statute is remedial, and orders to desist are civil; but even in criminal law convictions are upheld on statutory prohibitions of "rebates or concessions" or of "schemes to defraud," without any schedule of acts or specific definition of forbidden conduct, thus leaving the courts free to condemn new and ingenious ways that were unknown when the statutes were enacted. Why? Because the general ideas of "dishonesty" and "fraud" are so well, widely and uniformly understood that the general term "rebates or concessions" and "schemes to defraud" are sufficiently accurate measures of conduct.

On the face of this statute the legislative intent is apparent. The commissioners are not required to aver and prove that any competitor has been damaged or that any purchaser has been deceived. The commissioners, representing the government as parens patriae, are to exercise their common sense, as informed by their knowledge of the general idea of unfair trade at common law, and stop all those trade practices that have a capacity or a tendency to injure competitors directly or through deception of purchasers, quite irrespective of whether the specific practices in question have yet been denounced in common-law cases. . . .

With the increasing complexity of human activities many situations arise where governmental control can be secured only by the "board" or "commission" form of legislation. In such instances Congress declares the public policy, fixes the general principles that are to control, and charges an administrative body with the duty of ascertaining within particular fields from time to time the facts which bring into play the principles established by Congress. Though the action of the Commission in finding the facts and declaring them to be specific offenses of the character embraced within the general definition by Congress may be deemed to be quasi legislative, it is so only in the sense that it converts the actual legislation from a static into a dynamic condition. But the converter is not the electricity. And though the action of the commission in ordering disistance may be counted quasi judicial on account of its form, with respect to power it is not judicial, because a judicial determination is only that which is embodied in a judgment or decree of a court and enforceable by execution or other writ of the court. . . . [THE COURT DIRECTED THAT THE ORDER BE MODIFIED SLIGHTLY, BUT IN OTHER RESPECTS DENIED THE PETITION]

A very similar limitation to the definiteness requirement on the exercise of quasi-legislative authority is found in the requirement that the power of administrative agencies to make rules be limited. The limited-power concept means that delegations must contain standards by which a court can determine whether the limitations have been exceeded. The standards set must meet certain minimum requirements before the agency in question is validly empowered to act in a certain area, and the rules promulgated by the agency must follow these standards and limitations imposed by the law establishing the agency, if they are to be upheld.

Just as broad language has been approved as being sufficiently definite for a delegation to be valid, so also have broad standards been approved since the 1930s. In that era, delegations were held not to be subject to sufficient standards in two cases involving New Deal legislation. The Supreme Court held in these cases that the delegations were running riot. Since that time, however, very broad standards have been held constitutional. The cases which follow illustrate the problem of standards in delegation of quasi-legislative authority.

State v. Arizona Mines Supply Co.
484 P.2d 619 (Ariz., 1971)

The defendant was charged with violating rules of an agency pursuant to a statute on air pollution.

UDALL, JUSTICE: . . . [D]efendant-respondent has advanced . . . [the following] arguments . . . :

That the Information does not charge an Offense for the Reasons that the Procedure Employed in Setting Out and Adopting the Applicable Rules and

Regulations are Unconstitutional as being an Improper Delegation of Legislative Power Under Article III of Our Constitution.

Article III of our Constitution, A.R.S. provides for the separation of government into three separate and distinct departments:

The powers of the government of the State of Arizona shall be divided into three separate departments, the Legislative, the Executive, and the Judicial; and, except as provided in this Constitution, such departments shall be separate and distinct, and no one of such departments shall exercise the power properly belonging to either of the others.

The fundamental principle involved in Article III is that governmental powers are to be divided among the three departments of government; each to maintain its sovereignty within its own sphere. Yet,

. . . *[i]t is commonly said that it does not invariably follow that an entire and complete separation of power of the three branches of government is desirable or was ever intended. For example, the functions of public utility boards and workmen's compensation commissions are a blending of the recognized spheres of all three departments of government. The right is generally conceded to delegate to an administrative agency the power to adopt rules and regulations necessary to carry a law into effect. In some cases such as zoning and the licensing of professions, the discretion vested is so broad and the limitation so general that there is little essential difference between such generalities and no standard at all. We note also a distinct modern tendency to be more liberal in the granting of discretion in the administration of laws in fields where the complexities of economic and governmental conditions have increased, particularly where it is impractical to lay down a comprehensive rule.*

Under the doctrine of "separation of powers" the legislature alone possesses the lawmaking power and, while it cannot completely delegate this power to any other body, it may allow another body to fill in the details of legislation already enacted. Since the power to make a law includes discretion as to what it shall be, this particular power cannot be delegated. But the decisions display an increasing tendency, due to the complexity of our social and industrial activities, to hold as nonlegislative the authority conferred upon commissions and boards to formulate rules and regulations and to determine the state of facts upon which the law intends to make its action depend.

". . . We see, then, that while the Legislature may not divest itself of its proper functions, or delegate its general legislative authority, it may still authorize others to do those things which it might properly, yet cannot understandingly or advantageously do itself. Without this power legislation would become oppressive, and yet imbecile. *Local laws almost universally call into action, to a greater or less extent, the agency and discretion, either of the people or*

individuals, to accomplish in detail what is authorized or required in general terms. The object to be accomplished, or the thing permitted may be specified, and the rest left to the agency of others, with better opportunities of accomplishing the object, or doing the thing understandingly."

Delegation of "quasi-legislative" powers to administrative agencies, authorizing them to make rules and regulations, within proper standards fixed by the legislature, are normally sustained as valid, and, barring a total abdication of their legislative powers, there is no real constitutional prohibition against the delegation of a large measure of authority to an administrative agency for the administration of a statute enacted pursuant to a state's police power. And the standards which must accompany such grant of legislative power need not necessarily be set forth in express terms if they might reasonably be inferred from the statutory scheme as a whole.

When dealing with the question of standards, a court is not confined to the specific terms of the particular section in question, but must examine the entire act in the light of its surroundings and objectives. Standards may reasonably be implied from a consideration of the statutory scheme as a whole.

A statute need establish no more than a sufficient basic standard, i.e., a definite policy and rule of action which will serve as a guide for the administrative agency, in order for the delegation of legislative power to be deemed valid.

[T]he extent and character of the rules and regulations authorized to be adopted by the legislature must be fixed in accordance with common sense and the inherent necessities of governmental coordination. [I]t is not necessary for the legislature to lay down in advance an exact mathematical formula to which the administrative agency must adhere, for circumstances may vary which would serve to defeat the purpose of the legislative enactment.

Here we have two separate, distinct and adequate standards. The first is that the rules and regulations shall be such as are determined to be "necessary and feasible." In *Wacker,* . . . we upheld an act whose only standard was that the rules and regulations were to be such as were "necessary." The rules and regulations in the case at bar must, in addition to being necessary, be "feasible." In addition, the rules and regulations to be promulgated by the county board of supervisors, were to contain pollution standards "at least equal to or more restrictive than those adopted by the board of health." We find no difficulty in upholding the legislative delegation of authority since adequate standards were set up. [SO ORDERED]

Yakus v. United States
321 U.S. 414 (1944)

The Emergency Price Control Act, as amended by the Inflation Control Act, provided for the establishment of the Office of Price Administration and set up a scheme for the promulgation of regulations and orders fixing maximum prices of commodities and rents. These acts were adopted as wartime measures in the interest of national defense and security, with the avowed purposes of stabilizing prices and rents, eliminating speculation and hoarding, and protecting persons with fixed incomes and government from paying excessive prices because of shortages.

The standards which were to guide the Administrator's exercise of his authority to fix prices contained the following language: "The Administrator is authorized after consultation with representative members of the industry, to promulgate regulations fixing prices of commodities which in his judgment will be generally fair and equitable and will effectuate the purposes of this Act." Due consideration was to be given prevailing prices between October 1 and October 15, 1941. In addition, changes in costs of production, transportation, and distribution as well as increases or decreases in profits since 1941 were to be considered in making the regulations.

The petitioners were tried, convicted, sentenced to jail for six months, and fined $1,000 each on charges of violation of the act by the willful sale of wholesale cuts of beef at prices above the maximum prescribed by Revised Maximum Price Regulation No. 169, which had been promulgated by the Administrator. This was an appeal from their conviction.

STONE, CHIEF JUSTICE: Congress enacted the Emergency Price Control Act in pursuance of a defined policy and required that the prices fixed by the Administrator should further that policy and conform to standards prescribed by the Act. The boundaries of the field of the Administrator's permissible action are marked by the statute. It directs that the prices fixed shall effectuate the declared policy of the Act to stabilize commodity prices so as to prevent war-time inflation and its enumerated disruptive causes and effects. In addition the prices established must be fair and equitable, and in fixing them the Administrator is directed to give due consideration, so far as practicable, to prevailing prices during the designated base period, with prescribed administrative adjustments to compensate for enumerated disturbing factors affecting prices. In short the purposes of the Act specified in § 1 denote the objective to be sought by the Administrator in fixing prices—the prevention of inflation and its enumerated consequences. The standards set out in § 2 define the boundaries within which prices having that purpose must be fixed. It is enough to satisfy the statutory requirements that the Administrator finds that the prices fixed will tend to achieve that objective and will conform to those standards, and that the courts in an appropriate proceeding can see that substantial basis for those findings is not wanting.

The Act is thus an exercise by Congress of its legislative power. In it Congress has stated the legislative objective, has prescribed the method of achieving that objective—maximum price fixing—and has laid down standards to guide the administrative determination of both the occasions for the exercise of the price-fixing power, and the particular prices to be established. . . .

The Act is unlike the National Industrial Recovery Act of June 16, 1933, 48 Stat. 195, considered in *Schechter Poultry Corp. v. United States*, 295 U.S. 495, . . . which proclaimed in the broadest terms its purpose "to rehabilitate industry and to conserve natural resources." It prescribed no method of attaining that end save by the establishment of codes of fair competition, the nature of whose permissible provisions was left undefined. It provided no standards to which those codes were to conform. The function of formulating the codes was delegated, not to a public official responsible to Congress or the Executive, but to private individuals engaged in the industries to be regulated. . . .

The Constitution as a continuously operative charter of government does not demand the impossible or the impracticable. It does not require that Congress find for itself every fact upon which it desires to base legislative action or that it make for itself detailed determinations which it has declared to be prerequisite to the application of the legislative policy to particular facts and circumstances impossible for Congress itself properly to investigate. The essentials of the legislative function are the determination of the legislative policy and its formulation and promulgation as a defined and binding rule of conduct—here the rule, with penal sanctions, that prices shall not be greater than those fixed by maximum price regulations which conform to standards and will tend to further the policy which Congress has established. These essentials are preserved when Congress has specified the basic conditions of fact upon whose existence or occurrence, ascertained from relevant data by a designated administrative agency, it directs that its statutory command shall be effective. It is no objection that the determination of facts and the inferences to be drawn from them in the light of the statutory standards and declaration of policy call for the formulation of subsidiary administrative policy within the prescribed statutory framework. . . .

Nor does the doctrine of separation of powers deny to Congress power to direct that an administrative officer properly designated for that purpose have ample latitude within which he is to ascertain the conditions which Congress has made prerequisite to the operation of its legislative command. Acting within its constitutional power to fix prices it is for Congress to say whether the data on the basis of which prices are to be fixed are to be confined within a narrow or a broad range. In either case the only concern of courts is to ascertain whether the will of Congress has been obeyed. This depends not upon the breadth of the definition of the facts or conditions which the administrative officer is to find but upon the determination whether the definition sufficiently marks the field within which the Administrator is to act so that it may be known whether he has kept within it in compliance with the legislative will.

As we have said: "The Constitution has never been regarded as denying to the Congress the necessary resources of flexibility and practicality . . . to perform its function." *Currin v. Wallace, supra,* 306 U.S. at page 15. . . . Hence it is irrelevant that Congress might itself have prescribed the maximum prices or have provided a more rigid standard by which they are to be fixed; for example, that all prices should be frozen at the levels obtaining during a certain period or on a certain date. . . . Congress is not confined to that method of executing its policy which involves the least possible delegation of discretion to administrative officers. . . . It is free to avoid the rigidity of such a system, which might well result in serious hardship, and to choose instead the flexibility attainable by the use of less restrictive standards.

Only if we could say that there is an absence of standards for the guidance of the Administrator's action, so that it would be impossible in a proper proceeding to ascertain whether the will of Congress has been obeyed, would we be justified in over-riding its choice of means for effecting its declared purpose of preventing inflation.

The standards prescribed by the present Act, with the aid of the "statement of the considerations" required to be made by the Administrator, are sufficiently definite and precise to enable Congress, the courts and the public to ascertain whether the Administrator, in fixing the designated prices, has conformed to those standards. . . . Hence we are unable to find in them an unauthorized delegation of legislative power. The authority to fix prices only when prices have risen or threaten to rise to an extent or in a manner inconsistent with the purpose of the Act to prevent inflation is no broader than the authority to fix maximum prices when deemed necessary to protect consumers against unreasonably high prices, sustained in *Sunshine Anthracite Coal Co. v. Adkins, supra,* or the authority to take possession of and operate telegraph lines whenever deemed necessary for the national security or defense, upheld in *Dakota Cent. Tel. Co. v. State of South Dakota,* 250 U.S. 163, . . . or the authority to suspend tariff provisions upon findings that the duties imposed by a foreign state are "reciprocally unequal and unreasonable," held valid in *Field v. Clar, supra.* . . .

The directions that the prices fixed shall be fair and equitable, that in addition they shall tend to promote the purposes of the Act, and that in promulgating them consideration shall be given to prices prevailing in a stated base period, confer no greater reach for administrative determination than the power to fix just and reasonable rates, . . . or the power to regulate radio stations engaged in chain broadcasting "as public interest, convenience or necessity requires," upheld in *National Broadcasting Co. v. United States, supra,* 319 U.S. at page 225, . . . or the power to prohibit "unfair methods of competition" not defined or forbidden by the common law, *Federal Trade Commission v. R. F. Keppel & Bro.,* 291 U.S. 304, . . . or the direction that in allotting marketing quotas among states and producers due consideration be given to a variety of economic factors, sustained in *Mulford v. Smith, supra,* 307 U.S. at pages 48, 49, 59, . . . or the similar direction that in adjusting tariffs to meet differences in costs of production the President "take into consideration . . . in so far as he finds it practicable" a variety of economic matters, sustained in *Hampton Jr. & Co. v. United States, supra,* 276 U.S. 394, or the similar authority, in making classifications within an industry, to consider various named and unnamed "relevant factors" and determine the respective weights attributable to each, held valid in *Opp Cotton Mills v. Administrator, supra.* [AFFIRMED]

Since the *Yakus* case, it is generally agreed that delegations of authority to make rules may be in very broad language. For example, the delegation of authority to make such rules as the "public interest, convenience and necessity" may require is subject to a valid standard. Delegations which include a criterion that is as concrete as the field and factors involved permit will be held valid, since the law now recognizes that practical considerations often make definite standards impossible.

Statutes delegating authority to administrative agencies are usually liberally construed in order to accomplish the legislative goal. The trend of modern cases is to hold the delegations valid even though legislative power is given and standards are absent or are vague, as long as there are procedural safeguards or checks on the power which prevent an abuse of its exercise. As a practical matter, legislatures can deal only in generalities. Many of the problems which have arisen in connection with an area of regulation were not even considered by the legislature when it enacted the statute calling for regulation. It would not be possible to deal with all the present and future unforeseeable problems by specific statutes. The necessary flexibility is provided by delegation of the rule-making function to administrative agencies.

B   HAS THE AGENCY EXCEEDED ITS AUTHORITY?

While it is highly unlikely that a court would hold a delegation invalid because of indefiniteness or lack of standards, courts do find that agencies have exceeded their authority, as the following case illustrates.

Wolff v. Selective Service Local Board No. 16
372 F.2d 817 (1967)

MEDINA, CIRCUIT JUDGE: Peter Wolff and Richard Shortt, registrants of Selective Service Boards No. 66 in Queens County and No. 16 in New York County were classified II–S because of their status as full-time students at the University of Michigan. On October 15, 1965 these students and others participated in a demonstration to protest American involvement in Vietnam, at the offices of a Selective Service local board in Ann Arbor, Michigan. At the request of the New York City Director of Selective Service the local boards reclassified the two students I–A. The request was based upon the assertion that by participating in the demonstration the students became "delinquents" by reason of their alleged violation of Section 12(a) of the Universal Military Training and Service Act. Claiming that the local boards acted wholly without jurisdiction and in violation of their First Amendment rights of free speech and assembly and of their Sixth Amendment rights as well, Wolff and Shortt brought this action against the local boards and the Director to bring about a return of their student deferments.

Section 12 of the Act is a lengthy penal statute covering offenses committed by registrants and by members of local boards. Jurisdiction over these offenses is given to the United States District Courts. With respect to some of these offenses, however, such as the failure of any person knowingly to "fail or neglect or refuse to perform any duty required of him under or in execution of this title," to the extent that the statute affects registrants, the jurisdiction of the District Court is, in effect, concurrent with the administrative jurisdiction of the local boards. Thus a parallel clause of the regulations provides that if a registrant fails to produce certain requested information or to appear for questioning, he may . . . be declared a delinquent and classified or reclassified I-A. Also under Section 12 various draftees have been convicted in United States District Courts for failure to appear for induction.

The conduct of these New York students, registrants in Local Boards Nos. 16 and 66, in participating in the demonstration in Michigan on October 15, 1965 could, as Judge McLean assumed, be claimed to fall under another provision of Section 12 which makes it a federal criminal offense for any person to "knowingly hinder or interfere or attempt to do so in any way, by force or violence or otherwise, with the administration of this title" and no regulation authorizes a draft board to declare a registrant a delinquent or to reclassify him for such action. As jurisdiction over offenses of this character is exclusively granted to the District Courts, we hold that the Local Boards lacked authority to decide that Wolff and Shortt were "delinquents" by reason of their violation of the terms of this portion of Section 12. Accordingly, as these two students have never been indicted or tried or convicted of this offense in a District Court, the two Local Boards, appellees, exceeded their jurisdiction by reclassifying the two students I-A.

There is nothing to prevent the prosecution of registrants or others for conduct by them in violation of either federal or state criminal laws, subject to such defenses as may be alleged and established. What we hold in this case is that it is not the function of local boards in the Selective Service System to punish these registrants by reclassifying them I-A because they protested as they did over the Government's involvement in Vietnam. [REVERSED]

3 QUASI-JUDICIAL POWERS OF ADMINISTRATIVE AGENCIES

The doctrine of separation of powers, as was noted earlier, seemingly conflicts with administrative action in the exercise of judicial functions as well as legislative functions. The American Bar has long been concerned with the extent to which administrative agencies exercise judicial powers. The essay which follows indicates the attitude of many lawyers toward the adjudicating function of administrative bodies, and describes the various quasi-judicial activities of some of the many administrative agencies at the Federal level.

Administrative Agencies and Judicial Powers[1]
Roy L. Cole[2]

An administrative agency is customarily defined as any governmental authority, other than a court or legislature, which determines or directly affects the rights

[1] 44 *A.B.A.J.* 953 (Oct., 1958). Used by permission from the American Bar Association and the *American Bar Association Journal.*
[2] Mr. Cole is a member of the Texas Bar (Dallas).

and obligations of private parties through rule-making or adjudication. The First Congress in 1789 enacted three statutes granting administrative powers, two pertaining to customs and the third initiating the series of pension laws now administered by the Veterans' Administration. Of the fifty-one authorities classified as administrative agencies in 1941 by the Attorney General's Committee on Administrative Procedure, eleven trace their beginnings to legislation enacted prior to the end of the Civil War, but the tremendously powerful "independent" agencies, exercising broad control over nationwide activities, are largely a development of the twentieth century. The modern history of the administrative agency dates from the creation of the Interstate Commerce Commission in 1887. The Federal Reserve System was established in 1913, the Federal Trade Commission in 1914, the Federal Power Commission in 1920, and the Board of Tax Appeals in 1924. With the advent of the New Deal came such important agencies as the Federal Deposit Insurance Corporation, the Securities and Exchange Commission, the Social Security Board, and the National Labor Relations Board. World War II produced such powerful though temporary agencies as the Office of Price Administration, Office of Defense Transportation, the War Production Board and others. Still later came the tremendously important Atomic Energy Commission, and Congress seems sure to establish a space commission to control our relations with the rest of the universe.

A characteristic of these administrative authorities is their exercise of what are historically termed "judicial powers"—the adjudication of controversies directly affecting private individuals. The grant of these powers has often been attributed to a failure of the common law courts to meet the great social problems arising from late nineteenth and early twentieth century industrialization—the individual's inability as a practical matter to obtain legal redress for wrongs committed against him by the new gigantic industrial combines, and the transition from a *laissez-faire* government to one assuming many affirmative responsibilities for the social and economic well-being of the populace as a whole. Another and fairer analysis is that, while judicial failure was sometimes involved, administrative agencies have been created from time to time simply because in each particular situation such an authority seemed to practical men to be the most practical solution to the problem at hand. Certainly the expressed and accepted specific reasons for administrative exercise of traditionally judicial powers are practical and varied ones, among them being:

1 The need, in adjudication incidental to regulation of modern industrial complexes, for an expertise which can be developed only through the constant attention to a particular field which the courts are unable to give and with the assistance of large staffs whose combined skills cover all the various nonlegal areas pertinent to the industries to be regulated.

2 The necessity for intelligent coordination between policy-making and enforcement.

3 The necessity of deciding controversies in fields affected by the public interest as "rightly" as possible, taking into account all relevant facts, not

merely (as in the courts) those specially selected facts placed in the record by the adversary parties.

4 The tendency of the judiciary, drawn primarily from conservative, propertied classes, to resist legislative programs antipathetic to those classes even though clearly favored by the majority of the populace as a whole.

5 The tremendous volume of cases before some agencies which would so overwhelm the courts that they would find themselves unable to perform their normal and important tasks.

The American Bar . . . [has] constantly maintained [its] attack on all administrative exercise of judicial powers, on the ground that such exercise violates the fundamental doctrine of separation of powers and thus imperils the even more fundamental "rule of law."

These broadly based objections have had an almost astonishing lack of success in even retarding continual new and expanded grants of administrative judicial powers. . . .

There is room for doubt as to the correctness of classifying all adjudication as an exercise of judicial power. Although most of us fundamentally believe in a kind of natural law, we realize that the adjudicatory process in the courts is not merely a matter of "discovering" pre-existing law, as Blackstone and his contemporaries maintained, but in the judge's choice of available alternatives amounts actually to making law, and always has. In the words of Theodore Roosevelt, approved by Cardozo: "The chief lawmakers in our country may be, and often are, the judges, because they are the final seat of authority. Every time they interpret contract, property, vested rights, due process of law, liberty, they necessarily enact into law parts of a system of social philosophy; and as such interpretation is fundamental they give direction to all lawmaking."

Since making law is by definition an exercise of legislative power, it is logical to assert that what we call judicial powers are in many instances only adjudicatory techniques, which may as well be proper tools in the exercise of legislative powers as in the exercise of judicial ones. Furthermore, since the courts through judicial action actually make perhaps more law than legislatures, without complaint from the Bar, it appears to many persons that we are in poor position to clamor so strongly for complete abolition of the use of adjudicatory techniques by administrative agencies in the course of their congressional delegated lesiglative duties. . . .

There is widespread feeling that the judicial process has had its chance and muffed it, that the courts have failed, and would again fail, to meet the challenge posed by Theodore Roosevelt in the words immediately following those quoted above: "The decisions of the courts on economic and social questions depend upon their economic and social philosophy; and for the peaceful progress of our people during the twentieth century we shall owe most to those judges who hold to a twentieth century economic and social philosophy and not to a long outgrown philosophy which was itself the product of primitive economic conditions."

Even among those who do not view the judicial process as having failed, there is a feeling that the passive, impartial character of that process is unsuited to the accomplishment of the affirmative policies entrusted to many regulatory agencies in our complex modern existence. . . .

It is absolutely clear that the principle of complete divestiture of *all* adjudicatory powers of *all* administrative agencies is discredited beyond reasonable hope of revival. This discredit is merited, not only because the dogma is historically and logically unsound, but also because, from a coldly practical standpoint, "a government consisting of three (completely) separate powers would get no farther than a span of three horses without a driver. Our strength comes from the interplay of the powers and the checks and balances among them—our unity from the ultimate responsibility of all branches of government to the electorate and to the court-sustained fundamentals of Christian morality. . . .

If the demand for total abolition of all administrative adjudication is, as I believe, untenable, the opposite extreme is likewise indefensible. To allow Congress to provide for administrative use of adjudicatory techniques as incidental aids in implementing certain definite economic regulatory programs is one thing—to permit administrative adjudication of matters affecting life, liberty and basic individual rights, even with judicial review, is quite another. It is also a threat to our system of checks and balances to allow establishment or continuation of administrative adjudication in areas where there is no affirmative legislative policy to be implemented wholly or partly by the use of adjudicatory techniques; and a similar threat exists in the indefinite continuation of administrative adjudication in agencies of any type which use these techniques to the substantial exclusion of others, and which therefore actually constitute extra-judicial courts. Our solution to the basic problem of administrative exercise of judicial powers lies somewhere in the middle ground, and can be best approached through separate analysis of each class of agency.

Administrative agencies may be classified in various ways, *e.g.*, according to form, function, operational organization or degree of independence. For our purposes the functional analysis seems most fruitful. We have the following types:

1   Claims or "benefit" agencies such as the Veterans' Administration, the Social Security Board and the Bureau of Old Age and Survivors' Insurance, which do not set policy, but merely handle great numbers of small claims on the basis of approving those covered by comprehensive statutes and disapproving those not covered.
2   The Tax Court, formerly the Board of Tax Appeals, which adjudicates controversies under the tax laws between taxpayers and the Commissioner of Internal Revenue.
3   Authorities such as the Attorney General's Immigration and Naturalization Service and the Third Assistant Postmaster General, regulating matters involving life, liberty and freedom of speech and communication.
4   Agencies such as the ICC, SEC, FPC and FCC, which regulate and control nationwide industries in the public interest, and which bear a clear burden of

responsibility for their actions and for the success or failure of their efforts. These agencies act primarily through rules and use adjudicatory techniques as supplements to the rule-making power. In this class also fall such departmental divisions as the Commodity Stabilization Service in the Department of Agriculture, with broad regulatory power over certain aspects of nationwide industries, operating similarly to the independent agencies but having less easily identifiable responsibility.

5 Agencies such as the FTC and NLRB, which are regulatory in intent but prosecutory in form, which cut across all industries and fields of endeavor, have no clear burden of responsibility for the results of their efforts, and use adjudicatory techniques as a primary means of establishing and enforcing policy.

A. The clearest case for retention of adjudicatory powers by administrative agencies is in the first category—the claims or benefit agencies. Paradoxically, these are the authorities which make greatest use of adjudication in performing their functions. But the "controversies" which they determine are not really adversary in nature. Certain benefits are granted by Congress to those meeting carefully prescribed statutory conditions. In the vast majority of cases the determination of whether an individual meets those conditions calls merely for mechanical application of the rules to the undisputed facts. There is no real opposition to a claimant—agency personnel are charged with assisting him to obtain benefits to the full extent he is lawfully entitled. There is no necessity for the trial and evidentiary rules of a court. And as a practical matter the judicial system would quite surely be literally overwhelmed by the application of judicial procedures to the millions of claims involved.

B. The clearest case for removal of judicial powers from an administrative agency involves the Tax Court. As the name implies, it is a court, it operates as such, and should be transferred to the judicial branch. Its sole business is the adjudication of highly technical tax controversies between the government and individuals. In this process it deals with the ascertainment of facts of the type which judicial procedures are best fitted to ascertain, and with the interpretation of detailed statutory codes on a subject as to which lawyers are the experts. It has no regulatory, investigatory or policy-making authority, is charged only with the fair and impartial adjudication of cases, and clearly belongs in the judicial system.

C. An equally clear and more urgent case for transfer of adjudicatory functions from administrators to courts is in our third category—authorities exercising control over matters involving life, liberty and freedom of speech and communication. The most important agency in this field is the Immigration and Naturalization Service of the Department of Justice. A special inquiry officer first determines the question of exclusion or deportation. An appeal then lies to the nonstatutory quasi-judicial Board of Immigration Appeals. There is a further right of appeal to the courts in deportation cases and possible review through habeas corpus in exclusion proceedings. But in no case is full judicial review available, although we are here dealing with administrative power which can result, in

Justice Brandeis' words, "in loss of both property and life; or of all that makes life worth living." As pointed out by the Hoover Commission's Task Force on Legal Services and Procedure, the arbitrary exclusion of an alien not entitled to constitutional protection not only is inconsistent with humanitarian principles but also many times deeply affects citizens of the United States to whom the alien may be related. The problem in this field is infinitely complicated by what the Hoover Commission Task Force has correctly termed the absolute essentiality to the national security that unauthorized persons be stopped or ejected.

The delicate necessity of preserving both national security and individual liberty is too great to be left largely in the hands of administrators. This is a field in which the experts are the courts, trained in the traditions of the Constitution and the common law which has served so well whenever fundamentals are involved. The functions of the Board of Immigration Appeals must be transferred to the courts generally or to a special Immigration Court.

The allied rights of freedom of speech and expression are subject to several serious and largely unfettered administrative controls. Under a doubtful construction of the Foreign Agent's Registration Act of 1938, as amended in 1942, the Customs Bureau and the Post Office Department destroy, without notice to sender or addressee, any printed matter from other countries which they decide constitutes "foreign propaganda," a term subject to almost any definition. Both the above agencies have broad additional powers to prevent the transmission of material deemed seditious or obscene, and the Postmaster General also has the power to revoke the second-class mail privileges of periodical publications, revocation being the practical equivalent of suppression. Here again we are in a vital field where the judiciary has the expertise and where the dangers of arbitrary action are so vital that only the courts should have the right to act.

D. Our fourth category contains the powerful industry-wide independent regulatory agencies about which (together with the FTC and NLRB) most controversy arises. The highlights of their historical development have been outlined earlier in this article, as have the reasons for the grants to them of the right to exercise judicial powers or adjudicatory techniques. To recapitulate, each of these agencies was formed to cure certain evils which had not been alleviated by the existing branches of government, and to exercise an affirmative, continuing guidance over the future activities of the industry concerned. The Supreme Court aptly expressed the differing functions of administrative and judicial adjudication in this field as follows:

The Communications Act is not designed primarily as a new code for the adjustment of conflicting private rights through adjudication. Rather it expresses a desire on the part of Congress to maintain, through appropriate administrative control, a grip on the dynamic aspect of radio transmission. . . . To a large degree they (administrative agencies) have been a response to the felt need of governmental supervision over economic enterprise—a supervision which could effectively be exercised neither through self-executing legislation nor by the judicial process.

Effective regulation of a complex twentieth-century industry requires a cohesive, integrated instrumentality of control, having adequate staffs with as varied skills as the industry to be regulated, able to focus constant attention on that industry and to initiate action, and with the power to use all techniques, including the adjudicative, necessary to make its control meaningful and effective.

Apart from the complaint of violation of the separation of powers doctrine, already discussed, four main objections have been made to administrative control as represented by the industry-wide agencies:

1 The presence of an inherent "leftist" orientation;
2 A tendency toward totalitarianism, undermining "the rule of law";
3 Bias; and
4 Susceptibility to improper influence.

Certainly an antipathy toward a substantive program is not in itself a valid reason for criticizing the agency administering that program. However, in the early days of the independent regulatory agencies the administrative process was believed, with hope by some and with fear by others, to have an inherent political or social orientation. But "both the thrill and the chill failed to take into account basic factors limiting the managing and planning potentialities of the administrative process." Natural economic forces have in this country proved infinitely more potent than all the regulatory agencies combined in determining social and political orientation. Having observed the changes in aims and policies in the various agencies from time to time to meet the needs and demands of the people resulting from the development of new goods and services by industry, we must now realize that there is no such thing as a permanently built-in administrative viewpoint. The administrative process is instead a maneuverable device, shifting orientation as economic and social developments and varying legislative expressions may direct.

The complaint of totalitarianism is primarily directed at governmental regulation as such. Insofar as it constitutes an accusation that administrative use of adjudicatory techniques violates the principle of "rule of law," it is subject to the gibe that we are really advocating the rule of lawyers. The rule of law certainly must be preserved, but if for the term we accept perhaps the best modern definition—"a state of affairs in which there are legal barriers to governmental arbitrariness and legal safeguards for the protection of the individual"—we can through combined legislative and judicial control of administrative procedures and through judicial review achieve those ends without sacrificing the efficiency of the administrative process.

The accusations of bias seem largely unfair. The twentieth-century agency is created and from time to time revitalized to accomplish positive results—a bias in favor of the basic program is required by the legislative history and the terms of the governing statutes. Cardozo has reminded us that every person, every judge, necessarily views any given situation from a point where he is placed by his own heredity and environment—no one of us can look at the world out of another's eyes. Yet bias must not impair fair-mindedness, especially in adjudication. Careful scholarship seems to have shown that administrative agencies have been subject to isolated lapses in this respect, to no greater extent than have the courts. And charges of bias have been far less frequently heard since the agencies "went conservative" in the late 1940's, lending weight to the belief that many criticisms leveled at administrative authorities are in actuality motivated by antagonism to the substantive programs entrusted to their care.

The very real problem of agency exposure and susceptibility to improper influence is at this time of writing highlighted by congressional investigation of the Federal Communications Commission. This problem is best solved by (a) the formulation and enforcement of a code of ethics for administrators; (b) the enforcement of legislation imposing criminal penalties on persons exerting improper influence; and most importantly, (c) the development among legislators, members of the executive branch of government, politicians and the people generally of the realization that it is as immoral and destructive to attempt to influence administrative decisions as judicial ones. All branches of the government must co-operate to this end, since it is a joint problem of all. As yet, the drastic step of complete removal of administrative adjudicatory powers does not seem justified—if it later does, we can have confidence in the abilities of the judiciary to fill the gap.

On balance, the reasons for continuation of exercise of judicial powers in the industry-regulatory agencies outweigh the objections.

E. By far the greatest difficulty in determining whether judicial powers should be exercised by administrative agencies involves the Federal Trade Commission and the National Labor Relations Board. Most or all of the reasons advanced for the exercise of adjudicatory powers by industry-regulating agencies apply here, but there are far more powerful arguments against FTC and NLRB retention of such functions than apply to the others. The FTC and NLRB, while in a sense regulatory, differ from other independent agencies in the following important particulars.

First, they lack that most important essential of democratic government— precise accountability. It is comparatively easy to tell whether the SEC or the CAB is doing a good job in the public interest in the limited fields in which they function. It is far more difficult to determine the same question when the FTC and NLRB are involved, since their actions are but one of the many factors involved in the health of the general economy which they affect.

Second, instead of a defined and limited area where technical nonlegal expertness is essential, their inquiries involve a broad consideration of more intangible social and ethical factors—they deal with fields in which we may assert that courts are, or should be, the more expert.

Third, these agencies are not regulatory in the sense that they lay down rules of general application, but instead are solely investigatory and prosecutory. Here the use, or threat of use, of adjudicatory powers is not in aid of other, more clearly legislative processes, but is the sole technique. While it is noted above that the use of the adjudicatory technique may actually be an exercise of a legislative power, it is nevertheless true that all organisms, in the words of the Supreme Court, "represent an interplay of form and function." In the case of these two agencies, the forms are those of a court, the fundamental policies of their substantive programs have been established, and their adjudicatory functions should now be court-administered.

Finally, there is a widespread public distrust of the essential fairness of these agencies. This is probably explainable in the case of the NLRB as the "inevitable outcome of a statute which gives employers no affirmative rights, imposes no duties upon employees and places upon the Board a duty of acting as prosecutor as well as judge." This distrust has carried over in spite of the 1947 legislation imposing obligations on labor unions and providing complete internal separation of prosecuting and judging functions. The feeling with regard to the FTC, though less intense, arises from similar considerations. And, as Professor Davis has pointed out: "So long as detached and informed opinions differ as to what is justice, one objective in a democratic society is to appear to do justice. That ideal remains unrealized so long as significant groups, whether or not misled, firmly believe that justice is denied."

For the Bar to advocate the transfer to the courts of the adjudicatory functions of the NLRB and the FTC is a bold and self-challenging course. These are the two agencies which, so nearly identical in form to traditional courts, were established almost solely because of a belief that the judiciary's economic and social opinions were so far opposed to the prevailing ideals of the time that the courts would subvert the legislative purpose. This belief was largely justified and was widely held. If the judicial functions of these agencies are transferred to the courts, the Bar and judiciary must thereafter so act as to convince a still slightly suspicious people that their former causes for distrust are abated. In requesting such transfer we represent to the nation that the work of Holmes, Cardozo, Brandeis, Pound, and many others has had its effect—that American common law, attuning itself more closely to the convictions of the past, recognizes the necessity in its work for consideration of contemporary social, industrial and political conditions as well as historical factors, and is therefore entitled to exercise its traditional functions under the conditions of modern society. This is a strong representation and a magnificently challenging one, worthy of the best traditions of the Bench and Bar.

In summary, then, administrative exercise of judicial powers should be permitted in three instances:

1 In claims or "benefit" agencies, where the "adjudications" are not really controversial, do not need formal judicial techniques, and are of such volume as to be impossible of practicable administration by the courts.
2 In industry-regulatory agencies, where continuing supervision of complex industrial organizations requires the constant attention of specialists in the nonlegal fields and where the use of adjudicatory techniques is in addition and supplementary to rule making and other more usual forms of regulations.
3 In agencies (such as FTC and NLRB) administering new and untried economic and social policies cutting across many segments of the nation's

life, and which therefore of necessity must use a cautious case-by-case adjudicatory method in determining the proper implementation of such policies. In these instances, administrative adjudication should be permitted only for such period of time as is necessary to develop a generally accepted body of precedent. As soon as this has been done their adjudicatory powers should be transferred to the courts.

Administrative exercise of judicial powers should be denied, or if in existence should be removed, in all other cases, particularly where fundamentals of life, liberty and freedom of expression are involved. Even where administrative adjudication is permissible, judicial review should be preserved and strengthened, and the Bar should continue its efforts to assure that administrative procedures are conducted in accordance with the highest standards of fairness.

In immediate application these recommendations involve transfer to the present court system, or preferably to specialized courts, of the judicial functions of the Immigration and Naturalization Service, the National Labor Relations Board, the Federal Trade Commission, and certain authorities within the Post Office Department and the Customs Bureau. These changes should be specifically advocated—we only hurt our cause by continuing to demand the elimination of all administrative adjudication on the basis of an irretrievably discredited over-rigid application of the separation of powers doctrine.

Notwithstanding the objections of the organized bar indicated in the preceding essay, the exercise of judicial functions by administrative agencies continues to expand. The criticism is often made that in its judicial capacity an agency acts as prosecutor, finder of facts, and judge. However, similar to the current attitude on delegation of legislative power, the trend is to uphold the granting of judicial power to an administrative agency if the power is restricted by procedural safeguards preventing its abuse. Note that the right to a jury trial does not exist in either formal or informal hearings conducted by administrative bodies. However, the judicial power to hear and decide *criminal* cases cannot be granted to agencies other than courts, because of a stricter standard of procedural "due process of the law" in this area. In the exercise of the judicial function, the agency involved may issue an order requiring certain action or prohibiting certain conduct. The latter order is often referred to as a cease-and-desist order, which is the administrative-law version of a court injunction or decree. Such orders are usually complied with in the event that the affected party does not seek judicial review of the order. Failure to comply with the cease-and-desist order may result in fines, imprisonment, or other sanctions such as loss of a license or permit. Other orders are known as consent orders because they are entered by mutual agreement of the agency and the party involved. Cease-and-desist orders are entered only after the agency hears evidence and makes a finding of fact, but consent orders may be entered at any time.

4   JUDICIAL REVIEW OF ADMINISTRATIVE AGENCIES

It has already been noted that most aspects of the administrative process are subject to judicial review. The right of judicial review is the constitutional savior of the administrative process in that without it the whole administrative process might be unconstitutional. But what are the powers of courts in reviewing the quasi-legislative, quasi-judicial, and executive actions of administrative agencies? What chance does one who is aggrieved by a rule or decision of an agency have in obtaining a judicial reversal of the rule or decision? How much deference is given to the decision of the agency?

Judicial review of quasi-legislative rules raises different problems from those raised by judicial review of quasi-judicial decisions. In the latter case, many of the issues are factual, while the former involves more questions of law and policy. Insofar as the quasi-legislative function is concerned, we have already noted that courts, under the power of judicial review, will review the basic legislation to see if it is sufficiently definite and if it contains adequate standards as well as to determine if the agency has exceeded its delegated authority.

It must be recognized from the start that judicial review by its very nature is quite limited. Legislatures have delegated authority to agencies because of their expertise, etc., and courts usually exercise restraint and resolve doubtful issues in favor of the agency. For example, courts reviewing administrative interpretations of *law* do not always decide questions of law for themselves. It is not unusual for a court to accept an administrative interpretation of law as final if it has warrant in the record and rational basis in law. Administrative agencies are frequently called upon to interpret the statute governing the agency, and the agency's construction is persuasive to courts. However, courts frequently do replace administrative holdings with their own interpretations of law.

Administrative agencies develop their own rules of procedure. These procedures are far less formal than judicial procedures because one of the functions of the administrative process is to decide issues expeditiously. To proceed expeditiously usually means, for example, that administrative agencies are not restricted by the strict rules of evidence used by courts. This is not to say that such agencies can ignore all rules but only that some leeway shall be afforded. They cannot, for example, refuse to permit any cross-examination or unduly limit it. Because the agency "is frequently the accuser, the prosecutor, the judge and the jury," it must remain alert to observe accepted standards of fairness. Reviewing courts are, therefore, alert to ascertain that the true substance of a fair hearing is not denied to a party to an administrative hearing. However, the inordinate delay common in administrative hearings is a legitimate cause of public concern.

In reviewing the procedures of administrative agencies, courts are not empowered to substitute their judgment or their own procedures for those of the agency. Judicial responsibility is limited to ensuring consistency with statutes and compliance with the demands of the Constitution for a fair hearing.

The principle that Federal administrative agencies should be free to fashion their own rules of procedure and to pursue methods of inquiry capable of permitting them to discharge their multitudinous duties is an outgrowth of the view that administrative agencies and administrators will be familiar with the industries which they regulate and thus will be in a better position than courts or legislative bodies to design procedural rules adapted to the peculiarities of the industry and the tasks of the agency involved.

One important aspect of the broad area of judicial review of administrative action is that of "standing to sue." Standing to sue involves two important issues. First, is the action or decision of the agency subject to judicial review? Not all administrative decisions are reviewable. The Federal Administrative Procedure Act provides for judicial review except where "(1) statutes preclude judicial review or (2) agency action is committed to agency discretion by law." Few statutes actually preclude judicial review, and preclusion of judicial review by inference is rare.

The second issue is whether or not the plaintiff in any particular case is able to obtain judicial review. It is generally required that the plaintiff be "an aggrieved party" before he is allowed judicial review. For example, Ralph Nader was not allowed to challenge the ITT merger with Hartford Insurance Company because he lacked standing to sue. It is clear that persons who may suffer economic loss due to agency action have standing to sue. Recent decisions have expanded the group of persons with standing to sue to include those who have noneconomic interests, such as First Amendment rights, or an interest in the protection of the environment. The trend is to allow anyone with sufficient interest to conduct himself as an adversary to challenge the action of an administrative agency. Such decisions tend to make all members of society overseers of government. This concept has sometimes been referred to as the "private attorney general" principle. It should be noted that issues of standing to sue and the issues on the merits are not decided by the same standards. The case which follows is typical of the cases involving standing to sue.

Association of Data Processing Service Org., Inc. v. Camp
90 S.Ct. 827 (1970)

DOUGLAS, JUSTICE: Petitioners sell data processing services to businesses generally. In this suit they seek to challenge a ruling by respondent, Comptroller of the Currency, that as an incident to their banking services, national banks, including respondent American National Bank & Trust Company, may make data processing services available to other banks and to bank customers. The District Court dismissed the complaint for lack of standing of petitioners to bring the suit. The Court of Appeals affirmed. The case is here on a petition for writ of certiorari which we granted.

Generalizations about standing to sue are largely worthless as such. One generalization is, however, necessary and that is that the question of standing in the federal courts is to be considered in the framework of Article III which restricts judicial power to "cases" and "controversies." . . .

The first question is whether the plaintiff alleges that the challenged action has caused him injury in fact, economic or otherwise. There can be no doubt but that petitioners have satisfied this test. The petitioners not only allege that competition by national banks in the business of providing data processing services might entail some future loss of profits for the petitioners, they also allege that respondent American National Bank & Trust Company was performing or preparing to perform such services for two customers for whom petitioner Data Systems, Inc., had previously agreed or negotiated to perform such services.

. . . The question of standing concerns, apart from the "case" or "controversy" test, the question whether the interest sought to be protected by the complainant is arguably within the zone of interests to be protected or regulated by the statute or constitutional guarantee in question. Thus the Administrative Procedure Act grants standing to a person "aggrieved by agency action within the meaning of a relevant statute." That interest, at times, may reflect "aesthetic conservational, and recreational" as well as economic values. A person or a family may have a spiritual stake in First Amendment values sufficient to give him standing to raise issues concerning the Establishment Clause and the Free Exercise Clause. We mention these noneconomic values to emphasize that standing may stem from them as well as from the economic injury on which petitioner relies here. Certainly he who is "likely to be financially" injured may be a reliable private attorney general to litigate the issues of the public interest in the present case.

. . . Where statutes are concerned, the trend is toward enlargement of the class of people who may protest administrative action. The whole drive for enlarging the category of aggrieved "persons" is symptomatic of that trend. In a closely analogous case we held that an existing entrepreneur had standing to challenge the legality of the entrance of a newcomer into the business, because the established business was allegedly protected by a valid city ordinance which protected it from unlawful competition. In that tradition was *Hardin v. Kentucky Utilities Co.*, 390 U.S. 1, which involved a section of the TVA Act designed primarily to protect, through area limitations, private utilities against TVA competition. We held that no explicit statutory provision was necessary to confer standing, since the private utility bringing suit was within the class of persons which the statutory provision was designed to protect.

It is argued that . . . the *Hardin* case . . . [is] relevant here because of § 4 of the Bank Service Corporation Act of 1962, 76 Stat. 1132, 12 U.S.C. § 1864, which provides:

No bank service corporation may engage in any activity other than the performance of bank services for banks. . . .

We do think . . . that § 4 arguably brings a competitor within the zone of interests protected by it.

That leaves the remaining question, whether judicial review of the Comptroller's action has been precluded. We do not think it has been. There is great contrariety among administrative agencies created by Congress as respects "the extent to which, and the procedures by which, different measures of control afford judicial review of administrative action." The answer, of course, depends on the particular enactment under which review is sought. It turns on "the existence of courts and the intent of Congress as deduced from the statutes and precedents."

The Administrative Procedure Act provides that the provisions of the Act authorizing judicial review apply "except to the extent that—(1) statutes preclude judicial review; or (2) agency action is committed to agency discretion by law."

There is no presumption against judicial review and in favor of administrative absolutism, unless that purpose is fairly discernible in the statutory scheme.

We find no evidence that Congress in either the Bank Service Corporation Act or the National Bank Act sought to preclude judicial review of administrative rulings by the Comptroller as to the legitimate scope of activities available to national banks under those statutes. Both Acts are clearly "relevant" statutes within the meaning of § 702. The Acts do not in terms protect a specified group. But their general policy is apparent; and those whose interests are directly affected by a broad or narrow interpretation of the Act are easily identifiable. It is clear that petitioners, as competitors of national banks which are engaging in data processing services, are within that class of "aggrieved" persons who, under § 702, are entitled to judicial review of "agency action."

Whether anything in the Bank Service Corporation Act or the National Bank Act gives petitioners a "legal interest" which protects them against violations of those Acts, and whether the actions of respondents did in fact violate either of those Acts, are questions which go to the merits and remain to be decided below.

We hold that petitioners have standing to sue and that the case should be remanded for a hearing on the merits. [REVERSED]

A   THE DOCTRINE OF EXHAUSTION OF REMEDIES

In reviewing administrative decisions (which may involve both findings of fact and interpretations of rules), courts are reluctant to decide in advance of a hearing that it will not be conducted fairly by the agency in question. In general (although there are exceptions), courts refuse to review administrative actions until a complaining party has exhausted all the administrative remedies and procedures available to him for redress. For example, a Selective Service registrant must wait until he receives an induction order, and either obey it or be prosecuted for refusing to obey it, before the courts will review his classification. This is so because it is service in the armed forces and not the mere classification that constitutes the alleged injury. If it should develop that for independent reasons, such as physical disability, the registrant is not actually inducted into the armed forces, he will never have sustained a legally redressible injury. While a mere adverse classification may cause a disarray of plans and emotional upset, this is deemed by courts to be an acceptable price for a registrant to pay for the efficient functioning of the Selective Service System.

However, when there is nothing to be gained from the exhaustion of administrative remedies and the harm from the continued existence of the administrative ruling is great, the courts have not been reluctant to discard this doctrine. This is especially true when very fundamental constitutional guarantees such as freedom of speech or press are involved. In one draft classification case, exhaustion was not required when a person was reclassified for exercising his right of free speech to dissent. The Supreme Court in that case said that where basic constitutional rights are imperiled, the courts have not required a series of injured parties to litigate the permissible scope of a statute or administrative interpretation, but have nullified the unconstitutional action and required the government to start in the first instance with a statute or interpretation that will not so overhang free expression that the legitimate exercise of constitutionally protected rights is suppressed.

The following case illustrates the general concept of exhaustion of remedies, however.

McGee v. United States
91 S.Ct. 1565 (1971)

In 1966, petitioner McGee applied to his local Selective Service Board for a conscientious objector classification. He was told that his request would be passed on when his student deferment expired. In 1967, his board was told that McGee had been accepted for graduate school and that in petitioner's own view he would "probably qualify" for a theological exemption. At the time of his graduation, petitioner refused to fill out a current information questionnaire and announced that he would not cooperate with the Selective Service System. Petitioner was reclassified I-A, but he did not seek a personal appearance either before his local board or before an appeal board. Petitioner then refused induction and was convicted for violating the draft law. Petitioner in his defense claimed that he had been erroneously classified. The government contended that the petitioner's defense could not be raised as a matter of law because his classification was not in issue since he had not raised the issue with the Selective Service System and had not exhausted his administrative remedies.

MARSHALL, JUSTICE: . . . Two Terms ago, in *McKart v. United States*, 395 U.S. 185, the Court surveyed the place of the exhaustion doctrine in Selective Service cases, and the policies that underpin the doctrine. As it had evolved . . . , the doctrine when properly invoked operates to restrict judicial scrutiny of administrative action having to do with the classification of a registrant, in the case of a registrant who has failed to pursue normal administrative remedies and thus has side-stepped a corrective process which might have cured or rendered moot the very defect later complained of in court. *McKart* stands for the proposition that the doctrine is not to be applied inflexibly in all situations, but that decision also plainly contemplates situations where a litigant's claims will lose vitality because the litigant has failed to contest his rights in an administrative forum. The result in a criminal context is no doubt a substantial detriment to the defendant whose claims are barred. Still this unhappy result may be justified in particular circumstances by considerations relating to the integrity of the Selective Service classification process and the limited role of the courts in deciding the proper classification of draft registrants.

After *McKart* the task for the courts, in deciding the applicability of the exhaustion doctrine to the circumstances of a particular case, is to ask "whether allowing all similarly situated registrants to bypass [the administrative avenue in question] would seriously impair the Selective Service System's ability to perform its functions." *McKart* specified the salient interests that may be jeopardized by a registrant's failure to pursue administrative remedies. Certain failures to exhaust may deny the administrative system important opportunities "to make a factual record" for purposes of classification, or "to exercise its discretion or apply its expertise" in the course of decision-making. There may be a danger that relaxation of exhaustion requirements, in certain circumstances, would induce "frequent and deliberate flouting of administrative processes," thereby undermining the scheme of decision-making that Congress has created. And of course, a strict exhaustion requirement tends to ensure that the agency have additional opportunities "to discover and correct its own errors," and thus may help to obviate all occasion for judicial review.

To be weighed against the interests in exhaustion is the harsh impact of the doctrine when it is invoked to bar any judicial review of a registrant's claims. Surely an insubstantial procedural default by a registrant should not shield an invalid order from judicial correction, simply because the interest in time-saving self-correction by the agency is involved. That single interest is conceivably slighted by any failure to exhaust, however innocuous the bypass in other respects, and *McKart* recognizes that the exhaustion requirement is not to be applied "blindly in every case." *McKart* also acknowledges that the fear of "frequent and deliberate flouting" can easily be overblown, since in the normal case a registrant would be "foolhardy" indeed to withhold a valid claim from administrative scrutiny. Thus the contention that the rigors of the exhaustion doctrine should be relaxed is not to be met by mechanical recitation of the broad interests usually served by the doctrine but rather should be assessed in light of a discrete analysis of the particular default in question, to see whether there is "a governmental interest compelling enough" to justify the forfeiting of judicial review. . . .

In the present case . . . it is apparent that McGee's failure to exhaust did jeopardize the interest in full administrative fact-gathering and utilization of agency expertise, . . . McGee's claims to exempt status—as a ministerial student or a conscientious objector—depended on the application of expertise by administrative bodies in resolving underlying issues of fact. Fact-finding for purposes of Selective Service classification is committed primarily to the administrative process, with very limited judicial review to ascertain whether there is a "basis in fact" for the administrative determination.

McKart expressly noted that as to classification claims turning on the resolution of particularistic fact questions, "the Selective Service System and the courts may have a stronger interest in having the question decided in the first instance by the local board and then by the appeal board, which considers the question anew." This "stronger interest," in the circumstances of the present case, has become compelling and fully sufficient to justify invocation of the exhaustion doctrine.

Petitioner argues that denial of exemption as a ministerial student was erroneous, but he had never requested that classification nor had he submitted information that would have been pertinent to such a claim. In regard to his entitlement to this exempt status, McGee made no effort to invoke administrative processes for fact-finding, classification, and review. It is true that vagrant bits of information may have come to the attention of the local board raising a bare possibility that petitioner might qualify as a ministerial student, but this hardly changes the picture of a thoroughgoing attempt to sidestep the administrative process and make the first serious case for an exemption later in court.

Such a default directly jeopardizes the functional autonomy of the administrative bodies on whom Congress has conferred the primary responsibility to decide questions of fact relating to the proper classification of Selective Service registrants. Here the bypass was deliberate and without excuse, and this is not a case where entitlement to an exemption would be automatically made out given a minimal showing by the registrant or minimal investigatory effort by the local board. The exhaustion requirement is properly imposed where, as here, the claim to exemption depends on careful factual analysis and where the registrant has completely sidestepped the administrative process designed to marshal relevant facts and resolve factual issues in the first instance.

Petitioner did claim exemption as a conscientious objector to war. He filled out and returned the special form for conscientious objectors and appended a further statement of beliefs, thereby making out a prima facie case for the exempt status. Since at that time—1966—petitioner held an undergraduate student deferment, the board postponed consideration of the claim to a "higher" classification. In 1967, after petitioner had graduated, the pending conscientious objector claim was reviewed and rejected, and petitioner was classified 1–A. Petitioner contends that denial of conscientious objector status was erroneous but after the claim was rejected he did not invoke the administrative processes available to correct the error. He did not seek a personal appearance before the local board, nor did he take an administrative appeal to contest the denial before the appeal board, which classifies *de novo*.

That petitioner's failure to exhaust should cut off judicial review of his conscientious objector claim may seem too hard a result, assuming, as the Government admits, that the written information available to the board provided no basis in fact for denial of the exemption, and as the Court of Appeals ruled, that neither did petitioner's conduct in relation to the conscription system or other acts that came into view. But even assuming the above, petitioner's dual failure to exhaust—his failure either to secure a personal appearance or to take an administrative appeal—implicates decisively the policies served by the exhaustion requirement, especially the purpose of ensuring that the Selective Service System have full opportunity to "make a factual record" and "apply its expertise" in relation to a registrant's claims. When a claim to exemption depends ultimately on the careful gathering and analysis of relevant facts, the interest in full airing of the facts within the administrative system is prominent, and . . . the exhaustion requirement "cannot properly be limited to those persons whose claims would fail in court anyway."

Conscientious objector claims turn on the resolution of factual questions relating to the nature of a registrant's beliefs concerning war, the basis of the objection in conscience and religion, and the registrant's sincerity. Petitioner declined to contest the denial of his conscientious objector claim before the local board by securing a personal appearance, and the Selective Service System was thereby deprived of one opportunity to supplement the record of relevant facts. The opportunity would have been restored had petitioner sought review by the appeal board. While the local board apparently was satisfied that classification should be made on the basis of the record it confronted, the appeal board, which classifies *de novo*, might have determined that the record should be supplemented by the local board. In the circumstances of this case, petitioner's failure to take an administrative appeal not only deprived the appeal board of the opportunity to "apply its expertise" in fact-finding to the record that was available; it also removed an opportunity to supplement a record containing petitioner's own submissions but not containing the results of any specific inquiry into sincerity.

The Government contends that unless the exhaustion requirement is imposed to bar judicial review when the failure to exhaust has the present character, registrants would be encouraged to sidestep the administrative processes once a prima facie claim to conscientious objector status is made out by submission of a carefully drafted Form 150. Should the claim be denied at the local board level, the claimant might be tempted to circumvent further fact-gathering processes, and take a chance on showing in court that the only administrative record available contains no basis in fact for denial of the claim. This somewhat extreme situation is indeed presented by the circumstances of the present case, though of course there is no reason to question the bona fides of McGee's own supervening policy of noncooperation with the conscription system. It remains that McGee's failure to pursue his administrative remedies was deliberate and without excuse. And it is not fanciful to think that "frequent and deliberate flouting of the administrative process" might occur if McGee and others similarly situated were allowed to press their claims in court despite a dual failure to exhaust.

We conclude that petitioner's failure to exhaust administrative remedies bars the defense of erroneous classification, and therefore the judgment below is affirmed. [AFFIRMED]

B THE AGENCIES' DISCRETION

Delegation of quasi-legislative power usually involves grants of substantial discretion to the board or agency involved. It must be kept in mind that the delegation of discretion is to the agency and not to the courts. Therefore, courts cannot interfere with the discretion given to the agency and cannot substitute their judgment for that of the agency. The *Quaker Oats* case which follows is typical of cases in which business seeks to have the courts change an agency decision with which it disagrees.

Federal Security Administrator v. Quaker Oats Co.
318 U.S. 218 (1943)

STONE, CHIEF JUSTICE: The Federal Security Administrator, acting under §§ 401 and 701(e), of the Federal Food, Drug and Cosmetic Act, promulgated regulations establishing "standards of identity" for various milled wheat products, excluding vitamin D from the defined standard of "farina" and permitting it only in "enriched farina," which was required to contain vitamin B_1, riboflavin, nicotinic acid and iron. The question is whether the regulations are valid as applied to respondent. The answer turns upon (a) whether there is substantial evidence in support of the Administrator's finding that indiscriminate enrichment of farina with vitamin and mineral contents would tend to confuse and mislead consumers; (b) if so, whether, upon such a finding, the Administrator has statutory authority to adopt a standard of identity, which excludes a disclosed non-deleterious ingredient, in order to promote honesty and fair dealing in the interest of consumers; and (c) whether the Administrator's treatment, by the challenged regulations, of the use of vitamin D as an ingredient of a product sold as "farina" is within his statutory authority to prescribe "a reasonable definition and standard of identity." . . .

Respondent, The Quaker Oats Company, has for the past ten years manufactured and marketed a wheat product commonly used as a cereal food, consisting of farina as defined by the Administrator's regulation, but with vitamin D added. Respondent distributes this product in packages labeled "Quaker Farina Wheat Cereal Enriched with Vitamin D," or "Quaker Farina Enriched by the Sunshine Vitamin." The packages also bear the label "Contents 400 U.S.P. units of Vitamin D per ounce, supplied by approximately the addition of 1/5 of 1 percent irradiated dry yeast."

Respondent asserts, and the Government agrees, that the Act as supplemented by the Administrator's standards will prevent the marketing of its product as "farina" since, by reason of the presence of vitamin D as an ingredient, it does not conform to the standard of identity prescribed for "farina," and that respondent cannot market its product as "enriched farina" unless it adds the prescribed minimum quantities of vitamin B_1, riboflavin, nicotinic acid and iron. Respondent challenges the validity of the regulations. . . .

The court below . . . held that because there was no evidence that respondent's product had in fact confused or misled anyone, the Administrator's finding as to consumer confusion was without substantial support in the evidence. It thought that, if anything, consumer confusion was more likely to be created, and the interest of consumers harmed, by the sale of farinas conforming to the standard for "enriched farina," whose labels were not required to disclose their ingredients, than by the sale of respondent's product under an accurate and informative label such as that respondent was using.

The Act does not contemplate that courts should thus substitute their own judgment for that of the Administrator. As passed by the House it appears to have provided for a judicial review in which the court could take additional evidence, weigh the evidence, and direct the Administrator "to take such further action as justice may require." . . . But before enactment, the Conference Committee substituted for these provisions those which became § 701 (f) of the Act. While under that section the Administrator's regulations must be supported by findings based upon "substantial evidence" adduced at the hearing, the Administrator's findings as to the facts if based on substantial evidence are conclusive. In explaining these changes the chairman of the House conferees stated on the floor of the House that "there is no purpose that the court shall exercise the functions that belong to the executive or the legislative branches." . . .

The review provisions were patterned after those by which Congress has provided for the review of "quasi-judicial" orders of the Federal Trade Commission and other agencies, which we have many times had occasion to construe. Under such provisions we have repeatedly emphasized the scope that must be allowed to the discretion and informed judgment of an expert administrative body. . . . These considerations are especially appropriate where the review is of regulations of general application adopted by an administrative agency under its rule-making power in carrying out the policy of a statute with whose enforcement it is charged. . . . Section 401 calls for the exercise of the "judgment of the Administrator." That judgment, if based on substantial evidence of record, and if within statutory and constitutional limitations, is controlling even though the reviewing court might on the same record have arrived at a different conclusion. . . . Taking into account the evidence of public demand for vitamin-enriched foods, their increasing sale, their variable vitamin composition and dietary value, and the general lack of consumer knowledge of such values, there was sufficient evidence of "rational probative force" . . . to support the Administrator's judgment that, in the absence of appropriate standards of identity, consumer confusion would ensue. . . . Respondent's final and most vigorous attack on the regulations is that they fail to establish reasonable definitions and standards of identity, as § 401 requires, in that they prohibit the marketing, under the name "farina," of a wholesome and honestly labeled product consisting of farina with vitamin D added, and that they prevent the addition of vitamin D to products marketed as "enriched farina" unless accompanied by the other prescribed vitamin ingredients which do not coact with or have any dietary relationship to vitamin D. Stated in another form, the argument is that it is unreasonable to prohibit the addition to farina of vitamin D as an optional ingredient while permitting its addition as an optional ingredient to enriched farina, to the detriment of respondent's business.

Since the definition of identity of a vitamin-treated food, marketed under its common or usual name, involves the inclusion of some vitamin ingredients and the exclusion of others, the Administrator necessarily has a large range of choice in determining what may be included and what excluded. It is not necessarily a valid objection to his choice that another could reasonably have been made. The judicial judgment is not be substituted for the legislative judgment. It is enough that the Administrator has acted within the statutory bounds of his authority, and that his choice among possible alternative standards adapted to the statutory end is one which a rational person could have made. . . .

We conclude that the Administrator did not depart from statutory requirements in choosing these standards of identity for the purpose of promoting fair dealing in the interest of consumers, that the standards which he selected are adapted to that end, and that they are adequately supported by findings and evidence. [REVERSED]

C REVIEW OF FACTUAL ISSUES

When it reviews the findings of *fact* made by an administrative body, a court considers these to be prima facie correct. A court of review examines the evidence by analyzing the record of the agency's proceedings and upholds the agency's findings and conclusions on questions of fact if they are supported by substantial evidence in the record as a whole. In other words, the record must contain material evidence from which a reasonable person might reach the same conclusion as did the agency. If substantial evidence in support of the decision is present, the court will not disturb the agency's findings, even though the court itself might have reached a different conclusion on the basis of other conflicting evidence also in the record.

Thus it is apparent that on review (1) courts do not reweigh the evidence, (2) courts do not make independent determinations of fact, and (3) courts do not substitute their view of the evidence for that of the agency. However, courts do determine if there is substantial evidence to support the action taken, but in their examination of the evidence, all that is required is evidence sufficient to convince a reasonable mind to a fair degree of certainty. Thus, substantial evidence is such evidence as a reasonable mind might accept as adequate to support the conclusion.

The findings of an administrative body are not set aside unless the record clearly precludes the decision of the administrative body from being justified by a fair estimate of the worth and testimony of witnesses or its informed judgment on matters within its special competence, or both. The decision of the agency will be affirmed even if the court believes it to be erroneous, if a reasonable man could have reached the conclusion stated. Since it is the function of the agency to pass upon the weight to be accorded to the evidence and to make the choice, if necessary, between varying inferences which might be drawn therefrom, the possibility of drawing either of two inconsistent inferences from the evidence does not prevent the agency from drawing one of them. Courts, however, do not always agree with the administrative determination, and courts sometimes set aside a finding because it is not supported by substantial evidence.

The case which follows illustrates the "substantial evidence on the record as a whole" concept.

Universal Camera Corp. v. National Labor Relations Board
340 U.S. 474 (1951)

The NLRB ordered Universal Camera Corp. to reinstate, with back pay, an employee whom the Board found was discharged because he gave testimony in another proceeding under the National Labor Relations Act. This order was issued despite the fact the evidence concerning the reason the company dismissed the employee was conflicting, and the Board's examiner had found as a fact that the employee was discharged for some other reason and had recommended that the proceeding of the employee for reinstatement be dismissed. The Court of Appeals on reviewing the case held the Board's findings were "supported by substantial evidence" but the Court of Appeals did not consider the findings of the Hearing Examiner. This appeal to the Supreme Court resulted.

FRANKFURTER, JUSTICE: The essential issue raised by this case . . . is the effect of the Administrative Procedure Act and the legislation colloquially known as the Taft-Hartley Act, . . . on the duty of the Courts of Appeals when called upon to review orders of the National Labor Relations Board. . . .

Want of certainty in judicial review of Labor Board decisions partly reflects the intractability of any formula to furnish definiteness of content for all the impalpable factors involved in judicial review. But in part doubts as to the nature of the reviewing power and uncertainties in its application derive from history, and to that extent an elucidation of this history may clear them away.

The Wagner Act provided: "The findings of the Board as to the facts, if supported by evidence, shall be conclusive." . . . This Court read "evidence" to mean "substantial evidence," . . . and we said that "[s]ubstantial evidence is more than a mere scintilla. It means such relevant evidence as a reasonable mind might accept as adequate to support a conclusion." . . . Accordingly, it "must do more than create a suspicion of the existence of the fact to be established . . . it must be enough to justify, if the trial were to a jury, a refusal to direct a verdict when the conclusion sought to be drawn from it is one of fact for the jury." . . .

The very smoothness of the "substantial evidence" formula as the standard for reviewing the evidentiary validity of the Board's findings established its currency. But the inevitably variant applications of the standard to conflicting evidence soon brought contrariety of views and in due course bred criticism. Even though the whole record may have been canvassed in order to determine whether the evidentiary foundation of a determination by the Board was "substantial," the phrasing of this Court's process of review readily lent itself to the notion that it was enough that the evidence supporting the Board's result was "substantial" when considered by itself. It is fair to say that by imperceptible steps regard for the fact-finding function of the Board led to the assumption that the requirements of the Wagner Act were met when the reviewing court could find in the record evidence which, when viewed in isolation, substantiated the Board's findings. . . .

Criticism of so contracted a reviewing power reinforced dissatisfaction felt in various quarters with the Board's administration of the Wagner Act in the years preceding the war. . . .

Protests against "shocking injustices" and intimations of judicial "abdication" with which some courts granted enforcement of the Board's orders stimulated pressures for legislative relief from alleged administrative excesses. . . .

So far as the history of [the] movement for enlarged review reveals, the phrase "upon the whole record" makes its first appearance into the statute books when Congress with unquestioning—we might even say uncritical—unanimity enacted the Administrative Procedure Act.

One is tempted to say "uncritical" because the legislative history of that Act hardly speaks with that clarity of purpose which Congress supposedly furnishes courts in order to enable them to enforce its true will. On the one hand, the sponsors of the legislation indicated that they were reaffirming the prevailing "substantial evidence" test. But with equal clarity they expressed disapproval of the manner in which the courts were applying their own standard. The committee reports of both houses refer to the practice of agencies to rely upon "suspicion, surmise, implications, or plainly incredible evidence" and indicate that courts are to exact higher standards "in the exercise of their independent judgment" and on consideration of "the whole record."

Similar dissatisfaction with too restricted application of the "substantial evidence" test is reflected in the legislative history of the Taft-Hartley Act. . . . In order to clarify any ambiguity in that statute, however, the conference committee inserted the words "questions of fact, if supported by substantial evidence *on the record considered as a whole.* . . ."

This phraseology . . . became the law.

From the legislative story . . . two concrete conclusions do emerge. One is the identity of aim of the Administrative Procedure Act and the Taft-Hartley Act regarding the proof with which the Labor Board must support a decision. The other is that now Congress has left no room for doubt as to the kind of scrutiny which a court of appeals must give the record before the Board to satisfy itself that the Board's order rests on adequate proof. . . .

The standard of proof specifically required of the Labor Board by the Taft-Hartley Act is the same as that to be exacted by courts reviewing every administrative action subject to the Administrative Procedure Act.

Whether or not it was ever permissible for courts to determine the substantiality of evidence supporting a Labor Board decision merely on the basis of evidence which in and of itself justified it, without taking into account contradictory evidence or evidence from which conflicting inferences could be drawn, the new legislation definitively precludes such a theory of review and bars its practice. The substantiality of evidence must take into account whatever in the record fairly detracts from its weight. This is clearly the significance of the requirement in both statutes that courts consider the whole record. . . .

To be sure, the requirement for canvassing "the whole record" in order to ascertain substantiality does not furnish a calculus of value by which a reviewing court can assess the evidence. Nor was it intended to negative the function of the

Labor Board as one of those agencies presumably equipped or informed by experience to deal with a specialized field of knowledge, whose findings within that field carry the authority of an expertness which courts do not possess and therefore must respect. Nor does it mean that even as to matters not requiring expertise a court may displace the Board's choice between two fairly conflicting views, even though the court would justifiably have made a different choice had the matter been before it *de novo.* Congress has merely made it clear that a reviewing court is not barred from setting aside a Board decision when it cannot conscientiously find that the evidence supporting that decision is substantial, when viewed in the light that the record in its entirety furnishes, including the body of evidence opposed to the Board's view. . . .

But a standard leaving an unavoidable margin for individual judgment does not leave the judicial judgment at large even though the phrasing of the standard does not wholly fence it in. The legislative history of these Acts demonstrates a purpose to impose on courts a responsibility which has not always been recognized. Of course it is a statute and not a committee report which we are interpreting. But the fair interpretation of a statute is often "the art of proliferating a purpose" . . . revealed more by the demonstrable forces that produced it than by its precise phrasing. The adoption in these statutes of the judicially-constructed "substantial evidence" test was a response to pressures for stricter and more uniform practice, not a reflection of approval of all existing practices. To find the change so elusive that it cannot be precisely defined does not mean it may be ignored. We should fail in our duty to effectuate the will of Congress if we denied recognition to expressed Congressional disapproval of the finality accorded to Labor Board findings by some decisions of this and lower courts, or even of the atmosphere which may have favored those decisions.

We conclude, therefore, that the Administrative Procedure Act and the Taft-Hartley Act direct that courts must now assume more responsibility for the reasonableness and fairness of Labor Board decisions than some courts have shown in the past. Reviewing courts must be influenced by a feeling that they are not to abdicate the conventional judicial function. Congress has imposed on them responsibility for assuring that the Board keeps within reasonable grounds. That responsibility is not less real because it is limited to enforcing the requirement that evidence appear substantial when viewed, on the record as a whole, by courts invested with the authority and enjoying the prestige of the Courts of Appeals. The Board's findings are entitled to respect; but they must nonetheless be set aside when the record before a Court of Appeals clearly precludes the Board's decision from being justified by a fair estimate of the worth of the testimony of witnesses or its informed judgment on matters within its special competence or both. . . .

III

The Taft-Hartley Act provides that "The findings of the Board with respect to questions of fact if supported by substantial evidence on the record considered as a whole shall be conclusive." Surely an examiner's report is as much a part of the record as the complaint or the testimony. . . .

It is therefore difficult to escape the conclusion that the plain language of the statutes directs a reviewing court to determine the substantiality of evidence on the record including the examiner's report. The conclusion is confirmed by the indications in the legislative history that enhancement of the statutes and function of the trial examiner was one of the important purposes of the movement for administrative reform. . . .

We do not require that the examiner's findings be given more weight than in reason and in the light of judicial experience they deserve. The "substantial evidence" standard is not modified in any way when the Board and its examiner disagree. We intend only to recognize that evidence supporting a conclusion may be less substantial when an impartial, experienced examiner who has observed the witnesses and lived with the case has drawn conclusions different from the Board's than when he has reached the same conclusion. The findings of the examiner are to be considered along with the consistency and inherent probability of testimony. The significance of his report, of course, depends largely on the importance of credibility in the particular case. To give it this significance does not seem to us materially more difficult than to heed the other factors which in sum determine whether evidence is "substantial."

The direction in which the law moves is often a guide for decision of particular cases, and here it serves to confirm our conclusion. However halting its progress, the trend in litigation is toward a rational inquiry into truth, in which the tribunal considers everything "logically probative of some matter requiring to be proved." [CASE REMANDED TO COURT OF APPEALS]

On remand of the foregoing case, the Circuit Court of Appeals reexamined the record as a whole. Taking into account the recommendations and findings of the Board's examiner, the court found that the NLRB should have dismissed the complaint of the employee, because the record did *not* show substantially that he was discharged because he gave testimony, and accordingly denied enforcement of the Board's order.[3]

5 STATE ADMINISTRATIVE AGENCIES

It is frequently assumed that the only significant administrative agencies exist at the Federal level in government. While the importance of the Federal administrative agencies to the legal environment of business may stagger the imagination, the role of state and local agencies cannot be considered as anything less than very substantial.

At the local level every business will be regulated and controlled by such agencies as zoning boards, which determine the permissible locations of business enterprises, and various taxing boards, which play a major role in determining the "cost of doing business" in the community. State agencies exist to regulate

[3] 190 F.2d 429 (1951).

wages, hours, and working conditions of employees as well as to administer unemployment and workmen's compensation laws. Many states have Fair Employment Practice Commissions to prevent discrimination in hire, pay, or tenure of employment based on race, creed, sex, or national origin. As previously noted, other state agencies regulate rates charged by business in the fields of transportation, gas, water and power supply, and communications.

Clearly, there are not enough legally trained people in this country to staff all of these agencies. Agencies performing quasi-judicial functions are subject to constant criticism from lawyers because of "procedural errors" and related shortcomings as noted in the Cole article, set forth in section 3 of this chapter. The members of the bar have been attempting to bring reform to state administrative procedures to correct their weaknesses. The National Conference of Commissioners on Uniform State Laws prepared a Revised Model State Administrative Procedure Act in 1961. The act recognizes differences between Federal and state agencies. A major one is that state agencies operate in a much smaller area and on a more intimate basis. This means that state officials may have more preconceived ideas. In addition, states have more difficulty in hiring legally trained personnel. The following discussion outlines the nine basic principles of this model statute, which was designed to overcome some of the traditional objections to state administrative agency procedures.

Turning the Spotlight on State Administrative Procedure[4]
Frank E. Cooper[5]

. . . First, the Revised Model State Act requires a substantial degree of uniformity in procedure by defining "agency" in all-inclusive terms as meaning each state board, commission, department or officer (other than the legislature or the courts) authorized to make rules or determine contested cases. Many officers of state agencies are opposed to the principle of giving the act broad applicability. They prefer that their own agencies be exempted, because they believe they can work out a better code of procedure for their own agencies than can anyone else; and they are eager to improve on it from case to case, devising as they go along. A desire to obtain powers of self-direction, not to say self-determination, is the main reason agencies are generally opposed to administrative procedure acts; the desire that state agencies be denied such powers is the chief reason the Bar approves such legislation.

Second, the Revised Model State Act requires that each agency adopt well-defined courses of procedure, setting forth in formal rules a description of its organization, the method of its operations, the nature and requirements of all formal and informal procedures available and a description of all forms and instructions used by the agency. These requirements should result not only in

---

[4] 49 *A.B.A.J.* 29 (Jan., 1963). Used by permission from the American Bar Association and the *American Bar Association Journal.*
[5] Professor Cooper is chairman of the American Bar Association Section on Administrative Law and professor of law at the University of Michigan.

easing the task of respondents' counsel but also in improving the efficiency of the operations of the agencies.

Third, the Revised Model State Act implements the principle that agency actions should not be in the nature of secret, star-chamber proceedings but should be publicly known. All statements of policy or interpretations utilized by the agency are required to be made available for public inspection. No rule, order or decision may be invoked by the agency for any purpose until it has been made public in the manner prescribed.

Fourth, it is required that all interested parties have a voice in the adoption of agency rules. Except in the case of emergency rules (which may be effective only for a limited time) an agency proposing to adopt a rule must give at least twenty days' notice of its intended action, stating the terms or substance of the proposed rule. Further, the agencies must afford all interested persons reasonable opportunity to participate in the rule-making proceedings by submitting views and information. In stated cases, opportunity for oral hearing must be afforded (thus obviating the possibility that briefs may not be carefully considered). Provision is also made to assure the careful consideration of petitions for the adoption of rules.

Fifth, provisions are made for filing and prompt publication of all administrative rules. The provisions in this respect are skeletal in nature, experience having indicated that many states find it desirable to make detailed provisions, appropriate to their particular conditions, to assure that complete and current statements of all administrative rules are conveniently available. In Wisconsin, for example, a loose-leaf publication is issued monthly.

Sixth, the Revised Model State Act makes broad and explicit provision for obtaining declaratory relief, so that anyone who doubts either the validity or the applicability of an agency rule may obtain a speedy determination of such questions. To achieve these ends, agencies are required to provide by rule for the prompt disposition of petitions for declaratory rulings as to the applicability of any statutory provision or of any rule or order of the agency. Further, provision is made for the determination of the validity or applicability of a rule in a judicial proceeding for a declaratory judgment.

Seventh, ample provision is made to assure that all contested cases shall be decided fairly, on a complete and accurate record affording a basis for a fully informed decision by officers who have duly mastered the record. It is required that the notice initiating the proceeding include a short and plain statement of the matters asserted. Rules of evidence applied in civil cases in the state's courts are to be followed, except that when it is necessary to ascertain facts not reasonably susceptible of proof under such rules, agencies may relax the judicial standards of admissibility and hear evidence of a type commonly relied upon by reasonably prudent men in the conduct of their affairs. When an agency proposes to take official notice of facts within its asserted specialized knowledge, parties shall be notified of the facts which the agency proposes so to notice, and parties shall be given an opportunity to demonstrate that the actual facts are not what the agency had assumed.

Recognizing the dangers inherent in the institutional decision process, but recognizing also the necessity of utilizing it under some circumstances, the Revised Model State Act provides that when a majority of the agency officials who are to render the final decision have not heard the case or read the record, no decision adverse to a party other than the agency shall be made until a proposal for decision is served upon the parties, and an opportunity is afforded each party adversely affected to file exceptions and present briefs and oral argument before the officials who are to render the decision. In this way, parties respondent are guaranteed an opportunity of presenting their views as to the facts and law to the very individuals charged with ultimate responsibility for decision making.

As a further guarantee that decisions shall be carefully considered and fully informed, agencies are required to make specific rulings upon each proposed finding of fact submitted by any party in accordance with agency rules; and it is required that each final decision shall be accompanied by a concise and explicit statement of the underlying facts that support findings of ultimate fact set forth in the language of the applicable statute.

A final guarantee of fairness in the disposition of contested cases is contained in Section 13 of the Revised Model State Act, which places limitations upon resort to *ex parte* consultations as to either facts or law.

Eighth, express recognition is given to the principle that licensees have special rights and privileges of which they should not be summarily deprived. Appropriate provisions are made for the continuance of existing licenses pending application and final disposition of application for renewal. Limits are imposed on revocation or suspension of licenses.

Ninth, the Revised Model State Act provides for prompt, simple and effective judicial review. Appeals are heard in a trial court of general jurisdiction, thus avoiding the burdensome difficulties placed both upon the appellate courts and upon the parties when review is limited to the state supreme court. The reviewing courts are not limited to deciding questions of law, but are authorized to set aside agency findings and decisions which are clearly erroneous in view of the reliable, probative and substantial evidence on the whole record, or which are determined by the court to involve a clearly unwarranted exercise of discretion.

The Revised Model State Act provides a vehicle through which, with proper adaptation to local conditions, the state legislatures can achieve realistic and practical legal reform that will redound to the benefit of millions of American citizens.

6 CONTEMPORARY PROBLEMS

The vastness of the administrative process creates many problems other than those relating to the exercise of legislative or judicial powers by these agencies. For example, every rule-making agency publishes its rules, and so many are being published that no one person, company, or law firm can have them all available to *examine*, let alone *know* what they contain. The Federal Register prints these regulations so that persons and businesses will be charged with knowledge of them and will have at least an opportunity to discover what they are.

Not only are there so many rules and regulations that it is impossible to know them or sometimes to find them, the rules and regulations of different agencies are frequently in conflict with each other. One agency often does not know what others are doing, and there is today a tremendous overlapping of responsibilities. For example, at least forty-two Federal departments, agencies, and bureaus are involved with some aspect of education. Transportation problems are under the jurisdiction of the Department of Commerce, the Federal Aviation Agency (FAA), the Coast Guard, the Army Engineers, the Interstate Commerce Commission (ICC), the Civil Aeronautics Board (CAB), the Maritime Commission, and the Department of Housing and Urban Development. Senator Abraham Ribicoff, in a speech on October 20, 1965, on the floor of the Senate, illustrated the problems which result from such overlapping of administrative authority when he noted:

"In the pesticide field, the Department of Agriculture, the Food and Drug Administration, the Public Health Service and the Interior Department all vie with one another, not only in their day-to-day operations but in the policy area too. Interior forbids its constitutent agencies to use in National Forests the same poisons that the Agriculture Department urges the public to spray on lawns, trees and rose bushes. The Public Health Service spends public funds to study the possible connection between the cancer toll and the increased use of pesticides, while the Food and Drug Administration says the housewife's market-basket is 'safe' from pesticide residue."[6]

From the foregoing, it is clear that reorganization and elimination of duplication in the various agencies, as proposed by Senator Ribicoff, is urgently needed. The proliferation of agencies creates a difficult, if not incomprehensible, environment for business and constitutes a waste of the taxpayer's money as well. Even if the number of agencies and their functions were reduced to a minimum, it would still be difficult to keep abreast of the requirements imposed on business. Government, because of the vastness of administrative agencies, often appears "confused, diffused, and disorganized" in the words of Senator Ribicoff. Many people who are daily involved with the administrative process believe that government is in fact "confused, diffused, and disorganized."

Additional problems concerning the administrative process and administrative law will be further illustrated in subsequent chapters concerned with labor law, antitrust law, and other areas of regulation of business. It should be emphasized that this source of law comprises a substantial and probably the major portion of the legal environment of business.

REVIEW QUESTIONS—CHAPTER 7

1 Define the following legal terms introduced in this chapter: quasi-legislative; quasi-judicial; delegation; standing to sue; Administrative Procedure Act.

[6] III *Cong. Rec.* 27499 (1965).

2 What is the primary role of the following agencies: NLRB, FTC, ICC, FCC, FPC, AEC, and SEC?

3 What are the legal requirements and limitations on the delegation of legislative power to administrative agencies? Explain.

4 What are the two basic issues to be determined by a court hearing a challenge to the validity of a rule made by an administrative agency. Explain and give an example of each.

5 Give three examples of broad standards that have been constitutionally approved in delegations to administrative agencies.

6 Why do some administrative agencies exercise judicial powers?

7 Discuss three of the objections that many lawyers have to the exercise of judicial powers by administrative agencies.

8 Discuss the "standing to sue" concept as it affects judicial review of the decisions of administrative agencies. Your answer should illustrate the meaning of an "aggrieved person" as it relates to this issue.

9 Illustrate the doctrine of exhaustion of remedies and explain why such a doctrine is followed in administrative law.

10 Give an example of an exception to the doctrine of exhaustion of remedies.

11 Give reasons for the reluctance of courts to substitute their judgment for that of an administrative agency.

12 What is the significance to business of the principle that courts will not substitute their judgment on the facts for that of the agency?

13 Discuss the "substantial evidence on the record as a whole" concept and illustrate its application.

14 Name four administrative agencies of your state and local governments and indicate the primary role or function of each.

Chapter Eight

The Regulation of Business Activity

1   INTRODUCTION

Much of the legal environment of business consists of laws regulating and taxing business. The legislative and executive branches of government are actively engaged in the promulgation and execution of laws which regulate and control business activity and the economy. Much of this regulation is in the hands of administrative agencies who exercise rule-making, enforcing, and quasi-judicial powers. The determination of the legality of all regulatory activities is a problem for the courts. As a practical matter, then, all branches of government are actively engaged in placing limitations on business activity.

This chapter will discuss the nature of the power of Federal, state, and local governments to regulate commerce in general. Subsequent chapters deal with the tax power and single out for specific treatment some of the more important aspects of the legal environment of business, primarily in the areas of government regulation of competition, employment, and labor-management relations.

The power of the Federal government to regulate business activity is found in the so-called "commerce clause" of the Constitution. The commerce clause states one of the powers of Congress. Its interpretation and application are the primary issues discussed in this chapter.

The regulatory activities of the state governments are based on the "police power," which is the inherent power to control persons and property within the jurisdiction of the state for the purpose of promoting the general welfare. General welfare includes the public health, safety, and morals. The police power of the states was reserved to them by the Constitution and is vested in the legislatures, which have delegated portions of the power to municipalities. The United States has no general police power, but it has comparable authority to make laws which are necessary and proper for the exercise of any of the specific enumerated powers granted to it by the states in the Constitution. Thus, actions taken by the Federal government may not be objected to on the ground that they are an exercise of police power if they are an implementation of another power such as the regulation of commerce.

This chapter, in addition to discussing the Federal power to regulate commerce and the state police power, will discuss conflicts between these powers. It will also deal with some of the constitutional limitations on the exercise of these powers.

2 THE COMMERCE CLAUSE: FOREIGN COMMERCE

Article I, Section 8 of the Constitution provides that "Congress shall have Power . . . To regulate Commerce with foreign Nations, and among the several States, and with the Indian Tribes. . . ." Though the Constitution enumerates the powers of the Federal government, it does not define the terms used. Therefore, it was left to the courts to construe and define the power to regulate commerce. Chief Justice Marshall in *Gibbons v. Ogden*,[1] defining the power, said: "It is the power to regulate; that is, to prescribe the rules by which commerce is to be governed."

The commerce clause must be divided into its three component parts for understanding, i.e., the regulation of foreign commerce, the regulation of interstate commerce, and the regulation of commerce with the Indian tribes. This last power is relatively unimportant, although Congress is responsible for the laws applicable to Indian reservations. Commerce with the Indian tribes will not be discussed further, but foreign and interstate commerce will be treated in detail.

Chief Justice Marshall in *Gibbons v. Ogden, supra,* held that the power to regulate foreign commerce was vested exclusively in the Federal government and that it extended to all aspects of foreign trade. He stated in part:

Commerce, undoubtedly, is traffic, but it is something more—it is intercourse. . . . The word . . . comprehends . . . a power to regulate navigation. . . . The Constitution . . . comprehend[s] every species of commercial intercourse between the United States and foreign nations. No sort of trade can be carried on between this country and any other, to which this power does not extend. . . .
. . . [I]n regulating commerce with foreign nations, the power of Congress does not stop at the jurisdictional lines of the several states. It would be a very useless power, if it could not pass those lines. The commerce of the United States with foreign nations, is that of the whole United States; every district has a right to participate in it. The deep streams which penetrate our country in every direction, pass through the interior of almost every state in the Union, and furnish the means of exercising this right. If Congress has the power to regulate it, that power must be exercised whenever the subject exists. If it exists within the states, if a foreign voyage may commence or terminate at a port within a state, then the power of Congress may be exercised within a state. . . .
The power of Congress, then, whatever it may be, must be exercised within the territorial jurisdiction of the several states. . . .
The power over commerce with foreign nations, and among the several states, is vested in Congress as absolutely as it would be in a single government, having in its constitution the same restrictions on the exercise of the power as are found in the Constitution of the United States.

Notwithstanding this pronouncement, state and local governments frequently attempt directly or indirectly to regulate foreign commerce to some degree. The case which follows is typical of such cases.

22 U.S. (9 Wheat.) 1 (1824).

City of Columbus v. McGuire
195 N.E.2d 916 (Ohio, 1971)

The defendant was charged with violating a city ordinance which required persons who offered for sale merchandise from Communist countries to purchase and post a license authorizing the proprietor to sell such goods and to label them as to country of origin. Defendant alleged that the ordinance was unconstitutional under the commerce clause as an attempt to regulate foreign commerce. The defendant had sold baskets labeled "Made in Yugoslavia" without complying with the ordinance.

GILLIE, JUSTICE: . . . The leading case on importing and sale of foreign goods is *Brown v. Maryland*, 12 Wheat. 419, (decided in 1827).

A statute of the State of Maryland required all importers of foreign goods and all other persons selling the same by wholesale, bale or package, to take out a license to so import and/or sell, and pay therefore the sum of $50.00

The United States Supreme Court held that the Maryland statute was repugnant to the provisions of the Constitution with reference to laying an impost or duty on imports and regulating commerce with foreign nations.

In the decision in the *Brown v. Maryland* case, the Court said,

There is no difference, in effect, between a power to prohibit the sale of an article, and a power to prohibit its introduction into the country. The one would be a necessary consequence of the other. No goods would be imported if none could be sold. . . .

Brown v. Maryland set the rules for general application in the field of importing and selling foreign goods. Some of these are:

1 The commerce clause in the U.S. Constitution gives Congress the exclusive right to regulate commerce with foreign nations.
2 State or local laws regulating or interfering with federal regulation of commerce with foreign nations violate the Constitution and are invalid.
3 The right to import includes the right to sell the goods imported.
4 Federal regulatory power ceases as soon as the foreign goods become mixed or mingled with the mass of property in the country.

Since the *Brown v. Maryland* decision, commerce has undergone many far-reaching changes. The "complex society" to which Chief Justice Marshall referred in the opinion has utterly transcended in complexity the world of 1827. Federal and State courts at every level have rendered a flood of decisions on all aspects of commerce and the commerce clause.

Certain elements converge to form the decision herein. The cases permissible within the area of our inquiry come under three general headings:

Retail Sales

. . . [T]he commerce clause has been found to reserve to federal authority several types of retail transactions. . . .

[T]he exclusive power of regulation of foreign and interstate commerce goes beyond the handling of goods by importers and wholesalers.

Discriminatory Legislation

A long line of cases has been compiled in which statutes and ordinances based upon selective criteria have been held to conflict with the commerce clause.

Welton v. Missouri, 91 U.S. 275, reads in part, as follows:

The power which insures uniformity of commercial regulation must cover the property which is transported as an article of commerce from hostile or interfering legislation, until it has mingled with and become a part of the general property of the country, and subjected like it to similar protection, and to no greater burdens.

. . . *[We] hold now that the commercial power continues until the commodity has ceased to be the subject of discriminating legislation by reason of its foreign character.* That power protects it, even after it has entered the State, from any burdens imposed by reason of its foreign origin. . . .

Effect of Operation

In passing upon the validity of legislation the courts have long observed the necessity of ascertaining the total effect or result the law has or will have in operation. . . . The Court finds those set forth herein with reference to the relationship between the commerce clause of the United States Constitution and retail trade, the prohibition against laws which discriminate against foreign or interstate commerce, and the necessity of considering the effect in operation of any statute or ordinance tested, to be the compelling law on the subject.

Brown v. Maryland laid the foundation, pointed the direction, and left the way open for the future. In declaring the commerce clause a protection of the importer not only to import, but also to sell the Supreme Court used the argument . . . : "If this power reaches the interior of a State, and may be there exercised, it must be capable of authorizing the sale of those articles which it introduces. Commerce is intercourse; one of its most ordinary ingredients is traffic. It is inconceivable that the power to authorize this traffic, when given in the most comprehensive terms, with the intent that its efficacy should be complete, should cease at the point when its continuance is indispensable to its value. . . . Any charge on the introduction and incorporation of the articles into and with the mass of property in the country, must be hostile to the power given to Congress to regulate commerce, since an essential part of that regulation, and principal object of it, is to prescribe the regular means for accomplishing that introduction and incorporation."

The prosecution contends that the ordinance in question is simply a requirement that goods be identified for purchasers as to origin and the rest of the law an implementation of this purpose. In this identification, for special treatment, whether as products of Communist countries or any other, or as products of different States of the Union, lies the problem. The addition of a financial burden drives the point home with clarity.

Citizens of the United States tend to dislike, distrust, fear or shun the ideology of Communism, Communists, and the nations which embrace Communism as a form of government and philosophy. Hence, the ordinance requiring persons who offer for sale merchandise from Communist countries to post a license conspicuously authorizing the proprietor to sell Communist manufactured or processed goods, a sign announcing the fact that Communist goods are sold in the establishment or conspicuous labels on all such merchandise, would adversely affect the trade in these items.

In addition, the requirement that the merchant pay the license fee would reduce his profit from the sale of the merchandise. Selling less or none of such goods, the retail merchant will buy less or none such. This process spread even throughout this city imposes an obstacle across the flow of commerce such as is contemplated and prohibited by Article I, Section 8, of the United States Constitution. Thus frustrated, the stream of commerce stops. A regulation of commerce with foreign nations has been effected.

The ordinance thus stigmatizes the merchant and places a financial burden upon his handling of goods from the nations mentioned. To refer once again to *Brown v. Maryland,* "It is inconceivable that the power to authorize this traffic, when given in the most comprehensive terms, with the intent that its efficacy should be complete, should cease at the point when its continuance is indispensable to its value."

Seemingly, a convenient line of demarcation between foreign and local commerce is at the point at which the importer or wholesaler has disposed of items of commerce to retail dealers in local communities. Ordinarily, and for general purposes, this is a logical conclusion. Here, however, the ordinance in question specifically sets certain items of merchandise apart by reason of their foreign origin.

. . . [T]he City Code itself builds the wall which prevents the goods specified from being or becoming an indistinguishable part of the mass of property of the country or State. The ordinance by its terms recognizes the continued status of the merchandise as being in and part of commerce with a foreign nation.

This Court is not desirous of assisting any nation or person who would destroy this country politically, militarily, or economically. The within opinion is not and cannot be based on any foundation or reason other than those found in the constitutional law of the United States and the State of Ohio.

There is ample ground for action tending to thwart Communist aims by every available means. In the process, however, constitutional government must be not only maintained, but strengthened by the proper use of its powers. It is, therefore, with a sense of solemn responsibility that this Court has approached and determined the issue brought to bar.

The Court finds Sections 536.01 through 536.99 of the Columbus City Code violative of Article I, Section 8, of the United States Constitution and hence unconstitutional and invalid. Defendant's motion to quash the affidavit herein is well taken and is sustained. [AFFIDAVIT DISMISSED]

3   THE COMMERCE CLAUSE: INTERSTATE COMMERCE

In *Gibbons v. Ogden, supra,* Justice Marshall also had occasion to discuss the power to regulate commerce "among the several states." In holding that it was the power to regulate *inter*state commerce and not the power to regulate wholly *intra*state commerce, he noted:

The word "among" means intermingled with. A thing which is among others is intermingled with them. Commerce among the states, cannot stop at the external boundary line of each state, but may be introduced into the interior. It is not intended to say, that these words comprehend that (type of) commerce, which is completely internal, which is carried on between man and man in a state, or between different parts of the same state, and which does not extend to or affect other states. Such a power would be inconvenient, and is certainly unnecessary. Comprehensive as the word "among" is, it may very properly be restricted to that commerce which concerns more states than one. . . . The genius and character of the whole government seem to be, that its action is to be applied to all the external concerns of the nation, and to those internal concerns which affect the states generally; but not to those which are completely within a particular state, which do not affect other states, and with which it is not necessary to interfere, for the purpose of executing some of the general powers of the government. The completely internal commerce of a state, then, may be considered as reserved for the state itself.

Subsequent to *Gibbons v. Ogden*, there have been many cases further defining the power to regulate interstate commerce. These cases have expanded the commerce clause to encompass intrastate activities which have a substantial effect on interstate commerce. This effect may be negative or positive in the sense that the activity encourages interstate commerce or hinders it. The cases which follow in this section illustrate the extent of the power of Congress to regulate interstate commerce today.

Before turning to these cases, we should note that not all business or commercial activity is "commerce." For example, it has been held that the activity of accrediting institutions of higher learning is not commerce. Professional baseball has repeatedly been held to be a "sport" and not a business, but other professional sports have been held to be businesses and subject to Federal laws regulating business activity. As a practical matter, the trend is to consider that almost every business activity is a part of commerce, but there are still some noncommercial pursuits.

Subject to other constitutional restraints, such as those contained in the Bill of Rights, the net effect of the decisions construing the Federal power over commerce has been to make the power almost illimitable. The Supreme Court still indicates that some matters are exclusively local, but it is progressively more difficult to identify such areas. The Supreme Court's policy of aiding the development of a strong central government and fostering and encouraging regulation of activities which, while local in nature, have some effect on the country as a whole has given the Federal government powers not even dreamed of by the framers of the Constitution. Those in favor of such power laud the Court as being realistic and sensitive to the needs of the country growing out of changing conditions. Those opposed harshly criticize the Court's interpretations as aborting the original purpose and true meaning of the Constitution. Despite heated controversy on the matter, the power of the central government over commerce does extend to activities which are local in nature.

Burke v. Ford
88 S.Ct. 443 (1967)

PER CURIAM. Petitioners, Oklahoma liquor retailers, brought this action under § 1 of the Sherman Act to enjoin an alleged state-wide market division by all Oklahoma liquor wholesalers. The trial judge, sitting without a jury, found that there had in fact been a division of markets—both by territories and by brands. The court nevertheless entered judgment for the wholesalers because, among other reasons, it found that the interstate commerce prerequisite of the Sherman Act was not satisfied. The Court of Appeals affirmed upon the sole ground that "the proof was entirely insufficient to show that the activities complained of were in or adversely affected interstate commerce."

There are no liquor distilleries in Oklahoma. Liquor is shipped in from other States to the warehouses of the wholesalers, where it is inventoried and held until purchased by retailers. The District Court and the Court of Appeals found that the liquor "came to rest" in the wholesalers' warehouses and that interstate commerce ceased at that point. Hence, they concluded that the wholesalers' division of the Oklahoma market did not take place "in interstate commerce." But whatever the validity of that conclusion, it does not end the matter. For it is well established that an activity which does not itself occur *in* interstate commerce comes within the scope of the Sherman Act if it substantially *affects* interstate commerce.

Recognizing this, the District Court went on to find that the wholesalers' market division had no effect on interstate commerce, and the Court of Appeals agreed. The Court of Appeals held that proof of a state-wide wholesalers' market division in the distribution of goods retailed in substantial volume within the State but produced entirely out of the State was not by itself sufficient proof of an effect on interstate commerce. We disagree. Horizontal territorial divisions almost invariably reduce competition among the participants. When competition is reduced, prices increase and unit sales decrease. The wholesalers' territorial division here almost surely resulted in fewer sales to retailers—hence fewer purchases from out-of-state distillers—than would have occurred had free competition prevailed among the wholesalers. In addition the wholesalers' division of brands meant fewer wholesale outlets available to any one out-of-state distiller. Thus the state-wide wholesalers' market division inevitably affected interstate commerce. . . . [JUDGMENT OF COURT OF APPEALS REVERSED AND CASE REMANDED]

Maryland v. Wirtz
88 S.Ct. 2017 (1968)

By amendments enacted in 1961 and 1966, the coverage of the Fair Labor Standards Act was extended to include state hospitals, institutions, and schools. The State of Maryland sought to enjoin enforcement of the act, contending that its application to states was unconstitutional.

HARLAN, JUSTICE: . . . The plaintiffs argued that the expansion of coverage through the "enterprise concept" was beyond the power of Congress under the Commerce Clause. They contended that coverage of state-operated hospitals and schools was also beyond the commerce power. Finally, they urged that even if their constitutional arguments were rejected, the court should declare that schools and hospitals, as enterprises, do not have the statutorily required relationship to interstate commerce. . . .

We turn first to the adoption in 1961 of the "enterprise concept." Whereas the Act originally extended to every employee "who is engaged in commerce or in the production of goods for commerce," it now protects every employee who "is employed in an enterprise engaged in commerce or in the production of goods for commerce." Such an enterprise is defined as one which, along with other qualifications, "has employees engaged in commerce or in the production of goods for commerce . . . ." Thus the effect of the 1961 change was to extend protection to the fellow employees of any employee who would have been protected by the original Act, but not to enlarge the class of employ*ers* subject to the Act.

In *United States v. Darby*, 312 U.S. 100, this Court found the original Act a legitimate exercise of congressional power to regulate commerce among the States. Appellants accept the *Darby* decision, but contend that the extension of protection to fellow employees of those originally covered exceeds the commerce power. We conclude, to the contrary, that the constitutionality of the "enterprise concept" is settled by the reasoning of *Darby* itself and is independently established by principles stated in other cases.

Darby involved employees who were engaged in producing goods for commerce. Their employer contended that since manufacturing is itself an intrastate activity, Congress had no power to regulate the wages and hours of manufacturing employees. The first step in the Court's answer was clear:

"[Congress may] by appropriate legislation regulate intrastate activities where they have a substantial effect on interstate commerce."

The next step was to discover whether such a "substantial effect" existed. Congress had found that substandard wages and excessive hours, when imposed on employees of a company shipping goods into other States, gave the exporting company an advantage over companies in the importing States. Having so found, Congress decided as a matter of policy that such an advantage in interstate competition was an "unfair" one, and one that had the additional undesirable effect of driving down labor conditions in the importing States. This Court was of course concerned only with the finding of a substantial effect on interstate competition, and not with the consequent policy decisions. In accepting the congressional finding, the Court followed principles of judicial review only recently rearticulated in *Katzenbach v. McClung*, 379 U.S. 294:

Of course, the mere fact that Congress has said when particular activity shall be deemed to affect commerce does not preclude further examination by this Court. But where we find that the legislators . . . have a rational basis for finding a chosen regulatory scheme necessary to the protection of commerce, our investigation is at an end.

There was obviously a "rational basis" for the logical inference that the pay and hours of production employees affect a company's competitive position.

The logical inference does not stop with production employees. When a company does an interstate business, its competition with companies elsewhere is affected by all its significant labor costs, not merely by the wages and hours of those employees who have physical contact with the goods in question. . . .

The "enterprise concept" is also supported by a wholly different line of analysis. In the original Act, Congress stated its finding that substandard labor conditions tended to lead to labor disputes and strikes, and that when such strife disrupted businesses involved in interstate commerce, the flow of goods in commerce was itself affected. Congress therefore chose to promote labor peace by regulation of subject matter, wages, and hours, out of which disputes frequently arise. This objective is particularly relevant where, as here, the enterprises in question are significant importers of goods from other States. . . .

Whether the "enterprise concept" is defended on the "competition" theory or on the "labor dispute" theory, it is true that labor conditions in businesses having only a few employees engaged in commerce or production may not affect commerce very much or very often. Appellants therefore contend that defining covered enterprises in terms of their employees is sometimes to permit "the tail to wag the dog." However, while Congress has in some instances left to the courts or to administrative agencies the task of determining whether commerce is affected in a particular instance, *Darby* itself recognized the power of Congress instead to declare that an entire class of activities affects commerce. The only question for the courts is then whether the class is "within the reach of the federal power." The contention that in Commerce Clause cases the courts have power to excise, as trivial, individual instances falling within a rationally defined class of activities has been put entirely to rest. The class of employers subject to the Act was not enlarged by the addition of the enterprise concept. The definition of that class is as rational now as it was when *Darby* was decided.

Appellants' second contention is that the commerce power does not afford a constitutional basis for extension of the Act to schools and hospitals operated by the States or their subdivisions. Since the argument is made in terms of interference with "sovereign state functions," it is important to note exactly what the Act does. . . . The Act establishes only a minimum wage and a maximum limit of hours unless overtime wages are paid, and does not otherwise affect the way in which school and hospital duties are performed. Thus appellants' characterization of the question in this case as whether Congress may, under the guise of the commerce power, tell the States how to perform medical and educational functions is not factually accurate. Congress has "interfered with" these state functions only to the extent of providing that when a State employs people in performing such functions it is subject to the same restrictions as a wide range of other employers whose activities affect commerce, including privately operated schools and hospitals.

It is clear that labor conditions in schools and hospitals can affect commerce. The facts stipulated in this case indicate that such institutions are major users of goods imported from other States. . . . Strikes and work stoppages involving employees of schools and hospitals, events which unfortunately are not infrequent, obviously interrupt and burden this flow of goods across state lines. It is therefore clear that a "rational basis" exists for congressional action prescribing minimum labor standards for schools and hospitals, as for other importing enterprises.

Indeed, appellants do not contend that labor conditions in all schools and hospitals are without the reach of the commerce power, but only that the Act may not be constitutionally applied to state-operated institutions because that power must yield to state sovereignty in the performance of governmental functions. This argument simply is not tenable. There is no

[general] doctrine implied in the Federal Constitution that the two governments, national and state, are each to exercise its powers so as not to interfere with the free and full exercise of the powers of the other.

In the first place, it is clear that the Federal Government, when acting within a delegated power, may override countervailing state interests whether these be described as "governmental" or "proprietary" in character. . . . [T]he federal power over commerce is "superior to that of the States to provide for the welfare or necessities of their inhabitants."

There remains, of course, the question whether any particular statute is an "otherwise valid regulation of commerce." This Court has always recognized that the power to regulate commerce though broad indeed, has limits. . . . Mr. Chief Justice Hughes, . . . put the matter thus:

[T]he subject of federal power is still "commerce," and not all commerce but commerce with foreign nations and among the several states. The expansion of enterprise has vastly increased the interests of interstate commerce, but the constitutional differentiation still obtains.

The Court has ample power to prevent what the appellants purport to fear, "the utter destruction of the State as a sovereign political entity."

But while the commerce power has limits, valid general regulations of commerce do not cease to be regulations of commerce because a State is involved. If a State in engaging in economic activities that are validly regulated by the Federal Government when engaged in by private persons, the State too may be forced to conform its activities to federal regulation. . . .

This Court has examined and will continue to examine federal statutes to determine whether there is a rational basis for regarding them as regulations of commerce among the States. But it will not carve up the commerce power to protect enterprises indistinguishable in their effect on commerce from private businesses, simply because those enterprises happen to be run by the States for the benefit of their citizens. . . .

Appellants' remaining contention presents similar problems. In order to be covered by the Act, an employer hospital or school must in fact have

employees engaged in commerce or in the production of goods for commerce, including employees handling, selling, or otherwise working on goods that have been moved in or produced for commerce by any person. . . . 29 U.S.C. § 203(s).

Appellants ask us to declare that hospitals and schools simply have no such employees. The word "goods" is elsewhere defined to exclude "goods after their delivery into the actual physical possession of the ultimate consumer thereof other than a producer, manufacturer, or processor thereof." 29 U.S.C. § 203(i). Appellants contend that hospitals and schools are the ultimate consumers of the out-of-state products they buy, and hence none of their employees handles "goods" in the statutory sense.

We think the District Court was correct in declining to decide, in the abstract and in general, whether schools and hospitals have employees engaged in commerce or production. Such institutions, as a whole, obviously purchase a vast range of out-of-state commodities. These are put to a wide variety of uses, presumably ranging from physical incorporation of building materials into hospital and school structures, to over-the-counter sale for cash to patients, visitors, students, and teachers. . . . [AFFIRMED]

Perez v. United States
91 S.Ct. 1357 (1971)

The defendant was convicted of violating the "loan sharking" provisions of the Federal Consumer Credit Protection Act. It was proved beyond any doubt that the defendant as a part of organized crime had used extortion in collecting illegal rates of interest. He challenged the constitutionality of the statute on the ground that Congress has no power to control the local activity of loan sharking.

DOUGLAS, JUSTICE: . . . The constitutional question is a substantial one. . . .

The Commerce Clause reaches in the main three categories of problems. First, the use of channels of interstate or foreign commerce which Congress deems are being misused, as for example, the shipment of stolen goods or of persons who have been kidnapped. Second, protection of the instrumentalities of interstate commerce, as for example, the destruction of an aircraft, or persons or things in commerce, as for example, thefts from interstate shipments. Third, those activities affecting commerce. It is with this last category that we are here concerned.

Chief Justice Marshall in *Gibbons v. Ogden*, 9 Wheat. 1, 195, 6 L.Ed. 23, said:

The genius and character of the whole government seems to be, that its action is to be applied to all the external concerns of the nation, and to those internal concerns which affect the states generally; but not to those which are completely within a particular state, which do not affect other states, and with which it is not necessary to interfere, for the purpose of executing some of the general powers of the government. The completely internal commerce of a state, then, may be considered as reserved for the state itself. . . .

Chief Justice Stone wrote for a unanimous Court in 1942 that Congress could provide for the regulation of the price of intrastate milk, the sale of which, in competition with interstate milk, affects the price structure and federal regulation of the latter. The commerce power, he said, "extends to those activities intrastate which so affect interstate commerce, or the exertion of the power of Congress over it, as to make regulation of them appropriate means to the attainment of a legitimate end, the effective execution of the granted power to regulate interstate commerce."

Wickard v. Filburn, 317 U.S. 111, soon followed in which a unanimous Court held that wheat grown wholly for home consumption was constitutionally within the scope of federal regulation of wheat production because, though never marketed interstate, it supplied the need of the grower which otherwise would be satisfied by his purchases in the open market. We said:

. . . even if appellee's activity be local and though it may not be regarded as commerce, it may still, whatever its nature, be reached by Congress if it exerts a substantial economic effect on interstate commerce, and this irrespective of whether such effect is what might at some earlier time have been defined as 'direct' or 'indirect.' 317 U.S., at 125.

As pointed out in *United States v. Darby*, 312 U.S. 100, the decision sustaining an Act of Congress which prohibited the employment of workers in the production of goods "for interstate commerce" at other than prescribed wages and hours—*a class of activities*—was held properly regulated by Congress without proof that the particular intrastate activity against which a sanction was laid had an effect on commerce. A unanimous Court said:

> . . . *Congress has sometimes left it to the courts to determine whether the intrastate activities have the prohibited effect on the commerce, as in the Sherman Act. It has sometimes left it to an administrative board or agency to determine whether the activities sought to be regulated or prohibited have such effect, as in the case of the Interstate Commerce Act, and the National Labor Relations Act, or whether they come within the statutory definition of the prohibited Act, as in the Federal Trade Commission Act. And sometimes Congress itself has said that a particular activity affects the commerce, as it did in the present Act, the Safety Appliance Act and the Railway Labor Act. In passing on the validity of legislation of the class last mentioned the only function of courts is to determine whether the particular activity regulated or prohibited is within the reach of the federal power.*

That case is particularly relevant here because it involved a criminal prosecution, a unanimous Court holding that the Act was "sufficiently definite to meet constitutional demands." Petitioner is clearly *a member of the class* which engages in "extortionate credit transactions" as defined by Congress and the description of that class has the required definiteness.

It was the "class of activities" test which we employed in Heart of Atlanta Motel, Inc. v. United States, 379 U.S. 241, to sustain an Act of Congress requiring hotel or motel accommodations for Negro guests. The Act declared that " 'any inn, hotel, motel, or other establishment which provides lodging to transient guests' affects commerce *per se*." That exercise of power under the Commerce Clause was sustained.

> . . . *our people have become increasingly mobile with millions of people of all races traveling from State to State; that Negroes in particular have been the subject of discrimination in transient accommodations, having to travel great distances to secure the same; that often they have been unable to obtain accommodations and have had to call upon friends to put them up overnight . . . and that these conditions had become so acute as to require the listing of available lodging for Negroes in a special guidebook. . . .*

In a companion case, *Katzenbach v. McClung*, 379 U.S. 294, we ruled on the constitutionality of the restaurant provision of the same Civil Rights Act which regulated the restaurant "if . . . it serves or offers to serve interstate travelers or a substantial portion of the food which it serves . . . has moved in commerce." Apart from the effect on the flow of food in commerce to restaurants, we spoke of the restrictive effect of the exclusion of Negroes from restaurants on interstate travel by Negroes.

... there was an impressive array of testimony that discrimination in restaurants had a direct and highly restrictive effect upon interstate travel by Negroes. This resulted, it was said, because discriminatory practices prevent Negroes from buying prepared food served on the premises while on a trip, except in isolated and unkempt restaurants and under most unsatisfactory and often unpleasant conditions. This obviously discourages travel and obstructs interstate commerce for one can hardly travel without eating. Likewise, it was said, that discrimination deterred professional, as well as skilled, people from moving into areas where such practices occurred and thereby caused industry to be reluctant to establish there.

In emphasis of our position that it was the *class of activities* regulated that was the measure, we acknowledged that Congress appropriately considered the "total incidence" of the practice on commerce.

Where the *class of activities* is regulated and that *class* is within the reach of federal power, the courts have no power "to excise, as trivial, individual instances" of the class.

Extortionate credit transactions, though purely intrastate, may in the judgment of Congress affect interstate commerce. In an analogous situation, Mr. Justice Holmes, speaking for a unanimous Court, said ". . . when it is necessary in order to prevent an evil to make the law embrace more than the precise thing to be prevented it may do so." . . .

In the setting of the present case there is a tie-in between local loan sharks and interstate crime.

The findings by Congress are quite adequate on that ground. . . .

"Even where extortionate credit transactions are purely intrastate in character, they nevertheless directly affect interstate and foreign commerce." . . .

It appears . . . that loan sharking in its national setting is one way organized interstate crime holds its guns to the heads of the poor and the rich alike and syphons funds from numerous localities in finance its national operations. [AFFIRMED]

4   STATE REGULATION OF COMMERCE: GENERAL PRINCIPLES

The grant of power over commerce to Congress does not contain any provision which expressly excludes the states from exercising authority over commerce. The Supreme Court in *Cooley v. The Board of Wardens of Port of Philadelphia*[2] held that the nature of the commerce power did not by *implication* prohibit state action and that some state power over commerce is compatible with the Federal

[2] 53 U.S. 299 (1851).

power. Nevertheless there are definite limitations on the state powers over commerce because of the commerce clause.

The decisions of the Court have established three distinct subject areas of governmental regulation of commerce. Some areas are exclusively Federal, some are said to be exclusively local, and still others are such that regulation of them may be dual.

The subject area which is exclusively Federal, in addition to foreign commerce, pertains to those internal matters where uniformity on a nationwide basis is essential. Any state regulation of such subjects is void whether Congress has entered the field or not. In theory, those matters which are exclusively within the states' power are intrastate activities which do not have a substantial effect on interstate commerce. As previously noted, it is becoming more and more difficult, if not impossible, to find a subject matter which is truly exclusively local in the sense that it does not affect interstate commerce.

The third subject area between the above two extremes, where joint regulation is permissible, can be divided into three subparts. The first concerns those subjects over which the Federal government has preempted the field by express language or by comprehensive regulation showing an intent by Congress to exercise exclusive dominion over the subject matter. When a Federal statute has thus preempted the field, *any* state or local law pertaining to the same subject matter is unconstitutional under the commerce clause, and the state regulation is void. Absent the statute, however, the subject matter involved is of such a nature that state regulation could constitutionally exist. Second, in the area of possible joint regulation there may be some Federal regulation of a subject matter which is not comprehensive enough to preempt the field. Here state regulation is permitted, but when state law is inconsistent or in conflict with the Federal statute, it is unconstitutional and void. In addition, state laws are invalid if they discriminate against interstate commerce or impose an undue burden on it. Third, when no Federal statute exists, state regulation of interstate commerce is permissible, providing, of course, that it does not discriminate against interstate commerce in favor of local business and does not impose an undue burden on interstate commerce. Constitutional limitations, such as guarantees of due process, of equal protection of the laws, and of the basic freedoms in the Bill of Rights, in addition to other constitutional restraints, provide restrictions on both the Federal and state powers to regulate commerce.

While Federal statutes regulating commerce are enacted directly under the commerce clause, state laws are enacted pursuant to either the inherent police power or the taxing power, since the state government does not possess any commerce power as such. The police power has been defined as the power to enact laws protecting and promoting the public health, safety, morals, and general welfare. Conflicts between the state police power or taxing power and the commerce clause have resulted in extensive litigation. In the sections which follow, the cases will illustrate the foregoing principles and the extent of the use of the police power by states to regulate business activity.

5 STATE REGULATION AND THE COMMERCE CLAUSE

A THE AREA OF EXCLUSIVE FEDERAL CONTROL

As previously indicated, some matters are of such a character that their attempted regulation by states under the police power is unconstitutional. These are usually subjects where national uniformity is essential if there is to be any regulation at all. Frequently, the Federal government has taken no action with regard to a particular activity, but this fact does not necessarily allow the states to legislate on it. The case which follows is illustrative of a situation in which state regulation is not permissible.

Southern Pac. R.R. v. Arizona
325 U.S. 761 (1945)

Arizona enacted a statute which limited the length of passenger trains to fourteen cars and the length of freight trains to seventy cars. It was passed under the police power as a safety measure. The Southern Pacific Railroad challenged the constitutionality of the law under the commerce clause of the Federal Constitution. The Supreme Court of Arizona held the state law constitutional, and Southern Pacific appealed to the United States Supreme Court.

STONE, CHIEF JUSTICE: . . . Although the commerce clause conferred on the national government power to regulate commerce, its possession of the power does not exclude all state power of regulation. It has been recognized that, in the absence of conflicting legislation by Congress, there is a residuum of power in the state to make laws governing matters of local concern which nevertheless in some measure affect interstate commerce or even, to some extent, regulate it. . . . Thus the states may regulate matters which, because of their number and diversity, may never be adequately dealt with by Congress. . . . When the regulation of matters of local concern is local in character and effect, and its impact on the national commerce does not seriously interfere with its operation, and the consequent incentive to deal with them nationally is slight, such regulation has been generally held to be within state authority. . . .

But ever since *Gibbons v. Ogden,* 9 Wheat. 1, the states have not been deemed to have authority to impede substantially the free flow of commerce from state to state, or to regulate those phases of the national commerce which, because of the need of national uniformity, demand that their regulation, if any, be prescribed by a single authority. . . . Whether or not this long recognized distribution of power between the national and the state governments is predicated upon the implications of the commerce clause itself, or upon the presumed intention of Congress, where Congress has not spoken, . . . the result is the same.

In the application of these principles some enactments may be found to be plainly within and others plainly without state power. But between these extremes lies the infinite variety of cases in which regulation of local matters may also operate as a regulation of commerce, in which reconciliation of the conflicting claims of state and national power is to be attained only by some appraisal and accommodation of the competing demands of the state and national interests involved. . . .

For a hundred years it has been accepted constitutional doctrine that the commerce clause, without the aid of Congressional legislation, thus affords some protection from state legislation inimical to the national commerce, and that in such cases, where Congress has not acted, this Court, and not the state legislature, is under the commerce clause the final arbiter of the competing demands of state and national interests. . . .

Congress has undoubted power to redefine the distribution of power over interstate commerce. It may either permit the states to regulate the commerce in a manner which would otherwise not be permissible, . . . or exclude state regulation even of matters of peculiarly local concern. . . .

But in general Congress has left it to the courts to formulate the rules thus interpreting the commerce clause in its application, doubtless because it has appreciated the destructive consequences to the commerce of the nation if their protection were withdrawn, . . . and has been aware that in their application state laws will not be invalidated without the support of relevant factual material which will "afford a sure basis" for an informed judgment. . . . Meanwhile, Congress has accommodated its legislation, as have the states, to these rules as an established feature of our constitutional system. There has thus been left to the states wide scope for the regulation of matters of local state concern, even though it in some measure affects the commerce, provided it does not materially restrict the free flow of commerce across state lines, or interfere with it in matters with respect to which uniformity of regulation is of predominant national concern.

Hence the matters for ultimate determination here are the nature and extent of the burden which the state regulation of interstate trains, adopted as a safety measure, imposes on interstate commerce, and whether the relative weights of the state and national interests involved are such as to make inapplicable the rule, generally observed, that the free flow of interstate commerce and its freedom from local restraints in matters requiring uniformity of regulation are interests safeguarded by the commerce clause from state Interference. . . .

The findings show that the operation of long trains, that is trains of more than fourteen passenger and more than seventy freight cars, is standard practice over the main lines of the railroads of the United States, and that, if the length of trains is to be regulated at all, national uniformity in the regulation adopted, such as only Congress can prescribe, is practically indispensable to the operation of an efficient and economical national railway system. . . .

The unchallenged findings leave no doubt that the Arizona Train Limit Law imposes a serious burden on the interstate commerce conducted by appellant. It materially impedes the movement of appellant's interstate trains through that state and interposes a substantial obstruction to the national policy proclaimed by Congress, to promote adequate, economical and efficient railway transportation service. . . . The serious impediment to the free flow of commerce by the local regulation of train lengths and the practical necessity that such regulation, if any, must be prescribed by a single body having a nation-wide authority are apparent. . . .

The principle that, without controlling Congressional action, a state may not regulate interstate commerce so as substantially to affect its flow or deprive it of needed uniformity in its regulation is not to be avoided by "simply invoking the convenient apologetics of the police power." . . .

Here we conclude that the state does go too far. Its regulation of train lengths, admittedly obstructive to interstate train operation, and having a seriously adverse effect on transportation efficiency and economy, passes beyond what is plainly essential for safety since it does not appear that it will lessen rather than increase the danger of accident. Its attempted regulation of the operation of interstate trains cannot establish nation-wide control such as is essential to the maintenance of an efficient transportation system, which Congress alone can prescribe. The state interest cannot be preserved at the expense of the national interest by an enactment which regulates interstate train lengths without securing such control, which is a matter of national concern. To this the interest of the state here asserted is subordinate. . . . Here examination of all the relevant factors makes it plain that the state interest is outweighed by the interest of the nation in an adequate, economical, and efficient railway transportation service, which must prevail. [REVERSED]

In the following case the defendant raised the argument that a regulation by the city of Detroit requiring certain equipment on a ship which operated in interstate commerce was void, because if such requirements were to exist at all, they would have to be uniform nationwide. This case illustrates that many subjects do not require national uniformity and that it is legal for a state to burden interstate commerce so long as the burden is not an undue one in the constitutional sense.

Huron Portland Cement Co. v. City of Detroit, Michigan
362 U.S. 440 (1960)

STEWART, JUSTICE: This appeal from a judgment of the Supreme Court of Michigan draws in question the constitutional validity of certain provisions of Detroit's Smoke Abatement Code as applied to ships owned by the appellant and operated in interstate commerce.

The appellant is a Michigan corporation, engaged in the manufacture and sale of cement. It maintains a fleet of five vessels which it uses to transport cement from its mill in Alpena, Michigan, to distributing plants located in various states bordering the Great Lakes. Two of the ships, the S. S. Crapo and the S. S. Boardman, are equipped with hand-fired Scotch marine boilers. While these vessels are docked for loading and unloading it is necessary, in order to operate deck machinery, to keep the boilers fired and to clean the fires periodically. When the fires are cleaned, the ship's boiler stacks emit smoke which in density and duration exceeds the maximum standards allowable under the Detroit Smoke Abatement Code. Structural alterations would be required in order to insure compliance with the Code.

Criminal proceedings were instituted in the Detroit Recorder's Court against the appellant and its agents for violations of the city law during periods when the vessels were docked at the Port of Detroit. The appellant brought an action in the State Circuit Court to enjoin the city from further prosecuting the pending litigation in the Recorder's Court, and from otherwise enforcing the smoke ordinance against its vessels, "except where the emission of smoke is caused by the improper firing or the improper use of the equipment upon said vessels." The Circuit Court refused to grant relief, and the Supreme Court of Michigan affirmed, 355 Mich. 227. . . .

In support of the claim that the ordinance cannot constitutionally be applied to appellant's ships, two basic arguments are advanced. First, it is asserted that since the vessels and their equipment, including their boilers, have been inspected, approved and licensed to operate in interstate commerce in accordance with a comprehensive system of regulation enacted by Congress, the City of Detroit may not legislate in such a way as, in effect, to impose additional or inconsistent standards. Secondly, the argument is made that even if Congress has not expressly pre-empted the field, the municipal ordinance "materially affects interstate commerce in matters where uniformity is necessary." We have concluded that neither of these contentions can prevail, and that the Federal Constitution does not prohibit application to the appellant's vessels of the criminal provisions of the Detroit ordinance.

The ordinance was enacted for the manifest purpose of promoting the health and welfare of the city's inhabitants. Legislation designed to free from pollution the very air that people breathe clearly falls within the exercise of even the most traditional concept of what is compendiously known as the police power. In the exercise of that power, the states and their instrumentalities may act, in many areas of interstate commerce and maritime activities, concurrently with the federal government. . . .

The basic limitations upon local legislative power in this area are clear enough. The controlling principles have been reiterated over the years in a host of this Court's decisions. Evenhanded local regulation to effectuate a legitimate local public interest is valid unless pre-empted by federal action . . . or unduly burdensome on maritime activities or interstate commerce. . . .

In determining whether state regulation has been pre-empted by federal action, "the intent to supersede the exercise by the state of its police power as to matters not covered by the Federal legislation is not to be inferred from the mere fact that Congress has seen fit to circumscribe its regulation and to occupy a limited field. In other words, such intent is not to be implied unless the act of Congress, fairly interpreted, is in actual conflict with the law of the state." . . .

In determining whether the state has imposed an undue burden on interstate commerce, it must be borne in mind that the Constitution when "conferring upon Congress the regulation of commerce, . . . never intended to cut the States off from legislating on all subjects relating to the health, life, and safety of their citizens, though the legislation might indirectly affect the commerce of the country. Legislation, in a great variety of ways, may affect commerce and persons engaged in it without constituting a regulation of it, within the meaning of the Constitution." . . . But a state may not impose a burden which materially affects interstate commerce in an area where uniformity of regulation is necessary. . . .

Although verbal generalizations do not of their own motion decide concrete cases, it is nevertheless within the framework of these basic principles that the issues in the present case must be determined. . . .

By contrast, the sole aim of the Detroit ordinance is the elimination of air pollution to protect the health and enhance the cleanliness of the local community. . . . Congressional recognition that the problem of air pollution is peculiarly a matter of state and local concern is manifest. . . .

We conclude that there is no overlap between the scope of the federal ship inspection laws and that of the municipal ordinance here involved. For this reason we cannot find that the federal inspection legislation has preempted local action. To hold otherwise would be to ignore the teaching of this Court's decisions which enjoin seeking out conflicts between state and federal regulation where none clearly exists. . . .

The mere possession of a federal license, however, does not immunize a ship from the operation of the normal incidents of local police power, not constituting a direct regulation of commerce. Thus, a federally licensed vessel is not, as such, exempt from local pilotage laws . . . or local quarantine laws . . . safety inspections . . . or the local regulation of wharves and docks. . . . Indeed this court has gone so far as to hold that a state, in the exercise of its police power, may actually seize and pronounce the forfeiture of a vessel "licensed for the coasting trade, under the laws of the United States, while engaged in that trade." *Smith v. Maryland,* 18 How. 71, 74. . . . The present case obviously does not even approach such an extreme, for the Detroit ordinance requires no more than compliance with an orderly and reasonable scheme of community regulation. The ordinance does not exclude a licensed vessel from the Port of Detroit, nor does it destroy the right of free passage. We cannot hold that the local regulation so burdens the federal license as to be constitutionally invalid.

The claim that the Detroit ordinance, quite apart from the effect of federal legislation, imposes as to the appellant's ships an undue burden on interstate commerce needs no extended discussion. State regulation, based on the police power, which does not discriminate against interstate commerce or operate to disrupt its required uniformity, may constitutionally stand. . . .

It has not been suggested that the local ordinance, applicable alike to "any person, firm or corporation" within the city, discriminates against interstate commerce as such. It is a regulation of general application, designed to better the health and welfare of the community. And while the appellant argues that other local governments might impose differing requirements as to air pollution, it has pointed to none. The record contains nothing to suggest the existence of any such competing or conflicting local regulations. . . .

We conclude that no impermissible burden on commerce has been shown. [JUDGMENT AFFIRMED]

B PREEMPTION AND CONFLICTS BETWEEN FEDERAL AND STATE LAWS

A matter that is not an exclusively Federal problem may become so as a result of legislation. When Federal laws completely occupy a field, they are said to "preempt" it. In such cases, the state legislatures may not legally take action under their police powers, and the Federal laws are said to be exclusive. If a state does legislate on the subject, such legislation is unconstitutional as a violation of the commerce clause. However, Federal laws regulating business are not deemed to have preempted an area and thereby excluded state regulation of it unless the nature of the regulated subject matter permits no other conclusion or Congress has unmistakably so ordained. Many Federal statutes contain specific provisions on the issue of preemption. For example, the Civil Rights Act of 1964 provides that its public accommodation provisions do not preempt the field.

Clearly, not every Federal law regulating an activity preempts the field and thereby precludes the state from legislating on the same subject. State regulations may exist on the same matter, but they must not be in conflict with the Federal laws because of the supremacy clause of the United States Constitution. Difficult questions as to whether a conflict exists often are presented to the courts when the validity of a state rule is challenged and there is also a Federal rule in the same area. In deciding these issues, the courts have set forth certain guidelines. First of all, the state law cannot stand as an obstacle to the accomplishment and execution of the full purposes and objectives of Congress. If it does so, the courts will hold either that the Federal law preempted the field or is in irreconcilable conflict with the state law. In either case, the state law is unconstitutional. Another key guideline is found in the examination of the purposes of both laws. If the objectives are virtually identical, then the courts attempt to reconcile the laws and enforce both. If the purposes are in conflict, chances are that the state law cannot be enforced.

Irreconcilable conflicts exist when it is not possible for a business to comply with both statutes. If compliance with both is not possible, the state law must fall under the supremacy clause.

The case which follows is a typical challenge on the grounds of preemption and irreconcilable conflict. In such cases, if the courts find that the Federal law preempts the field, then they need go no further and need not decide the conflict issue. If they find that the Federal law does not preempt the field, then a finding on the second issue is required.

Swift & Co. v. Wickham
364 F.2d 241 (1966)

Plaintiffs, packers of frozen stuffed turkeys processed outside New York brought a suit in the Federal district court to have regulations by New York's Commissioner of Agriculture and Markets declared unconstitutional. A Federal statute required only that turkeys be labeled to show the net weight of the stuffed bird. New York's labeling requirements included a showing of the net weight of the unstuffed turkey. New York threatened to stop the sale of the turkeys unless both the stuffed and unstuffed weights were shown. The packers contended that the Federal act preempted the field, or, in the alternative, that the statutes were in conflict and therefore the Federal law was supreme. The lower court dismissed plaintiffs' suit and they appealed.

LUMBARD, CHIEF JUDGE: . . .

Federal Preemption

Appellants contend that the Poultry Products Inspection Act is a "broad comprehensive system of inspection and regulation of poultry and products moving in interstate commerce," that the labeling portions of this lesiglation are an essential and integral part of the system, and that state laws additionally regulating the labeling of poultry products are therefore preempted. In treating this question, we begin with the Supreme Court's caution that, "[F]ederal regulation of a field of commerce should not be deemed preemptive of state regulatory power in the absence of persuasive reasons—either that the nature of the regulated subject matter permits no other conclusion or that Congress has unmistakably so ordained."

The lower court dealt exhaustively with the history and content of the federal Act and concluded that Congress had not preempted more detailed state regulation of the manner in which poultry products are weighed, measured and labeled. We find several reasons for agreeing with this conclusion. First, the principal focus of the federal law was to combat the distribution of adulterated poultry through a uniform scheme of federal inspection. We find no basis for concluding that Congress intended the incidental and less exhaustive labeling provisions to preempt this particular area of state regulation. Second, the Poultry Products Inspection Act's labeling provisions are similar to those in the federal Pure Food, Drug, and Cosmetic Act, which are not preemptive of state regulation. Finally, we find nothing in the nature of the subject matter being regulated—the disclosure of the net weight of poultry products—that requires a uniform national standard. We agree with the district court and with the *amicus* brief of the Department of Justice that the Poultry Products Inspection Act does not preempt state regulation of the area in question.

Direct Conflict with Federal Law

A more difficult question is whether an irreconcilable conflict has arisen between the Poultry Products Inspection Act and the New York Agriculture and Markets Act, as interpreted. Federal law prohibits the shipment of appellants' turkeys in interstate commerce without an approved label. It is not practicable to thaw the birds after shipment to New York and make a supplemental weighing and labeling in conformance with state law at that time. Since the federal authorities have rejected a label showing the multiple weights required by New York law, and since the state will not permit the sale of stuffed turkeys absent such a label, at least the seeds of conflict are present.

The district court nonetheless held that an irreconcilable conflict had not been established. Starting with the premise that New York would accept a supplemental label showing the multiple weights required, Judge Friendly then noted that nothing in the federal Act indicated that such an additional label was necessarily unlawful. Conceding that construction of the statutory phrase "net weight" was primarily a task for the Administrator, Judge Friendly nevertheless held that the Poultry Division's rejection of the particular labels submitted by Swift and Armour for approval in 1963 did not constitute a broad ruling "that any supplementary labeling of weight in addition to that satisfying the Department would be unlawful." Given this path to reconciliation of the statutory schemes, Judge Friendly concluded that appellants had not discharged their burden of establishing conflict because they had not sought a full-fledged hearing before the Administrator at which the State of New York's interests could be presented and perhaps satisfied.

Appellants' first argument is that, contrary to the assumption of the district court, New York would not permit the multiple weights it requires to be displayed on a supplemental label. Therefore, appellants conclude, even the district court would now hold the New York scheme unlawful because the federal law, as interpreted by the Poultry Division, does not permit the multiple weights to be shown on the principal label which bears the federal markings.

One answer to this contention is that there is insufficient evidence that New York would insist upon enforcing this regulation in the face of federal opposition. But a more fundamental problem with the argument is that it still assumes that the decision of the Poultry Division rejecting appellants' proposed "principal labels" should be accepted as representing the policy of the Department of Agriculture. Like the district court, we cannot accept this assumption in view of the appellants' failure to request a hearing at which the decision of the lower-echelon officials could be more fully explored.

Appellants attack this last aspect of the district court's decision by arguing that the Act gives the right to a hearing to one who "does not accept" the initial administrative ruling and therefore that it is improper to require them to appeal rulings which they "accept." But appellants only accept the Poultry Division's rulings for the purpose of challenging the "contrary" state regulation. While they cannot be compelled to appeal from these rulings, the strong policy against invalidating state regulatory schemes in the absence of a clear showing of irreconcilable conflict with federal law requires that this court not accept the Poultry Division's rulings without a further inquiry into their propriety.

Appellants argue that, for a number of reasons, this is an inappropriate case to require them to pursue additional remedies within the federal agency. We disagree. As the lower court pointed out, uniform and accurate weights and measures are a traditional subject of state regulation. There is nothing in the federal Act or regulations that either requires the rejection of New York's definition of "net weight" or that condemns a labeling scheme that satisfies both current administrative interpretations. The reasons given by the Poultry Division in its letters rejecting appellants' proposed labels do not necessarily indicate that the two administrative positions are in hopeless conflict. In addition, the Deputy Director of the Poultry Division, called as a witness for the plaintiffs, testified that his department has as yet made no attempt to "straighten out any alleged differences" with the New York authorities. We conclude that on this record the two legislative schemes have not been shown to be in irreconcilable conflict.

Accordingly, we affirm the order of the district court. At the same time we suggest that the administrative agencies involved in this controversy should seek to resolve this unsettled situation without delay. [AFFIRMED]

C   THE PROHIBITION AGAINST UNDUE BURDENS ON INTERSTATE COMMERCE

The commerce clause does not prohibit the imposing of burdens on interstate commerce—only the imposition of *undue* burdens. Every regulatory measure is a burden to some degree. The cases which follow illustrate both a constitutional and unconstitutional burden. Note that in the second case, the parties were actually concerned with the issue of integration versus segregation but litigated their dispute on the undue-burden issue.

Commonwealth v. New York Cent. R.R. Co.
216 N.E.2d 870 (Mass. 1966)

The New York Central Railroad was prosecuted for obstructing a railroad crossing for more than five minutes. Defendant's train had taken seven minutes to pass a crossing but it had not stopped. Defendant contended that the statute was not applicable to moving trains and if applicable, that it was unconstitutional as contravening the commerce clause of the United States Constitution. The defendant was found guilty, and he then appealed.

WILKINS, CHIEF JUSTICE: . . . We have no doubt that the statute is intended to apply to moving trains as well as stationary ones. . . .

There is no violation of art. 1, § 8, of the Constitution of the United States. "The interstate commerce clause did not withdraw from the states the power to legislate with respect to their local concerns, even though such legislation may indirectly and incidentally affect interstate commerce and persons engaged in it."

Nothing in *Southern Pac. Co. v. Arizona ex rel. Sullivan,* 325 U.S. 761, 65 S.Ct. 1515, 89 L.Ed. 1915, persuades us to reverse the court below and to reach a different result. In that case an Arizona statute made it unlawful to operate a passenger train of more than fourteen cars or a freight train of more than seventy cars. The majority opinion recognized that there remained a large area for State regulation: "There has thus been left to the states wide scope for the regulation of matters of local state concern, even though it in some measure affects the commerce, provided it does not materially restrict the free flow of commerce across state lines, or interfere with it in matters with respect to which uniformity of regulation is of predominant national concern. . . ."

It is a far different situation from the consequences of the Arizona statute which is presented by the Massachusetts legislation in the case at bar. The latter is not directed at interstate commerce. Its purpose is "the safety of the public . . . and convenient use of its highways." There is no limitation of speed nor any direct restriction imposed on the length of trains. There is no confusing dislocation of interstate commerce over a distance of more than a thousand miles such that from Los Angeles to El Paso. The Waverly Street crossing is on a branch, and not on a main line. The particular train at this crossing was composed of newly arrived individual cars put together by the defendant at a Framingham classification yard for brief movement to nearby unloading areas. There is nothing to show that such a train could not reasonably be moved over the crossing in five minutes. In short, there is presented a local problem without effect on national or interstate uniformity and in a field where uniformity is not necessary or desirable. This is not a case for voluntary abandonment of municipal regulation. This is a critical moment in the State's right of control over highways at railroad crossings. Rights surrendered now will not be reacquired. Local authorities would be seriously crippled in their duty to preserve the public safety and to keep their highways free of obstructions which they could not control if they should be deprived of the benefit of the reasonable protection of c. 160, § 151. Should this statute be struck down, trains might occupy crossings indefinitely leaving the highways in a continuing state of chaos. [EXCEPTIONS OVERRULED. APPEAL DISMISSED]

Morgan v. Virginia
328 U.S. 373 (1946)

A Virginia statute required separation of the races in common carriers engaged in both interstate and intrastate commerce. If contiguous seats were occupied by persons of different races, the carrier, its employees, and the passengers involved could be found guilty of a misdemeanor. A Negro was convicted of violating the statute when she refused to change her seat on the request of a bus driver. The defendant contended that the statute was unconstitutional as violating the commerce clause, and the state argued that the statute was a valid exercise of the police power.

REED, JUSTICE: . . . This Court frequently must determine the validity of state statutes that are attacked as unconstitutional interferences with the national power over interstate commerce. This appeal presents that question as to a statute that compels racial segregation of interstate passengers in vehicles moving interstate.

The precise degree of a permissible restriction on state power cannot be fixed generally or indeed not even for one kind of state legislation, such as taxation or health or safety. There is a recognized abstract principle, however, that may be taken as a postulate for testing whether particular state legislation in the absence of action by Congress is beyond state power. This is that the state legislation is invalid if it unduly burdens that commerce in matters where uniformity is necessary—necessary in the constitutional sense of useful in accomplishing a permitted purpose. Where uniformity is essential for the functioning of commerce, a state may not interpose its local regulation. Too true it is that the principle lacks in precision. Although the quality of such a principle is abstract, its application to the facts of a situation created by the attempted enforcement of a statute brings about a specific determination as to whether or not the statute in question is a burden on commerce. Within the broad limits of the principle, the cases turn on their own facts.

In the field of transportation, there have been a series of decisions which hold that where Congress has not acted and although the state statute affects interstate commerce, a state may validly enact legislation which has predominantly only a local influence on the course of commerce. It is equally well settled that, even where Congress has not acted, state legislation or a final court order is invalid which materially affects interstate commerce. Because the Constitution puts the ultimate power to regulate commerce in Congress, rather than the states, the degree of state legislation's interference with that commerce may be weighed by federal courts to determine whether the burden makes the statute unconstitutional. The courts could not invalidate federal legislation for the same reason because Congress, within the limits of the Fifth Amendment, has authority to burden commerce if that seems to it a desirable means of accomplishing a permitted end.

This statute is attacked on the ground that it imposes undue burdens on interstate commerce. It is said by the Court of Appeals to have been passed in the exercise of the state's police power to avoid friction between the races. But this Court pointed out years ago "that a state cannot avoid the operation of this rule by simply invoking the convenient apologetics of the police power." Burdens upon commerce are those actions of a state which directly "impair the usefulness of its facilities for such traffic." That impairment, we think, may arise from other causes than costs or long delays. A burden may arise from a state statute which requires interstate passengers to order their movements on the vehicle in accordance with local rather than national requirements.

On appellant's journey, this statute required that she sit in designated seats in Virginia. Changes in seat designation might be made "at any time" during the journey when "necessary or proper for the comfort and convenience of passengers." This occurred in this instance. Upon such change of designation, the statute authorizes the operator of the vehicle to require, as he did here, "any passenger to change his or her seat as it may be necessary or proper." An interstate passenger must if necessary repeatedly shift seats while moving in Virginia to meet the seating requirements of the changing passenger group. On arrival at the District of Columbia line, the appellant would have had freedom to occupy any available seat and so to the end of her journey.

Interstate passengers traveling via motors between the north and south or the east and west may pass through Virginia on through lines in the day or in the night. The large buses approach the comfort of pullmans and have seats convenient for rest. On such interstate journeys the enforcement of the requirements for reseating would be disturbing.

Appellant's argument, properly we think, includes facts bearing on interstate motor transportation beyond those immediately involved in this journey under the Virginia statutory regulations. To appraise the weight of the burden of the Virginia statute on interstate commerce, related statutes of other states are important to show whether there are cumulative effects which may make local regulation impracticable. Eighteen states, it appears, prohibit racial separation on public carriers. Ten require separation on motor carriers. Of these Alabama applies specifically to interstate passengers with an exception for interstate passengers with through tickets from states without laws on separation of passengers. The language of the other acts, like this Virginia statute before the Court of Appeals' decision in this case, may be said to be susceptible to an interpretation that they do or do not apply to interstate passengers.

In states where separation of races is required in motor vehicles, a method of identification as white or colored must be employed. This may be done by definition. Any ascertainable Negro blood identifies a person as colored for purposes of separation in some states. In the other states which require the separation of the races in motor carriers, apparently no definition generally applicable or made for the purposes of the statute is given. Court definition or further legislative enactments would be required to clarify the line between the races. Obviously there may be changes by legislation in the definition.

The interferences to interstate commerce which arise from state regulation of racial association on interstate vehicles has long been recognized. Such regulation hampers freedom of choice in selecting accommodations. The recent changes in transportation brought about by the coming of automobiles does not seem of great significance in the problem. People of all races travel today more extensively than in 1878 when this Court first passed upon state regulation of racial segregation in commerce. . . . Other federal courts have looked upon racial separation statutes as applied to interstate passengers as burdens upon commerce.

In weighing the factors that enter into our conclusion as to whether this statute so burdens interstate commerce or so infringes the requirements of national uniformity as to be invalid, we are mindful of the fact that conditions vary between northern or western states such as Maine or Montana, with practically no colored population; industrial states such as Illinois, Ohio, New Jersey and Pennsylvania with a small, although appreciable, percentage of colored citizens; and the states of the deep south with percentages of from twenty-five to nearly fifty per cent colored, all with varying densities of the white and colored race in certain localities. Local efforts to promote amicable relations in difficult areas by legislative segregation in interstate transportation emerge from the latter racial distribution. As no state law can reach beyond its own border nor bar transportation of passengers across its boundaries, diverse seating requirements for the races in interstate journeys result. As there is no federal act dealing with the separation of races in interstate transportation, we must decide the validity of this Virginia statute on the challenge it interferes with commerce, as a matter of balance between the exercise of the local police power and the need for national uniformity in the regulations for interstate travel. It seems clear to us that seating arrangements for the different races in interstate motor travel require a single, uniform rule to promote and protect national travel. Consequently, we hold the Virginia statute in controversy invalid. [REVERSED]

D   THE PROHIBITION OF DISCRIMINATION AGAINST INTERSTATE COMMERCE

Olan Mills, Inc. v. City of Barre
194 A.2d 385 (Vt. 1963)

Plaintiff, an Ohio corporation, brought suit to obtain a declaratory judgment that an ordinance requiring the licensing of itinerant photographers was unconstitutional as violating the commerce clause. The ordinance in question required itinerant photographers to file performance bonds and to pay license fees. License fees and bonds were not required of resident photographers. The lower court entered a decree adverse to plaintiff and plaintiff appealed.

SMITH, JUSTICE: . . . The plaintiff has briefed two issues for our consideration:

1   Does the manner in which plaintiff conducts its business in the City of Barre constitute interstate commerce?
2   If plaintiff, Olan Mills, Inc. of Ohio is engaged in interstate commerce, does the Barre City Itinerant Photographer's Ordinance unduly burden that commerce in violation of the commerce clause of the Federal Constitution? . . .

Interstate commerce has been defined by the United States Supreme Court as:

The negotiation of the sales of goods which are in another state, for the purpose of introducing them into the state in which the negotiation is made, is interstate commerce.

The manner in which the plaintiff conducts its business in Barre has been held to be interstate commerce in decisions from other jurisdictions. We think the fact that the plaintiff, Olan Mills, was engaged in interstate commerce is inescapably inferable. . . .

The defendant does not, in its brief, contend that the plaintiff is not engaged in interstate commerce. Defendant contends that the only question presented for decision to this Court is whether its ordinance, as written, is unconstitutional by placing an undue burden upon interstate commerce in its requirement that a license fee be paid for the right to solicit in the City of Barre. . . .

The statutory authority to license and regulate itinerant photographers doing business within a municipality must be exercised without undue and unfair discrimination against such non-residents or the ordinance, so permitting, will be unconstitutional and void. . . .

While it may be that the Barre ordinance was not designed for the purpose of discriminating against the non-resident photographer, it clearly has that effect against one, such as the plaintiff, who is engaged in interstate commerce. . . .

The ordinance . . . requires that the plaintiff, as an itinerant photographer pay a license fee of $10 for one week, $20 for a period of more than one week and less than four weeks, and $75 for a period of more than four weeks. No license fee of any kind is required from resident photographers of Barre, nor are such photographers required to file a performance bond.

While interstate commerce may be required to pay its way, it must be placed on a plane of equality with local trade and commerce.

Such a plane of equality does not exist under the Barre ordinance between the resident photographer, who pays no license fees or regulatory costs, and the itinerant photographer, engaged in interstate commerce, subject to the various fees and costs stated above. The existing ordinance is both unfair and discriminatory. It requires little imagination to foresee that similar ordinances in each of the various municipalities of the state would constitute a burden and barrier on interstate commerce which could not be permitted.

It is the contention of the defendant municipality that because the licensing requirement in the ordinance is directed only to the soliciting of the making and selling of the photographs, such soliciting is local in character and distinct from the interstate commerce aspect of the business of the plaintiff.

If the only thing necessary to sustain a state tax bearing upon interstate commerce were to discover some local incident which might be regarded as separate and distinct from "the transportation or intercourse which is" the commerce itself and then to lay the tax on that incident, all interstate commerce could be subjected to state taxation and without regard to the substantial economic effects of the tax upon the commerce. For the situation is difficult to think of in which some incident of an interstate transaction taking place within a state could not be segregated by an act of mental gymnastics and made the fulcrum of the tax. All interstate commerce takes place within the confines of the states and necessarily involves "incidents" occurring within each state through which it passes or with which it is connected in fact. And there is no known limit to the human mind's capacity to carve out from what is an entire or integral economic process particular phases or incidents, label them as "separate and distinct" or "local," and thus achieve its desired result.

Where an order is solicited by an agent, and the filling of the order and delivery of goods require their transportation from one state to another the solicitation transaction is one of interstate commerce. This contention of the defendant cannot be sustained.

The "Itinerant Photographers" ordinance of the City of Barre being invalid for the reasons indicated, the order must be "Judgment Reversed and Judgment for the Plaintiff." [REVERSED]

Dean Milk Co. v. City of Madison, Wis.
340 U.S. 349 (1951)

CLARK, JUSTICE: This appeal challenges the constitutional validity of two sections of an ordinance of the City of Madison, Wisconsin, regulating the sale of milk and milk products within the municipality's jurisdiction. One section in issue makes it unlawful to sell any milk as pasteurized unless it has been processed and bottled at an approved pasteurization plant within a radius of five miles from the central square of Madison. . . .

Appellant is an Illinois corporation engaged in distributing milk and milk products in Illinois and Wisconsin. It contended below, as it does here, that . . . the five-mile limit on pasteurization plants . . . violates the Commerce Clause and the Fourteenth Amendment to the Federal Constitution. The Supreme Court of Wisconsin upheld the five-mile limit on pasteurization. . . .

The City of Madison is the county seat of Dane County. Within the county are some 5,600 dairy farms with total raw milk production in excess of 600,000,000 pounds annually and more than ten times the requirements of Madison. Aside from the milk supplied to Madison, fluid milk produced in the county moves in large quantities to Chicago and more distant consuming areas, and the remainder is used in making cheese, butter and other products. At the time of trial the Madison milkshed was not of "Grade A" quality by the standards recommended by the United States Public Health Service, and no milk labeled "Grade A" was distributed in Madison.

The area defined by the ordinance with respect to milk sources encompasses practically all of Dane County and includes some 500 farms which supply milk for Madison. Within the five-mile area for pasteurization are plants of five processors, only three of which are engaged in the general wholesale and retail trade in Madison. Inspection of these farms and plants is scheduled once every thirty days and is performed by two municipal inspectors, one of whom is full-time. The courts below found that the ordinance in question promotes convenient, economical and efficient plant inspection.

Appellant purchases and gathers milk from approximately 950 farms in northern Illinois and southern Wisconsin, none being within twenty-five miles of Madison. Its pasteurization plants are located at Chemung and Huntley, Illinois, about 65 and 85 miles respectively from Madison. Appellant was denied a license to sell its products within Madison solely because its pasteurization plants were more than five miles away.

It is conceded that the milk which appellant seeks to sell in Madison is supplied from farms and processed in plants licensed and inspected by public health authorities of Chicago, and is labeled "Grade A" under the Chicago ordinance which adopts the rating standards recommended by the United States Public Health Service.

Both the Chicago and Madison ordinances, though not the sections of the latter here in issue, are largely patterned after the Model Milk Ordinance of the Public Health Service. However, Madison contends and we assume that in some particulars its ordinance is more rigorous than that of Chicago.

Upon these facts we find it necessary to determine only the issue raised under the Commerce Clause, for we agree with appellant that the ordinance imposes an undue burden on interstate commerce.

This is not an instance in which an enactment falls because of federal legislation which, as a proper exercise of paramount national power over commerce, excludes measures which might otherwise be within the police power of the states. . . . There is no pertinent national regulation by the Congress, and statutes enacted for the District of Columbia indicate that Congress has recognized the appropriateness of local regulation of the sale of fluid milk. D.C.Code, 1940, §§ 33—301 *et seq.* It is not contended, however, that Congress has authorized the regulation before us.

Nor can there be objection to the avowed purpose of this enactment. We assume that difficulties in sanitary regulation of milk and milk products originating in remote areas may present a situation in which "upon a consideration of all the relevant facts and circumstances it appears that the matter is one which may appropriately be regulated in the interest of the safety, health and well-being of local communities. . . ." *Parker v. Brown*, 1943, 317 U.S. 341. . . . We also assume that since Congress has not spoken to the contrary, the subject matter of the ordinance lies within the sphere of state regulation even though interstate commerce may be affected . . . [cases cited].

But this regulation, like the provision invalidated in *Baldwin v. G. A. F. Selig, Inc., supra,* in practical effect excludes from distribution in Madison wholesome milk produced and pasteurized in Illinois. "The importer . . . may keep his milk or drink it, but sell it he may not." *Id.,* 294 U.S. at page 521, 55 Sup. Ct. at page 500. In thus erecting an economic barrier protecting a major local industry against competition from without the State, Madison plainly discriminates against interstate commerce. This it cannot do, even in the exercise of its unquestioned power to protect the health and safety of its people, if reasonable nondiscriminatory alternatives, adequate to conserve legitimate local interests, are available. . . . A different view, that the ordinance is valid simply because it professes to be a health measure, would mean that the Commerce Clause of itself imposes no limitations on state action other than those laid down by the Due Process Clause, save for the rare instance where a state artlessly discloses an avowed purpose to discriminate against interstate goods. . . . Our issue then is whether the discrimination inherent in the Madison ordinance can be justified in view of the character of the local interests and the available methods of protecting them. . . .

It appears that reasonable and adequate alternatives are available. If the City of Madison prefers to rely upon its own officials for inspection of distant milk sources, such inspection is readily open to it without hardship for it could charge the actual and reasonable cost of such inspection to the importing producers and processors. . . . Moreover, appellee Health Commissioner of Madison testified that as proponent of the local milk ordinance he had submitted the provisions here in controversy and an alternative proposal based on § 11 of the Model Milk Ordinance recommended by the United States Public Health Service. The model provision imposes no geographical limitation on location of milk sources and processing plants but excludes from the municipality milk not produced and pasteurized conformably to standards as high as those enforced by the receiving city. In implementing such an ordinance, the importing city obtains milk ratings based on uniform standards and established by health authorities in the jurisdiction where production and processing occur. The receiving city may determine the extent of enforcement of sanitary standards in the exporting area by verifying the accuracy of safety ratings of specific plants or of the milkshed in the distant jurisdiction through the United States Public Health Service, which routinely and on request spot checks the local ratings. The Commissioner testified that Madison consumers "would be safeguarded adequately" under either proposal and that he had expressed no preference. The milk sanitarian of the Wisconsin State Board of Health testified that the State Health Department recommends the adoption of a provision based on the Model Ordinance. Both officials agreed that a local health officer would be justified in relying upon the evaluation by the Public Health Service of enforcement conditions in remote producing areas.

To permit Madison to adopt a regulation not essential for the protection of local health interests and placing a discriminatory burden on interstate commerce would invite a multiplication of preferential trade areas destructive of the very purpose of the Commerce Clause. Under the circumstances here presented, the regulation must yield to the principle that "one state in its dealings with another may not place itself in a position of economic isolation."

For these reasons we conclude that the judgment below sustaining the five-mile provision as to pasteurization must be reversed.

The Supreme Court of Wisconsin thought it unnecessary to pass upon the validity of the twenty-five-mile limitation, apparently in part for the reason that this issue was made academic by its decision upholding the five-mile section. In view of our conclusion as to the latter provision, a determination of appellant's contention as to the other section is now necessary. As to this issue, therefore, we vacate the judgment below and remand for further proceedings not inconsistent with the principles announced in this opinion. It is so ordered. [JUDGMENT VACATED AND CAUSE REMANDED]

6   OTHER LIMITATIONS ON
THE POLICE POWER OF THE STATES

There are several limitations on the exercise of the police power by state government in addition to those imposed by the commerce clause. First, state laws regulating business must relate to public health, safety, morals, or general welfare. Second, they must not violate the due process and equal protection clauses of the United States Constitution. The objections based on due process and equal protection arguments are most frequently used to challenge a tax imposed on interstate commerce but may also be used to challenge a regulating or licensing statute. Third, while policy determination is the realm of the state legislature, it may not pass statutes which are unreasonable or arbitrary. Each of these rules will be further illustrated in the subsections below.

In many cases, the motive of the legislative body actually differs from the reason given for the exercise of the police power. For example, a law may be passed to create jobs, but a reason such as public safety may be given. The Arizona train length case previously set forth is an example of such a law. Thus, the police power, like the commerce power, is often just a convenient excuse for legislation. In those cases in which the actual reason differs from the stated purpose of a state law, the law is especially susceptible to challenge. It must be remembered that the police power may be used to regulate interstate as well as intrastate commerce without violating the Constitution. When courts review legislation to determine whether there is a valid constitutional objection, they are actually on occasion substituting their judgment for that of the legislative body. Such factors as the need for and desirability of the legislation, while purportedly immaterial, may in reality play a substantial role in forming the court's decision.

The cases which follow discuss the meaning of the police power and illustrate some of the grounds other than the commerce clause for challenging laws passed under it.

A RELATIONSHIP TO PUBLIC HEALTH, SAFETY, MORALS, OR GENERAL WELFARE

State v. Grimes
190 N.E.2d 588 (Ohio 1963)

Defendants were convicted of violating Ohio's Sunday closing law by operating their businesses on that day, and they appealed, challenging its constitutionality. The Sunday closing law had several exceptions but they did not include the type of business operated by defendants.

CARPENTER, JUSTICE: . . . To be a valid exercise of police power, there must be a substantial relationship to the health, safety and morals of the public.

To justify the state in interposing its authority in behalf of the public over the constitutional rights of the individual, it must appear that the interest of the public generally as distinguished from those of a particular class require such interference and that the means are reasonably necessary for the accomplishment of the desired purpose, and are not unduly oppressive against individuals. . . .

Considering the absolute necessity of maintaining at least a status quo of progress how can we conclude that the regulation is not unreasonable and discriminatory. . . .

". . . This act places an unreasonable and burdensome obligation upon persons engaged in a lawful business, and is an unwarranted exercise of the police power."

Police power is the inherent sovereignty which the people delegate to the legislature for regulation at large to guard the morals, safety, health and good order in accordance with needs.

Section 2, Art. I of the Constitution of Ohio provides: "All political power is inherent in the people. Government is instituted for their equal protections and benefit . . . no special privileges or immunities shall ever be granted."

The police power must be reasonable and necessary to secure the peace, safety, morals and best interests, of the commonwealth.

Such powers must be exercised for the interest of the public in general not unduly oppressive upon individuals. . . .

For the above reasons this court is of the opinion that Section 3773.24 of the Revised Code of Ohio is unconstitutional and void.

B   DUE PROCESS AND EQUAL PROTECTION

The Fourteenth Amendment provides that states shall not deprive any person of life, liberty, or property without due process of law; nor deny to any person the equal protection of the laws. The rights of an individual to engage in a lawful business are entitled to protection under the due process and equal protection clauses of the Fourteenth Amendment. This safeguard extends to corporations as well as to individuals. However, the protection afforded by the Fourteenth Amendment for corporations is not coextensive with that afforded individuals. For example, individuals may conduct certain businesses which corporations may not.

As previously noted, the due process and equal protection clauses are used primarily to challenge taxing laws. Historically, these clauses have also been used to challenge many regulating statutes that were "controversial." Due process served as a general form of challenge to be used in an attempt to convince a court that the law under attack was unwise. Today courts have abandoned the use of the "vague contours" of the due process clause to nullify laws which the Court believes to be economically unwise. In *Ferguson v. Skrupa*, 372 U.S. 726 (1962), the Court said: "We refuse to sit as a 'super legislature to weigh the wisdom of legislation,' and we emphatically refuse to go back to the time when courts used the Due Process Clause to strike down state laws, regulatory of business and industrial conditions, because they may be unwise, improvident, or out of harmony with a particular school of thought." The prohibition of the equal protection clause goes no further than to prohibit invidious discrimination. If there is a rational basis for a legislative distinction, the fact that there is discrimination, as for example between corporations and natural persons, is constitutionally immaterial.

City of Niles v. Dean
268 N.E.2d 275 (Ohio 1971)

A local ordinance confined through-truck traffic, not intending to discharge cargo within the city, to designated routes. It was challenged by nonresident truckers as a denial of equal protection.

O'NEILL, C. W., JUSTICE: . . . The basic question raised by this appeal is whether the ordinance enacted by the council of the city of Niles, regulating the use of its streets, is constitutional in its effect upon the appellants. . . .

[A] municipal corporation has the power, as part of its right to regulate and control its streets, to designate the routes which may be followed by trucks and to exclude them from all but designated streets, so long as such regulation is reasonable and does not constitute a denial of equal protection. . . .

The appellant contends that this ordinance is discriminatory, unreasonable and violates the equal-protection clause in relation to nonresident truckers.

An examination of the ordinance does not substantiate appellant's position. The ordinance confines through traffic, not intending to discharge cargo within the city, to designated state routes. It also provides that through trucks shall use the streets within the city designated by the Director of Public Safety. It permits any trucker, resident or nonresident, to service industrial and commercial firms in the city. The third part of the ordinance provides that trucks may use certain streets only for the servicing of designated businesses thereon. Such exception is necessary inasmuch as these streets constitute the only means of access to those businesses.

The ordinance does not deny access to or travel through the city. It merely regulates what streets trucks may use. It subjects both local and nonresident truckers to the same regulations. . . .

The appellants also urge that the ordinance constitutes a denial of equal protection and is not uniform in its operation in that it permits delivery to industrial and commercial businesses on nonexempt streets, but makes no provision for the use of such streets for delivery to agricultural, domestic or charitable institutions. They contend further that the part of the ordinance which permits the use of designated streets for delivery to and shipments from certain enumerated businesses thereon denies equal protection and lacks uniform operation in that it does not provide for delivery to and shipments from businesses which may come into existence after the enactment of the ordinance and, therefore, not named therein.

At the time of their arrest, appellants were operating their through trucks on Salt Springs Road, a street not mentioned in the ordinance as an exempt street under any conditions. They were using such street to get to Interstate 805. Appellants do not contend that they were on this street to make any delivery in the city of Niles. That part of the ordinance which they contend is invalid in this respect had no application to them and was not the reason for their arrest.

The validity of those portions of the ordinance is not in issue in relation to their arrest. Thus, the appellants have no standing to attack the validity of the ordinance on these grounds.

The regulation of truck taffic on municipal streets is necessary under today's traffic conditions, and a municipal ordinance regulating such use is a valid exercise of the police power so long as the ordinance is reasonable, is not discriminatory and is of uniform operation.

The ordinance in the instant case is non-discriminatory as between resident and non-resident truckers, has a uniform operation and does not constitute a denial of equal protection so far as appellants are concerned. [JUDGMENT AFFIRMED]

WHYY, Inc. v. Borough of Glassboro
89 S.Ct. 286 (1968)

PER CURIAM. The appellant is a nonprofit corporation organized under the laws of Pennsylvania. Under a license issued by the Federal Communications Commission, it operates a noncommercial television station which broadcasts cultural, recreational, and educational programs. The broadcasting facilities for one of the television channels allocated to the appellant are in New Jersey; on its 50-acre plot in the Borough of Glassboro in that State appellant has erected a transmittal station and a tower. Signals on this channel reach approximately 8,000,000 people in the Delaware Valley area, of whom 29.5% are estimated to live in New Jersey. Some of the programs are designed to appeal especially to the residents of New Jersey. In accordance with New Jersey law, the appellant has registered and qualified to transact business in the State.

In November of 1963 the appellant wrote to Glassboro Council requesting exemption, as a nonprofit organization, from state real and personal property taxes on its land and facilities for 1964. The request was denied, as was a similar petition to the Gloucester County Tax Board. The Division of Tax Appeals upheld the County Board, and the appellant took a further appeal to the Superior Court. That court held that while the appellant qualified for the exemption in all other respects, the statute exempted only those nonprofit corporations which were incorporated in New Jersey. On appeal to the Supreme Court of New Jersey, the appellant argued for the first time that the statute denied it equal protection of the laws in violation of the Fourteenth Amendment to the Constitution by discriminating against it solely on the basis of its foreign incorporation. The Supreme Court noted that it had discretion not to consider a question not raised in the lower court, but nevertheless proceeded to decide the constitutional question because of its widespread importance. It concluded that the classification was not wholly irrational and sustained the denial of exemption. We noted probable jurisdiction to consider the constitutional question thus raised.

This Court has consistently held that while a State may impose conditions on the entry of foreign corporations to do business in the State, once it has permitted them to enter, "the adopted corporations are entitled to equal protection with the state's own corporate progeny, at least to the extent that their property is entitled to an equally favorable *ad valorem* tax basis." Yet New Jersey has denied the appellant a tax exemption which it accords other nonprofit corporations solely because of the appellant's foreign incorporation. This is not a case in which the exemption was withheld by reason of the foreign corporation's failure or inability to benefit the State in the same measure as do domestic nonprofit corporations. . . . Nor has the appellee advanced any other distinction between this appellant and domestic nonprofit corporations which would justify the inequality of treatment.

The New Jersey Supreme Court concluded that the legislative purpose could reasonably have been to avoid the administrative burden which the taxing authorities would bear if they had to examine the laws of other jurisdictions in order to determine whether a corporation with nonprofit status under those laws would also satisfy New Jersey requirements. But this burden would exist only if a foreign corporation sought exemption in New Jersey on the basis of its nonprofit status at home. It is one thing for a State to avoid this extra burden by refusing to grant such an automatic exemption. It is quite another to deny a foreign corporation an opportunity equivalent to that of a domestic corporation to demonstrate that it meets the requirements for a nonprofit corporation under local law. Neither the New Jersey Supreme Court nor the appellee has suggested that there is any greater administrative burden in evaluating a foreign than a domestic corporation under New Jersey law. We must therefore conclude . . . that the appellant has not been "accorded equal treatment, and the inequality is not because of the slightest difference in [New Jersey's] relation to the decisive transaction, but solely because of the different residence of the owner." . . . [REVERSED AND REMANDED]

C   THE PROHIBITION OF UNREASONABLE, ARBITRARY REGULATION

Wasmuth v. Allen
200 N.E.2d 756 (N.Y., 1964)

A chiropractor brought suit on behalf of all chiropractors of New York to have certain provisions of the Education Law declared unconstitutional. These provisions required an examination of chiropractic examinees in basic subjects such as anatomy, physiology, chemistry, hygiene, bacteriology, pathology, and diagnosis and use and effects of X ray.

DYE, JUSTICE: . . . Requiring chiropractic examinees to pass an examination in the use and effects of X ray is denounced as being uneven and discriminatory in its application since others engaged in the field of public health—such as applicants for licenses to practice medicine, dentistry, podiatry and osteopathy—are not so required, thereby denying these plaintiffs and others similarly situated equal protection of the law. . . .

This phase of the constitutional challenge requires no lengthy comment. . . . Since the use of X ray relates to a field where chiropractors will be practicing, it is neither unreasonable nor inappropriate to require chiropractic license applicants to demonstrate a proficiency in that area. In short, the provisions requiring an examination in the use and effect of X ray are not violative of the equal protection clause.

The contention aimed at the unconstitutionality of the statute requiring examination in the basic subjects . . . is more subtle. Chiropractic—dealing as it does with the detection and correction of "structural imbalance, distortion, or subluxation in the human body for the purpose of removing nerve interference and the effects thereof" (§ 6550, subd. 4) on the nervous system—is intimately and inextricably connected with human health and well within the area of the State's police power. In fact, plaintiffs concede that the fields of healing art, medicine and chiropractic—though diverse—may and sometimes do overlap. Statutory validity is favored by a presumption of constitutionality. It is also a maxim of the judicial function that "courts do not substitute their social and economic beliefs for the judgment of legislative bodies." And, even when error is committed in the exercise of legislative discretion, the courts may not correct it. I do not apprehend, and neither did the courts below, that it is the function of this court to determine whether "the public policy that finds expression in legislation of this order is well or ill conceived."

The power of the legislature [as the learned Justice at Special Term put it,] to require proof of competence in a given field which will affect public interest has been adequately demonstrated. . . . subject always to judicial review to determine whether regulation by license serves the public interest, and to the prohibition against delegation of legislative powers to administrative officers.

Here, we are dealing with the sufficiency of the complaint to state unconstitutionality of a duly enacted statute for the licensing of the practice of chiropractic. It was enacted after we had said it did not transcend the police power of the State for the Public Health Council to rule that the unfamiliarity of chiropractors with the effects of radiation in the wholesale use of X ray constituted a danger to the public health. The conditions requisite to obtaining a license are specific, detailed and comprehensive. The imposition of a new requirement for the continued practice of a profession previously carried on without the need of such requirements does not violate the Constitution. . . . Neither can it reasonably be said that requiring an applicant for license to practice chiropractic to pass tests in basic subjects constitutes an arbitrary and unreasonable exercise of legislative power. While it is true that the statute draws a distinction between the practice of medicine, osteopathy or physiotherapy, as defined by the applicable statute, and the practice of chiropractic and in so doing, defines and limits the rights of licensed chiropractors in fields of practice deemed as belonging to the practice of medicine, osteopathy or physiotherapy (§ 6558), the practice of chiropractic is nonetheless one that deals with human health which has always been regarded and treated as a matter of public concern. "It is too well settled to require discussion at this day that the police power of the states extends to the regulation of certain trades and callings, particularly those which closely concern the public health."

Chiropractic, having to do with the health and well-being of the people, requires a high degree of general knowledge and technical skill and is a field where the power of the State may well be asserted to make sure that only properly qualified persons shall undertake its responsible and difficult duties. As the Justice

below pointed out, the challenged statute has conferred on chiropractors privileges which we have held they could not claim as a matter of constitutional right. This is ample to meet the challenge that the statute is unconstitutional. . . .
[ORDER AFFIRMED]

REVIEW QUESTIONS—CHAPTER 8

1 Define the following legal terms introduced in this chapter: police power; preemption; interstate commerce; intrastate commerce; enterprise concept.
2 What is the extent of the power of the Federal government to regulate foreign commerce? Explain.
3 What is the extent of the power of state and local governments to regulate foreign commerce? Explain.
4 What is the extent of the power of Congress under the commerce clause? Explain.
5 Can Congress regulate state government under the commerce clause? Explain.
6 Give three illustrations of subjects which are "exclusively Federal" for purposes of regulation.
7 What is the effect of a Federal regulating law which preempts the field? Explain.
8 To what extent may a state law conflict with a Federal law without the state law's being unconstitutional? Explain.
9 Is it legally and constitutionally permissible for a state law to burden interstate commerce? Explain.
10 Give three illustrations of state or local laws which discriminate against interstate commerce in favor of intrastate commerce.
11 Give examples of state or local laws which (1) violate the due process clause and (2) violate the equal protection clause of the Fourteenth Amendment.

Chapter Nine

Taxation of Business

1 INTRODUCTION

The taxing power is the power by which government raises revenue to defray its expenses. It is a method of apportioning the cost of government among those who receive its benefits. The purpose of taxation and the purposes and function of government are coextensive, in that the taxing power, in the broad sense, includes all charges and burdens imposed by government upon persons or property for the use and support of government. Government collects revenue from sources other than taxes. Such items as recording fees, filing fees, tolls, and license fees are charges for services or the use of facilities. Such revenues are not taxes in the strict sense of the term.

The taxing system is twofold in operation. The first part is concerned with the levy or imposition of the tax and the determination of the liability. The second is concerned with the collection of the tax. Our primary concern in this chapter is with the first aspect of taxation.

The taxing power can be exercised only for public purposes. A tax is not a contract based on assent but is a statutory liability based on force and authority. A tax is not a debt in the usual sense of the word and the constitutional prohibitions against imprisonment for debt are not applicable.

The theory supporting taxation is that since governmental functions are a necessity, the government has the right to compel persons and property within its jurisdiction to defray the costs of these functions. The payment of taxes gives no right to the taxpayer. The privilege of enjoying the protection and services of government is not based on taxes paid. As a matter of fact, there are many examples which illustrate that those who receive the most from the government pay the fewest taxes.

Taxes are paid by those able to do so, in order that all persons may share in the general benefits resulting from government. Thus property can be taxed without an obvious personal benefit to the property owner.

The power of taxation is in theory exclusively exercised by the legislative branch of the government. The only limitations on the exercise of the taxing power are found in Federal and state constitutions and the political power of the electorate to replace the legislators. Since the power of taxation is a legislative function, statutes dealing with taxation must be complete both as to the method of ascertaining the tax and its collection. The fact that a tax may destroy a business or the value of property is no basis for a judicial determination that the tax is unconstitutional. The court must find that the tax violates some specific provision of the Constitution before the tax can be held invalid. The decision as to the wisdom or propriety of the tax is left to the legislature.

2 CLASSIFICATION OF TAXES

There are many different ways of classifying taxes. Some taxes are referred to as direct taxes as contrasted with indirect taxes. Direct taxes are levied against a person who must bear their burden while the burden of indirect taxes may be passed on by the one paying them to someone else. Another common classification distinguishes specific from ad valorem taxes. A specific tax is fixed by some standard such as weight or measure and only requires a listing of the items to be taxed. For example, taxes on cigarettes are specific. An ad valorem tax is a fixed proportion of the value of the property and requires an appraisal of the property before the tax can be determined. Ad valorem means "according to the value" and an ad valorem tax is levied at a certain rate. For example, an automobile might be taxed at 4 percent of its fair market value. General property taxes on real estate and personal property are the most common examples of ad valorem taxes.

Frequently taxes are classified as general or special. A general tax is levied against all persons or property irrespective of any benefit received, while a special tax or assessment is levied only against those receiving direct benefits. Special assessments to pave streets are typical special taxes while real estate taxes are general.

The most common method of classifying taxes is based on the subject matter on which they are imposed. Taxes are imposed on (1) property, (2) privileges, or (3) persons. Under this method, there are property taxes, excise taxes, and capitation or poll taxes. A property tax is assessed on all property of a certain class within the territory, as of a certain time, and is based on value. Excise taxes are based on the exercise of a privilege, the doing of an act, or the engaging in an occupation. Many state constitutions contain certain limitations on property taxes and other limitations on excise taxes. A considerable amount of litigation has resulted as to whether a particular tax is a property tax or an excise tax to determine if the limitations of its classification have been exceeded. Excise taxes include all taxes not assessed on a person or his property and the term "privilege tax" is synonymous with excise tax. The sales tax and use tax are the most common of the excise taxes.

Capitation or poll taxes are levied upon persons of a certain class such as voters, without regard to property or occupation. The income tax is not a poll tax but an excise tax.

3 FEDERAL TAXATION

The Federal taxing power is a tool of government which is utilized as an aid in policy implementation as well as a means of raising revenue. The taxing power is used to assist governmental attempts to regulate the economy. For example, depreciation allowances have been accelerated in recent years to bolster the economy by making additional cash available for business investment. The periods over which property might be depreciated were varied as an economic tool. Tax laws are also used by the Federal government to equalize competition among different businesses. For example, the gasoline tax is an important part of the equalization of costs between truckers and other forms of transportation. The taxing power has been used to encourage uniform legislation among the states. States were encouraged to adopt inheritance taxes by a Federal law which gave persons an 80 percent credit on the Federal estate tax for death taxes paid to states. It should be noted that since the enactment of the original law, however, the Federal estate tax rates have been increased to such an extent that today only about 10 percent of all death taxes are paid to states. Similar pressure was put on the states by the Unemployment Compensation Act which allows, as a credit against the Federal tax, a certain portion of the tax paid to states. Import taxes imposed by the Federal government are also used as an economic tool. The protection from foreign competition they afforded domestic industries was a significant factor in the development of large manufacturing enterprises in this country. Under the Constitution, states may not impose import taxes[1] and neither the state nor Federal governments may impose direct export taxes.[2] However, note that the taxes on this country's imports are likely to be reciprocated by foreign nations with comparable taxes on imports from America, so that indirectly the Federal import tax policy results in a benefit or burden to American exporting.

The Federal taxing power is also used to implement social policies. For example, the Federal estate tax and the graduated income tax were in part adopted to break up large accumulations of wealth. In addition, the Federal government pays money to the states to encourage certain activities such as education, road building, and slum clearance. Persons in one part of the country may pay for social improvements in another as a direct result of the exercise of the taxing and spending powers of the Federal government. An examination of the implementation policies of the Federal government will reveal that many of them are tied directly to taxation.

Few questions are raised today concerning the *validity* of a federally imposed tax. The Sixteenth Amendment to the Constitution and the broad scope of the Federal taxing power which has been approved by the courts eliminates most such issues. Of course, there is a considerable amount of litigation involving the *interpretation* and *application* of the Federal tax laws and regulations. These regulations, as a rule of an administrative agency, the Internal Revenue Service (IRS), are subject to the general principles applicable to the quasi-legislative powers of administrative agencies as discussed in Chapter 7. Great deference is given to the position taken by the Commissioner of Internal Revenue, as the following case illustrates.

[1] United States Constitution, Art. I, §10.
[2] United States Constitution, Art. I, §§9, 10.

United States v. Correll
88 S.Ct. 445 (1967)

STEWART, JUSTICE: The Commissioner of Internal Revenue has long maintained that a taxpayer traveling on business may deduct the cost of his meals only if his trip requires him to stop for sleep or rest. The question presented here is the validity of that rule.

The respondent in this case was a traveling salesman for a wholesale grocery company in Tennessee. He customarily left home early in the morning, ate breakfast and lunch on the road, and returned home in time for dinner. In his income tax return for 1960 and 1961, he deducted the cost of his morning and noon meals as "traveling expenses" incurred in the pursuit of his business "while away from home" under § 162(a) (2) of the Internal Revenue Code of 1954. Because the respondent's daily trips required neither sleep nor rest, the Commissioner disallowed the deductions, ruling that the cost of the respondent's meals was a "personal, living" expense under § 262 rather than a travel expense under § 162(a) (2). The respondent paid the tax, sued for a refund in the District Court, and there received a favorable jury verdict. The Court of Appeals for the Sixth Circuit affirmed, holding that the Commissioner's sleep or rest rule is not "a valid regulation under the present statute." . . .

Under § 162(a) (2), taxpayers "traveling . . . away from home in the pursuit of a trade or business" may deduct the total amount "expended for meals and lodging." As a result, even the taxpayer who incurs substantial hotel and restaurant expenses because of the special demands of business travel receives something of a windfall, for at least part of what he spends on meals represents a personal living expense that other taxpayers must bear without receiving any deduction at all. Not surprisingly, therefore, Congress did not extend the special benefits of § 162(a) (2) to every conceivable situation involving business travel. It made the total cost of meals and lodging deductible only if incurred in the course of travel that takes the taxpayer "away from home." The problem before us involves the meaning of that limiting phrase.

In resolving that problem, the Commissioner has avoided the wasteful litigation and continuing uncertainty that would inevitably accompany any purely case-by-case approach to the question of whether a particular taxpayer was "away from home" on a particular day. Rather than requiring "every meal-purchasing taxpayer to take pot luck in the courts," the Commissioner has consistently construed travel "away from home" to exclude all trips requiring neither sleep nor rest, regardless of how many cities a given trip may have touched, how many miles it may have covered, or how many hours it may have consumed. By so interpreting the statutory phrase, the Commissioner has achieved not only ease and certainty of application but also substantial fairness, for the sleep or rest rule places all one-day travelers on a similar tax footing, rather than discriminating against intracity travelers and commuters, who of course cannot deduct the cost of the meals they eat on the road.

Any rule in this area must make some rather arbitrary distinctions, but at least the sleep or rest rule avoids the obvious inequity of permitting the New Yorker who makes a quick trip to Washington and back, missing neither his breakfast nor his dinner at home, to deduct the cost of his lunch merely because he covers more miles than the salesman who travels locally and must finance all his meals without the help of the Federal Treasury. And the Commissioner's rule surely makes more sense than one which would allow the respondent in this case to deduct the cost of his breakfast and lunch simply because he spends a greater percentage of his time at the wheel than the commuter who eats breakfast on his way to work and lunch a block from his office.

. . . The language of the statute—"meals and lodging . . . away from home"— is obviously not self-defining. . . . This case . . . comes within the settled principle that "Treasury regulations and interpretations long continued without substantial change, applying to unamended or substantially reenacted statutes, are deemed to have received congressional approval and have the effect of law."

Alternatives to the Commissioner's sleep or rest rule are of course available. Improvements might be imagined. But we do not sit as a committee of revision to perfect the administration of the tax laws. Congress has delegated to the Commissioner, not to the courts, the task of prescribing "all needful rules and regulations for the enforcement" of the Internal Revenue Code. 26 U.S.C. § 7805(a). In this area of limitless factual variations "it is the province of Congress and the Commissioner, not the courts, to make the appropriate adjustments." The rule of the judiciary in cases of this sort begins and ends with assuring that the Commissioner's regulations fall within his authority to implement the congressional mandate in some reasonable manner. Because the rule challenged here has not been shown deficient on that score, the Court of Appeals should have sustained its validity. The judgment is therefore reversed. [REVERSED]

4 STATE AND LOCAL TAXATION: GENERAL PRINCIPLES

State and local governments impose a variety of taxes on individuals and corporations. These commonly take the form of property taxes, income taxes, sales or use taxes, and license fees. State taxes may range from those on liquor, tobacco, and petroleum products to those on parimutuel betting. The variety and incidence of state taxation will depend on the economy and industry of the state. For example, a tourist state such as Florida may impose a higher tax on room rent receipts of motels and hotels than a non-tourist state does.

Local taxes are imposed by a multitude of municipal corporations in every locality. The boundaries of these municipal corporations overlap, and the local tax bill often is merely the sum total of the tax rates of all these taxing bodies. For example, local taxes may be paid to a (1) school district, (2) park district, (3) fire prevention and protection district, (4) sanitary district, (5) drainage district, (6) city or village, (7) township, (8) county, (9) mental health district, (10) library district, and (11) other public bodies given legislative responsibilities which need funds to carry out their functions. The general property tax is often used to raise money for local government. As the competition for revenue has increased, municipalities have become hard-pressed for sources of revenue. Some have imposed municipal sales or use taxes. Some have attempted and others are contemplating income taxes. Some are raising substantial sums by imposing large license fees on the privilege of doing business. The validity of many of the local revenue-raising schemes remains to be determined. Many of the decisions will depend on the constitutions of the various states, but issues under the Federal Constitution are also present.

Since a large number of businesses conduct interstate operations, complex legal questions arise as to the power of the various states to tax these business activities and the property involved. Taxes imposed on wholly intrastate activities raise no Federal constitutional issues, but there are limitations on the powers of state and local governments to tax interstate activities due to the commerce clause of the Federal Constitution. Courts are frequently faced with the delicate problem of determining the line between the state's power to tax activities occurring within its territorial jurisdiction and its lack of power to burden interstate commercial activity unduly in violation of the commerce clause.

In *Northwestern States Portland Cement Co. v. Minnesota,* 358 U.S. 450 (1959), the Supreme Court, speaking through Justice Clark, had occasion to review some of the general principles regarding the limitations placed on state taxing power by the commerce clause. He stated in part:

It has long been established doctrine that the Commerce Clause gives exclusive power to the Congress to regulate interstate commerce, and its failure to act on the subject in the area of taxation nevertheless requires that interstate commerce shall be free from any direct restrictions or impositions by the States. . . . In keeping therewith a State "cannot impose taxes upon persons passing through the state, or coming into it merely for a temporary purpose" such as itinerant drummers. . . . Moreover, it is beyond dispute that a State may not lay a tax on the "privilege" of engaging in interstate commerce. . . . Nor may a State impose a tax which discriminates against interstate commerce either by providing a direct commercial advantage to local business . . . or by subjecting interstate commerce to the burden of "multiple taxation." . . . Such impositions have been stricken because the States, under the Commerce Clause, are not allowed "one single tax-dollar worth of direct interference with the free flow of commerce."

On the other hand, it has been established since 1918 that a net income tax on revenues derived from interstate commerce does not offend constitutional limitations upon state interference with such commerce. . . . [T]he entire net income of a corporation, generated by interstate as well as intrastate activities, may be fairly apportioned among the States for tax purposes by formulas utilizing in-state aspects of interstate affairs. . . . [A] tax on net income from interstate commerce, as distinguished from a tax on the privilege of engaging in interstate commerce, does not conflict with the commerce clause. . . . It is axiomatic that the founders did not intend to immunize . . . [interstate] commerce from carrying its fair share of the costs of the state government in return for the benefits it derives from within the State. . . . "It is too late in the day to find offense to that [commerce] clause because a state tax is imposed on corporate net income of an interstate enterprise which is attributable to earnings within the taxing state. . . ."

The foregoing summary indicates that there are several distinct constitutional problems present when a state seeks to tax businesses engaged in interstate commerce. These issues are: (1) Is the tax properly apportioned? (2) Is there a sufficient minimum connection (nexus) between the activity being taxed and the tax to satisfy due process? (3) Does the tax discriminate against interstate commerce? and (4) Does the tax impose an unconstitutional burden on interstate commerce?

Each of these issues will be discussed more fully in the sections which follow. It must be kept in mind that the law views taxation as a method of distributing the burdens of government among those who benefit from governmental activities. Since interstate businesses receive benefits just as do intrastate businesses, there is no automatic exemption from taxation because of the commerce clause, and tax laws like other statutes are presumed to be constitutional.

5 APPORTIONMENT

Business which is conducted in more than one state may be subject to the burdens of multiple taxation unless some method is present for allocating its tax burden among the various taxing jurisdictions. For example, an airline receiving income in ten states could conceivably be required to file ten state income tax returns and to pay income tax in each state. In addition, each state that levies a property tax could seek to tax the airplanes of the airline. The concept of apportionment means that there must be some reasonable basis for calculating the percentage of income which each state may tax or the percentage of the value of the property each state may tax.

If a business engaged in interstate commerce were required to pay income taxes on its total income in more than one state, or to pay multiple property taxes on the same property, such taxes would be unconstitutional as a violation of the commerce clause. The concept of apportionment simply prevents the double taxation of businesses engaged in interstate commerce. It must be observed that the apportionment principle does not eliminate all problems which result from the imposition of taxes by more than one state. For example, each state determines its own apportionment formulas, and to date practically every state's formulas are different from those of other states. The total tax burden of a business engaged in interstate commerce may be in excess of that which would be imposed if it were only taxed by one state, such as the state of its domicile. The number of formulas which are reasonable is probably infinite, and the wide range of formulas used by the states is one major reason given in support of Federal legislation on the subject.

On occasion, the courts have approved taxes which are not apportioned. This usually occurs when the taxpayer fails to establish that another state is taxing the same property or activity. For example, in *Northwest Airlines v. Minnesota*, 322 U.S. 292 (1944), the Supreme Court allowed Minnesota, as the state of domicile, to tax the entire fleet of planes of Northwest Airlines because there was no evidence showing that any of them was permanently outside of Minnesota throughout the taxable year. This decision was modified later in *Standard Oil v. Peck*, 342 U.S. 382 (1952), in which the court held that "The rule which permits taxation by two or more states on an apportionment basis precludes taxation of all of the property by the state of the domicile. . . ." Otherwise there would be multiple taxation of interstate operations, and the tax would have no relation to the opportunities, benefits, or protection which the taxing state gives those operations.

The case which follows illustrates another situation in which an unapportioned tax was approved. The case also discusses the principle that there must be a constitutional connection between the tax and business activity within the taxing state.

General Motors Corporation v. Washington
84 S.Ct. 1564 (1964)

CLARK, JUSTICE: This appeal tests the constitutional validity, under the Commerce and Due Process Clauses, of Washington's tax imposed upon the privilege of engaging in business activities within the State. The tax is measured by the appellant's gross wholesale sales of motor vehicles, parts and accessories delivered in the State. Appellant claims that the tax is levied on unapportioned gross receipts from such sales and is, therefore, a tax on the privilege of engaging in interstate commerce; is inherently discriminatory; results in the imposition of a multiple tax burden; and is a deprivation of property without due process of law. The Washington Superior Court held that the presence of a branch office in Seattle rendered some of the Chevrolet transactions subject to tax, but, as to the remainder, held that the application of the statute would be repugnant to the Commerce and the Due Process Clauses of the United States Constitution. On appeal, the Supreme Court of Washington reversed the latter finding, holding that all of the appellant's transactions were subject to the tax on the ground that the tax bore a reasonable relation to the appellant's activities within the State. . . . We have concluded that the tax is levied on the incidents of a substantial local business in Washington and is constitutionally valid and, therefore, affirm the judgment.

We start with the proposition that "[i]t was not the purpose of the commerce clause to relieve those engaged in interstate commerce from their just share of state tax burden even though it increases the cost of doing the business." "Even interstate business must pay its way," as is evidenced by numerous opinions of this Court. For example, the Court has approved property taxes on the instruments employed in commerce; on property devoted to interstate transportation fairly apportioned to its use within the State; on profits derived from foreign or interstate commerce by way of a net income tax; by franchise taxes, measured by the net income of a commercially domiciled corporation from interstate commerce attributable to business done in the State and fairly apportioned; by a franchise tax measured on a proportional formula on profits of a unitary business manufacturing and selling ale, "the process of manufacturing resulting in no profits until it ends in sales"; by a personal property tax by a domiciliary State on a fleet of airplanes whose home port was in the taxing State, despite the fact that personal property taxes were paid on part of the fleet in other States; by a net income tax on revenues derived from interstate commerce where fairly apportioned to business activities within the State; and by a franchise tax levied on an express company, in lieu of taxes upon intangibles or rolling stock, measured by gross receipts, fairly apportioned, and derived from transportation within the State.

However, local taxes measured by gross receipts from interstate commerce have not always fared as well. Because every State has equal rights when taxing the commerce it touches, there exists the danger that such taxes can impose cumulative burdens upon interstate transactions which are not presented to local commerce. Such burdens would destroy interstate commerce and encourage the re-erection of those trade barriers which made the Commerce Clause necessary. And in this connection, we have specifically held that interstate commerce cannot be subjected to the burden of "multiple taxation." Nevertheless, as we have seen, it is well established that taxation measured by gross receipts is constitutionally proper if it is fairly apportioned.

A careful analysis of the cases in this field teaches that the validity of the tax rests upon whether the State is exacting a constitutionally fair demand for that aspect of interstate commerce to which it bears a special relation. For our purposes the decisive issue turns on the operating incidence of the tax. In other words, the question is whether the State has exerted its power in proper proportion to appellant's activities within the State and to appellant's consequent enjoyment of the opportunities and protections which the State has afforded. Where, as in the instant case, the taxing State is not the domiciliary State, we look to the taxpayer's business activities within the State, i.e., the local incidents, to determine if the gross receipts from sales therein may be fairly related to those activities. As was said in *Wisconsin v. J. C. Penney Co.*, 311 U.S. 435, "[t]he simple but controlling question is whether the state has given anything for which it can ask return."

Here it is admitted that General Motors has entered the State and engaged in activities therein. In fact, General Motors voluntarily pays considerable taxes on its Washington operations but contests the validity of the tax levy on four of its Divisions, Chevrolet, Pontiac, Oldsmobile and General Motors Parts. Under these circumstances appellant has the burden of showing that the operations of these divisions in the State are "dissociated from the local business and interstate in nature. The general rule, applicable here, is that a taxpayer claiming immunity from a tax has the burden of establishing his exemption." And, as we also [have] said, this burden is not met

by showing a fair difference of opinion which as an original matter might be decided differently. This corporation, by submitting itself to the taxing power . . . [of the State], likewise submitted itself to its judicial power to construe and apply its taxing statute insofar as it keeps within constitutional bounds. Of course, in constitutional cases, we have power to examine the whole record to arrive at an independent judgment as to whether constitutional rights have been invaded, but that does not mean that we will re-examine, as a court of first instance, findings of fact supported by substantial evidence.

With these principles in mind, we turn to the facts.

1   General Motors Corporate Organization and Sales Operation

General Motors . . . manufactures automobiles, trucks and other merchandise which are sold to dealers in Washington. However, all of these articles are manufactured in other States. In order to carry on the sale, in Washington, of the products of Chevrolet, Pontiac, Oldsmobile and General Motors Parts, the corporation maintains an organization of employees in each of these divisions on a national, regional and district level. . . .

2   Personnel Residing within the State and Their Activities

. . . The district managers lived within the State of Washington and their jobs were "the maintenance of a quality organization—dealer organization—and the follow-through and administration of programs, plans and procedures within their district, that will help to develop the dealer organization, for the best possible financial and sales results." . . .

In addition to the district manager, each of the Chevrolet, Pontiac and Oldsmobile Divisions also maintained service representatives who called on the dealers with regularity, assisting the service department in any troubles it experienced with General Motors products. These representatives also checked the adequacy of the service department inventory to make certain that the dealer's agreement was being complied with and to ensure the best possible service to customers. . . .

During the tax period involved here the Chevrolet, Oldsmobile and Pontiac Divisions had an average of about 20 employees resident or principally employed in Washington. General Motors Parts Division employed about 20 more. . . .

4   Activities of General Motors Parts Division

During the period of this tax, the General Motors Parts Division warehoused, sold and shipped parts and accessories to Washington dealers for Chevrolet,

Pontiac and Oldsmobile vehicles. It maintained warehouses in Portland and Seattle. No personnel of this division visited the dealers, but all of the Chevrolet, Pontiac and Oldsmobile dealers in Washington obtained their parts and accessories from the warehouses. Items carried by the Seattle warehouse were shipped from it, and those warehoused at Portland were shipped from there. The Seattle warehouse, which carried the items most often called for in Washington, employed from 20 to 28 people during the taxing period. The Portland warehouse carried the less frequently needed parts. The tax on the orders filled at the Seattle warehouse was paid but the tax on the Portland shipments is being protested.

[I]t is beyond dispute, "that a State may not lay a tax on the 'privilege' of engaging in interstate commerce." But that is not this case. To so contend here is to overlook a long line of cases, of this Court holding that an instate activity may be a sufficient local incident upon which a tax may be based. As was said in *Spector Motor Service, Inc., v. O'Connor*, 340 U.S. 602, (1951), "[t]he State is not precluded from imposing taxes upon other activities or aspects of this [interstate] business which, unlike the privilege of doing interstate business, are subject to the sovereign power of the State." This is exactly what Washington seeks to do here and we cannot say that appellant has shown that its activities within the State are not such incidents as the State can reach. . . .

Thus, in the bundle of corporate activity, which is the test here, we see General Motors' activity so enmeshed in local connections that it voluntarily paid taxes on various of its operations but insists that it was not liable on others. Since General Motors elected to enter the State in this fashion, we cannot say that the Supreme Court of Washington erred in holding that these local incidents were sufficient to form the basis for the levy of a tax that would not run contrary to the Constitution.

The tax that Washington levied is measured by the wholesale sales of the respective General Motors divisions in the State. It is unapportioned and, as we have pointed out, is, therefore, suspect. We must determine whether it is so closely related to the local activities of the corporation as to form "some definite link, some minimum connection, between a state and the person, property or transaction it seeks to tax." On the basis of the facts found by the state court we are not prepared to say that its conclusion was constitutionally impermissible. Here, . . . the corporation so mingled its taxable business with that which it claims nontaxable that we can only "conclude that, in the light of all the evidence, the judgment attributing . . . [the corporation's Washington sales to its local activity] was within the realm of permissible judgment. Petitioner has not established that such services as were rendered . . . [through in-state activity] were not decisive factors in establishing and holding this market." Although mere entry into a State does not take from a corporation the right to continue to do an interstate business with tax immunity, it does not follow that the corporation can channel its operations through such a maze of local connections as does General Motors, and take advantage of its gain on domesticity, and still maintain that same degree of immunity.

[The Court then noted that the issue of multiple taxation was not then before it.] [AFFIRMED]

It is apparent that states may impose a nondiscriminatory apportioned tax on businesses engaged in interstate commerce where a sufficient nexus exists. The next section gives additional insight into the nexus requirement.

6 NEXUS

The nexus limitation means that there must be a sufficient contact, connection, tie, or link with the taxing state to support the tax. In other words, there must be sufficient local activities to justify the tax in a constitutional sense. The constitutional requirements are stated in terms of the due process requirements of the Fourteenth Amendment. A business operating in a state directly benefits from its police and fire protection, use of its roads and the like. Indirectly it will be able to recruit employees more easily if they have easy access to good schools, parks, and civic centers. If the state gives anything for which it can reasonably expect payment, then the tax has a sufficient nexus. In cases involving property taxes, the term "taxable situs" is used in place of "nexus," but each is concerned with the adequacy of local activities to support the tax. The Braniff Airline case which follows is a typical "nexus" or "situs" case.

Braniff Airways v. Nebraska State Bd. of Eq. & A.
347 U.S. 590 (1954)

REED, JUSTICE: The question presented by this appeal from the Supreme Court of Nebraska is whether the Constitution bars the State of Nebraska from levying an apportioned ad valorem tax on the flight equipment of appellant, an interstate air carrier. Appellant is not incorporated in Nebraska and does not have its principal place of business or home port . . . in that state. Such flight equipment is employed as a part of a system of interstate air commerce operating over fixed routes and landing on and departing from airports within Nebraska on regular schedules. . . . It contends . . . that its flight equipment used in interstate commerce is immune from taxation by Nebraska because it is without situs in that state. . . .

The home port registered with the Civil Aeronautics Authority and the overhaul base for the aircraft in question is the Minneapolis–St. Paul Airport, Minnesota. All of the aircraft not undergoing overhaul fly regular schedules upon a circuit ranging from Minot, North Dakota, to New Orleans, Louisiana, with stops in fourteen states including Minnesota, Nebraska and Oklahoma. . . . The Nebraska stops are of short duration since utilized only for the discharge and loading of passengers, mail, express, and freight, and sometimes refueling. Appellant neither owns nor maintains facilities for repairing, reconditioning, or storing its flight equipment in Nebraska, but rents depot space and hires other services as required.

Required reports filed . . . for 1950 show that about 9% of its revenue and 11½% of the total system tonnage originated in Nebraska and about 9% of its total stops were made in that state. From these figures, using the statutory formula, the Tax Commissioner arrived at a valuation of $118,901 allocable to Nebraska, resulting in a tax of $4,280.44. . . . The Supreme Court of Nebraska held the statute not violative of the Commerce Clause. . . .

The argument upon which appellant depends ultimately, however, is that its aircraft never "attained a taxable situs within Nebraska" from which it argues that the Nebraska tax imposes a burden on interstate commerce. In relying upon the Commerce Clause on this issue and in not specifically claiming protection under the Due Process Clause of the Fourteenth Amendment, appellant names the wrong constitutional clause to support its position. While the question of whether a commodity en route to market is sufficiently settled in a state for purpose of subjection to a property tax has been determined by this Court as a Commerce Clause question, the bare question whether an instrumentality of commerce has tax situs in a state for the purpose of subjection to a property tax is one of due process. However, appellant timely raised and preserved its contention that its property was not taxable because such property had attained no taxable situs in Nebraska. Though inexplicit, we consider the due process issue within the clear intendment of such contention and hold such issue sufficiently presented. . . .

The limitation imposed by the Due Process Clause upon state power to impose taxes upon such instrumentalities was succinctly stated in the *Ott* case: "So far as due process is concerned the only question is whether the tax in practical operation has relation to opportunities, benefits, or protection conferred or afforded by the taxing State." 336 U.S. at page 174. . . . In *Curry v. McCanless*, 307 U.S. 357, . . . the evolution of such restriction on state power was reviewed and the rule stated thusly:

When we speak of the jurisdiction to tax land or chattels as being exclusively in the state where they are physically located, we mean no more than that the benefit and protection of laws enabling the owner to enjoy the fruits of his ownership and the power to reach effectively the interests protected, for the purpose of subjecting them to payment of a tax are so narrowly restricted to the state in whose territory the physical property is located as to set practical limits to taxation by others. . . .

Thus the situs issue devolves into the question of whether eighteen stops per day by appellant's aircraft is sufficient contact with Nebraska to sustain that state's power to levy an apportioned ad valorem tax on such aircraft. We think such regular contact is sufficient to establish Nebraska's power to tax even though the same aircraft do not land every day and even though none of the aircraft is continuously within the state. "The basis of the jurisdiction is the habitual employment of the property within the state." Appellant rents its ground facilities and pays for fuel it purchases in Nebraska. This leaves it in the position of other carriers such as rails, boats and motors that pay for the use of local facilities so as to have the opportunity to exploit the commerce, traffic, and trade that originates in or reaches Nebraska. Approximately one-tenth of appellant's revenue is produced by the pickup and discharge of Nebraska freight and passengers. Nebraska certainly affords protection during such stops and these regular landings are clearly a benefit to appellant. . . . [AFFIRMED]

After the foregoing decision, business reacted and encouraged legislation to reduce the burdens of multiple income taxation. The Interstate Income Law, passed by Congress, provides that a tax cannot be imposed on the net income of a person or corporation engaged in interstate business when the only business activity within the state is:

1 The solicitation of orders by such person, or his representative, in such state for sales of tangible personal property, which orders are sent outside the state for approval or rejection, and, if approved, are filled by shipment or delivery from a point outside the State; or

2 the solicitation of orders by such person, or his representative, in such State in the name of or for the benefit of a prospective customer of such person, if orders by such customer to such person to enable such customer to fill orders resulting from such solicitation are orders described in paragraph (1).

3 Selling or soliciting sales through one or more independent contractors, whether or not the latter have an office in the taxing state.

The area of nontaxable activities is obviously quite limited. In addition the act does not grant relief to corporations domiciled in the taxing state or individuals domiciled in the taxing state. For purposes of exception 3, an independent contractor is one who acts on behalf of "more than one principal and who holds himself out as such in the regular course of his business activities."

The State of Louisiana held the Interstate Income Tax Law to be constitutional and the Supreme Court of the United States refused to review this decision. This statute has not ended the clamor for additional laws to reduce the multiple tax burdens on interstate commerce. Some of the reasons for business dissatisfaction with taxation based on nexus and a reasonable apportionment formula are: (1) the major cost in compliance with the record-keeping rules of every state and municipal government (each is allowed to impose a tax using its own formula); (2) excessive taxation in the aggregate resulting from various formulas and procedures; (3) erroneous formulas particularly in sales tax apportionment when it is difficult to ascertain the state in which the sale is made; and (4) the need for uniformity in the law to ensure fairness and proper compliance.

To illustrate the complexity of the problem, at least thirty-eight states have corporate income tax laws and sales tax laws, thirty-seven states have capital stock tax laws, and eight states have gross receipts taxes. No two taxing states use identical formulas and there is even a wide variation in the factors included in the various formulas.

Many solutions are being advanced for the difficult problems caused by the "nexus" concept. Some would create a national formula which all taxing bodies would be required to follow. Others would limit the power to tax businesses actually located in the states. Time and the legislative process may provide a solution.

7 DISCRIMINATION AGAINST INTERSTATE COMMERCE

The discrimination limitation prohibits the tax burden from discriminating against interstate commerce in favor of intrastate commerce. Otherwise, the tax will violate the commerce clause, as the case which follows illustrates.

West Point Wholesale Groc. Co. v. City of Opelika
354 U.S. 390 (1957)

HARLAN, JUSTICE: This is a suit to recover taxes paid by the appellant to the City of Opelika, Alabama, on the ground that the taxes in question imposed a discriminatory burden on interstate commerce. The state court sustained a demurrer to the complaint, rejecting the appellant's federal contention, and we noted probable jurisdiction. . . .

Section 130(a), of Ordinance No. 101–53 of the City of Opelika, as amended by Ordinance No. 103–53, provides that an annual privilege tax of $250 must be paid by any firm engaged in the wholesale grocery business which delivers, at wholesale, groceries in the City from points without the City. Appellant is a Georgia corporation engaged in the wholesale grocery business in West Point, Georgia. It solicits business in the City of Opelika through salesmen; orders are transmitted to appellant's place of business in Georgia, where they are accepted and the groceries thereupon loaded on trucks and delivered to the City. Appellant has no place of business, office, or inventory in Opelika, its only contact with that City being the solicitation of orders and the delivery of goods.

We held in *Nippert v. City of Richmond*, 327 U.S. 416, . . . and in *Memphis Steam Laundry Cleaner, Inc. v. Stone*, 342 U.S. 389, . . . that a municipality may not impose a flat-sum privilege tax on an interstate enterprise whose only contact with the municipality is the solicitation of orders and the subsequent delivery of goods at the end of an uninterrupted movement in interstate commerce, such a tax having a substantial exclusory effect on interstate commerce. In our opinion the tax here in question falls squarely within the ban of those cases. This is particularly so in that Opelika places no comparable flat-sum tax on local merchants. Wholesale grocers whose deliveries originate in Opelika, instead of paying $250 annually, are taxed a sum graduated according to their gross receipts. Such an Opelika wholesaler would have to gross the sum of $280,000 in sales in one year before his tax would reach the flat $250 amount imposed on all foreign grocers before they may set foot in the City. The Commerce Clause forbids any such discrimination against the free flow of trade over state boundaries.

Since the present tax cannot constitutionally be applied to the appellant, the judgment must be reversed and the case remanded for proceedings not inconsistent with this opinion. [REVERSED]

8   BURDENS ON INTERSTATE COMMERCE

In many ways, any discussion of the burdens on interstate commerce as a result of state exercise of the taxing power actually involves other issues such as discrimination against interstate commerce. For example, issues of discrimination against interstate commerce are sometimes called the "burden of discrimination," and issues of failure to apportion the tax to local activities are sometimes called "multiple burdens." Since the courts frequently discuss burdens on interstate commerce as a separate grounds for challenge, it is helpful to examine a typical case discussing the burden on interstate commerce as a constitutional issue.

H & B Communications Corp. v. City of Richland
484 P.2d 1141 (Wash., 1971)

WRIGHT, JUSTICE: This case involves a challenge by the appellant, H & B Communications Corporation, to the constitutionality of a business and occupation tax levied by the respondent, City of Richland, Washington, on the gross revenues earned by appellant in said city.

The appellant operates a community antenna television system, known as CATV, in Richland. The CATV system began in Richland on December 8, 1953, when J. H. Whitney & Co., predecessor in interest of the appellant entered into a "license agreement" with the General Electric Company, predecessor in interest of respondent.

On June 6, 1960, the respondent enacted ordinance No. 5.20.090, which reads in material part as follows:

There is hereby levied upon and shall be collected from every person engaged in or carrying on the business of transmitting television by cable, a fee or tax equal to three (3) per cent of the total gross income from such business during the tax year for which the license is required.

On January 3, 1967, ordinance No. 5.20.090 was amended to increase the tax from three per cent to five per cent.

Appellant's CATV system does not broadcast, but transmits television programs to the listener-viewer via a coaxial cable which is suspended on utility poles. Appellant pays twenty-five cents per month for the use of each pole.

Appellant's CATV system, the only one in the Richland area, carries programs originating from eight television stations and three FM radio stations. The approximately four thousand subscribers pay appellant for this service at the rate of an initial $15 hook-up charge and $7.50 per month.

Programs carried over the CATV system include national and local news broadcasts, religious broadcasts, communications originating from governmental agencies, and educational programs. Educational television is federally subsidized.

The appellant contends that the Richland business and occupation tax on the CATV system places a burden on interstate commerce, and is therefore unconstitutional. Since the appellant's CATV system carries nationally transmitted broadcasts, there can be no question as to its interstate character.

The fact that the activity engaged in constitutes interstate commerce, does not free the activity from the tax being levied. Interstate business may pay its way. . . .

Since the decision in *Western Live Stock v. Bureau of Internal Revenue* (1938), 303 U.S. 250, the primary considerations for determining the limits of a state's power to tax activities connected with interstate commerce have been these: (1) Whether the tax places an extra burden on interstate commerce not borne by intrastate commerce, or erects barriers, placing out-of-state businesses at a disadvantage when competing locally; *the discrimination test*. (2) Whether the interstate commerce involved is subject to the risk of repeated exactions of the same nature from other states; *the multiple burden test*. . . . In the instant case, there is no burden on interstate commerce that is not placed on intrastate commerce. Under Richland City Ordinance No. 5.20.090, any person engaged in transmitting television by cable is subject to the gross receipts tax.

Appellant's CATV system is not subject to the risk of repeated taxation of the same nature since it only operates in the city of Richland. Therefore, respondent's business and occupation tax violates neither the "discrimination test" nor the "multiple burden test. . . .

Federal regulation does not preclude state taxation and state taxation does not preclude federal regulation. Numerous cases have upheld state levies where it is thought that the tax does not operate to discriminate against commerce or unduly burden it either directly or by the possibility of multiple taxation resulting from other taxes of the same sort being imposed by other states. . . . [AFFIRMED]

9   SALES AND USE TAXES: A SPECIAL PROBLEM

For many years the sales tax has been an important source of state revenue. However, problems of avoidance arose when one state imposed a sales tax and a neighboring state did not. For example, if the State of Illinois imposed a 5 percent sales tax and the State of Indiana did not, a new car buyer would save $200 on a $4,000 car if he purchased it in Indiana. To plug this gap, the use tax was developed. It taxes the user of personal property purchased outside the state and brought into it for use there in an amount equal to the sales tax.

The case which follows illustrates the breadth of the typical state law in this area and the types of transactions to which it is applied.

Sullivan v. United States
89 S.Ct. 1648 (1969)

STEWART, JUSTICE: The issue raised by this appeal is whether § 514 of the Soldiers' and Sailors' Civil Relief Act prohibits Connecticut from imposing its sales and use taxes on servicemen stationed there who are residents or domiciliaries of other States. The United States instituted this action in federal court against the appropriate Connecticut officials on behalf of the aggrieved servicemen. The District Court entered a declaratory judgment that the federal statute prevents collection of the sales and use taxes from such servicemen, and the Court of Appeals affirmed. We noted probable jurisdiction of this appeal.

The sales and use taxes imposed by the Connecticut Education, Welfare, and Public Health Tax Act are typical of those enacted by the vast majority of States. A tax of 3½% is levied on the gross receipts from sales of tangible personal property at retail within the State. Although the retailer is liable for payment of the tax, he is required to pass it on to purchasers by adding it to the original sales price of all items sold. The use tax is imposed at the same rate on "the storage, use or other consumption" in the State of tangible personal property purchased from any retailer. The use tax provisions—designed to reach the use or consumption in the State of property purchased outside it—exempt all transactions which are subject to the sales tax. And while the consumer is liable directly to the State for the use tax, he can discharge his liability by paying it to the retailer if the retailer is "engaged in business" within the State and therefore required to collect the use tax. The use tax is also imposed upon purchasers of motor vehicles, boats, or airplanes from nonretailers. The amount of any tax under the Act is reduced by whatever sales or use tax has already been collected "by any other state or political subdivision thereof." Finally, the Act commands that all proceeds of the sales and use taxes "shall be allocated to and expended for public health, welfare and education purposes only."

By stipulation and affidavits in the District Court, the parties offered some examples of the imposition of these taxes on naval personnel stationed in Connecticut but domiciled elsewhere. Lieutenant Schuman, a Nebraska domiciliary, and Commander Carroll, a Michigan domiciliary, bought used motorboats from nonretailers in Connecticut and were assessed a use tax. Schuman paid the tax under protest, and Carroll has refused to pay, each claiming that he is exempt under the Soldiers' and Sailors' Civil Relief Act. Lieutenant Commander Schaffer and Commander Foster, who are domiciled in Pennsylvania and Texas respectively, each purchased a new car; the Connecticut retailer collected and paid the sales tax. Foster registered his car in Texas, which also exacted a sales or use tax. Finally, Commander Roloff, whose home State is Wisconsin, purchased a used car in Florida and paid that State a 2% sales tax. When he registered the car in Connecticut, he was assessed and paid the use tax, with credit for the Florida sales tax.

As enacted in 1942, § 514 of the Soldiers' and Sailors' Civil Relief Act provided that for purposes of any state "taxation in respect of any person, or of his [personal] property, income, or gross income," he shall not be deemed to have lost his residence or domicile in his home State or acquired a residence in any other State "solely by reason of being absent [from home] in compliance with military or naval orders." Clarifying language was added in 1944 to provide that for purposes of taxation in respect of personal property, the "personal property shall not be deemed to be located or present in or to have a situs for taxation in such State." Also in 1944 Congress enacted a special subsection for automobiles: servicemen are exempt from "licenses, fees, or excises imposed in respect of motor vehicles or the use thereof" if they have paid such levies in their home States. Finally, in 1962, Congress added the provision that § 514 applies to property in any tax jurisdiction other than the serviceman's home State, "regardless of where the owner may be serving" in compliance with military orders.

We think it clear from the face of § 514 that state taxation of *sales* to servicemen is not proscribed. A tax on the privilege of selling or buying property has long been recognized as distinct from a tax on the property itself. And while § 514 refers to taxes "in respect of" rather than "on" personal property, we think it an overly strained construction to say that taxation of the sales transaction is the same as taxation "in respect of" the personal property transferred. . . . Had Congress intended to include sales taxes within the coverage of § 514, it surely would not have employed language so poorly suited to that purpose as "taxation in respect of the personal property."

It is contended on behalf of the servicemen that, even if § 514 does not encompass sales taxes, at least it prohibits taxation of the *use* of personal property. Not only are use taxes said to fall literally within the meaning of the phrase "taxation in respect of the personal property," but § 514 specifically refers in several places to property "or the use thereof." Moreover, it is argued, the sole jurisdictional basis of the use tax is the location of the personal property in Connecticut; yet imposition of a tax with such incidence on a serviceman contravenes the command of § 514 that his personal property "shall not be deemed to be located or present in or to have a situs for taxation in such State." While we agree that use taxes are not so clearly excluded by the language of § 514 as are sales taxes, neither do we believe that they are clearly included. And consideration of the purpose and legislative history of § 514 along with its language and other factors has led us to the conclusion that Congress did not intend to free servicemen stationed away from home from the sales *or* use taxes of the host State. . . .

Section 514 does not relieve servicemen stationed away from home from all taxes of the host State. It was enacted with the much narrower design "to prevent multiple State taxation of the property." And the substantial risk of double taxation under multi-state ad valorem property taxes does not exist with respect to sales and use taxes. Like Connecticut, nearly every State which levies such taxes provides a credit for sales or use taxes paid on the transaction to another State. . . . [T]he absence of any significant risk of double taxation under state sales and use taxes generally is therefore strong evidence of congressional intent not to include them in § 514. . . .

It is . . . evident that in subsection (2) (b) Congress was dealing solely with a unique form of state "tax"—the motor vehicle registration fee. Because such fees are not always clearly classifiable as property taxes, servicemen would not be exempted from many of them by subsection (1) of § 514. Since annually recurring license fees raise much the same risk of double taxation to transitory military personnel as do property taxes, Congress evidently decided in 1944 to extend the exemption of § 514 to include motor vehicle registration fees as well as property taxes. . . .

For these reasons we hold that § 514 of the Soldiers' and Sailors' Civil Relief Act does not exempt servicemen from the sales and use taxes imposed by Connecticut. Accordingly, the judgment is

Reversed. [REVERSED]

As might be suspected, there are many cases involving the collection of sales and use taxes on services and on goods which have moved or are moving in interstate commerce. Insofar as services are concerned, income from a ski tow was taxed in Wisconsin, and a Georgia case held that "slot machine" income is subject to the use tax.

An additional question arises of whether or not a businessman in one state must collect and remit sales and use taxes to all other states in which the goods he has sold may be delivered or used. To what extent must a seller inquire of the domicile of his buyer? These and other questions are involved in the following decisions.

Scripto, Inc. v. Carson
362 U.S. 207 (1960)

CLARK, JUSTICE: Florida, by statute, requires appellant, a Georgia corporation, to be responsible for the collection of a use tax on certain mechanical writing instruments which appellant sells and ships from its place of business in Atlanta to residents of Florida for use and enjoyment there. Upon Scripto's failure to collect the tax, the appellee Comptroller levied a use tax liability of $5,150.66 against it. Appellant then brought this suit to test the validity of the imposition, contending that the requirement of Florida's statute places a burden on interstate commerce and violates the Due Process Clause of the Fourteenth Amendment to the Constitution. It claimed, in effect, that the nature of its operations in Florida does not form a sufficient nexus to subject it to the statute's exactions. Both the trial court and the Supreme Court of Florida held that appellant does have sufficient jurisdictional contacts in Florida and, therefore, must register as a dealer under the statute and collect and remit to the State the use tax imposed on its aforesaid sales. We noted probable jurisdiction. . . . We agree with the result reached by Florida's courts.

Appellant operates in Atlanta an advertising specialty division trading under the name of Adgif Company. Through it, appellant is engaged in the business of selling mechanical writing instruments which are adapted to advertising purposes by the placing of printed material thereon. In its Adgif operation, appellant does not (1) own, lease, or maintain any office, distributing house, warehouse or other place of business in Florida, or (2) have any regular employee or agent there. Nor does it own or maintain any bank account or stock of merchandise in the State. Orders for its products are solicited by advertising specialty brokers or, as the Supreme Court of Florida called them, wholesalers or jobbers, who are residents of Florida. At the time of suit, there were 10 such brokers—each having a written contract and a specific territory. The somewhat detailed contract provides, *inter alia*, that all compensation is to be on a commission basis on the sales made, provided they are accepted by appellant; repeat orders, even if not solicited, also carry a commission if the salesman has not become inactive through failure to secure acceptable orders during the previous 60 days. The contract specifically provides that it is the intention of the parties "to create the relationship . . . of independent contractor." Each order is to be signed by the solicitor as a "salesman"; however, he has no authority to make collections or incur debts involving appellant. Each salesman is furnished catalogs, samples, and advertising material, and is actively engaged in Florida as a representative "of Scripto for the purpose of attracting, soliciting and obtaining Florida customers" for its mechanical advertising specialties. Orders for such products are sent by these salesmen directly to the Atlanta office for acceptance or refusal. If accepted, the sale is consummated there and the salesman is paid his commission directly. No money passes between the purchaser and the salesman—although the latter does occasionally accept a check payable to the appellant, in which event he is required to forward it to appellant with the order.

As construed by Florida's highest court, the impost levied by the statute is a tax "on the privilege of using personal property . . . which has come to rest . . . and has become a part of the mass of property" within the State. 105 So. 2d at page 781. It is not a sales tax, but "was developed as a device to complement [such a tax] in order to prevent evasion . . . by the completion of purchases in a nontaxing state and shipment by interstate commerce into a taxing forum." *Id.*, at page 779. The tax is collectible from "dealers" and is to be added to the purchase price of the merchandise "as far as practicable." In the event that a dealer fails to collect the tax, he himself is liable for its payment. The statute has the customary use tax provisions "against duplication of the tax, an allowance to the dealer for making the collection, and a reciprocal credit arrangement which credits against the Florida tax any amount up to the amount of the Florida tax which might have been paid to another state." *Id.*, at page 782. Florida held appellant to be a dealer under its statute. "The application by that Court of its local laws and the facts on which it founded its judgment are of course controlling here." . . .

The question remaining is whether Florida, in the light of appellant's operations there, may collect the State's use tax from it on the basis of property bought from appellant and shipped from its home office to purchasers in Florida for use there.

Florida has well stated the course of this Court's decisions governing such levies, and we need but drive home its clear understanding. There must be, as our

Brother Jackson stated in *Miller Bros. Co. v. State of Maryland,* 1954, 347 U.S. 340, 344–345, "some definite link, some minimum connection, between a state and the person, property or transaction it seeks to tax." We believe that such a nexus is present here. First, the tax is a nondiscriminatory exaction levied for the use and enjoyment of property which has been purchased by Florida residents and which has actually entered into and become a part of the mass of property in that State. The burden of the tax is placed on the ultimate purchaser in Florida and it is he who enjoys the use of the property, regardless of its source. We note that the appellant is charged with no tax—save when, as here, he fails or refuses to collect it from the Florida customer. Next, as Florida points out, appellant has 10 wholesalers, jobbers, or "salesmen" conducting continuous local solicitation in Florida and forwarding the resulting orders from that State to Atlanta for shipment of the ordered goods. The only incidence of this sales transaction that is nonlocal is the acceptance of the order. True, the "salesmen" are not regular employees of appellant devoting full time to its service, but we conclude that such a fine distinction is without constitutional significance. The formal shift in the contractual tagging of the salesman as "independent" neither results in changing his local function of solicitation nor bears upon its effectiveness in securing a substantial flow of goods into Florida. This is evidenced by the amount assessed against appellant on the statute's 3% basis over a period of but four years. To permit such formal "contractual shifts" to make a constitutional difference would open the gates to a stampede of tax avoidance. . . .

Moreover, we cannot see, from a constitutional standpoint, "that it was important that the agent worked for several principals." Chief Judge Learned Hand, in *Bomze v. Nardis Sportswear,* 2 Cir. 165 F.2d 33, 36. The test is simply the nature and extent of the activities of the appellant in Florida. In short, we conclude that this case is controlled by *General Trading Co., supra.* As was said there:

> *All these differentiations are without constitutional significance. Of course, no State can tax the privilege of doing interstate business. . . . That is within the protection of the Commerce Clause and subject to the power of Congress. On the other hand, the mere fact that property is used for interstate commerce or has come into an owner's possession as a result of interstate commerce does not diminish the protection which he may draw from a State to the upkeep of which he may be asked to bear his fair share.*

Nor do we believe that Florida's requirement that appellant be its tax collector on such orders from its residents changes the situation. As was pointed out in *General Trading Co.,* this is "a familiar and sanctioned device." Moreover, we note that Florida reimburses appellant for its service in this regard.

Appellant earnestly contends that *Miller Bros. Co. v. State of Maryland, supra,* is to the contrary. We think not. Miller had no solicitors in Maryland; there was no "exploitation of the consumer market"; no regular, systematic displaying of its products by catalogs, samples or the like. But, on the contrary, the goods on which Maryland sought to force Miller to collect its tax were sold to residents of Maryland when personally present at Miller's store in Delaware. True, there was an "occasional" delivery of such purchases by Miller into Maryland, and it did occasionally mail notices of special sales to former customers; but Marylanders went to Delaware to make purchases—Miller did not go to Maryland for sales. Moreover, it was impossible for Miller to determine that goods sold for cash to a customer over the counter at its store in Delaware were to be used and enjoyed in Maryland. This led the Court to conclude that Miller would be made "more vulnerable to liability for another's tax than to a tax on itself." 347 U.S. at page 346. . . . In view of these considerations, we conclude that the "minimum connections" not present in *Miller* are more than sufficient here.

The judgment is therefore affirmed. [AFFIRMED]

National Bellas Hess, Inc. v. Department of Rev.
87 S.Ct. 1389 (1967)

STEWART, JUSTICE: The appellant, National Bellas Hess, is a mail order house with its principal place of business in North Kansas City, Missouri. It is licensed to do business in only that State and in Delaware, where it is incorporated. Although the company has neither outlets nor sales representatives in Illinois, the appellee, Department of Revenue, obtained a judgment from the Illinois Supreme Court that National is required to collect and pay to the State the use taxes imposed by Ill.Rev.Stat. c. 120, § 439.3 (1965).

The facts bearing upon National's relationship with Illinois are accurately set forth in the opinion of the State Supreme Court:

[National] does not maintain in Illinois any office, distribution house, sales house, warehouse or any other place of business; it does not have in Illinois any agent, salesman, canvasser, solicitor or other type of representative to sell or take orders, to deliver merchandise, to accept payments, or to service merchandise it sells; it does not own any tangible property, real or personal, in Illinois; it has no telephone listing in Illinois and it has not advertised its merchandise for sale in newspapers, on billboards, or by radio or television in Illinois.

All of the contacts which National does have with the State are via the United States mail or common carrier. Twice a year catalogues are mailed to the company's active or recent customers throughout the Nation, including Illinois. This mailing is supplemented by advertising "flyers" which are occasionally mailed to past and potential customers. Orders for merchandise are mailed by the customers to National and are accepted at its Missouri plant. The ordered goods are then sent to the customers either by mail or by common carrier.

This manner of doing business is sufficient under the Illinois statute to classify National as a "[r]etailer maintaining a place of business in this State," since that term includes any retailer:

Engaging in soliciting orders within this State from users by means of catalogues or other advertising, whether such orders are received or accepted within or without this State. Ill. Rev.Stat. c. 120, § 439.2 (1965).

Accordingly, the statute requires National to collect and pay to the appellee Department the tax imposed by Illinois upon consumers who purchase the company's goods for use within the State. When collecting this tax, National must give the Illinois purchaser "a receipt therefor in the manner and form prescribed by the [appellee]," if one is demanded. It must also "keep such records, receipts, invoices and other pertinent books, documents, memoranda and papers as the [appellee] shall require, in such form as the [appellee] shall require," and must submit to such investigations, hearings, and examinations as are needed by the appellee to administer and enforce the use tax law. Failure to keep such records or to give required receipts is punishable by a fine of up to $5,000 and imprisonment of up to six months. Finally, to allow service of process on an out-of-state company like National, the statute designates the Illinois Secretary of State as National's appointed agent, and jurisdiction in tax collection suits attaches when process is served on him and the company is notified by registered mail.

National argues that the liabilities which Illinois has thus imposed violate the Due Process Clause of the Fourteenth Amendment and create an unconstitutional burden upon interstate commerce. These two claims are closely related. For the test whether a particular state exaction is such as to invade the exclusive authority of Congress to regulate trade between the States, and the test for a State's compliance with the requirements of due process in this area are similar. As to the former, the Court has held that "State taxation falling on interstate commerce . . . can only be justified as designed to make such commerce bear a fair share of the cost of the local government whose protection it enjoys." And in determining whether a state tax falls within the confines of the Due Process Clause, the Court has said that the "simple but controlling question is whether the state has given anything for which it can ask return."

The same principles have been held applicable in determining the power of a State to impose the burdens of collecting use taxes upon interstate sales. Here, too, the Constitution requires "some definite link, some minimum connection, between a state and the person, property or transaction it seeks to tax."

In applying these principles the Court has upheld the power of a State to impose liability upon an out-of-state seller to collect a local use tax in a variety of circumstances. Where the sales were arranged by local agents in the taxing State, we have upheld such power. We have reached the same result where the mail order seller maintained local retail stores. In those situations the out-of-state seller was plainly accorded the protection and services of the taxing State. The case in this Court which represents the furthest constitutional reach to date of a State's power to deputize an out-of-state retailer as its collection agent for a use tax is *Scripto, Inc. v. Carson*, 362 U.S. 207. There we held that Florida could constitutionally impose upon a Georgia seller the duty of collecting a state use tax upon the sale of goods shipped to customers in Florida. In that case the seller had "10 wholesalers, jobbers, or 'salesmen' conducting continuous local solicitation in Florida and forwarding the resulting orders from that State to Atlanta for shipment of the ordered goods."

But the Court has never held that a State may impose the duty of use tax collection and payment upon a seller whose only connection with customers in the State is by common carrier or the United States mail. Indeed, the Court [has] sharply differentiated such a situation from one where the seller had local retail outlets, . . . And in *Miller Bros. Co. v. State of Maryland,* 347 U.S. 340, the Court held that Maryland could not constitutionally impose a use tax obligation upon a Delaware seller who had no retail outlets or sales solicitors in Maryland. There the seller advertised its wares to Maryland residents through newspaper and radio advertising, in addition to mailing circulars four times a year. As a result, it made substantial sales to Maryland customers, and made deliveries to them by its own trucks and drivers.

In order to uphold the power of Illinois to impose use tax burdens on National in this case, we would have to repudiate totally the sharp distinction which these and other decisions have drawn between mail order sellers with retail outlets, solicitors, or property within a State, and those who do no more than communicate with customers in the State by mail or common carrier as part of a general interstate business. But this basic distinction, which until now has been generally recognized by the state taxing authorities, is a valid one, and we decline to obliterate it.

We need not rest on the broad foundation of all that was said in the *Miller Bros.* opinion, for here there was neither local advertising nor local household deliveries. . . . Indeed, it is difficult to conceive of commercial transactions more exclusively interstate in character than the mail order transactions here involved. And if the power of Illinois to impose use tax burdens upon National were upheld, the resulting impediments upon the free conduct of its interstate business would be neither imaginary nor remote. For if Illinois can impose such burdens, so can every other State, and so, indeed, can every municipality, every school district, and every other political subdivision throughout the Nation with power to impose sales and use taxes. The many variations in rates of tax, in allowable exemptions, and in administrative and record-keeping requirements could entangle National's interstate business in a virtual welter of complicated obligations to local jurisdictions with no legitimate claim to impose "a fair share of the cost of the local government."

The very purpose of the Commerce Clause was to ensure a national economy free from such unjustifiable local entanglements. Under the Constitution, this is a domain where Congress alone has the power of regulation and control. [REVERSED]

REVIEW QUESTIONS—CHAPTER 9

1 Define the following legal terms introduced in this chapter: poll tax; excise tax; ad valorem tax; property tax; nexus; apportionment; use tax.
2 Discuss five purposes for exercising the taxing power other than raising revenue.

3 Compare: direct and indirect taxes; general and special taxes; specific taxes and ad valorem taxes; property taxes and excise taxes.

4 Discuss the constitutional limitations imposed by the commerce clause on the power of state and local governments to tax business.

5 Under what circumstances have courts approved unapportioned gross income taxes? Explain.

6 Discuss the concept that interstate commerce must pay its fair share of the state and local tax burden.

7 How is it possible to tax the income of a company engaged in interstate commerce when it is not constitutional to tax the privilege of engaging in interstate commerce? Explain.

8 Discuss the role of the concept of "nexus" in cases involving the taxation of property and income of businesses engaged in interstate commerce.

9 Give examples of activities that do not constitute a sufficient "nexus" to justify taxation of a business engaged in interstate commerce.

10 Give examples of taxes that discriminate against interstate commerce and that impose an undue burden on interstate commerce.

11 Discuss the special constitutional problems involved in one state's attempting to collect its sales and use tax on sales in other states.

12 To what extent did the *National Bellas Hess* case reverse the *Scripto* case? Explain.

Chapter Ten

Introduction to Antitrust Law
—The Sherman Act

1 THE MEANING OF "ANTITRUST"

In the strict legal sense, a "trust" is a fiduciary relationship concerning property in which one person, known as the trustee, holds the legal title to the property for the benefit of another, known as the beneficiary. The trustee has the duty to manage and to preserve the property for the use and enjoyment of the beneficiary. Trusts are generally legal, and the so-called "antitrust laws" are not aimed at trusts which serve legitimate and socially desirable purposes, such as promoting education or caring for spendthrift or incompetent children. Such trusts are not within the scope of the antitrust laws.

In the last part of the nineteenth century, the trust device was used extensively for the purpose of gaining monopolistic control of different types of business. Through it, a group of corporations having the same type of business could unite in following common business policies and eliminating competition among themselves by controlling production, dividing the market, and establishing price levels. Yet the companies could remain individual, since no actual merger was necessary. Under this method, all or at least a majority of the stock in each company would be transferred to a certain board, consisting of various members of the top management of the companies, by common agreement of the stockholders involved. In exchange, the stockholders were issued trust certificates, naming them as beneficiaries of the trust and entitling them to dividends declared on the stock they had transferred. The board then was in a position to control the operation and policy making of all the companies, since it held the stock and could vote for directors of its own choosing in each. Technically, the companies were still separate businesses, but in substance they were united under one guiding hand.

Some of the first statutes attempting to control monopolistic combinations were enacted about the time this trust device was in vogue; hence these laws came to be known as "antitrust laws," although they were aimed at protecting the public from any type of monopoly. Today the term "trust," when not used in the strictly technical sense, has come to be generally applied to any monopolistic combination, whether it be by agreement, merger, holding company, interlocking directorate, or trade association.

This chapter and the next three deal with the major legislation enacted in the antitrust field, the roles of the Federal Trade Commission and the Justice Department in antitrust policy creation and enforcement, and some typical contemporary problems presented in business operation and decision making which have resulted from government involvement in regulating competition. However, before examining the *legal* requirements relative to competition, it will be beneficial to briefly note the goals of the antitrust laws and some of the economic theory upon which they are predicated.

2   THE REASONS FOR A COMPETITIVE ECONOMIC SYSTEM

Millions of words have been written about the virtues and vices of a competitive economic system as compared with other economic systems such as socialism. It is not our purpose here to review all the issues involved in such comparisons. However, we must recognize that ours *is* a competitive economic system and that the primary goal of the antitrust laws is to ensure that this competitive system works. Succinctly stated, workable competition is the goal of the antitrust laws. Thus the legal system has a primary duty to preserve, protect, and encourage our competitive economic system. The short discussion which follows summarizes the reasons for this goal.

From Report of the Attorney General's National Committee to Study the Antitrust Laws[1]
317-342 (1955)

Economic Benefits of Competition

Generally speaking, economists support competition for four series of reasons, which are of coordinate importance: (1) because the actual level of prices in competitive markets should in the short run more accurately reflect the influence of demand and of cost, and thus in the long run help guide the flow of capital and other resources toward the most productive possible uses; (2) because the goad of competition provides powerful and pervasive incentives for product innovations and product development, and for long-run cost-reduction, both through improved technology and improved management; these forces make themselves felt in the constant process of product variation, and through the

---

[1] The committee consisted of practicing attorneys, law professors, and economists, who were all specialists in antitrust or cognate fields. It was established by Attorney General Herbert Brownell, Jr., in 1953 with the commission to render a comprehensive report which he hoped would "provide an important instrument to prepare the way for modernizing and strengthening our laws to preserve American free enterprise against monopoly and unfair competition." After much study, debate, drafting, and redrafting of reports, the committee submitted the final draft of its overall report to the Attorney General on March 31, 1955. The vast bulk of this 393-page document deals with the antitrust laws: their concepts, policies, and enforcement. The one portion of the report which is concerned with the distinguishing earmarks of competition from the standpoint of economic theory rather than the antitrust law is what is presented here.

pressures implicit in the fact that competitive conditions offer an open opportunity to new entrants in a particular industry; (3) because competitive conditions in business should lead to an equitable diffusion of the resulting real income among consumers and factors of production; and (4) a view held with somewhat less unanimity than the others, because the more flexible prices of competitive markets should make it easier and cheaper for the economy to adjust to industrial fluctuations, and for the Federal Reserve System and the Government to carry through effective contracyclical programs of stabilization, primarily utilizing methods of monetary and fiscal policy.

Ours is not an exclusively competitive system. For example, the policy favoring competition has not been applied to public utilities. Public power, water, telephone, and transportation companies and other quasi-public businesses are granted exclusive or near exclusive markets by government. Permitting true monopoly power over such necessities would obviously be untenable, so, in lieu of the forces of competition, such industries are subjected to supervision of their rates and policies of operation by government agencies. The patent and copyright laws also represent a departure from a general policy favoring competition. Under the patent laws an inventor is given an exclusive monopoly to produce and sell his invention for seventeen years. Similarly, the copyright laws grant a monopoly to authors in that they have the exclusive right to multiply and sell copies of works resulting from their intellectual production for an initial period of twenty-eight years with one renewal permitted for an additional twenty-eight-year period. . . . Supposedly, the profit incentive given by these laws will induce the production of more inventions and literary works and in the end provide greater public benefit than unrestrained competition would.

(Sections 3 and 4 which follow are a continuation of the foregoing report of the Attorney General's committee.)

3   WORKABLE COMPETITION DEFINED

The concept of "workable" or "effective" competition can perhaps best be described as the economists' attempt to identify the conditions which could provide appropriate leads for policy in assuring society the substance of the advantages which competition should provide. It is a kind of economist's "Rule of Reason"—not, of course, to be confused with the legal rule of reason, but analogous to it in the sense that it is also an acknowledgment of the inevitability of the exercise of human judgment and discretion in classifying different forms of economic behavior.

The basic characteristic of effective competition in the economic sense is that no one seller, and no group of sellers acting in concert, has the power to choose its level of profits by giving less and charging more. Where there is workable competition, rival sellers, whether existing competitors or new or potential entrants into the field, would keep this power in check by offering or threatening to offer effective inducements, so long as the profits to be anticipated in the industry are sufficiently attractive in comparison with those in other employment, when all risks and other deterrents are taken into account. The result would be to force the seller who sought to increase his profits above this level by employing a high-price, limited-output monopoly policy either to give it up, or to lose ground to his rivals at a rate sufficient to reduce his profits, thus defeating his policy. In an effectively competitive market, the individual seller cannot control his rivals' offerings, and those offerings set narrow limits on his discretion as to price and production. He must, in the light of his own costs, adjust his offerings to a market scale of prices for offerings of different quality or attractiveness. In the moderately long run, he must accept market prices determined by changes in supply and demand beyond any effect which may be attributable to his own change in price or output. These market conditions inflict penalties on high costs or poor services. To bring this result about, it is necessary that rivals be free in fact to compete by lower prices and better service or products and selling activities, if they can achieve low enough costs to enable them to do so; and that no seller have power to limit this freedom of his rivals, and thus escape the pressures and penalties which effective competition imposes.

The market pressures which effective competition imposes upon each seller derive from the self-interested rivalry of his competitors. The essential character of this rivalry is to promote the competitor's economic interest by offering buyers inducements attractive enough to cause them to deal with him, in free bargaining, and in the face of inducements offered by his rivals.[a] The inducements consist of quantity, quality, time and place of delivery, incidental services, selling effort and price. The chief enabling condition is efficient operation. The rivalry may take the form of trying to enlarge one's share of the market by offering something more attractive than one's competitors, or to avoid a reduction of one's share of the business by offsetting the superior attractions of rivals' offers. In other words, competition includes both aggressive and defensive tactics.

Competitive rivalry in a given business situation may or may not be capable of developing enough force to deny any one seller or group of sellers acting in concert effective power to control the price they will charge, and other conditions of sale. Whether this condition is achieved normally depends on the character of the market. Active competition, for example, may involve initial moves by one competitor, the responses of the buyers, and the further responses of rival sellers. In some cases, the distinction between effective and ineffective competition may depend in part upon the speed of these responses, both the absolute and relative speed, and the certainty or uncertainty of buyers' responses and rivals' responses. The character of these responses may be affected not only by the agressiveness and business policies of the rival sellers and buyers, but by their number, relative size and the nature of their expectations.

---

[a] The wording is intentionally chosen to avoid stating or implying that the customers *prefer* to deal with him, or that he offers or tries to offer *superior* inducements, such as *lower* prices. The definition should not be read to imply that A is not competing with B unless he invariably offers a lower price than B's. But he must be free to do so.

The market pressures of effective competition can be, and should properly be, quite severe. The firm rendering service inferior to that of its rivals would be seriously handicapped; and a firm maintaining superiority over its rivals has a prospect of increasing its volume of trade progressively at their expense so long as it can maintain this superiority. The penalties of unsuccessful competition may take the form of either a positive shrinkage or a failure to expand, and may be viewed in a short-term or a long-run perspective. It is ordinarily poor business policy, to attempt to squeeze out the utmost profit that can be made in a single year, at least where other firms can enter the field, or where substitute goods or services are at all available. In an effectively competitive market, if one seller is shortsighted enough to attempt this, others will grow at his expense. The law need not concern itself with good managerial practice in this regard since it is sufficiently assured by the market itself, provided the conditions of market rivalry are sufficiently free, active, and healthy.

4 SUMMARY OF FACTORS BEARING ON IDENTIFICATION OF WORKABLE COMPETITION

What aspects of the market situation are significant in determining whether or not it is effectively competitive from the economic point of view? The short-hand legal definition of monopoly—"power . . . to raise prices or to exclude competition when it desired to do so" [b]—focuses directly on the ultimate economic elements of the problem. The economic definition of workable competition concentrates on the effective limits it sets on the power of a seller, or group of sellers acting in concert, over their price. That power cannot normally be retained for long without natural or imposed limitations on the opportunity for entry or growth of rivals. Restriction on the entry of rival firms is an integral part of the economic as it is of the legal definition of monopoly power, for competitive results are often less likely in a market where entry is not reasonably free. The factors listed below are considered some of the more important in summing up the economic aspects of workable competition. They indicate some of the types of information that may be used in determining whether, from an economic standpoint, effective competition exists. Of the 10 factors enumerated, the first 3 are the most general. But all the factors are in varying degrees elements of market situations which bear directly on the presence or absence of effective competition, in the sense in which that term is used in this section, i.e., a seller's power over his own price.

Several members emphasize that the first three factors are not only more general but overwhelmingly more important. Freedom of entry is basic but the ultimate test of freedom of entry is the appearance of new rivals; and independence of action of rivals is also basic but independence is highly correlated with the number of rivals—so the number (and relative size) of firms is especially

[b] *American Tobacco Co. v. United States,* 328 U.S. 781, 811 (1946).

strategic. The minor and equivocal information provided by the other factors should not obscure this broad verdict of economic analysis.

(1) A Number of Effective Competitive Sellers: The Issue of Relative Size The number and relative strength of firms necessary to effective competition cannot be compressed into a formula. The answer to the question depends also on other factors, including those hereafter discussed, so that a given number of firms might be compatible with effective competition in one industry and not in another. Size in the abstract is meaningless. Whatever significance it has exists only in relation to a particular market. Absolute size, as measured by number of employees, or dollars of assets, or similar formulae, has no significance in determining the presence or absence of workable competition. The interrelation and relative importance in different situations of the various factors bearing on the presence or absence of effective competition have not yet been fully isolated and measured by economics. However, where firms are few in number, special study would usually be needed to determine whether an industry were workably competitive.

For effective competition, in the economic sense, to exist, there should be that degree of self-interested independent rivalry in any given market that exists where there is no one firm or group of firms acting in concert which have effective monopoly power, as heretofore defined. By this we mean that no one firm or group of firms acting in concert could hold for long the power to choose its level of profits by giving less and charging more, or to exclude the entry into the market of alternate sources of supply.

Unless numbers are already large in a given market, a reduction of numbers may involve some reduction of competition, although not necessarily a lessening to the point of "effective" monopoly. Where genuine economies of large scale operations, or other considerations (including the capacity to innovate), permit only very small numbers of sellers, added vigilance is indicated as to other requisites of effective competition.

Effective competition may be affected not only by the total number of sellers; their relative size and strength must also be considered. This does not mean that close equality of size among the various firms is essential for workable competition to exist, but only that the rivalry should not depend entirely upon sellers who are so weak or inefficient as to exist by sufferance. For such firms are not independent, and are not properly counted among the number of effectively competitive sellers. And as the number of independent sellers reaches unity, the market obviously reaches monopoly. The presence in any market of a unit much stronger than the others is a factor to be closely examined for its bearing on the workably competitive character of that market, and on the issue of whether any firm in fact exists only by sufferance, but by itself is not indicative of the absence of workable competition.

Where the number of sellers is large, each one of them faces an impersonal market with a market price which he can take or leave. He can do little to affect total supply or to raise the market price.

When sellers are few, each producing a significant share of total market supply, each seller is aware of the fact that any substantial change in his price or his production will have an appreciable effect upon total market supply and market price, and will tend to elicit responsive changes in the prices and outputs of his rivals. Hence there is a mutual awareness rather than an impersonal market relationship. Where such a market is isolated from competitive pressures, the possibility of successful collusion is greater, to detect it is harder, and its rewards may be more immediate and tempting. Hence there is need for vigilance in scrutinizing such industries, without prejudging whether in fact any type of conspiracy exists. When sellers are few, even in the absence of conspiracy, the market itself may not show many of the characteristics of effective competition, and in fact may not be effectively competitive in the economic sense.

(2) Opportunity for Entry From the economic point of view, relative freedom of opportunity for entry of new rivals is a fundamental requisite for effective competition in the long run. Without this condition, it is idle to expect effective competition. The entry and withdrawal of firms, whether new firms or existing firms from other market areas, or other industries, or other stages of production and marketing, is the basic mechanism of the market for achieving its economic results. The cost of entry into the competitive area should not be impracticably high. This does not imply an absolute criterion for ease of entry in terms of a given number of dollars. Nor does it deny recognition to the fact that as a practical matter, the size of minimum adequate investment capital and other factors may make the entry of new firms into even a competitive industry a relatively slow or hazardous process. But it does mean that under prevailing conditions as to the availability of capital, an attempt by existing firms to raise prices considerably above the competitive norm would make it profitable and practicable for new firms or existing borderline firms to invade the field. In economic terms, this means that conditions of cost for a new firm should not be excessively higher, at least after a reasonable period of initial development, than conditions of cost for an existing member of the industry. In many cases, of course, the new firm may start with the cost advantage of being able to use the most advanced available techniques.

Reasonable opportunity of outsiders with requisite skill to enter the market may appear dispensable, for if there are a sufficient number of competitors, and they compete vigorously, what purpose would be served by additional numbers? But if energetic and imaginative rivals cannot enter, the boldest and most rewarding innovations may be excluded.

New firms entering an industry may not all survive. Some may be weeded out in the competitive struggle, sometimes indeed after making their contribution either to pricing or to business methods. But reasonable opportunity for entry is needed if there is to be assurance of a sufficient number of sellers to maintain effective competition and thus prevent markets from evolving gradually into a state of monopolistic stability. The exclusion of new rivals may be a major impairment of competition in itself, and the power to exclude rivals is usually associated with the power to eliminate rivalry between those already in the industry.

(3) Independence of Rivals A primary condition of workable competition in an economic sense is that there be genuine independence on the part of the business units in an industry, so that each firm pursues its own individual advantage. In industries with numerous sellers, concerted action is difficult to achieve without relatively visible machinery of cooperation. Where there are only a limited number of sellers, however, concerted action can be subtle and informal, and sometimes difficult to detect. In all industries, it is normal for sellers to try to take the reactions of rivals into account in determining their own competitive policies; where there are few sellers it may be easier to forecast such reactions. This may or may not impair competition, depending on whether or not the initiator of a competitive move can expect to retain an improved market position after his rivals have responded. Fewness of sellers does not necessarily lead to mutual interdependence of policies, but it may do so.

(4) Predatory Preclusive Practices There should be no predatory preclusive tactics, such that their natural effect would be to enable the user to eliminate rivals without regard to their efficiency, or at least to place them under serious handicaps irrelevant to their efficiency. It should be noted as a practical matter that predatory competition in this sense can usually only be waged where a considerable degree of market power already exists, or where an attempt is being made to use a long purse in order to destroy or coerce rivals. Such conduct is regarded therefore as symptomatic either of monopoly or the intent to monopolize, or both, although it may not be necessary for those possessing market power in high degree to use such methods in order to gain or to keep monopolistic advantages from their position. Conversely, the accusation of "predatory" or "cutthroat" practices often turns out on examination not to stem from the abuse of significant degrees of market power, but from the uncomfortably active pressures of competition itself. Only by examining the facts, including the market, is it possible to answer these important questions, among others: whether the low prices or other alleged predatory acts were temporary and for the purpose of destroying or coercing rivals; or whether they were undertaken to meet competition, or to increase profits under high level production at low-cost, or for some equally proper competitive purpose; whether the profit-seeking interests of the company under attack would have been served by predatory or oppressive tactics; and so forth. These facts bear not on the justification for predatory conduct—there is none—but on the issue of whether such conduct exists.

(5) Rate of Growth of the Industry or Market The speed with which an industry is growing is not a direct economic indicator of the state of competition within it. An industry may be actually in decline and yet be actively effectively competitive. For example, an industry may decline because the demand for its products is declining and yet there may still be competitive rivalry for shares of the remaining market. Rate of growth, however, is often important in determining the significance to be attached to other factors, and particularly to numbers and reasonable opportunity for entry.

The rate of growth or expansion of a market can, for example, strongly color the significance to competition of the number and relative size of the firms, and alter the effectiveness of barriers to entry. The expected rate of growth of the industry affects the attitudes and expectations of firms in the industry, the attractiveness of the industry to outside firms, and the possibility of maintaining positions of market power without severe restrictions on entry. In a new and rapidly expanding industry, the opening of new markets and the high rate of technical progress usually characteristic of such situations make for uncertainty as to the most profitable policies. The entrance of new firms, if it takes place, may lead to further unsettlement of industry policies and under these circumstances, firms may grow without imposing losses on their rivals. Insofar as any given number of firms find it possible to have a tight hold on a stable industry, they can hold their position more readily than the same firms in an industry that is open to rapid expansion. If such firms are not disposed to engage in competitive activity, they may, by their passivity, not only discourage the entry of rivals, but of new techniques which might, in turn, permit the industry to reduce costs and to expand. On the other hand, such passivity itself may well prove a substantial incentive to the entry of newcomers who might otherwise be deterred by the prospect of immediate, active stiff competition.

(6) Character of Market Incentives to Competitive Moves Competition may be effective or ineffective, depending upon how the market is organized and behaves, and according to what incentives there are for independent competitive actions: the hope of gain for the individual seller, and the risk of loss. The strength of these incentives may depend on factors which are in themselves neutral and become important only as they influence incentives. The intervals between a competitive move and the expected response, for example, are not themselves indicia of effective competition or its absence. But they come under study in seeking to determine whether incentives are relatively strong or weak.

In general, and outside of such specialized markets as organized exchanges and others of similar character, effective competition may hinge on the condition that the initiator of a competitive action can expect a gain in volume of business at least for a time. That is, the customers' response to an inducement may be quicker than rivals' responses for at least long enough to provide a pay-out period for the competitive action. The incentive to innovation, to price changes, or to other directly competitive moves is an interval during which an innovator may reasonably expect to have an advantage because his moves cannot be met and neutralized promptly enough by his rivals.

Where these competitive moves are not promptly matched and offset, therefore, or where uncertainty exists as to the pattern of rival responses, an influence exists which, *other things being equal*, provides inducements for effective competitive rivalry. Where uncertainty prevails—perhaps because of the presence of a company which refuses to follow prevailing patterns—sellers may be more likely to conclude that they have a chance to make a gain from a competitive innovation, than if the system of market responses had been securely built up by past habits, agreements, or experience. The mere existence and quick dissemination of information on price changes is not of itself evidence either way. But cooperative efforts by an industry to eliminate uncertainty and promote instant knowledge for everybody of everybody else's price may be a device to curb price cutting. Thus, a conviction that rivals will respond immediately may discourage any independent competitive action.

One circumstance that favors a time interval for gain through innovation or price reductions or other competitive moves is the fact that the initiator of a competitive move may gain business at the expense of all his competitors, thus gaining more than any one of them loses, so that they do not have the same decisive need to retaliate.

While information or continued price rigidities may be some indication of the existence or absence of incentives to competitive moves, such information cannot of itself be determinative from an economic standpoint of either effective monopoly or effective competition. Monopolies may change prices in their own interests, and competitive industries may have periods of stable demand and supply conditions. Price changes, or the absence thereof, must therefore be considered in their market settings in order to evaluate their significance.

(7) Product Differentiation and Product Homogeneity The definition of the word "market," and that of workable competition itself, both turn on the actual and direct competition a seller confronts from the closely related products of others. An important factor in determining the boundaries of the market is the knowledge of buyers as to the alternatives open to them. If other conditions are equal, it would seem for this reason to follow that the more homogeneous the product of rival sellers, the more easily buyers could switch from the output of one competitor to that of others; and therefore the wider the market and the greater the degree of competition in it.

The effect of product differentiation depends on the market setting in which it is placed. Extreme product differentiation, by tending to insulate the demand for one product against that for rival products, may allow real positions of monopoly to develop. Relatively mild differentiation of products within a market otherwise effectively competitive, however, may be a factor favorable to the intensiveness of competition, including price competition and competition in quality. This will tend to be most forcibly the case if the product differentiation reflects product rivalry, that is, product improvement, rather than mere heterogeneity of closely similar products. For product differentiation, especially if it constitutes or embodies a genuine innovation, may be a means whereby the seller can take advantage of the time interval the market allows within which he can expect to gain from a competitive move. Particularly if the situation is such as to justify uncertainty as to the speed and completeness with which rivals will counter the initial move, such a move, in the form of product differentiation, may contribute to the competitiveness of market behavior. This would not be the case if the innovation is fortified by obstacles to imitation by rival producers, or obstacles to the sale of cheaper and simpler models. Thus the impact of product differentiation on the effectiveness of competition will, as in the case of all the other factors mentioned, have to be judged in each case in its market setting, and in relation to more central indicia of effective competition. It is not, as such, evidence either way.

The fact that product homogeneity is the rule in a given market may be a significant element in determining the kind of market structure needed for effective competition. Product homogeneity may increase the zone of competition. Where the primary factors in the market situation indicate little question as to the effectiveness of competition, clearly this result will follow. The active and effective competition on organized exchanges and like markets depends upon product homogeneity within grades. But, in other markets, special inquiry may be required to determine whether product homogeneity tends to reduce any one seller's chance to gain through a competitive move. Where, in such markets, there is substantial product homogeneity, an open reduction of price is almost certain to be met instantly although, if not so met, a gain in volume as a result of the move is assured.

(8) Meeting or Matching the Prices of Rivals The above analysis of the varying effects which product homogeneity and differentiation may have on competition in the economic sense in different market settings has a bearing also on the question of meeting or matching the prices of competitors. It is of the essence of effective competition that competitors should try to meet, or offer an equivalent for, any superior inducement which one of them offers. Meeting a rival's inducements is the means whereby competition diffuses the gains of productive efficiency. To forbid a seller to meet his rival's price would involve a *reductio ad absurdum,* so long as the market structure itself is untouched. For example, in the case of homogeneous products, if A only part-way meets B's price, it does A no good—he still cannot sell his goods—and if A more than meets B's price, then B cannot sell his goods, or not until he in turn has more than met A's price. Under these circumstances, in the absence of a change in demand, there is no place where competitive price can level off, and no adjustment permitting a number of competitors to remain in the market in question, unless a seller is permitted to meet his competitor's price. This is the error in holding that a firm is not competing unless it is exceeding its rival's prices.

However, effective competition also involves freedom to undercut rivals' prices. Thus an inflexible requirement that any existing price may be met, but not undercut, would mean that when demand falls off, or when there is a reduction in cost, the decline in price which would follow under effective competition might be aborted, because it would be to no one's interest to make the first move, since it would be matched forthwith. In many such situations, it would be to everyone's interest not to cut prices.

Effective competition is therefore compatible either with meeting (or matching) the prices of rivals, or with undercutting them. Furthermore, prices uniform as among the respective sellers may under the pressure of falling demand give way to a period of undercutting, after which price again settles down to uniformity at a lower level. Hence these are not two mutually exclusive patterns, and price uniformity as of any given short period is not significant, even when the costs of various sellers are widely different from one another. But a rigid uniformity over periods of changing supply and demand, or a persistent failure by firms to increase or decrease prices when their independent self-interest would seem to dictate such a move, is not usually compatible with workable competition. This is a problem altogether distinct and apart from the legal question of whether a complex and rigid system of price-setting and price-changing can only be explained by an agreement or conspiracy. The legal problem transcends although it includes the economic. But any rule, public or private, which forbade the meeting of prices, or one which forbade the undercutting of prices, would be a rule against workable competition.

A climate more stimulating to effective competition might be introduced into such a market in several possible ways, including: new entry, if large profits were being made; price discrimination; variations in the product or in the other terms of the bargain; a change in the structure of the market, by an increase in the number of sellers; or utilization of other competitive devices such as product, service and customer relations improvement and more effective selling. This should not be interpreted as a general recommendation of a policy of discrimination, but is meant merely to point out some of the available alternatives in situations of this kind. Perhaps something could be accomplished by not preventing—and certainly by forbidding private groups the power to prevent—a reasonable variety and variability in pricing practices.

(9) Excess Capacity "Excess capacity" is a term difficult to define satisfactorily, and even more difficult to identify. The term is commonly used to describe capacity unused during a general depression, as well as "excesses" of capacity which may be generated by investment booms in competitive industries. Both these senses should be distinguished from the excess of capacity confronted by a declining industry. In a period of generally good business, for a growing or stable business, the existence of unused capacity, which could be utilized at or near prevailing costs, may help to demonstrate the presence of either effective monopoly or effective competition in connection with other facts. If the companies in an industry tend generally to pursue policies of making more money by charging high prices and restricting production, the industry may have chronic excess capacity as a result. The practice of a company purchasing and dismantling unused capacity in this sense—that is, capacity which could be utilized at normal costs—has always and rightly been considered strong evidence of attempt to monopolize. On the other hand, a moderate and varying amount of excess capacity naturally tends to develop from time to time as a result of expansion or in response to the rise and fall of demand in a competitive industry, or incident to competitive efforts of producers to increase their share of the market. And its presence is favorable to the effectiveness of competition, if other criteria of competition are present. It permits producers to handle added business at no great increase in unit cost of production, or even at a decrease in average unit costs, depending upon cost conditions at the time. And, as business approaches conditions in which efficient capacity is fully utilized at high profit, a failure on the part of the industry to expand in response to high levels of demand and profit

might suggest the possibility of some restrictive arrangement to prevent the normal response of a competitive market.

(10) Price Discrimination Some types of price discrimination may stimulate effective competition; others may be evidence of effective monopoly, in the economic sense. Before proceeding to examine the differences among the various types of price discrimination, a word of preliminary warning is in order.

Price discrimination as seen by an economist not only is not necessarily the same as "price discrimination" in the sense followed or applied in decisions under the Robinson-Patman Act, but it may be entirely antithetical. Furthermore, even when a price structure happens to be discriminatory in both senses, this may be evidence of either effectively monopolistic or effectively competitive forces, depending on its setting. Finally, even when price discrimination in an economic sense (whether or not in the sense proscribed under the Robinson-Patman Act) is evidence of departures from conditions of effective competition, it does not necessarily result in or denote violation of law.

Price discrimination, in the economic sense, occurs whenever and to the extent that there are price differences for the same product or service sold by a single seller, and not accounted for by cost differences or by changes in the level of demand; or when two or more buyers of the same goods and services are charged the same price despite differences in the cost of serving them. In order to know when there is or is not price discrimination, in the economic sense, between two or more buyers, it is necessary to know not only the price but also the total costs applicable to each class of transaction under comparison.

From the economic point of view, no particular definition of "price" is required; "price" is simply what the buyer has paid the seller as consideration for the goods and related services he has sought and purchased; nor is any close definition of the "goods" or "products" required except that there be some substantial elements of comparability. "Cost," for analysis of situations contemplated in this section of our Report, means average cost. The idea that the cost of serving a given buyer is less than that of serving other buyers, for no other reason than that this buyer's additional purchases spread the overhead, imputes arbitrarily to a particular buyer the savings of larger volume. And such cost differences as are relevant are those consistently characteristic of the categories of business being compared, not transitory or incidental differences. The actual lower costs of serving one or more buyers can arise from a great variety of circumstances. The product sold to some buyers may be physically somewhat different, in lacking certain appliances or finishing touches or quality. There may be differences in the services which go along with the goods to form the complete package for which consideration is given—such services as delivery, packaging, storage, credit extension, risk of default, handling, clerical attention, sales force attention, and many others. There may for these or other reasons be savings on large quantities sold, or on large volume over some time period (entirely apart from the savings arising from spreading the overhead); but large quantities or volumes, without more, are not necessarily more economical. These are all matters of factual detail.

Because many costs, particularly distribution costs, involve large elements of overhead, it may be difficult or impossible to estimate cost differentials with great precision. This is not to say, however, that the task should not be done, nor that cost differentials should be deemed not to exist, in the absence of precise estimates.

Occasional statements in the economic literature that price discrimination is proof of the existence of monopoly elements have been widely misunderstood, and as misunderstood, repeated by noneconomists. Under pure competition (and *a fortiori* under perfect competition) no price discrimination could exist. Every seller would sell at the going price and would have no power to charge more and no need to take less. But any attempt to infer from this that price discrimination, in the economic sense, is "inherently monopolistic" or presumptively anti-competitive, is implicit acceptance of pure or perfect competition as a workable goal of public policy. We have already shown that the terms "pure" and "perfect" mean merely precise or complete in the theoretical sense, not ideal or desirable. We therefore repudiate pure and perfect competition as direct goals of antitrust policy. We do, however, recognize that under workable competition there should exist substantial pressure driving the price of any given product or service toward uniformity, and toward its cost of production, so that there is a potent incentive for a business firm to maintain satisfactory profits over the long run by innovation in products or processes. The constant efforts of businessmen are and ought to be to get into new and higher-margin markets; and the constant effect of competition is to narrow margins in some markets as compared with others, for the leveling force is not felt with equal speed everywhere at the same time. Some amount of discrimination in the economic sense is therefore an inevitable part of the business scene. It remains to examine the circumstances under which it may be considered evidence of workable competition or of workable monopoly.

A single monopolist firm, or a group of firms exerting monopoly power in concert, would find it most profitable to divide up their customers and exact from each one the maximum that he could be made to pay. Such a scheme of discrimination would require that customers paying lower prices be prevented from reselling to those paying higher prices. The monopolist would need to control the product to point of final use, possibly by contract. If resale were practical, then competition among the customers would cause all the product to move through the lower-priced buyers, discrimination thus tending to disappear.

Price discimination may also take the form of predatory price cutting in selected areas or on selected products in order to eliminate competitors or to force them to follow a price or other policy. The essence of this conduct is its temporary nature; for it only exists in order that prices may eventually be raised once rivals are removed or coerced. Such predatory price discrimination must, however, be carefully distinguished from vigorous competition, where prices are not cut for such temporary purposes, but in order to permit more efficient firms to earn higher profits at low prices than at high prices, or for some other equally competitive reason.

A milder form of what might be regarded as price discrimination in the economic sense, although not in the Robinson-Patman Act sense, may be practiced by a seller who keeps his prices very low or barely remunerative on products facing competition, while maintaining higher prices and profit margins on other products free from competition or facing less competition. In *United States v. United Shoe Machinery Corp.,*[c] for example, the court considered this type of price discrimination as evidence of monopoly power, but it is significant that it did not attempt to extirpate such discrimination by its decree. Explaining its reasons therefor the court stated: "Some price discrimination, if not too rigid, is inevitable. Some may be justified as resting on patent monopolies. Some price discrimination is economically desirable, if it promotes competition in a market whose several multi-product firms compete."

Price discrimination, in the economic sense, may be practiced by a monopolist or by a group of sellers acting in concert, because they wish to build up or protect the position of certain customers, and weaken that of others. But price discrimination may serve to promote competition, and it may be relevant evidence that competition exists and is effective. While price discrimination of the type described above is therefore relevant to a determination of whether significant degrees of market power inhere in any individual company or group of companies acting in concert, further exploration is required to determine whether effective competition exists.

It is equally clear that in some cases differences in price not related to difference in cost may promote competition. Thus price discrimination may serve to disrupt or preclude any collusive or otherwise interdependent pricing. The very success of a concerted effort by a group of firms to raise prices above the competitive level by restricting output to less than the competitive level would make it attractive for some or all of the firms to offer better terms to some buyers. There is a tendency for such special bargains to be given more and more widely, as buyers try to play sellers off one against the other; and if the tendency is strong enough to make the special prices become the "regular" prices in the course of time, the discrimination has served to make the market more competitive.

These examples illustrate the diverse ways in which price discrimination in the economic sense appears in our market system. Where price discrimination is sustained, persistent and stable, it may throw light either on collusion in price-formation, or on the presence of market imperfections so fundamental as to constitute evidence of effective monopoly power. For, when price discriminations are sustained and substantial, they may have far-reaching effects at several levels of competition, and lead to significant departures from standards of workable competition. Price discrimination may be a means of making existing markets less effectively competitive.

As has been pointed out several times in the preceding analysis, price discrimination may be the force which can increase the number of effective sellers in a market, or disrupt an otherwise effective system of monopoly pricing. Thus

[c] 110 F. Supp. 295 (D. Mass. 1953), *aff'd per curiam* 347 U.S. 521 (1954).

price discrimination is a fact of significance, to be considered in relation to other facts, in determining whether a market is workably competitive.

Several members emphasize that such stable patterns of discrimination in the economic sense not only may throw light on collusion or market imperfections but are conclusive evidence that the market is behaving monopolistically.

5   THE SHERMAN ACT

States enacted the first antitrust laws, toward the end of the nineteenth century. These proved to be largely ineffective in preventing monopolistic practices, for a number of reasons. Among these were the lack of enforcement facilities and the fact that monopolies were really a national problem. The Federal government entered the scene in 1887 with the enactment of the Interstate Commerce Act to control the railroads, where the obvious danger of monopoly had first appeared. This was followed in 1890 by the Sherman Act, which was passed by Congress under its constitutional authority to regulate interstate commerce. Two of the pertinent provisions of this act appear below.

Section 1. Every contract, combination in the form of trust or otherwise, or conspiracy, in restraint of trade or commerce among the several States, or with foreign nations, is hereby declared to be illegal. . . . Every person who shall make any contract, or engage in any combination or conspiracy hereby declared to be illegal by Sections 1–7 of this title, shall be deemed guilty of a misdemeanor, and, on conviction thereof, shall be punished by fine not exceeding five thousand dollars, or by imprisonment not exceeding one year, or by both said punishments, in the discretion of the court.[2]

Section 2. Every person who shall monopolize, or attempt to monopolize, or combine or conspire with any other person or persons, to monopolize any part of the trade or commerce among the several States, or with foreign nations, shall be deemed guilty of a misdemeanor, and, on conviction thereof, shall be punished by fine not exceeding five thousand dollars, or by imprisonment not exceeding one year, or by both said punishments, in the discretion of the court.[3]

The Sherman Act represents an announcement by Congress of a policy favoring the preservation of competition. Congress attempted to enforce this policy by furnishing four separate legal remedies for violations of its provisions. First, as the above quotation from the act indicates, it is a Federal crime punishable by fine or imprisonment or both for any person (or corporation) to contract, combine, or participate in a conspiracy in restraint of trade; or to monopolize or attempt to monopolize or combine or conspire with some other person to monopolize some segment of trade. The original maximum fine for *each*

---

[2] 26 Stat. 209 (1890), 15 U.S.C. § 1 (1970).
[3] 26 Stat. 209 (1890), 15 U.S.C. § 2 (1970).

violation of Section 1 or 2 of the Act was $5,000, but the maximum was increased by Congress to $50,000 in 1955.[4] Second, the Sherman Act empowers courts to grant injunctions which will prevent and restrain violations or continued violations of its provisions. Failure to obey such injunctions subjects the defendant to contempt proceedings. A third remedy affords relief to those persons who have been injured by another's violation of the Act. Such victims are given the right, in a civil action, to collect three times the damages they have suffered, plus court costs and reasonable attorney's fees. Normally the objective of awarding money damages to an individual in a private lawsuit is to place him in the position he would have enjoyed, as nearly as this can be done with money, had his rights not been invaded. The treble damage provision of the Sherman Act, however, employs the remedy of damages as a means of punishing the defendant for his wrongful act in addition to compensating the plaintiff for his actual injury. Finally, any property owned in violation of Section 1 of the Act, which is being transported from one state to another, is made subject to seizure by and forfeiture to the United States. This last remedy has rarely been used.[5]

In criminal cases, the defendant has three possible pleas to enter to an indictment charging a violation. He may plead "guilty," "not guilty," or "nolo contendere." This last plea of "no contest" allows sentencing just as if the defendant had pleaded or been found guilty. It has the advantage to a defendant of avoiding the cost of trial and the effect of a guilty plea or finding in a subsequent civil suit. Criminal convictions create prima facie cases for treble damages, and this is the effect that can be avoided by the nolo contendere plea. The Sherman Act has provided that criminal convictions create a prima facie case for treble damages, because the burden of proof in a criminal case (beyond a reasonable doubt) is greater than the burden of proof in a civil case (by the preponderance or greater weight of the evidence). Acceptance of nolo contendere pleas (the plea is not a matter of right but discretionary with the trial court) tends to discourage treble damage suits, because of the difficulties that private parties face in proving Sherman Act violations. The cost of investigation and preparation of antitrust suits is usually substantial, and therefore private litigants benefit greatly from either a guilty plea or a conviction.

In *United States v. Aluminum Company of America*[6] Circuit Judge Learned Hand had occasion to comment on the purposes and philosophy of the Sherman Act. In holding that Alcoa was guilty of a violation of Section 2 for having intentionally acquired and maintained control of over 90 percent of the domestic "virgin" ingot market in aluminum, even though Alcoa had not misused such monopoly power to obtain exorbitant profits, Judge Hand said:

. . . it is no excuse for "monopolizing" a market that the monopoly has not been used to extract from the consumer more than a "fair" profit. The Act has wider purposes. Indeed, even though we disregarded all but economic considerations,

---

[4] 69 Stat. 282 (1955), 15 U.S.C. §§ 1, 2 (1970).
[5] For an example of a case in which forfeiture of property was involved, see *United States v. Addyston Pipe and Steel Co.*, 175 U.S. 2111 (1899).
[6] 148 F.2d 416 (1945).

it would by no means follow that such concentration of producing power is to be desired, when it has not been used extortionately. Many people believe that possession of unchallenged economic power deadens initiative. discourages thrift and depresses energy; that immunity from competition is a narcotic, and rivalry is a stimulant, to industrial progress; that the spur of constant stress is necessary to counteract an inevitable disposition to let well enough alone. Such people believe that competitors, versed in the craft as no consumer can be, will be quick to detect opportunities for saving and new shifts in production, and be eager to profit by them. In any event the mere fact that a producer, having command of the domestic market, has not been able to make more than a "fair" profit, is no evidence that a "fair" profit could not have been made at lower prices. . . . True, it might have been thought adequate to condemn only those monopolies which could not show that they had exercised the highest possible ingenuity, had adopted every possible economy, had anticipated every conceivable improvement, stimulated every possible demand. No doubt, that would be one way of dealing with the matter, although it would imply constant scrutiny and constant supervision, such as courts are unable to provide. Be that as it may, that was not the way that Congress chose; it did not condone "good trusts" and condemn "bad" ones; it forbade all. Moreover, in so doing, it was not necessarily actuated by economic motives alone. It is possible, because of its indirect social or moral effect, to prefer a system of small producers, each dependent for his success upon his own skill and character, to one in which the great mass of those engaged must accept the direction of a few. . . .

Continuing, Judge Hand indicated that, besides the economic reasons behind the Sherman Act's proscription of monopoly,

. . . there are others, based upon the belief that great industrial consolidations are inherently undesirable, regardless of their economic results. In the debates in Congress Senator Sherman himself . . . showed that among the purposes of Congress in 1890 was a desire to put an end to great aggregations of capital because of the helplessness of the individual before them. . . . Throughout the history of these statutes it has been constantly assumed that one of their purposes was to perpetuate and preserve, for its own sake and in spite of possible cost, an organization of industry in small units which can effectively compete with each other. . . .

In 1958 Justice Black in *Northern Pacific Ry. Co. v. United States*, 356 U.S. 1, discussed the purpose of the Sherman Act. He stated in part:

The Sherman Act was designed to be a comprehensive charter of economic liberty aimed at preserving free and unfettered competition as the rule of trade. It rests on the premise that the unrestrained interaction of competitive forces will yield the best allocation of our economic resources, the lowest prices, the highest quality and the greatest material progress, while at the same time providing an environment conducive to the preservation of our democratic political and social institutions.

6 THE RULE OF REASON

In 1897, in *United States v. Trans-Missouri Freight Association,*[7] the Court upheld the government's suit to have the Association (which included 18 carriers in its membership) dissolved and the agreement forming it declared null and void. In so doing, the Court had occasion to construe the statute and its scope, and stated as one of the issues, "Is [the Sherman Act] confined to a contract or combination which is only in unreasonable restraint of trade or commerce, or does it include what the language of the act plainly and in terms covers, all contracts of that nature?"[8] In answering the question posed, the court said,

Contracts in restraint of trade have been known and spoken of for hundreds of years both in England and in this country, and the term includes all kinds of those contracts, which in fact restrain or may restrain trade. Some of such contracts have been held void and unenforceable in the courts by reason of their restraint being unreasonable, while others have been held valid because they were not of that nature. A contract may be in restraint of trade and still be valid at common law. Although valid, it is nevertheless a contract in restraint of trade, and would be so described either at common law or elsewhere. By the simple use of the term "contract in restraint of trade," all contracts of that nature, whether valid or otherwise, would be included, and not alone that kind of contract which was invalid and unenforceable as being in unreasonable restraint of trade. When, therefore, the body of an act pronounces as illegal every contract or combination in restraint of trade or commerce among the several States, etc., the plain and ordinary meaning of such language is not limited to that kind of contract alone which is in unreasonable restraint of trade, but all contracts are included in such language, and no exception or limitation can be added without placing in the act that which has been omitted by Congress.[9]

The Court then considered the question of whether contractual restraints such as those ancillary to the sale of business (an agreement by the seller not to compete with the buyer), long recognized as valid at common law if reasonable in scope, should be excluded from the type of contract prohibited by the Act and reached the conclusion that:

A contract which is the mere accompaniment of the sale of property, and thus entered into for the purpose of enhancing the price at which the vendor sells it, which in effect is collateral to such sale, and where the main purpose of the

[7] 177 U.S. 290 (1897).
[8] *Id.*
[9] *Id.*

whole contract is accomplished by such sale, might not be included, within the letter or spirit of the statute in question. But we cannot see how the statute can be limited, as it has been by the courts below, without reading into its text an exception which alters the natural meaning of the language used, and that, too, upon a most material point, and where no sufficient reason is shown for believing that such alteration would make the statute more in accord with the intent of the law-making body that enacted it. . .[10]

However, the following year, in *United States v. Joint Traffic Association,*[11] the Court retreated somewhat from a strictly literal, all-encompassing construction of the meaning of the Sherman Act. And finally, in the case which follows, the Court gave up the literal approach altogether in announcing the so-called "rule of reason."

Standard Oil Co. v. United States
221 U.S. 1 (1911)

The United States brought this action for an injunction under the Sherman Antitrust Act to enforce its provisions against seventy-one corporations, including the Standard Oil Companies of New Jersey, California, Indiana, Iowa, Kansas, Kentucky, Nebraska, New York, and Ohio, and seven individuals, all of whom were engaged in purchasing, shipping, refining and selling petroleum and its products. The government charged that defendants had conspired to restrain the trade and commerce in petroleum among the several states, and claimed that the conspiracy was started around 1870 by three of the individual defendants, John D. Rockefeller, William Rockefeller and Henry M. Flagler, who along with Standard Oil of Ohio and others entered into agreements for the purpose of price fixing, limiting production, and controlling the transportation of oil and its products. It was further alleged that at a later time certain of the defendants turned over the managements of all aspects of their businesses to nine trustees in exchange for trust certificates, which constituted a restraint of trade in violation of the act. Finally it was alleged that in further pursuance of their conspiracy, the individual defendants, operating through Standard Oil Company of New Jersey as a holding corporation, caused that company to acquire a majority of the stocks of various corporations engaged in the oil business and in this fashion managed and controlled the corporations in violation of the act. The trial court found Standard Oil Company of New Jersey, thirty-seven of its corporate subsidiaries, and the seven individuals guilty of forming a combination in restraint of trade, of attempting to monopolize, and of a monopolization under the Sherman Act. The action was dismissed as to the thirty-three other corporations, because they were not proved to be parties to the combination. In its decree the court enjoined the Standard Oil Company of New Jersey from voting stocks or otherwise controlling

[10] *Id.*
[11] 171 U.S. 505 (1898).

the thirty-seven subsidiaries, and the individuals and thirty-eight corporations from entering into any similar combination to evade the decree. In addition, all guilty parties were enjoined *from engaging in the petroleum business at all* as long as their illegal combination continued. This appeal to the Supreme Court by the defendants resulted.

WHITE, CHIEF JUSTICE: . . . There can be no doubt that the sole subject with which the first section [of the Sherman Antitrust Act] deals is restraint of trade as therein contemplated, and that the attempt to monopolize and monopolization is the subject with which the second section is concerned. It is certain that those terms, at least in their rudimentary meaning, took their origin in the common law, and were also familiar in the law of this country prior to and at the time of the adoption of the act in question.

We shall endeavor then, first to seek their meaning, not by indulging in an elaborate and learned analysis of the English law and of the law of this country, but by making a very brief reference to the elementary and indisputable conceptions of both the English and American law on the subject prior to the passage of the Antitrust Act.

a. It is certain that at a very remote period the words "contract in restraint of trade" in England came to refer to some voluntary restraint put by contract by an individual on his right to carry on his trade or calling. Originally all such contracts were considered to be illegal, because it was deemed they were injurious to the public as well as to the individuals who made them. In the interest of the freedom of individuals to contract this doctrine was modified so that it was only when a restraint by contract was so general as to be coterminous with the kingdom that it was treated as void. That is to say, if the restraint was partial in its operation and was otherwise reasonable the contract was held to be valid.

b. Monopolies were defined by Lord Coke as follows:

A monopoly is an institution, or allowance by the king by his grant, commission, or otherwise to any person or persons, bodies politic or corporate, of or for the sole buying, selling, making, working, or using of anything, whereby any person or persons, bodies politic or corporate, are sought to be restrained of any freedom or liberty that they had before, or hindered in their lawful trade. . . .

Let us consider the language of the first and second sections, guided by the principle that where words are employed in a statute which had at the time a well-known meaning at common law or in the law of this country they are presumed to have been used in that sense unless the context compels to the contrary. . . .

As there is no room for dispute that the statute was intended to formulate a rule for the regulation of interstate and foreign commerce, the question is what was the rule which it adopted? . . .

The statute . . . evidenced the intent not to restrain the right to make and enforce contracts, whether resulting from combination or otherwise, which did not unduly restrain interstate or foreign commerce, but to protect that commerce from being restrained by methods, whether old or new, which would constitute an interference that is an undue restraint. . . .

[A]s the contracts or acts embraced in the provision were not expressly defined, since the enumeration addressed itself simply to classes of acts, those classes being broad enough to embrace every conceivable contract or combination which could be made concerning trade or commerce or the subjects of such commerce, and thus caused any act done by any of the enumerated methods anywhere in the whole field of human activity to be illegal if in restraint of trade, it inevitably follows that the provision necessarily called for the exercise of judgment which required that some standard should be resorted to for the purpose of determining whether the prohibitions contained in the statute had or had not in any given case been violated. Thus not specifying but indubitably contemplating and requiring a standard, it follows that it was intended that the standard of reason which had been applied at the common law and in this country dealing with subjects of the character embraced by the statute, was intended to be the measure used for the purpose of determining whether in a given case a particular act had or had not brought about the wrong against which the statute provided.

And a consideration of the text of the second section serves to establish that it was intended to supplement the first and to make sure that by no possible guise could the public policy embodied in the first section be frustrated or evaded. . . .

Undoubtedly, the words "to monopolize" and "monopolize" as used in the section reach every act bringing about the prohibited results. The ambiguity, if any, is involved in determining what is intended by monopolize. But this ambiguity is readily dispelled in the light of the previous history of the law of restraint of trade to which we have referred and the indication which it gives of the practical evolution by which monopoly and the acts which produce the same result as monopoly, that is, an undue restraint of the course of trade, all came to be spoken of as, and to be indeed synonymous with, restraint of trade. In other words, having by the first section forbidden all means of monopolizing trade, that is, unduly restraining it by means of every contract, combination, etc., the second section seeks, if possible, to make the prohibitions of the act all the more complete and perfect by embracing all attempts to reach the end prohibited by the first section, that is, restraints of trade by any attempt to monopolize, or monopolization thereof, even although the acts by which such results are attempted to be brought about or are brought about be not embraced within the general enumeration of the first section. And, of course, when the second section is thus harmonized with and made as it was intended to be the complement of the first, it becomes obvious that the criteria to be resorted to in any given case for the purpose of ascertaining whether violations of the section have been committed, is the rule of reason guided by the established law and by the plain duty to enforce the prohibitions of the act and thus the public policy which its restrictions were obviously enacted to subserve. And it is worthy of observation, as we have previously remarked concerning the common law, that although the statute by the comprehensiveness of the enumerations embodied in both the first and second sections makes it certain that its purpose was to prevent undue restraints of every kind or nature, nevertheless by the omission of any direct prohibition against monopoly in the concrete it indicates a consciousness that the freedom of the individual right to contract when not unduly or improperly exercised was the most efficient means for the prevention of monopoly, since the operation of the centrifugal and centripetal forces resulting from the right to freely contract was the means by which monopoly would be inevitably prevented if no extraneous or sovereign power imposed it and no right to make unlawful contracts having a monopolistic tendency were permitted. In other words that freedom to contract was the essence of freedom from undue restraint of the right to contract. . . .

Our conclusion is that the decree below was right, and should be affirmed, except as to the minor matters concerning which we have indicated the decree should be modified. . . . [Those matters were discussed in portions of the opinion which have been omitted here.] [AFFIRMED]

In the same year in *United States v. American Tobacco Co.*, 221 U.S. 106 (1911), the Court interpreted its own ruling in the above case and stated:

[In Standard Oil] . . . it was held not that acts which the statute prohibited could be removed from the control of its prohibitions by a finding that they were reasonable, but that the duty to interpret which inevitably arose from the general character of the term restraint of trade required that the words restraint of trade should be given a meaning which would not destroy the individual right to contract and render difficult if not impossible any movement of trade in the channels of interstate commerce—the free movement of which it was the purpose of the statute to protect.

The rule that contracts or conspiracies in restraint of trade were illegal only if they constituted undue or unreasonable restraints of trade, and that only unreasonable attempts to monopolize were covered by the Sherman Act, obviously gave the courts a great deal of power and discretion. In effect the courts were legislating in each case by determining what activities would be considered reasonable or unreasonable, as a matter of law. At this time in history, one of the Supreme Court's major concerns and emphases centered around the protection of individual constitutional rights, particularly property ownership and freedom of contract. Since the Sherman Act represented an attempt by Congress to make inroads into these two rights, particularly in the case of business activity, it is easy to see how the court in protecting such rights would seek a balance and not give as much sweeping effect to the Sherman Act as would literally have been possible under its broad, general language, even as modified by the rule of reason. Thus for many of its rulings in the antitrust area the court received heavy criticism from some quarters for being too conservative and too pro-business, and of course just for creating its rule of reason on the theory that the court was taking too much power, disregarding the true intent of Congress, and legislating the court's own philosophy instead.

7 FAIR TRADE: AN EXCEPTION TO THE SHERMAN ACT

In 1937, Congress passed the Miller-Tydings Act[12] which amended Section 1 of the Sherman Act to permit fair trade pricing of certain articles for retail sale and represented a retrenching of the effective application of the Sherman Act and the national policy favoring competition. By the Act, language was added to Section 1 of the Sherman Act to the effect that "nothing herein contained shall render illegal contracts or agreements prescribing minimum prices for the resale" of certain commodities when "contracts or agreements of that description are lawful as applied to intrastate transactions" under local law. In other words, in any state which had passed the requisite enabling fair trade statute, a manufacturer of a brand or trade name product was permitted to enter into a contract with a retailer whereby the retailer agreed to sell that product at no less than the minimum prices specified, without having the agreement constitute a violation of the Sherman Act. If the state in question had no fair trade legislation, any such contract would be unenforceable and would amount to a violation of the Act, as a contract, combination, or conspiracy in restraint of trade. The purpose of such legislation was to permit the states to allow the manufacturer of a brand or trade name product to protect that brand name and the aura of quality carried with it by a higher price.

In *Schwegmann Bros. v. Calvert Distillers Corp.*[13] the Supreme Court determined the legality of the Louisiana fair trade legislation, which not only permitted a manufacturer to contract to set minimum retail prices for the manufacturer's product but also made it unfair competition for *anyone* to sell at less than the price agreed, even though the seller was not a party to the contract which fixed the resale price. That is, the contract setting minimum retail prices was made enforceable both against parties to the contract and against nonsigners.

In this case, Calvert and Seagram brought suit against Schwegmann Brothers to prevent the defendant from continuing to sell products at cut-rate prices. Calvert and Seagram had executed price-fixing contracts with over 100 retailers in Louisiana, under which retailers promised not to sell at less than prices stated in the plaintiffs' schedules. However, Schwegmann Brothers was not a party to such a contract, so that the plaintiffs were attempting to invoke the nonsigner provisions of the Louisiana statute. The Supreme Court noted that the general concept of fair trade was legal under the Miller-Tydings amendment. However, the Court pointed out that under a literal interpretation of the Louisiana statute, if just one retailer signed, all others in the state would be compelled to abide by his contract to observe minimum resale prices under the nonsigner provision. The Court, in refusing the injunction, held that the noncontracting group was to be governed by the preexisting law (i.e., the Sherman Act, Section 1, forbidding contracts in restraint of trade) and ruled that the Louisiana statute was invalid to the extent of the nonsigner provision it contained.

In 1952, the year following the handing down of the *Schwegmann* decision, Congress responded by enacting the McGuire Fair Trade Act,[14] which amended

---

[12] 50 Stat. 693 (1937), 15 U.S.C. § 1 (1970).
[13] 341 U.S. 384 (1951).
[14] 66 Stat. 632 (1952), 15 U.S.C. 45 (a) (1)–(5) (1970).

Section 5(a) of the Federal Trade Commission Act[15] to permit fair trade pricing of articles for retail sale in those states with fair trade laws, without having the same constitute a violation of *any* of the antitrust laws. Pursuant to the McGuire Act, the State of Ohio enacted a fair trade law which also contained the nonsigner provisions. The case which follows involved the validity of the Ohio law.

Hudson Distributors, Inc. v. Upjohn Co. and Eli Lilly, Inc.
377 U.S. 386 (1964)

GOLDBERG, JUSTICE: These appeals raise the question of whether the McGuire Act . . . permits the application and enforcement of the Ohio Fair Trade Act against appellant in support of appellees' system of retail price maintenance. For the reasons stated below, we hold that the Ohio Act, as applied to the facts of these cases, comes within the provisions of the McGuire Act exempting certain resale price systems from the prohibitions of the Sherman Act. . . .

In June 1959, the Ohio Legislature enacted a new Fair Trade Act. . . . Subsequently Lilly sent letters to all Ohio retailers of Lilly products, including Hudson, to notify them of Lilly's intention to establish minimum retail resale prices for its trademarked products pursuant to the new Ohio Act and to invite the retailers to enter into written fair-trade contracts. More than 1,400 Ohio retailers of Lilly products (about 65% of all the retail pharmacists in Ohio) signed fair-trade contracts with Lilly. Hudson, however, refused to enter into a written contract with Lilly and ignored the specified minimum resale prices. Lilly formally notified Hudson that the Ohio Act required Hudson to observe the minimum retail resale prices for Lilly commodities. Hudson, nevertheless, continued to purchase and then to resell Lilly products at less than the stipulated minimum retail resale prices. . . .

Hudson contends that the provisions of the Ohio Act under which Lilly established minimum resale prices are not authorized by the McGuire Act. . . . Section 2 of the McGuire Act provides in pertinent part as follows:

Nothing contained in this section or in any of the Antitrust Acts shall render unlawful any contracts or agreements prescribing minimum or stipulated prices. . . . When contracts or agreements of that description are lawful as applied to intrastate transactions under any statute, law, or public policy now or hereafter in effect in any State. . . .

Section 3 of the McGuire Act reads as follows:

Nothing contained in this section or in any of the Antitrust Acts shall render unlawful the exercise or the enforcement of any right or right of action created by any statute, law, or public policy now or hereafter in effect in any State, Territory, or the District of Columbia, which in substance provides that willfully

[15] Section 5 prohibits unfair methods of competition, acts and practices.

and knowingly advertising, offering for sale, or selling any commodity at less than the price or prices prescribed in such contracts or agreements whether the person so advertising, offering for sale, or selling is or is not a party to such a contract or agreement, is unfair competition and is actionable at the suit of any person damaged thereby.

. . . The Report of the House Committee on Interstate and Foreign Commerce, which accompanied the McGuire Act, declared that:

The primary purpose of the [McGuire] bill is to reaffirm the very same proposition which, in the committee's opinion, the Congress intended to enact into law when it passed the Miller-Tydings Act . . . , to the effect that the application and enforcement of State fair-trade laws—including the nonsigner provisions of such laws—with regard to interstate transactions shall not constitute a violation of the Federal Trade Commission Act or the Sherman Antitrust Act. This reaffirmation is made necessary because of the decision of a divided Supreme Court in Schwegmann Bros. v. Calvert Distillers Corp. . . .

This authoritative report evinces the clear intention of Congress that, where sanctioned by a state fair-trade act, a trademark owner such as Lilly could be permitted to enforce, even against a nonsigning retailer such as Hudson, the stipulated minimum prices established by written contracts with other retailers. . . .

The price fixing authorized by the Ohio Fair Trade Act and involving goods moving in interstate commerce would be, absent approval by Congress, clearly illegal under the Sherman Act. . . . "Fixing minimum prices, like other types of price fixing, is illegal per se." *Schwegmann Bros. v. Calvert Distillers Corp., supra*. . . . Congress, however, in the McGuire Act has approved state statutes sanctioning resale price maintenance schemes such as those involved here. Whether it is good policy to permit such laws is a matter for Congress to decide. Where the statutory language and the legislative history clearly indicate the purpose of Congress that purpose must be upheld. . . . [AFFIRMED]

Notwithstanding the decision in the preceding case, the fair trade laws of many states have been held to be in violation of state constitutional provisions. The legislatures of some states have omitted the nonsigner provision, thus eliminating this constitutional objection.

Fair trade also suffers from another major difficulty. Most courts have held that a manufacturer who desires to maintain retail prices by use of fair trade contracts must enforce such contracts uniformly and consistently, or the contracts will not be enforced at all. Manufacturers cannot allow one retailer to violate the fair trade contract while seeking enforcement against other retailers. It is a defense to a suit brought to enforce the fair trade contract that others are or have been in violation of the same contract. Therefore, a manufacturer who seeks to fair-trade an item must police his contracts and require compliance by all retailers. The cost and difficulty of enforcing fair trade as a means of resale price maintenance have caused many manufacturers to abandon fair trade, but there still are numerous items such as luggage, cameras, and drugs which are fair-traded.

Contemporary Problems

8 RESALE PRICE MAINTENANCE

The purpose of a manufacturer of a brand or trade name product in having his product's retail price maintained at a minimum established by him may be based on the desire to create an image of high quality which consumers often relate to high prices. In addition he may desire to protect his regular retail outlets from price-cutting competition with discount houses, which frequently attract customers by offering a few products for sale as "loss-leaders." As was noted in the previous section, if a state has a fair trade law which permits a manufacturer to contract with retailers to maintain minimum prices for his brand name goods, such contracts are enforceable and are not in violation of the antitrust laws, because of the statutory provisions making fair trade an exception to them. Since fair trade laws have not been enacted in all states and some fair trade laws have been declared unconstitutional, many manufacturers have attempted other methods of maintaining minimum retail prices to protect their product's reputation and goodwill or its enhanced subjective value in the consumer's mind.

In *United States v. Colgate Co.*[16] the Supreme Court upheld a District Court decision to dismiss an indictment charging Colgate with violating the Sherman Act by entering into an unlawful combination in restraint of trade. The indictment alleged that Colgate had created a combination with wholesale and retail dealers of its products for the purpose of procuring their adherence to minimum resale prices fixed by the defendant. The court summarized the various things that Colgate was charged with doing in order to carry out its purposes with the following language:

Distribution among dealers of letters, telegrams, circulars and lists showing uniform prices to be charged; urging them to adhere to such prices and notices, stating that no sales would be made to those who did not; requests, often complied with, for information concerning dealers who had departed from specified prices; investigation and discovery of those not adhering thereto and placing their names upon "suspended lists"; requests to offending dealers for assurances and promises of future adherence to prices, which were often given; uniform refusals to sell to any who failed to give the same; sales to those who did; similar assurances and promises required of, and given by, other dealers followed by sales to them; unrestricted sales to dealers with established accounts who had observed specified prices, etc. . . .[17]

[16] 250 U.S. 300 (1919).
[17] *Id.* at 303.

In affirming the District Court's dismissal of the indictment, the Supreme Court stated:

Considering all said in the opinion (notwithstanding some serious doubts) we are unable to accept the construction placed upon it by the Government. We cannot, e.g., wholly disregard the statement that "The retailer, after buying, could, if he chose, give away his purchase, or sell it at any price he saw fit, or not sell it at all; his course in these respects being affected only by the fact that he might by his action incur the displeasure of the manufacturer, who could refuse to make further sales to him, as he had the undoubted right to do." And we must conclude that, as interpreted below, the indictment does not charge Colgate & Company with selling its products to dealers under agreements which obligated the latter not to resell except at prices fixed by the company. . . .
. . . In the absence of any purpose to create or maintain a monopoly, the Sherman act does not restrict the long recognized right of trader or manufacturer engaged in an entirely private business, freely to exercise his own independent discretion as to parties with whom he will deal. And, of course, he may announce in advance the circumstances under which he will refuse to sell.[18] *. . .*

The case which follows concerns a scheme of price maintenance very similar to Colgate's. In it the defendant, Parke Davis, argued that its activities were legal under the doctrine of the *Colgate* case.

United States v. Parke Davis & Co.
362 U.S. 29 (1960)

Parke Davis had announced the policy that it would sell its products only to those wholesalers and retailers who observed minimum resale prices suggested by the manufacturer. However, retailers in Washington, D.C., and Richmond, Virginia, began advertising and selling Parke Davis vitamins considerably below the suggested minimum retail price. To promote compliance with its price policy, Parke Davis informed the retailers and wholesalers in the area that it would refuse to sell to any *wholesaler* who *supplied* its products to any retailer who did not observe the suggested minimum retail prices. Several retailers continued to sell Parke Davis vitamins at a discount, and, when their names were furnished to the wholesalers, both Parke Davis and the wholesalers refused to fill their orders for *any* of the manufacturer's products. The government brought action for an injunction, which was dismissed by the District Court, and the government appealed.

BRENNAN, JUSTICE: . . . The District Court held that the Government's proofs did not establish a violation of the Sherman Act because "the actions of [Parke Davis] were properly unilateral and sanctioned by law under the doctrine laid down in the case of *United States v. Colgate & Co.*, 250 U.S. 300. . . . [in which the court on page 307 said:]

[18] *Id.* at 306, 307.

The purpose of the Sherman Act is to prohibit monopolies, contracts and combinations which probably would unduly interfere with the free exercise of their rights by those engaged, or who wish to engage, in trade and commerce— in a word to preserve the right of freedom to trade. In the absence of any purpose to create or maintain a monopoly, the act does not restrict the long recognized right of trader or manufacturer engaged in an entirely private business, freely to exercise his own independent discretion as to parties with whom he will deal; and, of course, he may announce in advance the circumstances under which he will refuse to sell. . . .

The Government concedes for the purposes of this case that under the *Colgate* doctrine a manufacturer, having announced a price maintenance policy, may bring about adherence to it by refusing to deal with customers who do not observe that policy. The Government contends, however, that subsequent decisions of this Court compel the holding that what Parke Davis did here by entwining the wholesalers and retailers in a program to promote general compliance with its price maintenance policy went beyond mere customer selection and created combinations or conspiracies to enforce resale price maintenance in violation of §§ 1 and 3 of the Sherman Act. . . . Judicial inquiry is not to stop with a search of the record for evidence of purely contractual arrangements. The Sherman Act forbids combinations of traders to suppress competition. True, there results the same economic effect as is accomplished by a prohibited combination to suppress price competition if each customer, although induced to do so solely by a manufacturer's announced policy, independently decides to observe specified resale prices. So long as *Colgate* is not overruled, this result is tolerated but only when it is the consequence of a mere refusal to sell in the exercise of the manufacturer's right "freely to exercise his own independent discretion as to parties with whom he will deal." [250 U.S. 330] When the manufacturer's actions, as here, go beyond mere announcement of his policy and the simple refusal to deal, and he employs other means which effect adherence to his resale prices, this countervailing consideration is not present and therefore he has put together a combination in violation of the Sherman Act. Thus, whether an unlawful combination or conspiracy is proved is to be judged by what the parties actually did rather than by the words they used. . . .

The program upon which Parke Davis embarked to promote general compliance with its suggested resale prices plainly exceeded the limitations of the *Colgate* doctrine and under *Beech-Nut* and *Bausch & Lomb* effected arrangements which violated the Sherman Act. Parke Davis did not content itself with announcing its policy regarding retail prices and following this with a simple refusal to have business relations with any retailers who disregarded that policy. Instead Parke Davis used the refusal to deal with the wholesalers in order to elicit their willingness to deny Parke Davis products to retailers and thereby help gain the retailers' adherence to its suggested minimum retail prices. The retailers who disregarded the price policy were promptly cut off when Parke Davis supplied the wholesalers with their names. The large retailer who said he would "abide" by the price policy, the multi-unit Peoples Drug chain, was not cut off. In thus involving the wholesalers to stop the flow of Parke Davis products to the retailers, thereby inducing retailers' adherence to its suggested retail prices, Parke Davis created a combination with the retailers and the wholesalers to maintain retail prices and violated the Sherman Act. Although Parke Davis' originally announced wholesalers' policy would not under *Colgate* have violated the Sherman Act if its action thereunder was the simple refusal without more to deal with wholesalers who did not observe the wholesalers' Net Price Selling Schedule, that entire policy was tainted with the "vice of . . . illegality" . . . when Parke Davis used it as the vehicle to gain the wholesalers' participation in the program to effectuate the retailers' adherence to the suggested retail price. [JUDGMENT REVERSED AND CASE REMANDED WITH DIRECTIONS TO ISSUE INJUNCTION]

In the case which follows, a gasoline company owned its retail outlets, but leased most of them, including the one in question. The lessee was required to sell only the oil of the company, Union Oil, and by a consignment agreement contracted to maintain minimum retail prices as set by Union Oil. The legality of the consignment provision as a means of resale price maintenance was challenged.

Simpson v. Union Oil Co.
377 U.S. 13 (1964)

Simpson was the lessee and operator of one of the retail filling stations owned by Union Oil Company. Union Oil followed the practice of leasing its stations out to dealers such as Simpson on a year-to-year basis, and also requiring the lessees to sign a consignment agreement valid for a one-year period and thereafter until canceled by either party or until termination of the lease. The consignment agreement provided that title to consigned gasoline would remain in Union Oil until sold by Simpson, and all property taxes would be paid by Union Oil. However, under it Simpson was required to carry personal liability and property damage insurance for losses which might arise from his possession of the gasoline and was responsible for all losses of the gasoline itself, except for those due to certain acts of God. Simpson paid all the costs of operating the station, and was compensated by a commission on sales made. Under the portion of the consignment agreement in question, Union Oil set the prices at which Simpson sold the gasoline. During a local "gas war," Simpson sold gasoline at 2 cents below the price set by the company, and because of this, it refused to renew Simpson's lease upon termination. This suit was an action for treble damages, alleging that Union Oil's consignment contract authorizing it to set prices violated the Sherman Act. The District Court granted summary judgment to the company, which was affirmed by the Circuit Court of Appeals. Simpson then appealed to the Supreme Court, which granted certiorari.

DOUGLAS, JUSTICE: . . . If the "consignment" agreement achieves resale price maintenance in violation of the Sherman Act, it and the lease are being used to injure interstate commerce by depriving independent dealers of the exercise of free judgment whether to become consignees at all, or remain consignees, and, in any event, to sell at competitive prices. The fact that a retailer can refuse to deal does not give the supplier immunity if the arrangement is one of those schemes condemned by the antitrust laws.

There is actionable wrong whenever the restraint of trade or monopolistic practice has an impact on the market; and it matters not that the complainant may be only one merchant.

Congress has, by legislative fiat, determined that such prohibited activities are injurious to the public and has provided sanctions allowing private enforcement of the antitrust laws by an aggrieved party. These laws protect the victims of the forbidden practices as well as the public.

The fact that, on failure to renew a lease, another dealer takes Simpson's place and renders the same service to the public is no more an answer here than it was in *Poller v. Columbia Broadcasting System*, 368 U.S. 464, 473. For Congress, not the oil distributor, is the arbiter of the public interest; and Congress has closely patrolled price fixing whether effected through resale price maintenance agreements or otherwise. The exclusive requirements contracts struck down in *Standard Oil Co. and Standard Stations v. United States*, 337 U.S. 293, were not saved because dealers need not have agreed to them, but could have gone elsewhere. If that were a defense, a supplier could regiment thousands of otherwise competitive dealers in resale price maintenance programs merely by fear of nonrenewal of short-term leases.

We made it clear in *United States v. Parke, Davis & Co.* 362 U.S. 29, that a supplier may not use coercion on its retail outlets to achieve resale price maintenance. We reiterate that view, adding that it matters not what the coercive device is. . . . Here we have such an agreement; it is used coercively, and, it promises to be equally if not more effective in maintaining gasoline prices than were the Parke, Davis techniques in fixing monopoly prices on drugs.

Consignments perform an important function in trade and commerce, and their integrity has been recognized by many courts, including this one. Yet consignments, though useful in allocating risks between the parties and determining their rights *inter se*, do not necessarily control the rights of others, whether they be creditors or sovereigns. Thus the device has been extensively regulated by the States. . . .

One who sends a rug or a painting or other work of art to a merchant or a gallery for sale at a minimum price can, of course, hold the consignee to the bargain. A retail merchant may, indeed, have inventory on consignment, the terms of which bind the parties *inter se*. Yet the consignor does not always prevail over creditors in case of bankruptcy, where a recording statute or a "traders act" or a "sign statute" is in effect. The interests of the Government also frequently override agreements that private parties make. Here we have an antitrust policy expressed in Acts of Congress. Accordingly, a consignment, no matter how lawful it might be as a matter of private contract law, must give way before the federal antitrust policy. Thus a consignment is not allowed to be used as a cloak to avoid § 3 of the Clayton Act. Nor does § 1 of the Sherman Act tolerate agreements for retail price maintenance. . . .

Dealers, like Simpson, are independent businessmen; and they have all or most of the indicia of entrepreneurs, except for price fixing. The risk of loss of the gasoline is on them, apart from acts of God. Their return is affected by the rise and fall in the market price, their commissions declining as retail prices drop. Practically the only power they have to be wholly independent businessmen, whose service depends on their own initiative and enterprise, is taken from them by the proviso that they must sell their gasoline at prices fixed by Union Oil. By reason of the lease and "consignment" agreement dealers are coercively laced into an arrangement under which their supplier is able to impose noncompetitive prices on thousands of persons whose prices otherwise might be competitive. The evil of this resale price maintenance program is its inexorable potentiality for and even certainty in destroying competition in retail sales of gasoline by these nominal "consignees" who are in reality small struggling competitors seeking retail gas customers.

As we have said, an owner of an article may send it to a dealer who may in turn undertake to sell it only at a price determined by the owner. There is nothing illegal about that arrangement. When, however, a "consignment" device is used to cover a vast gasoline distribution system, fixing prices through many retail outlets, the antitrust laws prevent calling the "consignment" an agency, for then the end result of *United States v. Socony-Vacuum Oil Co.*, supra, would be avoided merely by clever manipulation of words, not by differences in substance. The present, coercive "consignment" device if successful against challenge under the antitrust laws, furnishes a wooden formula for administering prices on a vast scale. . . .

To allow Union Oil to achieve price fixing in this vast distribution system through this "consignment" device would be to make legality for anti-trust purposes turn on clever draftsmanship. We refuse to let a matter so vital to a competitive system rest on such easy manipulation.

Hence on the issue of resale price maintenance under the Sherman Act there is nothing left to try, for there was an agreement for resale price maintenance, coercively employed. . . .

. . . [W]e hold only that resale price maintenance through the present, coercive type of "consignment" agreement is illegal under the anti-trust laws, and that petitioner suffered actionable wrong or damage. . . . [REVERSED AND REMANDED]

9   PRICE-FIXING

The Sherman Act's proscription of contracts or combinations in restraint of trade or commerce obviously applies to agreements among competitors whereby they establish minimum or maximum prices for their goods or services. Notwithstanding the rule of reason, all price-fixing agreements are illegal, that is, price-fixing is said to be illegal per se. Since price-fixing is illegal per se, it is no defense that the prices fixed are fair or reasonable. It also is no defense that price-fixing is engaged in by small competitors to allow them to compete with larger competitors. In 1927, the Supreme Court held all price-fixing to be unreasonable and thus illegal per se in the case of *United States v. Trenton Potteries, 273 U.S. 392.* The Court in that case stated in part:

That only those restraints upon interstate commerce which are unreasonable are prohibited by the Sherman Law was the rule laid down by the opinions of this Court in the Standard Oil *and* Tobacco Cases. *But it does not follow that agreements to fix or maintain prices are reasonable restraints and therefore permitted by the statute, merely because the prices themselves are reasonable. Reasonableness is not a concept of definite and unchanging content. Its meaning necessarily varies in the different fields of law, because it is used as a convenient summary of the dominant considerations which control in the application of legal doctrines. Our view of what is a reasonable restraint of commerce is controlled by the recognized purpose of the Sherman Law itself. Whether this type of restraint is reasonable or not must be judged in part at least in the light of its effect on competition, for whatever difference of opinion there may be among economists as to the social and economic desirability of an unrestrained competitive system, it cannot be doubted that the Sherman Law and the judicial decisions interpreting it are based upon the assumption that the public interest is best protected from the evils of monopoly and price control by the maintenance of competition. . . .*

The aim and result of every price-fixing agreement, if effective, is the elimination of one form of competition. The power to fix prices, whether reasonably exercised or not, involves power to control the market and to fix arbitrary and unreasonable prices. The reasonable price fixed today may through economic and business changes become the unreasonable price of tomorrow. Once established, it may be maintained unchanged because of the absence of competition secured by the agreement for a price reasonable when fixed. Agreements which create such potential power may well be held to be in themselves unreasonable or unlawful restraints, without the necessity of minute inquiry whether a particular price is reasonable or unreasonable as fixed and without placing on the Government in enforcing the Sherman Law the burden of ascertaining from day to day whether it has become unreasonable through the mere variation of economic conditions. . . . Thus viewed, the Sherman Law is not only a prohibition against the infliction of a particular type of public injury. It "is a limitation of rights, . . . which may be pushed to evil consequences and therefore restrained. . . ."

[I]t has since often been decided and always assumed that uniform price-fixing by those controlling in any substantial manner a trade or business in interstate commerce is prohibited by the Sherman Law, despite the reasonableness of the particular prices agreed upon. . . .

It is clear from the foregoing that price-setting arrangements among competitors are considered to be unreasonable per se, or in themselves. In other words, an unreasonable contract or combination in restraint of trade is established by simply proving the existence of a price-fixing agreement. Other cases have indicated that the per se rule makes such a combination illegal whether the parties to it have control of the market or not, and whether they are trying to raise *or lower* the market price.

Similar contracts to those fixing the price at which conspirators sell their product have been held unreasonable per se. Thus, agreements to divide up territories among competitors, or to fix the market price of a product or service they are buying, or to limit the supply of a commodity are outlawed without proof of any unreasonable effects. It is clear from these per se rules that the Sherman Act does not, as might erroneously be assumed, apply only where the public at large is injured by conspiracies or monopolistic practices, and is not of sole interest to big business.

Other violations of the Sherman Act are not illegal per se. For example, group boycotts, or concerted refusals by traders to deal with other traders, have long been held to be violations of the Sherman Act, but only where they are on the facts unreasonable. A single trader may refuse to deal with another, and a manufacturer and a dealer may agree to an exclusive distributorship. However, if manufacturers, distributors, and retailers combine and agree not to deal with a particular business, a violation may exist. Such a combination may take from the excluded business its freedom to buy in an open competitive market and could drive it out of business as a dealer in the products of the conspirators. The combination could deprive the manufacturers and distributors of their freedom to sell to one business at the same prices and conditions made available to others. Such agreements could interfere with the natural flow of interstate commerce and could be contrary to the Sherman Act. Group boycotts may be a violation, even though the victim is just one merchant whose business is so small that its destruction makes little difference to the economy.[19] The case which follows illustrates the application of the Sherman Act to activities in setting maximum prices.

Lester J. Albrecht, Petitioner v. The Herald Company, etc.
88 S.Ct. 869 (1968)

WHITE, JUSTICE: . . . Respondent publishes the Globe-Democrat, a morning newspaper distributed in the St. Louis metropolitan area by independent carriers who buy papers at wholesale and sell them at retail. There are 172 home delivery routes. Respondent advertises a suggested retail price in its newspaper. Carriers have exclusive territories which are subject to termination if prices exceed the suggested maximum. Petitioner, who had Route 99, adhered to the advertised price for some time but in 1961 raised the price to customers. After more than once objecting to this practice, respondent wrote petitioner on May 20, 1964, that

---

[19] See *Klor's Inc. v. Broadway-Hale Stores, Inc.* 359 U.S. 207 (1959).

because he was overcharging and because respondent had reserved the right to compete should that happen, subscribers on Route 99 were being informed by letter that respondent would itself deliver the paper to those who wanted it at the lower price. In addition to sending these letters to petitioner's customers, respondent hired Milne Circulation Sales, Inc., which solicited readers for newspapers, to engage in telephone and house-to-house solicitation of all residents on Route 99. As a result, about 300 of petitioner's 1,200 customers switched to direct delivery by respondent. Meanwhile respondent continued to sell papers to petitioner but warned him that should he continue to overcharge, respondent would not have to do business with him. Since respondent did not itself want to engage in home delivery, it advertised a new route of 314 customers as available without cost. Another carrier, George Kroner, took over the route knowing that respondent would not tolerate overcharging and understanding that he might have to return the route if petitioner discontinued his pricing practice. On July 27 respondent told petitioner that it was not interested in being in the carrier business and that petitioner could have his customers back as long as he charged the suggested price. Petitioner brought this lawsuit on August 12. In response, petitioner's appointment as a carrier was terminated and petitioner was given 60 days to arrange the sale of his route to a satisfactory replacement. Petitioner sold his route for $12,000, $1,000 more than he had paid for it but less than he could have gotten had he been able to turn over 1,200 customers instead of 900.

Petitioner's complaint charged a combination . . . in restraint of trade under § 1 of the Sherman Act. . . . The case went to the jury on this theory, the jury found for respondent, and judgment in its favor was entered on the verdict. The court denied petitioner's motion for judgment notwithstanding the verdict, which asserted that . . . the undisputed facts showed as a matter of law a combination to fix resale prices of newspapers which was *per se* illegal under the Sherman Act. The Court of Appeals affirmed. In its view "the undisputed evidence fail[ed] to show a Sherman Act violation," because respondent's conduct was wholly unilateral and there was no restraint of trade. The previous decisions of this Court were deemed inapposite to a situation in which a seller establishes maximum prices to be charged by a retailer enjoying an exclusive territory and in which the seller, who would be entitled to refuse to deal, simply engages in competition with the offending retailer. We disagree with the Court of Appeals and reverse its judgment.

On the undisputed facts recited by the Court of Appeals respondent's conduct cannot be deemed wholly unilateral and beyond the reach of § 1 of the Sherman Act. That section covers combinations in addition to contracts and conspiracies, express or implied. . . . There can be no doubt that a combination arose between respondent, Milne, and Kroner to force petitioner to conform to the advertised retail prices. When respondent learned that petitioner was overcharging, it hired Milne to solicit customers away from petitioner in order to get petitioner to reduce his price. It was through the efforts of Milne, as well as because of respondent's letter to petitioner's customers, that about 300 customers were obtained for Kroner. Milne's purpose was undoubtedly to earn its fee, but it was aware that the aim of the solicitation campaign was to force petitioner to lower his price. Kroner knew that respondent was giving him the customer list as part of a program to get petitioner to conform to advertised price, and he knew that he might have to return the customers if petitioner ultimately complied with respondent's demands. He undertook to deliver papers at the suggested price and materially aided in the accomplishment of respondent's plan. Given the uncontradicted facts recited by the Court of Appeals, there was a combination within the meaning of § 1 between respondent, Milne, and Kroner, and the Court of Appeals erred in holding to the contrary.

The Court of Appeals also held there was no restraint of trade, despite the long-accepted rule in § 1 cases that resale price fixing is a *per se* violation of the law whether done by agreement or combination. . . .

Agreements to fix maximum prices no less than those to fix minimum prices, cripple the freedom of traders and thereby restrain their ability to sell in accordance with their own judgment. . . .

Maximum and minimum price fixing may have different consequences in many situations. But schemes to fix maximum prices, by substituting the perhaps erroneous judgment of a seller for the forces of the competitive market, may severely intrude upon the ability of buyers to compete and survive in that market. Competition, even in a single product, is not cast in a single mold. Maximum prices may be fixed too low for the dealer to furnish services essential to the value which goods have for the consumer or to furnish services and conveniences which consumers desire and for which they are willing to pay. Maximum price fixing may channel distribution through a few large or specifically advantaged dealers who otherwise would be subject to significant nonprice competition. Moreover, if the actual price charged under a maximum price scheme is nearly always the fixed maximum price, which is increasingly likely as the maximum price approaches the actual cost of the dealer, the scheme tends to acquire all the attributes of an arrangement fixing minimum prices. It is our view, therefore, that the combination formed by the respondent in this case to force petitioner to maintain specified prices for the resale of the newspapers which he had purchased from respondent constituted, without more, an illegal restraint of trade under § 1 of the Sherman Act.

. . . In sum, the evidence cited by the Court of Appeals makes it clear that a combination in restraint of trade existed. . . . [REVERSED AND REMANDED]

Another important area of contemporary concern is price-fixing by persons performing services such as lawyers, real estate dealers, accountants, and physicians. Recent decisions have held that the Sherman Act is as applicable to contracts involving services as it is to contracts concerning goods. Cases involving real estate dealers' agreements to share listings and split agreed-upon commissions have been litigated, and such conduct has been held violative of the Sherman Act. While problems of establishing the requisite effect on commerce are present, it is believed that the 1970s will see application of the Sherman Act prohibition to fee-setting practices of those rendering professional services.

10 CONCERTED ACTIVITES BY COMPETITORS

Concerted activities among competitors take a variety of forms and appear in diverse circumstances. Some arise out of a desire to protect a channel of distribution or a marketing system. Others result from attempts to keep marginal competitors in business, which is in fact one goal of the antitrust laws. Thus, some cases dealing with concerted activities actually involve conflicts between various competing goals of the antitrust laws. For example, the case which follows involves attempts by General Motors and a majority of its franchised dealers in a certain geographical area to protect themselves from the price-cutting tactics of automobile discount sales houses in the Los Angeles area. The alleged illegal activity resulted from an attempt to protect a substantial number of competitors.

United States v. General Motors Corp.
384 U.S. 127 (1966)

The United States brought action for injunction against General Motors and the three associations of the Chevrolet dealers located in the Los Angeles, California, area, to prevent the defendants from continuing an alleged conspiracy in restraint of trade in violation of the Sherman Act. All Chevrolet dealers in the locality belonged to at least one of the associations. The alleged conspiracy came about as a result of an attempt by the vast majority of the dealers and General Motors to prevent a small minority of the franchised dealers from participating with nonfranchised "discount houses" in retail sales of new Chevrolets. These discount houses claimed to the public that they could sell new cars at bargain prices. Although their relationships with franchised dealers were varied, there were two main methods of dealing. First, the discounter might refer his customer directly to the dealer, who would sell at a price previously agreed upon and pay a commission to the discounter, typically around $50, for supplying the customer. Second, the discounter himself might make the sale, with the dealer transferring title to the customer upon receiving an order from the discounter. Under this type of arrangement one dealer charged the discounter $85 more than invoice cost for the car, and the discounter tried to make the best deal he could with the buyer. About 12 of the 85 dealers in the area were in league with the discounters in some similar fashion. The others began to "feel the pinch" because of these discount sales. Many "potential customers received or thought they would receive a more attractive deal from a discounter who obtained his Chevrolets from a distant dealer." The discounters advertised alleged price savings widely. Besides losing sales, the nonparticipating dealers were often obliged to back up new-car warranties and furnish free service to the purchasers through discounters, because of General Motors' requirements concerning these warranties and services. These dealers and the dealers' associations prevailed upon General Motors to do something about bringing those who were doing business with discount houses into line.

General Motors co-operated with the dealers' associations in obtaining the agreement of each dealer to have nothing more to do with discounters and in enforcing said agreements. The District Court gave judgment to the defendants and the Government appealed to the Supreme Court.

Among other things, General Motors argued that its actions were justified as simply enforcing the "location clause" contained in its franchise agreements, by which dealers promised they would not move to or establish "a new or different location, branch sales office, branch service station, or place of business including any used car lot or location without the prior written approval of Chevrolet."

FORTAS, JUSTICE: . . . By mid-January General Motors had elicted from each dealer a promise not to do business with the discounters. But such agreements would require policing—a fact which had been anticipated. General Motors earlier had initiated contacts with firms capable of performing such a function. This plan, unilaterally to police the agreements, was displaced, however, in favor of a joint effort between General Motors, the three defendant associations, and a number of individual dealers.

On December 15, 1960, the three defendant associations had met and appointed a joint committee to study the situation and to keep in touch with Chevrolet's O'Connor. Early in 1961, the three associations agreed jointly to finance the "shopping" of the discounters to assure that no Chevrolet dealer continued to supply them with cars. Each of the associations contributed $5,000, and a professional investigator was hired. He was instructed to try to purchase new Chevrolets from the proscribed outlets, to tape record the transactions, if any, and to gather all the necessary documentary evidence—which the associations would then lay "at the doorstep of Chevrolet." These joint associational activities were both preceded and supplemented by similar "shopping" activities by individual dealers and by defendant Losor Chevrolet Dealers Association.

General Motors collaborated with these policing activities. There is evidence that zone manager O'Connor and a subordinate, Jere Faust, actively solicited the help of individual dealers in uncovering violations. Armed with information of such violations obtained from the dealers or their associations, O'Connor or members of his staff would ask the offending dealer to come in and talk. The dealer was then confronted with the car purchased by the "shopper," the documents of sale, and in most cases a tape recording of the transaction. In every instance, the embarrassed dealer repurchased the car, sometimes at a substantial loss, and promised to stop such sales. At the direction of O'Connor or a subordinate, the checks with which the cars were repurchased were made payable to an attorney acting jointly for the three defendant associations. . . .

By the Spring of 1961, the campaign to eliminate the discounters from commerce in new Chevrolet cars was a success. Sales through the discount outlets seem to have come to a halt. . . .

We have here a classic conspiracy in restraint of trade: joint, collaborative action by dealers, the defendant associations, and General Motors to eliminate a class of competitors by terminating business dealings between them and a minority of Chevrolet dealers and to deprive franchised dealers of their freedom to deal through discounters if they so choose. . . .

It is of no consequence, for purposes of determining whether there has been a combination or conspiracy under § 1 of the Sherman Act, that each party acted in its own lawful interest. Nor is it of consequence for this purpose whether the "location clause" and franchise system are lawful or economically desirable. . . . [I]t has long been settled that explicit agreement is not a necessary part of a Sherman Act conspiracy—certainly not where, as here, joint and collaborative action was pervasive in the initiation, execution, and fulfillment of the plan.

Neither individual dealers nor the associations acted independently or separately. The dealers collaborated, through the associations and otherwise, among themselves and with General Motors, both to enlist the aid of General Motors and to enforce dealers' promises to forsake the discounters. The associations explicitly entered into a joint venture to assist General Motors in policing the dealers' promises, and their joint proffer of aid was accepted and utilized by General Motors. . . .

General Motors sought to elicit from each dealer agreements, substantially interrelated and interdependent, that none of them would do business with the discounters. These agreements were hammered out in meetings between non-conforming dealers and officials of General Motors' Chevrolet Division, and in telephone conversations with other dealers. It was acknowledged from the beginning that substantial unanimity would be essential if the agreements were to be forthcoming. And once the agreements were secured, General Motors both solicited and employed the assistance of its alleged co-conspirators in helping to police them. What resulted was a fabric interwoven by many strands of joint action to eliminate the discounters from participation in the market, to inhibit the free choice of franchised dealers to select their own methods of trade and to provide multilateral surveillance and enforcement. This process for achieving and enforc-ing the desired objective can by no stretch of the imagination be described as "unilateral" or merely "parallel." .

There can be no doubt that the effect of the combination or conspiracy here was to restrain trade and commerce within the meaning of the Sherman Act. Elimination, by joint collaborative action, of discounters from access to the market is a *per se* violation of the Act. . . .

The principle of . . . [law applicable] is that where businessmen concert their actions in order to deprive others of access to merchandise which the latter wish to sell to the public, we need not inquire into the economic motivation underlying their conduct. Exclusion of traders from the market by means of combination or conspiracy is so inconsistent with the free-market principles embodied in the Sherman Act that it is not to be saved by reference to the need for preserving the collaborators' profit margins or their system for distributing automobiles, any more than by reference to the allegedly tortious conduct against which a combination or conspiracy may be directed—as in *Fashion Originators' Guild of America, Inc. v. FTC, supra*, 312 U.S., at 468.

We note, moreover, that inherent in the success of the combination in this case was a substantial restraint upon price competition—a goal unlawful *per se* when sought to be effected by combination or conspiracy. And the *per se* rule applies even when the effect upon prices is indirect.

There is in the record ample evidence that one of the purposes behind the concerted effort to eliminate sales of new Chevrolet cars by discounters was to protect franchised dealers from real or apparent price competition. The discounters advertised price savings. . . . Some purchasers found and others believed that discount prices were lower than those available through the franchised dealers. Certainly, complaints about price competition were prominent in the letters and telegrams with which the individual dealers and salesmen bombarded General Motors in November 1960. . . .

The protection of price competition from conspiratorial restraint is an object of special solicitude under the antitrust laws. We cannot respect that solicitude by closing our eyes to the effect upon price competition of the removal from the market, by combination or conspiracy, of a class of traders. Nor do we propose to construe the Sherman Act to prohibit conspiracies to fix prices at which competitors may sell, but to allow conspiracies or combinations to put competitors out of business entirely.

Accordingly, we reverse and remand to the United States District Court for the Southern District of California in order that it may fashion appropriate equitable relief. [REVERSED AND REMANDED]

In the next case, the concerted activity among competitors took the form of an exchange of information. Economic theory was used to support the assumption that prices would be more unstable and lower if the information had not been exchanged.

United States v. Container Corporation of America
89 S.Ct. 510 (1969)

DOUGLAS, JUSTICE: This is a civil antitrust action charging a price-fixing agreement in violation of § 1 of the Sherman Act. . . .

The case as proved is unlike any of other price decisions we have rendered. There was here an exchange of price information but no agreement to adhere to a price schedule. . . . There was here an exchange of information concerning specific sales to identified customers, not a statistical report on the average cost to all members, without identifying the parties to specific transactions. . . . While there was present here, as in *Cement Manufacturers Protective Assn. v. United States*, 268 U.S. 588, an exchange of prices to specific customers, there was absent the controlling circumstance, *viz.*, that cement manufacturers, to protect themselves from delivering to contractors more cement than was needed for a specific job and thus receiving a lower price, exchanged price information as a means of protecting their legal rights from fraudulent inducements to deliver more cement than needed for a specific job.

Here all that was done was a request by each defendant from its competitor for information as to the most recent price charged or quoted, whenever it needed such information and whenever it was not available from another source. Each defendant on receiving that request usually furnished the data with the expectation that he would be furnished reciprocal information when he wanted it. That concerted action is of course sufficient to establish the combination or conspiracy, the initial ingredient of a violation of § 1 of the Sherman Act.

There was of course freedom to withdraw from the agreement. But the fact remains that when a defendant requested and received price information, it was affirming its willingness to furnish such information in return.

There was to be sure an infrequency and irregularity of price exchanges between the defendants; and often the data was available from the records of the defendants or from the customers themselves. Yet the essence of the agreement was to furnish price information whenever requested.

Moreover, although the most recent price charged or quoted was sometimes fragmentary, each defendant had the manuals with which it could compute the price charged by a competitor on a specific order to a specific customer.

Further, the price quoted was the current price which a customer would need pay in order to obtain products from the defendant furnishing the data.

The defendants account for about 90% of the shipment of corrugated containers from plants in the southeastern United States. While containers vary as to dimensions, weight, color, and so on, they are substantially identical, no matter who produces them, when made to particular specifications. The prices paid depend on price alternatives. Suppliers when seeking new or additional business or keeping old customers, do not exceed a competitor's price. It is common for purchasers to buy from two or more suppliers concurrently. A defendant supplying a customer with containers would usually quote the same price on additional orders, unless costs had changed. Yet where a competitor was charging a particular price, a defendant would normally quote the same price or even a lower price.

The exchange of price information seemed to have the effect of keeping prices within a fairly narrow ambit. Capacity has exceeded the demand from 1955 to 1963, the period covered by the complaint, and the trend of corrugated container prices has been downward. Yet despite this excess capacity and the downward trend of prices, the industry has expanded in the Southeast from 30 manufacturers with 49 plants to 51 manufacturers with 98 plants. An abundance of raw materials and machinery makes entry into the industry easy with an investment of $50,000 to $75,000.

The result of this reciprocal exchange of prices was to stabilize prices though at a downward level. Knowledge of a competitor's price usually meant matching that price. The continuation of some price competition is not fatal to the Government's case. The limitation or reduction of price competition brings the case within the ban, for . . . interference with the setting of price by free market forces is unlawful *per se*. Price information exchanged in some markets may have no effect on a truly competitive price. But the corrugated container industry is dominated by relatively few sellers. The product is fungible and the competition for sales is price. The demand is inelastic, as buyers place orders only for immediate, short-run needs. The exchange of price data tends toward price uniformity. For a lower price does not mean a larger share of the available business but a sharing of the existing business at a lower return. Stabilizing prices as well as raising them is within the ban of § 1 of the Sherman Act. As we said in United States v. Socony Vacuum Oil Co., supra, at 223, 60 S.Ct. at 844, "in terms of market operations, stabilization is but one form of manipulation." The inferences are irresistible that the exchange of price information has had an anticompetitive effect in the industry, chilling the vigor of price competition. . . .

Price is too critical, too sensitive a control to allow it to be used even in an informal manner to restrain competition. [REVERSED]

11 PROOF OF SHERMAN ACT VIOLATIONS

There are obvious difficulties which may arise in connection with proving the existence of a contract, combination, or conspiracy among competitors when they indulge in cooperative action to control the market in some fashion. Must an actual oral or written offer and acceptance be established? If the market behavior of competitors is consciously parallel will it be implied that they are conspiring together? The case which follows deals with the nature of the evidence which is required to prove that a conspiracy or contract in restraint of trade does in fact exist.

Theatre Enterprises v. Paramount Film Distrib. Corp.
346 U.S. 537 (1954)

The plaintiff, Theatre Enterprises, owned and operated the Crest Theatre, a modern motion picture theatre located in a shopping center in Baltimore, Maryland, six miles from the downtown area. The plaintiff brought this action for treble damages and an injunction against defendant motion picture producers and distributors, claiming that they had conspired in violation of the antitrust laws to restrict first-run motion pictures to the theatres downtown, thereby limiting the Crest to only subsequent runs. The evidence disclosed that although the plaintiff had asked each of the defendants on different occasions for first-run motion pictures, no one would furnish it these but all uniformly limited their showing to the downtown theatres, of which there were eight. The jury returned a verdict for the defendants, and the trial court entered judgment in their favor. The Circuit Court of Appeals affirmed. On appeal to the Supreme Court, the plaintiff contended that, on the evidence, the trial judge should have directed the jury to find that there was an unlawful conspiracy, and that the only determination of fact the jury should have been permitted to make was the amount of damages suffered.

CLARK, JUSTICE: . . . Admittedly there is no direct evidence of illegal agreement between the respondents and no conspiracy is charged as to the independent exhibitors in Baltimore, who account for 63% of first-run exhibitions. The various respondents advanced much the same reasons for denying petitioner's offers. Among other reasons they asserted that day and date first-runs are normally granted only to noncompeting theatres. Since the Crest is in "substantial competition" with the downtown theatres, a day and date arrangement would be economically unfeasible. And even if respondents wished to grant petitioner such a license, no downtown exhibitor would waive his clearance rights over the Crest and agree to a simultaneous showing. As a result, if petitioner were to receive first-runs, the license would have to be an exclusive one. However, an exclusive license would be economically unsound because the Crest is a suburban theatre, located in a small shopping center, and served by limited public transportation facilities; and, with a drawing area of less than one-tenth that of a downtown theatre, it cannot compare with those easily accessible theatres in the power to draw patrons. Hence the downtown theatres offer far greater opportunities for the widespread advertisement and exploitation of newly released features, which is thought necessary to maximize the overall return from subsequent runs as well as first-runs. The respondents, in the light of these conditions, attacked the guaranteed offers of petitioner, one of which occurred during the trial, as not being made in good faith. Respondents Loew's and Warner refused petitioner an exclusive license because they owned the three downtown theatres receiving their first-run product.

The crucial question is whether respondents' conduct toward petitioner stemmed from independent decision or from an agreement, tacit or express. To be sure, business behavior is admissible circumstantial evidence from which the fact finder may infer agreement. But this Court has never held that proof of parallel business behavior conclusively establishes agreement or, phrased differently, that such behavior itself constitutes a Sherman Act offense. Circumstantial evidence of consciously parallel behavior may have made heavy inroads into the traditional judicial attitude toward conspiracy; but "conscious parallelism" has not yet read conspiracy out of the Sherman Act entirely. Realizing this, petitioner attempts to bolster its argument for a directed verdict by urging that the conscious unanimity of action by respondents should be "measured against the background and findings in the Paramount case." In other words, since the same respondents had conspired in the Paramount case to impose a uniform system of runs and clearances without adequate explanation to sustain them as reasonable restraints of trade, use of the same device in the present case should be legally equated to conspiracy. But the Paramount decrees, even if admissible, were only prima facie evidence of a conspiracy covering the area and existing during the period there involved. Alone or in conjunction with the other proof of the petitioner, they would form no basis for a directed verdict. Here each of the respondents had denied the existence of any collaboration and in addition had introduced evidence of the local conditions surrounding the Crest operation which, they contended, precluded it from being a successful first-run house. They also attacked the good faith of the guaranteed offers of the petitioner for first-run pictures and attributed uniform action to individual business judgment motivated by the desire for maximum revenue. This evidence, together with other testimony of an explanatory nature, raised fact issues requiring the trial judge to submit the issue of conspiracy to the jury. . . . [AFFIRMED]

The language in the foregoing case should be compared with that in *American Tobacco Co. v. United States,*[20] where the American, Liggett and Myers, and Reynolds tobacco companies were found guilty of conspiring or combining in an unlawful restraint of trade in controlling both the market and prices of leaf tobacco they purchased and the market and prices of the manufactured cigarettes they sold. On appeal the Supreme Court upheld the convictions, stating in part:

It is not the form of the combination or the particular means used but the result to be achieved that the statute condemns. It is not of importance whether the means used to accomplish the unlawful objective are in themselves lawful or unlawful. Acts done to give effect to the conspiracy may be in themselves wholly innocent acts. Yet, if they are part of the sum of the acts which are relied upon to effectuate the conspiracy which the statute forbids, they come within its prohibition. No formal agreement is necessary to constitute an unlawful conspiracy. Often crimes are a matter of inference deduced from the acts of the person accused and done in pursuance of a criminal purpose. Where the conspiracy is proved, as here, from the evidence of the action taken in concert by the parties to it, it is all the more convincing proof of an intent to exercise the power of exclusion acquired through that conspiracy. The essential combination or conspiracy in violation of the Sherman Act may be found in a course of dealings or other circumstances as well as in any exchange of words. . . . Where the circumstances are such as to warrant a jury in finding that the conspirators had a unity of purpose or a common design and understanding, or a meeting of minds in an unlawful arrangement, the conclusion that a conspiracy is established is justified. Neither proof nor exertion of the power to exclude nor proof of actual exclusion of existing or potential competitors is essential to sustain a charge of monopolization under the Sherman Act. . . .

REVIEW QUESTIONS—CHAPTER 10

1 Define the following terms introduced in this chapter: trust; workable competition; price discrimination; nolo contendere; monopoly; fair trade laws; resale price maintenance; consignment.
2 Briefly state the advantages of a competitive economic system.

[20] 328 U.S. 781 (1946).

3 List the ten factors used by courts in determining whether or not workable competition exists from an economic point of view. Briefly illustrate each factor.

4 What is the basic characteristic of workable competition in the economic sense?

5 What sanctions are imposed for violation of the Sherman Act?

6 Under what circumstances would a plea of "nolo contendere" be advisable?

7 Define the "rule of reason" and discuss its effect on the application of the Sherman Act.

8 Give the reasons for the enactment of the Sherman Act provisions relating to monopolies and attempts to monopolize.

9 Give reasons why some manufacturers desire to maintain retail prices. List some techniques which had been used to accomplish this objective and discuss the legality of each.

10 What is a "nonsigner" clause in a fair trade law? What is its effect?

11 Why are relatively few items fair-traded today?

12 What is the *Colgate* doctrine? How was it modified by the *Parke-Davis* case?

13 What is meant by the statement: "Price-fixing is illegal per se"?

14 Why are some activities per se violations of the Sherman Act whereas others which are not may nevertheless be in violation of the Act anyway?

15 Why is it a violation of the Sherman Act to set maximum prices? Isn't such a legal result actually contrary to public policy and the public interest? Explain.

16 Give examples of three concerted activities which could constitute violations of the Sherman Act.

Chapter Eleven

The Clayton Act and Its Amendments

1   INTRODUCTION

After it had been in effect for a time, the Sherman Act was criticized as being inadequate. For one thing, the Act did little to prevent practices which only *tended* to reduce competition or were simply *conducive* to creating monopolies. As interpreted with the rule of reason announced in the *Standard Oil* case, it did not apply to situations which were *likely* to lead to the destruction of competition but which fell short of an actual monopoly or combination in unreasonable restraint of trade. Also, the rule of reason and the lack of specificity in the Sherman Act practically required that courts decide each alleged violation on its own merits on a case-by-case basis. It was felt by many that this gave the courts undue power and further that the interpretations which they were placing on the Act in exercising that power made it much less effective in preserving competition than Congress had intended. There were even a few interpretations that were contrary to the will of Congress. For example, the Supreme Court held that the law was applicable to labor unions. In addition, some common business practices which were destructive of competition had been held outside the purview of the Sherman Act by the courts.

The foregoing were among the factors underlying the passage of the Clayton Act and Federal Trade Commission Act in 1914, which both represent major developments in antitrust law. One additional purpose of the Clayton Act was to exclude labor unions along with nonprofit agricultural organizations from the scope of antitrust legislation.

The Clayton Act was more specific than the Sherman Act in declaring certain enumerated practices in commerce to be illegal, practices which might have an adverse effect on competition but were not themselves contracts, combinations, or conspiracies in restraint of trade and did not go far enough to constitute actual monopolization or attempts to monopolize. Further, the enumerated practices did not have to actually injure competition to be wrongful; they were outlawed if their effect *might* be to substantially lessen competition or *tend* to create a monopoly. Thus, the burden of proving a violation was eased, and the rule of reason was circumvented to some extent in certain cases. It would be much easier, for example, for a court to find that certain practices *tended* toward monopoly, than to find that they *amounted* to a monopoly. The Clayton Act made it possible to attack many practices in their incipiency which, if continued, eventually could destroy competition or create monopoly. The idea was to remedy these matters before the full harm was done. Some of the more pertinent provisions of the

Clayton Act are discussed in this chapter. Section 7 on corporate mergers and acquisitions is the subject matter of Chapter 12.

Violations of the original Clayton Act were not crimes and the Act contained no sanction for forfeiture of property. However, it did provide that the Justice Department might obtain injunctions to prevent violations of it. Those persons who were injured by a violation could obtain injunctive relief in their own behalf and, in addition, were given the right to collect treble the damages they suffered plus court costs and reasonable attorney's fees. Also, the Federal Trade Commission (FTC) was authorized to enforce the substantive provisions of the Clayton Act for businesses other than common carriers, broadcasting media, airlines, and banks. Those businesses are regulated by the Interstate Commerce Commission, Federal Communications Commission, Civil Aeronautics Board, and Federal Reserve Board, respectively. If the commission, in a proper hearing before it, determined that a violation existed, it was empowered to issue a cease and desist order, which is, of course, subject to review and to being set aside or enforced by the Circuit Courts of Appeals of the United States.

While persons guilty of acts proscribed by the Clayton Act were not subject to a criminal sanction, Section 14 imposed criminal liability on *directors* and *agents* of corporations which violated penal provisions of the antitrust laws (such as those found in Sections 1 and 2 of the Sherman Act), if they had a part in the prohibited activity.

The Act expanded the Sherman Act provisions by allowing private individuals to obtain injunctions in cases of *threatened* loss due to violations by another person or corporation of any of the antitrust laws. It also greatly eased the burden of proof which normally must be shouldered by a plaintiff; a final decision in favor of the United States to the effect that a defendant has violated the antitrust laws was made prima facie evidence of such violation in a suit brought by a person who was injured by it against the same defendant.

2   THE PROHIBITION OF INTERLOCKING DIRECTORATES

Section 8 of the Clayton Act is aimed at interlocking directorates. It prohibits a person from being a member of the board of directors of two or more corporations at the same time, when one of them has capital, surplus, and undivided profits totaling more than $1,000,000, where elimination of competition by agreement between such corporations would amount to a violation of any of the antitrust laws. Portions of Section 8 which deal exclusively with banks, and Section 10, which deals exclusively with common carriers, are not discussed here. The case which follows is an example of the application of Section 8.

United States v. Sears, Roebuck & Co.
111 F. Supp. 614 (S.D.N.Y., 1953)

These proceedings were brought by the Government against Sears, Roebuck & Co., The B.F. Goodrich Company, and Sidney J. Weinberg, seeking an order under Section 8 of the Clayton Act directing that Weinberg resign from the board of directors of one or both of the corporate defendants. The defendants admitted to the following facts: that Sears and Goodrich are New York corporations, each having capital, surplus, and undivided profits in excess of 1 million dollars; that Weinberg was and had been for many years a director of both companies; that each corporation was engaged in interstate commerce; that the two were competitors at retail in ninety-seven communities in the sale of appliances, hardware, automotive supplies, sporting goods, tires, radios, television sets, and toys; and that for 1951 the total volume of sales of the foregoing items in the ninety-seven communities by Sears was over 65 million dollars compared to total sales of 16 million dollars by Goodrich. This case was one of first impression, involving the first judicial construction of Section 8 since it was passed in 1914, almost forty years earlier.

WEINFELD, DISTRICT JUDGE: . . . The relevant portion of § 8 provides: ". . . No person at the same time shall be a director in any two or more corporations, any one of which has capital, surplus, and undivided profits aggregating more than $1,000,-000, engaged in whole or in part in commerce . . . if such corporations are or shall have been theretofore, by virtue of their business and location of operation, competitors, so that the elimination of competition by agreement between them would constitute a violation of any of the provisions of any of the antitrust laws. . . ."

The basic issue presented for decision under the admitted facts is whether Sears and Goodrich are "competitors, so that the elimination of competition by agreement between them would constitute a violation of any of the provisions of any of the antitrust laws." If so, then § 8 forbids Weinberg to be a director of both. The case is one of novel impression involving the first construction of this section of the Clayton Act since its passage in 1914.

Defendants in substance contend that the clause just quoted severely limits the scope of the prohibition upon interlocking directorates; that it requires a finding that a hypothetical merger between the two corporations would violate the antitrust laws before the same director is forbidden them; that plaintiff has not demonstrated that the combined position of the two corporate defendants in the sale of the particular commodities is such that there is a "reasonable probability that they could together substantially restrain trade or create a monopoly" and that, therefore, the plaintiff cannot succeed since a merger would not be violative of the antitrust laws without such a showing. In essence, the defendants would apply the merger test as spelled out in § 7 of the Clayton Act, 15 U.S.C.A. § 18.

The plaintiff urges to the contrary that "a violation of any of the provisions of any of the antitrust laws" is not limited to a merger or acquisition situation; that it includes agreements to fix prices or divide markets; that such agreements are illegal per se; and that, therefore, Sears and Goodrich may not retain in their service the same director since an agreement between them to fix prices or to divide territories would constitute a per se violation of § 1 of the Sherman Act, 15 U.S.C.A. § 1.

The Senate and House Reports on the various proposals antecedent to the passage of § 8 of the Clayton Act and the Congressional Debates shed little light on the precise point at issue. However, the broad purposes of Congress are unmistakably clear. Section 8 was but one of a series of measures which finally emerged as the Clayton Act, all intended to strengthen the Sherman Act, which, through the years, had not proved entirely effective. Congress had been aroused by the concentration of control by a few individuals or groups over many gigantic corporations which in the normal course of events should have been in active and unrestrained competition. Instead, and because of such control, the healthy competition of the free enterprise system had been stifled or eliminated. Interlocking directorships on rival corporations had been the instrumentality of defeating the purpose of the antitrust laws. They had tended to suppress competition or to foster joint action against third party competitors. The continued potential threat to the competitive system resulting from these conflicting directorships was the evil aimed at. Viewed against this background, a fair reading of the legislative debates leaves little room for doubt that, in its efforts to strengthen the antitrust laws, what Congress intended by § 8 was to nip in the bud incipient violations of the antitrust laws by removing the opportunity or temptation to such violations through interlocking directorates. The legislation was essentially preventative.

It is in the context of this history that defendants' argument must be evaluated. . . .

Defendants also rely on the asserted necessity for reading § 8 in connection with § 7 of the Clayton Act, 38 Stat. 731, as amended, 64 Stat. 1125, 15 U.S.C.A. § 18, which deals with mergers and interdicts the acquisition by one corporation of the stock or the assets of another where the effect of such acquisition "may be substantially to lessen competition, or to tend to create a monopoly."

Defendants argue, as set forth above, that § 8 does not prohibit defendant Weinberg's directorship on the two Boards, absent a showing that the effect of an assumed consolidation between Sears and Goodrich "may be substantially to lessen competition, or to tend to create a monopoly," as set forth in § 7. The vital distinction between § 7 and § 8, however, is that the latter omits the § 7 test and promulgates its own substantiality standard in the form of the one million dollar size requirement. The omission of "substantially to lessen competition, or to tend to create a monopoly" from § 8 in contradistinction to its inclusion in § 7 and other sections of the same Act may not be deemed inadvertent. Were the defendants' construction to be adopted, it would require the application under § 8 of a test which Congress appears deliberately to have omitted. . . .

Further, the defendants' construction would denude of meaning the phrase "*any* of the provisions of *any* of the antitrust *laws*." [EMPHASIS ADDED] This language is broad enough to cover all methods of violating antitrust legislation. At the time of the passage of § 8, price fixing and division of territory agreements were in common use to effect such violations. Merger or acquisition was not the sole means used to achieve this result. There is no logical basis upon which to infer that the all-inclusive language was intended to exclude the other known methods from the reach of § 8.

Finally, defendants urge that no policy reasons have been advanced to show that the public interest is affected by the dual directorship of the defendant

Weinberg on the Boards of the corporate defendants. They say that the government has failed to show that there exists between Sears and Goodrich any agreement fixing prices, restricting territories or otherwise restraining competition between them or that there is a likelihood of any such agreement; further, that no contention is made that the individual defendant's dual directorship has had the effect, or has the potentiality, of restraining competition. But this argument ignores the preventative nature of § 8. The instant case presents a good example of what the section was intended to avert.

The defendants have conceded that they are competitors in the sale of the seven categories of items at retail in commerce as the term is used in the Clayton Act. The sales of the seven items in the 97 communities amounted to $80,000,000 for 1951. The fact that this volume of sales may represent but a small percentage of either or both of the corporate defendants' annual sales, or a fraction of the annual retail sales volume of all distributors in the country of those commodities, does not militate against the undesirability of directorates common to both corporations. Actually, commerce in a particular product, using refrigerators as an example, while perhaps insignificant as related to the corporate defendants' total sales of all their other products or infinitesimal compared to the national retail volume, may, nonetheless, represent the total absorptive capacity of a given community within which they are competitors.

Assume that Sears and Goodrich are selling refrigerators competitively in a town of 30,000 population, the effective and easy means is at hand, through a price fixing agreement or the withdrawal of either Sears or Goodrich from the territory or an agreement not to sell the refrigerators in the same area, to eliminate or lessen competition. While the government does not charge that any such agreement has been made or is contemplated, a director serving in a dual capacity might, if he felt the interest of an interlocking corporation so required, either initiate or support a course of action resulting in price fixing or division of territories or a combination of his competing corporations as against a third competitive corporation. The fact that this has not happened up to the present does not mean that it may not happen hereafter.

In summary, an agreement between Sears and Goodrich which fixed the prices at which they would sell the seven categories of items would eliminate competition, as would an agreement by which they allocated as between themselves the territories in which they would sell those items. Price fixing and territorial division between competitors are per se violations of § 1 of the Sherman Act, 26 Stat. 209, 15 U.S.C.A. § 1, without regard to the amount of commerce affected. No showing of industry domination is required. It is the character of the restraint and not the amount of commerce affected that taints the transactions. . . .

Since Sears and Goodrich are competitors, since a price fixing or division of territory agreement would eliminate competition between them, and since such an agreement would per se violate at least one "of the provisions of . . . the antitrust laws," namely § 1 of the Sherman Act, it follows that § 8 forbids defendant Weinberg to be a director of both corporations.

The government's motion for summary judgment is granted. . . . [MOTION GRANTED]

3 PRICE DISCRIMINATION—GENERALLY

The Clayton Act as enacted in 1914 contained provisions in Section 2 relating to price discrimination. Section 2 as originally adopted declared that it was unlawful for a seller to discriminate in the price charged different purchasers of commodities where the effect *might* be to substantially lessen competition or *tend* to create a monopoly in any line of commerce. However, "discrimination in price . . . on account of differences in the grade, quality, or quantity of the commodity sold, or that makes only due allowance for difference in the cost of selling or transportation. . . ." was not illegal. This latter provision, which allowed quantity discounts among other things, so weakened Section 2 that it was very difficult if not impossible to prevent price discrimination.

In the 1920s and early 1930s, various techniques were used by large-volume retailers and especially chain stores to obtain more favorable prices than those available to smaller competitors. In addition to obtaining quantity discounts, some large businesses created subsidiary corporations which received brokerage allowances as wholesalers. Another method used by big business to obtain price advantages was demanding and obtaining larger promotional allowances than were given to smaller businesses. The prevalence of the foregoing practices, which were not prohibited by the Clayton Act, led to the enactment in 1936 of the Robinson-Patman amendment. This statute attempted to eliminate the advantage that a large buyer could secure over a small buyer solely because of the large buyer's quantity purchasing ability. The Robinson-Patman amendment was passed to deprive a large buyer of such advantage except to the extent that a lower price could be justified by reason of a seller's diminished costs due to quantity manufacture, delivery, or sale, or by reason of the seller's good-faith effort to meet a competitor's equally low price.

The goal of the Robinson-Patman amendment was to ensure equality of treatment to all customers of a seller, where the result of unequal treatment may be to substantially lessen competition or tend to create a monopoly in any line of commerce. This latter language means that in price discrimination cases, a determination of fact is required as to the relevant market and the probable anticompetitive effects of the discrimination. The relevant market determination has two aspects—product market and geographic market. A finding as to the applicable product and the area in which buyers compete is required because it would be unreasonable to prohibit a seller from price differentials in different areas. For example, a seller should be able to charge a different price in California than in Florida, when the buyers of the product are not in competition with each other and the price difference will therefore have no anticompetitive effect.

The law applies to both buyers and sellers. It is just as illegal to receive the benefit of price discrimination as it is to give a lower price to one of two buyers.

The original Clayton Act required a showing of general injury to competitive conditions. The 1936 amendment provided that there could be a finding of injury to competition by a showing of "injury to the competitor" victimized by the discrimination. This proviso gave additional protection to small businessmen.

The Robinson-Patman amendment made it a crime for a seller to sell at lower prices in one geographical area than elsewhere in the United States in order to eliminate competition or a competitor, or to sell at unreasonably low prices to drive out a competitor. This provision has been held constitutional even though it contains the words "unreasonably low prices." Such words are not so vague as to amount to a denial of due process. The statutory language means that it is illegal to sell goods below cost for illegitimate purposes. Not every sale below cost constitutes a violation. For example, sales for legitimate purposes such as liquidation of excess, obsolete, or perishable merchandise may be legal. It is illegal to charge the low price where the intention is to drive out a competitor.

The Robinson-Patman amendment also gave the Federal Trade Commission jurisdiction and authority to eliminate quantity discounts and to forbid brokerage allowances, except to independent brokers, and also prohibited promotional allowances, except on an equal basis.

To summarize Section 2 of the Clayton Act as amended by Robinson-Patman, it is unlawful for any person to discriminate in price between different purchasers of commodities of like grade and quality where the effect of such discrimination may be substantially to lessen competition or tend to create a monopoly in any line of commerce or to injure competition with any person. It is a violation to knowingly receive a benefit of such discrimination. The statute recognizes certain exceptions: (1) price differentials based on differences in the cost of manufacture, sale, or delivery of commodities are permitted, except that the Federal Trade Commission may fix and establish quantity limits on particular commodities where it finds so few purchasers as to render differentials owing to quantity unjustly discriminatory or promotive of monopoly; (2) persons engaged in selling goods, wares, or merchandise in commerce may select their own customers in bona fide transactions and not in restraint of trade; and (3) price changes may be made in response to changing conditions such as actual or imminent deterioration of perishable goods, obsolescence of seasonal goods, distress sales under court process, or sales in good faith in discontinuance of business in the goods concerned. These exceptions and the defenses available to one charged with a violation will be discussed more fully later.

The burden of showing cost justification is upon the person charged with a violation once there has been proof of discrimination in price; and, unless justification is affirmatively shown, the Federal Trade Commission is authorized to issue an order terminating the discrimination. A seller is also permitted to justify a discrimination by showing that his lower price of services or facilities to any purchaser was made in good faith to meet an equally low price of a competitor.

Various indirect price discriminations are also prohibited. For example, it is unlawful to pay or receive a commission or discount on sales or purchases except for actual services rendered; to pay a customer for any services or facilities he furnishes in connection with a transaction unless such payment is available to all customers on equal terms; and to favor one purchaser of a commodity over another by furnishing him services or facilities in connection with a sale which are not available to all purchasers on equal terms.

On its face, the Robinson-Patman amendment purports to have the objective of preserving competition. However, in fact, it represents to some degree a withdrawal or modification of that policy. For example, the amendment does not allow a supplier to encourage those who are able to buy his product in very large quantities by giving them price concessions or discounts. The net result of such provisions is to partially remove the small, individual business from some of the forces of competition. Partially insulating such businesses from competition and preserving them may have the effect of rewarding less efficient operations and keeping prices artificially high for the consumer. Thus higher prices may result from attempts to preserve competition even though one reason for preserving competition is to obtain lower prices for consumers. The Robinson-Patman amendment has as at least one of its purposes the preservation of small *competitors* at the cost of competition.

The price discrimination provisions relate to commodities. They do not relate to services or the sale of advertising such as television time.

The cases which follow illustrate some of the problems of interpreting and applying the provisions of Section 2 of the Clayton Act as amended by Robinson-Patman.

FTC v. The Borden Co.
383 U.S. 637 (1966)

WHITE, JUSTICE: The Borden Company, respondent here, produces and sells evaporated milk under the Borden name, a nationally advertised brand. At the same time Borden packs and markets evaporated milk under various private brands owned by its customers. This milk is physically and chemically identical with the milk it distributes under its own brand but is sold at both the wholesale and retail level at prices regularly below those obtained for the Borden brand milk. The Federal Trade Commission found the milk sold under the Borden and the private labels to be of like grade and quality as required for the applicability of § 2(a) of the Robinson-Patman Act, held the price differential to be discriminatory within the meaning of the section, ascertained the requisite adverse effect on commerce, rejected Borden's claim of cost justification and consequently issued a cease-and-desist order. The Court of Appeals set aside the Commission's order on the sole ground that as a matter of law, the customer label milk was not of the same grade and quality as the milk sold under the Borden brand. Because of the importance of this issue, which bears on the reach and coverage of the Robinson-Patman Act, we granted certiorari. We now reverse the decision of the Court of Appeals and remand the case to that court for the determination of the remaining issues raised by respondent Borden in that court.

The position of Borden and of the Court of Appeals is that the determination of like grade and quality, which is a threshold finding essential to the applicability of § 2(a), may not be based solely on the physical properties of the products without regard to the brand names they bear and the relative public acceptance these brands enjoy—"consideration should be given to all commercially significant distinctions which affect market value, whether they be physical or promotional." . . . Here, because the milk bearing the Borden brand regularly sold at a higher price than did the milk with a buyer's label, the court considered the products to be "commercially" different and hence of different "grade" for the purposes of § 2(a), even though they were physically identical and of equal quality. Although a mere difference in brand would not in itself demonstrate a difference in grade, decided consumer preference for one brand over another, reflected in the willingness to pay a higher price for the well-known brand, was, in the view of the Court of Appeals, sufficient to differentiate chemically identical products and to place the price differential beyond the reach of § 2(a).

We reject this construction of § 2(a), as did both the examiner and the Commission in this case. The Commission's view is that labels do not differentiate products for the purpose of determining grade or quality, even though the one label may have more customer appeal and command a higher price in the marketplace from a substantial segment of the public. . . .

Obviously there is nothing in the language of the statute indicating that grade, as distinguished from quality, is not to be determined by the characteristics of the product itself, but by consumer preferences, brand acceptability or what customers think of it and are willing to pay for it. Moreover, what legislative history there is concerning this question supports the Commission's construction of the statute rather than that of the Court of Appeals.

The Commission's construction of the statute also appears to us to further the purpose and policy of the Robinson-Patman Act. Subject to specified exceptions and defenses, § 2(a) proscribes unequal treatment of different customers in comparable transactions, but only if there is the requisite effect upon competition, actual or potential. But if the transactions are deemed to involve goods of disparate grade or quality, the section has no application at all and the Commission never reaches either the issue of discrimination or that of anticompetitive impact. We doubt that Congress intended to foreclose these inquiries in situations where a single seller markets the identical product under several different brands, whether his own, his customers or both. Such transactions are too laden with potential discrimination and adverse competitive effect to be excluded from the reach of § 2(a) by permitting a difference in grade to be established by the label alone or by the label and its consumer appeal.

If two products, physically identical but differently branded, are to be deemed of different grade because the seller regularly and successfully markets some quantity of both at different prices, the seller could, as far as § 2(a) is concerned, make either product available to some customers and deny it to others, however discriminatory this might be and however damaging to competition. Those who were offered only one of the two products would be barred from competing for those customers who want or might buy the other. The retailer who was permitted to buy and sell only the more expensive brand would have no chance to sell to those who always buy the cheaper product or to convince others, by experience or otherwise, of the fact which he and all other dealers already know—that the cheaper product is actually identical with that carrying the more expensive label.

The seller, to escape the Act, would have only to succeed in selling some unspecified amount of each product to some unspecified portion of his customers, however large or small the price differential might be. The seller's pricing and branding policy, by being successful, would apparently validate itself by creating a difference in "grade" and thus take itself beyond the purview of the Act.

Our holding neither ignores the economic realities of the marketplace nor denies that some labels will command a higher price than others, at least from some portion of the public. But it does mean that "the economic factors inherent in brand names and national advertising should not be considered in the jurisdictional inquiry under the statutory 'like grade and quality' test. . . . And it does mean that transactions like those involved in this case may be examined by the Commission under § 2(a). The Commission will determine, subject to judicial review, whether the differential under attack is discriminatory within the meaning of the Act, whether competition may be injured, and whether the differential is cost justified or is defensible as a good-faith effort to meet the price of a competitor. "[T]angible consumer preferences as between branded and unbranded commodities should receive due legal recognition in the more flexible 'injury' and 'cost justification' provisions of the statute." This, we think, is precisely what Congress intended. The arguments for exempting private brand selling from § 2(a) are, therefore, more appropriately addressed to the Congress than to this Court. . . .

The judgment of the Court of Appeals is reversed and the case is remanded for further proceedings consistent with this opinion. It is so ordered. [REVERSED AND REMANDED]

STEWART, JUSTICE, dissenting (joined by JUSTICE HARLAN): There is nothing intrinsic to the concepts of grade and quality that requires exclusion of the commercial attributes of a product from their definition. The product purchased by a consumer includes not only the chemical components that any competent laboratory can itemize, but also a host of commercial intangibles that distinguish the product in the market place. The premium paid for Borden brand milk reflects the consumer's awareness, promoted through advertising, that these commercial attributes are part and parcel of the premium product he is purchasing. The record in the present case indicates that wholesale purchasers of Borden's private label brands continued to purchase the premium brand in undiminished quantities. The record also indicates that retail purchasers who bought the premium brand did so with the specific expectation of acquiring a product of premium quality. Contrary to the Court's suggestion, ante, this consumer expectation cannot accurately be characterized as a misapprehension. Borden took extensive precautions to insure that a flawed product did not reach the consumer. None of these precautions was taken for the private brand milk packed by Borden. An important ingredient of the premium brand inheres in the consumer's belief, measured by past satisfaction and the market reputation established by Borden for its products, that tomorrow's can will contain the same premium product as that purchased today. . . .

Perkins v. Standard Oil Company of California
89 S.Ct. 1871 (1969)

Plaintiff, Perkins, brought suit for treble damages under Section 2 of the Clayton Act as amended by the Robinson-Patman Act. He alleged that Standard Oil was guilty of price discrimination in two ways: (1) that it sold gasoline to its own branded dealers at prices lower than it sold to plaintiff and (2) that it sold gasoline at a lower price to another oil company, which in turn sold it to a wholesaler, who in turn sold it to a competitor of the plaintiff at a price that was still lower than the price paid by the plaintiff for similar gasoline. The jury awarded plaintiff $333,404.57, which when trebled gave plaintiff $1,298,213.71. The Court of Appeals reversed. The issue on this appeal is whether or not the second type of price discrimination which was alleged is within the coverage of the Act.

BLACK, JUSTICE: We disagree with the Court of Appeals conclusion that Sec. 2 of the Clayton Act, as amended by the Robinson-Patman Act, does not apply to the damages suffered by Perkins as a result of the price advantage granted by Standard to Signal, then by Signal to Western, then by Western to Regal. The Act, in pertinent part, provides:

(a) It shall be unlawful for any person engaged in commerce, . . . either directly or indirectly, to discriminate in price between different purchasers of commodities of like grade and quality, . . . where the effect of such discrimination may be substantially to lessen competition or tend to create a monopoly in any line of commerce, or to injure, destroy, or prevent competition with any person who either grants or knowingly receives the benefit of such discrimination, or with customers of either of them: . . . .

The Court of Appeals read this language as limiting "the distributing levels on which a supplier's price discrimination will be recognized as potentially injurious to competition." According to that court, the coverage of the Act is restricted to injuries caused by an impairment of competition with (1) the seller ["any person who . . . grants . . . such discrimination"], (2) the favored purchaser ["any person who . . . knowingly receives the benefit of such discrimination"] and (3) customers of the discriminating seller or favored purchaser ["customers of either of them"]. Here, Perkins' injuries resulted in part from impaired competition with a customer (Regal) of a customer (Western Hyway) of the favored purchaser (Signal). The Court of Appeals termed these injuries "fourth level" and held that they were not protected by the Robinson-Patman Act. We conclude that this limitation is wholly an artificial one and is completely unwarranted by the language or purpose of the Act.

In *FTC v. Fred Meyer, Inc.*, 390 U.S. 341, 88 S.Ct. 904, 19 L.Ed.2d 1222 (1968), we held that a retailer who buys through a wholesaler could be considered a "customer" of the original supplier within the meaning of § 2(d) of the Robinson-Patman Act, a section dealing with discrimination in promotional allowances which is closely analogous to § 2(a) involved in this case. In *Meyer*, the Court stated that to read "customer" narrowly would be wholly untenable when viewed in light of the purposes of the Robinson-Patman Act. Similarly, to read "customer" more narrowly in this section than we did in the section involved in *Meyer* would allow price discriminators to avoid the sanctions of the Act by the simple expedient of adding an additional link to the distribution chain. Here, for example, standard supplied gasoline and oil to Signal. Signal, allegedly because it furnished

Standard with part of its vital supply of crude petroleum, was able to insist upon a discriminatorily lower price. Had Signal then sold its gas directly to the Regal stations, giving Regal stations a competitive advantage, there would be no question, even under the decision of the Court of Appeals in this case, that a clear violation of the Robinson-Patman Act had been committed. Instead of selling directly to the retailer Regal, however, Signal transferred the gasoline first to its subsidiary, Western Hyway, who in turn supplied the Regal stations. Signal owned 60% of the stock of Western Hyway; Western in turn owned 55% of the stock of the Regal stations. We find no basis in the language or purpose of the Act for immunizing Standard's price discriminations simply because the product in question passed through an additional formal exchange before reaching the level of Perkins' actual competitor. From Perkins' point of view, the competitive harm done him by Standard is certainly no less because of the presence of an additional link in this particular distribution chain from the producer to the retailer. Here Standard discriminated in price between Perkins and Signal, and there was evidence from which the jury could conclude that Perkins was harmed competitively when Signal's price advantage was passed on to Perkins' retail competitor Regal. These facts are sufficient to give rise to recoverable damages under the Robinson-Patman Act. . . . [VERDICT AND JUDGMENT REINSTATED]

4 SPECIAL FORMS OF PRICE DISCRIMINATION

The Clayton Act as amended by the Robinson-Patman Act proscribes certain hidden or indirect discriminations by sellers in favor of certain buyers. Section 2(c) prohibits an unearned brokerage or commission related to a sale of goods. Section 2(d) outlaws granting promotional allowances or payments on goods bought for resale, unless they are available to all competing customers. Section 2(e) prohibits the giving of promotional facilities or services on goods bought for resale, unless they are available to all competing customers. Note that the Act does not *expressly* require that any anticompetitive effects be demonstrated to prove a violation of these provisions. Further, it does not *expressly* avail the seller who has committed any of the prohibited acts the three defenses, already discussed, which he has to a charge of out and out *price* discrimination under Section 2(a). Obviously, Sections 2(c), (d), and (e) leave many business practices open to question and many issues regarding their application in doubt. In the case which follows, the legality under Section 2(c) of certain discriminatory brokerage allowances granted by the defendant to some of his customers was brought into issue.

Empire Rayon Yarn Co. v. American Viscose Corp.
364 F.2d 491 (1966)

Empire Rayon Yarn Co. brought action for treble damages against the defendant, American Viscose Corporation, alleging a violation of Sections 2(c), (d), and (e) of the amended Clayton Act, because of American's allowing 5 percent brokerage allowances to certain jobbers but refusing the same privilege to the plaintiff. American was in the business of manufacturing and selling unprocessed rayon yarn, while American's jobbers as well as the plaintiff, Empire, were in the business of buying unprocessed rayon yarn and either reselling it in its original state as received from the manufacturer, or converting and selling it for use in the textile trade.

An outline of the method of distribution chosen by American was given by its general sales manager, as follows:

Many years ago American established a distribution policy for the sale of viscose rayon yarn by direct sales to consumers of most of the product and sales to two jobbers, the defendants Malina and Gutner, of a small percentage of the product. These two jobbers were able to sell and service smaller units of the textile trade at lower selling costs than American and for that reason American established the jobber relation. These jobbers performed such services as the maintenance of substantial inventories of yarn in their plants as well as in warehouses, maintenance of an experienced selling organization, assumption of all risk of loss and credit, advertising American products, assumption of all risk of price fluctuation and furnishing of technical assistance to users of rayon. For acting as such jobbers American allowed a discount from list price on all viscose rayon yarn resold by the jobbers. On all sales to these jobbers for processing (not for resale) they pay the current price just the same as the plaintiff [Empire] or any other customer.

As the reason for refusing a similar discount to Empire, American's general sales manager stated that American's "offices . . . in the exercise of their own business judgment decided that the volume of yarn sold by the jobbing trade did not, and does not (as of January, 1958) . . . justify the appointment by American of more . . . jobbers." The District Court granted summary judgment to the defendant American. However, on appeal, the Court of Appeals, Second Circuit (three judges) held that the payments in question violated Section 2(c) and reversed, remanding the case to the District Court to ascertain the plaintiff's damages and to enter summary judgment for the plaintiff. The defendant petitioned the Court of Appeals, Second Circuit, for a rehearing before them, *in banc* (nine circuit judges), and the court granted the rehearing.

MOORE, CIRCUIT JUDGE: This opinion supersedes the previous opinion of a panel of this Court wherein that panel reversed an order which had granted defendants' motion for summary judgment. Thereafter defendants petitioned for a rehearing *in banc* which by order dated March 31, 1966 was granted, reconsideration to be had on the record and briefs. Because of the importance of the issue involved, the Court, *sua sponte*, requested the Federal Trade Commission "to submit a brief *amicus curiae* on the issues raised by this case." The Commission filed such brief to which appellants and appellee replied. After due consideration of the briefs filed originally, of the briefs filed in the *in banc* rehearing and of the position taken by the Commission in its *amicus* brief, we unanimously affirm the order granting summary judgment for the defendants and denying the cross motion therefor.

The facts are set forth adequately in the panel opinion, 354 F.2d 182. Nor need the arguments *pro* and *con* therein stated be repeated. The Court adopts the statutory interpretation set forth in the dissenting opinion, 354 F.2d, pages 188–192. Brief reference, however, should be made to the views of the Federal Trade Commission, the agency which to a considerable extent is charged with the administration of the Robinson-Patman Act.

The issue, as before, is whether the payment by American of a 5% discount from list price to Malina and Gutner, which together with Shawmut had been acting for special factual reasons as jobbers for American, was an illegal brokerage payment within the compass of, and in violation of, Section 2(c).

The Commission has taken the position that upon the facts here presented this 5% discount was not "an unlawful 'brokerage' payment, or allowance or discount in lieu thereof, violative of Section 2(c)" and that these facts "preclude[s] a finding that it constituted a violation of Section 2(c)." The Commission noted that Malina and Gutner were not "dummy" brokers; that they were not powerful buyers able to compel because of economic power the payment of discounts in lieu of brokerage; that American did not utilize brokers in selling its rayon yarn; and that Malina and Gutner did not fall into the buying broker category. The Commission further noted that Malina and Gutner took title and resold to small manufacturers; solicited and obtained their own customers; assumed all risks of loss and credit; operated warehouses; maintained inventories; employed selling organizations; advertised; and furnished technical assistance to their customers. The factual conclusion reached by the Commission was that Malina and Gutner were "independent business men who operated as jobbers at a level of distribution between the manufacturers of the yarn and the processor who found it economically difficult to buy direct"; that they "satisfied an economic need by facilitating the movement of American's rayon yarn to the small units in the textile trade"; and that the 5% discount "bears all the characteristics of a functional discount, the validity of which should be judged under Section 2(a)."

Reliance upon Section 2(c) might well, in the Commission's view, "render all functional discounts illegal *per se*" and prevent the recognition of price differentials at non-competing business levels.

It is our conclusion that if plaintiff has any grievance, it must find its remedy under Section 2(a) and not as here under Section 2(c), (d) and (e). [AFFIRMED]

5   DEFENSES TO PRICE DISCRIMINATION CHARGES

In a price discrimination case under Section 2 of the amended Clayton Act, when the plaintiff has introduced proof of differential pricing of the same kind of goods by the defendant and proof of the requisite injury to competition which resulted, he has established a prima facie case. Sections 2(a) and 2(b) provide for several instances in which a price discrimination is not violative of the law. However, these are affirmative defenses, since the Act imposes the burden of proving them on the defendant, rather than making it the obligation of the plaintiff to negate their existence.

The first justification for a price discrimination is the cost-justification defense. Section 2(a) provides that nothing "shall prevent differentials which make only due allowance for *differences in the cost of manufacture, sale, or delivery* resulting from the differing methods or quantities in which . . . commodities are . . . sold or delivered." [EMPHASIS ADDED] This would appear to be a significant excuse which would permit cost savings to be passed on to customers. However, according to the Attorney General's Committee "the cost defense has proved largely illusory in practice."[1] Because of the complexities in determining what is "cost" very rarely has this defense been successful in the past. One obvious problem is that of bringing forth acceptable *evidence* of cost. As the Supreme Court noted in *Automatic Canteen Co. v. FTC,* "Proof of a cost justification being what it is, too often no one can ascertain whether a price is cost justified."[2] The Attorney General's Committee notes two other reasons why the cost defense is "illusory." The first of these is ". . . the failure of past adjudications to evolve workable criteria by which the cost defense can attain its intended role."[3] The other is "[t]he absence of officially sanctioned accounting standards [which] has provoked needless dispute over easily reconcilable disparities in technique."[4] The Committee concludes that the circumstances are such that "only the most prosperous and patient business firms could afford pursuit of [this] often illusory defense. Pressure builds to gain legal safety by withholding price differentials from more efficient buyers, thus denying to the public the benefits of mass production and economical distribution processes which Congress intended to preserve by enacting the cost proviso in Section 2(a)."[5]

In addition to the foregoing, price differentials due to savings resulting from larger quantity sales may be further limited by the FTC, which is authorized under certain circumstances to "fix and establish quantity limits."

A second affirmative defense is afforded those who discriminate in price due to changing conditions. Section 2(a) also exempts "price changes from time to time where in response to changing conditions affecting the market for or the marketability of the goods concerned, such as but not limited to actual or imminent deterioration of perishable goods, obsolescence of seasonal goods, distress sales under court process or sales in good faith in discontinuance of business in the goods concerned." The Attorney General's Committee recommended a liberal interpretation of this provision "to promote competitors' freedom to react realistically to the spontaneous movements of a dynamic market."[6] However, the extent to which this exemption actually is available to justify

[1] Report of the Attorney General's National Committee to Study the Antitrust Laws 171 (1955).
[2] 346 U.S. 61, 79 (1953).
[3] Report of the Attorney General's National Committee to Study the Antitrust Laws 171 (1955).
[4] *Id.* at 172, 173.
[5] *Id.* at 173.
[6] *Id.* at 178.

changes in pricing due to changes in *market conditions,* apart from the types of changes in *marketability of goods* specifically enumerated is not clear.

A final affirmative defense justifying price discrimination is the good faith meeting of competition. Section 2(b) of the Act permits a defendant to demonstrate that a given price discrimination was not unlawful by "showing that his lower price or the furnishing of services or facilities to any purchaser or purchasers was made in good faith to meet an equally low price of a competitor, or the services or facilities furnished by a competitor."

"Good faith" is not easily defined. In one case, the Federal Trade Commission found good faith where the company involved proved that (1) for a period of time it had refrained from granting any discriminating discounts and had changed its policy only after its market position had deteriorated; (2) competitive allowances were given to existing customers who otherwise would have switched; (3) the lower price bestowed matched and never beat that extended by competitors; (4) in every instance customer claims that they were receiving discounts from competitors of respondent were adequately verified by respondent's on-the-spot sales representatives.

In this same case, the Federal Trade Commission in discussing good faith as it is used in Section 2(b) of the Robinson-Patman amendment stated:

This is a flexible and pragmatic, not technical or doctrinaire, concept. The standard of good faith is simply the standard of the prudent businessman responding fairly to what he reasonably believes is a situation of competitive necessity. . . . Such a standard, whether it be considered "subjective" or "objective" is inherently ad hoc. Rigid rules and inflexible absolutes are especially inappropriate in dealing with the 2(b) defense; the facts and circumstances in the particular case, not abstract theories or remote conjectures, should govern its interpretation and application. Thus, the same method of meeting competition may be consistent with an inference of good faith in some circumstances, inconsistent with such an inference in others.

While the term "good faith" cannot be quantified, it is clear that this defense cannot be established where the purpose of a seller's price discrimination is to eliminate competition. The seller may offer discriminatory prices to customers whether or not he has done business with them in the past, but these discriminatory prices must not be lower than those offered by competitors.

The timing of the price offers must be such that it is apparent that they are made to meet an individual competitive situation and are not a part of a general system of competition. The seller must also have knowledge of the prices he is meeting, to the extent that a reasonable man would believe that these prices were lawful.

The overriding consideration concerning the good-faith proviso is the motive of the discriminating seller. The good-faith concept should be used solely to test the seller's adherence to the basic objectives of the meeting-competition proviso: facilitating price reductions in genuine response to competitive market pressures in order to equalize a competitive opportunity. In practice, this will disqualify the seller to whom meeting of competition is only an incidental by-product of a scheme to monopolize or of any other objective contrary to the purposes of the overall antitrust policy.

In *FTC v. A. E. Staley Mfg. Co.*,[7] the defendant company manufactured corn syrup in Decatur, Illinois, but sold it for list price plus freight from Chicago, Illinois, to the delivery point. Staley was held to be in violation of Section 2(a), even though it argued it should be exempt under Section 2(b), since it was merely meeting the same prices charged by its competitors. The court upheld the Commission's finding that Staley was not meeting competition in good faith by using the same basing point pricing system as that used by the other competitors, which was unlawful on its face. The Supreme Court also had occasion to consider the application of the "meeting competition" defense to a price discrimination in the case which follows.

Standard Oil Co. v. FTC
340 U.S. 231 (1951)

BURTON, JUSTICE: In this case the Federal Trade Commission challenged the right of the Standard Oil Company, under the Robinson-Patman Act, to sell gasoline to four comparatively large "jobber" customers in Detroit at a less price per gallon than it sold like gasoline to many comparatively small service station customers in the same area. The company's defenses were that (1) the sales involved were not in interstate commerce and (2) its lower price to the jobbers was justified because made to retain them as customers and in good faith to meet an equally low price of a competitor. The Commission, with one member dissenting, ordered the company to cease and desist from making such a price differential. The Court of Appeals slightly modified the order and required its enforcement as modified. . . .

For the reasons hereinafter stated, we agree with the court below that the sales were made in interstate commerce but we agree with petitioner that, under the Act, the lower price to the jobbers was justified if it was made to retain each of them as a customer and in good faith to meet an equally low price of a competitor. . . .

Petitioner presented evidence tending to prove that its tank-car price was made to each "jobber" in order to retain that "jobber" as a customer and in good faith to meet a lawful and equally low price of a competitor. Petitioner sought to show that it succeeded in retaining these customers, although the tank-car price which it offered them merely approached or matched, and did not undercut, the lower prices offered them by several competitors of petitioner. The trial examiner made findings on the point but the Commission declined to do so, saying: "Based on the record in this case the Commission concludes as a matter of law that it is not material whether the discriminations in price granted by the respondent to the said four dealers were made to meet equally low prices of competitors. The

[7] 324 U.S. 746 (1945).

Commission further concludes as a matter of law that it is unnecessary for the Commission to determine whether the alleged competitive prices were in fact available or involved gasoline of like grade or quality or of equal public acceptance. Accordingly the Commission does not attempt to find the facts regarding those matters because, even though the lower prices in question may have been made by respondent in good faith to meet the lower prices of competitors, this does not constitute a defense in the face of affirmative proof that the effect of the discrimination was to injure, destroy and prevent competition with the retail stations operated by the said named dealers and with stations operated by their retailer-customers."

The court below affirmed the Commission's position. . . .

The defense relating to the meeting of the price of a competitor appears only in subsection (b). There it is applied to discrimination in services or facilities as well as to discriminations in price, which alone are expressly comdemned in subsection (a). In its opinion in the instant case, the Commission recognizes that it is an absolute defense to a charge of price discrimination for a seller to prove, under § 2(a), that its price differential makes only due allowances for differences in cost or for price changes made in response to changing market conditions. Each of these three defenses is introduced by the same phrase "nothing . . . shall prevent," and all are embraced in the same word "justification" in the first sentence of § 2(b). It is natural, therefore, to conclude that each of these defenses is entitled to the same effect, without regard to whether there also appears an affirmative showing of actual or potential injury to competition at the same or a lower level traceable to the price differential made by the seller. The Commission says, however, that the proviso in § 2(b) as to a seller meeting in good faith a lower competitive price is not an absolute defense if an injury to competition may result from such price reduction. We find no basis for such a distinction between the defenses in § 2(a) and (b). . . .

This right of a seller, under § 2(b), to meet in good faith an equally low price of a competitor has been considered here before. Both in *Corn Prod. Ref. Co. v. FTC*, 324 U.S. 726, and in *FTC v. A. E. Staley Mfg. Co.*, 324 U.S. 746, evidence in support of this defense was reviewed at length. While this Court did not sustain the seller's defense in either case, it did unquestionably recognize the relevance of the evidence in support of that defense. The decision in each case was based upon the insufficiency of the seller's evidence to establish its defense, not upon the inadequacy of its defense as a matter of law.

In the *Corn Products* case, *supra*, after recognizing that the seller had allowed differentials in price in favor of certain customers, this Court examined the evidence presented by the seller to show that such differentials were justified because made in good faith to meet equally low prices of a competitor. It then said: "Examination of the *testimony* satisfies us, as it did the court below, that it was *insufficient* to sustain a finding that the lower prices allowed to favored customers were in fact made to meet competition. Hence petitioners *failed to sustain the burden* of showing that the price discriminations were granted for the purpose of meeting competition." [EMPHASIS ADDED]

In the *Staley* case, *supra,* most of the Court's opinion is devoted to the consideration of the evidence introduced in support of the seller's defense under § 2(b). The discussion proceeds upon the assumption, applicable here, that if a competitor's "lower price" is a lawful individual price offered to any of the seller's customers, then the seller is protected, under § 2(b), in making a counteroffer provided the seller proves that its counteroffer is made to meet in good faith its competitor's equally low price. On the record in the *Staley* case, a majority of the Court of Appeals, in fact, declined to accept the findings of the Commission and decided in favor of the accused seller. This Court, on review, reversed that judgment but emphatically recognized the availability of the seller's defense under § 2(b) and the obligation of the Commission to make findings upon issues material to that defense. It said:

Congress has left to the Commission the determination of fact in each case whether the person, charged with making discriminatory prices, acted in good faith to meet a competitor's equally low prices. The determination of this fact from the evidence is for the Commission. In the present case, the Commission's finding that respondents' price discriminations were not made to meet a "lower" price and consequently were not in good faith, is amply supported by the record, and we think the Court of Appeals erred in setting aside this portion of the Commission's order to cease and desist. . . .

All that petitioner asks in the instant case is that its evidence be considered and that findings be made by the Commission as to the sufficiency of that evidence to support petitioner's defense under § 2(b). . . .

We need not now reconcile, in its entirety, the economic theory which underlies the Robinson-Patman Act with that of the Sherman and Clayton Acts.

It is enough to say that Congress did not seek by the Robinson-Patman Act either to abolish competition or so radically to curtail it that a seller would have no substantial right of self-defense against a price paid by a competitor. For example, if a large customer requests his seller to meet a temptingly lower price offered to him by one of his seller's competitors, the seller may well find it essential, as a matter of business survival, to meet that price rather than to lose the customer. It might be that this customer is the seller's only available market for the major portion of the seller's product, and that the loss of this customer would result in forcing a much higher unit cost and higher sales price upon the seller's other customers. There is nothing to show a congressional purpose, in such a situation, to compel the seller to choose only between ruinously cutting its prices to all its customers to match the price offered to one, or refusing to meet the competition and then ruinously raising its prices to its remaining customers to cover increased unit costs. There is, on the other hand, plain language and established practice which permits a seller, through § 2(b), to retain a customer by realistically meeting in good faith the price offered to that customer, without necessarily changing the seller's price to its other customers.

In a case where a seller sustains the burden of proof placed upon it to establish its defense under § 2(b), we find no reason to destroy that defense indirectly, merely because it also appears that the beneficiaries of the seller's price reductions may derive a competitive advantage from them or may, in a natural course of events, reduce their own resale prices to their customers. It must have been obvious to Congress that any price reduction to any dealer may always affect competition at that dealer's level as well as at the dealer's resale level, whether or not the reduction to the dealer is discriminatory. Likewise, it must have been obvious to Congress that any price reductions initiated by a seller's competitor would, if not met by the seller, affect competition at the beneficiary's level or among the beneficiary's customers just as much as if those reductions had been met by the seller. The proviso in § 2(b), as interpreted by the Commission, would not be available when there was or might be an injury to competition at a resale level. So interpreted, the proviso would have such little, if any, applicability as to be practically meaningless. We may, therefore, conclude that Congress meant to permit the natural consequences to follow the seller's action in meeting in good faith a lawful and equally low price of its competitor.

. . . The judgment of the Court of Appeals, accordingly, is reversed and the case is remanded to that court with instructions to remand it to the Federal Trade Commission to make findings in conformity with this opinion. It is so ordered.
[REVERSED AND REMANDED]

In the preceding case, the Supreme Court clarified the defense of meeting an equally low price of a competitor by holding that it is available to one charged with selling at discriminatory prices, even if the discrimination might have anticompetitive effects otherwise prohibited. In doing so, however, it raised other questions by occasionally using the word "lawful" in referring to the "equally low prices of competitors" which the defense permits one to meet. Is, then, a seller justified in discriminating in price between his customers because he is meeting an equally low price offered one of them by a competitor *only if the competitor's price is "lawful"?* If a competitor's lower price amounts to a forbidden price discrimination by him in favor of the customer, can a seller meet it in "good faith" if doing so would result in his charging discriminatory prices for his product also? While some Federal court decisions seem to indicate that the defense is available in spite of the fact that the competitor's lower price is not a "lawful" one, some FTC rulings appear to hold otherwise.[8]

6   TYING CONTRACTS AND EXCLUSIVE DEALINGS

A "tying contract" is one in which a commodity is sold or leased for use only on condition that the buyer or lessee purchase certain additional products or services from the seller or lessor. An "exclusive dealing," however, does not necessarily

---

[8] For a thorough discussion of the problem, see Johnston and Day, Meeting Competitive Prices? Must They Be Lawful? 52 *Ill. B.J.* 828 (June, 1964).

involve more than one product and the terms of its sale. An exclusive dealing may be a requirements contract, whereby the buyer agrees to purchase all his business needs of a product supplied by the seller during a certain period of time. The buyer may be a manufacturer who has a reasonably ascertainable need for the raw materials or parts agreed to be supplied, or he may be a retailer who needs goods for resale. An exclusive dealing also is present in a contract whereby a buyer agrees not to purchase an item or items of merchandise from competitors of the seller. Such a contract might take the form of a franchise, in which a dealer agrees to sell only the product manufactured or distributed by the seller—a particular make of automobile, for instance. Either tying contracts or exclusive dealings may be in violation of the antitrust laws.

Section 3 of the Clayton Act made it unlawful for a person engaged in commerce to lease or sell commodities (whether patented or unpatented) or to fix a price charged on the condition that the lessee or purchaser should not use or deal in the commodities of a competitor of the lessor or seller where the effect *may* be to substantially lessen competition or *tend* to create a monopoly in any line of commerce. Taken literally, then, the same issues concerning the *relevant market* and *probable anticompetitive effects* are involved in the determination of a violation of Section 3 of the Clayton Act as may be in issue in a case on mergers or on price discrimination. Section 3 of the Clayton Act attempts to eliminate anticompetitive activity which might not be a violation of the Sherman Act.

Typical of the cases involving a tying contract in violation of Section 3 are those where the monopoly power of a patent is used to tie in the promise to buy an unpatented item if the amount of business in question is not "insignificant or insubstantial." In *Times-Picayune Publishing Co. v. United States*,[9] the court said, "The essence of illegality in tying agreements is the wielding of monopolistic leverage." It went on to state that when a seller or lessor "enjoys a monopolistic position in the market for the tying product, *or* if a substantial volume of commerce in the 'tied' product is restrained, a tying agreement violates the narrower standards expressed in Section 3 of the Clayton Act because from either factor, the requisite potential lessening of competition is inferred."

One form of tying arrangement is known as "full-line forcing." In full-line forcing the buyer or lessee is compelled to take a complete product line from the seller. Under these arrangements the buyer cannot purchase only the main product of the line. A typical illegal agreement under this concept is one in which a gasoline company requires its dealers to buy its tires, batteries, and accessories as a condition to obtaining the gasoline. If the contract prohibited the sale of other tires, batteries, and accessories, it would also be an exclusive dealing contract.

A defense which has been raised frequently in tying contract cases is debasement. For example, IBM in one case contended that it could legally require lessees of its machines to agree to use only its punch cards because the use of inferior punch cards would debase IBM's goodwill. This argument was rejected because competitors could produce punch cards of equal quality.

[9] 345 U.S. 594, 608, 611 (1953).

The case which follows is one of the leading decisions involving the legality of exclusive dealings under Section 3.

Standard Oil Co. of California v. United States
337 U.S. 293 (1949)

As of March, 1947, Standard Oil Company of California had entered into exclusive supply or requirements contracts with the operators of 5,937 independent stations in the seven Western states in which it was doing business. These amounted to 16 percent of the total retail gasoline outlets in that area. Several types of contracts were involved, but in all of them, the dealer had undertaken to purchase from Standard Oil either his business requirements of petroleum products, or his business requirements of petroleum products plus tubes, tires, and batteries. They were either to last for a specified period or to run from year to year, being terminable by either party upon giving thirty days' notice in the latter case. In 1947 these independent dealers purchased roughly $58,000,000 worth of gasoline and $8,200,000 worth of other products from Standard. In 1946, Standard sold 6.8 percent of the total sales of gasoline in the area involved through its company-owned service stations, and 6.7 percent of that total to the independent operators under the exclusive dealings contracts. Standard's six leading competitors, who employed similar contracts, sold 42.5 percent of the total sales of gasoline in the area through service stations during the same year. Only 1.6 percent of the stations in the seven-state region sold the gasoline of more than one supplier. The United States brought this action against Standard Oil and its wholly owned subsidiary, Standard Stations, Inc., for an injunction preventing the defendants from enforcing or entering into exclusive supply contracts with any independent dealer, alleging that these contracts violated § 1 of the Sherman Act and § 3 of the Clayton Act. The District Court granted the injunction, and the defendants appealed.

FRANKFURTER, JUSTICE: . . . . Since § 3 of the Clayton Act was directed to prohibiting specific practices even though not covered by the broad terms of the Sherman Act, it is appropriate to consider first whether the enjoined contracts fall within the prohibition of the narrower Act. The relevant provisions of § 3 are:

It shall be unlawful for any person engaged in commerce, in the course of such commerce, to lease or make a sale or contract for sale of goods, wares, merchandise, machinery, supplies, or other commodities, whether patented or unpatented, for use, consumption, or resale within the United States . . . on the condition, agreement, or understanding that the lessee or purchaser thereof shall not use or deal in the goods . . . of a competitor or competitors of the . . . seller, where the effect of such lease, sale, or contract for sale or such condition, agreement, or understanding may be to substantially lessen competition or tend to create a monopoly in any line of commerce.

Obviously the contracts here at issue would be proscribed if § 3 stopped short of the qualifying clause beginning, "where the effect of such lease, sale, or contract for sale. . . ." If effect is to be given that clause, however, it is by no means obvious, in view of Standard's minority share of the "line of commerce" involved, of the fact that that share has not recently increased, and of the claims of these contracts to economic utility, that the effect of the contracts may be to lessen competition or tend to create a monopoly. It is the qualifying clause, therefore, which must be construed.

The District Court held that the requirement of showing an actual or potential lessening of competition or a tendency to establish monopoly was adequately met by proof that the contracts covered "a substantial number of outlets and a substantial amount of products, whether considered comparatively or not." Given such quantitative substantiality, the substantial lessening of competition—so the court reasoned—is an automatic result, for the very existence of such contracts denies dealers opportunity to deal in the products of competing suppliers and excludes suppliers from access to the outlets controlled by those dealers. . . .

The issue before us, therefore, is whether the requirement of showing that the effect of the agreements "may be to substantially lessen competition" may be met simply by proof that a substantial portion of commerce is affected or whether it must also be demonstrated that competitive activity has actually diminished or probably will diminish. . . .

International Salt Co. v. United States, 332 U.S. 392, . . . at least as to contracts tying the sale of a nonpatented to a patented product, rejected the necessity of demonstrating economic consequences once it has been established that "the volume of business affected" is not "insignificant or insubstantial" and that the effect of the contracts is to "foreclose competitors from [a] substantial market." Upon that basis we affirmed a summary judgment granting an injunction against the leasing of machines for the utilization of salt products on the condition that the lessee use in them only salt supplied by defendant. It was not established that equivalent machines were unobtainable, it was not indicated what proportion of the business of supplying such machines was controlled by defendant, and it was deemed irrelevant that there was no evidence as to the actual effect of the tying clauses upon competition. It is clear, therefore, that unless a distinction is to be drawn for purposes of the applicability of § 3 between requirements contracts and contracts tying the sale of a nonpatented to a patented product, the showing that Standard's requirements contracts affected a gross business of $58,000,000 comprising 6.7% of the total in the area goes far toward supporting the inference that competition has been or probably will be substantially lessened.

In favor of confining the standard laid down by the International Salt case to tying agreements, important economic differences may be noted. Tying agreements serve hardly any purpose beyond the suppression of competition. The justification most often advanced in their defense—the protection of the good will of the manufacturer of the tying device—fails in the usual situation because specification of the type and quality of the product to be used in connection with the tying device is protection enough. In the usual case only the prospect of reducing competition would persuade a seller to adopt such a contract and only his control of the supply of the tying device, whether conferred by patent monopoly or otherwise obtained, could induce a buyer to enter one. The existence of market control of the tying device, therefore, affords a strong foundation for the presumption that it has been or probably will be used to limit competition in the tied product also.

Requirements contracts, on the other hand, may well be of economic advantage to buyers as well as to sellers, and thus indirectly of advantage to the consuming public. In the case of the buyer, they may assure supply, afford protection against rises in price, enable long-term planning on the basis of known costs, and obviate the expense and risk of storage in the quantity necessary for a commodity having a fluctuating demand. From the seller's point of view, requirements contracts may make possible the substantial reduction of selling expenses, give protection against price fluctuations, and—of particular advantage to a newcomer to the field to whom it is important to know what capital expenditures are justified—offer the possibility of a predictable market. They may be useful, moreover, to a seller trying to establish a foothold against the counterattacks of entrenched competitors. Since these advantages of requirements contracts may often be sufficient to account for their use, the coverage by such contracts of a substantial amount of business affords a weaker basis for the inference that competition may be lessened than would similar coverage by tying clauses, especially where use of the latter is combined with market control of the tying device. A patent, moreover, although in fact there may be many competing substitutes for the patented article, is at least prima facie evidence of such control. And so we could not dispose of this case merely by citing *International Salt Co. v. United States*, 332 U.S. 392.

Thus, even though the qualifying clause of § 3 is appended without distinction of terms equally to the prohibition of tying clauses and of requirements contracts, pertinent considerations support, certainly as a matter of economic reasoning, varying standards as to each for the proof necessary to fulfill the conditions of that clause. If this distinction were accepted, various tests of the economic usefulness or restrictive effect of requirements contracts would become relevant. Among them would be evidence that competition has flourished despite use of the contracts, and under this test much of the evidence tendered by appellant in this case would be important. Likewise bearing on whether or not the contracts were being used to suppress competition, would be the conformity of the length of their term to the reasonable requirements of the field of commerce in which they were used. Still another test would be the status of the defendant as a struggling newcomer or an established competitor. Perhaps most important, however, would be the defendant's degree of market control, for the greater the dominance of his position, the stronger the inference that an important factor in attaining and maintaining that position has been the use of requirements contracts to stifle competition rather than to serve legitimate economic needs.

Yet serious difficulties would attend the attempt to apply these tests. We may assume, as did the court below, that no improvement of Standard's competitive position has coincided with the period during which the requirements-contract system of distribution has been in effect. We may assume further that the duration of the contracts is not excessive and that Standard does not by itself dominate the market. But Standard was a major competitor when the present system was adopted, and it is possible that its position would have deteriorated but for the adoption of that system. When it is remembered that all the other major suppliers have also been using requirements contracts, and when it is noted that the relative share of the business which fell to each has remained about the same during the period of their use, it would not be farfetched to infer that their effect has been to enable the established suppliers individually to maintain their own standing and at the same time collectively, even though not collusively, to prevent a late arrival from wresting away more than an insignificant portion of the market. If, indeed, this were a result of the system, it would seem unimportant that a short-run by-product of stability may have been greater efficiency and lower costs, for it is the theory of the antitrust laws that the long-run advantage of the community depends upon the removal of restraints upon competition.

Moreover, to demand that bare inference be supported by evidence as to what would have happened but for the adoption of the practice that was in fact adopted or to require firm predication of an increase of competition as a probable result of ordering the abandonment of the practice, would be a standard of proof if not virtually impossible to meet, at least most ill-suited for ascertainment by courts. Before the system of requirements contracts was instituted, Standard sold gasoline through independent service-station operators as its agents, and it might revert to this system if the judgment below were sustained. Or it might, as opportunity presented itself, add service stations now operated independently to the number managed by its subsidiary, Standard Stations, Inc. From the point of view of maintaining or extending competitive advantage, either of these alternatives would be just as effective as the use of requirements contracts, although of course insofar as they resulted in a tendency to monopoly they might encounter the anti-monopoly provisions of the Sherman Act. As appellant points out, dealers might order petroleum products in quantities sufficient to meet their estimated needs for the period during which requirements contracts are now effective, and even that would foreclose competition to some degree. So long as these diverse ways of restricting competition remain open, therefore, there can be no conclusive proof that the use of requirements contracts has actually reduced competition below the level which it would otherwise have reached or maintained. . . . It seems hardly likely that, having with one hand set up an express prohibition against a practice thought to be beyond the reach of the Sherman Act, Congress meant, with the other hand, to reestablish the necessity of meeting the same tests of detriment to the public interest as that Act had been interpreted as requiring. Yet the economic investigation which appellant would have us require is of the same broad scope as was adumbrated with reference to unreasonable restraints of trade in *Chicago Bd. of Trade v. United States*, 246 U.S. 231. To insist upon such an investment would be to stultify the force of Congress' declaration that requirements contracts are to be prohibited wherever their effect "may be" to substantially lessen competition. . . .

We conclude, therefore, that the qualifying clause of § 3 is satisfied by proof that competition has been foreclosed in a substantial share of the line of commerce affected. It cannot be gainsaid that observance by a dealer of his requirements contract with Standard does effectively foreclose whatever opportunity there might be for competing suppliers to attract his patronage, and it is clear that the affected proportion of retail sales of petroleum products is substantial. In view of the widespread adoption of such contracts by Standard's competitors and the availability of alternative ways of obtaining an assured market, evidence that competitive activity has not actually declined is inconclusive. Standard's use of the contracts creates just such a potential clog on competition as it was the purpose of § 3 to remove wherever, were it to become actual, it would impede a substantial amount of competitive activity.

Since the decree below is sustained by our interpretation of § 3 of the Clayton Act, we need not go on to consider whether it might also be sustained by § 1 of the Sherman Act. . . .

The judgment below is affirmed. [AFFIRMED]

The Attorney General's Committee, discussing the foregoing decisions, noted:[10]

While postulating "foreclosure" of competitors from a significant market as the index of illegality, the Court never analyzed the factual arrangements at bar. Without explaining what "foreclosure" meant, the Court assumed rather than demonstrated that Standard's requirements contracts actually "foreclosed" competitors from market access. Hence its affirmance of the District Court's "quantitative substantiality" ruling intimated that exclusive arrangements violated the Clayton Act merely if covering a substantial number of outlets or volume of trade.

Sequels to Standard Stations *have, however, retreated from any "quantitative substantiality" criterion. . . .*

. . . [S]ubsequent interpretations of Section 3 and the Standard Oil *ruling— both in Supreme Court opinions and Federal Trade Commission determinations—have refrained from a strict "quantitative substantiality" test. Rather than subjecting exclusive arrangements to rigid criteria tantamount to* per se *illegality, they have accorded thorough scrutiny to the specific factual pattern of each case. This inquiry is evidently directed to determine whether the challenged practice menaces competition in the distribution process by actually "foreclosing" competitors from access to a substantial share of the consuming market.*

The legality of both tying and exclusive arrangements is thus tested by criteria adapted to their special characteristics in measuring adverse market effects. . . .

---

[10] Report of the Attorney General's National Committee to Study the Antitrust Laws 142, 143–144 (1955).

It should not be forgotten that tying arrangements and exclusive dealings may also run afoul of § 1 of the Sherman Act as contracts in unreasonable restraint of trade. However, proof is easier under Section 3 of the Clayton Act, and most challenges to tying and exclusive contracts will be brought under that Act rather than the Sherman Act. If a criminal sanction is to be imposed, however, the action will be brought under the Sherman Act with its greater burden of proof.

A third provision in the antitrust laws under which a tying arrangement or exclusive dealing may be found illegal is Section 5 of the Federal Trade Commission Act, which prohibits "unfair methods of competition . . . and unfair or deceptive acts or practices. . . ." The subject of exclusive and tying contracts should be kept in mind when studying Chapter 13, which deals with the Federal Trade Commission.

REVIEW QUESTIONS—CHAPTER 11

1 Define the following terms introduced in this chapter: interlocking director-ates; quantity discount; tying contract; exclusive dealing contract; require-ments contract; full-line forcing; debasement.
2 Discuss the defects or weaknesses in the Sherman Act which led to the adoption of the Clayton Act.
3 Explain the reasons for the prohibition against interlocking directorates.
4 Under what circumstances is it legal to sell to different purchasers for resale at different prices?
5 What weaknesses in the Clayton Act prompted the enactment of the Robinson-Patman amendment?
6 What are the two basic aspects to the decision on the determination of the relevant market?
7 Is it illegal to benefit from price discrimination or only to grant it? Explain.
8 Does the law require an injury to competition for price discrimination to be illegal? Explain.
9 Give three illustrations of price discrimination other than simply charging different prices, i.e., three examples of indirect price discrimination.
10 Does the Robinson-Patman amendment favor price competition? Explain.
11 To what extent can the price discrimination provision of the Clayton Act as amended be avoided by injecting wholesalers and other intermediate parties or levels in a scheme of product distribution? Explain.
12 Discuss the problems inherent in the cost justification defense to a price discrimination allegation.
13 Discuss the problem inherent in the "meeting a competitor's price in *good faith*" defense to a price discrimination allegation.
14 Under what circumstances are exclusive dealing contracts illegal? Explain.
15 Are requirements contracts always legal? Explain.
16 What is a full-line forcing contract? Give an example of such a contract. Is it legal or illegal? Why?

Chapter Twelve

Legal Aspects of Mergers, Consolidations, and Acquisitions

1   INTRODUCTION

Many businesses have accumulated millions and even billions of dollars in assets and substantial economic power. The legal restraints on the methods by which business may acquire such assets and economic power are the subject matter of this chapter. Internal growth is generally regarded as a proper means of expanding total resources and income, but growth to large size by means of acquisition of other companies is legally subject to question under the provisions of the antitrust laws.

A corporation may acquire other businesses in a variety of ways. For example, two corporations may join together and create a third corporation, with the two original companies being dissolved. This is technically known as a "consolidation." One business may acquire and absorb another business, with the acquired business being dissolved. This is technically known as a "merger." Another method for one company to acquire another is for the former to purchase a controlling interest in the stock of the latter. The subsidiary is controlled by the parent company's electing the board of directors and controlling policy. When the stock of a company is controlled, both companies continue to exist, and no dissolution occurs. A fourth method of acquisition is for one business to purchase the assets of another. The selling company then ceases to continue its former business activities, and the purchased assets are integrated into the buying company.

There are numerous means of financing the various methods for gaining control of subsidiary organizations. For example, stock and warrants of the parent company may be used in lieu of cash for acquisition.

In the material which follows, technical consolidations, mergers, and other acquisitions are generally referred to as mergers. Mergers are usually classified as horizontal, vertical, or conglomerate. A "horizontal merger" combines two businesses which formerly competed with each other in a particular line of commerce. Such mergers lead to greater concentration in that industry. A "vertical merger" brings together a company which is the *customer* of the other in one of the lines of commerce in which the other is a supplier. Such a combination ordinarily removes or has the potential to remove the merged customer from the market as far as other suppliers are concerned. A "conglomerate merger" is one in which the businesses involved neither compete nor are related as customer and supplier in any given line of commerce.

Any of these types of mergers, however accomplished, can amount to a violation of the Sherman Act as a combination in unreasonable restraint of trade or a monopolization or attempted monopolization. However, mergers are more apt to run afoul of Section 7 of the Clayton Act as amended, which provides essentially that no corporation engaged in commerce shall acquire any of the stock or assets of another such corporation if the effect may be to substantially lessen competition or to tend to create a monopoly in any line of commerce in any section of the country. The Sherman Act requires a finding of actual anticompetitive effects before a violation can be demonstrated. As previously noted, the limited application of the Sherman Act and its resultant incapability to curtail practices which were deemed likely to adversely affect competition, or monopoly in its incipiency, were the main reasons underlying the passage of the Clayton Act. Section 7 of the Clayton Act only requires a finding and conclusion that a given acquisition has a reasonable *probability* of lessening competition or *tendency* toward monopoly.

This chapter is limited to a discussion of the legality of mergers under Section 7 of the Clayton Act as amended. Since that section is so much broader than the Sherman Act in its application, it is difficult to conceive of a merger which would violate the Sherman Act without also violating Section 7 of the Clayton Act. As a practical matter, since the burden of proof required to demonstrate a violation of Section 7 is considerably less, Section 7 is usually employed by the Justice Department and Federal Trade Commission when the legality of a merger is challenged. Of course, if a criminal sanction is sought, the Justice Department will proceed under the more rigorous requirements of the Sherman Act.

The application of Section 7 to any given merger is discretionary with the Justice Department and the Federal Trade Commission. While both have issued guidelines to industry as to which mergers are likely to be challenged, both agencies have reserved the right to bring action against mergers and acquisitions which they feel will have the prohibited effect of probably lessening competition or tending to create a monopoly. The decade of the sixties saw a rising tide of mergers and acquisitions and more action against them by government than at any time in our history. Thousands of mergers and acquisitions were effected, and the validity of many has not yet been finally determined. However, it should be observed that when mergers were challenged, either by the Federal Trade Commission or the Justice Department, the challenges were almost without exception upheld. Enforcement, then, to a large degree depends upon the attitude of the administration in power and the attitude of the Federal Trade Commission. The early seventies saw a decline in the number of mergers and acquisitions, due in part to the more active enforcement policy of the Federal government.

As the materials in the following sections are studied, special attention should be paid to discussions of product markets, geographic markets, and the economic issues raised. The question is often asked: Are the courts the proper place to resolve these types of economic issues?

2 SECTION 7 OF THE CLAYTON ACT AS AMENDED

In 1950 Congress enacted the Celler-Kefauver amendment to Section 7 of the Clayton Act. Section 7 as amended prohibits the acquisition by a corporation engaged in commerce of the *stock or assets* of other such corporations, where the effect may be to *lessen competition substantially or tend to create a monopoly in any line of commerce in any section of the country.* In spite of the original provisions of the Clayton Act which prohibited the acquisitions of the stock of a competitor, corporate mergers were showing an alarming increase in the late 1940s. The 1950 amendment was motivated by Congress' concern about this increase and the effect such mergers were having on the competitive situation in many industries and geographical areas. The Celler-Kefauver amendment substantially broadened the application of the Clayton Act to corporate mergers and acquisitions. First of all, the amendment plugged a loophole in that the original Section 7 only prohibited certain acquisitions of *stock* by one corporation of another. Technically, the same end could be accomplished and was permitted under it through an acquisition of *assets*. Therefore, this was also prohibited. Secondly, the original statute prohibited acquisitions "where the effect . . . may be to substantially lessen competition *between the corporation whose stock is so acquired and the corporation making the acquisition, or to restrain such commerce in any section or community.*" (Emphasis added.) This language led to the contention that only horizontal mergers were outlawed. The amendment broadens the prohibition by deleting the "acquired-acquiring" language so as to outlaw all acquisitions where the effect may be to lessen competition substantially *in any line of commerce* in any section of the country. The case which follows is one of the first Supreme Court decisions interpreting Section 7 of the Clayton Act after the 1950 Celler-Kefauver amendment. Note that it involves a merger with both vertical and horizontal aspects.

Brown Shoe Co. v. United States
370 U.S. 294 (1962)

In 1956, Brown Shoe Company, Inc., acquired the G. R. Kinney Company, Inc., through an exchange of Kinney for Brown Stock. The government brought suit in the Federal District Court, charging that the merger of Brown (the third largest seller of shoes in the United States by dollar volume) and Kinney (the eighth largest seller among those engaged primarily in selling shoes) constituted a violation of the amended Section 7 of the Clayton Act. The District Court found in favor of the government and, among other things, ordered Brown to divest itself completely of all stock, share capital, assets, or other interests it held in Kinney. Brown Shoe Company appealed directly to the Supreme Court.

WARREN, CHIEF JUSTICE: . . . In order fully to understand and appraise . . . [Brown's contentions on appeal], it is necessary to set out . . . the District Court's findings concerning the nature of the shoe industry and the place of Brown and Kinney within that industry.

The Industry

The District Court found that although domestic shoe production was scattered among a large number of manufacturers, a small number of large companies occupied a commanding position. Thus, while the 24 largest manufacturers produced about 35% of the Nation's shoes, the top 4—International, Endicott-Johnson, Brown (including Kinney) and General Shoe—alone produced approximately 23% of the Nation's shoes or 65% of the production of the top 24.

In 1955, domestic production of nonrubber shoes was 509.2 million pairs. . . .

The public buys these shoes through about 70,000 retail outlets, only 22,000 of which, however, derive 50% or more of their gross receipts from the sale of shoes and are classified as "shoe stores" by the Census Bureau. These 22,000 shoe stores were found generally to sell (1) men's shoes only, (2) women's shoes only, (3) women's and children's shoes, or (4) men's, women's, and children's shoes.

The District Court found a "definite trend" among shoe manufacturers to acquire retail outlets. . . . Brown, itself, with no retail outlets of its own prior to 1951, had acquired 845 such outlets by 1956. . . .

And once the manufacturers acquired retail outlets, the District Court found there was a "definite trend" for the parent-manufacturers to supply an ever increasing percentage of the retail outlets' needs, thereby foreclosing other manufacturers from effectively competing for the retail accounts. Manufacturer-dominated stores were found to be "drying up" the available outlets for independent producers.

Another "definite trend" found to exist in the shoe industry was a decrease in the number of plants manufacturing shoes. And there appears to have been a concomitant decrease in the number of firms manufacturing shoes. In 1947, there were 1,077 independent manufacturers of shoes, but by 1954 their number had decreased about 10% to 970.

Brown Shoe

Brown Shoe was found not only to have been a participant, but also a moving factor, in these industry trends. . . .

As a result, in 1955, Brown was the fourth largest shoe manufacturer in the country, producing about 25.6 million pairs of shoes or about 4% of the Nation's total footwear production.

Kinney

Kinney is principally engaged in operating the largest family-style shoe store chain in the United States. At the time of trial, Kinney was found to be operating over 400 such stores in more than 270 cities. These stores were found to make about 1.2% of all national retail shoe sales by dollar volume. Moreover, in 1955 the Kinney stores sold approximately 8 million pairs of nonrubber shoes or about 1.6% of the national pairage sales of such shoes. Of these sales, approximately 1.1 million pairs were of men's shoes or about 1% of the national pairage sales of men's shoes; approximately 4.2 million pairs were of women's shoes or about

1.5% of the national pairage sales of women's shoes; and approximately 2.7 million pairs were of children's shoes or about 2% of the national pairage sales of children's shoes.

In addition to this extensive retail activity, Kinney owned and operated four plants which manufactured men's, women's, and children's shoes and whose combined output was 0.5% of the national shoe production in 1955, making Kinney the twelfth largest shoe manufacturer in the United States.

Kinney stores were found to obtain about 20% of their shoes from Kinney's own manufacturing plants. At the time of the merger, Kinney bought no shoes from Brown; however, in line with Brown's conceded reasons for acquiring Kinney, Brown had, by 1957, become the largest outside supplier of Kinney's shoes, supplying 7.9% of all Kinney's needs.

It is in this setting that the merger was considered and held to violate § 7 of the Clayton Act. . . .

III Legislative History

This case is one of the first to come before us in which the Government's complaint is based upon allegations that the appellant has violated § 7 of the Clayton Act, as that section was amended in 1950. . . .

As enacted in 1914, § 7 of the original Clayton Act prohibited the acquisition by one corporation of the *stock* of another corporation when such acquisition would result in a substantial lessening of competition *between the acquiring and the acquired* companies, or tend to create a monopoly in any line of commerce. The Act did not, by its explicit terms, or as construed by this Court, bar the acquisition by one corporation of the *assets* of another. Nor did it appear to preclude the acquisition of stock in any corporation other than a direct competitor. . . .

The dominant theme pervading congressional consideration of the 1950 amendments was a fear of what was considered to be a rising tide of economic concentration in the American economy. Apprehension in this regard was bolstered by the publication in 1948 of the Federal Trade Commission's study on corporate mergers. Statistics from this and other current studies were cited as evidence of the danger to the American economy in unchecked corporate expansions through mergers. Other considerations cited in support of the bill were the desirability of retaining "local control" over industry and the protection of small businesses. Throughout the recorded discussion may be found examples of Congress' fear not only of accelerated concentration of economic power on economic grounds, but also of the threat to other values a trend toward concentration was thought to pose.

What were some of the factors, relevant to a judgment as to the validity of a given merger, specifically discussed by Congress in redrafting § 7?

First, there is no doubt that Congress did wish to "plug the loophole" and to include within the coverage of the Act the acquisition of assets no less than the acquisition of stock.

Second, by the deletion of the "acquiring-acquired" language in the original text, it hoped to make plain that § 7 applied not only to mergers between actual competitors, but also to vertical and conglomerate mergers whose effect may tend to lessen competition in any line of commerce in any section of the country.

Third, it is apparent that a keystone in the erection of a barrier to what Congress saw was the rising tide of economic concentration, was its provision of authority for arresting mergers at a time when the trend to a lessening of competition in a line of commerce was still in its incipiency.

Fourth, and closely related to the third, Congress rejected, as inappropriate to the problem it sought to remedy, the application to § 7 cases of the standards for judging the legality of business combinations adopted by the courts in dealing with cases arising under the Sherman Act, and which may have been applied to some early cases arising under original § 7.

Fifth, at the same time that it sought to create an effective tool for preventing all mergers having demonstrable anti-competitive effects, Congress recognized the stimulation to competition that might flow from particular mergers. When concern as to the Act's breadth was expressed, supporters of the amendments indicated that it would not impede, for example, a merger between two small companies to enable the combination to compete more effectively with larger corporations dominating the relevant market, nor a merger between a corporation which is financially healthy and a failing one which no longer can be a vital competitive factor in the market. The deletion of the word "community" in the original Act's description of the relevant geographic market is another illustration of Congress' desire to indicate that its concern was with the adverse effects of a given merger on competition only in an economically significant "section" of the country. Taken as a whole, the legislative history illuminates congressional concern with the protection of *competition*, not *competitors*, and its desire to restrain mergers only to the extent that such combinations may tend to lessen competition.

Sixth, Congress neither adopted nor rejected specifically any particular tests for measuring the relevant markets, either as defined in terms of product or in terms of geographic locus of competition, within which the anti-competitive effects of a merger were to be judged. Nor did it adopt a definition of the word "substantially," whether in quantitative terms of sales or assets or market shares or in designated qualitative terms, by which a merger's effects on competition were to be measured.

Seventh, while providing no definite quantitative or qualitative tests by which enforcement agencies could gauge the effects of a given merger to determine whether it may "substantially" lessen competition or tend toward monopoly, Congress indicated plainly that a merger had to be functionally viewed, in the context of its particular industry. That is, whether the consolidation was to take place in an industry that was fragmented rather than concentrated, that had seen a recent trend toward domination by a few leaders or had remained fairly consistent in its distribution of market shares among the participating companies, that had experienced easy access to markets by suppliers and easy access to suppliers by buyers or had witnessed foreclosure of business, that had witnessed the ready entry of new competition or the erection of barriers to prospective entrants, all were aspects, varying in importance with the merger under consideration, which would properly be taken into account.

Eighth, Congress used the word *"may* be substantially to lessen competition" [EMPHASIS SUPPLIED], to indicate that its concern was with probabilities, not certainties. Statutes existed for dealing with clear-cut menaces to competition; no statute was sought for dealing with ephemeral possibilities. Mergers with a probable anti-competitive effect were to be proscribed by this Act.

It is against this background that we return to the case before us.

IV The Vertical Aspects of the Merger

Economic arrangements between companies standing in a supplier-customer relationship are characterized as "vertical." The primary vice of a vertical merger or other arrangement tying a customer to a supplier is that, by foreclosing the competitors of either party from a segment of the market otherwise open to them, the arrangement may act as a "clog on competition," which "deprive[s] . . . rivals of a fair opportunity to compete." Every extended vertical arrangement by its very nature, for at least a time, denies to competitors of the supplier the opportunity to compete for part or all of the trade of the customer-party to the vertical arrangement. However, the Clayton Act does not render unlawful all such vertical arrangements, but forbids only those whose effect "may be substantially to lessen competition, or to tend to create a monopoly" "in any line of commerce in any section of the country." Thus, as we have previously noted,

[d]etermination of the relevant market is a necessary predicate to a finding of a violation of the Clayton Act because the threatened monopoly must be one which will substantially lessen competition "within the area of effective competition." Substantiality can be determined only in terms of the market affected.

The "area of effective competition" must be determined by reference to a product market (the "line of commerce") and a geographic market (the "section of the country").

The Product Market

The outer boundaries of a product market are determined by the reasonable interchangeability of use or the cross-elasticity of demand between the product itself and substitutes for it. However, within this broad market, well-defined submarkets may exist which, in themselves, constitute product markets for antitrust purposes. The boundaries of such a submarket may be determined by examining such practical indicia as industry or public recognition of the submarket as a separate economic entity, the product's peculiar characteristics and uses, unique production facilities, distinct customers, distinct prices, sensitivity to price changes, and specialized vendors. Because § 7 of the Clayton Act prohibits any merger which may substantially lessen competition "in *any* line of commerce" [EMPHASIS SUPPLIED], it is necessary to examine the effects of a merger in each such economically significant submarket to determine if there is a reasonable probability that the merger will substantially lessen competition. If such a probability is found to exist, the merger is proscribed.

Applying these considerations to the present case, we conclude that the record supports the District Court's finding that the relevant lines of commerce are men's, women's, and children's shoes. These product lines are recognized by the public; each line is manufactured in separate plants; each has characteristics peculiar to itself rendering it generally noncompetitive with the others; and each is, of course, directed toward a distinct class of customers.

Appellant, however, contends that the District Court's definitions fail to recognize sufficiently "price/quality" and "age/sex" distinctions in shoes. Brown argues that the predominantly medium-priced shoes which it manufactures occupy a product market different from the predominantly low-priced shoes which Kinney sells. But agreement with that argument would be equivalent to holding that medium-priced shoes do not compete with low-priced shoes. We think the District Court properly found the facts to be otherwise. . . .

The Geographic Market

We agree with the parties and the District Court that insofar as the vertical aspect of this merger is concerned, the relevant geographic market is the entire Nation. . . .

The Probable Effect of the Merger

Once the area of effective competition affected by a vertical arrangement has been defined, an analysis must be made to determine if the effect of the arrangement "may be substantially to lessen competition, or to tend to create a monopoly" in this market.

Since the diminution of the vigor of competition which may stem from a vertical arrangement results primarily from a foreclosure of a share of the market otherwise open to competitors, an important consideration in determining whether the effect of a vertical arrangement "may be substantially to lessen competition, or to tend to create a monopoly" is the size of the share of the market foreclosed. However, this factor will seldom be determinative. If the share of the market foreclosed is so large that it approaches monopoly proportions, the Clayton Act will, of course, have been violated; but the arrangement will also have run afoul of the Sherman Act. And the legislative history of § 7 indicates clearly that the tests for measuring the legality of any particular economic arrangement under the Clayton Act are to be less stringent than those used in applying the Sherman Act. On the other hand, foreclosure of a *de minimis* share of the market will not tend "substantially to lessen competition."

Between these extremes, in cases such as the one before us, in which the foreclosure is neither of monopoly nor *de minimis* proportions, the percentage of the market foreclosed by the vertical arrangement cannot itself be decisive. In such cases, it becomes necessary to undertake an examination of various economic and historical factors in order to determine whether the arrangement under review is of the type Congress sought to proscribe.

A most important such factor to examine is the very nature and purpose of the arrangement. . . .

The importance . . . attached to economic purpose is . . . demonstrated by the . . . intention to preserve the "failing company" doctrine. . . . Similarly, Congress foresaw that the merger of two large companies or a large and a small company might violate the Clayton Act while the merger of two small companies might not, although the share of the market foreclosed be identical, if the purpose of the small companies is to enable them in combination to compete with larger corporations dominating the market.

The present merger involved neither small companies nor failing companies. . . .

Another important factor to consider is the trend toward concentration in the industry. . . .

The existence of a trend toward vertical integration . . . is well substantiated by the record. . . . It is against this background of continuing concentration that the present merger must be viewed.

Brown argues, however, that the shoe industry is at present composed of a large number of manufacturers and retailers, and that the industry is dynamically competitive. But remaining vigor cannot immunize a merger if the trend in that industry is toward oligopoly. It is the probable effect of the merger upon the future as well as the present which the Clayton Act commands the courts and the Commission to examine.

Moreover, as we have remarked above, not only must we consider the probable effects of the merger upon the economics of the particular markets affected but also we must consider its probable effects upon the economic way of life sought to be preserved by Congress. Congress was desirous of preventing the formation of further oligopolies with their attendant adverse effects upon local control of industry and upon small business. Where an industry was composed of numerous independent units, Congress appeared anxious to preserve this structure. The Senate Report . . . states explicitly that amended § 7 is addressed, *inter alia,* to the following problem:

Under the Sherman Act, an acquisition is unlawful if it creates a monopoly or constitutes an attempt to monopolize. Imminent monopoly may appear when one large concern acquires another, but it is unlikely to be perceived in a small acquisition by a large enterprise. As a large concern grows through a series of such small acquisitions, its accretions of power are individually so minute as to make it difficult to use the Sherman Act tests against them. . . .

Where several large enterprises are extending their power by successive small acquisitions, the cumulative effect of their purchases may be to convert an industry from one of intense competition among many enterprises to one in which three or four large concerns produce the entire supply.

The District Court's findings, and the record facts, . . . convince us that the shoe industry is being subjected to just such a cumulative series of vertical mergers which, if left unchecked, will be likely "substantially to lessen competition."

We reach this conclusion because the trend toward vertical integration in the shoe industry, when combined with Brown's avowed policy of forcing its own shoes upon its retail subsidiaries, may foreclose competition from a substantial share of the markets for men's, women's, and children's shoes, without producing any countervailing competitive, economic, or social advantages.

V The Horizontal Aspects of the Merger

An economic arrangement between companies performing similar functions in the production or sale of comparable goods or services is characterized as "horizontal." The effect on competition of such an arrangement depends, of course, upon its character and scope. Thus, its validity in the face of the antitrust laws will depend upon such factors as: the relative size and number of the parties to the arrangement; whether it allocates shares of the market among the parties; whether it fixes prices at which the parties will sell their product; or whether it absorbs or insulates competitors. Where the arrangement effects a horizontal merger between companies occupying the same product and geographic market, whatever competition previously may have existed in that market between the parties to the merger is eliminated. Section 7 of the Clayton Act, prior to its amendment, focused upon this aspect of horizontal combinations by proscribing acquisitions which might result in a lessening of competition between the acquiring and the acquired companies. The 1950 amendments made plain Congress' intent that the validity of such combinations was to be gauged on a broader scale: their effect on competition generally in an economically significant market.

Thus, again, the proper definition of the market is a "necessary predicate" to an examination of the competition that may be affected by the horizontal aspects of the merger. . . .

The Product Market

. . . In . . . this opinion we hold that the District Court correctly defined men's, women's, and children's shoes as the relevant lines of commerce in which to analyze the vertical aspects of the merger. For the reasons there stated we also hold that the same lines of commerce are appropriate for considering the horizontal aspects of the merger.

The Geographic Market

The criteria to be used in determining the appropriate geographic market are essentially similar to those used to determine the relevant product market. Moreover, just as a product submarket may have § 7 significance as the proper "line of commerce," so may a geographic submarket be considered the appropriate "section of the country." Congress prescribed a pragmatic, factual approach to the definition of the relevant market and not a formal, legalistic one. The geographic market selected must, therefore, both "correspond to the commercial realities" of the industry and be economically significant. Thus, although the geographic market in some instances may encompass the entire Nation, under other circumstances it may be as small as a single metropolitan area. The fact that two merging firms have competed directly on the horizontal level in but a fraction of the geographic markets in which either has operated, does not, in itself, place their merger outside the scope of § 7. That section speaks of "any . . . section of the country," and if anticompetitive effects of a merger are probable in "any" significant market, the merger—at least to that extent—is proscribed.

. . . The District Court found that the effects of this aspect of the merger must be analyzed in every city with a population exceeding 10,000 and its immediate contiguous surrounding territory in which both Brown and Kinney sold shoes at retail through stores they either owned or controlled.

We . . . agree that the District Court properly defined the relevant geographic markets in which to analyze this merger as those cities with a population exceeding 10,000 and their environs in which both Brown and Kinney retailed shoes through their own outlets. Such markets are large enough to include the downtown shops and suburban shopping centers in areas contiguous to the city, which are the important competitive factors, and yet are small enough to exclude stores beyond the immediate environs of the city, which are of little competitive significance.

The Probable Effect of the Merger

. . . Brown objects that the District Court did not examine the competitive picture in each line of commerce and each section of the country it had defined as appropriate. . . .

However, we believe the record is adequate to support the findings of the District Court. While it is true that the court concentrated its attention on the structure of competition in the city in which it sat and as to which detailed evidence was most readily available, it also heard witnesses from no less than 40 other cities in which the parties to the merger operated. . . .

The market share which companies may control by merging is one of the most important factors to be considered when determining the probable effects of the combination on effective competition in the relevant market. In an industry as fragmented as shoe retailing, the control of substantial shares of the trade in a city may have important effects on competition. If a 5% control were now approved, we might be required to approve future merger efforts by Brown's competitors seeking similar market shares. The oligopoly Congress sought to avoid would then be furthered and it would be difficult to dissolve the combinations previously approved. Furthermore, in this fragmented industry, even if the combination controls but a small share of a particular market, the fact that this share is held by a large national chain can adversely affect competition. . . . A third significant aspect of this merger is that it creates a large national chain which is integrated with a manufacturing operation. The retail outlets of integrated companies, by eliminating wholesalers and by increasing the volume of purchases from the manufacturing division of the enterprise, can market their own brands at prices below those of competing independent retailers. Of course, some of the results of large integrated or chain operations are beneficial to consumers. Their expansion is not rendered unlawful by the mere fact that small independent stores may be adversely affected. It is competition, not competitors, which the Act protects. But we cannot fail to recognize Congress' desire to promote competition through the protection of viable, small, locally owned businesses. Congress appreciated that occasional higher costs and prices might result from the maintenance of fragmented industries and markets. It resolved these competing considerations in favor of decentralization. We must give effect to that decision.

Other factors to be considered in evaluating the probable effects of a merger in the relevant market lend additional support to the District Court's conclusion that this merger may substantially lessen competition. One such factor is the history of tendency toward concentration in the industry. As we have previously pointed out, the shoe industry has, in recent years, been a prime example of such a trend. . . . We cannot avoid the mandate of Congress that tendencies toward concentration in industry are to be curbed in their incipiency, particularly when those tendencies are being accelerated through giant steps striding across a hundred cities at a time. In the light of the trends in this industry we agree with the Government and the court below that this is an appropriate place at which to call a halt.

At the same time appellant has presented no mitigating factors, such as the business failure or the inadequate resources of one of the parties that may have prevented it from maintaining its competitive position, nor a demonstrated need for combination to enable small companies to enter into a more meaningful competition with those dominating the relevant markets. . . . We hold that the District Court was correct in concluding that this merger may tend to lessen competition substantially in the retail sale of men's, women's, and children's shoes in the overwhelming majority of those cities and their environs in which both Brown and Kinney sell through owned or controlled outlets. [AFFIRMED]

The *Brown Shoe* case set the pattern for subsequent litigation concerning Section 7 of the Clayton Act as amended. Each case involves three questions:

1 What is the relevant "line of commerce" (product market) affected by the merger?
2 What is the relevant "section of the country" (geographic market) affected by the merger?
3 What are the *likely* or *probable* future anticompetitive effects which will result in that market from the merger?

Since it is within the relevant market that the substantiality of future anticompetitive effects of the merger will be measured, it is obvious that a definition by the court which narrows or enlarges the "line of commerce" affected may be critical to its decision as to whether a violation exists or not. Equally important to the outcome may be a determination that the effects are to be measured nationwide, in only one state, in just one metropolitan area, or in some other geographical area. In the sections which follow, the three determinations of fact which must be made before a Section 7 violation can be demonstrated are discussed in more detail.

3 THE PRODUCT MARKET

In the case below the importance of the definition of the product market to the legality of a merger is dramatically illustrated.

Reynolds Metals Co. v. FTC
309 F.2d 223 (1962)

In 1956, Reynolds Metals Company acquired the stock and assets of Arrow Brands, Inc., a company which converted aluminum foil and sold it nationally to wholesale florist supply houses for decorative purposes. The FTC instituted a proceeding against Reynolds under Section 7 of the Clayton Act and ordered its divestiture of the stock and assets of Arrow, after finding that the acquisition might "have the effect of substantially lessening competition or tending to create a monopoly in the production and sale of decorative aluminum foil to the florist trade." Reynolds brought this proceeding to have the Commission's order reviewed and set aside by the Circuit Court of Appeals.

BURGER, JUDGE: . . . It is urged on appeal that the Commission erred in its conclusion that the "production and sale of decorative aluminum foil *to the florist trade*" is the "relevant line of commerce" within the meaning of Sec. 7 of the Clayton Act; . . .

Reynolds is the largest producer of aluminum foil in the world. . . . The record indicates that the large foil producers such as Reynolds find it both impracticable and unprofitable to accept small orders from small buyers of foil to be used for specific and limited end purposes such as the decoration of flower pots or foodstuffs. Consequently, Reynolds and other major raw foil producers sell in quantity to intermediaries known in the trade as converters, who have come into existence precisely to meet the needs of these small foil markets, which individually do not require a sufficiently large amount of raw foil to purchase it in the minimum quantities sold by the manufacturers. These converters purchase large quantities of foil from the producers in so-called "jumbo" rolls, and after breaking these down and processing them with decorative or other features sought by the end users, sell in limited quantities to the several smaller markets.

Arrow, prior to and since its acquisition by Reynolds in 1956, has been engaged in converting "jumbo" rolls of raw foil into such limited quantities of a specialized kind which are then sold, in decorated form, almost exclusively to the florist trade. While roughly 200 foil converters are active in the United States, only eight (approximately) including Arrow, served the florist industry when this proceeding began. In 1956, these eight firms sold not more than an estimated 1,500,000 pounds of florist foil altogether, of which Arrow accounted for approximately 33%. Several of the firms competing with Arrow in converting foil for the florist industry purchased their plain or raw foil from Reynolds prior to the acquisition. Raw foil costs to an unintegrated florist foil converter, such as Arrow was, account for 70% of the total cost of production.

The remainder of the 200 converters process aluminum foil for all its many other uses, including usage as tape, candy box liners, covers for takeout foodstuffs, condensers and many others. The uses are almost endless. The government concedes that theoretically all 200 converters could supply florist foil, but observes that in fact only the eight firms comprise the domestic *florist* foil converting industry. The record supports this view and we must assume for this discussion that the florist trade is supplied almost exclusively by the eight firms listed. . . . The problem of market definition in the present case centers only on the determination of the "line of commerce," since Reynolds does not disagree with the Commission's finding that the geographical area for measuring the competitive effects of the acquisition is the entire United States. . . .

. . . It is . . . clear that mere potential interchangeability or cross-elasticity may be insufficient to mark the legally pertinent limits of a "relevant line of commerce." The "outer limits" of a general market may be thus determined, but sharply distinct submarkets can exist within these outer limits which may henceforth be the focal point of administrative and judicial inquiry under Section 7. . . .

Analyzing the facts of the present case makes it abundantly clear that under these standards the production and sale of florist foil may rationally be defined by the Commission as comprising the relevant line of commerce in terms of (1) public and industrial recognition of it as a separate economic entity, (2) its distinct customers and (3) its distinct prices. . . .

. . . [W]e must affirm the Commission on the . . . bases of (1) distinct pricing and purchaser identity, and (2) indisputable industry and consumer recognition of the florist foil converting industry as a separate economic entity.

First, the identity of purchasers of florist foil is distinct and limited. With insignificant exception, the sole purchasers of florist foil are the nation's 700 wholesale florist outlets and, through these, the 25,000 retail florists throughout the country. Despite a clearly lower price for florist foil, . . . other end users of decorative foil have not joined the identifiable mass of florist foil purchasers in noticeable numbers. . . . [T]he identity of the florist foil converters who *alone* serve these florist purchasers is clearly limited to eight firms including Arrow, with some minor and as yet undefined competition from a few foreign firms. . . .

Secondly, both producer and consumer recognition of the florist foil submarket as a definite economic entity is clearly demonstrated by what appears to have been the election of other decorative foil converters not to serve the florist industry, by the habit and practice of the extensive florist industry itself in purchasing only from florist foil converters like Arrow and not from other decorative foil converters, and again, by the failure of decorative foil users other than florists to purchase the lower priced florist foil.

Pricing forms the final point. Substantial evidence discloses a markedly lower price for florist foil compared with the price of other colored or embossed aluminum foil sold in comparable weight units and gauged at approximately the same thickness. We think price differentials have an important if not decisive bearing in the quest to delimit a submarket. No prudent businessman (the ordinary end user of foil), would purchase colored or embossed foil at prices on this record of $1.15 to $1.22 per unit when another foil converter market offers florist foil, similarly colored or embossed, and of similar gauge and weight, at a cost of only $.75 to $.85 per unit. The fact that prudent businessmen do so supports the inference, drawn in the negative since as we have noted the record lacks affirmative evidence on the point, that florist foil must be distinct and separable from aluminum foil generally or the many users of the latter would have long ago begun to substitute the former at the lower price. Such a difference in price as appears on this record must effectively preclude comparison, and inclusion in the same market, of products as between which the difference exists, at least for purposes of inquiry under Sec. 7 of the Clayton Act.

It appears, therefore, that the florist foil market probably is a distinguishable product market, and therefore the production and sale of decorative aluminum foil to the florist trade is a "line of commerce" within the meaning of Sec. 7.

The effect of the acquisition of Arrow on this line of commerce was . . . justifiably predicated as substantially anti-competitive. While as many as eight or more firms converted foil for the florist industry, we have observed that roughly 33% of this business had been captured by Arrow alone prior to the 1956 transaction tying Arrow into Reynolds. When Arrow was vertically integrated through the Reynolds' acquisition, one minor anti-competitive effect foreseeable was the exclusion of other manufacturers of raw foil (Reynolds' competitors) from selling to approximately 33% of the florist foil converting industry. . . . Arrow's assimilation into Reynolds' enormous capital structure and resources gave Arrow an immediate advantage over its competitors who were contending for a share of the market for florist foil. The power of the "deep pocket" or "rich parent" for one of the florist foil suppliers in a competitive group where previously no company was very large and all were relatively small opened the possibility and power to sell at prices approximating cost or below and thus to undercut and ravage the less affluent competition. The Commission is not required to establish that the Reynolds' acquisition of Arrow did in fact have anti-competitive consequences. It is sufficient if the Commission shows the acquisition had the capacity or potentiality to lessen competition. That such a potential emerged from the combination of Reynolds and Arrow was enough to bring it within Sec. 7. But the Commission on substantial evidence has additionally provided us with a finding of *actual* anti-competitive effect, where as an apparent consequence of retroactive price reductions for Arrow foil after the acquisition of florist foil sales of 5 of Arrow's 7 competitors had by 1957 dropped from 14% to 47% below 1955 sales. Arrow's sales over the same period increased by 18.9%.

The necessary probability of anti-competitive effect has . . . been shown. In agreeing with the Commission, however, we do not, nor could we intimate, that the mere intrusion of "bigness" into a competitive economic community otherwise populated by commercial "pygmies" will *per se* invoke the Clayton Act. Each factual situation under judicial review has its own atmosphere of economic freedom and viability or lack thereof; occasion may well arise where an acquisition superficially similar to the one here condemned by the Commission may be encouraged as necessary to *preserve* competition, to maintain production levels adequate to meet consumer demand or otherwise to produce "countervailing competitive, economic or social advantages." . . .

Affirmed and order will be enforced. [AFFIRMED]

4   THE GEOGRAPHIC MARKET

While in the *Reynolds* case above, defining the product market was all-important to the finding of a violation of the Clayton Act, in the case which follows, identifying the "line of commerce" seems somewhat secondary to the determination of the geographical market or the "section of the country" involved. Besides illustrating the importance of such determinations in merger cases, the decision is significant because the Supreme Court held that the merger provisions of the antitrust laws were applicable to the commercial banking industry and, in effect, to those who provide services generally.

United States v. Philadelphia Nat'l Bank
374 U.S. 321 (1963)

The United States brought this action under the antitrust laws to enjoin a merger which was planned by two Philadelphia Banks, the Philadelphia National Bank (PNB) and the Girard Trust Corn Exchange Bank (Girard). The District Court gave judgment for the defendants and the government appealed.

BRENNAN, JUSTICE: . . . Commercial banking in this country is primarily unit banking. That is, control of commercial banking is diffused throughout a very large number of independent, local banks—13,460 of them in 1960—rather than concentrated in a handful of nationwide banks, as, for example, in England and Germany. There are, to be sure, in addition to the independent banks, some 10,000 branch banks; but branching, which is controlled largely by state law—and prohibited altogether by some States—enables a bank to extend itself only to state lines and often not that far. It is also the case, of course, that many banks place loans and solicit deposits outside their home area. But with these qualifications, it remains true that ours is essentially a decentralized system of community banks. Recent years, however, have witnessed a definite trend toward concentration. Thus, during the decade ending in 1960, the number of commercial banks in the United States declined by 714, despite the chartering of 887 new banks and a very substantial increase in the Nation's credit needs during the period. Of the 1,601 independent banks which thus disappeared, 1,503, with combined total resources of well over $25,000,000,000, disappeared as the result of mergers. . . .

The Philadelphia National Bank and Girard Trust Corn Exchange Bank are, respectively, the second and third largest of the 42 commercial banks with head offices in the Philadelphia metropolitan area, which consists of the City of Philadelphia and its three contiguous counties in Pennsylvania. The home county of both banks is the city itself; Pennsylvania law, however, permits branching into the counties contiguous to the home county, and both banks have offices throughout the four-county area. PNB, a national bank, has assets of over $1,000,000,000, making it (as of 1959) the twenty-first largest bank in the Nation. Girard, a state bank, is a member of the FRS and is insured by the FDIC; it has assets of about $750,000,000. Were the proposed merger to be consummated, the resulting bank would be the largest in the four-county area, with (approximately) 36% of the area banks' total assets, 36% of deposits, and 34% of net loans. It and the second largest (First Pennsylvania Bank and Trust Company, now the largest) would have between them 59% of the total assets, 58% of deposits, and 58% of the net loans, while after the merger the four largest banks in the area would have 78% of total assets, 77% of deposits, and 78% of net loans.

The present size of both PNB and Girard is in part the result of mergers. Indeed, the trend toward concentration is noticeable in the Philadelphia area generally, in which the number of commercial banks has declined from 108 in 1947 to the present 42. Since 1950, PNB has acquired nine formerly independent banks and Girard six; and these acquisitions have accounted for 59% and 85% of the respective banks' asset growth during the period, 63% and 91% of their deposit growth, and 12% and 37% of their loan growth. During this period, the seven largest banks in the area increased their combined share of the area's total commercial bank resources from about 61% to about 90%.

In November 1960 the boards of directors of the two banks approved a proposed agreement for their consolidation under the PNB charter. . . . Such a consolidation is authorized, subject to the approval of the Comptroller of the Currency, by 12 U.S.C. (1958 ed., Supp. IV) § 215. But under the Bank Merger Act of 1960, the Comptroller may not give his approval until he has received reports from the other two banking agencies and the Attorney General respecting the probable effects of the proposed transaction on competition. All three reports advised that the proposed merger would have substantial anticompetitive effects in the Philadelphia metropolitan area. However, on February 24, 1961, the Comptroller approved the merger. . . .

[T]he Comptroller explained the basis for his decision to approve the merger in a statement to be included in his annual report to Congress. As to effect upon competition, he reasoned that "[s]ince there will remain an adequate number of alternative sources of banking service in Philadelphia, and in view of the beneficial effects of this consolidation upon international and national competition it was concluded that the over-all effect upon competition would not be unfavorable." He also stated that the consolidated bank "would be far better able to serve the convenience and needs of its community by being of material assistance to its city and state in their efforts to attract new industry and to retain existing industry." The day after the Comptroller approved the merger, the United States commenced the present action. No steps have been taken to consummate the merger pending the outcome of this litigation. . . . Upon . . . [the] record the District Court held that: (1) the passage of the Bank Merger Act of 1960 did not repeal by implication the antitrust laws insofar as they may apply to bank mergers; (2) § 7 of the Clayton Act is inapplicable to bank mergers because banks are not corporations "subject to the jurisdiction of the Federal Trade Commission"; (3) but assuming that § 7 is applicable, the four-county Philadelphia metropolitan area is not the relevant geographical market because PNB and Girard actively compete with other banks for bank business throughout the greater part of the northeastern United States; (4) but even assuming that § 7 is applicable and that the four-county area is the relevant market, there is no reasonable probability that competition among commercial banks in the area will be substantially lessened as the result of the merger; (5) since the merger does not violate § 7 of the Clayton Act, *a fortiori* it does not violate § 1 of the Sherman Act; (6) the merger will benefit the Philadelphia metropolitan area economically. The District Court also ruled that for the purposes of § 7, commercial banking is a line of commerce; the appellees do not contest this ruling. . . .

We have no difficulty in determining the "line of commerce" (relevant product or services market) and "section of the country" (relevant geographical market) in which to appraise the probable competitive effects of appellees' proposed merger. We agree with the District Court that the cluster of products (various kinds of credit) and services (such as checking accounts and trust administration) denoted by the term "commercial banking," composes a distinct line of commerce. . . .

We part company with the District Court on the determination of the appropriate "section of the country." The proper question to be asked in this case is not where the parties to the merger do business or even where they compete, but where, within the area of competitive overlap, the effect of the merger on competition will be direct and immediate. This depends upon "the geographic structure of supplier-customer relations." . . . In banking, as in most service industries, convenience of location is essential to effective competition. Individuals and corporations typically confer the bulk of their patronage on banks in their local community; they find it impractical to conduct their banking business at a distance. The factor of inconvenience localizes banking competition as effectively as high transportation costs in other industries. Therefore, since, as we recently said in a related context, the "area of effective competition in the known line of commerce must be charted by careful selection of the market area in which the seller operates, *and to which the purchaser can practicably turn for supplies.*" [T]he four-county area in which appellees' offices are located would seem to be the relevant geographical market. In fact, the vast bulk of appellees' business originates in the four-county area. . . .

We recognize that the area in which appellees have their offices does not delineate with perfect accuracy an appropriate "section of the country" in which to appraise the effect of the merger upon competition. Large borrowers and large depositors, the record shows, may find it practical to do a large part of their banking business outside their home community; very small borrowers and depositors may, as a practical matter, be confined to bank offices in their immediate neighborhood; and customers of intermediate size, it would appear, deal with banks within an area intermediate between these extremes. . . . So also, some banking services are evidently more local in nature than others. But that in banking the relevant geographical market is a function of each separate customer's economic scale means simply that a workable compromise must be found; some fair intermediate delineation which avoids the indefensible extremes of drawing the market either so expansively as to make the effect of the merger upon competition seem insignificant, because only the very largest bank customers are taken into account in defining the market, or so narrowly as to place appellees in different markets, because only the smallest customers are considered. We think that the four-county Philadelphia metropolitan area, which state law apparently recognizes as a meaningful banking community in allowing Philadelphia banks to branch within it, and which would seem roughly to delineate the area in which bank customers that are neither very large nor very small find it practical to do their banking business, is a more appropriate "section of the country" in which to appraise the instant merger than any larger or smaller or different area. We are helped to this conclusion by the fact that the three federal banking agencies regard the area in which banks have their offices as an "area of effective competition." Not only did the FDIC and FRB, in the reports they submitted to the Comptroller of the Currency in connection with appellees' application for permission to merge, so hold, but the Comptroller, in his statement approving the merger, agreed: "With respect to the effect upon competition, there are three separate levels and effective areas of competition involved. These are the national level for national accounts, the regional or sectional area, and the local area of the City of Philadelphia and the immediately surrounding area."

Having determined the relevant market, we come to the ultimate question under § 7: whether the effect of the merger "may be substantially to lessen competition" in the relevant market. Clearly, this is not the kind of question which is susceptible of a ready and precise answer in most cases. It requires not merely an appraisal of the immediate impact of the merger upon competition, but a prediction of its impact upon competitive conditions in the future; this is what is meant when it is said that the amended § 7 was intended to arrest anticompetitive tendencies in their "incipiency." Such a prediction is sound only if it is based upon a firm understanding of the structure of the relevant market; yet the relevant economic data are both complex and elusive. And unless businessmen can assess the legal consequences of a merger with some confidence, sound business planning is retarded. So also, we must be alert to the danger of subverting congressional intent by permitting a too-broad economic investigation. And so in any case in which it is possible, without doing violence to the congressional objective embodied in § 7, to simplify the test of illegality, the courts ought to do so in the interest of sound and practical judicial administration. This is such a case.

We noted in *Brown Shoe Co. v. United States* 370 U.S., at 315, that "[t]he dominant theme pervading congressional consideration of the 1950 amendments (to § 7) was a fear of what was considered to be a rising tide of economic concentration in the American economy." This intense congressional concern with the trend toward concentration warrants dispensing, in certain cases, with elaborate proof of market structure, market behavior, or probable anticompetitive effects. Specifically, we think that a merger which produces a firm controlling an undue percentage share of the relevant market, and results in a significant increase in the concentration of firms in that market is so inherently likely to lessen competition substantially that it must be enjoined in the absence of evidence clearly showing that the merger is not likely to have such anticompetitive effects.

Such a test lightens the burden of proving illegality only with respect to mergers whose size makes them inherently suspect in light of Congress' design in § 7 to prevent undue concentration. Furthermore, the test is fully consonant with economic theory. That "[c]ompetition is likely to be greatest when there are many sellers, none of which has any significant market share," is common ground among most economists, and was undoubtedly a premise of congressional reasoning about the antimerger statute.

The merger of appellees will result in a single bank's controlling at least 50% of the commercial banking business in the four-county Philadelphia metropolitan area. Without attempting to specify the smallest market share which would still be considered to threaten undue concentration, we are clear that 30% presents that threat. Further, whereas presently the two largest banks in the area (First Pennsylvania and PNB) control between them approximately 44% of the area's commercial banking business, the two largest after the merger (PNB-Girard and First Pennsylvania) will control 59%. Plainly, we think, this increase of more than 33% in concentration must be regarded as significant. . . .

. . . A fundamental purpose of amending § 7 was to arrest the trend toward concentration, the *tendency* to monopoly, before the consumer's alternatives disappeared through merger, and that purpose would be ill-served if the law stayed its hand until 10, or 20, or 30 more Philadelphia banks were absorbed. This is not a fanciful eventuality, in view of the strong trend toward mergers evident in the area; and we might note also that entry of new competitors into the banking field is far from easy. . . .

. . . [I]t is suggested that the increased lending limit of the resulting bank will enable it to compete with the large out-of-state bank, particularly the New York banks, for very large loans. We reject this application of the concept of "countervailing power." If anticompetitive effects in one market could be justified by procompetitive consequences in another, the logical upshot would be that every firm in an industry could, without violating § 7, embark on a series of mergers that would make it in the end as large as the industry leader. For if all the commercial banks in Philadelphia area merged into one, it would be smaller than the largest bank in New York City. This is not a case, plainly, where two small firms in a market propose to merge in order to be able to compete more successfully with the leading firms in that market. Nor is it a case in which lack of adequate banking facilities is causing hardships to individuals or businesses in the community. The present two largest banks in Philadelphia have lending limits of $8,000,000 each. The only businesses located in the Philadelphia area which find such limits inadequate are large enough to obtain bank credit in other cities.

This brings us to appellees' final contention, that Philadelphia needs a bank larger than it now has in order to bring business to the area and stimulate its economic development. We are clear, however, that a merger the effect of which "may be substantially to lessen competition" is not saved because, on some ultimate reckoning of social or economic debits and credits, it may be deemed beneficial. A value choice of such magnitude is beyond the ordinary limits of judicial competence, and in any event has been made for us already, by Congress when it enacted the amended § 7. Congress determined to preserve our traditionally competitive economy. It therefore proscribed anticompetitive mergers, the benign and the malignant alike, fully aware, we must assume, that some price might have to be paid. . . .

The judgment of the District Court is reversed and the case remanded with direction to enter judgment enjoining the proposed merger. It is so ordered.
[REVERSED AND REMANDED]

5 SUBSTANTIALLY LESSENING COMPETITION AND TENDING TO CREATE A MONOPOLY

In addition to determining the relevant market affected by a given merger, courts must also find that within that market the effect of the merger "may be substantially to lessen competition, or to tend to create a monopoly" before a violation of Section 7 of the Clayton Act is established.

In the florist foil case and the bank merger case, *supra*, this effect was readily apparent because of the size of the relevant markets involved. The case which follows illustrates the fact that justices of the Supreme Court frequently disagree as to the probable effects of some mergers. These disagreements together with the difficulties of economic analysis and differences of opinion as to the interpretation of such analyses have created great uncertainty as to the legality of many mergers and acquisitions.

United States v. Von's Grocery Co.
384 U.S. 270 (1966)

The United States brought an action which charged that the acquisition by Von's Grocery Company of Shopping Bag Food Stores violated Section 7 of the Clayton Act. After the District Court refused the request of the Government for a temporary injunction. Von's immediately took over Shopping Bag's capital stock and assets. Then, after hearing the evidence, the District Court entered judgment for the defendants, ruling as a matter of law that there was "not a reasonable probability" that the acquisition would tend "substantially to lessen competition" or tend to "create a monopoly." The Government appealed.

BLACK, JUSTICE: . . . The record shows the following facts relevant to our decision. The market involved here is the retail grocery market in the Los Angeles area. In 1958 Von's retail sales ranked third in the area and Shopping Bag's ranked sixth. In 1960 their sales together were 7.5% of the total two and one-half billion dollars of retail groceries sold in the Los Angeles market each year. For many years before the merger both companies had enjoyed great success as rapidly growing companies. From 1948 to 1958 the number of Von's stores in the Los Angeles area practically doubled from 14 to 27, while at the same time the number of Shopping Bag's stores jumped from 15 to 34. During that same decade, Von's sales increased fourfold and its share of the market almost doubled while Shopping Bag's sales multiplied seven times and its share of the market tripled. The merger of these two highly successful, expanding and aggressive competitors created the second largest grocery chain in Los Angeles with sales of almost $172,488,000 annually. In addition the findings of the District Court show that the number of owners operating a single store in the Los Angeles retail grocery market decreased from 5,365 in 1950 to 3,818 in 1961. By 1963, three years after the merger, the number of single-store owners had dropped still further to 3,590. During roughly the same period from 1953 to 1962 the number of chains with two or more grocery stores increased from 96 to 150. While the grocery business was being concentrated into the hands of fewer and fewer owners, the small companies were continually being absorbed by the larger firms through mergers. According to an exhibit prepared by one of the Government's expert witnesses, in the period from 1949 to 1958 nine of the top 20 chains acquired 126 stores from their smaller competitors. Figures of a principal defense witness, . . . illustrate the many acquisitions and mergers in the Los Angeles grocery industry from 1953 through 1961 including acquisitions made by Food Giant, Alpha Beta, Fox and Mayfair, all among the 10 leading chains in the area. Moreover, a table prepared by the Federal Trade Commission appearing in the Government's reply brief, but not a part of the record here, shows that acquisitions and mergers in the Los Angeles retail grocery market have continued at a rapid rate since the merger. These facts alone are enough to cause us to conclude contrary to the District Court that the Von's-Shopping Bag merger did violate § 7. Accordingly, we reverse. . . .

Like the Sherman Act in 1890 and the Clayton Act in 1914, the basic purpose of the 1950 Celler-Kefauver Bill was to prevent economic concentration in the American economy by keeping a large number of small competitors in business. In stating the purposes of the bill, both of its sponsors, Representative Celler and Senator Kefauver, emphasized their fear, widely shared by other members of

Congress, that this concentration was rapidly driving the small businessman out of the market. The period from 1940 to 1947, which was at the center of attention throughout the hearings and debates on the Celler-Kefauver Bill, had been characterized by a series of mergers between large corporations and their smaller competitors resulting in the steady erosion of the small independent business in our economy. . . .

The facts of this case present exactly the threatening trend toward concentration which Congress wanted to halt. The number of small grocery companies in the Los Angeles retail grocery market had been declining rapidly before the merger and continued to decline rapidly afterwards. This rapid decline in the number of grocery store owners moved hand in hand with a large number of significant absorptions of the small companies by the larger ones. In the midst of this steadfast trend toward concentration, Von's and Shopping Bag, two of the most successful and largest companies in the area, jointly owning 66 grocery stores merged to become the second largest chain in Los Angeles. This merger cannot be defended on the ground that one of the companies was about to fail or that the two had to merge to save themselves from destruction by some larger and more powerful competitor. What we have on the contrary is simply the case of two already powerful companies merging in a way which makes them even more powerful than they were before. If ever such a merger would not violate § 7, certainly it does when it takes place in a market characterized by a long and continuous trend toward fewer and fewer owner-competitors which is exactly the sort of trend which Congress, with power to do so, declared must be arrested.

Appellee's primary argument is that the merger between Von's and Shopping Bag is not prohibited by § 7 because the Los Angeles grocery market was competitive before the merger, has been since, and may continue to be in the future. Even so, § 7 "requires not merely an appraisal of the immediate impact of the merger upon competition, but a prediction of its impact upon competitive conditions in the future; this is what is meant when it is said that the amended § 7 was intended to arrest anticompetitive tendencies in their 'incipiency.'" *United States v. Philadelphia Nat'l Bank,* 374 U.S., at p. 362. It is enough for us that Congress feared that a market marked at the same time by both a continuous decline in the number of small businesses and a large number of mergers would, slowly but inevitably gravitate from a market of many small competitors to one dominated by one or a few giants, and competition would thereby be destroyed. Congress passed the Celler-Kefauver Bill to prevent such a destruction of competition. Our cases since the passage of that bill have faithfully endeavored to enforce this congressional command. We adhere to them now.

Here again as in *United States v. El Paso Gas Co.,* 376 U.S. 651, 662, . . . since appellees "have been on notice of the anti-trust charge from almost the beginning . . . we not only reverse the judgment below but direct the District Court to order divestiture without delay." [REVERSED]

[Two of the Justices issued a strong dissent from the majority opinion above, stating in effect that the court was holding that the existence of certain superficial facts which were unrelated to any actual anticompetitive effects lead to a conclusion that the merger violated Section 7, per se. They argued that there should be demonstrated at least a reasonable probability of a substantial reduction in competition before a merger is outlawed, and that an examination of the economic facts in the relevant market did not establish such a probability in the *Von's Grocery* case. Excerpts from their dissent follow.]

STEWART, JUSTICE, dissenting (joined by JUSTICE HARLAN): . . . The concept of arresting restraints of trade in their "incipiency" was not an innovation of the 1950 amendment. The notion of incipiency was part of the report on the original Clayton Act by the Senate Committee on the Judiciary in 1914, and it was reiterated in the Senate report in 1950. That notion was not left undefined. The legislative history leaves no doubt that the applicable standard for measuring the substantiality of the effect of a merger on competition was that of a "reasonable probability" of lessening competition. The standard was thus more stringent than that of a "mere possibility" on the one hand and more lenient than that of a "certainty" on the other. I cannot agree that the retail grocery business in Los Angeles is in an incipient or any other stage of a trend toward a lessening of competition, or that the effective level of concentration in the industry has increased. Moreover, there is no indication that the present merger, or the trend in this industry as a whole, augurs any danger whatsoever for the small businessman. The Court has substituted bare conjecture for the statutory standard of a reasonable probability that competition may be lessened.

The Court rests its conclusion on the "crucial point" that, in the 11-year period between 1950 and 1961, the number of single-store grocery firms in Los Angeles decreased 29% from 5,365 to 3,818. Such a decline should, of course, be no more than a fact calling for further investigation of the competitive trend in the industry. For the Court, however, that decline is made the end, not the beginning, of the analysis. In the counting-of-heads game played today by the Court, the reduction in the number of single-store operators becomes a yard-stick for automatic disposition of cases under § 7.

I believe that even the most superficial analysis of the record makes plain the fallacy of the Court's syllogism that competition is necessarily reduced when the bare number of competitors has declined. In any meaningful sense, the structure of the Los Angeles grocery market remains unthreatened by concentration. Local competition is vigorous to a fault, not only among chain stores themselves but also between chain stores and single store operators. The continuing population explosion of the Los Angeles area, which has outrun the expansion plans of even the largest chains, offers a surfeit of business opportunity for stores of all sizes. Affiliated with cooperatives that give the smallest store the buying strength of its largest competitor, new stores have taken full advantage of the remarkable ease of entry into the market. And, most important of all, the record simply cries out that the numerical decline in the number of single-store owners is the result of transcending social and technological changes that positively preclude the inference that competition has suffered because of the attrition of competitors.

Section 7 was never intended by Congress for use by the Court as a charter to roll back the supermarket revolution. Yet the Court's opinion is hardly more than a requiem for the so-called "Mom and Pop" grocery stores—the bakery and butcher shops, the vegetable and fish markets—that are now economically and technologically obsolete in many parts of the country. No action by this Court can resurrect the old single-line Los Angeles food stores that have been run over by the automobile or obliterated by the freeway. The transformation of American society since the Second World War has not completely shelved these specialty stores, but it has relegated them to a much less central role in our food economy. Today's dominant enterprise in food retailing is the supermarket. Accessible to the housewife's automobile from a wide radius, it houses under a single roof the entire food requirements of the family. Only through the sort of reactionary philosophy that this Court long ago rejected in the Due Process Clause area can the Court read into the legislative history of § 7 its attempt to make the automobile stand still, to mold the food economy of today into the market pattern of another era.[a]

The District Court's finding of fact that there was no increase in market concentration before or after the merger is amply supported by the evidence if concentration is gauged by any measure other than that of a census of the number of competing units. Between 1948 and 1958, the market share of Safeway, the leading grocery chain in Los Angeles, declined from 14% to 8%. The combined market shares of the top two chains declined from 21% to 14% over the same period; for the period 1952–1958, the combined shares of the three, four, and five largest firms also declined. It is true that between 1948 and 1958, the combined shares of the top 20 firms in the market increased from 44% to 57%. The crucial fact here, however, is that seven of these top 20 firms in 1958 were not even in existence as chains in 1948. Because of the substantial turnover in the membership of the top 20 firms, the increase in market share of the top 20 as a group is hardly a reliable indicator of any tendency toward market concentration.

In addition, statistics in the record for the period 1953–1962 strongly suggest that the retail grocery industry in Los Angeles is less concentrated today than it

---

[a] [footnote by Justice Stewart] ". . . Plenty of living American men and women remember an era when virtually all groceries were sold through very small stores none of which had 'any significant market share.' Was this era the high point of competition in food retailing? Many little towns had, in fact, only one place where a given kind of food could be bought. In a typical city neighborhood, defined by the range of a housewife's willingness to lug groceries home on foot, there might be three or four relaxed 'competitors.' If she did not like the price or quality offered by them, she should take her black-string market bag, board a trolley car, and try her luck among the relaxed 'competitors' of some other neighborhood." Ways, a New "Worst" in Antitrust, Fortune, April 1966, pp. 111–112. . . .

In the present case, the District Court found that in the era preceding the rise of the supermarkets, "the area from which the typical store drew most of its customers was limited to a block or two in any direction and if a particular grocery store happened to be the only one in its immediate neighborhood, it had a virtual monopoly of local trade." Thus, the Court's aphorism in *United States v. Philadelphia Nat'l Bank*, 374 U.S. 321, 363—that "[c]ompetition is likely to be greatest when there are many sellers, none of which has any significant market share"—is peculiarly maladroit in the historic context of the retail food industry.

was a decade ago. During this period, the number of chain store firms in the area rose from 96 to 150, or 56%. That increase occurred overwhelmingly among chains of the very smallest size, those composed of two or three grocery stores. Between 1953 and 1962, the number of such "chains" increased from 56 to 104, or 86%. Although chains of 10 or more stores increased from 10 to 24 during the period, seven of these 24 chains were not even in existence as chains in Los Angeles in 1953.

Yet even these dramatic statistics do not fully reveal the dynamism and vitality of competition in the retail grocery business in Los Angeles during the period. The record shows that at various times during the period 1953–1962, no less than 269 separate chains were doing business in Los Angeles, of which 208 were two- or three-store chains. During that period, therefore, 173 new chains made their appearance in the market area, and 119 chains went out of existence as chain stores. The vast majority of this market turbulence represented turnover in chains of two or three stores; 143 of the 173 new chains born during the period were chains of this size. Testimony in the record shows that, almost without exception, these new chains were the outgrowth of successful one-store operations. There is no indication that comparable turmoil did not equally permeate single-store operations in the area. In fashioning its *per se* rule, based on the net arithmetical decline in the number of single-store operators, the Court completely disregards the obvious procreative vigor of competition in the market as reflected in the turbulent history of entry and exit of competing small chains. . . .

The Court's reliance on the fact that nine of the top 20 chains acquired 120 stores in the Los Angeles area between 1949 and 1958 does not withstand analysis in light of the complete record. Forty percent of these acquisitions, representing 48 stores with gross sales of more than $71,000,000, were made by Fox, Yor-Way, and McDaniels, which ranked 9th, 11th, and 20th, respectively, according to 1958 sales in the market. Each of these firms subsequently went into bankruptcy as a result of over-expansion, under-capitalization, or inadequate managerial experience. This substantial post-acquisition demise of relatively large chains hardly comports with the Court's tacit protrayal of the inexorable march of the market toward oligopoly. . . .

With regard to the "plight" of the small businessman, the record is unequivocal that his competitive position is strong and secure in the Los Angeles retail grocery industry. The most aggressive competitors against the larger retail chains are frequently the operators of single stores. The vitality of these independents is directly attributable to the recent and spectacular growth in California of three large cooperative buying organizations. Membership in these groups in unrestricted; through them, single-store operators are able to purchase their goods at prices competitive with those offered by suppliers even to the largest chains. The rise of these cooperative organizations has introduced a significant new source of countervailing power against the market power of the chain stores, without in any way sacrificing the advantages of independent operation. In the face of the substantial assistance available to independents through membership in such cooperatives, the Court's implicit equation between the market power and the market share resulting from the present merger seems completely invalid. . . .

The harsh standard now applied by the Court to horizontal mergers may prejudice irrevocably the already difficult choice faced by numerous successful small and medium-sized businessmen in the myriad smaller markets where the effect of today's decision will be felt, whether to expand by buying or by building additional facilities. And by foreclosing future sale as one attractive avenue of eventual market exit, the Court's decision may over the long run deter new market entry and tend to stifle the very competition it seeks to foster.

In a single sentence and an omnibus footnote at the close of its opinion, the Court pronounces its work consistent with the line of our decisions under § 7 since the passage of the 1950 amendment. The sole consistency that I can find is that in litigation under § 7, the Government always wins. . . .

The emotional impact of a merger between the third and sixth largest competitors in a given market, however fragmented, is understandable, but that impact cannot substitute for the analysis of the effect of the merger on competition that Congress required by the 1950 amendment. Nothing in the present record indicates that there is more than an ephemeral possibility that the effect of this merger may be substantially to lessen competition. Section 7 clearly takes "reasonable probability" as its standard. That standard has not been met here, and I would therefore affirm the judgment of the District Court.

The conglomerate merger—one between companies that neither compete directly nor stand in a seller-buyer relationship—became a significant legal problem in the 1960s. Such mergers and acquisitions also created problems for accountants and financial experts. The accountant found it difficult, if not impossible, to prepare consolidated financial statements for conglomerates which would accurately set forth the financial condition and earnings of the organization. The financial expert found it difficult to judge the earnings and value of companies that were pooling their interests and reporting substantial paper growth.

The number of conglomerate organizations grew rapidly in the 1960s for a variety of reasons. Among these were (1) economies of scale in production, sales, research and development, etc.; (2) diversification and all its advantages such as reduction of the risk in one industry caused by economic cycles and the ability to deploy capital into new areas which may be developing rapidly; (3) capacity to join a company with substantial liquid assets with one in need of cash for expansion and growth; (4) the desire of many managers for power; and (5) the positive effect on the market price of the corporate stock involved in such transactions. Such companies as Gulf and Western Industries, International Telephone and Telegraph (ITT), Ling-Temco-Vought (LTV), Inc., Litton, and Leasco were developed during this period.

To illustrate a typical conglomerate, LTV at one time could have been charted as shown on page 396.

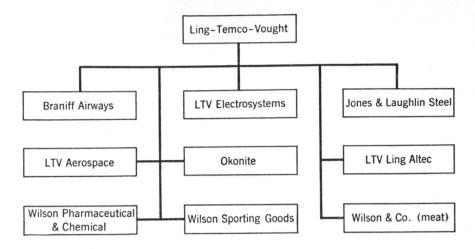

To further illustrate the diversification of conglomerates, consider that ITT, in addition to its telephone operation, owned Canteen Corporation; Avis, Inc.; Continental Banking Co.; Sheraton Hotel Corp.; and Leavitt and Sons. It then acquired Hartford Fire Insurance Co., and the Justice Department sought to intervene.

Before the ITT challenge, the Justice Department brought suit against LTV to require divestiture of Jones and Laughlin Steel Co. under Section 7 of the Clayton Act, contending that this provision covered conglomerate mergers. LTV denied that Section 7 was applicable to conglomerate mergers. The case nevertheless was settled with LTV's keeping Jones & Laughlin but agreeing to divest itself of Braniff Airways, Inc., and Okonite Co. LTV further agreed that it would not make any major acquisition for ten years without governmental approval. The ITT case was later settled with ITT's keeping the Hartford Fire Insurance Co. but divesting itself of other companies such as Avis, Inc.

While there is no Supreme Court decision *specifically* holding that Section 7 covers conglomerates, it is being applied to such acquisitions by the Justice Department. Notwithstanding these cases, some congressmen and legal scholars contend that additional legislation is needed to make it clear that the Clayton Act is applicable to conglomerates. In any event, the rising tide of mergers and acquisitions and the growing influence of conglomerates have focused the attention of those responsible for antitrust enforcement on such businesses.

Some reasons for the growing concern over conglomerates are: (1) economies of scale will allow large companies to drive out smaller, less-efficient competitors; (2) diversified companies can absorb losses in some areas of operations while driving out competitors; (3) large companies serve as a barrier to entry into a market by small companies; (4) smaller companies will be less competitive in their activities because of fear of retaliation; (5) a potential entrant to an area of competition is eliminated when an industry is entered by acquisition; (6) all the anticompetitive effects of reciprocity are potentially present; and (7) excessive concentrations of economic power can result. Some of these objections will be discussed further in the merger guidelines in this chapter.

In the *Procter & Gamble* case, below, the FTC challenged Procter's acquisition of a company whose product did not directly compete with those of Procter but was in the same general market category—laundry products. The acquisition could not be labeled horizontal, vertical, or conglomerate, according to the FTC and the Supreme Court. The Court seems to have created a fourth category called "product extension" mergers. It is doubtful whether there are substantive distinctions between conglomerate and product extension mergers. Using the product extension category actually provides a method of proving a substantial lessening of competition or a tendency toward monopoly. This case also illustrates the "incipiency" rule.

FTC v. Procter & Gamble Co.
87 S.Ct. 1224 (1967)

DOUGLAS, JUSTICE: This is a proceeding initiated by the Federal Trade Commission charging that respondent, Procter & Gamble Co., had acquired the assets of Clorox Chemical Co. in violation of § 7 of the Clayton Act, as amended. The charge was that Procter's acquisition of Clorox may substantially lessen competition or tend to create a monopoly in the production and sale of household liquid bleaches.

Following evidentiary hearings, the hearing examiner rendered his decision in which he concluded that the acquisition was unlawful and ordered divestiture. On appeal, the Commission reversed, holding that the record as then constituted was inadequate, and remanded to the examiner for additional evidentiary hearings. After the additional hearings, the examiner again held the acquisition unlawful and ordered divestiture. The Commission affirmed the examiner and ordered divestiture. The Court of Appeals for the Sixth Circuit reversed and directed that the Commission's complaint be dismissed. We find that the Commission's findings were amply supported by the evidence, and that the Court of Appeals erred.

As indicated by the Commission in its painstaking and illuminating report, it does not particularly aid analysis to talk of this merger in conventional terms, namely, horizontal or vertical or conglomerate. This merger may most appropriately be described as a "product-extension merger," as the Commission stated. The facts are not disputed, and a summary will demonstrate the correctness of the Commission's decision.

At the time of the merger, Clorox was the leading manufacturer in the heavily concentrated household liquid bleach industry. It is agreed that household liquid bleach is the relevant line of commerce. The product is used in the home as a germicide and disinfectant, and more importantly, as a whitening agent in washing clothes and fabrics. It is a distinctive product with no close substitutes. Liquid bleach is a low-price, high-turnover consumer product sold mainly through grocery stores and supermarkets. The relevant geographical market is the Nation and a series of regional markets. Because of high shipping costs and low sales price, it is not feasible to ship the product more than 300 miles from its point of manufacture. Most manufacturers are limited to competition within a single region since they have but one plant. Clorox is the only firm selling nationally; it has 13 plants distributed throughout the Nation. Purex, Clorox's closest competitor in size, does not distribute its bleach in the northeast or middle-Atlantic States; in 1957 Purex's bleach was available in less than 50% of the national market.

At the time of the acquisition, Clorox was the leading manufacturer of household liquid bleach, with 48.8% of the national sales. . . . Its market share had been steadily increasing for the five years prior to the merger. Its nearest rival was Purex. . . . Purex accounted for 15.7% of the household liquid bleach market. The industry is highly concentrated; in 1957 Clorox and Purex accounted for almost 65% of the Nation's household liquid bleach sales, and, together with four other firms, for almost 80%. The remaining 20% was divided among over 200 small producers. . . .

Since all liquid bleach is chemically identical, advertising and sales promotion is vital. In 1957 Clorox spent almost $3,700,000 on advertising, imprinting the value of its bleach in the mind of the consumer. In addition, it spent $1,700,000 for other promotional activities. The Commission found that these heavy expenditures went far to explain why Clorox maintained so high a market share despite the fact that its brand, though chemically indistinguishable from rival brands, retailed for a price equal to or, in many instances, higher than its competitors.

Procter is a large, diversified manufacturer of low-price, high-turnover household products sold through grocery, drug, and department stores. Prior to its acquisition of Clorox, it did not produce household liquid bleach. Its 1957 sales were in excess of $1,100,000,000 from which it realized profits of more than $67,000,000; its assets were over $500,000,000. Procter has been marked by rapid growth and diversification. It has successfully developed and introduced a number of new products. Its primary activity is in the general area of soaps, detergents, and cleansers; in 1957, of total domestic sales, more than one-half (over $500,000,000) were in this field. Procter was the dominant factor in this area. It accounted for 54.4% of all packaged detergent sales. The industry is heavily concentrated—Procter and its nearest competitors, Colgate-Palmolive and Lever Brothers, account for 80% of the market.

In the marketing of soaps, detergents and cleansers, as in the marketing of household liquid bleach, advertising and sales promotion are vital. In 1957, Procter was the Nation's largest advertiser, spending more than $80,000,000 on advertising and an additional $47,000,000 on sales promotion. Due to its tremendous volume, Procter receives substantial discounts from the media. As a multi-product producer Procter enjoys substantial advantages in advertising and sales promotion. Thus, it can and does feature several products in its promotions, reducing the printing, mailing, and other costs for each product. It also purchases network programs on behalf of several products, enabling it to give each product network exposure at a fraction of the cost per product that a firm with only one product to advertise would incur.

Prior to the acquisition, Procter was in the course of diversifying into product lines related to its basic detergent-soap-cleanser business. Liquid bleach was a distinct possibility since packaged detergents—Procter's primary product line—

and liquid bleach are used complementarily in washing clothes and fabrics, and in general household cleaning. . . .

The decision to acquire Clorox was the result of a study conducted by Procter's promotion department designed to determine the advisability of entering the liquid bleach industry. The initial report noted the ascendancy of liquid bleach in the large and expanding household bleach market, and recommended that Procter purchase Clorox rather than enter independently. Since a large investment would be needed to obtain a satisfactory market share, acquisition of the industry's leading firm was attractive, "Taking over the Clorox business . . . could be a way of achieving a dominant position in the liquid bleach market quickly, which would pay out reasonably well." The initial report predicted that Procter's "sales distribution and manufacturing setup" could increase Clorox's share of the markets in areas where it was low. The final report confirmed the conclusions of the initial report and emphasized that Procter would make more effective use of Clorox's advertising budget and that the merger would facilitate advertising economies. A few months later, Procter acquired the assets of Clorox in the name of a wholly owned subsidiary, the Clorox Company, in exchange for Procter stock.

The Commission found that the acquisition might substantially lessen competition. The findings and reasoning of the Commission need be only briefly summarized. The Commission found that the substitution of Procter with its huge assets and advertising advantages for the already dominant Clorox would dissuade new entrants and discourage active competition from the firms already in the industry due to fear of retaliation by Procter. The Commission thought it relevant that retailers might be induced to give Clorox preferred shelf space since it would be manufactured by Procter, which also produced a number of other products marketed by the retailers. There was also the danger that Procter might underprice Clorox in order to drive out competition, and subsidize the underpricing with revenue from other products. The Commission carefully reviewed the effect of the acquisition on the structure of the industry, noting that "the practical tendency of the . . . merger . . . is to transform the liquid bleach industry into an arena of big business competition only, with the few small firms falling by the wayside, unable to compete with their giant rivals." Further, the merger would seriously diminish potential competition by eliminating Procter as a potential entrant into the industry. Prior to the merger, the Commission found that Procter was the most likely prospective entrant, and absent the merger would have remained on the periphery, restraining Clorox from exercising its market power. If Procter had actually entered, Clorox's dominant position would have been eroded and the concentration of the industry reduced. The Commission stated that it had not placed reliance on postacquisition evidence in holding the merger unlawful. . . .

Section 7 of the Clayton Act was intended to arrest the anticompetitive effects of market power in their incipiency. The core question is whether a merger may substantially lessen competition, and necessarily requires a prediction of the merger's impact on competition, present and future. The section can deal only with probabilities, not with certainties. And there is certainly no requirement that the anticompetitive power manifest itself in anticompetitive action before § 7 can be called into play. If the enforcement of § 7 turned on the existence of actual anticompetitive practices, the congressional policy of thwarting such practices in their incipiency would be frustrated.

All mergers are within the reach of § 7, and all must be tested by the same standard, whether they are classified as horizontal, vertical, conglomerate or other. As noted by the Commission this merger is neither horizontal, vertical, nor conglomerate. Since the products of the acquired company are complementary to those of the acquiring company and may be produced with similar facilities, marketed through the same channels and in the same manner, and advertised by the same media, the Commission aptly called this acquisition a "product-extension merger"; . . .

The anticompetitive effects with which this product-extension merger is fraught can easily be seen; (1) the substitution of the powerful acquiring firm for the smaller, but already dominant, firm may substantially reduce the competitive structure of the industry by raising entry barriers and by dissuading the smaller firms from aggressively competing; (2) the acquisition eliminates the potential competition of the acquiring firm.

. . . The acquisition may also have the tendency of raising the barriers to new entry. The major competitive weapon in the successful marketing of bleach is advertising. Clorox was limited in this area by its relatively small budget and its inability to obtain substantial discounts. By contrast, Procter's budget was much larger; and, although it would not devote its entire budget to advertising Clorox, it could divert a large portion to meet the short-term threat of a new entrant. Procter would be able to use its volume discounts to advantage in advertising Clorox. Thus, a new entrant would be much more reluctant to face the giant Procter than it would have been to face the smaller Clorox.

Possible economies cannot be used as a defense to illegality. Congress was aware that some mergers which lessen competition may also result in economies but it struck the balance in favor of protecting competition.

. . . It is clear that the existence of Procter at the edge of the industry exerted considerable influence on the market. First, the market behavior of the liquid bleach industry was influenced by each firm's predictions of the market behavior of its competitors, actual and potential. Second, the barriers to entry by a firm of Procter's size and with its advantages were not significant. There is no indication that the barriers were so high that the price Procter would have to charge would be above the price that would maximize the profits of the existing firms. Third, the number of potential entrants was not so large that the elimination of one would be insignificant. Few firms would have the temerity to challenge a firm as solidly entrenched as Clorox. Fourth, Procter was found by the Commission to be the most likely entrant. These findings of the Commission were amply supported by the evidence.

The judgment of the Court of Appeals is reversed and remanded with instructions to affirm and enforce the Commission's order. . . . [REVERSED AND REMANDED]

6 MERGER GUIDELINES

In 1968, the Department of Justice issued Merger Guidelines which it would use in deciding whether or not to oppose corporate acquisitions or mergers. Because the actual legality as a practical matter depends on whether or not the merger is challenged (the government almost always wins if suit is brought), the guidelines are important to the business community and other interested parties since they show, in a general way, which mergers probably will be challenged. While the guidelines were issued by the Johnson Administration, subsequent administrations may tend to follow them generally. Any Attorney General may question the legality of mergers and acquisitions which do not violate the guidelines or may cause new guidelines to be issued from time to time. Also, the FTC may challenge mergers under its authority to enforce Section 7, even though the Justice Department does not decide to do so. The guidelines are too extensive to be set forth in full, but the following excerpts illustrate their approach to the enforcement of Section 7.

Merger Guidelines, Department of Justice (May 30, 1968)

. . . [T]he primary role of Section 7 enforcement is to preserve and promote market structures conducive to competition. Market structure is the focus of the Department's merger policy chiefly because the conduct of the individual firms in a market tends to be controlled by the structure of that market, i.e., by those market conditions which are fairly permanent or subject only to slow change (such as, principally, the number of substantial firms selling in the market, the relative sizes of their respective market shares, and the substantiality of barriers to the entry of new firms into the market). Thus, for example, a concentrated market structure, where a few firms account for a large share of the sales, tends to discourage vigorous price competition by the firms in the market and to encourage other kinds of conduct, such as use of inefficient methods of production or excessive promotional expenditures, of an economically undesirable nature. Moreover, not only does emphasis on market structure generally produce economic predictions that are fully adequate for the purposes of a statute that requires only a showing that the effect of a merger "may be substantially to lessen competition, or to tend to create a monopoly," but an enforcement policy emphasizing a limited number of structural factors also facilitates both enforcement decision-making and business planning which involves anticipation of the Department's enforcement intent. Accordingly, the Department's enforcement activity under Section 7 is directed primarily toward the identification and prevention of those mergers which alter market structure in ways likely now or eventually to encourage or permit non-competitive conduct. . . .

I Horizontal Mergers

With respect to mergers between direct competitors (i.e., horizontal mergers), the Department's enforcement activity under Section 7 of the Clayton Act has the following interrelated purposes: (i) preventing elimination as an independent business entity of any company likely to have been a substantial competitive influence in a market; (ii) preventing any company or small group of companies from obtaining a position of dominance in a market; (iii) preventing significant increases in concentration in a market; and (iv) preserving significant possibilities for eventual deconcentration in a concentrated market.

In enforcing Section 7 against horizontal mergers, the Department accords primary significance to the size of the market share held by both the acquiring and the acquired firms. . . . The larger the market share held by the acquired firm, the more likely it is that the firm has been a substantial competitive influence in the market or that concentration in the market will be significantly increased. The larger the market share held by the acquiring firm, the more likely it is that an acquisition will move it toward, or further entrench it in, a position of dominance or of shared market power. Accordingly, the standards most often applied by the Department in determining whether to challenge horizontal mergers can be stated in terms of the sizes of the merging firms' market shares.

In a market in which the shares of the four largest firms amount to approximately 75% or more (highly concentrated), the Department will ordinarily challenge mergers between firms accounting for, approximately, the following percentages of the market:

Acquiring Firm	Acquired Firm
4%	4% or more
10%	2% or more
15% or more	1% or more

In a market in which the shares of the four largest firms amount to less than approximately 75% (trend toward concentration), the Department will ordinarily challenge mergers between firms accounting for, approximately, the following percentages of the market:

Acquiring Firm	Acquired Firm
5%	5% or more
10%	4% or more
15%	3% or more
20%	2% or more
25% or more	1% or more

The Department applies an additional, stricter standard in determining whether to challenge mergers occurring in any market, not wholly unconcentrated, in which there is a significant trend toward increased concentration. Such a trend is considered to be present when the aggregate market share of any grouping of the largest firms in the market from the two largest to the eight largest has increased by approximately 7% or more of the market over a period of time extending from any base year 5–10 years prior to the merger (excluding any year in which some abnormal fluctuation in market shares occurred) up to the time of the merger. The Department will ordinarily challenge any acquisition, by any firm in a grouping of such largest firms showing the requisite increase in market share, of any firm whose market share amounts to approximately 2% or more. . . .

[The guidelines then recognized that some horizontal mergers may be challenged that do not fit within the guidelines and that the failing company doctrine may create exceptions to mergers within the guidelines.]

II Vertical Mergers

With respect to vertical mergers . . . the Department's enforcement activity . . . , is intended to prevent change in market structure that [is] likely to lead over the course of time to significant anticompetitive consequences. In general, the Department believes that such consequences can be expected to occur whenever a particular vertical acquisition, or series of acquisitions, by one or more of the firms in a supplying or purchasing market, tends significantly to raise barriers to entry in either market or to disadvantage existing non-integrated or partly integrated firms in either market in ways unrelated to economic efficiency.

. . . [V]ertical mergers tend to raise barriers to entry in undesirable ways, particularly the following: (i) by foreclosing equal access to potential customers, thus reducing the ability of non-integrated firms to capture competitively the market share needed to achieve an efficient level of production, or imposing the burden of entry on an integrated basis (i.e., at both the supplying and purchasing levels) even though entry at a single level would permit efficient operation; (ii) by foreclosing equal access to potential suppliers, thus either increasing the risk of a price or supply squeeze on the new entrant or imposing the additional burden of entry as an integrated firm; or (iii) by facilitating promotional product differentiation, when the merger involves a manufacturing firm's acquisition of firms at the retail level.

. . . The Department believe[s] . . . that the most important aims of its enforcement policy on vertical mergers can be satisfactorily stated by guidelines framed primarily in terms of the market shares of the merging firms and the conditions of entry which already exist in the relevant markets. . . . With all vertical mergers it is necessary to consider the probable competitive consequences of the merger in both the market in which the supplying firm sells and the market in which the purchasing firm sells, although a significant adverse effect in either market will ordinarily result in a challenge by the Department. ("Supplying firm" and "purchasing firm," as used herein, refer to the two parties to the vertical merger transaction, the former of which sells a product in a market in which the latter buys that product.)

In determining whether to challenge a vertical merger on the ground that it may significantly lessen existing or potential competition in the supplying firm's market, the Department attaches primary significance to (i) the market share of the supplying firm, (ii) the market share of the purchasing firm or firms, and (iii) the conditions of entry in the purchasing firm's market. Accordingly, the Department will ordinarily challenge a merger or series of mergers between a supplying firm, accounting for approximately 10% or more of the sales in its market, and one or more purchasing firms, accounting *in toto* for approximately 6% or more of the total purchases in that market, unless it clearly appears that there are no significant barriers to entry into the business of the purchasing firm or firms.

Although the standard [previously stated] is designed to identify vertical mergers having likely anticompetitive effects in the supplying firm's market, adherence by the Department to that standard will also normally result in challenges being made to most of the vertical mergers which may have adverse effects in the purchasing firm's market (i.e., that market comprised of the purchasing firm and its competitors engaged in resale of the supplying firm's product or in the sale of a product whose manufacture requires the supplying firm's product) since adverse effects in the purchasing firm's market will normally occur only as the result of significant vertical mergers involving supplying firms with market shares in excess of 10%. . . . [V]ertical mergers which . . . account for less than 6% of the purchases in the supplying firm's market . . . [may also] be challenged by the Department on the ground that they raise entry barriers in the purchasing firm's market, or disadvantage the purchasing firm's competitors, by conferring upon the purchasing firm a significant supply advantage over unintegrated or partly integrated existing competitors or over potential competitors. . . .

[Among the factors listed which may cause a challenge when the 6% test is not met is the ability to apply a price or supply squeeze. Such a squeeze is possible when the product involved is (1) complex, (2) a scarce raw material, or (3) one in which ability of supply to expand to meet demand is not present.] [T]he Department believes that the increase in barriers to entry in the purchasing firm's market arising simply from the increased risk of a possible squeeze is sufficient to warrant prohibition of any merger between a supplier possessing significant market power and a substantial purchaser of any product meeting the above description. Accordingly, where such a product is a significant feature or ingredient of the end-product manufactured by the purchasing firm and its competitors, the Department will ordinarily challenge a merger or series of mergers between a supplying firm, accounting for approximately 20% or more of the sales in its market, and a purchasing firm or firms, accounting *in toto* for approximately 10% or more of the sales in the market in which it sells the product whose manufacture requires the supplying firm's product. . . . [C]hallenge by the Department can [also] ordinarily be anticipated [in] acquisitions of suppliers or customers by major firms in an industry in which (i) there has been, or is developing, a significant trend toward vertical integration by merger such that the trend, if unchallenged, would probably raise barriers to entry or impose a competitive disadvantage on unintegrated or partly integrated firms, and (ii) it does not clearly appear that the particular acquisition will result in significant economies of production or distribution unrelated to advertising or other promotional economies.

A less common special situation in which a challenge by the Department can ordinarily be anticipated is the acquisition by a firm of a customer or supplier for the purpose of increasing the difficulty of potential competitors in entering the market of either the acquiring or acquired firm, or for the purpose of putting competitors of either the acquiring or acquired firm at an unwarranted disadvantage. . . .

[The guidelines then note that the failing company doctrine is an exception to the rules and that the concept of economies of scale is no defense to an action brought to enforce Section 7.]

III Conglomerate Mergers

. . . At the present time, the Department regards two categories of conglomerate mergers as having sufficiently identifiable anti-competitive effects as to be the subject of relatively specific structural guidelines: mergers involving potential entrants and mergers creating a danger of reciprocal buying.

Another important category of conglomerate mergers that will frequently be the subject of enforcement action [is]—mergers which for one or more of several reasons threaten to entrench or enhance the market power of the acquired firm. . . .

[In discussing mergers involving potential entrants the guidelines provide in part:]

(a) Since potential competition . . . may often be the most significant competitive limitation on the exercise of market power by leading firms, as well as the most likely source of additional actual competition, the Department will ordinarily challenge any merger between one of the most likely entrants into the market and:

(i) any firm with approximately 25% or more of the market;

(ii) one of the two largest firms in the market in which the shares of the two largest firms amount to approximately 50% or more;

(iii) one of the four largest firms in a market in which the shares of the eight largest firms amount to approximately 75% or more, provided the merging firm's share of the market amounts to approximately 10% or more; or

(iv) one of the eight largest firms in a market in which the shares of these firms amount to approximately 75% or more, provided either (A) the merging firm's share of the market is not insubstantial and there are no more than one or two likely entrants into the market, or (B) the merging firm is a rapidly growing firm. . . .

[In discussing mergers creating the danger of reciprocal buying, the guidelines provide in part:]

Since reciprocal buying . . . is an economically unjustified business practice which confers a competitive advantage on the favored firm unrelated to the merits of its product, the Department will ordinarily challenge any merger which creates a significant danger of reciprocal buying. Unless it clearly appears that some special market factor makes remote the possibility that reciprocal buying behavior will actually occur, the Department considers that a significant danger of reciprocal buying is present whenever approximately 15% or more of the total purchases in a market in which one of the merging firms ("the selling firm") sells are accounted for by firms which also make substantial sales in markets where the other merging firm ("the buying firm") is both a substantial buyer and a more substantial buyer than all or most of the competitors of the selling firm.

The Department will also ordinarily challenge (i) any merger undertaken for the purpose of facilitating the creation of reciprocal buying arrangements, and (ii) any merger creating the possibility of any substantial reciprocal buying where one (or both) of the merging firms has within the recent past, or the merged firm has after consummation of the merger, actually engaged in reciprocal buying, or attempted directly or indirectly to induce firms with which it deals to engage in reciprocal buying, in the product markets in which the possibility of reciprocal buying has been created. . . .

[In discussing mergers which entrench market power and other grounds for challenge of conglomerate mergers, the guidelines state:]

The Department will ordinarily investigate the possibility of anti-competitive consequences, and may in particular circumstances bring suit, where an acquisition of a leading firm in a relatively concentrated or rapidly concentrating market may serve to entrench or increase the market power of that firm or raise barriers to entry in that market. Examples of this type of merger include: (i) a merger which produces a very large disparity in absolute size between the merged firm and the largest remaining firms in the relevant markets, (ii) a merger of firms producing related products which may induce purchasers, concerned about the merged firm's possible use of leverage, to buy products of the merged firm rather than those of competitors, and (iii) a merger which may enhance the ability of the merged firm to increase product differentiation in the relevant markets.

Generally speaking, the conglomerate merger area involves novel problems that have not yet been subjected to as extensive or sustained analysis as those presented by horizontal and vertical mergers. It is for this reason that the Department's enforcement policy regarding the foregoing category of conglomerate mergers cannot be set forth with greater specificity. . . .

The Federal Trade Commission also has issued guidelines for several industries such as grocery stores and cement. These guidelines are just that—guidelines. Mergers which appear not to be in violation may be challenged, and those which appear to be in violation have not always been challenged. The fact that a merger or acquisition has not yet been challenged does not mean that it cannot or will not be in the future. Many of the thousands of mergers that were effected in the 1960s may be questioned in the seventies or eighties.

All guidelines have been criticized on many grounds. First, they are only advisory documents published by government administrative bodies and do not have the impact of law. Second, the words "undue concentrations of economic power" are not defined. Third, the guidelines are really an oversimplification and admittedly may not be followed by subsequent administrations. Fourth, there is insufficient evidence of the impact of conglomerates on competition. Fifth, the guidelines establish a *structure* for each market as the standard for judging the legality of a merger rather than judging it on its effect on competition. Mergers beneficial to competition that hurt structure are subject to challenge, despite the fact that the intention is to benefit competition. Sixth, the Commerce Department and the Census Bureau cannot always come up with the market share data needed to apply the guidelines. Seventh, the guidelines may not prevent certain harmful effects of mergers such as those that: (*a*) are made solely to gain size and satisfy the ego of top management; (*b*) spread management too thin; (*c*) concentrate corporate management in a few cities and away from smaller communities; (*d*) create labor problems of nationwide proportions because of the refusal of all workers of a large company to cross picket lines; or (*e*) deceive investors by showing growth of income where none actually exists.

7   MERGERS AND ACQUISITIONS CAN BE CHALLENGED AT ANY TIME

The case which follows is one of the landmark decisions involving Section 7 of the Clayton Act. Note that the government brought suit in 1949. Thus, the decision was rendered on the basis of the Act as it existed prior to the broadening 1950 amendment. Also note that the government's action was commenced thirty years after the acquisitions in question occurred. This was due at least in part to the fact that almost all authorities, including the FTC, had held the view that the original Section 7 was applicable only to horizontal mergers. In addition the case is significant in that it illustrates these principles: that an acquisition of stock or assets may be perfectly legal at the time, but later may become illegal because it "threatens to ripen into a prohibited effect;" and that proof of a wrongful intent is not required to demonstrate a Section 7 violation.

United States v. E. I. du Pont de Nemours & Co.
353 U.S. 586 (1957)

Du Pont acquired 23 percent of the stock of General Motors in 1917 to 1919. Subsequently, in 1949, the government brought action charging that this acquisition violated Section 7 of the Clayton Act. The District Court dismissed the action and the government appealed. One of the arguments of du Pont was that Section 7 did not apply, since this was a vertical, not horizontal, combination; that is, du Pont and General Motors were not in competition with each other.

BRENNAN, JUSTICE: The primary issue is whether du Pont's commanding position as General Motors' supplier of automotive finishes and fabrics was achieved on competitive merit alone, or because its acquisition of General Motors' stock, and the consequent close intercompany relationship, led to the insulation of most of the General Motors' market from the competition, with the resultant likelihood, at the time of suit, of the creation of a monopoly of a line of commerce. . . .

Section 7 is designed to arrest in its incipiency not only the substantial lessening of competition from the acquisition by one corporation of the whole or any part of the stock of a competing corporation, but also to arrest in their incipiency restraints or monopolies in a relevant market which, as a reasonable probability, appear at the time of suit likely to result from the acquisition by one corporation of all or any part of the stock of any other corporation. The section is violated whether or not actual restraints or monopolies, or the substantial lessening of competition, have occurred or are intended. Acquisitions solely for investment are excepted, but only if, and so long as, the stock is not used by voting or otherwise to bring about, the substantial lessening of competition.

We are met at the threshold with the argument that § 7, before its amendment in 1950, applied only to an acquisition of the stock of a competing corporation, and not to an acquisition by a supplier corporation of the stock of a customer corporation—in other words, that the statute applied only to horizontal and not to vertical acquisitions. . . .

The first paragraph of § 7, written in the disjunctive, plainly is framed to reach not only the corporate acquisition of stock of a competing corporation, where the effect may be substantially to lessen competition between them, but also the corporate acquisition of stock of any corporation, competitor or not, where the effect may be either (1) to restrain commerce in any section or community, or (2) tend to create a monopoly of any line of commerce. The amended complaint does not allege that the effect of du Pont's acquisition may be to restrain commerce in any section or community but alleges that the effect was ". . . to tend to create a monopoly in particular lines of commerce. . . ."

Appellees argue that there exists no basis for a finding of a probable restraint or monopoly within the meaning of § 7 because the total General Motors market for finishes and fabrics constituted only a negligible percentage of the total market for these materials for all uses, including automotive uses. It is stated in the General Motors brief that in 1947 du Pont's finish sales to General Motors constituted 3.5% of all sales of finishes to industrial users, and that its fabrics sales to General Motors comprised 1.6% of the total market for the type of fabric used by the automobile industry.

Determination of the relevant market is a necessary predicate to a finding of a violation of the Clayton Act because the threatened monopoly must be one which will substantially lessen competition "within the area of effective competition." Substantiality can be determined only in terms of the market affected. The record shows that automotive finishes and fabrics have sufficient peculiar characteristics and uses to constitute them products sufficiently distinct from all other finishes and fabrics to make them a "line of commerce" within the meaning of the Clayton Act. . . . Thus, the bounds of the relevant market for the purpose of this case are not coextensive with the total market for finishes and fabrics, but are coextensive with the automobile industry, the relevant market to automotive finishes and fabrics.

The market affected must be substantial. . . . Moreover, in order to establish a violation of § 7 the Government must prove a likelihood that competition may be "foreclosed in a substantial share of . . . [that market]." Both requirements are satisfied in this case. The substantiality of a relevant market comprising the automobile industry is undisputed. The substantiality of General Motors' share of that market is fully established in the evidence.

General Motors is the colossus of the giant automobile industry. It accounts annually for upwards of two fifths of the total sales of automotive vehicles in the nation.

In 1955 General Motors ranked first in sales and second in assets among all United States industrial corporations and became the first corporation to earn over a billion dollars in annual net income. In 1947 General Motors' total purchases of all products from du Pont were $26,628,274, of which $18,938,229 (71%) represented purchases from du Pont's Finishes Division. . . . Expressed in percentages, du Pont supplied 67% of General Motors' requirements for finishes in 1946 and 68% in 1947. In fabrics du Pont supplied 52.3% of requirements in 1946, and 38.5% in 1947. Because General Motors accounts for almost one-half of the automobile industry's annual sales, its requirements for automotive finishes and fabrics must represent approximately one-half of the relevant market for these materials. Because the record clearly shows that quantitatively and percentage-wise du Pont supplies the largest part of General Motors' requirements, we must conclude that du Pont has a substantial share of the relevant market.

The appellees argue that the Government could not maintain this action in 1949 because § 7 is applicable only to the acquisition of stock and not to the holding or subsequent use of the stock. This argument misconceives the objective toward which § 7 is directed. The Clayton Act was intended to supplement the Sherman Act. Its aim was primarily to arrest apprehended consequences of inter-corporate relationships before those relationships could work their evil, which may be at or any time after the acquisition, depending upon the circumstances of the particular case. The Senate declared the objective of the Clayton Act to be as follows:

. . . *Broadly stated, the bill, in its treatment of unlawful restraints and monopolies, seeks to prohibit and make unlawful certain trade practices which, as a rule, singly and in themselves, are not covered by the Act of July 2, 1890 [the Sherman Act], or other existing anti-trust acts, and thus, by making these practices illegal, to arrest the creation of trusts, conspiracies, and monopolies in* their incipiency and before consummation. . . . *S. Rep. No. 698, 63d Cong., 2d Sess. 1. [emphasis added]*

"Incipiency" in this context denotes not the time the stock was acquired, but any time when the acquisition threatens to ripen into a prohibited effect. See *Transamerica Corp. v. Board of Governors*, 3 Cir., 206 F.2d 163, 166. To accomplish the congressional aim, the Government may proceed at any time that an acquisition may be said with reasonable probability to contain a threat that it may lead to a restraint of commerce or tend to create a monopoly of a line of commerce. Even when the purchase is solely for investment, the plain language of § 7 contemplates an action at any time the stock is used to bring about, or in attempting to bring about, the substantial lessening of competition.

Prior cases under § 7 were brought at or near the time of acquisition. . . . None of these cases holds, or even suggests, that the Government is foreclosed from bringing the action at any time when a threat of the prohibited effects is evident.

Related to this argument is the District Court's conclusion that 30 years of nonrestraint negated "any reasonable probability of such a restraint" at the time of the suit. While it is, of course, true that proof of a mere *possibility* of a prohibited restraint or tendency to monopoly will not establish the statutory requirement that the effect of an acquisition "may be" such restraint or tendency, the basic facts found by the District Court demonstrate the error of its conclusion. . . .

The fact that sticks out in this voluminous record is that the bulk of du Pont's production has always supplied the largest part of the requirements of the one customer in the automobile industry connected to du Pont by a stock interest. The inference is overwhelming that du Pont's commanding position was promoted by its stock interest and was not gained solely on competitive merit.

We agree with the trial court that considerations of price, quality and service were not overlooked by either du Pont or General Motors. Pride in its products and its high financial stake in General Motors' success would naturally lead du Pont to try to supply the best. But the wisdom of this business judgment cannot obscure the fact, plainly revealed by the record, that du Pont purposely employed its stock to pry open the General Motors market to entrench itself as the primary supplier of General Motors' requirements for automotive finishes and fabrics.

Similarly, the fact that all concerned in high executive posts in both companies acted honorably and fairly, each in the honest conviction that his actions were in the best interests of his own company and without any design to overreach anyone, including du Pont's competitors, does not defeat the Government's right to relief. It is not requisite to the proof of a violation of § 7 to show that restraint or monopoly was intended.

The statutory policy of fostering free competition is obviously furthered when no supplier has an advantage over his competitors from an acquisition of his customer's stock likely to have the effects condemned by the statute. We repeat, that the test of a violation of § 7 is whether, at the time of suit, there is a reasonable probability that the acquisition is likely to result in the condemned restraints. The conclusion upon this record is inescapable that such likelihood was proved as to this acquisition. The fire that was kindled in 1917 continues to smolder. It burned briskly to forge the ties that bind the General Motors market to du Pont, and if it has quieted down, it remains hot, and, from past performance, is likely at any time to blaze and make the fusion complete.

The judgment must therefore be reversed and the cause remanded to the District Court for a determination, after further hearing, of the equitable relief necessary and appropriate in the public interest to eliminate the effects of the acquisition offensive to the statute. [REVERSED]

Upon remand, the District Court divested du Pont of the right to vote its 63 million shares of General Motors stock, prohibited du Pont from attempting to influence General Motors in any way, and canceled preferential trade arrangements or understandings and requirements contracts between the two companies.[1] Additional relief included a ruling that officers of one of the companies could not henceforth be members of the board of directors of the other.

However, on petition by the government, the Supreme Court of the United States reviewed the District Court's disposition and agreed with the government that partial divestiture by transfer of voting rights would not be an effective remedy. The Supreme Court then directed the District Court to enter a decree requiring the du Pont company to divest itself *completely* of the General Motors stock, no later than ten years after the decree's effective date.[2]

8 THE FUTURE

In spite of the numerous cases interpreting Section 7 and of the guidelines issued by the Justice Department and the FTC, the business community is still unable to accurately determine in advance the legality or illegality of proposed acquisitions. Several other allied issues pertinent to mergers remain, including the following: (1) What are the proper methods and principles to use in the preparation of financial reports of conglomerates? (2) Are labor contracts negotiated before a merger binding on the merged entity? (3) Should mergers which enable basic industries such as steel to meet foreign competition be treated as exceptions to the general principles of Section 7? (4) Are additional laws regulating the sale of securities of conglomerates needed? (5) Does strict enforcement of Section 7 tend to lower productivity? Some of the these issues are economic and others are within the problem sphere of administrative agencies other than the FTC such as the Securities and Exchange Commission. Their breadth illustrates the extent of unresolved problems inherent in growth by merger and acquisition.

Insofar as Section 7 enforcement is concerned, it appears that mergers by and among any of the top 200 manufacturing firms or firms of comparable size will probably be challenged. In addition, any acquisition by any leading producer in

[1] 177 F. Supp. 1 (1959).
[2] 366 U.S. 316 (1961).

any industry that is highly concentrated or tending toward high concentration will probably be challenged. Finally, the principals to any merger which in the opinion of either the Justice Department or the FTC may substantially lessen potential competition or which may develop a substantial potential for reciprocity should expect it to be challenged.

Superconcentration will be challenged especially in conglomerates because: (1) they tend to eliminate competition, both existing and potential; (2) they create nationwide corporate structures whose enormous physical and psychological resources pose substantial barriers to entry by small firms; (3) they increase the possibility for reciprocity and other forms of unfair buyer-seller leverage; (4) they create a climate in the marketplace which encourages more and more mergers; (5) they may lead to the situation in which residents of smaller communities lose influence over local industries; (6) they establish a trend in which the nation's financial and productive assets are in the hands and under the control of fewer and fewer people; and (7) they tend to concentrate political power.

Actual reciprocity and the potential for reciprocity will be a danger signal because: (1) reciprocity eliminates a supplier or a customer from the competitive market, and considerations of price, quality, and service—so essential to the functioning of a free market—cease to exist; (2) in industries where reciprocity is the rule, potential entrants find it difficult to enter the market; (3) there is an increase in market concentration; and (4) reciprocity has a cyclical effect—it is both a cause and consequence of conglomeration, since business reciprocity is a natural motive to conglomerate.

While economies of scale, the ability to commit more resources to research and development, and the theoretical efficiencies in the allocation of capital and personnel have encouraged thousands of mergers in recent years, the law is now discouraging such activity by large companies, and it may be used to divorce some of the corporate marriages of the fifties and sixties. The goal remains as stated by Justice Learned Hand in *U.S. v. Alcoa* 148 F.2d 416 (1945): "Throughout the history of these [antitrust] statutes it has been consistently assumed that one of their purposes was to perpetuate and preserve, for its own sake, and in spite of possible cost, an organization of industry in small units which can effectively compete with each other."

REVIEW QUESTIONS—CHAPTER 12

1 Define the following terms introduced in this chapter: horizontal merger; vertical merger; conglomerate merger; product extension merger; and consolidation.

2 Why do businesses seek to grow externally by acquisition rather than internally?

3 What is the effect of the "failing company" doctrine on Section 7 of the Clayton Act?

4 To what extent is enforcement of Section 7 of the Clayton Act discretionary with the Justice Department? With the FTC? Explain.

5 Could a merger which was consummated in the 1960s be challenged this year? Explain.

6 List the basic issues of any case brought under Section 7 of the Clayton Act as amended.

7 Is it possible that a merger might stimulate competition? Explain.

8 List several key terms in merger and acquisition litigation which Congress failed to define in the applicable statutes.

9 What factors are considered by courts in determining the applicable product market in a Section 7 case? The applicable geographic market? Give examples.

10 Why do we seek to stop trends toward economic concentration in their incipiency?

11 Give reasons for conglomerate mergers and discuss the possible anticompetitive effects of conglomerates.

12 Is Section 7 of the Clayton Act applicable to all kinds of mergers? Explain.

13 If a merger or acquisition does not violate the merger guidelines, under what circumstances may it nevertheless be challenged by the Justice Department? Explain.

14 What two categories of conglomerate mergers have sufficiently identifiable anticompetitive effects to be likely to be challenged? Explain.

15 Why is reciprocity and the potential for reciprocity a basis for challenging mergers and acquisitions?

Chapter Thirteen

The Federal Trade Commission

1 INTRODUCTION

The Federal Trade Commission Act of 1914 was enacted with the Clayton Act in order to create an "independent" administrative agency with expertise to assist in the enforcement of the Clayton Act and other laws. This independent agency has the usual functions and powers of administrative agencies as discussed in Chapter 7. The FTC has five commissioners appointed by the President, with the advice and consent of the Senate, in staggered terms of seven years each. A maximum of three of them may belong to the same political party. Commissioners are not permitted to engage in any other business or employment during their terms, and may be removed from office by the President only for inefficiency, neglect of duty, or malfeasance in office.

One of the major functions of the FTC is to enforce Section 5 of the Federal Trade Commission Act. This Act originally declared that "unfair methods of competition in commerce" were unlawful, and empowered and directed the Commission (exclusively) "to prevent persons, partnerships, or corporations . . . from using unfair methods of competition in commerce." This was amended later to make both "unfair methods of competition in commerce" and "unfair or deceptive acts or practices in commerce" unlawful.[1] (Emphasis added.) The Commission has broad, sweeping powers and a mandate to determine what methods, acts, or practices fall within the vague category of being "unfair or deceptive" and are thus unlawful. Such decisions are made on a case-by-case basis. A more detailed discussion of unfair methods of competition and unfair or deceptive trade practices is presented in sections which follow.

A second major function of the FTC is to supervise and enforce Sections 2, 3, 7, and 8 of the Clayton Act with regard to all businesses not regulated by the Interstate Commerce Commission, Federal Communications Commission, Civil Aeronautics Board, or Federal Reserve Board. The FTC has the power to enforce these provisions by restraining future violations of them through use of "cease and desist orders." The Commission has no power to punish defendants for past misconduct.

In theory, the commissioners, with expertise in business and economics, are able to apply their training and experience to solving specific problems of

---

[1] Wheeler-Lee Amendments, 52 Stat. 111 (1938), 15 U.S.C. § 45 (1970).

preserving or restoring competition in a better manner and with more desirable results than the courts, which lack this technical background. In a real sense, Congress in creating the Commission created a form of competition between the courts, the Commission, and Congress itself in the matter of preserving competition.

By use of the independent agency system, the President is able to appoint persons who may take a more vigorous approach to the problems of making the competitive economic system work, so that more progress is possible than if such problems were left to the courts or Congress. However, it should be noted that Congress did not express its complete distrust of the courts (as it did in the case of the enforcement of later labor legislation—the Wagner Act) since actions under the Clayton Act can also be brought by private individuals who are injured by violations thereof in the regular court system or by the Attorney General in the Federal District Courts.

In addition to the foregoing responsibilities, the FTC has that of administering several other Federal statutes. Among these are: the Export Trade Act; the Lanham Trade Mark Act (which provides for the registration and protection of trade marks in commerce); the Wool Products Labeling Act (which is designed to protect manufacturers, distributors, and consumers from substitutes and mixtures in wool products which are not revealed by their labels); the Fur Products Labeling Act (which protects consumers and others from the misbranding and false advertising of fur products and furs); the Flammable Fabrics Act (which prohibits the movement in interstate commerce of articles of wearing apparel and fabrics which are so highly flammable as to be dangerous when worn by individuals or used for other purposes); the Textile Fiber Products Identification Act (which protects consumers against the misbranding and false advertising of the fiber content of textile fiber products); the Fair Packaging and Labeling Act (which prohibits the use of unfair or deceptive methods of packaging or labeling of consumer commodities); and the Consumer Credit Protection Act, also known as "Truth-in-Lending" (which requires the full disclosure of terms and conditions of finance charges and restricts the garnishment of wages).

2 ORGANIZATION AND PROCEDURES OF THE FTC

Reorganized in the early 1970s, part of the staff of the FTC is divided into three bureaus: the Bureau of Competition, the Bureau of Consumer Protection, and, the Bureau of Economics. The FTC also has a number of regional offices throughout the country. These have the power to proceed without prior approval of the commission itself in enlarging consumer protection and public-information activities in their respective regions. They have been given subpoena power and the authority to bring legal actions in the courts on their own motion. The Commission staff also includes an Executive Director and the Offices of General Counsel, Hearing Examiners, Secretary, and Policy Planning and Evaluation. In addition, Consumer Protection Coordinating Committees have been established in several large metropolitan areas to assist the FTC in coordinating its consumer protection activities with those of state and local authorities and other Federal agencies. These committees meet often and exchange information. For example, the membership of the Chicago committee includes representatives of the FTC; the Illinois Attorney General's Bureau of Consumer Fraud and Protection; the City of Chicago's Department of Consumer Sales, Weights and Measures; the Food and Drug Administration; and the Postal Inspector's Office of the U.S. Postal Service. All consumer complaints received by any of the member agencies are computerized, and the resulting data are compiled into reports for use by all agencies on enforcement trends and problems. These reports are also used for planning purposes. When one of the agencies receives a consumer complaint over which it does not have jurisdiction and statutory authority, it refers the complaint to the proper agency instead of requiring the complaining consumer to shuttle from one office to another.

Because of its investigating power, the FTC can gather and compile information concerning the organization and business practices of any corporation engaged in commerce to determine whether there has been a violation of any of the laws it administers. In exercising this power, the Commission may utilize its subpoena power and require reports, examine witnesses under oath, and examine and copy documents, or it may obtain information from other governmental offices. This power of investigation complements and permits the exercise of the other powers of the FTC such as giving advice, prosecuting violations, issuing rules, and entering cease and desist orders.

An investigation by the FTC may indicate that it should use its expertise and exercise its advisory power. This may be accomplished by making reports to the President or to Congress. For example, the FTC may propose new legislation to Congress, or it may inform the Attorney General of the need for court decrees restraining violations of the law. It may also report to the general public concerning information which should be known in the public interest. Such announcements usually involve unfair and deceptive practices.

In exercising its prosecuting and quasi-judicial powers, the FTC issues a cease and desist order upon finding that a violation of the law over which it has jurisdiction exists. Violations of final cease and desist orders are punished by a fine of $5,000 per day, with each day being a new violation. A cease and desist order is the administrative agency equivalent of an injunction issued by a court of equity. However, there are several stages to the formal adjudicative process before a cease and desist order is issued.

An alleged violation may come to the attention of the Commission in a variety of ways. A businessman may complain about acts of another which are injurious to his ability to compete, or a consumer may direct the attention of the FTC to acts of a business which he claims are unfair or deceptive. Such complaints are filed informally. A letter signed by the complaining party is sufficient if it identifies the one about whom he is complaining, contains all the evidence in his possession, and states the relief he desires. Of course, other government agencies, Congress, or the FTC itself may discover business conduct which is alleged to be illegal.

Before a formal complaint is issued by the FTC against a business, the allegations are examined to determine if the matter is within its jurisdiction. If jurisdiction exists, the matter is assigned to a staff member to gather the evidence.

The FTC itself is the official complaining (prosecuting) party, and the original applicant has no legal status before the Commission since the proceedings involved are not adversary in nature. They are not designed to resolve private disputes but to end illegal practices. The name of the complaining party is not disclosed in the proceedings. The person against whom the informal complaint was made is given a complete statement of the allegations and evidence and is permitted (or in some cases required) to submit evidence in explanation of his defense. After this preliminary investigation and preparation of a report by some staff members, the case is reviewed and evaluated. At this stage several recommendations are possible. For example, the reviewing personnel may recommend to the Commission that it dismiss the case for lack of evidence, that it dismiss if the proposed respondent agrees to cease and desist from continuing the alleged unlawful practice, or that a formal complaint should be issued. The preliminary investigation, of course, is not made with a view to making actual determinations of fact, other than that probable cause has been shown to justify holding a formal hearing. If a majority of the Commission has reason to believe from the report submitted that a violation of the law has taken place and that further action by it would be in the public interest, a formal complaint is issued and served on the alleged violator. Such a complaint includes a recital of the facts concerning the practices alleged to be illegal, a proposed form of the order to be issued, and notice of the time and place of the hearing (which must be set at least thirty days after service of the complaint).

After the formal complaint is served, the respondent files an answer to the charges and allegations. The case is then assigned to a hearing examiner, whose role is similar to that of a trial judge who hears a case without a jury. He is in charge of the proceedings. At the hearing, counsel for the FTC and the respondent produce evidence in an effort to prove or disprove the allegations of fact in the complaint and answer. The hearing examiner rules on the admissibility of evidence, rules on motions made by counsel, and renders an initial decision which includes a statement of his findings and conclusions, along with reasons for them, as to all material issues of fact and law. His ruling also includes an order which he deems to be appropriate in view of the evidence in the record. This order becomes final if neither the FTC nor the respondent challenge it within thirty days after it is filed. However, either of these parties may appeal the decision of the hearing examiner within the thirty-day period to the full Commission. On the appeal the Commission reviews the record of the initial decision rendered by the hearing examiner and has all the powers it could have exercised if it rendered that decision itself. It may adopt, modify, or set aside the decision of the hearing examiner, and it must state the reasons for its actions. If the FTC finds that a violation exists, it issues an order to the respondent to cease and desist from continuing the practice found to be illegal. Such an order becomes final sixty days after it is served on the respondent, unless the respondent petitions the United States Circuit Court of Appeals to set it aside within that period. On appeal, the court reviews the decision of the FTC as it does those of other administrative agencies which are challenged, as discussed in Chapter 7. If the Court of Appeals upholds the order of the Commission, the order in effect becomes an injunction which may be enforced by contempt-of-court proceedings.

As previously noted, the penalty for disobeying a final cease and desist order is a fine of $5,000 *per day* for each day the violation continues. There is no punishment for offenses committed prior to a final order but only for violations after the order is entered.

At any stage in the formal proceedings before the hearing itself (including the period before the formal complaint is issued during the preliminary investigation), a settlement may be negotiated between the FTC and the respondent. Such a settlement results in the issuance of a "consent order," after which formal proceedings are dropped. The settlement requires that the respondent admit to the jurisdiction of the FTC and waive all rights to seek a review. However, the respondent does not have to admit that it has been guilty of a violation of the law; but it does agree that it will not engage in the business activities which were the subject of the complaint. A consent order has the same legal force and effect as a final cease and desist order issued after a full hearing. One obvious advantage of such a settlement to both the business charged and the FTC is that the considerable expense of pursuing formal proceedings to their conclusion is thereby saved. Another advantage is that the business is not found guilty, but only agrees that it will not do the act complained of. The Commission encourages the use of consent orders, and the majority of proceedings which are initiated result in the issuance of consent orders instead of the more formal procedures.

The Commission sometimes uses the consent order on an industry-wide basis to restrain practices which are found to be unfair or anticompetitive. To assist the making of such orders, the Commission utilizes its special authority to conduct "mail order investigations." For example, if the FTC suspects that a violation of the law exists in an industry, it may require the firms in that industry to submit a special report concerning certain of their business practices. In one case, 400 suppliers in the food industry were required to reveal the facts about promotional food allowances given by them to grocery chains. Other reports have required the manufacturers of certain products to submit answers from which the Commission could determine whether their advertising claims were exaggerated or not. When the reports have been evaluated, the Commission sends proposed complaints, charging violations of certain laws, and proposed consent orders to the members of the industry. Usually most of the members of the industry sign the orders and agree to cease and desist from continuing the practice in question. Those who do not may have charges filed against them and may ultimately be restrained by a formal cease and desist order.

Using the industry-wide procedure has a number of advantages. It is inexpensive, expeditious, and capable of discovering a wide range of illegal acts being committed in an Industry. Moreover, simultaneous consent orders which are issued on an industry-wide basis ensure that no one firm is placed at a competitive disadvantage or singled out for unfavorable publicity. Finally, it should be noted that a formal cease and desist order directed against one firm does not restrain others in the same industry which were not a party to the proceedings. Thus the overall remedial effect of such an order may be minimal. Sole reliance on formal proceedings might require the Commission to attack industry practice on a piecemeal basis, which would involve considerable delay in effectively restraining illegal practices and deplete Commission resources.

The use of advisory opinions is another technique employed by the FTC. A firm may request advice as to whether a proposed course of action might violate any of the laws which the Commission administers. After conferences, the Commission's staff may recommend a certain opinion regarding that specific issue. Or it may recommend that an opinion be withheld, as in a case where the legality of the act may not be capable of determination without an extensive investigation. While an advisory opinion is not binding on the Commission as a formal ruling, it does give a business a reasonably certain indicator of the view the FTC would take if the practice in question were challenged formally. The advisory opinion is a unique device generally not available in the judicial system: courts are concerned only with actual cases and controversies. Only about one-third of the Commission's advisory opinions lend themselves to publication, since confidential information cannot be disclosed in many cases, and thus the fact situations on which these opinions were based cannot be given in adequate detail. Those which are published furnish guidelines for other businesses which are considering similar courses of action.

The FTC exercises its quasi-legislative power by issuing "trade regulation rules" which have the force and effect of law. A trade regulation rule which is relevant to any issue involved in an adjudicative proceeding may be used by the Commission to resolve that issue. Respondents are entitled to a hearing on the applicability of the rule to their particular case. Before trade rules are promulgated, interested parties are given an opportunity to be heard on the desirability and legality of the proposed rule. Trade rules are issued by the FTC on its own motion. They usually deal with a single practice in a single industry. For example, trade regulation rules have been issued which restrict size representations on tablecloths and sleeping bags, forbid claims that dry-cell batteries are leakproof, and prohibit marking belts made of split, ground, or shredded leather as being "leather." Also, the Commission promulgated the rule which required that cigarette ads and packages contain certain health-hazard disclosures. It would appear that the future will bring a wider reliance by the Commission on the use of rules rather than on the formal hearing process.

Finally, the FTC periodically issues "trade practice rules and guides." The rules are the result of a trade practice conference of the members of a given industry. These conferences provide a forum for the discussion of the problems and practices of an industry and the formulation of proposals for their solution. They culminate in the Commission's issuing of a set of rules which constitute its informal opinion of the legal requirements applicable to the particular industry's practices. Although compliance with the rules is voluntary, they provide the basis for the informal and simultaneous abandonment by the industry members of practices which are thought to be unlawful. "Guidelines" are also issued by the FTC to supplement the trade practice rules. These are administrative interpretations of the statutes which the Commission is responsible for enforcing, and they provide guidance to both the FTC staff and businessmen in evaluating the legality of certain practices. They deal with a particular practice and may cut across industry lines. While formal complaints do not charge violations of trade practice rules or guides, they do charge violation of a particular statute to which the rules or guidelines relate.

From the foregoing, it is apparent that many of the procedures employed by the FTC are informal in nature and are designed to achieve voluntary compliance with the law, with a minimum of delay and expense. The increasing use of such procedures should result in a more effective and efficient utilization of the resources of the FTC than would be possible by relying solely on the formal hearing procedures.

3   UNFAIR METHODS OF COMPETITION

While the original Section 5 of the Federal Trade Commission Act outlawed unfair methods of competition in commerce and directed the FTC to prevent the use of such, it offered no definition of the specific practices which were unfair. The term "unfair methods of competition" was designed by Congress as a flexible concept, the exact meaning of which could evolve on a case-by-case basis. It is capable of application to a variety of unrelated activities. The case which follows discusses the problem of defining "unfair methods of competition" and contains some of the legislative history pertaining to the final choice by Congress of these words in the Federal Trade Commission Act.

FTC v. R. F. Keppel & Bro., Inc.
291 U.S. 304 (1934)

After conducting a hearing, the Federal Trade Commission issued a cease and desist order forbidding certain practices engaged in by R. F. Keppel & Bro., Inc., in pursuing the business of manufacturing and distributing penny candy as unfair methods of competition under Section 5 of the Federal Trade Commission Act. On review, the Circuit Court of Appeals set aside the commission's order on the ground that the practices in question were not unfair methods of competition within the meaning of the statute. The FTC then sought and obtained a writ of certiorari from the Supreme Court to review the adverse decree of the Circuit Court of Appeals.

STONE, JUSTICE: . . . The Commission found that respondent, one of numerous candy manufacturers similarly engaged, manufactures, sells, and distributes, in interstate commerce, package assortments of candies known to the trade as "break and take" packages, in competition with manufacturers of assortments known as "straight goods" packages. Both types are assortments of candies in packages in convenient arrangement for sale by the piece at a small price in retail stores in what is known as the penny candy trade. The break and take assortments are so arranged and offered for sale to consumers as to avail of the element of chance as an inducement to the retail purchasers. One assortment, consisting of 120 pieces retailing at 1 cent each, includes four pieces, each having concealed within its wrapper a single cent, so that the purchasers of those particular pieces of candy receive back the amount of the purchase price and thus obtain the candy without cost. Another contains 60 pieces of candy, each having its retail price marked on a slip of paper concealed with its wrapper; 10 pieces retail at 1 cent each, 10 at 2 cents, and 40 at 3 cents. The price paid for each piece is that named on the price ticket, ascertained only after the purchaser has selected the candy and the wrapper has been removed. A third assortment consists of 200 pieces of candy, a few of which have concealed centers of different colors, the remainder having white centers. The purchasers of the candy found to have colored centers are given prizes, packed with the candy, consisting of other pieces of candy or a package containing lead pencils, penholder and ruler. Each assortment is accompanied by a display card, attractive to children, prepared by respondent for exhibition and use by the dealer in selling the candy, explaining the plan by which either the price or the amount of candy or other merchandise which the purchaser receives is affected by chance. The pieces of candy in the break and take packages are either smaller than those of the competing straight goods packages, which are sold at a comparable price without the aid of any chance feature, or they are of inferior quality. Much of the candy assembled in the break and take packages is sold by retailers, located in the vicinity of schools, to school children.

The Commission found that the use of the break and take package in the retail trade involves the sale or distribution of the candy by lot or chance; that it is a lottery or gambling device which encourages gambling among children; that children, enticed by the element of chance, purchase candy so sold in preference to straight goods candy; and that the competition between the two types of package results in a substantial diversion of trade from the manufacturers of the straight goods package to those distributing the break and take type. It found further that in some states lotteries and gaming devices are penal offenses; that the sale or distribution of candy by lot or chance is against public policy; that many manufacturers of competing candies refuse to engage in the distribution of the break and take type of package because they regard it as a reprehensible encouragement of gambling among children; and that such manufacturers are placed at a disadvantage in competition. The evidence shows that others have reluctantly yielded to the practice in order to avoid loss of trade to their competitors.

The court below held as the respondent argues here, that respondent's practice does not hinder competition or injure its competitors, since they are free to resort to the same sales method; that the practice does not tend to create a monopoly or involve any deception to consumers or the public and hence is not an unfair method of competition within the meaning of the statute. . . .

[W]e pass . . . to the decisive question whether the practice itself is one over which the Commission is given jurisdiction because it is unfair. . .

Neither the language nor the history of the act suggests that Congress intended to confine the forbidden methods to fixed and unyielding categories. The common law afforded a definition of unfair competition and, before the enactment of the Federal Trade Commission Act, the Sherman Anti-Trust Act had laid its inhibition upon combinations to restrain or monopolize interstate commerce which the courts had construed to include restraints upon competition in interstate commerce. It would not have been a difficult feat of draftsmanship to have restricted the operation of the Trade Commission Act to those methods of competition in interstate commerce which are forbidden at common law or which are likely to grow into violations of the Sherman Act, if that had been the purpose of the legislation.

The act undoubtedly was aimed at all the familiar methods of law violation which prosecutions under the Sherman Act had disclosed. . . . But, as this Court has pointed out it also had a broader purpose. . . .

As proposed by the Senate Committee on Interstate Commerce and as introduced in the Senate, the bill which ultimately became the Federal Trade Commission Act declared "unfair competition" to be unlawful. But it was because the meaning which the common law had given to those words was deemed too narrow that the broader and more flexible phrase "unfair methods of competition" was substituted. Congress, in defining the powers of the Commission, thus advisedly adopted a phrase which, as this Court has said, does not "admit of precise definition, but the meaning and application of which must be arrived at by what this court elsewhere has called the gradual process of judicial inclusion and exclusion." . . . It is true that the statute does not authorize regulation which has no purpose other than that of relieving merchants from troublesome competition or of censoring the morals of business men. But here the competitive method is shown to exploit consumers, children, who are unable to protect themselves. It employs a device whereby the amount of the return they receive from the expenditure of money is made to depend upon chance. Such devices have met with condemnation throughout the community. Without inquiring whether, as respondent contends, the criminal statutes imposing penalties on gambling, lotteries and the like, fail to reach this particular practice In most or any of the states, it is clear that the practice is of the sort which the common law and criminal statutes have long deemed contrary to public policy. For these reasons a large share of the industry holds out against the device, despite ensuing loss in trade, or bows reluctantly to what it brands unscrupulous. It would seem a gross perversion of the normal meaning of the word, which is the first criterion of statutory construction, to hold that the method is not "unfair." . . .

We hold that the Commission correctly concluded that the practice was an unfair method of competition within the meaning of the statute. It is unnecessary to attempt a comprehensive definition of the unfair methods which are banned, even if it were possible to do so. We do not intimate either that the statute does not authorize the prohibition of other and hitherto unknown methods of competition or, on the other hand, that the Commission may prohibit every unethical competitive practice regardless of its particular character or consequences. New or different practices must be considered as they arise in the light of the circumstances in which they are employed. [REVERSED]

Business conduct which is in violation of *any* provision of the antitrust laws may also be ruled illegal under Section 5 of the FTC Act and subject to a cease and desist order. For example, either a tying arrangement or an exclusive dealing may be found to be illegal under the Sherman Act, under Section 3 of the Clayton Act, under Section 5 of the FTC Act, or under all or a combination of these. Further, anticompetitive acts or practices which *fall short* of transgressing the Sherman or Clayton Acts may be restrained by the FTC as being "unfair methods of competition." When an unfair trade practice is alleged to exist, the choice of the law under which to proceed will depend upon the nature of the relief being sought, the nature of the violation, and the status of the party seeking it. Thus, if criminal sanctions are desired, the Justice Department must initiate the action in the regular Federal courts on behalf of the United States and generally must proceed under the Sherman Act. The burden of proof in such cases is beyond a reasonable doubt, and as a result, such cases are successfully brought only where the business practice involved is clearly unfair. On the other hand, if the business practice is a violation of the Clayton Act, such as a tying contract, the Justice Department may seek and obtain an injunction. The proof required in such a case is less than is required for a Sherman Act conviction. If the practice is such that it is not only questionable that the Sherman Act is violated but also doubtful that the proof is sufficient to prove a Clayton Act violation, the FTC may nevertheless proceed and find that the business practice is unfair. Thus, business practices may be stopped by FTC cease and desist orders which could not be prevented in a judicial proceeding.

The case below involves the activities of the same Brown Shoe Company which was the defendant in the 1962 case already presented in Chapter 12. There, the reader will recall, Brown Shoe's acquisition of Kinney, a chain of shoe stores, was successfully challenged by the Justice Department as a violation of Section 7 of the Clayton Act, and divestiture was ordered by the Court. In the decision which follows, Brown Shoe Company had attempted to accomplish the same end (namely to obtain additional retail outlets which would handle Brown Shoe products exclusively) but by entering into franchise agreements for the sale of its products. These arrangements were challenged by the Federal Trade Commission under Section 5 of the FTC Act. It may be assumed that the activities in this case would not be a violation of either the Sherman or Clayton Acts.

FTC v. Brown Shoe Co.
384 U.S. 316 (1966)

BLACK, JUSTICE: Section 5(a) (6) of the Federal Trade Commission Act empowers and directs the Commission "to prevent persons, partnerships, or corporations . . .

from using unfair methods of competition in commerce and unfair or deceptive acts or practices in commerce." Proceeding under the authority of § 5, the Federal Trade Commission filed a complaint against the Brown Shoe Co., Inc., one of the world's largest manufacturers of shoes with total sales of $236,946,078 for the year ending October 31, 1957. The unfair practices charged against Brown revolve around the "Brown Franchise Stores' Program" through which Brown sells its shoes to some 650 retail stores. The complaint alleged that under this plan Brown, a corporation engaged in interstate commerce, had "entered into contracts or franchises with a substantial number of its independent retail shoe store operator customers which require said customers to restrict their purchases of shoes for resale to the Brown lines and which prohibit them from purchasing, stocking or reselling shoes manufactured by competitors of Brown." Brown's customers who entered into these restrictive franchise agreements, so the complaint charged, were given in return special treatment and valuable benefits which were not granted to Brown's customers who did not enter into the agreements. In its answer to the Commission's complaint Brown admitted that approximately 259 of its retail customers had executed written franchise agreements and that over 400 others had entered into its franchise program without execution of the franchise agreement. Also in its answer Brown attached as an exhibit an unexecuted copy of the "Franchise Agreement" which, when executed by Brown's representative and a retail shoe dealer, obligates Brown to give to the dealer but not to other customers certain valuable services, including among others, architectural plans, costly merchandising records, services of a Brown field representative, and a right to participate in group insurance at lower rates than the dealer could obtain individually. In return, according to the franchise agreement set out in Brown's answer, the retailer must make this promise:

In return I will:

1. Concentrate my business within the grades and price lines of shoes representing Brown Shoe Company Franchises of the Brown Division and will have no lines conflicting with Brown Division Brands of the Brown Shoe Company.

Brown's answer further admitted that the operators of "such Brown Franchise Stores in individually varying degrees accept the benefits and perform the obligations contained in such franchise agreements or implicit in such Program," and that Brown refuses to grant these benefits "to dealers who are dropped or voluntarily withdraw from the Brown Franchise Program. . . ." The foregoing admissions of Brown as to the existence and operation of the franchise program were buttressed by many separate detailed fact findings of a trial examiner, one of which findings was that the franchise program effectively foreclosed Brown's competitors from selling to a substantial number of retail shoe dealers. Based on these findings and on Brown's admissions the Commission concluded that the restrictive contract program was an unfair method of competition within the meaning of § 5 and ordered Brown to cease and desist from its use.

On review the Court of Appeals set aside the Commission's order. In doing so the court said:

By passage of the Federal Trade Commission Act, particularly § 5 thereof, we do not believe that Congress meant to prohibit or limit sales programs such as Brown Shoe engaged in in this case. . . . The custom of giving free service to those who will buy their shoes is widespread, and we cannot agree with the Commission that it is an unfair method of competition in commerce.

In addition the Court of Appeals held that there was a "complete failure to prove an exclusive dealing agreement which might be held violative of Section 5 of the Act." We are asked to treat this general conclusionary statement as though the court intended it to be a rejection of the Commission's findings of fact. We cannot do this. Neither this statement of the court nor any other statement in the opinion indicate a purpose to hold that the evidence failed to show an agreement between Brown and more than 650 franchised dealers which restrained the dealers from buying competing lines of shoes from Brown's competitors. Indeed, in view of the crucial admissions in Brown's formal answer to the complaint we cannot attribute to the Court of Appeals a purpose to set aside the Commission's findings that these restrictive agreements existed and that Brown and most of the franchised dealers in varying degrees lived up to their obligations. Thus the question we have for decision is whether the Federal Trade Commission can declare it to be an unfair practice for Brown, the second largest manufacturer of shoes in the Nation, to pay a valuable consideration to hundreds of retail shoe purchasers in order to secure a contractual promise from them that they will deal primarily with Brown and will not purchase conflicting lines of shoes from Brown's competitors. We hold that the Commission has power to find, on the record here, such an anticompetitive practice unfair, subject of course to judicial review.

In holding that the Federal Trade Commission lacked the power to declare Brown's program to be unfair the Court of Appeals was much influenced by and quoted at length from this Court's opinion in *FTC v. Gratz*, 253 U.S. 421. That case, decided shortly after the Federal Trade Commission Act was passed, construed the Act over a strong dissent by Mr. Justice Brandeis as giving the Commission very little power to declare any trade practice unfair. Later cases of this Court, however, have rejected the *Gratz* view and it is now recognized in line with the dissent of Mr. Justice Brandeis in *Gratz* that the Commission has broad powers to declare trade practices unfair. This broad power of the Commission is particularly well established with regard to trade practices which conflict with the basic policies of the Sherman and Clayton Acts even though such practices may not actually violate these laws. The record in this case shows beyond doubt that Brown, the country's second largest manufacturer of shoes, has a program, which requires shoe retailers, unless faithless to their contractual obligations with Brown, substantially to limit their trade with Brown's competitors. This program obviously conflicts with the central policy of both § 1 of the Sherman Act and § 3 of the Clayton Act against contracts which take away freedom of purchasers to buy in an open market. Brown nevertheless contends that the Commission had no power to declare the franchise program unfair without proof that its effect "may be to substantially lessen competition or tend to create a monopoly" which of course would have to be proved if the Government were proceeding against Brown under § 3 of the Clayton Act rather than § 5 of the Federal Trade Commission Act. We reject the argument that proof of this § 3 element must be made for as we pointed out above our cases hold that the Commission has power under § 5 to arrest trade restraints in their incipiency without proof that they amount to an outright violation of § 3 of the Clayton Act or other provisions of the antitrust laws. This power of the Commission was emphatically stated in *FTC v. Motion Picture Advertising Co.*, 334 U.S. 392, at pp. 394–395:

It is . . . clear that the Federal Trade Commission Act was designed to supplement and bolster the Sherman Act and the Clayton Act . . . to stop in their incipiency acts and practices which, when full blown, would violate those Acts . . . as well as to condemn as "unfair methods of competition" existing violations of them.

We hold that the Commission acted well within its authority in declaring the Brown franchise program unfair whether it was completely full blown or not. [REVERSED]

4 UNFAIR OR DECEPTIVE TRADE PRACTICES

As was previously noted, in 1938 the Wheeler-Lee amendments to the Federal Trade Commission Act changed Section 5 so that in addition to outlawing unfair methods of competition, "unfair or deceptive acts or practices in commerce" are also prohibited. Thus, the FTC is empowered to issue cease and desist orders restraining acts or practices which are *deceptive or otherwise unfair to consumers,* in addition to those which are injurious to competition. In fact, the greater percentage of the cases of the Commission involve protecting the consumer from "unfair or deceptive" business practices. In determining which cases to select for formal action, the FTC has stated that it places "a high priority on those matters which relate to the basic necessities of life, and to situations in which the impact of false and misleading advertising, or other unfair and deceptive practices, falls with cruelest impact upon those least able to survive the consequences—the elderly and the poor."[2] Often the type of false advertising attacked by the FTC is designed to make a prospective purchaser believe he will be getting a "good deal" in terms of price if he buys the product in question. Such a price representation was in issue in *Giant Food Inc. v. FTC,*[3] in which the defendant was ordered to refrain from advertising its products for sale by use of a price comparison in which its actual price was compared to a higher "regular" price or a manufacturer's list price. The Commission ruled that it was deceptive to refer to "regular price" unless the defendant had usually sold the items at that price

[2] *Annual Report of the Federal Trade Commission,* 17 (1967).
[3] 322 F.2d 977 (1963), *cert. denied* 376 U.S. 967 (1963).

recently in the regular course of business. Also, it was held deceptive to refer to the "manufacturer's list price" when that list price was not the ordinary and customary retail sales price of the item in the locality. This was in spite of the fact that manufacturers themselves had suggested the retail prices to which the seller compared its lower selling price. In ordering enforcement of the Commission's cease and desist order, the Court of Appeals said, "We do not understand the Commission to hold that use of the term 'manufacturer's list price' is unlawful *per se;* rather it is unlawful only if it is not the usual and customary retail price in the area."

The case below also involved a type of price representation as a deceptive practice.

FTC v. Mary Carter Paint Co.
382 U.S. 46 (1965)

BRENNAN, JUSTICE: Respondent manufactures and sells paint and related products. The Federal Trade Commission ordered respondent to cease and desist from the use of certain representations found by the Commission to be deceptive and in violation of § 5 of the Federal Trade Commission Act. The representations appeared in advertisements which stated in various ways that for every can of respondent's paint purchased by a buyer, the respondent would give the buyer a "free" can of equal quality and quantity. The Court of Appeals for the Fifth Circuit set aside the Commission's order. We granted certiorari. We reverse.

Although there is some ambiguity in the Commission's opinion, we cannot say that its holding constituted a departure from Commission policy regarding the use of the commercially exploitable word "free." Initial efforts to define the term in decisions were followed by "Guides Against Deceptive Prices." These informed businessmen that they might advertise an article as "free," even though purchase of another article was required, so long as the terms of the offer were clearly stated, the price of the article required to be purchased was not increased, and its quality and quantity were not diminished. With specific reference to two-for-the-price-of-one offers, the Guides required that either the sales price for the two be "the advertiser's usual and customary retail price for the single article in the recent, regular course of his business," or where the advertiser has not previously sold the article, the price for two be the "usual and customary" price for one in the relevant trade areas. These, of course, were guides, not fixed rules as such, and were designed to inform businessmen of the factors which would guide Commission decisions. Although Mary Carter seems to have attempted to tailor its offer to come within their terms, the Commission found that it failed; the offer complied in appearance only.

The gist of the Commission's reasoning is in the hearing examiner's finding, which it adopted, that

. . . the usual and customary retail price of each can of Mary Carter paint was not, and is not now, the price designated in the advertisement ($6.98) but was,

and is now substantially less than such price. The second can of paint was not, and is not now, "free," that is, was not, and is not now, given as a gift of gratuity. The offer is, on the contrary, an offer of two cans of paint for the price advertised as or purporting to be the list price or customary and usual price of one can.

In sum, the Commission found that Mary Carter had no history of selling single cans of paint; it was marketing twins, and in allocating what is in fact the price of two cans to one can, yet calling one "free," Mary Carter misrepresented. It is true that respondent was not permitted to show that the quality of its paint matched those paints which usually and customarily sell in the $6.98 range, or that purchasers of paint estimate quality by the price they are charged. If both claims were established, it is arguable that any deception was limited to a representation that Mary Carter has a usual and customary price for single cans of paint, when it has no such price. However, it is not for courts to say whether this violates the Act. "[T]he Commission is often in a better position than are courts to determine when a practice is 'deceptive' within the meaning of the Act." There was substantial evidence in the record to support the Commission's finding; its determination that the practice here was deceptive was neither arbitrary nor clearly wrong. The Court of Appeals should have sustained it. . . .

Judgment of Court of Appeals reversed. . . . [REVERSED]

Similar to price representations which offer "free" goods for the purchase of others is a "bait-and-switch" promotion. Here, the seller intends to use a product advertised at a low price only as bait to capture the interest of consumers and then to switch their attention from it to products which the baiter really desired to sell from the beginning.

Besides involving misleading price representations, deceptive practices may result from fraudulent, false, or misleading advertising or other representations concerning the performance capability of goods or services being sold. The decision which follows illustrates this kind of representation as well as the limitations on the use of "mock-ups" for purposes of television commercials.

FTC v. Colgate-Palmolive Co.
380 U.S. 379 (1965)

WARREN, CHIEF JUSTICE: . . . [This] case arises out of an attempt by respondent Colgate-Palmolive Company to prove to the television public that its shaving cream, "Rapid Shave," outshaves them all. Respondent Ted Bates & Company, Inc., an advertising agency, prepared for Colgate three one-minute commercials designed to show that Rapid Shave could soften even the toughness of sandpaper. Each of the commercials contained the same "sandpaper test." The announcer informed the audience that, "To prove RAPID SHAVE'S super-moisturizing power, we put it right from the can onto this tough, dry sandpaper.

It was apply . . . soak . . . and off in a stroke." While the announcer was speaking, Rapid Shave was applied to a substance that appeared to be sandpaper, and immediately thereafter a razor was shown shaving the substance clean.

The Federal Trade Commission issued a complaint against respondents Colgate and Bates charging that the commercials were false and deceptive. The evidence before the hearing examiner disclosed that sandpaper of the type depicted in the commercials could not be shaved immediately following the application of Rapid Shave, but required a substantial soaking period of approximately 80 minutes. The evidence also showed that the substance resembling sandpaper was in fact a simulated prop, or "mock-up," made of plexiglass to which sand had been applied. However, the examiner found that Rapid Shave could shave sandpaper, even though not in the short time represented by the commercials, and that if real sandpaper had been used in the commercials the inadequacies of television transmission would have made it appear to viewers to be nothing more than plain, colored paper. The examiner dismissed the complaint because neither misrepresentation—concerning the actual moistening time or the identity of the shaved substance—was in his opinion a material one that would mislead the public.

The Commission . . . reversed the hearing examiner. It found that since Rapid Shave could not shave sandpaper within the time depicted in the commercials, respondents had misrepresented the product's moisturizing power. Moreover, the Commission found that the undisclosed use of a plexiglass substitute for sandpaper was an additional material misrepresentation that was a deceptive act separate and distinct from the misrepresentation concerning Rapid Shave's underlying qualities. Even if the sandpaper could be shaved just as depicted in the commercials, the Commission found that viewers had been misled into believing they had seen it done with their own eyes. As a result of these findings the Commission entered a cease-and-desist order against the respondents.

. . . The Court of Appeals . . . found unsatisfactory that portion of the order dealing with simulated props and refused to enforce it.

We granted certiorari . . .

. . . Both respondents were ordered to cease and desist from:

Unfairly or deceptively advertising any . . . product by presenting a test, experiment or demonstration that (1) is represented to the public as actual proof of a claim made for the product which is material to inducing its sale, and (2) is not in fact a genuine test, experiment or demonstration being conducted as represented and does not in fact constitute actual proof of the claim, because of the undisclosed use and substitution of a mock-up or prop instead of the product, article, or substance represented to be used therein. . . .

In reviewing the substantive issues in the case, it is well to remember the respective roles of the Commission and the courts in the administration of the Federal Trade Commission Act. When the Commission was created by Congress in 1914, it was directed by § 5 to prevent "[u]nfair methods of competition in commerce." Congress amended the Act in 1938 to extend the Commission's jurisdiction to include "unfair or deceptive acts or practices in commerce"—a significant amendment showing Congress' concern for consumers as well as for competitors. It is important to note the generality of these standards of illegality; the proscriptions in § 5 are flexible, "to be defined with particularity by the myriad of cases from the field of business."

This statutory scheme necessarily gives the Commission an influential role in interpreting § 5 and in applying it to the facts of particular cases arising out of unprecedented situations. Moreover, as an administrative agency which deals continually with cases in the area, the Commission is often in a better position than are courts to determine when a practice is "deceptive" within the meaning of the Act. This Court has frequently stated that the Commission's judgment is to be given great weight by reviewing courts. This admonition is especially true with respect to allegedly deceptive advertising since the finding of a § 5 violation in this field rests so heavily on inference and pragmatic judgment. Nevertheless, while informed judicial determination is dependent upon enlightenment gained from administrative experience, in the last analysis the words "deceptive practices" set forth a legal standard and they must get their final meaning from judicial construction. . . .

We granted certiorari to consider the Commission's conclusion that even if an advertiser has himself conducted a test, experiment or demonstration which he honestly believes will prove a certain product claim, he may not convey to television viewers the false impression that they are seeing the test, experiment or demonstration for themselves, when they are not because of the undisclosed use of mock-ups.

We accept the Commission's determination that the commercials involved in this case contained three representations to the public: (1) that sandpaper could be shaved by Rapid Shave; (2) that an experiment had been conducted which verified this claim; and (3) that the viewer was seeing this experiment for himself. . . . For the purposes of our review, we can assume that the first two representations were true; the focus of our consideration is on the third which was clearly false. The parties agree that § 5 prohibits the intentional misrepresentation of any fact which would constitute a material factor in a purchaser's decision whether to buy. They differ, however, in their conception of what "facts" constitute a "material factor" in a purchaser's decision to buy. Respondents submit, in effect, that the only material facts are those which deal with the substantive qualities of a product. The Commission on the other hand, submits that the misrepresentation of *any* fact so long as it materially induces a purchaser's decision to buy is a deception prohibited by § 5.

The Commission's interpretation of what is a deceptive practice seems more in line with the decided cases than that of respondents. . . . It has long been considered a deceptive practice to state falsely that a product ordinarily sells for an inflated price but that it is being offered at a special reduced price, even if the offered price represents the actual value of the product and the purchaser is receiving his money's worth. Applying respondents' arguments to these cases, it would appear that so long as buyers paid no more than the product was actually worth and the product contained the qualities advertised, the misstatement of an inflated original price was immaterial.

It has also been held a violation of § 5 for a seller to misrepresent to the public that he is in a certain line of business, even though the misstatement in no way affects the qualities of the product. . . .

Respondents claim that all these cases are irrelevant to our decision because they involve misrepresentations related to the product itself and not merely to the manner in which an advertising message is communicated. This distinction misses the mark for two reasons. In the first place, the present case is not concerned with a mode of communication, but with a misrepresentation that viewers have objective proof of a seller's product claim over and above the seller's word. Secondly, all of the above cases, like the present case, deal with methods designed to get a consumer to purchase a product, not with whether the product, when purchased, will perform up to expectations.

We agree with the Commission, therefore, that the undisclosed use of plexiglass in the present commercials was a material deceptive practice, independent and separate from the other misrepresentation found. . . . Respondents claim that it will be impractical to inform the viewing public that it is not seeing an actual test, experiment or demonstration, but we think it inconceivable that the ingenious advertising world will be unable, if it so desires, to conform to the Commission's insistence that the public be not misinformed. If, however, it becomes impossible or impractical to show simulated demonstrations on television in a truthful manner, this indicates that television is not a medium that lends itself to this type of commercial, not that the commercial must survive at all costs. Similarly unpersuasive is respondents' objection that the Commission's decision discriminates against sellers whose product claims cannot be "verified" on television without the use of simulations. All methods of advertising do not equally favor every seller. If the inherent limitations of a method do not permit its use in the way a seller desires, the seller cannot by material misrepresentation compensate for those limitations. . . .

We turn our attention now to the order issued by the Commission. It has been repeatedly held that the Commission has wide discretion in determining the type of order that is necessary to cope with the unfair practices found, and that Congress has placed the primary responsibility for fashioning orders upon the Commission. For these reasons the courts should not "lightly modify" the Commission's orders. However, this Court has also warned that an order's prohibitions "should be clear and precise in order that they may be understood by those against whom they are directed," and that "[t]he severity of possible penalties prescribed . . . for violations of orders which have become final underlines the necessity for fashioning orders which are, at the outset, sufficiently clear and precise to avoid raising serious questions as to their meaning and application."

The Court of Appeals has criticized the reference in the Commission's order to "test, experiment or demonstration" as not capable of practical interpretation.

It could find no difference between the Rapid Shave commercial and a commercial which extolled the goodness of ice cream while giving viewers a picture of a scoop of mashed potatoes appearing to be ice cream. We do not understand this difficulty. In the ice cream case the mashed potato prop is not being used for additional proof of the product claim, while the purpose of the Rapid Shave commercial is to give the viewer objective proof of the claims made. If in the ice cream hypothetical the focus of the commercial becomes the undisclosed potato prop and the viewer is invited, explicitly or by implication, to see for himself the truth of the claims about the ice cream's rich texture and full color, and perhaps compare it to a "rival product," then the commercial has become similar to the one now before us. Clearly, however, a commercial which depicts happy actors delightedly eating ice cream that is in fact mashed potatoes or drinking a product appearing to be coffee but which is in fact some other substance is not covered by the present order.

The crucial terms of the present order—"test, experiment or demonstration . . . represented . . . as actual proof of a claim"—are as specific as the circumstances will permit. If respondents in their subsequent commercials attempt to come as close to the line of misrepresentation as the Commission's order permits, they may without specifically intending to do so cross into the area proscribed by this order. However, it does not seem "unfair to require that one who deliberately goes perilously close to an area of proscribed conduct shall take the risk that he may cross the line." In commercials where the emphasis is on the seller's word, and not on the viewer's own perception, the respondents need not fear that an undisclosed use of props is prohibited by the present order. On the other hand, when the commercial not only makes a claim, but also invites the viewer to rely on his own perception, for demonstrative proof of the claim, the respondents will be aware that the use of undisclosed props in strategic places might be a material deception. We believe that respondents will have no difficulty applying the Commission's order to the vast majority of their contemplated future commercials. If, however, a situation arises in which respondents are sincerely unable to determine whether a proposed course of action would violate the present order, they can, by complying with the Commission's rules, oblige the Commission to give them definite advice as to whether their proposed action, if pursued, would constitute compliance with the order.

Finally, we find no defect in the provision of the order which prohibits respondents from engaging in similar practices with respect to "any product" they advertise. The propriety of a broad order depends upon the specific circumstances of the case, but the courts will not interfere except where the remedy selected has no reasonable relation to the unlawful practices found to exist. In this case the respondents produced three different commercials which employed the same deceptive practice. This we believe gave the Commission a sufficient basis for believing that the respondents would be inclined to use similar commercials with respect to the other products they advertise. We think it reasonable for the Commission to frame its order broadly enough to prevent respondents from engaging in similarly illegal practices in future advertisements. As was said in *FTC v. Ruberoid Co.*, 343 U.S. 470: "[T]he Commission is not limited to prohibiting the illegal practice in the precise form in which it is found to have existed in the past." Having been caught violating the Act, respondents "must expect some fencing in."

The judgment of the Court of Appeals is reversed and the case remanded for the entry of a judgment enforcing the Commission's order. [REVERSED AND REMANDED]

False representations of the composition, quality, character, or source of products, by misbranding or otherwise, have been barred as deceptively misleading. For example, lumber dealers have been barred from advertising under names such as "California White Pine" and "Western White Pine" when their products were inferior to genuine "White Pine," even though these terms were accepted and understood in the trade.[4] Other cases falling into this category of violation are one in which a seller suggested that a beauty aid "restored natural moisture necessary for a lively healthy skin," a claim which was false,[5] and one in which cigars made of domestic tobacco were labeled "Havana."[6]

False statements which neither misrepresent a product or its price have also been ruled unfair or deceptive. Typical of these is one in which a product is endorsed by one who is misrepresented to be a "doctor" or "scientific expert." Disparaging the goods of others in an attempt to promote the sale of one's own is also an unfair practice. For example, the FTC restrained a manufacturer of stainless steel cooking utensils from publishing questions like "Do you know that aluminum pans may be full of the most deadly bacteria known to science?" and "Did you ever find maggots in your aluminum pans?"[7]

Other cases have involved no actual misstatement but representations which, while true in themselves, were intended to mislead. Using a word while having a hidden or unusual interpretation in mind for the purpose of promoting sales is an example. If a manufacturer states that his product is "guaranteed for life," most persons would probably believe that the guarantee was to run for the life of the purchaser. However, Parker Pen Company used this phrase in its advertising with the undisclosed intention that the lives in question were those of the pens they manufactured, thus making the statement a nullity. Parker was restrained from making such "guarantees."[8]

The use of the technique of product name simulation is also unfair. This occurs when a manufacturer or seller uses either the same name or one that is deceptively similar to another product of another manufacturer which has acquired consumer acceptance. This conduct, whether undertaken with the intent of exploiting the goodwill of a competitor or not, may confuse consumers. If the

---

[4] *FTC v. Algoma Lumber Co.*, 291 U.S. 67 (1934).
[5] *Ritz Distrib. Corp. v. FTC*, 143 F.2d 89 (1962).
[6] *El Moro Cigar Co. v. FTC*, 107 F.2d 429 (1939).
[7] *Perma-Maid Co. v. FTC*, 121 F.2d 282 (1941).
[8] *Parker Pen Co. v. FTC*, 149 F.2d 509 (1946).

name selected is close enough to that of the established product, its use may be restrained by the FTC as being deceptive.

Even silence by a seller may result in deception of consumers, and the Commission may require that positive disclosures be made before further sales of the goods in question are permissible. For example, nondisclosure that books published were abridged or condensed was ruled as deceptive. In addition, distributing secondhand or rebuilt goods without indicating them as such and selling foreign goods without disclosing their origin have been restrained by the Commission in its efforts to protect consumers from unfair or deceptive trade practices.

5 THE EXTENT OF THE FTC'S POWER

It is clear from the foregoing discussions that a particular business activity may be prohibited by the FTC if it amounts to an "unfair method of competition" or an "unfair or deceptive act or practice." However, the question remains as to whether it is the province of the Federal courts to ultimately define the legislative intent of Congress in using the term "unfair," or whether the power to do so is that of the FTC. As has been noted, Congress itself did not undertake to define the terms it used in Section 5 of the FTC Act. Further, that section does not expressly refer to a "relevant market" or "line of commerce" and does not expressly restrict the prohibited trade practices to those whose effect "may be substantially to lessen competition or tend to create a monopoly" as Sections 2, 3, and 7 of the Clayton Act do. Justice Black's words in *FTC v. Brown Shoe Co.*, 384 U.S. 316 (1966), bear repeating here: ". . . the Commission has broad power to declare trade practices unfair. This broad power is particularly well established with regard to trade practices which conflict with the basic *policies* of the Sherman and Clayton Acts *even though such practices may not actually violate these laws.*" (Emphasis added.) Thus, the Commission may outlaw practices which it feels are injurious to competition but do not exactly fall within the categories of activities proscribed by the other antitrust laws.

In the case which follows, the Commission attacked a business arrangement as being unfair under Section 5. The practice in question was not a tying lease or sale within the meaning of Section 3 of the Clayton Act, but did bear some resemblance to tying arrangements. The case illustrates the broad powers of the Commission and the deference given by courts to the decisions of the Commission.

Atlantic Ref. Co. v. FTC
381 U.S. 357 (1965)

CLARK, JUSTICE: The Federal Trade Commission has found that an agreement between the Atlantic Refining Company (Atlantic) and the Goodyear Tire & Rubber Company (Goodyear), under which the former "sponsors" the sale of the tires, batteries and accessory products of the latter to its wholesale outlets and its retail service station dealers, is an unfair method of competition in violation of § 5 of the Federal Trade Commission Act. Under the plan Atlantic sponsors the sale of Goodyear products to its wholesale and retail outlets on an overall commission basis. Goodyear is responsible for its sales and sells at its own price to Atlantic wholesalers and dealers for resale; it bears all of the cost of distribution through its warehouses, stores and other supply points and carries on a joint sales promotion program with Atlantic. The latter, however, is primarily responsible for promoting the sale of Goodyear products to its dealers and assisting them in their resale; for this it receives a commission on all sales made to its wholesalers and dealers. The hearing examiner, with the approval of the Commission and the Court of Appeals, enjoined the use of direct methods of coercion on the part of Atlantic toward its dealers in the inauguration and promotion of the plan. Atlantic does not seek review of this phase of the case. However, the Commission considered the coercive practices to be symptomatic of a more fundamental restraint of trade and found the sales-commission plan illegal in itself as "a classic example of the use of economic power in one market . . . to destroy competition in another market. . . ." It prohibited Atlantic from participating in any such commission arrangement. Similarly, it forbade Goodyear from continuing the arrangement with Atlantic or any other oil company. Goodyear and Atlantic filed separate appeals. The Court of Appeals approved the findings of the Commission and affirmed its order. "Appraising the broader aspects of the system (used by Atlantic and Goodyear) as a tying arrangement," it agreed with the Commission that it injured "competition in the distribution of tires, batteries and accessories at the manufacturing, wholesale, and retail levels." We granted certiorari. . . .

The Goodyear-Atlantic agreement required Atlantic to assist Goodyear "to the fullest practicable extent in perfecting sales, credit, and merchandising arrangements" with all of Atlantic's outlets. This included announcement to its dealers of its sponsorship of Goodyear products followed by a field representative's call to "suggest . . . the maintenance of adequate stocks of merchandise" and "maintenance of proper identification and advertising" of such merchandise. Atlantic was to instruct its salesmen to urge dealers to "vigorously" represent Goodyear, and to "cooperate with and assist" Goodyear in its "efforts to promote and increase the sale" by Atlantic dealers of Goodyear products. And it was to "maintain adequate dealer training programs in the sales of tires, batteries and accessories." In addition, the companies organized joint sales organization meetings at which plans were made for perfecting the sales plan. One project was a "double teaming" solicitation of Atlantic outlets by representatives of both companies to convert them to Goodyear products. They were to call on the dealers together, take stock orders, furnish initial price lists and project future quotas of purchases of Goodyear products. Goodyear also required that each Atlantic dealer be assigned to a supply point maintained by it, such as a warehouse, Goodyear store, independent dealer or designated Atlantic distributor or retail dealer. Atlantic would not receive any commission on purchases made outside of an assigned supply point. Its commission of 10% on sales to Atlantic dealers and 7.5% on sales to its wholesalers was paid on the basis of a master sheet prepared by Goodyear and furnished Atlantic each month. . . .

Section 5 of the Federal Trade Commission Act declares "[u]nfair methods of competition in commerce, and unfair . . . acts or practices in commerce . . . unlawful." In a broad delegation of power it empowers the Commission, in the first instance, to determine whether a method of competition or the act or practice complained of is unfair. The Congress intentionally left development of the term "unfair" to the Commission rather than attempting to define "the many and variable unfair practices which prevail in commerce. . . ." . . . As the House Report stated, unfair competition could best be prevented "through the action of an administrative body of practical men . . . who will be able to apply the rule enacted by Congress to particular business situations, so as to eradicate evils with the least risk of interfering with legitimate business operations." H.R.Rep. No. 1142, 63d Cong., 2d Sess., 19 (conference report). In thus divining that there is no limit to business ingenuity and legal gymnastics the Congress displayed much foresight. . . . Where the Congress has provided that an administrative agency initially apply a broad statutory term to a particular situation, our function is limited to determining whether the Commission's decision "has 'warrant in the record' and a reasonable basis in law." While the final word is left to the courts, necessarily "we give great weight to the Commission's conclusion. . . ."

Certainly there is "warrant in the record" for the findings of the Commission here. Substantial evidence supports the conclusion that notwithstanding Atlantic's contention that it and its dealers are mutually dependent upon each other, they simply do not bargain as equals. . . .

With this background in mind, we consider whether there was a "reasonable basis in law" for the Commission's ultimate conclusion that the sales-commission plan constituted an unfair method of competition.

At the outset we must stress what we do not find present here. We recognize that the Goodyear-Atlantic contract is not a tying arrangement. . . . As our cases hold, all that is necessary in § 5 proceedings to find a violation is to discover conduct that "runs counter to the public policy declared in the Act." But this is of necessity, and was intended to be, a standard to which the Commission would give substance. In doing so, its use as a guideline of recognized violations of the antitrust laws was, we believe, entirely appropriate. It has long been recognized that there are many unfair methods of competition that do not assume the proportions of antitrust violations. When conduct does bear the characteristics of recognized antitrust violations it becomes suspect, and the Commission may properly look to cases applying those laws for guidance.

Although the Commission relied on such cases here, it expressly rejected a mechanical application of the law of tying arrangements. Rather it looked to the entire record as a basis for its conclusion that the activity of Goodyear and Atlantic impaired competition at three levels of the tires, batteries and accessories industry. It found that wholesalers and manufacturers of competing brands, and even Goodyear wholesalers who were not authorized supply points, were foreclosed from the Atlantic market. In addition, it recognized the obvious fact that

Firestone and Goodyear were excluded from selling to Atlantic's dealers in each other's territories. Both of these effects on competition flowed from the contract itself. It also found that the plight of Atlantic wholesalers and retailers was equally clear. They had to compete with other wholesalers and retailers who were free to stock several brands, but they were effectively foreclosed from selling brands other than Goodyear. This restraint is in this respect broader than the one found in *International Salt Co. v. United States*, 332 U.S. 392, where the dealers could stock other salt if they could buy it at lower prices. Here the dealers could buy only at Goodyear's price.

Thus the Commission was warranted in finding that the effect of the plan was *as though* Atlantic had agreed with Goodyear to require its dealers to buy Goodyear products and had done so. It is beyond question that the effect on commerce was not insubstantial. . . .

Goodyear and Atlantic contend that the Commission should have made a far more extensive economic analysis of the competitive effect of the sales-commission plan, examining the entire market in tires, batteries and accessories. But just as the effect of this plan is similar to that of a tie-in, so is it unnecessary to embark upon a full-scale economic analysis of competitive effect. We think it enough that the Commission found that a not insubstantial portion of commerce is affected. . . .

Nor can we say that the Commission erred in refusing to consider evidence of economic justification for the program. While these contracts may well provide Atlantic with an economical method of assuring efficient product distribution among its dealers they also amount to a device that permits suppliers of tires, batteries and accessories, through the use of oil company power, to effectively sew up large markets. Upon considering the destructive effect on commerce that would result from the widespread use of these contracts by major oil companies and suppliers, we conclude that the Commission was clearly justified in refusing the participants an opportunity to offset these evils by a showing of economic benefit to themselves.

The short of it is that Atlantic with Goodyear's encouragement and assistance, has marshaled its full economic power in a continuing campaign to force its dealers and wholesalers to buy Goodyear products. The anticompetitive effects of this program are clear on the record and render unnecessary extensive economic analysis of market percentages or business justifications in determining whether this was a method of competition which Congress has declared unfair and therefore unlawful. . . . [AFFIRMED]

The foregoing case exemplifies the deference the Court displays to the judgment of the Commission when it comes to defining what business practices are "unfair." It is clear that in this area, the Court is very hesitant to substitute its judgment (or to permit the Circuit Courts of Appeal to substitute their judgments) for that of the Commission.

The question posed by the case which follows is the extent to which the Circuit Court of Appeals may encroach upon the power of the FTC by postponing the operation of one of its cease and desist orders. In it, the appellate court delayed the effective date of the Commission's order and instructed it to conduct an investigation of alleged industry-wide violations of the price discrimination provisions of Section 2 of the Clayton Act. The Supreme Court granted certiorari on petition by the FTC.

FTC v. Universal-Rundle Corporation
87 S.Ct. 1622 (1967)

WARREN, CHIEF JUSTICE: . . . Respondent Universal-Rundle produces a full line of china and cast-iron plumbing fixtures which it sells to customers located throughout the United States. In 1960, the Federal Trade Commission issued a complaint charging that for more than three years Universal-Rundle's sales to some of these customers had been made "at substantially higher prices than the prices at which respondent sells such products of like brand and quality to other purchasers, some of whom are engaged in competition with the less favored purchasers in the resale of such products." The effect of the discriminations, the complaint alleged, "may be to substantially lessen competition" in violation of § 2(a) of the Clayton Act, as amended. In its answer, Universal-Rundle denied the essential allegations of the complaint. . . .

After evidentiary hearings . . . the Commission found that during 1957 Universal-Rundle had offered "truckload discounts" averaging approximately 10% to all of its customers. Because some of these customers could not afford to purchase in truckload quantities, and thus were unable to avail themselves of the discounts, the Commission held that the offering of the truckload discounts constituted price discrimination within the meaning of § 2(a) of the Clayton Act, as amended. Since some Universal-Rundle customers who were able to purchase in truckload quantities were found to be in competition with customers unable to take advantage of the discounts, the Commission concluded that Universal-Rundle's price discrimination had the anticompetitive effect proscribed by § 2(a). . . .

[O]ne month after the issuance of the cease-and-desist order, Universal-Rundle petitioned the Commission to stay its cease-and-desist order for a time sufficient "to investigate and institute whatever proceedings are deemed appropriate by the Commission to correct the industry-wide practice by plumbing fixture manufacturers of granting discounts in prices on truckload shipments." In support of its petition, Universal-Rundle submitted affidavits and documents tending to show (1) that its principal competitors were offering truckload discounts averaging approximately 18%; (2) that Universal-Rundle's share of the plumbing fixture market, exclusive of its sales to Sears, Roebuck and Co., was 5.75% whereas the five leading plumbing manufacturing concerns enjoyed market shares of 6 to 32%; and (3) that each of these five competitors had reported profits within the preceding two years whereas Universal-Rundle had sustained substantial losses during each of the preceding three years. . . .

In a unanimous decision denying the petition for the stay, the Commission held that a general allegation that competitors were offering truckload discounts was not a sufficient basis for instituting industry-wide proceedings or for withholding enforcement of the cease-and-desist order. . . . "Moreover," the Commission wrote, "the fact that respondent may have incurred losses prior to the issuance of the order does not support the contention that enforcement of the order will cause it financial hardship."

Following denial of its petition for a stay, Universal-Rundle instituted review proceedings in the Court of Appeals for the Seventh Circuit. Without reaching the merits of the petition to set aside the cease-and-desist order, the court below set aside the Commission's order denying the stay and remanded the cause with instructions that the Commission conduct an industry investigation. The court conceded that under *Moog Industries v. Federal Trade Commission*, 355 U.S. 411 (1958), the Federal Trade Commission's discretionary determination to refuse to stay a cease-and-desist order "should not be overturned in the absence of a patent abuse of discretion." But it considered that Universal-Rundle's evidentiary offering was sufficient to demonstrate that the refusal to grant the requested stay constituted a patent abuse of discretion. The premises upon which the court below based its conclusion may be briefly restated: (1) "it is apparent," the court wrote with reference to the evidentiary offering, "that the Commission has directed its attack against a general practice which is prevalent in the industry"; (2) enforcement would lead to the "sacrifice" of one of the "smallest participants" in the industry; and, consequently, (3) approval of the enforcement sanctions would be contrary to the purposes of the Clayton Act since "the giants in the field would be the real benefactors—not the public."

In *Moog Industries v. Federal Trade Commission, supra*, we set forth the principles which must govern our review of the action taken by the court below: The decision as to whether to postpone enforcement of a cease-and-desist order "depends upon a variety of factors peculiarly within the expert understanding of the Commission." Thus, "although an allegedly illegal practice may appear to be operative throughout an industry, whether such appearances reflect fact" is a question "that call[s] for discretionary determination by the administrative agency." Because these determinations require the specialized experienced judgment of the Commission, they cannot be overturned by the courts "in the absence of a patent abuse of discretion." Consequently, the reviewing court's inquiry is not whether the evidence adduced in support of a petition for a stay tends to establish certain facts, such as that the industry is engaged in allegedly illegal price discrimination practices; rather, the court's review must be limited to determining whether the Commission's evaluation of the merit of the petition for a stay was patently arbitrary and capricious.

Viewed in the light of these principles, the decision below must be reversed. . . . Universal-Rundle's truckload discounts were held to be illegal only because the corporation sold fixtures to one group of customers who were unable to purchase in truckload quantities while simultaneously selling fixtures at a discount to another group of customers who were in competition with the nonfavored group. Since the evidence presented in the petition for a stay did not tend to show that the discounts offered by Universal-Rundle's competitors had such an anticompetitive effect, there was no basis for a conclusion that the practice held illegal by the Commission was prevalent throughout the plumbing industry. . . . It follows that Universal-Rundle has failed to demonstrate that enforcement would be contrary to the purposes of the Clayton Act.

We note that even if a petitioner succeeded in demonstrating to the Commission that all of its competitors were engaged in illegal price-discrimination practices identical to its own, and that enforcement of a cease-and-desist order might cause it substantial financial injury, the Commission would not necessarily be obliged to withhold enforcement of the order. As we stated in *Moog Industries:*

It is clearly within the special competence of the Commission to appraise the adverse effect on competition that might result from postponing a particular order prohibiting continued violations of the law. Furthermore, the Commission alone is empowered to develop the enforcement policy best calculated to achieve the ends contemplated by Congress and to allocate its available funds and personnel in such a way as to execute its policy efficiently and economically.

On the other hand, as the *Moog Inudstries* case also indicates, the Federal Trade Commission does not have unbridled power to institute proceedings which will arbitrarily destroy one of many law violators in an industry. This is not such a case. The Commission's refusal to withhold enforcement of the cease-and-desist order against respondent was based upon a reasonable evaluation of the merits of the petition for a stay; thus it was not within the scope of the reviewing authority of the court below to overthrow the Commission's determination. Consequently, we reverse the judgment below, set aside the stay, and remand the cause for further proceedings consistent with this opinion. It is so ordered. [REVERSED AND REMANDED]

Commenting on the intent of Congress regarding the scope of authority it granted the FTC, the Court in *Grand Union Co. v. FTC* stated that the purpose was "to give the Commission power to hit at *every trade practice, then existing or thereafter contrived,* which restrained competition or *might lead* to such restraint." [9] (Emphasis added.)

6 CRITICISMS OF THE FEDERAL TRADE COMMISSION

In spite of (or perhaps because of) the broad range of power granted to the FTC, many persons for some time have felt that it has failed to fulfill its twofold mission of preserving competition and protecting consumers. Most of the criticisms leveled at the Commission were summarized in the late 1960s in the reports of two

[9] 300 F.2d 92 (1962).

studies—one made by the American Bar Association and the other by a group headed by the consumer advocate and lawyer Ralph Nader.

The American Bar Association Commission Report was made at the request of President Nixon by sixteen lawyers and economists, who described the FTC as being a model of bureaucratic inertia and timidity which was torn with internal dissension, and concluded that it needed a complete overhauling. Among other things, the report noted that the FTC was suffering from the operation of "Parkinson's Law" in that it apparently had been doing less with more people. In 1962, it opened up 1,795 investigations of alleged abuses of the law by businesses but in 1968 commenced only 611. Yet in this same period, the Commission's staff increased by over 100 from 1,126 to 1,230.

In addition, the report noted that those cases which the FTC had undertaken often involved trivial matters. For example, the FTC attacked the label on an 89.9% wool blanket which stated 90% Wool" and the label on fur from South Africa which abbreviated the origin to "S. W. Africa." The report charged that indeed too much effort had been spent on fur and textile labels. At the same time, it noted, the Commission had done little or nothing at all to screen local TV and radio commercials for fraudulent or misleading practices. This was in spite of the fact that the Commission had an Office of Program Review charged with the responsibility of setting priorities.

A third criticism leveled in the ABA report cited an apparent lack of enforcement. The report noted that there had been a shift in emphasis from the issuing of cease and desist orders to a reliance on voluntary compliance such as merely securing written—or frequently only oral—promises from businesses that they would discontinue deceptive practices. For example, the Commission only issued guidelines concerning gas station prize games instead of forbidding them outright. Among the conclusions reported by the ABA committee was that many of the FTC staff members were incompetent. To explain this trend toward incompetence, it was noted that one of the senior staff members preferred to hire lawyers who had been in practice for ten years or so and who realized that they were not going to be much of a success on their own. These were favored over recent graduates because the older, unsuccessful lawyer tended to be loyal to the FTC and more of them remained with it.

It is not surprising that there is a degree of similarity in the criticisms leveled at the FTC by the Nader report and the ABA group's report. For one thing, Nader and "Nader's Raiders" (which his volunteer group of law students and graduates has been called) charged misdirection of the activities of the Commission's staff and inactivity in important areas. Particularly stressed was Commission inactivity in the area of deceptive advertising. The Nader report noted that detergent makers were mislabeling old products by calling them new, that certain menthol cigarette ads were implying that smoking their brand was similar to "fresh air, spring, and cool mountain brooks," and that a manufacturer claimed that butchers could not distinguish between his dog food and table beef (implying it was fit for human consumption)—all without interference by the FTC. The report also concluded that the Commission did not display enough concern for consumers, while often permitting questionable activities of large corporations to go unchallenged. In reaching such a conclusion, the Nader report said that the Commission was permitting flagrant violations of the law to exist, specifically stating that the FTC "has failed to detect violations systematically," and "has failed to establish efficient priorities for its enforcement energy."

Second, Nader was critical, as was the ABA group, of the trend of the FTC to rely on voluntary codes and compliance instead of prosecuting through formal hearings. Third, Nader also noted that the FTC staff contained too many persons at the top and that many of these were ineffective and had overlapping and conflicting duties. His report stated that some of the agency's members were guilty of "alcoholism, spectacular lassitude and office absenteeism, incompetence by the most modest standards, and lack of commitment." He noted that the FTC staff included an unusually high number of top-grade, well-paying civil service positions, which were used for patronage purposes and often filled by assistants of retiring congressional leaders. The report further stated that former Chairman Paul Dixon had gone so far as to open a branch office of the FTC in Oak Ridge so that an old friend of his who was washed up in local politics would have a conveniently located job.

Among the other points made by the Nader report was a charge that the actions of the FTC were too mindful of politics and motivated by political considerations. It claimed that due to political manipulation, an FTC report on auto warranties was withheld "at least until after the election [of 1968], to avoid alienating Henry Ford II and other business interests who were contributing to Hubert Humphrey's campaign." Nader also hit the failure of the Commission to follow up and effectively check on compliance with its consent orders. His report noted that the FTC did require companies to report in writing every six months with regard to their compliance but questioned the effectiveness of this procedure. The Nader report further stated that "the FTC has failed to enforce the powers it has with energy and speed" and that "the FTC had failed to seek sufficient statutory authority to make its work effective."

Criticisms of the past operation of the FTC have also come from other sources and have concerned other matters. For one thing, there has been all too often a protracted delay in granting relief because of the cumbersome procedures employed by the agency. The lack of fast, efficient enforcement has resulted in a backlog of cases and in the impossibility of effectively granting relief in some. Advertising cases, often involving seemingly endless scientific testimony, may take years to litigate to a final order. Meanwhile, advertisers may change their campaigns in many different ways, or keep employing the one being challenged. It took the FTC sixteen years to require the manufacturer of Carter's Little Liver Pills to drop "Liver" from the advertising and labeling of this product. In merger challenges, by the time the case has passed through all the Commission's machinery, it is often too late for relief of any value to be ordered so that a tendency toward monopoly can be averted. In this interim, the assets involved often have become so intertwined or the competitive situation has changed to such an extent that practical action is difficult. The suggestion has been made that the field of activity of the Commission is so broad and undefined and its discretionary power so great that these factors keep it from formulating rules which are sound and recognizable.

Of course, many recommendations have been made as a result of the criticisms of the FTC, and some of them have been implemented. Among those that are still under consideration are the following: that the judicial function of the FTC be transferred to a "Trade Court"; that special offices of the FTC be set up in ten major cities to carry on a model program for law enforcement; that legislation be passed to enable consumers to bring a class action for damages against a violator of the law on the basis of a Commission holding; that the FTC be authorized to obtain preliminary injunctions against deceptive practices which it has challenged; and that the FTC leave routine cases of antitrust violations to the Justice Department if it has jurisdiction, thus allowing the Commission to concentrate on the more novel and complicated ones.

7 CONTEMPORARY ASPECTS OF THE FTC

In spite of the criticism of the FTC's heavy reliance on notice and voluntary compliance with its policies rather than on the more time-consuming and expensive formal hearing process, it appears that the Commission will continue this approach to the enforcement of the antitrust laws.

Many and diverse kinds of trade regulation rules have been adopted or proposed by the FTC. For example, the *"Games of Chance in the Food Retailing and Gasoline Industry"* regulation establishes requirements which must be met when games of chance are used as promotional devices. This rule requires users of such games in the food retailing and gasoline industries to clearly disclose in their advertising the exact number of prizes available and the odds of winning each prize with a value of $25 or more. The odds stated must be revised each week the game extends over thirty days, so that they will reflect the odds then existing. Among other things, advertisers may not terminate any game (regardless of its announced schedule) before distributing all game prizes to the public, and may not add new game prizes during the course of a contest. Any violation is an unfair and deceptive trade practice.

Recently *proposed* rules include one which would prohibit retail food stores from advertising merchandise for sale at a stated price and failing to make it conspicuously available for sale at or below the advertised price in any store in the area where the advertisement was disseminated. The FTC also has suggested a rule which would require that textile products have a permanently attached label containing clear and proper instructions for their laundering and cleaning. Still another proposal of the Commission would require clear and prominent disclosure of the tar and nicotine content per cigarette in all advertising of any particular brand of cigarettes.

To further illustrate the new active role of the FTC, it has recently proposed a rule which would not only alter a business practice long accepted as perfectly legitimate but, in effect, amount to the Commission's amending the private law of practically every state. Under the Uniform Commercial Code, a good-faith purchaser before maturity of commercial paper, such as a check or a note, may collect on it even if the drawer or maker has certain defenses against the payee to whom he issued it. This is known as the "holder-in-due-course principle." For example, assume seller delivers goods to buyer for which buyer gives his installment note in payment. Seller then indorses the note to bank, which pays seller for it. Even if the goods are so defective that they are useless to buyer, he will have to pay the holder-in-due-course bank, as agreed in the note, assuming that bank was not aware of the defect when it purchased the note. Buyer's remedy under the law is to sue seller for damages for breach of contract. If the debtor's obligation were a simple contract instead of a negotiable instrument, the transfer would not give any assignee such as bank better rights than seller had. The reason the law gives a holder in due course his superior position is to permit commercial paper to pass more freely from hand to hand in the economy as a substitute for money. The proposed FTC rule in question would change this by preserving buyers' claims and defenses in *consumer* installment sales. In such sales where the buyer executes a promissory note, it would require the following to appear on the face of the note in ten-point boldface type: *"NOTICE: Any holder of this instrument takes this instrument subject to all defenses and claims of the maker hereof which would be available to the maker in any action arising out of the contract which gave rise to the execution of this instrument, notwithstanding any agreement to the contrary."* The rule also would prohibit a waiver by the buyer in the sales contract itself of any of his claims or defenses arising out of the sale.

Other proposed rules include the regulation of door-to-door sales, new-automobile pricing practices, and private vocational and home study schools.

While the foregoing trade regulation rules are only proposed as of this writing, it can be expected that most if not all of them will be promulgated by the FTC substantially as initially worded.

In other action, the Commission has stated that under its investigating powers to require businesses to submit evidence and information, it would require documented proof of advertising claims in regard to the safety, performance, efficacy, quality, or comparative price of products being advertised. Although the FTC started with the automobile industry, because that industry has a very large advertising budget and purchasing an auto requires a substantial investment, the Commission indicated that it planned to cover all major industries which engage in advertising. In its resolution, the FTC stated that "[p]ublic disclosure can enhance competition by encouraging competitors to challenge advertised claims which have no basis in fact. . . . The knowledge that documentation or the lack thereof will be made public will encourage advertisers to have on hand adequate substantiation before claims are made."

Of course, the FTC also has continued to utilize the formal complaint and hearing procedure. In one recent case, complaints were filed against Mattel, Inc., and Topper Corp. because they had made advertising suggestions that playing with their toys gave more enjoyment than the Commission believed it actually did. In so doing, the FTC embarked upon a new program to protect consumers from deceptive or misleading advertising. In the past, the literal truth of advertising claims was considered a defense to a charge of deceptive advertising. Under its new policy, the Commission also will consider the educational level and sophistication of the audience at whom the advertising is aimed, in determining whether it might be deceptive to that particular group or not. The FTC's chief of consumer protection stated that the Commission would be more strict in challenging advertising directed at those who are "more vulnerable because they are sick, or bald, or unmarried at 45."

The FTC has been responsive to many of the prior criticisms of it and has become more active in policing the business community. The Commission's activities will have a substantial effect on the marketing process and will continue to be a major factor in the legal environment of business.

REVIEW QUESTIONS—CHAPTER 13

1 Define the following terms introduced in this chapter: unfair method of competition; cease and desist order; Truth-in-Lending; consent order; hearing examiner; advisory opinion; trade regulation rule; deceptive trade practice; bait-and-switch.

2 What are the most important functions of the Federal Trade Commission?

3 What is a cease and desist order, and how is it used by the FTC?

4 Trace a case through the FTC procedures from the filing of the complaint to the final decision.

5 What is the penalty for violating a cease and desist order of the FTC?

6 What is a consent order, and how is it used by the FTC?

7 What are the advantages to the business community of consent orders?

8 Explain how the FTC uses advisory opinions and trade regulation rules to accomplish its function.

9 Give five examples of unfair methods of competition.

10 Give five examples of deceptive trade practices.

11 Are all TV advertising mock-ups illegal? Explain.

12 How much latitude does the FTC have in correcting unfair methods of competition and deceptive practices? Explain.

13 Discuss some of the criticisms that were leveled against the FTC in the late 1960s and early 1970s, and note the extent to which such criticisms have led to changes and improvements in the agency.

14 Does the FTC have the authority to require documented proof of advertising claims as a condition for allowing an ad to continue to be used?

Chapter Fourteen

The Law of Employment

1 INTRODUCTION

This and the following chapter will examine the legal problems which arise as a result of the fact that a business usually employs people to carry on its work. In many ways, people are the most important single factor in the conduct of a business, and in the social sense they are the very reason for its existence. Corporations, being intangible legal entities, must always act through agents and employees. A partnership is essentially an agency relationship among the partners and often employs additional persons to assist in its operation. Most sole proprietorships also employ other persons. It is not surprising, therefore, that a substantial body of law exists to determine the rights and duties of employers with respect to their employees as well as to third parties.

The common law contains a body of principles which governs the rights and duties between employers and employees, and between them and third parties, both in contract and in tort. This field of the private law is known as the "law of agency." In addition, the law of employment includes numerous statutes regulating business and labor both on the state and the Federal level. State legislation controls such matters as (1) child labor, (2) hours of work, particularly for women and minors, (3) minimum wages, (4) unemployment compensation, (5) workmen's compensation, (6) safety appliances and conditions of work, (7) factory inspection, (8) wage assignments, (9) employment agencies, and (10) discriminatory practices with regard to hire and tenure of employees. The more significant labor legislation by the Federal government includes statutes dealing with hours and wages, employers' liability for injuries of employees, civil rights, and labor-management relations.

This chapter on employment will discuss the law of agency, the law as it relates to hours of work and wages, workmen's compensation, unemployment compensation, and fair employment practices legislation. The next chapter will discuss labor-management relations.

2 AGENCY

The law of agency in the narrow sense is concerned with questions of contractual liability when an alleged agent enters into a contract with a third party on behalf of a purported principal. The liability of the principal, the liability of the agent, and the rights of third parties are frequent subjects of agency litigation. While it is not our purpose to explore the substantive law of agency in detail, the general rule is that a principal has liability on all contracts entered into by the agent within the scope of the actual or apparent authority of the agent. Before the person dealing with the agent can hold the principal to the contract, he must prove the existence of this authority of the agent, although such factors as trade custom and emergencies may be used to establish it. When "apparent authority" or "ostensible authority" exists, there is no actual authority, but the law binds the principal as if it did because, by his conduct, he has led third persons to believe that the agent has authority, and to rely on that belief. In *Reusche v. California Pac. Title Ins. Co.*,[1] the court said: Ostensible authority is defined ". . . as such authority . . . as a principal, intentionally or by want of ordinary care, causes or allows a third person to believe the agent to possess." Liability of the principal for the ostensible agent's acts rests on the doctrine of "estoppel," and its essential elements are representation by the principal, justifiable reliance thereon by the third party, and change of position or injury resulting from such reliance.

The case which follows is typical of those in which issues of apparent authority are raised.

Debentures, Inc. v. Zech
73 P.2d 1314 (Wash. 1937)

Canny had purchased an apartment building and had mortgaged it to Debentures, Inc., the plaintiff, to secure payment of a loan made to him for the purchase price. When Canny experienced difficulty in keeping up with the payments, he assigned the rent of the building and full power to manage it to the mortgagee, Debentures, Inc., until the loan was repaid. However, the mortgagee permitted Canny to remain in possession of the building, operate it, and collect the rents for Debentures, Inc., as they fell due, in spite of the assignment. Canny later entered into a contract for repairs and redecoration of the building with defendant, Zech, without actual authority from plaintiff. The agreement provided that Zech and his wife were to be allowed to occupy one apartment, rent-free, in payment for both the labor and materials expended by him, until the rental value matched the amount due Zech for his work. Zech performed as agreed and for a time was permitted by Canny to live in an apartment rent-free. Debentures, Inc., foreclosed on the mortgage after Canny defaulted in repaying the loan. When Debentures, Inc., attempted to collect rent from the defendant, Zech, he refused to pay, contending the plaintiff was bound by the agreement Canny made with Zech and that the debt due defendant for his work was not yet fully satisfied. Debentures, Inc., denied any liability for Canny's acts and sued Zech and his wife for wrongful detainer of their apartment. The jury found for the defendants, and judgment was entered by the trial court in their favor. Plaintiff appealed.

HOLCOMB, JUSTICE: . . . In the ultimate, the question to be determined which is decisive of this case is whether or not the assignment of rents or any other acts

[1] 42 Cal. Rpt. 262 (1965).

of appellant . . . created a principal and agent relationship between appellant and Canny so that Canny was clothed with sufficient authority to authorize the execution of the contract in question for redecoration.

The instrument for assignment of rents and the policy adopted by the mortgagee subsequent to its execution clothed Canny with authority to act for the mortgagee since, notwithstanding the broad language of the assignment, he was left in possession and continued to have authority to collect rents, to manage and operate, and to maintain the Apartments, and therefore was vested with implied authority as a necessary incident to the exercise of his powers, to order and to direct that reasonable expenditures be made for the purpose of redecoration. The mere fact that the mortgagee had sufficient confidence in him so as to find it unnecessary to exercise any appreciable amount of supervision over him is immaterial.

An agent in possession of buildings or business properties has implied authority to make the necessary repairs on the premises, and in doing so may bind his principal.

"An agent to manage, supervise, or oversee the business or property of his principal has powers coextensive in scope with the business intrusted to him, that is to say, implied authority to do in the business or with the property whatever is usually and customarily done in businesses or with property of the same kind in the same locality. . . .

"Authority exists sufficient to bind the principal by acts or contracts of such an agent if they are reasonably necessary to keep the property in good repair, or the business a going concern, or requisite to the protection of the interests intrusted to the agent's management." 2 C.J.S., Agency, pp. 1241, 1242, § 103.

It is unfortunate that respondents [the Zechs] did not have the mortgagee join in the contract, but we are convinced the mortgagee was bound thereby even though it did not sign the same. By reason of the execution of the assignment of rents . . . , coupled with the fact that Canny was left in possession with authority to collect rents, to manage and operate the Apartments, and the surrounding circumstances, Canny had implied authority to enter into a contract for redecoration with respondents. Canny had this authority to act by reason of the fact that he had divested himself of practically all authority which he could exercise over the Apartments and by reason of the fact that he had been left in possession to operate and to maintain the Apartments, and so stated to respondents.

Agency may be inferred from a course of dealing or of conduct by parties or may be established by estoppel. . . .

"The apparent authority of an agent to act as the representative of his principal is to be gathered from all the facts and circumstances in evidence, and ordinarily this is a question of fact for the jury's determination." 21 R.C.L. 856, 857, § 34.

"The liability of the principal for the acts and contracts of his agent is not limited to such acts and contracts of the agent as are expressly authorized, necessarily implied from express authority, or otherwise actually conferred by implication from the acts and conduct of the principal. All such acts and contracts of the agent as are within the apparent scope of the authority conferred on him, although no actual authority to do such acts or to make such contracts has been conferred, are also binding upon the principal. . . ." 2 Am.Jur. pp. 82, 83, § 101.

"Apparent authority is the power of an apparent agent to affect the legal relations of an apparent principal with respect to a third person by acts done in accordance with such principal's manifestations of consent to such third person that such agent shall act as his agent." 1 Restatement of the Law of Agency, page 25, § 8. . . .

The judgment is affirmed. [AFFIRMED]

A principal who puts an agent in a position that enables the agent, while apparently acting within his authority, to commit a fraud upon third persons is subject to liability to such third persons for the fraud. The principal is liable although he is entirely innocent, although he has received no benefit from the transaction, and although the agent acts solely for his own purposes. Liability is based upon the fact that the agent's position facilitates the consummation of the fraud, in that, from the point of view of the third persons, the transaction seems regular on its face and the agent appears to be acting in the ordinary course of the business entrusted to him. The law reasons that in such a case, where one of two innocent parties must suffer, the loss should be accepted by the principal who is responsible for the selection of the agent and for the definition of his authority.

The principal-agent relationship is used to describe the nature of the employment where the employee has power to contract. In those situations where he has no such power, the relationship is usually characterized as master-servant. A principal is liable for the torts of his agent just as a master is liable for the torts of his servant if the agent or servant is acting within the course of his employment or is engaged in work for the employer. Essentially, the rule is that both the agent or servant and the principal or master have tort liability if the course-of-employment test is met.

The law of agency also deals with the duties an agent owes his employer, such as the duty of undivided loyalty. Conflict-of-interest questions, which frequently arise, are decided under this principle. The duty of loyalty arises because the agency relationship is a fiduciary one (one of high trust and confidence) and any benefits other than those agreed upon, which the agent receives because of his position, actually belong to the principal. Many acts of disloyalty involve so-called "trade secrets." The case which follows illustrates the length to which courts will go in protecting employers from disloyalty by employees relating to business trade secrets.

Albert B. Cord Co. v. S & P Management Servs., Inc.
194 N.E.2d 173 (Ohio C.P. 1963)

LEIS, JUSTICE: . . . The plaintiff, Albert B. Cord Company, Inc., is an Ohio corporation engaged in management consulting. Mr. Albert B. Cord is the president of said corporation.

The defendant, S & P Management Services, Inc., is, likewise, a management consulting business and was organized some time after May 30, 1961. The individual defendants, Mr. Anthony M. Schummer and Mr. J. Paul Pickering, S & P's principal shareholders, were employed by the plaintiff prior to May 30, 1961. Mr. Schummer, an engineer, became a member of plaintiff's staff as a Staff Engineer at or about June 1948. In January 1950, he was promoted to the supervisory staff as Chief Engineer. In this capacity Mr. Schummer was recognized as Assistant General Manager with full power and authority to act in the event anything happened to the General Manager (Mr. Albert Cord), and he had full force and power to perform anything that, in his discretion, he saw fit. Mr. J. Paul Pickering was employed by the plaintiff as its Sales Manager prior to his resignation.

Management consulting firms offer assistance to business concerns in solving various problems in such areas as labor relations, shop operations, wage plans, production, administration, sales promotion and related problems peculiar to modern business. Service is rendered upon a fee basis. One of the chief assets of a management consulting firm is its staff of well-trained engineers, accountants, administrators and salesmen; men who are qualified and trained both technically and through years of experience in all the phases of business activity in production control, sales and sales promotion, administration, accounting and cost control, statistics, engineering, etc. These assets are "human assets" and, as experts, their minds and mentality, and their ability to analyze the problems presented to them, apply their technical knowledge, experience and imagination and recommend a workable remedy to cure the business ailment are of intangible value to the management consulting firm. Another asset of relative and equal importance to the management consulting company is a knowledge of, and access to, companies which are likely to need its services.

In the case at bar Mr. Pickering was the person most relied upon to secure the clientele. He was continually "on the road" making business calls in the midwest—Ohio, Indiana, Michigan, Illinois, Missouri, Pennsylvania and West Virginia. Whenever he made a call he submitted a report to the office for filing in the customer's file (if the call merited such a file). The contents of the reports included . . . D & B credit rating of the client or prospect and many other items and facts pertinent and helpful to the plaintiff, for the present and for the future, in ascertaining whether or not the prospect is in need, or will be in need of service and if repeat calls should be made. All this data and these comprehensive reports were accumulated in the plaintiff's confidential file with the hope that at some future time it would or will be available in securing an engagement for the plaintiff. Much time, effort and money was spent by the plaintiff through its sales representatives, under the leadership of Mr. Pickering.

This Court recognizes the unique character of this type of business as compared to the type of business which offers a commodity or product, or a common service. The Court also recognizes the fact that repeat business can result from a successful initial engagement. Another element of this business that entered into this Court's consideration is the fact that Cord Company personnel had to work closely with their client's management and personnel. Such close contact can result in relationships of confidence and trust in the personnel of the plaintiff. For this reason the plaintiff, in its contracts, included the following statement:

In order to maintain a professional atmosphere it is our policy to consider your personnel ineligible for employment with our organization, and we require your commitment to similar conditions regarding the employment or engagement of our personnel by your organization.

All of these factors emphasize the unique character of the plaintiff's business service and of its intangible value, a value which cannot be measured accounting-wise in money, but which is a valuable asset to the corporation in the nature of good will.

The defendants, Mr. Schummer and Mr. Pickering, were the top men in the plaintiff company. The evidence shows that while other employees had written contracts of employment none were required of Mr. Schummer and Mr. Pickering. Evidence was presented to show that Mr. Cord and the defendants worked closely together and freely interchanged information at all times and, as a result of membership in this "inner circle" the defendants had unlimited access to confidential information contained in the locked files of the Cord Company. The defendants had keys to all the locked confidential files except two drawers which contained private papers of Mr. Cord.

This case is categorized under the topic in law entitled "Trade Secrets." The Restatement of Torts, Section 757, comment (b) (1939) defines a "Trade Secret" as follows:

A trade secret may consist of any formula, pattern, device, or compilation of information which is used in one's business, and which gives him an opportunity to obtain an advantage over competitors who do not know or use it. It may be a formula for a chemical compound, a process of manufacturing, treating or preserving materials, a pattern for a machine or other device, or a list of customers. . . .

A trade secret, therefore, is almost anything and everything useful or advantageous in business activity that is not generally known or easily or immediately ascertainable to members of the trade. . . .

The plaintiff in its Second Amended Petition alleges that the defendants

. . . have solicited on behalf of S & P Management Services, Inc. the following clients or prospective clients of plaintiff, among others, with whom said individual defendants had dealt on behalf of plaintiff during the last three years of their employment by plaintiff and with respect to whom defendants possessed information secured in the course of their confidential employment by plaintiff and regarded as confidential: . . .

The plaintiff then lists twenty-six company names. Included in the list is the Frick-Gallagher Mfg. Co., Wellston, Ohio, a client of the plaintiff and with whom the plaintiff had been negotiating additional service when defendants were plaintiff's employees, which company plaintiff alleges the defendants induced to retain defendant S & P Management Services, Inc., to perform management-consulting service on the basis of information available to Mr. Schummer and Mr. Pickering as a result of their confidential employment by plaintiff.

The Supreme Court of Ohio stated in *Curry v. Marquart*, 133 Ohio St. 77, 11 N.E.2d 868 (1937):

The authorities are quite uniform that disclosures of trade secrets by an employee secured by him in the course of confidential employment will be restrained by the process of injunction, and in numerous instances attempts to use for himself or for a new employer information relative to the trade or business in which he has been engaged, such as lists of customers regarded as confidential, have been restrained. . . .

This Court concludes that the information available to the defendants Mr. Schummer and Mr. Pickering was confidential information and was the property of the plaintiff, secured and paid for by the plaintiff with the aid and assistance of the defendants while they were employed by the plaintiff in a confidential capacity. The defendants were confidential employees intrusted with information, in the regular course of their employment, of such a nature that it was not necessary that there be a written customer list for an injunction to issue. The defendants are men of high intelligence and this Court concludes that their memories are as good as any written list. The information about the clients and prospective clients was available to the defendants up until the day of their termination of employment.

This Court grants the temporary injunction per the plaintiff's motion filed November 27, 1961. [TEMPORARY INJUNCTION GRANTED]

3 WAGES AND HOURS OF WORK

Statutes setting minimum wages per hour and maximum hours of work are found both on the state and the Federal level. Early state legislation of this type mainly concerned labor by children and women. At first such legislation was successfully attacked as being an unconstitutional invasion of the freedom of contract. While today we recognize that state government possesses the power to enact statutes of this type for social and economic purposes, such was not always the case. *West Coast Hotel v. Parrish*[2] was the landmark decision upholding the regulation

---

[2] 300 U.S. 379 (1936).

of the minimum employment contract by state government. In that case the Supreme Court, speaking through Chief Justice Hughes, said in part:

The principle which must control our decision is not in doubt. The constitutional provision invoked is the due process clause of the Fourteenth Amendment governing the states. . . . [T]he violation alleged by those attacking minimum wage regulation for women is deprivation of freedom of contract. It speaks of liberty and prohibits the deprivation of liberty without due process of law. In prohibiting that deprivation, the Constitution does not recognize an absolute and uncontrollable liberty. Liberty in each of its phases has its history and connotation. But the liberty safeguarded is liberty in a social organization which requires the protection of law against the evils which menace the health, safety, morals, and welfare of the people. Liberty under the Constitution is thus necessarily subject to the restraints of due process, and regulation which is reasonable in relation to its subject and is adopted in the interests of the community is due process.

This essential limitation of liberty in general governs freedom of contract in particular. More than twenty-five years ago we set forth the applicable principle in these words. . . .

". . . [F]reedom of contract is a qualified, and not an absolute, right. There is no absolute freedom to do as one wills or to contract as one chooses. The guaranty of liberty does not withdraw from legislative supervision that wide department of activity which consists of the making of contracts, or deny to government the power to provide restrictive safeguards. Liberty implies the absence of arbitrary restraint, not immunity from reasonable regulations and prohibitions imposed in the interests of the community. . . ."

The point that has been strongly stressed that adult employees should be deemed competent to make their own contracts was decisively met nearly forty years ago in Holden v. Hardy, *supra, where we pointed out the inequality in the footing of the parties. We said . . . :*

"The legislature has also recognized the fact, which the experience of legislators in many states has corroborated, that the proprietors of these establishments and their operatives do not stand upon an equality, and that their interests are, to a certain extent, conflicting. The former naturally desire to obtain as much labor as possible from their employés, while the latter are often induced by the fear of discharge to conform to regulations which their judgment, fairly exercised, would pronounce to be detrimental to their health or strength. In other words, the proprietors lay down the rules, and the laborers are practically constrained to obey them. In such cases self-interest is often an unsafe guide, and the legislature may properly interpose its authority."

And we added that the fact

". . . that both parties are of full age, and competent to contract, does not necessarily deprive the state of the power to interfere, where the parties do not stand upon an equality, or where the public health demands that one party to the contract shall be protected against himself. . . . The state still retains an

interest in his welfare, however reckless he may be. The whole is no greater than the sum of all the parts, and when the individual health, safety, and welfare are sacrificed or neglected, the state must suffer. . . ."

There is an additional and compelling consideration which recent economic experience has brought into a strong light. The exploitation of a class or workers who are in an unequal position with respect to bargaining power and are thus relatively defenseless against the denial of a living wage is not only detrimental to their health and well being, but casts a direct burden for their support upon the community.

The foregoing case rather effectively eliminated most constitutional objections to social legislation regulating employment. Today, approximately 70 percent of the states have minimum wage laws.

The Federal government also regulates wages and hours. The Fair Labor Standards Act, which was originally enacted in 1938, has been amended several times to increase the minimum wage, decrease maximum hours, and to broaden its coverage. Originally, the FLSA required covered employers to pay their employees at least 25 cents an hour for a regular work week of 44 hours, to pay such employees at least time and one-half for all work performed over the 44-hour week, and to keep certain records for each worker which would demonstrate compliance or noncompliance with the Act. It also restricted the use of child labor. This statute was held to be a constitutional exercise of the power of Congress under the commerce clause.

As this is written in late 1972, the minimum hourly wage of $1.60 is in the process of being raised to at least $2. The standard work week is 40 hours, with overtime pay at a rate of not less than one and one-half times the employee's regular rate of pay. While this regular rate may not be less than the minimum wage, it can be and usually is more. If it is, the time and one-half is at the higher rate. For example, an employee whose hourly rate is $4 receives $6 per hour for overtime. The wage and overtime provisions apply whether an employee is paid on a time, piece, job, incentive, or other basis. In addition, the Act now requires payment of time and one-half the regular rate for work of over eight hours in any given day. Of course, record-keeping requirements remain.

Not all types of employment were covered by the original FLSA, nor are they today. However, the amendments have expanded coverage greatly along with the minimum wage, so that now most workers are protected by it. While there are still some exempt businesses, their number is decreasing, and the trend is to require the minimum wage for all. Categories of persons who are presently not covered include many who do not need the protection such as those engaged in the practice of a profession, managerial and supervisory personnel, and outside salesmen. Most of the time persons engaged in such employment earn incomes far in excess of the FLSA minimums, anyway. Also not covered are certain governmental employees and workers employed by small farms and small businesses such as retail establishments which are mainly intrastate in operation. In addition, learners, apprentices, messengers, handicapped workers, and full-time students employed in similar service operations or agriculture may be paid lower minimum wages, provided the employer first obtains special certificates from the Administrator of the Wage and Hour Division of the Department of Labor. Each business must examine its particular operations to determine whether it is covered or whether it comes under any of the exceptions.

Besides its wage and hour provisions, the FLSA contains sections which regulate the employment of child labor. Under these, eighteen is the minimum age for employment in occupations which are declared hazardous by the Secretary of Labor. These include such work as that involving exposure to radioactivity, the operation of various kinds of dangerous machinery, mining, and roofing. Generally these restrictions do not apply to employment in agriculture. Otherwise the basic minimum age for employment is sixteen, at which children may be employed in any nonhazardous work. The employment of fourteen- and fifteen-year-olds is limited to certain occupations such as sales and clerical work, under specific conditions of work, for limited hours, and outside school time only. Children under fourteen may not be employed except for a few jobs which are specifically exempt. For example, children employed in agriculture outside of school hours, children employed by their parents in nonhazardous occupations, child actors, and newspaper deliverers are exempt. State laws on child labor must also be followed if more strict than the Federal standards.

One who violates any of the provisions of the Fair Labor Standards Act may be prosecuted criminally by the Attorney General, and if found guilty, he may be punished by a fine of up to $10,000 for the first offense and, for subsequent offenses, a fine of up to $10,000 or imprisonment for up to six months, or both. The Act also empowers the Federal district courts, upon showing of cause, to issue injunctions restraining violations of it. Finally, employees who are injured by a violation may bring a civil suit against their employer and recover unpaid wages or overtime compensation and punitive damages, plus reasonable attorney's fee and costs of the action. However, if the employer shows the court that he acted in good faith and had reasonable grounds to believe that he was not violating the law, the court may, in its discretion, award no punitive damages, or limit them. The Administrator of the Wage and Hour Division of the Department of Labor may supervise the payment of back wages, or the Secretary of Labor may, upon the written request of an employee, bring suit himself for back pay due the employee. The agreement by any employee to accept payment obtained by either of the two foregoing methods constitutes a waiver by him of his right to bring suit against the employer in his own behalf and a waiver of any damages in addition to his back pay. Any action to recover back pay or damages must be commenced within two years after it has accrued, or it is forever barred by the statute of limitations. Back wages illegally withheld and due under the Equal Pay Act (discussed below) may be recovered by the same means as other wages due under the FLSA.

The Equal Pay Act of 1963 amended the FLSA by prohibiting employers from discriminating on the basis of sex in paying wages for equal work performed. Under it, employers may not pay employees of one sex at rates lower than those of the opposite sex for doing equal work on jobs which require equal skill, effort, and responsibility when such jobs are performed under similar working conditions. The provisions apply only to employees who are covered by the minimum wage provision of the FLSA. An exception is provided in cases where it can be shown that the wage differential is based on a seniority system, a merit system, a system measuring wages by quantity or quality of production, or any other factor except sex. An employer in violation of the Act may not *reduce* the wage rate of any employee in order to avoid a violation. The Equal Pay Act also prohibits labor organizations and their agents from causing or attempting to cause any employer whose employees they represent to discriminate because of sex.

In addition to setting minimum wages and forbidding discrimination in pay on account of sex, the Federal government also has recently controlled maximum wages. This was done by President Nixon pursuant to the authority given him by Congress under the Economic Stabilization Act of 1970 as a move to help curb runaway inflation. The first segment of the economy to be so affected was the construction industry when, in March of 1971, the President issued an Executive order providing for the stabilization of wages and prices in it. Then, in August of the same year, the President imposed a 90-day freeze on wages, prices, and rents generally. Its purpose was to halt inflation and also provide time for the Federal government to develop a long-range plan for economic stabilization. The more flexible Phase Two of the plan began in November 1971 when the President appointed the Cost of Living Council to establish broad economic goals and created both the Pay Board and the Price Commission to control wage increases and price increases, respectively. The Internal Revenue Service was given the responsibility of administering the program and informing the public of its details. The Pay Board, as originally constituted, was appointed to include members representing the interests of labor, business, and the general public.

4 WORKMEN'S COMPENSATION

Workmen's compensation laws are state statutes which are designed to protect employees and their families from the risks of accidental injury, death, or disease resulting from their employment. They have been enacted because the common law was viewed as deficient in the protection it afforded employees from the hazards of their work. At common law, anyone was liable in tort for the money damages resulting from injuries caused to another as a proximate result of negligence. Thus, if an employer acted unreasonably and his carelessness was the proximate cause of physical injury suffered by one of his employees, the latter theoretically could sue and recover damages from the employer. However, the common law also provided the employer with the means of escaping this tort liability in most cases. It provided him with three defenses known as (1) assumption of the risk, (2) contributory negligence, and (3) the fellow-servant doctrine.

For example, assume that employer E knowingly instructed workers to operate dangerous machinery not equipped with any safety devices, even though he realized injury to them was likely. W, a worker, had his arm mangled when it was caught in the gears of one of these machines. Even though E was negligent in permitting this hazardous condition to persist, if W were cognizant of the inherent dangers which existed, he would be unable to recover damages because he knowingly *assumed the risk* of his injury. In addition, if the injury were caused by *contributory negligence* of the employee, as well as the negligence of the employer, the action was defeated. And if the injury occurred because of the negligence of another employee, the negligent employee rather than the employer was liable because of the *fellow-servant rule*.

Other obstacles hindered employees from obtaining adequate relief under the common law for their on-the-job injuries. For one thing, even if the defenses of the employer could be overcome and judgment obtained against him, the time which elapsed between the injury itself and the receipt of payment after trial or after exhaustion of appeals by the employer could amount to many years. The employee often was destitute during this period and unable to afford the medical treatment he needed, let alone support himself and his family. His only recourse then was to turn to public aid or charity, which was usually inadequate even if it was available. In addition, the contingent-fee system which was (and still is) customarily employed in tort cases could work to the recovering employee's disadvantage. Under it, of course, the attorney's fee is contingent on his winning the case for his client. The employee would pay nothing if the suit were lost, but anywhere from 25 percent to 50 percent of the amount recovered would go to his attorney when the suit was won. The jury assessed the damages, however, with a view to adequate compensation and not to covering expenses of suit.

Perhaps at one time the common-law rules were adequate. But the industrial revolution brought with it larger plants, with poorer working conditions and more hazardous machinery. These were conducive to many more industrial accidents resulting in a sharp increase in serious injuries. In addition, employers no longer worked side by side with their employees, sharing their risks. As manufacturing businesses became larger, the employment relationship became more and more impersonal. Employers were much less apt to think of the welfare of individual employees rather than keeping their costs to a minimum. This was particularly true in industries where investment in plant and equipment had exceeded demand and thus had resulted in high total fixed costs, operation at much less than capacity, and cutthroat competition. For these reasons, the common-law rules were seen as incapable of coping with the social needs of an industrial society.

The English Parliament passed the first workmen's compensation statute. Today, all states have such legislation, modeled to a greater or lesser degree on the English act. These laws vary a great deal from state to state as to the industries which are subject to them, the employees they cover, the nature of the injuries or diseases which are compensable, the rates of compensation, and the means of administration. Because of this diversity, difficult conflicts-of-law questions often are present in a workmen's compensation case. Which law would apply to the case of an employee who resides in State X but who is injured in State Y while working for an employer located in State Z? In spite of the wide variances in the laws of the states in this area, certain general observations can be made about them.

State workmen's compensation statutes provide a system to pay workers or their families in the event the worker is accidentally killed or injured or incurs an occupational disease while employed. To be compensable, the death, illness, or injury must arise out of and in the course of the employment. Under these acts, the negligence or fault of the employer in causing an on-the-job injury is not an issue. Instead these laws recognize the fact of life that a certain number of injuries, deaths, and diseases are bound to occur in a modern industrial society as a result of the attempts of businesses and their employees to provide the goods and services demanded by the consuming public. Therefore, it is deemed more equitable that the consuming public should bear the monetary costs of such mishaps rather than impose the total expense on the unfortunate workers who suffer them. This is done by imposing strict liability on the employer for such accidents, regardless of his lack of negligence or fault, provided the necessary association between the injuries and the business of the employer is present. The three defenses the employer had at common law are eliminated. The employers, treating the costs of these injuries as part of the costs of production, pass them on to the consumers who created the demand for the product or service being furnished.

Even though all states have some form of workmen's compensation, the statutes exclude certain types of employment from their coverage. Generally, domestic and agricultural employees are not covered. In addition, the law may not provide compensation for specified kinds of accidents or diseases. In about one-half of the states the statutes are compulsory. In the other half, employers may elect to be subject to the act or to lawsuits by employees or their survivors for damages. If the latter course is chosen, an employee seeking compensation for injuries must prove they resulted proximately from the negligence of the employer, as at common law, but is not subject to the common-law defenses discussed above. In such a case, there is no statutory limit to the amount of damages recoverable.

The workmen's compensation acts give covered employees the right to certain cash payments for their loss of income due to accidental on-the-job injuries. In the event of an employee's death, benefits are provided for his widow and minor children. The amount of such awards usually is subject to a stated maximum and is calculated by using a percentage of the wages of the employee. If the employee suffers permanent partial disability, most states provide compensation both for injuries which are scheduled in the statute and those which are nonscheduled. As an example of the former, a worker who loses a hand might be awarded 100 weeks of compensation at $50 per week. Besides scheduling specific compensation for certain specific injuries, most acts also provide compensation for nonscheduled ones based upon the earning power the employee lost due to his injury. In addition to the above payments, all statutes provide for medical benefits.

In some states the employers have a choice of covering their workmen's compensation risk with insurance or of being self-insured (i.e., paying all claims directly) if they can demonstrate their capability to do so. In other states, employers pay into a state fund used to compensate workers entitled to benefits. In these states, the amounts of the payments are based on the size of the payroll and the experience of the employer in having claims filed against him.

Workmen's compensation laws are usually administered exclusively by an administrative agency called the industrial commission or board which has quasi-judicial powers, formal court action being dispensed with. Of course, the ruling of such boards is subject to review by the courts of the jurisdiction in the same manner as the actions of other administrative agencies.

As was noted, the right to recovery of workmen's compensation benefits is given without regard to the negligence or fault of either the employer or the employee in the traditional sense, being predicated on the employment relationship and the fact that the injury arose out of and in the course of the employment. Thus, the tests for determining whether an employee is entitled to workmen's compensation are simply: (1) "Was the injury accidental?" and (2) "Did the injury arise out of and in the course of the employment?" Since workmen's compensation laws are remedial in nature, they have been very liberally construed under rules of statutory interpretation. However, an intentionally inflicted self-injury would usually not be considered accidental and would not be compensable under the first test. But cases in recent years have tended to expand coverage and the scope of the employer's liability. It has been held that heart attacks as well as other common ailments where the employee either had a preexisting disease or a physical condition likely to lead to the disease were compensable as "accidental injuries." Likewise, the courts have been more and more liberal in upholding awards which have been challenged on the ground that the injury did not arise out of and in the course of the employment. The following case is a fairly typical example of these.

Cavalcante v. Lockheed Electronics Co.
204 A.2d 621 (N.J. 1964)

This was an appeal by Lockheed Electronics Company from an award of statutory compensation benefits to the petitioner, who was the widow of a former Lockheed employee. The deceased employee had been working long and odd hours on a special "cleanup" job for Lockheed in New London, Connecticut, about 150 miles from his regular place of employment. After dinner, at about 10 P.M. of the third day of this job, he and four co-workers decided to leave their motel and to "go out and see what New London was like." They drove to "a bar and a restaurant and dance hall" where they were "drinking beer, listening to the music and talking over our work and what had to be done and what we had accomplished so far." They were also dancing and drinking scotch and soda, decedent included. Driving back at 12:30 A.M. the next morning, decedent failed to negotiate a hidden curve in the road and died as a result of the accident.

HOPKINS, JUDGE: . . . In its appeal Lockheed argues strenuously that decedent's accident and death did not arise out of and in the course of his employment, that there was no causal connection between the conditions of the work and the resulting injury, and that the injury did not have its origin in a risk connected with the employment, nor did it flow from that source as a natural consequence. . . .

Lockheed argues that the acts of the decedent and his associates in the present case were not reasonably necessary to serve their basic subsistence needs, and that in fact the decedent had finished his work for the day, had had his evening meal, and from that time on his time was his own, just as if he had finished a long overtime session at the Plainfield plant at home. It contends that the evening trip from its start to its unfortunate finish was clearly an abandonment of and departure from the employment on a purely personal matter, having no connection whatever with the duties of his employment, his meals, his travel or his living conditions.

It is basic that an accident arises "in the course of" employment when it occurs (a) within the period of employment, (b) at a place where the employee may reasonably be, and (c) while he is fulfilling the duties of the employment, or doing something incidental to it. It arises "out of" the employment when the risk of such an occurrence is reasonably incident to the employment. Such a risk is one that grows out of or is connected with what a workman has to do in fulfilling his contract of service. It immediately becomes evident that the standard always is reasonableness. . . .

Where an employee is traveling on a business trip away from his home, "reasonableness" . . . is given a very liberal construction. In *Robinson v. Federal Telephone & Radio*, the court quoted with approval from *Thornton v. Hartford Accident & Indemnity Co.*, when it said:

The eating of meals, while a pleasure indulged in by a traveling salesman and all mankind, is as necessary to the continuance of his duties as the breath of life; and where his duties take him away from his home, his acts of ministration to himself should not—and we believe do not—take him outside the scope of his employment, so long as he performs these acts in a normal and prudent manner. Such activities, the performance of which are necessary to his health and comfort, while in a sense personal to himself are nevertheless incidents of his employment.

It therefore becomes necessary to examine what acts, which "are reasonably necessary to serve the basic subsistence needs of the employee," and are to be "reasonably included within the scope of the employment," come within the meaning of the *Robinson* case. . . .

It must be kept in mind that "work-connected activity goes beyond the direct services performed for the employer and includes at least some ministration to the personal comfort and human wants of the employee." . . .

In *Schneider v. United Whelan Drug Stores*, decedent and his superior were in Miami, Florida on business. Because they had about 24 hours to await the return flight for which they had reservations, they accepted the invitation of a local employee to go boating. Decedent drowned when the boat capsized. The court reversed the denial of the award and held this act of boating was reasonable to engage in.

The facts of *Hancock v. Ingersoll-Rand Co.*, are clearly distinguishable (from those of the case at bar). . . . In *Hancock* recovery was denied because the court was of the opinion that the frequenting of cocktail lounges with unknown female companions was completely unreasonable. There is no difference in the principle or rule to be applied, as it is only a question of degree. In the instant case the visit to the tavern was with fellow employees simply seeking some reasonable relaxation. Reasonableness is the key to recovery. . . .

In *Lewis v. Knappen Tippetts Abbett Engineering Co.*, decedent had been sent to Israel as a consultant to the Israeli Government. Before his work was fully completed, he went from Tel Aviv to Jerusalem with a United Nations convoy for the sole purpose of sight-seeing. The convoy was attacked by unknown Arabs, who broke a period of truce then in effect and decedent was fatally shot. The Court of Appeals of New York found that this employee was acting within the scope of his employment and that the accident occurred during the course of his employment because he was acting in a reasonable manner and the accident happened at a place where he might reasonably have been expected to have been. . . .

Because it is reasonable for a traveling employee to seek some physical relaxation, and because this was done in a reasonable manner, this accident and the consequent death did arise out of and in the course of decedent's employment.

The judgment below is affirmed. [AFFIRMED]

There are many other examples of the tendency of industrial commissions and the courts to be liberal in allowing workmen's compensation awards. In one case, a teacher who was injured on the way home from school in an automobile accident was found to be in the course of her employment under the "dual purpose" doctrine. She was held to be furthering her employer's interest at the time, even though also furthering her own, since she had no other time to correct papers and prepare lessons except when at home. In another case, a sales manager of a dairy store who was one of the prize winners in a company competition was offered either a cash amount or a trip to New Orleans. He chose the trip, and was awarded workmen's compensation for injuries sustained while on it. In still another case, a worker filed a claim for injuries he received from being beaten by a fellow employee. The latter was angered because he believed that the claimant was moving ahead of him in the line at a drinking fountain provided by the employer. In allowing an award for total, permanent incapacity, the court ruled that the injury was "accidental" as that term was used in the workmen's compensation statute, and that it happened when the claimant was about his employer's business.

The system of separate and varying state workmen's compensation laws as they exist today has been subjected to much criticism. The laws have been attacked as inadequate because of their restrictive coverage and limited benefits. Not all types of employment or occupational risks are covered. And about half the states exempt businesses which do not employ a certain minimum number of workers (ranging from two to fifteen). Much criticism has also been leveled at the quality of administration of most workmen's compensation programs. The weaknesses in the present laws, and the fact that there are wide variations in the workmen's compensation acts (as well as case law) from state to state, have led to suggestions that workmen's compensation be modernized and reformed to better meet the social needs of today and that it be made uniform from state to state. Some have proposed a Federal Workmen's Compensation Act which would replace the state ones. Others have called for a Uniform Workmen's Compensation Act to be drafted by the National Conference of Commissioners on Uniform State Laws.

5 FEDERAL COMPENSATION ACTS

Several statutes have been enacted by the Federal government which pertain to the liability of certain kinds of employers for injuries, diseases, and deaths arising out of the course of employment. Railroad workers are covered by the Federal Employers' Liability Act. This statute does not provide for liability without fault as in the case of workmen's compensation, but it greatly increases the chances of a worker's winning a lawsuit against his employer by eliminating the defenses the latter would have had at common law. In a suit for damages based upon the negligence of the officers, agents, or employees of a carrier, the contributory negligence of the injured employee is not a bar to recovery. If it is present, however, the claimant's damages will be diminished in proportion to the amount of negligence attributable to him, except when the carrier's violation of a statute enacted for the safety of the employee contributed to the injury. Also the common-law defense of assumption of the risk is not available to an employer. The Act further provides that a term in a contract of employment which attempts to exempt a carrier from liability or prevent enforcement of the FELA is void. In addition, the legal rights of a deceased employee which are created by the statute survive for the benefit of his widow and children. While fault of the carrier must be proved for an employee to recover for his injuries under the FELA, and a regular law suit must be filed in court, the Act provides the worker with a distinct advantage over many workmen's compensation systems. There is no limit or ceiling to the amount an employee can recover for his injuries. It is clear that juries are often sympathetic to the injured worker. The Jones Act gives maritime employees the same rights against their employers as railway workers have against theirs under the FELA. The case below involved the application of the Jones Act.

Hopson v. Texaco, Inc.
383 U.S. 262 (1966)

PER CURIAM: These actions were brought under the Jones Act . . . to recover damages for injuries sustained by one seaman and for the death of another, as a result of an automobile accident on the Island of Trinidad. Judgment on the jury's verdict was entered in United States District Court in favor of the plaintiffs, but the Court of Appeals reversed. . . . We granted a writ of certiorari and reverse.

The facts are not in dispute. The two seamen were members of the crew of respondent's tanker which was docked at respondent's refinery at Pointe-a-Pierre on the Island of Trinidad. Both fell ill and it was determined that they would be unable to continue the voyage. In order to discharge an incapacitated seaman in a foreign port, federal law requires that he be taken to a United States Consul where arrangements for his return to the United States can be made. The United States Consul's Office was located in Port-of-Spain, some 38 miles distant. Although respondent had a fleet of motor vehicles used for transportation in the immediate vicinity of the refinery and docking areas, its practice was to utilize either of two local taxi companies for journeys to more distant points. The ship's Master procured one of these cabs, which set out for Port-of-Spain with the two ill seamen. En route, the taxi collided with a truck, killing the Master and one of the seamen; the other seaman was seriously injured. The jury found that the taxi driver had been negligent—a finding challenged neither in the Court of Appeals nor here. The Court of Appeals reversed the District Court's determination that respondent is liable to petitioners for this negligence of the taxi operator.

The Jones Act incorporates the standards of the Federal Employers' Liability Act which renders an employer liable for the injuries negligently inflicted on its employees by its "officers, agents, or employees." We noted in *Sinkler v. Missouri Pac. R. Co.*, 356 U.S. 326, . . . that the latter Act was "an avowed departure from the rules of the common law," . . . which, recognizing "[t]he cost of human injury, and inescapable expense of railroading," undertook to "adjust that expense equitably between the worker and the carrier." . . . In order to give "an accommodating scope . . . to the word 'agents'" we concluded that "when [a]n . . . employee's injury is caused in whole or in part by the fault of others performing, under contract, operational activities of the employer, such others are 'agents' of the employer within the meaning of § 1 of FELA." . . .

We think those principles apply with equal force here. These seamen were in the service of the ship and the ill-fated journey to Port-of-Spain was a vital part of the ship's total operations. The ship could not sail with these two men, nor could it lawfully discharge them without taking them to the United States Consul. Indeed, to have abandoned them would have breached the statutory duty to arrange for their return to the United States. Getting these two ill seamen to the United States Consul's office was, therefore, the duty of respondent. And it was respondent—not the seamen—which selected, as it had done many times before, the taxi service. Respondent—the law says—should bear the responsibility for the negligence of the driver which it chose. This is so because, as we said in *Sinkler*, "justice demands that one who gives his labor to the furtherance of the enterprise should be assured that all combining their exertions with him in the common pursuit will conduct themselves in all respects with sufficient care that his safety while doing his part will not be endangered." . . . [REVERSED]

Other Federal statutes require awards for on-the-job injuries or deaths of certain employees in the manner of state workmen's compensation laws without regard to the fault of the employer. These provide formulas to use in computing the amounts of the awards for various kinds and degrees of disability, along with upper and lower limits for such awards. One such statute is the Longshoremen's and Harbor Workers' Compensation Act. The coverage of this statute was extended to workers for private employers on United States defense bases by the Defense Bases Act.

6 UNEMPLOYMENT COMPENSATION

Unemployment compensation is a Federal-state program which provides for payments for temporary periods to workers who are unemployed through no fault of their own. It is a classic example of the use of the Federal taxing power as a tool to pressure the states into adopting legislation deemed desirable by the Federal government. The Social Security Act of 1935 imposed a 3 percent Federal tax on the wages paid by all employers who were not exempted. However, the Act provided that taxed employers were entitled to a credit of up to 2.7 percent or 90 percent of this tax for any contributions they paid to an approved state unemployment insurance plan. Although only Wisconsin had an unemployment compensation law in 1935, all the states, needless to say, enacted such statutes shortly after the Social Security Act of 1935.

The Federal policy to encourage state unemployment insurance was a result of the mass unemployment in the depression during the 1930s. Then, millions were out of work for long periods, with about 25 percent of the labor force being unemployed. Today, the Federal unemployment tax is imposed on any person, with respect to any calendar year, who during any quarter in that or the preceding calendar year paid wages of $1,500 or more. It is also levied on those who, on each of 20 days during the current or preceding calendar year, each day being in a different week, employed at least one person for some portion of the day regardless of the amount of wages paid. However, the law grants a series of exemptions from the tax. Among the exempted are: agricultural labor; family labor; labor for the United States government or for a state; and labor for a religious, charitable, or educational organization. The states may provide for wider coverage if they desire.

Only a worker in a covered business can collect unemployment compensation, and then only if he meets certain tests. If he qualifies, he draws payments as a matter of right, regardless of his financial position, since need is not a factor. The laws require him either to have worked for a certain minimum number of weeks in a covered industry or to have earned a certain minimum amount of wages. These times and amounts vary from state to state. Generally he must wait one week before applying and must register with the state employment agency and be ready, willing, and able to undertake suitable employment.

Some states disqualify employees if they leave jobs to get married, to go into business for themselves, to go to school, or because they are pregnant. The Social Security Act does not permit the states to disqualify a worker from receiving unemployment benefits if he refuses to accept a job because it is left vacant by reason of a labor dispute, because the wages and conditions of employment are substantially below those for similar jobs, or because he is required to join a company union or to agree not to join a union as a condition of his employment.

Generally a worker is disqualified if he refuses other work which is suitable, if he was discharged for proper cause, or if he quit work voluntarily. In the case below, the issue was whether the claimant had disqualified herself from receiving benefits.

Layton v. Bureau of Unemployment Compensation
218 N.E.2d 767 (Ohio 1965)

McCRYSTAL, JUSTICE: This matter is before the court on appeal from the decision of the Board of Review of the Bureau of Unemployment Compensation.

The appellant, Susan A. Layton, had been employed at the Fanny Farmer Candy shop in Norwalk, Ohio, from August 11, 1958, until March 17, 1965, when she was separated by reason of a voluntary quit. On March 18, 1965, she was employed by the Clevite Harris Products Company, Milan, Ohio, and was laid off March 26, 1965, due to lack of work. Appellant subsequently filed application for unemployment benefits, which application was disallowed by the Board of Review. Basis for the decision of the Board of Review was Section 4141.29(D)(2)(a), Revised Code, which reads in part as follows:

(D). . . no individual may serve a waiting period or be paid benefits under the following conditions: . . . (2) For the duration of his unemployment if the administrator finds that: (a) He quit his work without just cause . . .

The record discloses that the appellant, with some six and a half years steady employment with Fanny Farmer, where she was earning at a pay rate of $1.65 per hour, applied for employment with Clevite Harris and was offered a position paying $2.37 per hour. After giving a week's notice to Fanny Farmer, she was separated and on the following day went to work for Clevite Harris. Her position at Clevite Harris lasted one week and two days, when she was separated due to lack of work.

The record also discloses that the reason for the appellant's switch in jobs was the 40% increase in pay, plus the fact that the Clevite Harris plant was 3 or 4 miles closer to her home.

The question raised in this appeal is whether, under the facts so stated, the appellant quit the job with Fanny Farmer "without just cause." It is the opinion of this court that the appellant's separation from Fanny Farmer was "with just cause." The sections of the Revised Code pertaining to the Unemployment Compensation Act do not define "just cause" and, hence, each case must be decided on its individual facts. To hold that an employee who leaves one job to take on a better paying job automatically disqualifies himself from unemployment compensation until employed a sufficient time under the new employment would be a harsh rule and contrary to the liberal intent and purpose of the Unemployment Compensation Act. While there may be cases where the quitting of one job to secure another might well be "without just cause," as where the reason for such move was based on personal whims or for insufficient cause, the facts in this case are not of that nature.

The appellant here had been steadily employed for six and a half years with a long established and well known candy manufacturer. When a position with another well known and established manufacturing company was offered to her with an approximate 40% increase in pay, she accepted it. To rule that such a transfer of jobs in a period of rising living costs would be a quit "without just cause" would put a penalty on one's desire to better one's financial position and a premium on being satisfied with more security at less pay. Such interpretation of the Unemployment Compensation Act could not be reconciled with the intent of the Legislature or with one's inherent desire to improve his standard of living.

It is, therefore, the conclusion of the court that the decision of the Board of Review was unlawful, unreasonable and against the manifest weight of the evidence and is, therefore, reversed and vacated. [DECISION REVERSED]

A worker is disqualified from receiving payments if he is on strike because of a labor dispute. In one case, a nonstriking employee honored the picket lines of striking employees of the employer and filed for unemployment compensation. The court held that he would have been entitled to payments if he had been in actual fear that there probably would be violence or that he would suffer bodily harm if he attempted to cross the picket line. His refusal to go to work in such a case would have been involuntary. However, in ruling against the claimant, the court found that he had entertained no real fear but had voluntarily refused to cross the picket line out of conscience and sympathy with the striking union, which constituted active participation in the dispute.

The maximum period during which benefits are payable varies from state to state and generally has ranged from twenty-six to thirty-nine weeks. Both in 1958 and 1961, because of recessions, Congress temporarily authorized extension of the period that benefits would be available by up to one-half of the maximum provided by the states. In 1961, all states elected to participate in the program since the financing was accomplished by a temporary increase in the Federal payroll tax. The maximum amount of weekly payments for unemployment also varies widely from state to state. Usually it is computed as a percentage of the highest quarterly earnings in a base period.

As of this writing, the Federal unemployment tax has been increased from the original 3 percent to 3.2 percent of payroll paid by covered industries. However, the maximum credit permitted employers for contributions to the state remains at 2.7 percent. All money received by a state unemployment fund is required to be turned over to the Secretary of the Treasury, who deposits it in the Federal

Unemployment Trust Fund on account for that state. The state may make withdrawals only for the payment of unemployment benefits. Annually, the Federal portion of the tax (0.5 percent) is used first to appropriate funds to the states to cover all of their costs of administration of unemployment compensation and state employment agencies. Any balance remaining is automatically transferred to the Federal Unemployment Trust Fund.

All states have adopted experience rating systems which excuse employers who have a good record of maintaining stable employment from paying part or all of the state unemployment tax. Such systems were adopted as a result of the Federal Unemployment Tax Act, which now allows employers a credit against the Federal tax not only for amounts paid the state but also for such amounts as they are excused from paying because of a good experience rating. Thus, those businesses with a good rating pay less unemployment taxes than the ones with a higher unemployment experience. As a result of the credit permitted by the experience rating system, the average unemployment tax rate nationwide has been considerably less than the 3.2 percent provided for in the Social Security Act, as amended. In 1967 it averaged only 1.6 percent. Experience rating has given employers the incentive to attempt to control their unemployment record and to detect fraudulent claims filed by former employees. On the minus side it means that taxes will be lower during times when the economy is in good condition and higher when general conditions are bad.

7 FAIR EMPLOYMENT PRACTICES

The most important legislation relating to fair employment practices on the Federal level is found in the Civil Rights Act of 1964. The provisions of the Act which affect labor law are applicable to employers with twenty-five or more employees, labor unions with twenty-five or more members, all labor unions which operate a hiring hall, and employment agencies. They are not applicable to governmental units, corporations wholly owned by the United States government, Indian tribes, and private membership clubs. Exemptions are also provided for religious corporations, associations, or societies with respect to the employment of individuals of a particular religion to perform work connected with the carrying on of their religious activities, and educational institutions with respect to the employment of persons connected with the educational activities of the institutions.

One of the major purposes of the Act is to eliminate job discrimination based on race, color, religion, sex, or national origin. Discrimination for any of these reasons is a violation of the law, except that:

1 Employers, employment agencies, and labor unions, can discriminate on the basis of religion, sex, or national origin in those certain instances where the above categories are bona fide occupational qualifications.
2 Employers who are working under government security programs can deny employment to individuals because of their inability to obtain security clearance. (This may be unconstitutional.)

3 Employers can deny employment to individuals who are members of the Communist party of the United States or of any other organization which is required to register as a Communist action or Communist-front organization. (This may be unconstitutional.)

4 Employers can establish different standards, compensation, terms, or conditions of employment if they are applied pursuant to a bona fide seniority or merit system.

The types of employer action in which discrimination is prohibited include discharge; refusal to hire; compensation; and terms, conditions or privileges of employment. Additionally, employers are not permitted to segregate or classify employees on any of these bases where the result tends to affect employee status or opportunity adversely. The Act also prevents employers who have or share control of apprenticeship or training programs from discriminating in the admissions to or operations of such programs.

Employment *agencies* are prohibited from either *failing to refer* or from *actually referring* an individual for employment on the basis of race, color, religion, sex, or national origin. This provision is in marked contrast to that binding *employers* where it is unlawful only to fail or refuse to hire on discriminatory grounds—the affirmative act of hiring for a discriminatory reason is apparently not illegal. For example, assume that a contractor with a government contract, in order to improve his compliance reports, seeks a qualified black engineer and requests an employment agency to refer such an individual. The agency complies with the request and a black is referred and hired. Unless a white applicant was discriminated against, the employer probably did not commit an unlawful practice; but the employment agency, by referring an individual on the basis of his color, unquestionably did commit an unlawful practice under the Act.

Note that regarding general hiring, referrals, advertising, and admissions to apprenticeship programs, the Act allows discrimination only on the basis of religion, sex, or national origin and only where these considerations are bona fide occupational qualifications. The omission of *race* and *color* from this exception must mean the Congress does not feel that these two factors are ever bona fide occupational qualifications.

Additional exemptions exist with respect both to laws creating preferential treatment for veterans and to hiring on the basis of professionally developed ability tests. In the following case the requirement by a company of a high school education and the passing of a general intelligence test as a condition of employment and promotion was challenged.

Griggs v. Duke Power Company
91 S.Ct. 849 (1971)

BURGER, CHIEF JUSTICE: We granted the writ in this case to resolve the question whether an employer is prohibited by the Civil Rights Act of 1964, Title VII, from requiring a high school education or passing of a standardized general intelligence test as a condition of employment in or transfer to jobs when (a) neither standard Is shown to be significantly related to successful job performance, (b) both requirements operate to disqualify Negroes at a substantially higher rate than white applicants, and (c) the jobs in question formerly had been filled only by white employees as part of a long-standing practice of giving preference to whites.

. . . All the petitioners are employed at the Company's Dan River Steam Station, a power generating facility located at Draper, North Carolina. At the time this action was instituted, the Company had 95 employees at the Dan River Station, 14 or whom were Negroes; 13 of these are petitioners here.

The District Court found that prior to July 2, 1965, the effective date of the Civil Rights Act of 1964, the Company openly discriminated on the basis of race in the hiring and assigning of employees at its Dan River plant. The plant was organized into five operating departments: (1) Labor, (2) Coal Handling, (3) Operations, (4) Maintenance, and (5) Laboratory and Test. Negroes were employed only in the Labor Department where the highest paying jobs paid less than the lowest paying jobs in the other four "operating" departments in which only whites were employed. Promotions were normally made within each department on the basis of job seniority. Transferees into a department usually began in the lowest position.

In 1955 the Company instituted a policy of requiring a high school education for initial assignment to any department except Labor, and for transfer from the Coal Handling to any "inside" department (Operations, Maintenance, or Laboratory). When the Company abandoned its policy of restricting Negroes to the Labor Department in 1965, completion of high school also was made a prerequisite to transfer from Labor to any other department. From the time the high school requirement was instituted to the time of trial, however, white employees hired before the time of the high school education requirement continued to perform satisfactorily and achieve promotions in the "operating" departments. Findings on this score are not challenged.

The Company added a further requirement for new employees on July 2, 1965, the date on which Title VII became effective. To qualify for placement in any but the Labor Department it became necessary to register satisfactory scores on two professionally prepared aptitude tests, as well as to have a high school education. Completion of high school alone continued to render employees eligible for transfer to the four desirable departments from which Negroes had been excluded if the incumbent had been employed prior to the time of the new requirement. In September 1965 the Company began to permit incumbent employees who lacked a high school education to qualify for transfer from Labor or Coal Handling to an "inside" job by passing two tests—the Wonderlic Personnel Test, which purports to measure general intelligence, and the Bennett Mechanical Aptitude Test. Neither was directed or intended to measure the ability to learn to perform a particular job or category of jobs. The requisite scores used for both initial hiring and transfer approximated the national median for high school graduates.

The District Court had found that while the Company previously followed a policy of overt racial discrimination in a period prior to the Act, such conduct had ceased. The District Court also concluded that Title VII was intended to be prospective only and, consequently, the impact of prior inequities was beyond the reach of corrective action authorized by the Act.

The Court of Appeals was confronted with a question of first impression, as are we, concerning the meaning of Title VII. After careful analysis a majority of that court concluded that a subjective test of the employer's intent should govern, particularly in a close case, and that in this case there was no showing of a discriminatory purpose in the adoption of the diploma and test requirements. On this basis, the Court of Appeals concluded there was no violation of the Act. . . .

The objective of Congress in the enactment of Title VII is plain from the language of the statute. It was to achieve equality of employment opportunities and remove barriers that have operated in the past to favor an identifiable group of white employees over other employees. Under the Act, practices, procedures, or tests neutral on their face, and even neutral in terms of intent, cannot be maintained if they operate to "freeze" the status quo of prior discriminatory employment practices.

The Court of Appeals' opinion, and the partial dissent, agreed that, on the record in the present case, "whites fare far better on the Company's alternative requirements" than Negroes. This consequence would appear to be directly traceable to race. Basic intelligence must have the means of articulation to manifest itself fairly in a testing process. Because they are Negroes, petitioners have long received inferior education in segregated schools and this Court expressly recognized these differences in *Gaston County v. United States*. There, because of the inferior education received by Negroes in North Carolina, this Court barred the institution of a literacy test for voter registration on the ground that the test would abridge the right to vote indirectly on account of race. Congress did not intend by Title VII, however, to guarantee a job to every person regardless of qualifications. In short, the Act does not command that any person be hired simply because he was formerly the subject of discrimination, or because he is a member of a minority group. Discriminatory preference for any group, minority or majority, is precisely and only what Congress has proscribed. What is required by Congress is the removal of artificial, arbitrary, and unnecessary barriers to employment when the barriers operate invidiously to discriminate on the basis of racial or other impermissible classification.

. . . The Act proscribes not only overt discrimination but also practices that are fair in form, but discriminatory in operation. The touchstone is business necessity. If an employment practice which operates to exclude Negroes cannot be shown to be related to job performance, the practice is prohibited.

On the record before us, neither the high school completion requirement nor the general intelligence test is shown to bear a demonstrable relationship to successful performance of the jobs for which it was used. Both were adopted, as the Court of Appeals noted, without meaningful study of their relationship to job-performance ability. Rather, a vice president of the Company testified, the requirements were instituted on the Company's judgment that they generally would improve the overall quality of the work force.

The evidence, however, shows that employees who have not completed high school or taken the tests have continued to perform satisfactorily and make progress in departments for which the high school and test criteria are now used. The promotion record of present employees who would not be able to meet the new criteria thus suggests the possibility that the requirements may not be needed even for the limited purpose of preserving the avowed policy of advancement within the Company. In the context of this case, it is unnecessary to reach the question whether testing requirements that take into account capability for the next succeeding position or related future promotion might be utilized upon a showing that such long range requirements fulfill a genuine business need. In the present case the Company has made no such showing.

The Court of Appeals held that the Company had adopted the diploma and test requirements without any "intention to discriminate against Negro employees." We do not suggest that either the District Court or the Court of Appeals erred in examining the employer's intent; but good intent or absence of discriminatory intent does not redeem employment procedures or testing mechanisms that operate as "built-in headwinds" for minority groups and are unrelated to measuring job capability. . . .

The facts of this case demonstrate the inadequacy of broad and general testing devices as well as the infirmity of using diplomas or degrees as fixed measures of capability. History is filled with examples of men and women who rendered highly effective performance without the conventional badges of accomplishment in terms of certificates, diplomas, or degrees. Diplomas and tests are useful servants, but Congress has mandated the common-sense proposition that they are not to become masters of reality.

The Company contends that its general intelligence tests are specifically permitted by § 703(h) of the Act. That section authorizes the use of "any professionally developed ability test" that is not "designed, intended, *or used* to discriminate because of race . . . ." (Emphasis added.)

The Equal Employment Opportunity Commission, having enforcement responsibility, has issued guidelines interpreting § 703(h) to permit only the use of job-related tests. The administrative interpretation of the Act by the enforcing agency is entitled to great deference. Since the Act and its legislative history support the Commission's construction, this affords good reason to treat the Guidelines as expressing the will of Congress. . . .

Nothing in the Act precludes the use of testing or measuring procedures; obviously they are useful. What Congress has forbidden is giving these devices and mechanisms controlling force unless they are demonstrably a reasonable measure of job performance. Congress has not commanded that the less qualified be preferred over the better qualified simply because of minority origins. Far from disparaging job qualifications as such, Congress has made such qualifications the controlling factor, so that race, religion, nationality, and sex become irrelevant. What Congress has commanded is that any tests used must measure the person for the job and not the person in the abstract.

The judgment of the Court of Appeals is, as to that portion of the judgment appealed from, reversed. [REVERSED]

The ban contained in the Civil Rights Act of 1964 on sex discrimination is a result of an amendment proposed by a former Representative from Virginia in the hope that such a provision would make the bill unsavory enough overall to spell its defeat. Thus the blow the Act struck for equal treatment for women was almost happenstance. The case below challenged the validity of a state law prohibiting women from being employed for certain work as being in conflict with the Federal law.

Sail'er Inn, Inc. v. Kirby
485 P.2d 529 (Cal. 1971)

PETERS, JUSTICE: Petitioners, holders of on-sale liquor licenses, seek a writ of mandate to prevent the Department of Alcoholic Beverage Control from revoking their licenses because they hired women bartenders, contrary to the prohibition contained in section 25656 of the Business and Professions Code. Section 25656 prohibits women from tending bar except when they are licensees, wives of licensees or are, singly or with their husbands, the sole shareholders of a corporation holding the license. Petitioners . . . contend that the code section violates . . . the 1964 Federal Civil Rights Act. . . .

Petitioners challenge the constitutionality of the statute on its face; no material facts are disputed. They raise important legal issues of statewide significance. Two of them are placed in the untenable situation of having to choose whether to obey possibly conflicting federal and state laws and face a penalty under the one they choose to disobey. . . .

Petitioners urge that section 25656 conflicts with the nondiscriminatory hiring provision contained in Title VII of the Federal Civil Rights Act of 1964. A state law, however clearly within a state's acknowledged power, which interferes with or is contrary to federal law is void under the supremacy clause of the United States Constitution (U.S.Const., art. VI, cl.2).

The Attorney General urges, however, that the Federal Civil Rights Act does not apply because section 2 of the Twenty-first Amendment to the United States Constitution precludes federal interference with state regulation of alcoholic beverages. Section 2 provides that *"[t]he transportation or importation into any State, Territory, or possession* of the United States for delivery or use therein of intoxicating liquors, *in violation of the laws thereof,* is hereby prohibited." (Italics added.) The Attorney General contends that this amendment "cedes vast plenary powers" to the states to regulate alcoholic beverages "unfettered" by the commerce clause. Since the 1964 Civil Rights Act was passed pursuant to Congress' commerce clause power, it is contended that a state's power to regulate liquor is also unfettered by the 1964 Civil Rights Act.

This argument must fail. The Twenty-first Amendment clearly was not intended to work such a wholesale "repeal" of the commerce clause in the area of alcoholic beverage control. When national prohibition was terminated by section 1 of the Twenty-first Amendment, section 2 was added as a "saving clause" to protect the laws of states which chose to retain prohibition against a possible conflict with the commerce clause. The language of the amendment clearly reflects the purpose, since it prohibits the importation or transporting of liquor only into states where such importation will be in violation of the laws thereof. . . .

"'Since the Twenty-first Amendment . . . the right of a state to prohibit or regulate the *importation* of intoxicating liquor is not limited by the commerce clause.'" . . . "To draw a conclusion . . . that the Twenty-first Amendment has somehow operated to 'repeal' the Commerce Clause wherever regulation of intoxicating liquors is concerned . . . be an absurd oversimplification. If the Commerce Clause had been *pro tanto* 'repealed,' then Congress would be left with no regulatory power over interstate or foreign commerce in intoxicating liquor. Such a conclusion would be patently bizarre and is demonstrably incorrect." . . .

Section 25656 is not even tangentially related to "transportation or importation" of liquor into California, and therefore does not fall within the literal language of the Twenty-first Amendment. The statute merely regulates employment at the retail level, and has nothing to do with the flow of alcoholic beverages into the state.

But even if the amendment were broadly construed to cover all state laws regulating the liquor business, the interests and issues at stake in employment discrimination cases present no conflict with the intent and purposes of the Twenty-first Amendment. Title VII of the Civil Rights Act was passed to prevent the impact of racial and sexual discrimination in employment on interstate commerce. It was not enacted to regulate the flow of alcohol as a commodity in interstate commerce. Since the aim of the Civil Rights Act is so wholly different from that of the Twenty-first Amendment, the two provisions in no way clash with each other. . . .

We turn to the question whether section 25656 is in direct conflict with . . . the Civil Rights Act of 1964.

Section 2000e-2(a) makes it unlawful to hire or to "limit, segregate or classify" employees in any way which would tend to deprive an employee of employment opportunities on the basis of sex. Section 2000e-2(e) permits an exception only where there is a "bona fide occupational qualification reasonably necessary to the normal operation of that particular business or enterprise, . . .

. . . [W]e . . . hold that that statute is not based upon a bona fide occupational qualification necessary to the operation of a bar and is therefore in direct conflict with section 2000e-2 of the Civil Rights Act.

Certainly . . . women as a class are as capable as men of mixing drinks and are permitted to do so in many states. The technical capabilities of women are not, however, at issue here. The Legislature concedes this point when it exempts women licensees and wives of male licensees from the general prohibition without regard to their capacity to prepare spirits for consumption by patrons of liquor establishments.

The more serious contention that a bartender must be physically strong enough to protect himself against inebriated customers and to maintain order in the bar, and that women as a class are unable to do so, must also be rejected. Whether a condition constitutes "a bona fide occupational qualification reasonably necessary to the normal operation of that particular business or enterprise" is a matter of evidence. The state has made no showing whatever that bartenders are endangered by their work and require physical strength, not possessed by women, for self defense and to maintain order.

The reason for the lack of such a showing is apparent. As we have pointed out, the saloon days of the Wild West are long gone. Nowadays the typical bar does not provide a setting for violence and danger, if in fact it ever did. At most, the dangers feared by the Attorney General may justify discrimination only in a particular establishment where, first, the employer can prove that such problems arise, and, second, that "substantially all women" lack the requisite strength to deal with such problems. Such perils cannot serve as the basis for a blanket statewide statutory prohibition against the employment of women bartenders.

We conclude that section 25656 conflicts with section 2000e-2 of the Civil Rights Act. As to those liquor licensees who employ the requisite 25 employees and otherwise come within the prohibition of section 2000e-2, section 25656 is invalid and must fall. . . .

For the reasons stated, we find section 25656 invalid. Let the peremptory writ of mandate issue compelling the Director of the Department of Alcoholic Beverage Control to cease license revocation proceedings based upon section 25656 of the Business and Professions Code and to cease enforcement of the section. [SO ORDERED]

Original enforcement of those provisions of the Civil Rights Act outlined above is in the hands of a special Federal administrative agency known as the Equal Employment Opportunity Commission. Its powers are largely restricted to conducting investigations and to moral persuasion. In the course of its investigations, the Commission has broad authority to examine and copy evidence, require the production of documentary evidence, hold hearings, and subpoena and examine witnesses under oath. Upon finding reasonable cause, any member of the Commission may individually file unlawful employment practice charges; but the Commission has no power to issue cease and desist orders or make binding determinations against respondents. Faced with what it considers to be an unlawful employment practice, its authority to resolve the matter is restricted to the sphere of conciliation and persuasion in informal efforts to achieve voluntary compliance.

If it is unsuccessful in its efforts, the Commission can merely so advise the aggrieved person. The Commission itself cannot institute a civil action for enforcement. Its authority to commence civil proceedings is limited to two narrow cases: it may institute legal action to compel compliance with a *prior court order* in the case of a defaulting employer, employment agency, or labor union; and it may obtain a court order requiring recalcitrant respondents to produce records or to appear as witnesses or otherwise to cooperate with the Commission in the exercise of its investigatory powers.

Ancillary powers of the Commission include promulgating record-keeping and report-making requirements, controlling the posting of required notices, establishing procedural regulations, furnishing those persons covered by the Act with technical assistance, cooperating with and utilizing state and other agencies, and making appropriate studies.

While it appears that the power of the Commission is substantially limited to that of moral persuasion, it must be kept in mind that Commission *members* have the right to file charges, and can advise and counsel individuals to institute civil actions which the Commission itself cannot bring. Moreover, while the Commission itself cannot commence civil actions, the Attorney General, in proper cases, may either intervene in actions brought by individuals, or himself institute proceedings. The Commission is expressly authorized to refer matters with recommendations for action and otherwise advise and assist the Attorney General in such suits.

The Congressional intent of preserving the vitality of local fair employment laws finds its expression in the enforcement procedures. Section 706(b) of the Act provides that where the unlawful practice alleged, if true, is violative of a state or local law, no charge may be filed with the Commission until sixty days after the proceedings have been commenced under that law. Similarly, when a charge is filed by a Commission member where a local law provides relief, the Commission must notify the appropriate officials and defer all action until the local authority has had, in general, at least sixty days to resolve the matter. In either case, the sixty-day waiting requirement is dispensed with if the local proceeding is terminated before that time.

The Federal enforcement procedure can be summarized as follows:

1 Proceedings are commenced by the filing of a written charge by either an individual claiming to be aggrieved or a member of the Commission.
2 The Commission must furnish respondent with a copy of the charge—which cannot be made public—and make an investigation.
3 If the Commission determines there is reasonable cause to believe the charge is true, it endeavors to eliminate the alleged unlawful practices by informal methods of conference, conciliation and persuasion.
4 If the Commission is unable to obtain voluntary compliance within thirty days after the charge was filed (this period may be expanded to sixty days) the Commission so notifies the aggrieved.
5 Within thirty days after being so notified, the aggrieved may commence a civil action against respondent in a District Court. In the court's discretion, the Attorney General may intervene upon certification that the case is of general public importance.

6 The court may grant injunctive relief or order affirmative remedial action only if it finds that respondent *intentionally* engaged in an unlawful employment practice. Such relief may consist of an injunction ordering, among other things, the reinstatement or hiring of the aggrieved employee, with or without back pay. Interim earnings reduce the back pay allowable. The court may further award attorney's fees as part of the costs to any prevailing party other than the Commission or the United States. Either of these, however, may be held liable for costs including attorney's fees. Appeals are taken, as usual, to the United States Courts of Appeals.

7 In the event that a respondent fails to comply with a court order, the Commission may commence proceedings to compel such compliance. The courts retain their usual civil contempt powers but respondents are entitled to jury trials for criminal contempt charges based on conduct outside the court room.

As indicated above, the Attorney General may, upon certification of the general public importance of a civil action brought by an aggrieved person, intervene in it. But beyond this power of intervention, the Attorney General may himself initiate a civil action where he "has reasonable cause to believe that any person or group of persons is engaged in a pattern or practice of resistance to the full enjoyment of any of the rights secured by . . . [the Act], and that the pattern or practice is of such a nature and intended to deny the full exercise of the rights . . . [therein] described. . . ." In such a case, there is no requirement that any charges have been filed by an aggrieved person; neither need the state nor Commission machinery be utilized before the action is instituted directly in a district court and given preferential treatment.

If a person who charges a violation of the Act first follows state procedure, he must file a charge with the Fair Employment Practices Commission within 210 days after the alleged discrimination took place or within 30 days after he receives notice that the state agency has terminated proceedings, whichever is sooner. Where there is no state fair employment law, charges must be filed with the FEPC within 90 days after the alleged unfair practice occurred.

After the first six years in operation of the Equal Employment Opportunities Commission, action was taken in fewer than half of the 30,000 or so cases in which it found discrimination. As of this writing it would appear that the Commission will be given new powers in the near future. Two bills with this objective have been introduced. The House passed a measure in September of 1971 which would empower the EEOC to bring suits itself against employers or unions it finds to be guilty of discriminatory practices. A Senate bill would go even further and give the EEOC quasi-judicial powers to issue cease and desist orders, similar to those of the FTC and NLRB.

Besides the EEOC, the Office of Federal Contract Compliance (OFCC) of the Department of Labor is actively engaged in preventing job discrimination by those performing contracts which use Federal funds. The OFCC was created to enforce an Executive order of the President prohibiting discrimination in such contracts on the basis of race, religion, color, national origin, or sex. This agency has issued guidelines for compliance with the order which requires contractors to take *affirmative action* to avoid unlawful discrimination in the recruitment, employment, promotion, training, rate of compensation, or layoff of workers.

The affirmative-action requirement means that contractors must actively recruit members of minority groups which are being underutilized. That is, members of such groups must be recruited when there are fewer of them working in a given job category than one would reasonably expect there should be, considering their availability. Compliance reports must be filed with the agency, and failure to supply the information required by it constitutes a violation of the Executive order. Anyone who feels aggrieved may file a complaint with the agency within 180 days of the alleged violation. If after a fair hearing it is found that a contractor is in violation of the Executive order, his contract can be cancelled by the OFCC, or it may simply be suspended pending compliance. Contractors are expected to guarantee compliance by their subcontractors with the order.

Other Federal legislation which pertains to fair employment practices includes the Equal Pay Act of 1963 (discussed in section 3 as an amendment to the Fair Labor Standards Act), which requires that women be paid wages equivalent to those paid men for equivalent work (or vice versa), and the Age Discrimination in Employment Act of 1967, which affords protection to persons between forty and sixty-five years old from job discrimination against them because of their age. Executive personnel are exempt from the Equal Pay Law. Thus, an employer is permitted to pay a female executive less than a male holding an equivalent position. Also exempted are differentials based on factors other than sex as well as those based on merit, seniority, and piece rates. It should be noted that if a pay differential is permitted under the Equal Pay Act, then it is not in violation of the Civil Rights Act either.

In recent years, fair employment practices legislation has been introduced and passed by many state legislatures. The purpose of this legislation is to ensure equal job opportunities to all persons, regardless of race, creed, or color. To date, the goals of these laws have not been obtained even in those states which have adopted the statutes, primarily because equal opportunity requires equal background and ability, and compliance with the spirit as well as the letter of the law. Until educational opportunities are equal, it is not likely that job opportunities will be equal. A typical act provides that it is an unfair employment practice for any employer to refuse to hire or otherwise discriminate against any individual because of his race, color, religion, national origin, or ancestry. If employment agencies or labor organizations discriminate against an individual in any way because of one of the foregoing reasons, they are also guilty of an unfair employment practice. Such acts usually establish an administrative body, generally known as the Fair Employment Practices Commission, which is given the power to promulgate rules and regulations to effectuate the purposes of the act and hear and decide charges of violations filed by complainants. If conciliation fails and the commission after a formal hearing sustains the charge, it is empowered to issue an order requiring the person charged to cease and desist from the unfair employment practice complained of. The Commission may also take such other action as is necessary to eliminate the effect of the original unfair act.

In addition, many states have enacted equal pay statutes which are similar to the Federal one, but these have not proved to be very effective.

REVIEW QUESTIONS—CHAPTER 14

1 Define the following terms introduced in this chapter: agency; workmen's compensation; unemployment compensation; fair employment practices legislation; apparent authority; estoppel; trade secrets; contributory negligence; assumption of the risk; and fellow-servant doctrine.

2 Under what circumstances is a principal liable on contracts entered into by an agent?

3 Under what circumstances is a master or principal liable for the torts of a servant or agent? Explain.

4 Is the principal-agent relationship fiduciary in character? Explain.

5 Review the basic requirements of the Fair Labor Standards Act and the scope of its coverage.

6 Give examples of jobs that are not covered by the Fair Labor Standards Act.

7 What common-law defenses have been eliminated by workmen's compensation legislation?

8 When is an employer liable for the accidental injuries, diseases, or deaths of his employees?

9 List the elements of loss used in computing workmen's compensation benefits.

10 Compare the workmen's compensation law of your state with the Federal Employer's Liability Act.

11 Under what circumstances is there a waiting period before a person is entitled to receive unemployment compensation?

12 What are the limitations on the use of general ability or intelligence tests in the hiring and promotion of employees?

13 Under what circumstances is it legally permissible to discriminate in the hiring of an employee?

14 Discuss the weaknesses in Federal laws aimed at eliminating job discrimination.

Chapter Fifteen

Legal Aspects of Labor-Management Relations

1 INTRODUCTION

Management and labor are mutually dependent for their continued existence, but an inherent conflict exists between them. One of management's main objectives is to keep costs at a minimum, while labor naturally seeks the highest wages and fringe benefits possible. Management frequently believes that it has the duty and responsibility to make all decisions respecting the business, while labor argues that it should participate in them. Management's view is based on the argument that the ownership of capital carries with it the right and responsibility to decide how that capital is to be used. If the capital is used unwisely, the owners point to the fact that *they* bear the risk of its loss.

Labor, on the other hand, bases its claim of right to participate in business decision making on the philosophy espousing industrial democracy as the proper way of economic life. This doctrine urges that employees have an inherent right to participate in arriving at decisions which greatly affect their lives, especially those directly involving wages, hours of work, and employment conditions. Labor argues that capital owned by a business is of little value to its operation as a going concern without the services of its employees and that if risk of loss is a criterion, workers also bear their share, since they may lose their jobs in the event their employer suffers business reverses.

Individual workers have little if any bargaining power to obtain a role in business decision making. Therefore, employees have sought to unite in organizations which could bargain effectively with employers to obtain this participation. Historically employers have viewed such attempts to unionize as a threat to their rights to manage and frequently have resisted the creation of labor organizations or have refused to deal with such organizations unless compelled to do so by law.

Historically, too, the basic conflicts between labor and management have led to the disruption of the free flow of commerce and many social and economic problems for society. In disputes between management and labor, one real party in interest in addition to the owners of the business and its employees is the general public. Thus, the law as it affects labor must be designed to reflect the conflicting concerns of all three of these parties directly affected by labor-management relations.

The law has been of prime importance in the resolution of disputes between labor and management and in seeking to produce a proper balance between their conflicting interests. Much of the more important legislation in this regard has the avowed purpose of encouraging free collective bargaining and the settlement of disagreements by negotiation. This chapter will examine the legal environment of labor-management relations and the collective-bargaining process as it has developed and as it exists today.

2   HISTORY OF THE UNION MOVEMENT

In the colonial period, there was a great shortage of labor in America. This was due in part to the low cost of land, which made it easy for a person to acquire a farm and work it for himself. Those who worked for someone else were mainly members of the family, apprentices, indentured servants (including a great many convicts), and Negro slaves. The hours of labor for these people were long, generally from sunrise to sunset. After the Revolutionary War, this shortage still prevailed. Most of the able-bodied men were engaged in agriculture and those who were not so occupied were mainly self-employed craftsmen.

During the nineteenth century, the population grew (partially because of a large number of immigrants) and the labor force increased, becoming overplentiful. This growth accompanied the dramatic change in the economy from basically agrarian to mass-production industrial. By the end of the century, instead of farming or working for themselves, most men were wage earners, dependent upon their employer and his business for a livelihood. In many instances newly developed machines made it possible to break down production steps and replace unskilled workmen altogether, or substitute unskilled workmen for the skilled. The change in the economy and methods of production brought about far-reaching changes in the relationship of laborer to employer. Independent craftsmen who produced goods which they sold directly to the consumer became rare or nonexistent. The employer and employee no longer worked together but seemingly had conflicting interests. Instead of being a master craftsman working alongside his journeymen, an employer furnished the capital for the business, became more involved in management and selling, and no longer belonged to the same social sphere.

A major problem in the distribution of finished goods and merchandise was brought about by great increases in productive capacity. Instead of marketing finished products himself, the factory owner was forced to look to middlemen to perform this function. Consumers naturally sought lower prices from competing retailers, who in turn sought lower prices from competing middlemen, who also sought lower prices from competing manufacturers. This cutthroat competition, while distinctly beneficial from the customer's point of view, was distinctly disadvantageous from the wage earner's standpoint. The answer to the manufacturer was to produce more for less. To meet prices which had been forced down by overcapacity and to protect and make some profit on his capital invested in plant and machinery, the factory owner had to reduce his costs and naturally sought to reduce the cost of labor. This was done in a number of ways: simply reducing the hourly wage or piece rate paid to present employees; employing women, children, or convicts who were available at a lower wage; or increasing the output per man-hour by utilizing machines developed through technological advances. Of course, faced with these economic pressures, employers were not prone to raise their costs to make working conditions more comfortable and enjoyable, or even to eliminate hazardous and unhealthful conditions which existed in many factories. This economic situation naturally led to attempts on the part of workingmen to organize and defend themselves. As individuals they were in a very weak bargaining position because of their oversupply. United, their ever-increasing number would give them strength, especially in a democracy, for their votes outnumbered those of the employers.

It should be noted that the labor movement did make some progress in the nineteenth century. The hours of work per day were shorter, although they still averaged eleven around 1860; in some industries such as steel, they remained at twelve a day, six days a week, until well into the twentieth century. Increased production brought increased wealth, and wages in terms of their purchasing power rose. But a greater percentage of this wealth was being retained by the owners of businesses. This caused resentment by the workers, since in their eyes they were largely responsible for the production of the business. In addition, working in a factory was degrading. The dignity of labor declined. The social gap between workman and owner widened greatly, and within the wage-earner class skilled workmen lost ground economically and socially compared to the unskilled.

For more than one hundred years, until the latter part of the nineteenth century, the attempts by laborers to organize resulted in no strong, lasting unions. During this period, membership in unions brought about some wage increases. However, during periodic depressions, times of unemployment and falling prices, wages were lowered to cut costs and nonunion workers were hired by employers. Previous members of unions abandoned their organizations because they were willing to work at any price to escape privation and hunger, and their unions had no funds for relief during bad times. Organizations were wiped out by this understandable lack of loyalty by workmen and consequent drop in membership. As a result, the union movement showed little progress during this period.

The pattern began to change from one of failure to success with the appearance of unions on the national scale. Among the first of the national unions were the Railway Brotherhoods, starting with the Engineers, who were organized in 1854, and followed by the Conductors, Firemen, and Trainmen. The Knights of Labor was organized in 1869 as a secret society at first. Anyone who worked could become a member. For a time, this union was of importance, but it disintegrated, among other reasons, because of internal dissension between skilled and unskilled workers, loss of prestige in the workingmen's eyes due to a number of strike failures, and loss of public support from occasional violence in strikes. The American Federation of Labor began in 1866 as a loose association of twenty-five almost independent national unions organized along trade lines, such as carpenters, miners, iron molders, and cigar makers. The national union concerned itself with problems which were general in nature, and avoided unskilled labor, useless strikes, and violence. After its founding, it attracted many of the skilled members from the Knights of Labor. The Industrial Workers of the World, one of the most notorious labor unions, was organized in 1905 by two socialists and indulged in strikes, physical force, and sabotage to better the lot of the unskilled. The IWW had as its ultimate aim the socialistic goal of placing the direction and control of industry in the hands of laborers by direct, violent means, and seriously damaged the cause of labor in the eyes of the public. Its demise occurred during World War I as a result of internal conflict and its inherent unpatriotic qualities.

World War I brought prosperity which enhanced union expansion, so that by 1920, the AFL numbered 4 million members. However, for a number of reasons, total union membership dropped back to about 3.5 million during the 1920s. The attempt to organize workers in the steel industry and the steel strike of 1919–1920 failed, losing prestige for labor and the hope of organizing mass-production industries for some time to come. The general public became alarmed for fear of influence by Communists and other radical left-wing elements in the labor movement. Management actively combated union activity by fighting organization or by improving working conditions so that union membership seemed unnecessary to workers. The Federal government's attitude during this period was generally antiunion, influenced no doubt by business pressures, public reaction, and a sentiment that subversive radicals had too much to do with labor.

The Great Depression caused a further setback to unions and membership dropped to less than 3 million. However, the election of Franklin D. Roosevelt with his New Deal program, including the Wagner Act, resulted in a governmental climate favoring union growth, so that by 1939 union membership increased by threefold to 9 million. Because of the influence of certain strong craft unions of skilled laborers, which were concerned with the prospect of losing control to the industrial unions of essentially unskilled laborers, the AFL in 1935 stood opposed to encouraging further organization of workers in mass-production industries. As a result, eight former AFL unions with a membership of 1 million, including the United Mine Workers, formed a separate organization which was to become the Congress of Industrial Organizations, and set about organizing such industries as steel, oil, automobile, and rubber.

World War II brought an end to the unemployment which had existed despite the New Deal and further stimulated union growth, so that by 1946 the total union membership reached 15 million, 7.2 million of these belonging to the AFL and 6 million to the CIO. After World War II, unions flexed their muscles in a series of crippling strikes which were felt by the whole nation. The obvious control that unions had gained over the economy and their great power in getting their own way resulted in a loss of support for organized labor from the general public. It became apparent that too much power in the hands of the leaders of large unions would result in exploitation just as *laissez faire* had resulted in business combination and monopoly inimical to the public interest. Since the need for control of big labor was demonstrated to be as essential as the need for control of big business, in 1947 Congress passed the Taft-Hartley Labor Management Relations Act, which still is the law essentially as enacted originally. In 1956, the rift between the AFL and the CIO was mended and the two giant unions merged, having a total membership of around 15 million. One factor causing merger no doubt was a desire to become more effective politically. Unions had been unable to procure the repeal of the Taft-Hartley Act and had not acquired any significant legislation favoring labor at the expense of management since the days of the New Deal.

Throughout their history, the prime goals of unions generally have been related to bettering labor's economic position and providing economic security for members. Labor organizations have more or less continuously placed pressures on the owners of capital to reduce the hours of employment and increase the amount of wages paid employees, so that wage earners would obtain a larger proportionate share of the fruits of their work and would have more leisure time for the enjoyment of these increased benefits. Other economic goals of unions have included payments to the unemployed during periods of recession or depression and some form of pension payments to elderly, retired members. Another objective of organized labor was to improve working conditions by eliminating hazardous and unhealthy situations and to shift the losses incurred in industrial accidents from the injured employee to the employer. The latter was accomplished with the adoption of workmen's compensation statutes previously discussed.

Unions have used political and economic pressures as weapons to achieve their objectives. They have exerted political pressure by placing their case before the general public in an attempt to gain sympathetic support. And, as was noted, the voting power of the union members themselves could not be ignored by politicians. Unions have exerted economic pressure through strikes (which also made the public aware of their complaints) and through boycotts.

Employers have combated union action with their own political and economic pressures. They, too, have formed organizations and have sought general public support of their point of view through the media, to which they generally have had better access than the unions. The main economic weapons which employers used early in this century were related to their bargaining superiority. With an overabundance of labor, employers maintained an open shop and refused to hire union members. So-called "yellow-dog contracts" were used, in which the worker agrees when he is hired that he will not join a union, and can be fired in the event that he does. To locate union members and organizers, employers shared their information by circulating "black lists," and utilized employees who were "labor spies" in their own plants. If labor trouble were brewing, an employer could take the initiative by using the device of a "lock-out," or, in other words, closing his factory and stopping production for a time. This permitted the owner to choose the time of inactivity and made the workers aware of the importance of their jobs to them, since they could earn and receive no wages during the period of shutdown. Unions without relief funds could be destroyed by loss of members during a lock-out. If the unionized employees of a business went out on strike, the employer could fire and replace them with nonunion laborers or "scabs." Often the use of "scabs" to take the place of strikers would lead to retaliation by the union members in the form of violence which resulted in damage to property, injury to persons, and sometimes death.

The common law placed a very powerful weapon in the hands of employers whose workers were on strike—the court injunction. An injunction is an order of a court of equity directing the defendant to do or refrain from doing certain specific acts. Its issuance is largely within the discretion of the court, but generally an injunction will lie where irreparable damage to the plaintiff or his property is likely and the law offers no adequate remedy. If the defendant persists in committing the enjoined acts, he is subject to fine and incarceration for contempt of court. Toward the end of the nineteenth century, courts became increasingly liberal in granting injunctive relief to employers whose workers were on strike. Of course, where actual violence by the strikers was resulting in loss of property and life and was likely to continue, courts were very sympathetic to the employer. The right of workers to strike included the right to leave their jobs in protest and peacefully voice their complaints and grievances but did not extend to actual force, violence, and destruction, which were illegal. Some courts took the view that such a thing as peaceful picketing did not exist, that *all* picketing was likely to result in violence and destruction, and issued injunctions forbidding picketing even where no physical force had been used by the strikers. Other courts favored factory owners even more by holding that any *strike* could be enjoined because it was certain to cause irreparable damage.

It is easy to see that prior to the 1930s the bargaining position of the employer was vastly superior to that of his workers. In the absence of statutory restriction, the employer was free to hire and fire whom he pleased and discriminate against union members. He could import nonunion help during a strike and generally had the court injunction available as a weapon. Thus, the unions had as secondary goals the enactment of remedial statutes which would neutralize the bargaining position of employers. Only by doing this could the unions make effective use of their main weapons—the strike and the boycott—and attain their primary economic goals. Unions sought a closed shop, legislation prohibiting discrimination against their members, the outlawing of yellow-dog contracts and the use of scab labor, and, of course, statutes prohibiting the use of court injunctions in labor disputes. The sections which follow reflect the extent to which unions have been successful in attaining many of their economic and political objectives.

3   FEDERAL LAWS AFFECTING LABOR RELATIONS PRIOR TO 1935

Prior to the twentieth century, there were no Federal statutes dealing directly with labor-management relations. The law was developed in the individual cases and was based essentially on contract principles rather than on economic or social policies.

The first Federal statute of any importance was the Clayton Act, passed in 1914. Besides its antitrust provisions, it contained two sections relating to labor. The first attempted to prohibit Federal courts from enjoining activities such as strikes and picketing in a dispute over terms or conditions of employment. However, its language was narrowly construed by the Supreme Court, adversely affecting the interests of organized labor. The second section stated that the antitrust laws did not apply to labor unions or their members in lawfully carrying out their legitimate objects. Although the Sherman Antitrust Act had been aimed at business combinations, in practice it was sometimes applied by courts to the activities of those in the labor movement. However, in spite of the Clayton Act's exemption of labor activities, union action can be in violation of the antitrust laws if it is not undertaken in the course of a labor dispute. Such would be the case if a nonlabor and a labor group combine to accomplish some direct commercial restraint. Also not exempted are acts by a union undertaken with the intent primarily to achieve some commercial restraint rather than that of advancing its own causes as a labor organization.

In 1926, Congress enacted the Railway Labor Act, which had as an avowed purpose the encouragement of collective bargaining in the railroad industry to resolve labor disputes that might otherwise disrupt transportation. The Act, which provided machinery for dealing with both major and minor disputes, was later extended to airlines and is applicable to both air and rail transportation today. It established the three-man National Mediation Board, on which it imposed the duty to designate the bargaining representative for any given bargaining unit of employees in the railway or air transport industries. The Board generally does this by holding representation elections. The Act also outlawed certain unfair labor practices such as refusing to bargain collectively.

The National Mediation Board, unlike the National Labor Relations Board, has no judicial power to hold hearings and issue cease and desist orders. Willful violations of the Railway Labor Act are punishable through criminal proceedings initiated by the Department of Justice in the regular Federal court system. However, convictions under it are almost impossible to obtain due to the extreme difficulty of proving beyond any reasonable doubt that the commission of a given unfair labor practice was intentional.

When the parties to a dispute over proposed contract terms in the transportation industry cannot reach an agreement concerning rates of pay or working conditions, it is the function of the National Mediation Board to attempt mediation of their differences. In the event that mediation does not resolve their differences, the Board encourages voluntary arbitration. If the parties refuse arbitration and the dispute is likely to disrupt interstate commerce in a substantial manner, the Board informs the President, who then appoints a special emergency board. This emergency board also lacks any judicial power, but it encourages the parties to reach agreement by investigating the dispute and publishing its findings of fact and recommendations for settlement. During the investigation and for thirty days after the report is issued, neither party to the dispute can unilaterally change the conditions out of which it arose, such as by striking. The parties, however, have no duty to comply with the special board's proposals. Thus, if no new collective-bargaining agreement is reached after the thirty day period, lockouts and strikes are legal.

In several cases since 1940, the Railway Labor Act has failed to resolve major disputes, necessitating special action by the President or the Congress. The transportation industry has frequently had its labor problems presented to the government for solution because the procedures of the Railway Labor Act are not such that all disputes can be resolved without irreparable damage to the public. It should be noted that the provisions previously discussed apply to assisting employers and unions to arrive at a collective-bargaining agreement where none currently is in force. The Act requires compulsory arbitration of disputes concerning the interpretation of existing contracts between the parties. This requirement is peculiar to the transportation industry.

In 1932, the Norris-La Guardia Act, sometimes referred to as the Anti-Injunction Statute, was passed by Congress. The Clayton Act had not provided sufficient protection for labor, and attempts were still being made to prevent union growth in the courts through injunctions. The Norris-La Guardia Act attempted to encourage collective bargaining by severely limiting the jurisdiction and authority of Federal courts in enjoining union activity. The Act recognized that "under prevailing economic conditions, developed with the aid of governmental authority for owners of property to organize in the corporate and other forms of ownership association, the individual unorganized worker is commonly helpless to exercise actual liberty of contract and to protect his freedom of labor, and thereby to obtain acceptable terms and conditions of employment." It then stated a national public policy that although a worker "should be free to decline to associate with his fellows, it is necessary that he have full freedom of association, self-organization and designation of representatives of his own choosing, to negotiate the terms and conditions of his employment, and that he shall be free from the interference, restraint, or coercion of employers of labor, or their agents, in the designation of such representatives or in self-organization or in other concerted activities for the purpose of collective bargaining or other mutual aid or protection. . . ."

The first major limitation of the Norris-La Guardia Act was to make "yellow dog" contracts (those forbidding union membership) unenforceable. The second was to enumerate specific acts of persons participating in labor disputes which were not subject to Federal restraining orders or injunctions. These included:

1 Striking or quitting work.
2 Being a member of a labor organization.
3 Paying strike or unemployment benefits to participants in a labor dispute.
4 Giving publicity to the existence of a labor dispute or the facts related to it (including by picketing).
5 Peaceably assembling to act in promotion of their interests in a labor dispute.
6 Agreeing with others or advising or causing them to do any of the above acts without fraud or violence.

A labor dispute under the Act includes any controversy concerning terms or conditions of employment or the representation of persons in arranging such terms, even if the disputants do not stand in the proximate relationship of employer and employee. Thus, labor organizations have a legally recognized interest in the terms and conditions of employment, even where they do not represent any employees.

It should be emphasized that while Norris-La Guardia greatly restricts the use of injunctions in labor disputes, it does not prohibit them altogether. However, a restraining order may be issued only when the court makes certain findings of fact after an open hearing of the testimony of witnesses both in favor of and opposed to allegations in the complaint asking for such relief. The required findings are: (1) that unlawful acts have been threatened (or committed) and will be committed unless they are restrained; (2) that there will be substantial, irreparable damage to the complainant's property; (3) that greater injury will be inflicted on the complainant by denying the order than will be inflicted on the defendants by granting it; (4) that complainant does not have an adequate remedy at law; and (5) that the public authorities who have the duty to protect the complainant's property cannot furnish him adequate protection, or are unwilling to do so. In addition, one seeking an injunction in a labor dispute must meet the test of a stringent "clean hands" rule. No restraining order will be granted to any person "who has failed to comply with any obligation imposed by law which is involved in the labor dispute in question, or who has failed to make every reasonable effort to settle such dispute either by negotiation or with the aid of any available governmental machinery of mediation or voluntary arbitration." Temporary injunctions may be issued without notice to the defendants and without a full, open hearing of testimony of witnesses for both sides in an emergency situation. Such orders are effective for a maximum of five days, however. Appeals from orders granting *or* denying injunctions in labor disputes are expedited and given precedence by the Act over all other matters.

The case which follows involved the application of provisions of both the Railway Labor Act and the Norris-La Guardia Act.

Chicago & North Western Ry. Co. v. United Transportation Union
91 S.Ct. 1731 (1971)

HARLAN, JUSTICE: The Chicago and North Western Railway Co., petitioner in this action, brought suit in the United States District Court for the Northern District of Illinois to enjoin a threatened strike by the respondent, the United Transportation Union. The substance of the complaint was that in the negotiations between the parties over work rules, the Union had failed to perform its obligation under § 2 First of the Railway Labor Act, "to exert every reasonable effort to make and maintain agreements concerning rates of pay, rules, and working conditions." The Union in its answer contended that the Norris-LaGuardia Act deprived the District Court of jurisdiction to issue a strike injunction and that in any event the complaint failed to state a claim upon which relief could be granted. The District Judge . . .

ruled that the Norris-LaGuardia Act deprived the court of jurisdiction to issue an injunction against the Union's threatened strike. The Court of Appeals for the Seventh Circuit affirmed, construing § 2 First as a statement of the purpose and policy of the subsequent provisions of the Act, and not as a specific requirement anticipating judicial enforcement. Rather, in that court's view, the enforcement of § 2 First was solely a matter for the National Mediation Board. We granted certiorari to consider this important question under the Railway Labor Act, on which the lower courts had expressed divergent views. For reasons that follow we reverse. . . .

The narrow questions presented to us are whether § 2 First imposes a legal obligation on carriers and employees or is a mere exhortation; whether the obligation is enforceable by the judiciary; and whether the Norris-LaGuardia Act strips the federal courts of jurisdiction to enforce the obligation by a strike injunction. . . .

This Court has previously observed that "[t]he heart of the Railway Labor Act is the duty, imposed by § 2 First upon management and labor, 'to exert every reasonable effort to make and maintain agreements concerning rates of pay, rules, and working conditions, and to settle all disputes . . . in order to avoid any interruption to commerce or to the operation of any carrier growing out of any dispute between the carrier and the employees thereof.' " It is not surprising that such is the case. As one leading commentator has said, in connection with the duty under the National Labor Relations Act to bargain in good faith, "[i]t was not enough for the law to compel the parties to meet and treat without passing judgment upon the quality of the negotiations. The bargaining status of a union can be destroyed by going through the motions of negotiating almost as easily as by bluntly withholding recognition." Cox, "The Duty To Bargain in Good Faith," 71 Harv.L.Rev. 1401, 1412–1413 (1958). . . .

Virginian Railway v. System Federation No. 40, 300 U.S. 515, (1937), furnishes an early illustration of this principle in connection with the duty to "exert every reasonable effort" under the Railway Labor Act. In that case, the railroad refused to recognize a union certified by the National Mediation Board as the duly authorized representative of its shop workers, and instead sought to coerce these employees to join a company union. The employees sought and obtained an injunction requiring the railroad to perform its duty under § 2 Ninth to "treat with" their certified representative; the injunction also compelled the railroad "to exert every reasonable effort" to make and maintain agreements with the union. This Court affirmed that decree, explicitly rejecting the argument that the duty to exert every reasonable effort was only a moral obligation. This conclusion has been repeatedly referred to without criticism in subsequent decisions. . . .

[W]e think it plain that § 2 First was intended to be more than a mere statement of policy or exhortation to the parties; rather, it was designed to be a legal obligation, enforceable by whatever appropriate means might be developed on a case-by-case basis. . . .

[The Court next concluded that the legal obligation imposed by § 2 First of the Railway Labor Act was one which was enforceable by the judiciary. It noted that

§ 2 First "is central to the working" of the Act, and since the National Mediation Board was given no adjudicatory function, Congress must have intended that that section be "overseen by appropriate judicial means."]

We turn finally to the question whether § 4 of the Norris-LaGuardia Act prohibits the use of a strike injunction in all cases of violation of § 2 First. The fundamental principles in this area were epitomized in *International Association of Machinists v. Street,* 367 U.S. 740 (1961):

The Norris-LaGuardia Act expresses a basic policy against the injunction of activities of labor unions. We have held that the Act does not deprive the federal courts of jurisdiction to enjoin compliance with various mandates of the Railway Labor Act. However, the policy of the Act suggests that the courts should hesitate to fix upon the injunctive remedy for breaches of duty owing under the labor laws unless that remedy alone can effectively guard the plaintiff's right.

Similar statements may be found in many of our opinions. We consider that these statements properly accommodate the conflicting policies of our labor laws, and we adhere to them. We find it quite impossible to say that no set of circumstances could arise where a strike injunction is the only practical, effective means of enforcing the command of § 2 First. Accordingly, our prior decisions lead us to hold that the Norris-LaGuardia Act did not forbid the District Court from even considering whether this is such a case. If we have misinterpreted the congressional purpose, Congress can remedy the situation by speaking more clearly. In the meantime we have no choice but to trace out as best we may the uncertain line of appropriate accommodation of the two statutes with purposes that lead in opposing directions. . . .

[W]eighty considerations indeed counsel restraint in the issuance of strike injunctions based on violations of § 2 First. Nevertheless, the result reached today is unavoidable if we are to give effect to all our labor laws—enacted as they were by Congresses of differing political makeup and differing views on labor relations—rather than restrict our examination to those pieces of legislation which are in accord with our personal views of sound labor policy. . . . [REVERSED AND REMANDED]

While the Norris-LaGuardia Act restricted the use of Federal Court injunctions in labor disputes, it did not limit the jurisdiction of state courts in issuing them. State injunctions were still valid unless outlawed by a state statute or issued in violation of the state or Federal Constitution. As an example of the latter, state injunctions prohibiting peaceful picketing have been held unconstitutional under the First Amendment's guarantee of freedom of speech.

Although Norris-LaGuardia stated the policy that employees should be free to organize and bargain collectively through their chosen representatives without interference or coercion on the part of employers, it did nothing to impose any duty on management to deal with or even recognize unions. Its essentially negative approach did not furnish the impetus for a tremendous growth of unions and union power. Further, at this time union development was hampered by the depression and the overabundant labor supply.

4 THE WAGNER ACT

The labor movement received its greatest stimulus for growth with the enactment in 1935 of the National Labor Relations Act (Wagner Act). This statute did for unions representing employees of businesses engaged in interstate commerce what the Railway Labor Act had done for unions in the transportation industry. It announced as a finding of Congress that "The denial by some employers of the right of employees to organize and the refusal by some employers to accept the procedure of collective bargaining lead to strikes and other forms of industrial strife which have the intent or necessary effect of burdening or obstructing commerce. . . ." It further noted as a cause of this industrial strife the inequality of bargaining power between employees and employers. The Act stated that its policy was to protect by law the right of employees to organize and bargain collectively and thereby encourage the "friendly adjustment of industrial disputes" by restoring equality in their bargaining positions with that of employers. In summary, the Wagner Act:

1 Outlawed certain conduct by employers which generally had had the effect of either preventing the organization of employees or emasculating their unions where they did exist. The forbidden acts were defined as "unfair labor practices."
2 Provided for the selection by employees of a union with exclusive power to act as their collective bargaining representative.
3 Created a three-man agency, the National Labor Relations Board (NLRB) to administer the Act and gave it broad powers to prevent employers from engaging in unfair labor practices by issuing cease and desist orders. The NLRB, which was increased in size to five members by the Taft-Hartley Act, is discussed in section 6 of this chapter.

Section 7 of the Wagner Act states the rights of employees in general. It provides: "Employees shall have the right to self organization, to form, join, or assist labor organizations, to bargain collectively through representatives of their own choosing, and to engage in concerted activities for the purpose of collective bargaining or other mutual aid or protection." Section 8 of the statute secures the rights granted in Section 7 by describing and prohibiting five practices by employers declared to be unfair to labor:

1 Interference with efforts of employees to form, join, or assist labor organizations, or to engage in concerted activities for mutual aid or protection. Section 8(a)(1).

2 Domination of a labor organization or contribution of financial or other support to it. Section 8(a)(2).
3 Discrimination in hire or tenure of employees for reason of union affiliation. Section 8(a)(3).
4 Discrimination against employees for filing charges or giving testimony under the Act. Section 8(a)(4).
5 Refusal to bargain collectively with a duly designated representative of the employees. Section 8(a)(5).

The above unfair labor practices are discussed in sections 7 and 9 of this chapter. Unions and employees are entitled to cease and desist orders, injunctions, and awards for damages if any of these unfair labor practices are committed.

The selection of a union as collective bargaining representative is made by a vote of a majority of the employees "in a unit appropriate for such purposes." Elections are by secret ballot and are supervised by the NLRB. The Board decides what unit of employees is appropriate for purposes of collective bargaining and therefore which employees are entitled to vote in an election. Except for a few minor limitations, it may select the total employer unit, craft unit, plant unit, or any subdivision of the foregoing. Obviously, how the Board exercises its discretion in this regard may be crucial to the outcome of a given election. If all 100 workers at one plant operated by an employer desire to organize, but 400 out of 500 at another of the employer's plants do not, designation of the total employer unit as appropriate would ensure that both plants would remain nonunion.

Before a representation election is conducted by the NLRB, a petition for such election must be filed with it by either an employee, labor organization, or employer. If the petition is filed by either an employee or labor organization, it must allege: that a substantial number of employees desire to have a collective bargaining representative, but their employer refuses to recognize their representative; or that a substantial number of employees assert that the union which has been certified by the Board or which the employer currently recognizes as their bargaining representative is no longer such. If the petition is filed by an employer, it must allege that one or more unions have claimed to him that they are the representative of his employees. The NLRB investigates the petition and upon finding reasonable cause provides for a hearing on the matter of whether a question of representation exists. If the Board determines from the record of the hearing that there is such a question, it directs that a representation election be held by secret ballot. After the results are tallied, the Board certifies either that no union has been selected by the employees or that a given one has. In some cases, two or more unions compete to qualify as the legal representative of the bargaining unit. Employees may also withdraw authority from a previously designated bargaining representative by secret ballot. If at least 30 percent of those in a bargaining unit allege that they desire their union's authority be rescinded, the Board must hold an election to that effect. However, after any valid election has been conducted by the NLRB, another is not permitted for one year.

A union seeking designation as the representative of certain employees may solicit cards from each of them indicating their willingness that it act in that capacity. In a few isolated cases, the Board has certified a representative because it has obtained such union authorization cards from a majority of the employees in the bargaining unit instead of holding an election by secret ballot or using the results of one in which the majority voted "no union." These rare rulings of the NLRB have been issued in cases where it found that the employer has requested an election as a delaying tactic and not because he doubted in good faith that the union was the majority choice, or because he was guilty of committing an unfair labor practice prior to the election, which made its outcome a nullity. The drawbacks of utilizing authorization cards as a means of determining the representative of employees are obvious. Since such authorizations are not secret, they may be obtained by coercion or misrepresentation. In addition, many employees may believe that the card they sign is simply a request that a representation election be held.

Although those subject to the provisions of the Wagner Act are many, certain employers and employees are exempted from its coverage. These include the Federal and state governments, political subdivisions of the states, nonprofit hospitals, and persons subject to the Railway Labor Act. Also excluded are independent contractors, individuals employed as agricultural laborers or as domestic servants in a home, and those employed by their spouse or a parent.

In *NLRB v. Jones & Laughlin Steel Corp.*, the Supreme Court held that the Wagner Act was constitutional and applicable to manufacturing enterprises. Its constitutionality was affirmed as a valid exercise of power by Congress under the commerce clause. Chief Justice Hughes, in discussing the right of employees to bargain collectively, said:[1]

That is a fundamental right. Employees have as clear a right to organize and select their representatives for lawful purposes as the respondent has to organize its business and select its own officers and agents. Discrimination and coercion to prevent the free exercise of the right of employees to self-organization and representation is a proper subject for condemnation by competent legislative authority. Long ago we stated the reason for labor organizations. We said that they were organized out of the necessities of the situation; that a single employee was helpless in dealing with an employer; that he was dependent ordinarily on his daily wage for the maintenance of himself and family; that if the employer refused to pay him the wages that he thought fair, he was nevertheless unable to leave the employ and resist arbitrary and unfair treatment; that union was essential to give laborers opportunity to deal on an equality with their employer. . . . We reiterated these views when we had under consideration the Railway Labor Act of 1926. Fully recognizing the legality of collective action on the part of employees in order to safeguard their proper interests, we said that Congress was not required to ignore this right but could

---

[1] 301 U.S. 1 (1937).

safeguard it. Congress could seek to make appropriate collective action of employees an instrument of peace rather than of strife. We said that such collective action would be a mockery if representation were made futile by interference with freedom of choice. Hence the prohibition by Congress of interference with the selection of representatives for the purpose of negotiation and conference between employers and employees, "instead of being an invasion of the constitutional right of either, was based on the recognition of the rights of both." . . .

The Act was also challenged under the due process clause and for being one-sided in its application since there was no provision relating to unfair labor practices by unions. Chief Justice Hughes disposed of these agruments by saying:

The Act does not compel agreements between employers and employees. It does not compel any agreement whatever. It does not prevent the employer "from refusing to make a collective contract and hiring individuals on whatever terms" the employer "may by unilateral action determine." The Act expressly provides in § 9(a) that any individual employee or a group of employees shall have the right at any time to present grievances to their employer. The theory of the Act is that free opportunity for negotiation with accredited representatives of employees is likely to promote industrial peace and may bring about the adjustments and agreements which the Act in itself does not attempt to compel. . . . The Act does not interfere with the normal exercise of the right of the employer to select its employees or to discharge them. The employer may not, under cover of that right, intimidate or coerce its employees with respect to their self-organization and representation, and, on the other hand, the Board is not entitled to make its authority a pretext for interference with the right of discharge when that right is exercised for other reasons than such intimidation and coercion. The true purpose is the subject of investigation with full opportunity to show the facts. It would seem that when employers freely recognize the right of their employees to their own organizations and their unrestricted right of representation there will be much less occasion for controversy in respect to the free and appropriate exercise of the right of selection and discharge.

The Act has been criticized as one-sided in its application; that it subjects the employer to supervision and restraint and leaves untouched the abuses for which employees may be responsible; that it fails to provide a more comprehensive plan,—with better assurances of fairness to both sides and with increased chances of success in bringing about, if not compelling, equitable solutions of industrial disputes affecting interstate commerce. But we are dealing with the power of Congress, not with a particular policy or with the extent to which policy should go. We have frequently said that the legislative authority, exerted within its proper field, need not embrace all the evils within its reach. The Constitution does not forbid "cautious advance, step by step," in dealing with the evils which are exhibited in activities within the range of legislative power.

. . . The question in such cases is whether the legislature, in what it does prescribe, has gone beyond constitutional limits. . . .

5   THE TAFT-HARTLEY ACT

The Wagner Act provided the open door for the rapid growth of the union movement. From 1935 to the end of World War II the strength and influence of unions grew by leaps and bounds. Where prior to the Wagner Act the employers had the greater advantage in bargaining power, by 1946 many persons felt the pendulum had shifted and the unions with their ability to call nationwide crippling strikes had the better bargaining position. It may be stated that the general desire of government has been for equality of bargaining power between labor and management so that fair and equitable employment contracts are agreed upon. The individual employee did not have equality with the large corporation which could discharge him and hire someone else. On the other hand, one company or one industry did not necessarily have an equal bargaining position with a union which represented all employees in an industry.

As an attempt to balance the scale, the Labor Management Relations Act of 1947 (the Taft-Hartley Act) was enacted to amend the Wagner Act. Its purposes were to ensure the free flow of commerce by eliminating practices of unions which burden commerce and to provide procedures for avoiding disputes which jeopardize the public health, safety, or interest. It recognized that both parties to collective bargaining need protection from wrongful interference by the other and that employees sometimes need protection from the union itself. Finally, the Taft-Hartley Act recognized the need for protection of the public in labor disputes which affect commerce.

In adding the other side to the coin, the Taft-Hartley Act:

1   Outlawed certain conduct by unions as unfair labor practices.
2   Provided for an eighty-day cooling-off period in strikes which imperil the national health or safety.
3   Restricted the right of unions to insist on a union shop.
4   Created the Federal Mediation and Conciliation Service to assist in the settlement of labor disputes.

The following is a summary of the actions and omissions by unions which are unfair labor practices as specified in Section 8(b) of the Taft-Hartley Act:

1   Restraining or coercing an employee to join a union or an employer in selecting his representatives to bargain with the union.
2   Causing or attempting to cause the employer to discriminate against an employee who is not a union member, unless there is a legal union-shop agreement in effect. (This outlawed the closed shop.)

3 Refusing to bargain with the employer if it is the NLRB-designated representative of his employees.
4 Striking, picketing, and engaging in secondary boycotts for illegal purposes.
5 Charging new members excessive or discriminatory initiation fees where there is a union-shop agreement.
6 Causing an employer to pay for work not performed (featherbedding).

Taft-Hartley gave the NLRB the same broad powers to prevent unions from engaging in unfair labor practices as it has to prevent employers from doing so. The above practices by unions are discussed in sections 8 and 9 of this chapter.

Employers had complained that the Wagner Act violated the employer's right of free speech. To meet this objection, Congress added Section 8(c), which reads as follows:

(c) The expressing of any views, argument, or opinion, or the dissemination thereof, whether in written, printed, graphic, or visual form, shall not constitute or be evidence of an unfair labor practice under any of the provisions of this Act, if such expression contains no threat of reprisal or force or promise of benefit.

The provision of the Taft-Hartley Act calling for an eighty-day "cooling-off period" after certain procedures have been followed begins, "Whenever in the opinion of the President of the United States, a threatened or actual strike or lockout affecting an entire industry or substantial part thereof engaged in trade, commerce, transportation, transmission, or communication among the several states or with foreign nations, or engaged in the production of goods for commerce, will, if permitted to occur or to continue, imperil the national health or safety, he may appoint a board. . . ." Thus the procedure starts with the President, recognizing the emergency characteristics of a strike, appointing a board of inquiry to obtain facts about the strike. The board then makes a study of the strike and reports back to the President. If the board finds that the national health is indeed affected by the strike, then the President, through the Attorney General, goes to the Federal District Court for an injunction ordering the union to suspend the strike (or company to suspend the lockout) for eighty days. During the eighty-day period, the Federal Mediation Service works with the two parties to try to achieve an agreement. If during this time the reconciliation effort fails, the presidential board holds new hearings and receives the company's final offer. The members of the union are then allowed to vote on this final proposal by the company. If they vote for the new proposal, the dispute is over and work continues as usual. If they vote against the proposal, the workers may again be called out on strike. At this point, the strike may continue indefinitely until the disagreement causing it is resolved by collective bargaining, or unless there is additional legislation by Congress to solve the problem. Experience has shown that many disputes are settled during the eighty-day period. The injunction provided for in the Taft-Hartley Act may not be used for all strikes but is limited to "national emergency" strikes. These must involve national defense or key industries, or must have a substantial effect on the economy.

One of the most distasteful sections of Taft-Hartley to unions is 14(b), which outlaws the union shop in states which have adopted a "right-to-work" law. Right-to-work laws prohibit agreements requiring membership in a labor organization as a condition of employment. Nineteen states have enacted such prohibitions.

6   THE NATIONAL LABOR RELATIONS BOARD

The National Labor Relations Board was created as an independent three-man administrative agency by the Wagner Act to enforce its provisions. The NLRB was given the functions and powers usually possessed by administrative agencies as was discussed in Chapter 7. The Board was increased in size to five members by the Taft-Hartley Act. Members are appointed by the President, with the advice and consent of the Senate, in staggered terms of five years each. The President designates one member to serve as chairman. In order to preserve the independence of this agency from the executive branch once appointments have been made, members may be removed from the Board by the President for neglect of duty or malfeasance in office only, and then only after notice and after a hearing. Members may not engage in any other business, vocation, or employment while in office.

The NLRB has two major tasks. First, it supervises elections to determine whether the majority of the employees in an appropriate unit wish to select a collective-bargaining representative or not and, if they do, to certify as their exclusive representative the union chosen by the majority. (Representation elections were discussed in section 4 of this chapter.) The second major function of the NLRB is to hear and adjudicate charges that unfair labor practices have been committed by either employers or unions. (These are discussed in sections 7, 8, and 9 of this chapter.) In the event that it finds such a violation of the law, the Board is given extensive powers to fashion remedial orders.

As it was first structured, the Board was not only the *judge* and *jury* in exercising its quasi-judicial powers, but also had the function of *investigator* and *prosecutor* when unfair labor practice charges were filed with it. This led to many complaints by employers that performing all these roles at once was bound to bias the Board's rulings and was contrary to fundamental concepts of justice in our legal system, which requires that both the finder of fact and judge in a controversy be free of prejudice. In response to such charges, the Taft-Hartley Act divested the Board members of direct control of the investigating and prosecuting functions. It established the position of General Counsel of the Board and charged him with supervising all attorneys employed by the Board (except those who are legal assistants to Board members or are trial examiners) as well as the officers and employees in the thirty-one regional offices, who conduct the operations in the field. The General Counsel is appointed by the President with the advice and consent of the Senate for a term of four years. He has *final* authority regarding the investigation of charges, the issuance of complaints, and the prosecution of such complaints as well as the dismissal of charges.

The General Counsel also is responsible for the conduct of representation elections, since the Board has delegated this function to its regional directors subject to a review of their actions. (The Board still determines policy questions such as what types of employers and groups of employees are covered by the labor laws.) In addition, the General Counsel is responsible for seeking court orders requiring compliance with the Board's orders, and represents the Board in miscellaneous litigation. The organizational changes brought about by Taft-Hartley left the Board with full authority over the Division of Trial Examiners. The trial examiners perform a judicial function, being responsible for the initial conduct of hearings in unfair labor practices cases. Of course, each member of the Board controls his own chief counsel and legal assistants.

In establishing the NLRB and giving it, rather than the district courts, jurisdiction over the interpretation and application of the unfair labor practices provision of the Wagner Act, Congress deemed it desirable to put the development and enforcement of labor law in the hands of a body of men who could be sympathetic with the cause of labor. Although employers argued that such a tribunal would prejudge cases brought against them, those who supported labor organizations contended that a bias of Board members in favor of achieving the ends of the new program was essential if it were to be implemented as intended.

Congress gave the NLRB jurisdiction over any business "affecting commerce," with a few exceptions. Because of Supreme Court interpretations of the nature and extent of the commerce power (discussed in Chapter 8), this was a broad grant indeed. However, the Board has never been able to fully exercise the powers given it, because of budget and time considerations. Although it could act in almost any case covered by the Wagner Act as amended, it has limited its own jurisdiction to cases which it deems to be more significant because they meet certain minimum standards. Under present guidelines the Board will generally exercise jurisdiction over labor disputes involving the following types of businesses:

1 *Nonretail operations* with an annual outflow or inflow across state lines of at least $50,000.
2 *Retail enterprises* with a gross volume of $500,000 or more a year.
3 *Enterprises operating office buildings* if the gross revenues are at least $100,000 per year.
4 *Transportation enterprises* furnishing interstate services.
5 *Local transit systems* with an annual gross volume of at least $250,000.
6 *Newspapers* which subscribe to interstate news services, publish nationally syndicated features, or advertise nationally sold products with a minimum annual gross volume of $250,000.
7 *Communication enterprises* which operate radio or television stations or telephone or telegraph services with a gross volume of $100,000 or more per year.

8 *Local public utilities* with an annual gross volume of $250,000 per year, or an outflow or an inflow of goods or services across state lines of $50,000 or more per year.

9 *Hotel and motel enterprises* serving transient guests which gross at least $500,000 in revenues per year.

10 All enterprises whose operations have a substantial impact on *national defense*.

Because of its self-imposed jurisdictional limits, the Board has denied the protection of Federal labor law to small employers, their employees, and self-employed persons. In early decisions, the Supreme Court ruled that Congress had preempted the field of labor-management relations. Thus *any* state legislative or judicial action in this area was outlawed. These two factors created a jurisdictional no-man's-land. Small employers were unable to obtain NLRB relief from coercive union tactics because of its refusal to act, and from the state government because it was constitutionally prohibited from acting. In 1959, the Landrum-Griffin Act attempted to alleviate this problem. It provided that nothing in the Wagner Act as amended by Taft-Hartley prevents any agency or the courts of any state from asserting jurisdiction over labor disputes which the Board has declined to hear. In addition, while this amendment recognized the right of the NLRB to adopt rules which limit its jurisdiction, it was prohibited from setting more restrictive standards than those prevailing on August 1, 1959. Of course, the jurisdiction of the Board may be expanded by it to include labor disputes in all business subject to the Wagner Act. Thus, the limited jurisdiction that states have over labor disputes is subject to reduction by action of the Board. In spite of the congressional authorization that states control labor-management relations to the extent that the NLRB does not, the legislatures of over two-thirds of them have not taken advantage of this privilege. Therefore, in the vast majority of states to date, the result of Landrum-Griffin has been to reinstate the power of state courts to apply common-law doctrines in resolving disputes over which the NLRB has refused to assert jurisdiction.

In the event there is a labor dispute over which the NLRB will take jurisdiction, certain procedures are followed. The one claiming that an unfair labor practice has been committed must file charges within six months at the proper regional office. Field examiners of the Board then investigate. The charge may be disposed of informally by its withdrawal, dismissal by the regional director, or adjustment by the parties. Dismissal is subject to review by the General Counsel. The field examiner may obtain a formal adjustment in a settlement stipulation. If the charge appears to have merit and efforts to settle the case fail, the regional director issues a formal complaint and notice of hearing which is served on all parties. The person complained of has the right to file an answer, appear, and give testimony and evidence at the hearing as fixed by the complaint. A public hearing is then conducted by a trial examiner. At this point, the General Counsel no longer has control over the case. He or his staff appear before the examiner and the Board as a party litigant.

It is the responsibility of the trial examiner to conduct a fair and orderly hearing, preserve the rights of all parties, and see that a proper record of the proceeding is made. The General Counsel's staff is responsible for presenting evidence to prove the allegations in the complaint. The proceeding must be conducted in accordance with the rules of evidence applicable in district courts as adopted by the Supreme Court of the United States if practicable. For purposes of conducting all investigations and hearings, the Board and its agents have access to any evidence of any person being investigated, and the right to copy it. In addition, any member of the Board generally is required to issue subpoenas requiring the testimony of evidence in any proceeding or investigation upon application by any party to it. (Any member of the Board or agent designated by it may administer oaths, examine witnesses, and receive evidence. Subpoenas may be enforced by orders of Federal district courts, if necessary.) After hearing all the evidence produced at the hearing by the parties, along with their arguments, the trial examiner recommends a decision. His report contains findings of fact, conclusions of law, and a recommended order, which may be for dismissal of the complaint or for suggested remedies. If neither party contests his decision within twenty days, his recommendations have the effect of an order of the Board itself. The parties can appeal from this report of the trial examiner by filing exceptions to it with the Board. In such a case, the NLRB reviews the entire transcript of the hearing and may decide to adopt, modify, or reject the findings and recommendations of the trial examiner.

The Wagner Act directs the Board, upon finding that a person has committed an unfair labor practice, to issue an order requiring him to cease and desist and to take such affirmative action as will effectuate the Act's policies. The courts have held that this power to devise appropriate orders is a broad discretionary one which is peculiarly a matter for administrative competence and subject only to limited judicial review. On such a review, the remedy fashioned by the Board will not be disturbed "unless it can be shown that the order is a patent attempt to achieve ends other than those which can fairly be said to effectuate the policies of the Act."[2]

The NLRB may order the reinstatement of an employee who has been discharged wrongfully, with back pay and restoration of full seniority rights. (However, the Act specifies that it is not within the Board's power to order the reinstatement of an employee who was discharged for proper cause.) The NLRB may require an employer to bargain collectively with the appropriate union, or vice versa. It may even order an employer to post notices at his plant assuring his employees that he will no longer commit a particular unfair labor practice of which he has been found guilty. If an employer or union has committed an unfair labor practice which may have influenced the outcome of a representation election, the NLRB may hold another election, free of such improper pressures on the employees. It should be noted that the cease and desist orders of the Board, like

[2] *Virginia Electric & Power Co. v. NLRB,* 319 U.S. 533, 540 (1943).

those of the Federal Trade Commission, are not self-enforcing. If a respondent fails to comply voluntarily with such an order, the NLRB may petition any appropriate Court of Appeals of the United States for enforcement of it. The court then has the power to review the record of the proceedings and to enter a decree enforcing, modifying, or setting aside the order of the Board in whole or part. Similarly, any person aggrieved by an order of the Board granting or denying relief may petition the Court of Appeals for a review of it. Often the record of the proceedings before the NLRB will contain contradictory evidence introduced by the petitioner and respondent before it. Even so, the findings of fact of the Board shall be conclusive if they are supported by substantial evidence on the record considered as a whole.[3] This strictly limits the reviewing court's power to set aside such findings.

Since its creation, there have been many criticisms of the NLRB. One of these has concerned the period of delay between the time of filing of a complaint and its final resolution. While Landrum-Griffin permitted delegation of the function of conducting representation elections to regional directors, such has not been allowed in unfair labor practices cases. The Board has tried to remedy this situation by relying more heavily on the voluntary settlement of these cases by the parties.

It has already been noted that many labor disputes affecting smaller businesses are not handled by the Board because it has refused to take jurisdiction of them. It would seem improper, however, to place the blame for this deficiency at its door. Since it has only a limited budget and amount of time, it has been forced to choose to act only in those cases which have a more substantial effect on commerce.

One of the most serious (and justified) criticisms of the Board has been its disregard of the principle of stare decisis. Scholars in the labor law area recognize without question that the Board's changing membership (brought about by the periodic appointments of different Presidents from different parties with different philosophies) has resulted in frequent changes in its rulings from being prolabor to proemployer, or vice versa. For example, the Eisenhower Board broadened the right of employers to speak freely before a representation election without being guilty of interfering with the rights of their employees to organize and bargain collectively. However, the Kennedy and Johnson Boards restricted such statements by employers, ruling that the free speech guarantees of the Taft-Hartley amendment did not apply to representation elections but only to unfair labor practices cases. Because of the NLRB's disregard of precedents, some argue that its judicial function should be divested and put in the hands of a labor court, whose members are appointed as judges are, for the purpose of being judges.

Mr. Henry L. Browne[4] expressed the view of many that the NLRB should be more consistent, and adhere to its own policy decisions, so that both management

---

[3] See *Universal Camera Corp. v. NLRB,* page 220.
[4] Mr. Browne has had extensive experience in the field of labor law as a private practitioner, as an attorney for the NLRB, and as cochairman of an American Bar Association panel that deals with Federal agencies on labor law.

and labor leaders may predict the legality of their conduct with greater certainty. Commenting on decisions which had failed to follow previous NLRB rulings, he stated in his article "Is The Labor Board Biased?":[5]

What is the conclusion we draw from the Board's new decisional doctrines? The Board, we submit, has fallen before the temptation to rewrite policies of the body of our national labor law rather than only to interpret it. Our basic labor policies are determined by Congress, to be interpreted and applied by the administrative tribunal "in accordance with its design and purpose."

Congress has established the policy that equality of bargaining power is a condition for collective bargaining to function in the national interest, and it has legislated to that end.

It must be conceded, we believe, that the weight of Board decisions since the passage of the Landrum-Griffin Act, the reversals in precedent and the construction of critical provisions of the law have been on the side of organized labor.

Board decisions, we submit, have thwarted the policy and have upset the equality Congress provided as a condition precedent for collective bargaining to serve in the national interest.

To criticisms of Board decisions, the answer by Board spokesmen that Board decisions are subject to review and can be reversed when inappropriate begs the fundamental issue, because the Board, not the courts, is the tribunal set up to administer our national labor policy.

The Board has been given wide latitude under the Act in making its findings of fact and in fashioning remedies and, while courts may disagree with Board decisions, they are most reluctant to interfere where Board decisions may have support in the record and are not clearly erroneous.

Today, as a result, free collective bargaining is on trial, and the Board, as the chief administrator of our national labor policy, cannot escape the consequences. . . .

Amidst the outcry, indignation and demands for remedial legislation, many will suggest that, whatever the cause, the cure lies in such remedies as compulsory arbitration, or "cooling off" periods, or the application of antitrust laws to labor organizations, or to increasing the "arsenal of weapons" available to the Chief Executive.

But we would submit that an area for correction in both the cause and the cure may well lie in the Board's reversal of a policy that has upset the balance of power so essential to make collective bargaining work in the public interest, thereby giving our labor statutes a chance to work as Congress originally intended.

If equality is restored, free collective bargaining may yet be made to work in the national interest without federal controls imposed on a free bargaining

---

[5] Reprinted from *U.S. News & World Report* 72 (Nov. 28, 1966), published at Washington.

*process that all—the public, labor and management, and the Congress alike—
would abjure. [Copyright 1966 U.S. News & World Report, Inc.]*

7   UNFAIR LABOR PRACTICES BY EMPLOYERS

Through the years, there have been numerous allegations of unfair labor practices
against employers. A great many of these have been judicially reviewed, so that
there is a substantial body of case law on what conduct by employers is an unfair
labor practice. The Wagner Act, being remedial in nature and intended to improve
the bargaining position of unions, has been liberally construed. This section
discusses some of the precedents defining the scope and application of unfair
labor practices by employers.

A   *Interference with efforts of employees to form, join, or assist labor
organizations, or to engage in concerted activities for mutual aid or
protection* [Section 8(a)(1)]

This unfair labor practice is a catchall intended to guarantee the rights to organize
and bargain collectively. It forbids such practices as utilizing yellow-dog contracts
and blacklists. Clearly, it prohibits "scare" tactics such as threats by employers
to fire those involved in an attempt to organize employees or to cut back on
employee benefits if they succeed in unionizing. Taft-Hartley amended the
Wagner Act to also give employees the right to *refrain* from joining or assisting
labor organizations or from bargaining collectively, *except* where this right is
affected by a valid union-shop agreement between their employer and a union.

   Not every violation of 8(a)(1) is obvious. A conferring of benefits may be an
unfair labor practice as the following case illustrates.

NLRB v. Exchange Parts Co.
375 U.S. 405 (1964)

HARLAN, JUSTICE: . . . This case presents a question concerning the limitations
which § 8(a)(1) of the National Labor Relations Act, . . . places on the right of an
employer to confer economic benefits on his employees shortly before a
representation election. The precise issue is whether that section prohibits the
conferral of such benefits, without more, where the employer's purpose is to affect
the outcome of the election. . . .

   The respondent, Exchange Parts Company, is engaged in the business of
rebuilding automobile parts in Fort Worth, Texas. Prior to November 1959 its
employees were not represented by a union. On November 9, 1959, the
International Brotherhood of Boilermakers, Iron Shipbuilders, Blacksmiths, Forg-
ers and Helpers, AFL-CIO, advised Exchange Parts that the union was conducting
an organizational campaign at the plant and that a majority of the employees had
designated the union as their bargaining representative. On November 16 the

union petitioned the Labor Board for a representation election. The Board conducted a hearing on December 29, and on February 19, 1960, issued an order directing that an election be held. The election was held on March 18, 1960.

At two meetings on November 4 and 5, 1959, C. V. McDonald, the Vice-President and General Manager of Exchange Parts, announced to the employees that their "floating holiday" in 1959 would fall on December 26 and that there would be an additional "floating holiday" in 1960. On February 25, six days after the Board issued its election order, Exchange Parts held a dinner for employees at which Vice-President McDonald told the employees that they could decide whether the extra day of vacation in 1960 would be a "floating holiday" or would be taken on their birthdays. The employees voted for the latter. McDonald also referred to the forthcoming representation election as one in which in the words of the trial examiner, the employees would "determine whether . . . [they] wished to hand over their right to speak and act for themselves." He stated that the union had distorted some of the facts and pointed out the benefits obtained by the employees without a union. He urged all the employees to vote in the election.

On March 4 Exchange Parts sent its employees a letter which spoke of "the *Empty Promises* of the Union" and "the *fact* that *it is the Company that puts things in your envelope.* . . ." After mentioning a number of benefits, the letter said: "The Union can't put any of those things in your envelope—*only the Company can do that.*" Further on, the letter stated: ". . . [I]t didn't take a Union to get any of those things and . . . it won't take a Union to get additional improvements in the future." Accompanying the letter was a detailed statement of the benefits granted by the company since 1949 and an estimate of the monetary value of such benefits to the employees, included in the statement of benefits for 1960 were the birthday holiday, a new system for computing overtime during holiday weeks which had the effect of increasing wages for those weeks and a new vacation schedule which enables employees to extend their vacations by sandwiching them between two weekends. Although Exchange Parts asserts that the policy behind the latter two benefits was established earlier, it is clear that the letter of March 4 was the first general announcement of the changes to the employees. In the ensuing election the union lost.

The Board, affirming the findings of the trial examiner, found that the announcement of the birthday holiday and the grant and announcement of overtime and vacation benefits were arranged by Exchange Parts with the intention of inducing the employees to vote against the union. It found that this conduct violated § 8(a)(1) of the National Labor Relations Act and issued an appropriate order. On the Board's petition for enforcement of the order, the Court of Appeals rejected the finding that the announcement of the birthday holiday was timed to influence the outcome of the election. . . . However, noting that "the benefits were put into effect unconditionally on a permanent basis, and no one has suggested that there was any implication the benefits would be withdrawn if the workers voted for the union," . . . the court denied enforcement of the Board's order. It believed that it was not an unfair labor practice under § 8(a)(1) for an employer to grant benefits to its employees in these circumstances. . . .

We think the Court of Appeals was mistaken in concluding that the conferral of employee benefits while a representation election is pending, for the purpose of inducing employees to vote against the union, does not "interfere with" the protected right to organize.

The broad purpose of § 8(a)(1) is to establish "the right of employees to organize for mutual aid without employer interference." We have no doubt that it prohibits not only intrusive threats and promises but also conduct immediately favorable to employees which is undertaken with the express purpose of impinging upon their freedom of choice for or against unionization and is reasonably calculated to have that effect. In *Medo Photo Supply Corp. v. NLRB,* 321 U.S. 678, this Court said: "The action of employees with respect to the choice of their bargaining agents may be induced by favors bestowed by the employer as well as by his threats or domination." Although in that case there was already a designated bargaining agent and the offer of "favors" was in response to a suggestion of the employees that they would leave the union if favors were bestowed, the principles which dictated the result there are fully applicable here. The danger inherent in well-timed increases in benefits is the suggestion of a fist inside the velvet glove. Employees are not likely to miss the inference that the source of benefits now conferred is also the source from which future benefits must flow and which may dry up if it is not obliged. The danger may be diminished if, as in this case, the benefits are conferred permanently and unconditionally. But the absence of conditions or threats pertaining to the particular benefits conferred would be of controlling significance only if it could be presumed that no question of additional benefits or renegotiation of existing benefits would arise in the future; and, of course, no such presumption is tenable. . . .

We cannot agree with the Court of Appeals that enforcement of the Board's order will have the "ironic" result of "discouraging benefits for labor." . . . The beneficence of an employer is likely to be ephemeral if prompted by a threat of unionization which is subsequently removed. Insulating the right of collective organization from calculated good will of this sort deprives employees of little that has lasting value. [REVERSED]

Another area of employer activities that can amount to an unfair labor practice under Section 8(a)(1) is that of discharging employees for breaking company rules. Many problems have arisen over such company policies as rules prohibiting the solicitation of union members during working hours. The first case on this subject to be decided by the Supreme Court was *Republic Aviation Corp. v. NLRB.*[6] Republic had adopted a plant policy long before any union activity began that read: "Soliciting of any type cannot be permitted in the factory or offices." One employee persisted, after being warned of the rule, in soliciting union membership in the plant and was subsequently discharged for infraction of the rule. This action was taken without discrimination by Republic against union

[6] 324 U.S. 793 (1945).

activity. Three other employees were discharged for wearing UAW-CIO union steward buttons after being asked to remove the insignia. Republic claimed the union was not the duly designated representative of the employees, that the insignia represented an acknowledgment of the authority of the stewards to represent the employees, and it might thus infringe on Republic's policy of strict neutrality in union matters.

The NLRB ruled, and the Supreme Court agreed, that the enforcement of the no-solicitation rule violated Section 8(a)(1) of the Wagner Act, as it interfered with, restrained, and coerced employees in their rights under Section 7 and discriminated against the discharged employee under Section 8(a)(3). The Board directed reinstatement of the four discharged employees with back pay and also the recission of ". . . the rule against solicitation in so far as it prohibits union activity and solicitation on company property during the employees' own time."

Another rule frequently used in industry is that a worker may not leave work without permission. In *NLRB v. Washington Aluminum Co.*,[7] the employer discharged seven employees for violating this rule. The employees on a particularly cold day had walked off the job from an uninsulated machine shop which on that day had no heat. On other occasions protests had been made about the poor heat. The employees claimed to have acted as a group in protest against unfit working conditions, hoping that their concerted action would cause the employer to heat the shop properly. The employer justified the discharge action by claiming the men left work without permission.

The NLRB ruled that the action of the employees was protected concerted activity under Section 7 of the Wagner Act as amended and that their discharge amounted to an unfair labor practice under Section 8(a)(1). The Supreme Court agreed in a unanimous decision that employees do not

> . . . *necessarily lose their right to engage in concerted activities under Section 7 merely because they do not present a specific demand upon their employer to remedy a condition which they find objectionable. The language of Section 7 is broad enough to protect concerted activities whether they take place before, after, or at the same time such a demand is made. . . . Having no bargaining representative and no established procedure . . . the men took the most direct course to let the company know they wanted a warmer place in which to work.*

A most difficult aspect of Section 8(a)(1) is presented in those cases in which an employer is accused of an unfair labor practice as a result of something he has said or written. Such allegations pose a direct conflict between the labor laws and the First Amendment, which guarantees freedom of speech and the press. Some early decisions under Section 8(a)(1) held that employers could not make speeches or distribute letters or circulars of certain kinds to employees before a representation election to discourage them from voting for a union. Employers

[7] 370 U.S. 9 (1962).

contended that this was a direct violation of their constitutional rights of freedom of speech. They pointed out the unfairness of permitting union organizers to vigorously encourage their selection as collective bargaining representative while requiring employers to sit by silently, preventing them from supplying antiunion information. As was noted in section 5 of this chapter, the Taft-Hartley Act [Section 8(c)] seems to have met this objection by providing that the expression of views, arguments, or opinions should not be evidence of an unfair labor practice if it contains no threats of reprisal or promises of benefits.

An employer may even predict that the consequences of unionization will be unfavorable if he does so in a way which contains no threat. The statement that "it is our definite view that if the union were to come in here, it would work to your serious harm" was held privileged and noncoercive.[8] However, if the employer predicts dire economic events as a result of unionization, such may be an illegal threat if he has it within his power to make the prediction come true. Whether particular language is coercive or not often depends on the analysis of the total background of facts and circumstances in which it was uttered. To be forbidden, the statements of an employer need not be proved to have been coercive in fact but only to have had a reasonable tendency under all the circumstances to intimidate employees. In *NLRB v. Bush Hog, Inc.*,[9] the employer stated that the union had donated funds to advance racial integration. The court ruled that this statement might be privileged if considered alone, but when evaluated in the totality of conduct by the employer, it implied that plant segregation would be preserved by him, while a union victory would mean that blacks would have to be hired. Therefore, it was unprivileged, amounting to a promise of what was considered a benefit to present employees. Clearly, threats by an employer to withdraw existing benefits of employees if they unionize is not speech protected by 8(c). However, mere predictions and prophecies are protected. For example, in *NLRB v. Herman Wilson Lumber Co.*,[10] the employer's speeches and handbills during the union's organizational campaign stated its intention to fight the union in every legal way possible, to "deal hard" with the union at arm's length if voted in, and warned that employees could be permanently replaced if the union called an economic strike. This language was held to fall within the protection of Section 8(c). The right of free speech guaranteed by the Taft-Hartley Act applies to labor unions as well as employers. However, there is a rule prohibiting either from making election speeches on company time to massed assemblies of employees within twenty-four hours before an election.

It is extremely difficult to draw a clear-cut line between those statements of employers which are coercive and those which are noncoercive and thus privileged by Section 8(c). Interpretations of the Board have varied with its membership over the years. The case which follows is typical of those involving statements of management which were challenged as interfering with the rights of its employees under Section 8(a)(1).

---

[8] *Wellington Mill Division, West Point Mfg. Co. v. NLRB*, 330 F.2d 579 (1964).
[9] 405 F.2d 755 (1968).
[10] 355 F.2d 426 (1966).

NLRB v. Deutsch Company
445 F.2d 902 (1971)

BYRNE, DISTRICT JUDGE: The National Labor Relations Board ("the Board") found, in agreement with the Trial Examiner, that The Deutsch Company, Metal Components Division ("the Company"), violated Section 8(a)(1), of the National Labor Relations Act ("the Act"), 29 U.S.C. § 158(a)(1) by coercively interrogating employees concerning their union activity at its Los Angeles plant, by invoking an invalid prohibition against union solicitation and by soliciting employees to revoke their union authorization cards. . . .

In March, 1968, the Union began an organizing campaign at the Company's Los Angeles plant. Shortly thereafter, Peter Hanly, the Company's personnel director, engaged three employees in a conversation during their lunch break. According to Ray Rodriguez, a former employee of the Company described by the Trial Examiner as "one of the leading adherents of the union among the employees," Hanly stated "that he heard there was going to be a union meeting and that he heard that the union organizers were giving $25.00" for each signed authorization card. Albert Matas, one of the employees to whom Hanly addressed his remarks, corroborated Rodriguez' account of this conversation.

Hanly admitted inquiring of these employees about the place of the purported union meeting and whether they were being paid for submitting signed authorization cards, but maintained these inquiries were made in a jesting fashion. Because of the surrounding circumstances the Board found this conversation to be neither amusing nor lawful.

Viewed as an isolated incident, Hanly's innocuous questions, which apparently were directed at learning whether these employees supported the Union's organizational efforts, would not be considered violative of Section 8(a)(1) of the Act. . . .

It is well settled that an employer's interrogation of employees constitutes an unfair labor practice under Section 8(a)(1) when it is associated with threats, be they express or implied, or promises, or "form(s) part of an overall pattern tending to restrain or coerce employees with regard to their protected activities." Here, the conversation in question, which included a patently unlawful statement regarding the prohibition of union solicitation on Company property, must be viewed as another dimension in the panorama of unlawful antiunion activity which served as the Company's response to the organization campaign. In this context, it is clear that Hanly's interrogation comes within the well settled rule.

According to Rodriguez and Matas, during the conversation now in controversy, Hanly stated that Company policy prohibited any kind of solicitation on Company property. Hanly denied this account of the conversation claiming instead that he "told them it was against Company rules to distribute or to solicit, solicitation of any kind during working hours on Company premises." The Company's personnel director also asserted that he referred the employees to the booklet, "Employees Handbook, Deutsch," for further guidance as to the Company's rules regarding on premises solicitation. The Trial Examiner found that

Hanly gave a mistakenly restrictive statement of the Company's "no-solicitation rule" and thus concluded that the Company had invoked "an invalid no-solicitation rule," a violation of Section 8(a)(1) of the Act. The Board adopted the Trial Examiner's finding and conclusion. . . .

On April 1, 1968, the Company mailed to its employees a letter informing them that a union authorization card could be revoked if it were signed due to misinformation, coercion or intimidation. The employees were also told that a forged authorization card was ground for revocation. In order to facilitate revocation, the Company enclosed a post card addressed to the Board which contained a statement which rescinded the union authorization card.

Approximately seven weeks later, May 20, 1968, Philip Holzman, the Company's president, sent a letter to the employees which again afforded them, by way of enclosed post cards, similar to those which were a part of the April 1 mailing, the opportunity to "withdraw" their authorization cards. The Company president concluded his letter with the following observation:

In my opinion the relationship as it presently exists at Deutsch is much better than the promises being made by these Union organizers which everyone knows will not be kept.

To those of you who support my position and continue to do so, and have not signed a card—many thanks.

The Board's finding that the Company's letter of May 20, 1968, violated Section 8(a)(1) is completely consistent with the established rule that an employer cannot engage in conduct calculated to erode employee support for the union.

In the instant case it is readily apparent that the thrust of the Company's mailing was to undermine employee support for the union. Given the state of the law, the Board's action of condemning this practice as a violation of Section 8(a)(1) is beyond reproach. [THE ORDER OF THE BOARD SHALL BE ENFORCED IN FULL]

B   *Domination of a labor organization or contribution of financial or other support to it* [Section 8(a)(2)]

Before the Wagner Act was passed, it was a fairly common practice for employers to sidetrack the desires and efforts of employees to organize by forming a "union" which was in fact controlled by the employer. The prohibition of this unfair labor practice put an end to the use of such company unions.

Under the Wagner Act, any organization of employees must be completely independent of the employer. Neither he nor his supervisory personnel may promote or sponsor a particular organization for collective bargaining. In the case of a controversy between competing unions, the employer must remain strictly neutral, unless he already has a union-shop agreement in force with one of them. This section of the law was violated when it was agreed that an employee representative plan could not be amended if the employer disapproved. Such control of the form and structure of the employees' representative committee deprived them of the guaranteed freedom from control by their employer. Section 8(a)(2) also proscribes such support to a union as giving it a meeting place. An employer's agreement to pay initiation fees and dues to a union for member employees was found to be in violation of this section when such was an inducement to join the union.

c Discrimination in hire or tenure of employees for reason of union affiliation [Section 8(a)(3)]

Under this section, an employer may neither discharge nor refuse to hire an employee either to *encourage* or *discourage* membership in any labor organization. Nor may he discriminate in regard to any term or condition of employment for such purposes. However, the Wagner Act provided that the employer who had a closed-shop agreement with a union was not in violation of the Act by insisting upon union membership as a condition of employment. The Taft-Hartley Act outlawed the closed shop but permitted the union shop in those states which did not outlaw it by enacting right-to-work legislation. In a closed-shop contract the employer agrees that he will not *hire* any person who is not a member of the union. In a union-shop contract, the employer agrees to require membership in the union sometime after an employee has been hired, as a condition of his continued employment. Under Taft-Hartley such a requirement may not be imposed until the thirtieth day after employment begins. In addition, an employer may not compel union membership of an employee (1) if such was not available to him on the same terms and conditions applicable to other members or (2) if the employee's membership was denied or terminated for reasons other than his failure to pay dues and fees. Section 8(a)(3) does not oblige an employer to favor union members in hiring employees. It also does not restrict him in the normal exercise of the right of an employer to select or discharge employees. However, he may not abuse that right by discriminatory action based on union membership or activities which encourages or discourages membership in a labor organization. The following case involves the right of an employer to go out of business because his employees have organized.

Textile Workers Union v. Darlington Manufacturing Company
85 S.Ct. 994 (1965)

HARLAN, JUSTICE: We here review judgments of the Court of Appeals setting aside and refusing to enforce an order of the National Labor Relations Board which found respondent Darlington guilty of an unfair labor practice by reason of having permanently closed its plant following petitioner union's election as the bargaining representative of Darlington's employees.

Darlington Manufacturing Company was a South Carolina corporation operating one textile mill. A majority of Darlington's stock was held by Deering Milliken & Co., a New York "selling house" marketing textiles produced by others. Deering Milliken in turn was controlled by Roger Milliken, president of Darlington, and by other members of the Milliken family. The National Labor Relations Board found that the Milliken family, through Deering Milliken, operated 17 textile manufacturers, including Darlington, whose products manufactured in 27 different mills, were marketed through Deering Milliken.

In March 1956 petitioner Textile Workers Union initiated an organizational campaign at Darlington which the company resisted vigorously in various ways, including threats to close the mill if the union won a representation election. On September 6, 1956, the union won an election by a narrow margin. When Roger Milliken was advised of the union victory, he decided to call a meeting of the Darlington board of directors to consider closing the mill. Mr. Milliken testified before the Labor Board:

I felt that as a result of the campaign that had been conducted and the promises and statements made in these letters that had been distributed [favoring unionization], that if before we had had some hope, possible hope of achieving competitive [costs] . . . by taking advantage of new machinery that was being put in, that this hope had diminished as a result of the election because a majority of the employees had voted in favor of the union. . . .

The board of directors met on September 12 and voted to liquidate the corporation, action which was approved by the stockholders on October 17. The plant ceased operations entirely in November, and all plant machinery and equipment was sold piecemeal at auction in December.

The union filed charges with the Labor Board claiming that Darlington had violated §§ 8(a)(1) and 8(a)(3) of the National Labor Relations Act by closing its plant, and § 8(a)(5) by refusing to bargain with the union after the election. The Board, by a divided vote, found that Darlington had been closed because of the anti-union animus of Roger Milliken, and held that to be a violation of § 8(a)(3). The Board also found Darlington to be part of a single integrated employer group controlled by the Milliken family through Deering Milliken; therefore Deering Milliken could be held liable for the unfair labor practices of Darlington. Alternatively, since Darlington was a part of the Deering Milliken enterprise, Deering Milliken had violated the Act by closing part of its business for a discriminatory purpose. The Board ordered back pay for all Darlington employees until they obtained substantially equivalent work or were put on preferential hiring lists at the other Deering Milliken mills. Respondent Deering Milliken was ordered to bargain with the union in regard to details of compliance with the Board order.

On review, the Court of Appeals, sitting *in banc*, set aside the order and denied enforcement by a divided vote. The Court of Appeals held that even accepting *arguendo* the Board's determination that Deering Milliken had the status of a single employer, a company has the absolute right to close out a part or all of its business regardless of anti-union motives. The court therefore did not review the Board's finding that Deering Milliken was a single integrated employer. We granted certiorari to consider the important questions involved. We hold that so far as the Labor Act is concerned, an employer has the absolute right to terminate his entire business for any reason he pleases, but disagree with the Court of Appeals that such right includes the ability to close part of a business no matter what the reason. We conclude that the cause must be remanded to the Board for further proceedings.

The AFL-CIO suggests in its *amicus* brief that Darlington's action was similar to a discriminatory lockout, which is prohibited "because designed to frustrate organizational efforts, to destroy or undermine bargaining representation, or to evade the duty to bargain." One of the purposes of the Labor Act is to prohibit the discriminatory use of economic weapons in an effort to obtain future benefits. The discriminatory lockout designed to destroy a union, like a "runaway shop," is a lever which has been used to discourage collective employee activities in the future. But a complete liquidation of a business yields no such future benefit for the employer, if the termination is *bona fide*. It may be motivated more by spite against the union than by business reasons, but it is not the type of discrimination which is prohibited by the Act. The personal satisfaction that such an employer may derive from standing on his beliefs or the mere possibility that other employers will follow his example are surely too remote to be considered dangers at which the labor statutes were aimed. Although employees may be prohibited from engaging in a strike under certain conditions, no one would consider it a violation of the Act for the same employees to quit their employment *en masse*, even if motivated by a desire to ruin the employer. The very permanence of such action would negate any future economic benefit to the employees. The employer's right to go out of business is no different.

We are not presented here with the case of a "runaway shop," whereby Darlington would transfer its work to another plant or open a new plant in another locality to replace its closed plant. Nor are we concerned with a shutdown where the employees, by renouncing the union, could cause the plant to reopen. Such cases would involve discriminatory employer action for the purpose of obtaining some benefit in the future from the new employees. We hold here only that when an employer closes his entire business, even if the liquidation is motivated by vindictiveness towards the union, such action is not an unfair labor practice.

While we thus agree with the Court of Appeals that viewing Darlington as an independent employer the liquidation of its business was not an unfair labor practice, we cannot accept the lower court's view that the same conclusion necessarily follows if Darlington is regarded as an integral part of the Deering Milliken enterprise.

The closing of an entire business, even though discriminatory, ends the employer-employee relationship; the force of such a closing is entirely spent as to that business when termination of the enterprise takes place. On the other hand, a discriminatory partial closing may have repercussions on what remains of the business, affording employer leverage for discouraging the free exercise of § 7 rights among remaining employees of much the same kind as that found to exist in the "runaway shop" and "temporary closing" cases. Moreover, a possible remedy open to the Board in such a case, like the remedies available in the "runaway shop" and "temporary closing" cases, is to order reinstatement of the discharged employees in the other parts of the business. No such remedy is available when an entire business has been terminated. By analogy to those cases involving a continuing enterprise we are constrained to hold, in disagreement with the Court of Appeals, that a partial closing is an unfair labor practice under § 8(a)(3) if motivated by a purpose to chill unionism in any of the remaining plants of the single employer and if the employer may reasonably have foreseen that such closing will likely have that effect.

While we have spoken in terms of a "partial closing" in the context of the Board's finding that Darlington was part of a larger single enterprise controlled by the Milliken family, we do not mean to suggest that an organizational integration of plants or corporations is a necessary prerequisite to the establishment of such a violation of § 8(a)(3). If the persons exercising control over a plant that is being closed for anti-union reasons (1) have an interest in another business, whether or not affiliated with or engaged in the same line of commercial activity as the closed plant, of sufficient substantiality to give promise of their reaping a benefit from the discouragement of unionization in that business; (2) act to close their plant with the purpose of producing such a result; and (3) occupy a relationship to the other business which makes it realistically foreseeable that its employees will fear that such business will also be closed down if they persist in organizational activities, we think that an unfair labor practice has been made out. . . .

Judgments of Court of Appeals vacated and cases remanded with instruc-. tions. [VACATED]

D *Discrimination against employees for filing charges or giving testimony under the Act* [Section 8(a)(4)]

The banning of this unfair labor practice protects employees from being discharged or from other reprisals by their employers because they have sought to enforce their rights under the Act. In so doing, it prevents the NLRB's channels of information from being dried up by employers' intimidation of complainants and witnesses. The forbidden discrimination includes the refusal to hire a prospective employee because charges were filed by him. Although supervisors are not regarded as "employees" within the meaning of the Act, they have been held to be protected from discharge or reprisal for testifying in a labor proceeding where such would coerce those who are employees in the exercise of their rights to organize.

The main line of defense of any employer accused under Section 8(a)(4) is that he discharged or discriminated against the employee for some reason other than the filing of charges or giving of testimony. Thus, most often the cases here boil down to a question of proof of what motivated the employer in pursuing his course of action. If he can convince the NLRB that he discharged the employee because of misconduct, low production, personnel cutbacks necessitated by economic conditions, or other legitimate considerations, he will be exonerated. Otherwise, he will be found guilty of this unfair labor practice. The decision in the case below turned on the scope of the language of Section 8(a)(4).

NLRB v. Scrivener
92 S.Ct. 798 (1972)

BLACKMUN, JUSTICE: . . . This case presents the issue whether an employer's retaliatory discharge of an employee who gave a written sworn statement to a National Labor Relations Board field examiner investigating an unfair labor practice charge filed against the employer, but who had not filed the charge or testified at a formal hearing on it, constitutes a violation of § 8(a)(1) or of § 8(a)(4) of the [Wagner] Act. The Board, with one member not participating, unanimously held that it was. The United States Court of Appeals for the Eighth Circuit, by a unanimous panel vote, held otherwise and denied enforcement. . . .

The Board, in agreement with the trial examiner, concluded that the April 18 dismissal of the four employees was "in retaliation against them for having met with and given evidence to a Board field examiner investigating unfair labor practice charges which had been filed against" Scrivener; that "[t]he investigation of charges filed is an integral and essential stage of Board proceedings"; and that this conduct violated § 8(a)(1) and § 8(a)(4). The customary orders to cease and desist, to reinstate the four employees with back pay, and to post notices were issued.

The view of the Court of Appeals is that § 8(a)(4) of the Act serves to protect an employee against an employer's reprisal only for *filing* an unfair labor practice charge or for giving *testimony* at a formal hearing, and that it affords him no protection for otherwise participating in the investigative stage or, in particular, for giving an affidavit or sworn statement to the investigating field examiner.

We disagree for several reasons.

1. Construing § 8(a)(4) to protect the employee during the investigative stage as well as in connection with the filing of a formal charge or the giving of formal testimony comports with the objective of that section. Mr. Justice Black, in no uncertain terms, spelled out the congressional purpose:

. . . Congress has made it clear that it wishes all persons with information about such practices to be completely free from coercion against reporting them to the Board. This is shown by its adoption of § 8(a)(4) which makes it an unfair labor practice for an employer to discriminate against an employee because he has filed charges. And it has been held that it is unlawful for an employer to seek to restrain an employee in the exercise of his right to file charges" [citations omitted].

This complete freedom is necessary, it has been said, "to prevent the Board's channels of information from being dried up by employer intimidation of prospective complainants and witnesses." It is also consistent with the fact that the Board does not initiate its own proceedings; implementation is dependent "upon the initiative of individual persons."

The Act's reference in § 8(a)(4) to an employee who "has filed charges or given testimony," could be read strictly and confined in its reach to formal charges and formal testimony. It can also be read more broadly. On textual analysis alone, the presence of the preceding words "to discharge or otherwise discriminate" reveals, we think particularly by the word "otherwise," an intent on the part of Congress to afford broad rather than narrow protection to the employee. . . .

This interpretation, in our view, also squares with the practicalities of appropriate agency action. An employee who participates in a Board investigation may not be called formally to testify or may be discharged before any hearing at which he could testify. His contribution might be merely cumulative or the case may be settled or dismissed before hearing. Which employees receive statutory protection should not turn on the vagaries of the selection process or on other events that have no relation to the need for protection. It would make less than complete sense to protect the employee because he participates in the formal inception of the process (by filing a charge) or in the final, formal presentation, but not to protect his participation in the important developmental stages that fall between these two points in time. This would be unequal and inconsistent protection and is not the protection needed to preserve the integrity of the Board process in its entirety.

The Board's subpoena power also supports this interpretation. Section 11 of the Act, 29 U.S.C. § 161, gives the Board this power for "the purpose of all hearings and investigations." Once an employee has been subpoenaed he should be protected from retaliatory action regardless of whether he has filed a charge or has actually testified. Judge Lumbard pertinently described it:

It is, we think, a permissible inference that Congress intended the protection to be as broad as the [subpoena] power.

Under this reasoning, if employees of Scrivener had been subpoenaed, they would have been protected. There is no basis for denying similar protection to the voluntary participant. . . .

We are aware of no substantial countervailing considerations. We therefore conclude that an employer's discharge of an employee because the employee gave a written sworn statement to a Board field examiner investigating an unfair labor practice charge filed against the employer constitutes a violation of § 8(a)(4) of the National Labor Relations Act.

The judgment of the Court of Appeals is reversed and the case is remanded for further proceedings. [REVERSED AND REMANDED]

E *Refusal to bargain collectively with a duly designated representative of the employees* [Section 8(a)(5)]

The law today imposes a requirement on both employers and unions to bargain collectively with each other. The unfair labor practice of refusing to do so is discussed in section 9 of this chapter.

F *Agreeing with a labor organization to engage in a secondary boycott*
[Section 8(e)]

This unfair labor practice by employers was not one of the original five forbidden under the Wagner Act and has not been mentioned before. Taft-Hartley attempted to limit the use by unions of the secondary boycott as an indirect weapon in a campaign to organize employees. It was an unfair labor practice for a union to induce the *employees* of any employer to strike, or engage in a concerted refusal to use, handle, or work on any goods or to perform any services, in order to force the employer to stop doing business with any other person. For example, assume that employer A sells supplies to manufacturer B, which are transported by trucking firm C, whose employees are nonunion. This Taft-Hartley provision made it illegal for either a union attempting to organize the employees of C or the union representing the employees of A to induce the employees of A to strike or refuse to load C's trucks with supplies in order to require A to stop shipping his goods by C. This represented a swing of the pendulum back from the Norris-LaGuardia Act's liberalization of the use of secondary boycotts toward the policy of the law as it existed before that Act. Then, secondary boycotts were viewed as illegal combinations in restraint of trade under the Sherman Act, or as illegal conspiracies under the common law.

Taft-Hartley, however, was not successful in eliminating all secondary boycotts. Loopholes appeared in its proscriptions. For example, a "hot cargo" contract, in which an employer *voluntarily* agreed with a union not to handle, use, or deal in nonunion-produced goods of another person were held to be legal. The union was prevented only from inducing the *employees* of the employer to strike or otherwise act to force their employer not to handle such goods. The Landrum-Griffin Act (the major provisions of which are discussed more fully in section 11 of this chapter) plugged this loophole and outlawed hot-cargo contracts. Its amendment to Taft-Hartley states in Section 8(e): "It shall be an unfair labor practice for any labor organization and any employer to enter into any contract or agreement . . . whereby such employer . . . agrees to refrain from handling, using, selling, transporting or otherwise dealing in any of the products of any other employer, or to cease doing business with any other person. .. ." Further, such contract provisions are made unenforceable and void.

8 UNFAIR LABOR PRACTICES BY UNIONS

The Wagner Act did not contain any provisions relating to unfair labor practices by labor unions. It was in its effect one-sided. The Taft-Hartley Act covered the missing side by declaring that certain conduct or activities by labor unions also were unfair labor practices and thus illegal. Six such activities were specified. The Landrum-Griffin Act in 1959 added two additional unfair labor practices by unions to those declared illegal by Taft-Hartley. These unfair labor practices will be discussed in this section.

A   *Restraining or coercing an employee in joining a union, or an employer in selecting his representatives to bargain with the union* [Section 8(b)(1)]

This unfair labor practice includes misconduct by unions directed toward employees and misconduct directed toward employers. Most allegations of unfair labor practices filed against unions are brought under this provision. The first part of Section 8(b)(1) makes it illegal for a union to restrain or coerce employees in the exercise of their right to bargain collectively, just as it is an unfair labor practice by employers to interfere with the same rights. Employees also are guaranteed the right to *refrain* from union activities unless required by a legal union-shop agreement in force between their employer and a labor organization.

Mass picketing, threats of physical violence aimed at employees or their families, and blocking of entrances to plants to physically bar employees from going in have all been held to be conduct in violation of this section. Picketing to coerce an employer to have his employees join a union by whatever means he might use in order to save his business from harm, physical or economic, also is an unfair labor practice. In one case a union was found guilty of this unfair practice because it insisted upon the discharge of a *supervisor* for failure to comply with union rules. The court noted that this would inevitably tend to coerce nonsupervisory personnel into observing such rules.

The phrase to "restrain or coerce" has the same meaning when used in reference to union activity as it does when used in reference to activities by employers. The test is whether words or conduct by the union was reasonably likely to have restrained the free choice of the employees. The intent is to ensure that the decision of the employees as to whether or not to be represented by a union in bargaining and also the choice of that representative are arrived at freely without coercion. A union violated this section by executing and maintaining a contract with an employer which covered its office and sales employees where they unanimously opposed the union and none desired to join it.

Although most cases brought under Section 8(b)(1)(A) charge that a union has restrained or coerced employees in their right to *organize* and *bargain* collectively or refrain from doing so, the scope of this unfair labor practice is actually much broader, as the following case illustrates.

Local Union No. 12, United Rubber, C. L. & P. Workers v. NLRB
368 F.2d 12 (1966)

Negro members of the defendant union filed charges with the NLRB against the union for committing an unfair labor practice by summarily refusing to process certain grievances they had. The employer, Goodyear Tire & Rubber Company of East Gadsden, Alabama, had maintained three separate seniority rolls—white male, black male, and female. By reason of custom and interpretation, black employees with greater seniority had no rights over white employees with less seniority, and vice versa, with respect to promotions, transfers, layoffs, and recalls. Also, as a matter of custom, segregated lunchrooms, restrooms, and showers were maintained at the plant, although nothing in the bargaining contract dealt with these matters. The complainants had been laid off and executed affidavits that during the time of their layoff, new workers had been hired in violation of plant seniority rules. These were given to the president of the union asking for an investigation and remedial action. Before the grievance committee, the complainants charged that their layoff was improper under contract-stated seniority. They demanded reinstatement with back wages and the right to all plant privileges without color barriers. The committee determined that "no contract violation exists, therefore, the Union has no ground on which to base a complaint against the company." Later appeals to the union executive board and the full membership were denied. And in spite of a recommendation by the International President, the local union continued to refuse to process and file a formal grievance against the company. The NLRB found that the union, by this refusal, had restrained or coerced the complainants in their Section 7 right to be represented without invidious discrimination and had refused to bargain in complainant's behalf in violation of Section 8(b)(1)(A) of the Taft-Hartley Act. Accordingly the Board ordered the local union to process the grievances through arbitration and to propose to Goodyear contract provisions prohibiting racial discrimination in terms and conditions of employment. The union petitioned the Court of Appeals for review of the Board's order.

THORNBERRY, CIRCUIT JUDGE: . . . The vital issue . . . resolves itself into that of determining at what point the exclusive bargaining agent's duty to represent fairly the interests of each individual employee must bow to the equally comprehensive obligation of negotiating and administering the bargaining contract in accordance with the act's primary policy of fostering union-employer relations. While the Supreme Court has declared that an exclusive bargaining agent "is responsible to, and owes complete loyalty to, the interests of all whom it represents," it has at the same time recognized the inherent burden this mandate serves to impose upon a union obliged to exercise good faith in adjusting the numerous competing interests of its individual members:

Inevitably differences will arise in the manner and degree to which the terms of any negotiated agreement affect individual employees and classes of employees. The mere existence of such differences does not make them invalid. The complete satisfaction of all who are represented is hardly to be expected. A wide range of reasonableness must be allowed a statutory bargaining representative in serving the unit it represents, subject always to complete good faith and honesty of purpose in the exercise of its discretion.

Nevertheless, when the individual employee, pursuant to federal law aimed at preserving industrial harmony, is required to surrender completely his right of self-representation in deference to an "exclusive" bargaining agent designated by a majority of his coworkers, both logic and equity dictate that such agent be impressed with a reciprocal duty to "represent all its members, the majority as well as the minority, and . . . to act for and not against those whom it represents." Indeed, the Supreme Court has indicated that any statute purporting to bestow upon a union the exclusive right to represent all employees would be unconstitutional if it failed to impose upon the union this reciprocal duty of fair representation. . . . Therefore, we are not here called upon to establish such duty but rather to face the issue of what conduct represents a breach of that duty, together with its appropriate remedy. More specifically, we must determine whether a breach of the duty of fair representation in itself constitutes an unfair labor practice within contemplation of the National Labor Relations Act, as amended. We are convinced that the duty of fair representation implicit in the exclusive-representation requirement in section 9(a) of the act comprises an indispensable element of the right of employees "to bargain collectively through representatives of their own choosing" as guaranteed in section 7. We therefore conclude that by summarily refusing to process the complainants' grievances concerning back wages and segregated plant facilities, petitioner thereby violated section 8(b)(1)(A) of the act by restraining those employees in the exercise of their section 7 rights.

At the outset it must be reiterated that every union decision which may in some way result in overriding the wishes . . . of . . . , even an appreciable number of employees, does not in and of itself constitute a breach of the fiduciary duty of fair representation. Even in the administration stage of the bargaining contract . . . , the union must necessarily retain a broad degree of discretion in processing individual grievances. Thus, where the union, after a good faith investigation of the merits of a grievance, concludes that the claim is insubstantial and refuses to encumber further its grievance channels by continuing to process the unmeritorious claim, its duty of fair representation may well be satisfied. Such good-faith effort to represent fairly the interests of individual employees, however, is not evidenced in this controversy. To the contrary, Local 12 in open disregard of the recommendations of its International President has continued to refuse to represent the vital interests of a segment of its membership. . . . Undoubtedly, the duty of fair representation can be breached by discriminatory inaction in refusing to process a grievance as well as by active conduct on the part of the union. The Supreme Court has declared that

The bargaining representative's duty . . . does not come to an abrupt end . . . with the making of an agreement between union and employer. Collective bargaining is a continuous process. Among other things, it involves day-to-day adjustments in the contract and other working rules, resolution of new problems not covered by existing agreements, and the protection of employee rights already secured by contract. The bargaining representative can no more unfairly discriminate in carrying out these functions than it can in negotiating a collective agreement.

. . . As the Board properly concluded, had the claims been allowed to proceed to arbitration, an arbitrator would not have been bound by the prior invalid interpretation of the contract and might well have awarded back wages. We thus conclude that where the record demonstrates that a grievance would have been processed to arbitration but for arbitrary and discriminatory reasons, the refusal to so process it constitutes a violation of the union's duty to represent its members "without hostile discrimination, fairly, impartially, and in good faith."

Similarly, with respect to the grievances concerning the segregated nature of plant facilities, the union not only refused to process such claims but actively opposed desegregation of shower and toilet facilities. It is impossible for us to look upon such conduct as anything other than an effort to discriminate against Negro employees with respect to conditions of employment. . . . As the Board properly concluded, "whatever may be the bases on which a statutory representative may properly decline to process grievances, the bases must bear a reasonable relation to the Union's role as bargaining representative or its functioning as a labor organization; manifestly racial discrimination bears no such relationship."

. . . Local 12, in refusing to represent the complainants in a fair and impartial manner, thereby violated section 8(b)(1)(A) by restraining them in the exercise of their section 7 right to bargain collectively through their chosen representatives. The mere fact that Local 12's conduct may not have directly resulted in encouraging or discouraging union membership does not persuade us to alter our determination, for the language of section 8(b)(1)(A), unlike certain other provisions of section 8, is not restricted to discrimination which encourages or discourages union membership.

. . . To adopt a narrow interpretation of section 8(b)(1)(A) which would only protect the comprehensive section 7 right of employees to bargain collectively in those cases involving union conduct which encourages or discourages union membership would to a large degree render such right meaningless in the area of union administration of the bargaining agreement. Indeed, it is only through the day-to-day administration of individual grievances that employee rights achieved in the negotiated bargaining contract are placed in a definitive context, and through which specific individual claims find a vital means of protection. . . .

[ENFORCEMENT GRANTED]

The second part of Section 8(b)(1), which prohibits a union from restraining or coercing an employer in the selection of his representatives for collective bargaining, is violated if a union refuses to bargain with a proper representative of an employer and yet threatens a strike if bargaining does not succeed. However, if a strike called by a union is an economic one with the sole objective of obtaining certain contractual terms and is not based on the refusal to deal with the employer's representative, it is not coercion of the employer forbidden by this subsection.

B   *Causing or attempting to cause the employer to discriminate against an employee who is not a union member, unless there is a legal union-shop agreement in effect* [Section 8(b)(2)]

This section made union security contracts calling for a closed shop illegal, even if both the employer and his employees were in favor of one. And even where a legal union-shop contract is in effect, this section prohibits a union from attempting to cause an employer to discriminate against an employee who has been denied membership, or had his membership terminated, for some reason other than his failure to pay the dues and initiation fees uniformly required of all members. This prohibition was designed to prevent the use of the union shop as a means of intimidating employees who were at odds with union officials over their policies.

c Refusing to bargain with the employer [Section 8(b)(3)]

This unfair labor practice, along with that of an employer's refusal to bargain collectively with the union representing his employees, is discussed in section 9 of this chapter.

D Striking, picketing, and engaging in secondary boycotts for illegal purposes [Section 8(b)(4)]

Under this section of the original Taft-Hartley Act it was unfair for a union to engage in or induce the employees of any person to engage in certain *concerted* activities, such as secondary boycotts. Because of the use of the word "concerted," it was found legal for unions to induce single employees to perform the acts forbidden by the section. Thus, it was not an unfair labor practice for pickets of a striking union to induce the *individual* truck drivers of a customer of their employer not to pick up goods from him. The Landrum-Griffin Act (discussed more fully in section 11 of this chapter) contained an amendment which plugged this loophole. Under the amended 8(a)(4), it is an unfair labor practice for a union to engage in or induce any *individual* employed to engage in a strike or in a refusal in the course of his employment to use, process, or otherwise handle any goods or to perform any services, or for a union to threaten or coerce any employer where an object of doing any of the foregoing is one of the four outlined below.

(1) Requiring an Employer or Self Employed Person to Join a Union or Employer Organization or to Enter into a "Hot Cargo" Contract Hot-cargo contracts were discussed in section 7 of this chapter.

(2) Forcing Any Person to Engage in a Secondary Boycott This section made it illegal to require an employer or any other person to stop using or dealing in the products of another or to stop doing business with another. Forcing any other employer to recognize or bargain with a union as the representative of his employees was also outlawed, unless it has been certified by the NLRB as such. The use of primary strikes or picketing is not restricted by this section. Thus, if the union representing the employees of X induces them to strike in order to force X to grant them a pay increase, there is no violation. However, it would be forbidden for the union of X's employees in the course of a dispute with X to induce any employees of Y to strike to coerce Y to stop buying the products of X. Likewise, it would be a violation for the union of X's employees to induce them not to work on goods which were produced by "scab" labor at the nonunion plant of Z, in order to induce X to use union-made goods instead. Secondary boycotts can

result in an undue disruption of commerce by adversely affecting businesses which are only indirectly related to the one with which a labor dispute exists. Their use can make a union too powerful, is unfair to the remote employer, and can be detrimental to the public interest.

(3) Forcing an Employer to Recognize or Bargain with One Union if Another One Has Been Certified as the Representative of His Employees   This provision was made to protect employers (and their employees) from the destructive rivalry between unions competing to be the bargaining representative of the employees in a unit where they had already chosen one. Under the Wagner Act, the employer could not bargain with the uncertified union, but was prevented by the Norris-LaGuardia Act from obtaining an injunction to prevent its picketing.

(4) Forcing an Employer to Assign Work to the Employees in One Particular Union or Craft Rather than Another   The purpose of this section was to make so-called "jurisdictional" strikes illegal. Before Taft-Hartley, it was common, especially in the construction industry, for strikes to result from a dispute between two different crafts, such as brickmasons and cement workers, as to who should be assigned certain work by the employer. Such strikes could cause irreparable damage to an employer who had no antiunion bias whatsoever. If he would submit to the demands of one of the crafts, the other would stop work. *NLRB v. Radio and Television Broadcast Engineers' Union*[11] involved a dispute between a union of stage employees and one of television employees as to which would be assigned the job of handling electric lighting for CBS television programs. In that case, the Supreme Court ruled that the Taft-Hartley Act required the NLRB to hear charges of jurisdictional disputes filed with it under this provision and to make an affirmative award of the disputed work where the parties were unable to reach an agreement among themselves. Of course, it is not a violation of this section for a union which has been certified by the Board to represent the employees performing the particular work involved to force the employer to assign it to them.

The Act specifically excludes certain conduct from being a violation of (1), (2), (3), or (4) above. First, if the properly designated union of the employees of employer A is engaged in a primary strike against A, any person may refuse to enter the premises of A. Second, if a union has a primary dispute with an employer, it may give publicity (other than picketing) to truthfully inform the public that a product is produced by the employer with whom they have a dispute and is distributed by another business. However, such publicity may not induce any employee (other than those of the primary employer) to refuse to pick up or deliver any goods or perform any services at the business of the one engaged in the distribution.

Any person who suffers injury to his business or property because of a violation of (1), (2), (3), or (4) above may recover damages from the guilty union in the Federal district court, or any other court which has jurisdiction of the parties, without regard to the amount claimed. In addition, when a charge of a violation of (1), (2), or (3) is filed, and there is reasonable cause to believe it is true, the

---

[11] 364 U.S. 573 (1961).

appropriate officer of the Board is required to seek a temporary court order enjoining any further violation by the union until final adjudication of the matter by the NLRB.

E   *Requiring employees to pay excessive fees* [Section 8(b)(5)]

This unfair labor practice was included to protect employees who were required to join a union as a condition of employment by reason of a union-shop agreement. It prohibits the charging of an excessive or discriminatory initiation fee as a requirement of becoming a member of the union.

F   *Causing an employer to pay for work not to be performed* [Section 8(b)(6)]

This unfair labor practice was designed to prevent "featherbedding" but is quite limited in actual operation. The issue is: What are "services not performed or not to be performed?" Make-work rules have been approved by the courts as being outside the prohibition of this provision. It is not violated as long as some services are performed, even if they are of little or no actual value to the employer. In *NLRB v. Gamble Enterprises*[12] the Supreme Court held that it was permissible for a musician's union to require a theatre to employ a local orchestra to play overtures and intermissions as a condition of its consent to local appearances of traveling big-name bands. And in *American Newspaper Publisher's Association v. NLRB*[13] the Court approved the insistence by a union that newspaper publishers who used advertising mats as molds for metal castings from which to print advertisements pay union printers for setting up in type duplicates of these advertisements. The payments were found to be for work actually done, in spite of the fact that the duplicates were not used and ordinarily were just melted down.

G   *Picketing to require an employer to recognize or bargain with a union which is not currently certified as representing his employees, in certain cases* [Section 8(b)(7)]

This unfair labor practice was prohibited by the Landrum-Griffin Act. The purpose was to reinforce the effectiveness of the election procedures employed by the NLRB by outlawing certain tactics which have been used by unions that were backed by only a minority of the employees of a particular employer. By reason of it, picketing to force an employer to recognize an uncertified union became illegal in the following cases:

1   Where the employer lawfully has recognized another union as the collective-bargaining representative of his employees.
2   Where a valid representation election has been conducted by the NLRB within the past twelve months.

[12] 345 U.S. 117 (1953).
[13] 345 U.S. 100 (1953).

3 Where picketing has been conducted for a reasonable time, not in excess of thirty days, without a petition for a representation election being filed with the NLRB.

Under (3) above, however, the Act does not prohibit so-called "informational" picketing. That is, picketing or publicity to truthfully advise the public (including consumers) that an employer has a nonunion business, unless the effect of the picketing is to induce employees of another person to observe the picket line.

Certain kinds of "organizational" picketing are made unfair by this amendment. Before Landrum-Griffin, it was possible for a minority union to picket an employer for recognition as the collective-bargaining representative of his employees, when it was illegal for him to accept it as such. While Congress felt that unions should be able to publicize the fact that certain employers are nonunion, they also felt that unions should not be permitted to attempt to force employers to violate the law. Purely recognitional picketing under the circumstances stated above is illegal. Purely informational picketing probably is legal.

The fact is, however, that often picketing has both purposes. Such dual-purpose picketing under the facts stated in cases (1) or (2) listed above is literally unlawful. However, dual-purpose picketing in case (3) is probably legal unless it inhibits deliveries of goods to the employer being picketed, or the like. Even if it does, the NLRB has ruled that such interruptions must be substantial enough to curtail the employer's business. The rules concerning the application of this provision of the statute have not been clearly enunciated by the NLRB (which has taken several positions) or the courts.

This part of the Act also prohibits picketing by an uncertified union (in the situations enumerated) in order to force the *employees* of an employer to select that union as their collective-bargaining representative. As in the case of certain violations under Section 8(b)(4), when a charge of a violation is filed under Section 8(b)(7) and there is reasonable cause to believe it is true, the proper officer of the Board must seek a temporary injunction restraining further violation until the NLRB disposes of the matter.

H *Agreeing with an employer to engage in a secondary boycott* [Section 8(e)]

Banning of this unfair labor practice, added by Landrum-Griffin to the Taft-Hartley Act, outlawed hot-cargo contracts between unions and employers. It was discussed in section 7 of this chapter.

Section 8(c) of the Taft-Hartley Act, quoted in section 5 of this chapter, benefits unions as well as employers. Under it, the expression of views, arguments, or opinions by anyone is not evidence of *any* unfair labor practice if it contains no threats of reprisal or promises of benefits.

9   THE REQUIREMENT TO BARGAIN COLLECTIVELY

As previously noted, it is now an unfair labor practice for both an employer and the representatives of his employees to refuse to bargain collectively with each other. The Wagner Act did not define the term "to bargain collectively." Judicial decisions have added the concept "good faith" to it, so that it actually means to bargain in good faith. Thus, while an employer need not agree to all union demands, such conduct as the failure to make counterproposals to union demands may be evidence of bad faith. In order to comply with the requirement that they bargain collectively in good faith, employers and unions must approach the bargaining table with fair and open minds and a sincere purpose to find a basis of agreement. Refusing to meet at reasonable times with representatives of the other party, refusing to reduce agreements to writing, and designating persons with no authority to negotiate as representatives at meetings are examples of conduct which constitute this unfair labor practice.

A more fundamental issue than "good faith" is also inherent in the requirement that the parties bargain collectively. That issue simply stated is: About what? Must the employer bargain with the union about all subjects and all management decisions in which the union or the employees are interested? Are there subjects and issues upon which management is allowed to act unilaterally?

The Taft-Hartley Act contained language which attempted to answer these questions. It stated in part:

. . . to bargain collectively is the performance of the mutual obligation of the employer and the representative of the employees to meet at reasonable times and confer in good faith with respect to wages, hours and other terms and conditions of employment, or the negotiation of an agreement, or any question arising thereunder, and the execution of a written contract incorporating any agreement reached if requested by either party. . . .

Thus the law requires or compels bargaining on issues concerned with *wages, hours and other terms and conditions of employment.* While the parties may *voluntarily* consider other issues raised by their adversary, the refusal by either to bargain in good faith on such other matters is not an unfair labor practice.

It follows that management decisions affecting labor fall into two categories, those which concern *mandatory* or *compulsory* bargaining issues and those which involve *voluntary* or *permissive* bargaining issues. Classifications must be made on a case-by-case basis. For example, do questions relating to fringe benefits such as stock options or pension plans concern compulsory bargaining issues? If stock options and pension plans are "wages," then they do. If not, then decisions affecting stock options and pension plans may be made unilaterally by management, even if the union seeks to bargain about these matters. The NLRB and the courts are called on to decide if management and labor must bargain with each other on a multitude of issues, as the case which follows illustrates.

Westinghouse Electric Corporation v. NLRB
387 F.2d 542 (1967)

Westinghouse Electric Corporation (the company) owned cafeterias housed at several of its plants which were operated by an independent contractor, the Baltimore Catering Company (the caterer). Under the contract, the caterer paid the company rental of only $1 per year for the space and capital equipment necessary to operate the facilities. The caterer also agreed that "the quality and prices of the meals served, and the hours of service thereof, in said cafeterias shall at all times be reasonable." Either party had the right to terminate the agreement upon giving sixty days' written notice. Between 40 and 45 percent of Westinghouse's employees ate lunch at the cafeterias. Few left the premises for lunch because of the shortness of the lunch periods. The caterer announced an increase in food prices (5 cents for entrees and 1 cent for carry-out coffee) which it attributed to rising costs caused by wage increases granted to its own union employees through collective bargaining. One of the unions representing some of the Westinghouse employees (2,500 of 7,500) attempted to negotiate with Westinghouse concerning the cafeteria price increases made by the caterer, but Westinghouse refused to discuss the matter. The union then filed a complaint with the NLRB contending that the company's refusal to bargain constituted an unfair labor practice. The Board issued an order requiring the company to bargain with the union.

BOREMAN, CIRCUIT JUDGE: . . . The statutory phrase—"terms and conditions of employment"—according to the Board, is intended by Congress to be used in its "broadest sense" and encompasses virtually everything which bears on the employment relationship and to which workers seek management's agreement. However, the legislative history does not support the Board's view of congressional intent and design. At best, the history merely shows that Congress did not desire to enumerate specific bargaining subjects; it does not show that the phrase was meant to embrace every issue that might be of interest to unions or employers. To the contrary, as Mr. Justice Stewart stressed, in his concurring opinion in *Fibreboard Paper Products Corp. v. NLRB,* 379 U.S. 203,

It is important to note that the words of the statute are words of limitation. The National Labor Relations Act does not say that the employer and employees are bound to confer upon any subject which interests either of them; the specification of wages, hours, and other terms and conditions of employment defines a limited category of issues subject to compulsory bargaining. The limiting purpose of the statute's language is made clear by the legislative history of the present Act. . . .

The phrase "condition of employment" is no doubt susceptible of diverse interpretations. At the extreme, the phrase could be construed to apply to any subject which is insisted upon as a prerequisite for continued employment. Such an interpretation, which would in effect place the compulsion of the Board behind any and all bargaining demands, would be contrary to the intent of Congress, as reflected in this legislative history. . . . If, as I think clear, the purpose of § 8(d) is to describe a limited area subject to the duty of collective bargaining, those management decisions which are fundamental to the basic direction of a corporate enterprise or which impinge only indirectly upon employment security should be excluded from that area.

In *Fibreboard,* the company operated a manufacturing plant at which United Steel Workers of America represented the company's maintenance employees working on the premises. The agreement with the union was about to expire when the company informed the union that after a study it had decided to engage an independent contractor to perform these maintenance services. The company expressed the view that in the light of its decision, negotiation of a new contract would be pointless. At the termination of the contract the employment of the maintenance workers was ended and a subcontractor's employees began doing this work. The Board held that under those circumstances the company was under a duty to bargain with the union; the Court of Appeals for the District of Columbia Circuit decreed enforcement of the Board's order and the Supreme Court affirmed. The Court pointed to the fact that it was a widespread industrial practice to include the subject of "contracting out" within the collective bargaining process and that the contracting out of work performed by members of the bargaining unit might appropriately be called a condition of employment.

. . .[I]t appears that the Supreme Court's decision in *Fibreboard* was limited to a particular situation involving the job security of members of the bargaining unit which was threatened not merely by the transfer of work to other employees but by the transfer of work to be done on the premises. However, Mr. Justice Stewart noted: "[I]t surely does not follow that every decision which may affect job security is a subject of compulsory collective bargaining."

In its briefing and arguing the instant case, the Board is apparently unwilling to acknowledge that in determining whether a given matter should be deemed a mandatory bargaining subject, the courts, as well as the Board itself, have recognized a legal distinction between those subjects which have a material or significant impact upon wages, hours, or other conditions of employment, and those which are only indirectly, incidentally, or remotely related to those subjects.

It is interesting to note that *Fibreboard Paper Products Corp. v. NLRB,* supra, . . . was decided in 1964. Subsequently, the subject of "contracting out" was considered by this court in *District 50 United Mine Workers v. NLRB,* 358 F.2d 234 (1966). We there held that an employer's decision to subcontract work was *not* a mandatory bargaining subject because there was no evidence of a significant impact on the employees from which the Board could find that the employer, by deciding to subcontract, violated its duty to bargain. It was pointed out that no employees in the maintenance department had been laid off and that some employees had refused additional overtime assignments. The court agreed with the Board that the record failed to show any substantial loss of work which might create a significant adverse impact on the employees. "We add, however, that were the impact substantial, the full-scale bargaining contended for by the union would not necessarily be appropriate. There is a difference between a decision to close a department with consequent layoffs, and decisions to subcontract which may result in less serious deprivations. It is a matter of degree and the statutory bargaining requirements should be flexibly administered to meet the needs of the particular case."

In the instant case we arrive at the conclusion, one which we believe is not inconsistent with past pronouncements of this court, that since practically every managerial decision has some impact on wages, hours, or other conditions of employment, the determination of which decisions are mandatory bargaining subjects must depend upon whether a given subject has a significant or material relationship to wages, hours, or other conditions of employment.

The case before us does not even remotely involve any question of job security or any other issue which employees could traditionally consider "vital." Nor is there any evidence that the inclusion of this issue here within the collective bargaining framework is a widespread industrial practice.

In the circumstances, we reach the conclusion that the Board's order should not be enforced. . . . [ENFORCEMENT DENIED]

Sometimes the requirement to bargain collectively is violated by an employer who bestows benefits on his employees beyond those which the union has demanded or requested. For example, in *NLRB v. Katz*,[14] the union for Katz's technical employees notified the employer of its desire to bargain about merit increases, general wage levels and increases, and a sick-leave proposal. During the course of the negotiations, the company unilaterally announced a change in sick-leave policy, granted numerous merit increases, and instituted a new system of wage increases which were to be automatic, all with no strings attached. Katz was held guilty of the unfair labor practice of refusing to bargain collectively. The grants by the employer to the employees were greater than offers which had been made to and rejected by the union at the bargaining table and so showed his bad faith in the negotiations. The Court said, ". . . an employer is not required to lead with his best offer and he is free to bargain, but even after an impasse is reached, the employer has no license to grant wage increases greater than those offered to the union at the bargaining table."

While either party may refuse to negotiate on a voluntary bargaining subject, what if one party insists upon including a provision on such a matter in the collective-bargaining agreement? In *NLRB v. Wooster Division of Borg Warner Corporation*[15] the employer conditioned its approval of a collective-bargaining contract on the inclusion of a "ballot" clause. This clause would have required an opportunity for the employees (both union and nonunion) to vote by secret ballot on whether to accept or reject the employer's last offer before striking. The NLRB

---

[14] 369 U.S. 736 (1962).
[15] 356 U.S. 342 (1958).

ruled that the employer's insistence upon this clause amounted to a refusal to bargain in good faith. In upholding the Board's decision, the Supreme Court reiterated the rule that the statutory obligation of the employer and representative of the employees is to bargain with each other in good faith with respect to "wages, hours, and other terms and conditions of employment." It continued:

The duty is limited to those subjects, and within that area neither party is legally obligated to yield. As to other matters, however, each party is free to bargain or not to bargain, and to agree or not to agree.

The company's good faith has met the requirements of the statute as to the subjects of mandatory bargaining. But that good faith does not license the employer to refuse to enter into agreements on the ground that they do not include some proposal which is not a mandatory subject of bargaining. We agree with the Board that such conduct is, in substance, a refusal to bargain about the subjects that are within the scope of mandatory bargaining. This does not mean that bargaining is to be confined to the statutory subjects. . . . But it does not follow that, because the company may propose [a clause], it can lawfully insist upon [one] as a condition to any agreement.

Since it is lawful to insist upon matters within the scope of mandatory bargaining and unlawful to insist upon matters without, the issue here is whether . . . the "ballot" . . . clause is a subject within the phrase "wages, hours, and other terms and conditions of employment" which defines mandatory bargaining. The "ballot" clause is not within that definition. It relates only to the procedure to be followed by the employees among themselves before their representative may call a strike or refuse a final offer. It settles no term or condition of employment—it merely calls for an advisory vote of the employees. . . . The "ballot" clause . . . deals only with relations between the employees and their unions. It substantially modifies the collective bargaining system provided for in the statute by weakening the independence of the "representative" chosen by the employees. It enables the employer, in effect, to deal with its employees rather than with their statutory representative. . . .

Thus, a party to labor negotiations may present a demand relating to a nonmandatory bargaining issue, as long as its resolution is not a condition precedent to the resolution of mandatory bargaining issues. The tying of a voluntary bargaining issue to a compulsory bargaining issue results in a failure to bargain in good faith and is in effect an unfair labor practice.

Courts tend to defer to the special expertise of the NLRB in classifying collective-bargaining subjects, especially in the area of "terms or conditions of employment." The courts have affirmed Board rulings holding that issues such as union dues checkoff, health and accident insurance, merit pay increases, incentive-pay plans, Christmas and other bonuses, stock purchase plans, pensions, paid vacations and holidays, proposals for effective arbitration and grievance procedures, and no-strike and no-lockout clauses are compulsory bargaining issues. Industry practice is a major factor in many decisions.

As noted, there are many disputes and questions between labor and management which do not involve compulsory bargaining matters. This is true even if layoffs may result from a management decision. For example, steps taken by an employer to make loading and unloading procedures at its terminal more efficient do not directly affect wages, hours, and other terms and conditions of employment.[16] Such action is viewed merely as a change in ordinary day-to-day operating procedures. Another nonmandatory issue is the fixing of the price of the employer's product. This is not only a subject about which the employer need not bargain; it is also one toward which union activities may not be directed without violating the antitrust laws.[17]

Taft-Hartley made the union selected by the majority of the employees in a unit their *exclusive* representative for purposes of collective bargaining in respect to mandatory bargaining issues. It also gave individual employees or groups of them the right to present grievances directly to their employer at any time. Further, they were given the right to have such grievances adjusted *without* the intervention of the union. However, their union bargaining representative has the right to be present at the adjustment, and one cannot be made which is inconsistent with the terms of the collective-bargaining agreement then in effect.

It should be reemphasized that neither the employer nor the union is required to make concessions to the other concerning a mandatory subject of bargaining. The law only demands that each negotiate such matters in good faith with the other before making a decision and taking unilateral action. If the parties fail to reach an agreement after discussing these problems, each may take steps which are against the wishes and best interests of the other party. For example, the employer may refuse to grant a wage increase requested by the union, and the union is free to strike.

10 THE COLLECTIVE-BARGAINING AGREEMENT

The ultimate goal of collective bargaining is an agreement between management and labor on wages, hours, and conditions of employment. It may be achieved without resort to strikes or lockouts. Or this goal may be reached only after substantial economic pressure has been exerted by one or both sides.

Collective-bargaining agreements typically contain contract clauses dealing with wages and hours of work. These include provisions concerning such matters as job classifications, production standards and wage rates for each classification, shifts and hours of work, and premium pay for overtime. Conditions of employment are covered by contract terms relating to rest periods, health and safety, shop and work rules, the discipline and discharge of employees, and the like. Other provisions in many agreements regulate job and income security including promotions, seniority, layoff and recall procedures, and severance pay. Clauses concerning vacations, sick leave, and personal leave are ordinarily present.

[16] *NLRB v. Dixie Ohio Express Co.,* 409 F.2d 10 (1969).
[17] *Carroll v. American Federation of Musicians,* 372 F.2d 155 (1967).

Some collective-bargaining agreements go so far as to spell out the extent to which management may make decisions without union approval about the subcontracting of work, utilization of technological advances in machinery, and the change of plant locations. These may or may not be compulsory bargaining matters.

Contract terms which deal with the rights of employees and union leaders to engage in union activities on company time and on the company's premises often appear. "Union security" provisions may be inserted by which the employer agrees to a union shop.

Of course, the typical contract includes a statement as to its duration, a promise of no strikes or lockouts during its term, and details of employee grievance procedures.

When a collective-bargaining agreement is currently in force, a labor dispute may arise over its interpretation and application. Frequently the management and the union are able to resolve their differences by themselves. Sometimes a dispute is settled by conciliation or *mediation,* where, by mutual agreement, a neutral third party is called upon to assist the employer and the union in their deliberations and help them find a solution which is acceptable to both. A mediator does not make a decision which is binding on the parties but helps them in reaching their agreement. Another method of settling a dispute is by *arbitration,* where the employer and the union select a third party to make a decision for them. If arbitration is employed, the parties present evidence and arguments to the arbitrator and agree in advance to accept his decision as final and binding on each. If arbitration is not used and agreement cannot be reached, a strike may result. Then, when the public interest is involved, the dispute may be resolved, at least temporarily, by government intervention and force, such as the invoking of the Taft-Hartley Act by obtaining an injunction forbidding the strike for the statutory eighty-day cooling-off period.

Arbitration may be agreed to by the parties sometime after a dispute arises, or it may be required by the collective-bargaining contract itself. In *Textile Workers Union v. Lincoln Mills of Alabama*[18] the parties had included an arbitration clause in their agreement, but the employer had denied several grievances of union employees concerning workloads and assignments and had refused a union request for arbitration. In an action by the union to compel arbitration, the Supreme Court held in favor of the union, ruling that specific performance of an arbitration provision may be granted. However, in *Sinclair Refining Co. v. Atkinson*[19] the Supreme Court held that a union which went on strike in spite of its agreement to arbitrate all disputes (and *not* to strike) could not be compelled by injunction to abide by its agreement. The Court ruled that the Norris-LaGuardia (Anti-Injunction) Act prevented the Federal courts from taking jurisdiction over such cases. Thus, the extent to which an agreement to arbitrate will be specifically enforced is not clearly resolved.

[18] 353 U.S. 449 (1957).
[19] 82 S.Ct. 1328 (1962).

Often an agreement contains a so-called "management rights" clause. Such a clause typically states in broad language that the employer has the *exclusive* right to manage the business and direct its working forces, but still shall observe the provisions of the collective-bargaining agreement. Naturally, a great deal of the agreement's provisions severely inhibit the "exclusive" authority of the management to make business decisions, so the contradiction inherent in management-rights clauses is evident. It would seem that they are inserted in an attempt to persuade arbitrators to construe narrowly those more specific provisions in the agreement which restrict the employer's rights, in case a dispute arises over their meaning. The trend has been for the scope of bargaining to expand, and thus for collective-bargaining agreements to restrict more and more the areas of decision making which are exclusively within the purview of management.

The Taft-Hartley Act provides that suits for breach of a contract between an employer and a labor organization can be filed in the Federal district courts, without regard to the amount in question. A labor organization is responsible for the acts of its agents and may sue or be sued. Any money judgment against it is enforceable only against its assets and not against any individual member. Thus, while an employer may not enforce a "no-strike" clause in a collective-bargaining agreement by obtaining an injunction, he may recover money damages from the union if it breaches such a contract clause. In addition, employees may sue their union and recover the money damages they suffer because of an illegal strike.

The Taft-Hartley Act states that the duty to bargain collectively also means that no party to a collective-bargaining agreement which is in force shall *terminate* or *modify* it without following certain procedures. Failure to follow these requirements is, therefore, an unfair labor practice. A party desiring to modify or terminate a collective-bargaining contract must: (1) notify the other party of his desire to do so at least sixty days before the expiration date of the contract; (2) offer to meet in order to negotiate a new contract; (3) notify the Federal Mediation and Conciliation Service (and any similar agency of the state where the dispute occurred) within thirty days of giving the foregoing notice; and (4) continue to perform the terms of the existing contract fully, without a strike or lockout, until its expiration date (at least sixty days after notice of the dispute was given to the other party). Any employee who strikes within the required sixty-day notice period shall lose his status as an "employee" and the protection of the Act. Such persons may be discharged because of their union activity (the strike), without the employer's being guilty of an unfair labor practice.

11 THE LANDRUM-GRIFFIN ACT

In the 1950s corruption in labor unions was revealed in testimony before congressional investigating committees. This corruption included embezzlement from union treasuries, engaging in "juice" loans, and converting union resources to the personal interests of union officials. Violence at union meetings was commonplace, and the administrative procedures of some unions could hardly be called "democratic." It was also established that some union officials had extensive criminal records and others were members of the Communist party.

In 1959, the Labor-Management Reporting and Disclosure Act (Landrum-Griffin Act) was passed under the commerce clause. It contained the following statement in Section 2(b) as to the reasons for the statute:

The Congress . . . finds, from recent investigations in the labor and management fields, that there have been a number of instances of breach of trust, corruption, disregard of the rights of individual employees, and other failures to observe high standards of responsibility and ethical conduct which require further and supplementary legislation that will afford necessary protection of the rights and interests of employees and the public generally as they relate to the activities of labor organizations, employers, labor relations consultants, and their officers and representatives.

Title I of the Act has been called the "Bill of Rights" of union members. These provisions give union members the following rights:

1 To nominate candidates, to vote in elections, to attend membership meetings, and to have a voice in business transactions, subject to reasonable union rules and regulations.
2 To have free expression in union meetings, business discussions, and conventions subject to reasonable rules and regulations.
3 To vote on an increase of dues or fees.
4 To sue and testify against the union.
5 To receive written, specific charges; to be given a reasonable time for defense; and to be accorded a full and fair hearing before any disciplinary action is taken by the union against them.
6 To be given a copy of the collective-bargaining agreement that they work under, upon request.

An exception to provision 5 above is made in the case of disciplinary action for nonpayment of dues. The rights and remedies granted to union members by the statute are in addition to any other rights that the members may have under other laws or under union constitutions and bylaws. In the event that a member's rights are violated, the statute allows him to bring civil action for relief, including injunction, in the United States District Court where the violation occurred or where the principal office of the union is located. For example, it has been held that the expulsion of union members for advocating right-to-work laws was forbidden under their guarantee of free expression.

In the case which follows, a union member claimed he had been expelled in violation of the rights granted him by Landrum-Griffin. The court discusses the role of the judiciary in such cases.

International Brotherhood of Boilermakers v. Hardeman
91 S.Ct. 609 (1971)

The respondent, Hardeman, had been charged with violations of the constitution and by-laws of the union of which he was a member. He was tried by the union, found "guilty as charged" and expelled for an indefinite period. He later brought suit for damages in the District Court, which awarded him $152,150 after holding that he had been deprived of a "full and fair hearing" as guaranteed by the Landrum-Griffin Act. The Court of Appeals affirmed, and the union appealed to the Supreme Court.

BRENNAN, JUSTICE: . . . Two charges were brought against Hardeman in the union disciplinary proceedings. He was charged with violation of Article 13, § 1, of the Subordinate Lodge Constitution, which forbids attempting to create dissension or working against the interest and harmony of the union, and carries a penalty of expulsion. He was also charged with violation of Article 12, § 1, of the Subordinate Lodge By-Laws, which forbids the threat or use of force against any officer of the union in order to prevent him from properly discharging the duties of his office; violation may be punished "as warranted by the offense." Hardeman's conviction on both charges was upheld in internal union procedures for review.

The trial judge instructed the jury that "whether or not he [respondent] was rightfully or wrongfully discharged or expelled is a pure question of law for me to determine." He assumed, but did not decide, that the transcript of the union disciplinary hearing contained evidence adequate to support conviction of violating Article 12. He held, however, that there was no evidence at all in the transcript of the union disciplinary proceedings to support the charge of violating Article 13. . . . Since the union tribunals had returned only a general verdict, and since one of the charges was thought to be supported by no evidence whatsoever, the trial judge held that Hardeman had been deprived of the full and fair hearing guaranteed by [the Act].

We find nothing in either the language or the legislative history of [the Act] that could justify such a substitution of judicial for union authority to interpret the union's regulations in order to determine the scope of offenses warranting discipline of union members. . . .

After [an amendment to the original bill] passed the Senate, Senator Goldwater explained it to the House Committee on Labor and Education as follows:

[T]he bill of rights in the Senate bill require[s] that the union member be served with written charges prior to any disciplinary proceedings but it does not require that these charges, to be valid, must be based on activity that the union had proscribed prior to the union member having engaged in such activity.

And Senator McClellan's testimony was to the same effect.

We think that this is sufficient to indicate that [the Act] was not intended to authorize courts to determine the scope of offenses for which a union may discipline its members. And if a union may discipline its members for offenses not proscribed by written rules at all, it is surely a futile exercise for a court to construe the written rules in order to determine whether particular conduct falls within or without their scope.

Of course, [the Act] requires that a member subject to discipline be "served with written specific charges." These charges must be, in Senator McClellan's words, "specific enough to inform the accused member of the offense that he has allegedly committed." Where, as here, the union's charges make reference to specific written provisions, [the Act] obviously empowers the federal courts to examine those provisions and determine whether the union member had been misled or otherwise prejudiced in the presentation of his defense. But it gives courts no warrant to scrutinize the union regulations in order to determine whether particular conduct may be punished at all.

Respondent does not suggest, and we cannot discern, any possibility of prejudice in the present case. Although the notice of charges with which he was served does not appear as such in the record, the transcript of the union hearing indicates that the notice did not confine itself to a mere statement or citation of the written regulations that Hardeman was said to have violated: the notice appears to have contained a detailed statement of the facts relating to the fight which formed the basis for the disciplinary action.

There remains only the question whether the evidence in the union disciplinary proceeding was sufficient to support the finding of guilt. [The] LMRDA guarantees union members a "full and fair" disciplinary hearing, and the parties and the lower federal courts are in full agreement that this guarantee requires the charging party to provide some evidence at the disciplinary hearing to support the charges made. This is the proper standard of judicial review. We have repeatedly held that conviction on charges unsupported by any evidence is a denial of due process. . . .

Applying this standard to the present case, we think there is no question that the charges were adequately supported. Respondent was charged with having attacked Wise without warning, and with continuing to beat him for some time. Wise so testified at the disciplinary hearing, and his testimony was fully corroborated by one other witness to the altercation. Even Hardeman, although he claimed he was thereafter held and beaten, admitted having struck the first blow. On such a record there is no question but that the charges were supported by "some evidence." [REVERSED]

The Landrum-Griffin Act also contains several provisions relating to the Secretary of Labor and reports which he may require of unions. The purpose of these reports is to reveal practices detrimental to union members. For example, each union must adopt a constitution and by-laws and file them with the Secretary of Labor together with the following information:

1 The name and address of the union office and the place where records are kept.

2 The names and titles of officers.
3 The amount of initiation fees required.
4 The amount of dues charged.
5 A detailed statement of procedures for (*a*) qualification for office, (*b*) levying fees, (*c*) insurance plans, (*d*) disbursement of funds, (*e*) audits, (*f*) selection of officers, (*g*) removal of officers, (*h*) determining bargaining demands, (*i*) fines, (*j*) approval of contracts, (*k*) calling strikes, and (*l*) issuance of work permits.

In addition, yearly financial reports must be filed which indicate:

1 Assets and liabilities.
2 Receipts and sources of funds.
3 Salaries of officers.
4 Loans to members greater than $250.
5 Loans to business enterprises.
6 Other disbursements.

Note that the above reports do not concern the operation of union welfare and pension plan funds, which involve a great deal more money than the union treasuries. The Welfare and Pension Plans Disclosure Act of 1958 (as amended in 1962), also known as the Teller Act, governs such funds. This Act requires filing with the Secretary of Labor a description of every employee pension and welfare plan covered by it as well as annual reports detailing the operations of the funds. The Act also gives the Secretary broad investigative and enforcing powers.

The Landrum-Griffin Act also requires reports on trusteeships. A trusteeship is a method of supervision or control whereby a labor union suspends the autonomy otherwise available to a subordinate body under its constitution and by-laws. In this report the union must state the names and addresses of subordinate organizations, the date of establishing trusteeship, and the reasons for establishing the trusteeship.

In addition to the foregoing reports, union employees and officials must file a yearly report with the Secretary of Labor containing information on possible areas of conflict of interest such as holdings of stock in companies with which the union has dealings, and payments personally received from employers. Employers must file yearly reports with the Secretary containing information concerning payments made to unions or union officials. An employer must also report on payments made to consultants whom he engages to deal with unions. Reports made to the Secretary of Labor become public information. Records supporting the reports must be kept for five years, and the Secretary of Labor is given broad powers to investigate the reports filed with him. He is empowered to delegate this power to a commission, such as the Bureau of Labor-Management Reports, if he desires.

The Landrum-Griffin Act provides for an elaborate system of regulation of internal union activities. It will be seen that most of these regulations cover activities that are supposed to be revealed in the reports. They cover union election procedures, management of union funds, trusteeships, and union personnel. The Secretary is given power to investigate alleged violations of any of the regulations and may institute criminal proceedings through the Attorney General.

The Act requires that elections be held at minimum regular intervals to promote democracy. National unions must hold elections at least every five years, locals every three years, and intermediate bodies every four years. Elections must be by secret ballot of members, or of delegates who were chosen by secret ballot of members. Every candidate for union office must have access to membership lists. The union must provide adequate safeguards to ensure a fair election and every candidate is given the right to post observers at the polls and counting place. This provision is enforceable by civil action instituted by candidates. All candidates must have equal opportunity to run for office without penalty or punishment by the organization or any member thereof, subject to reasonable rules. Union funds may not be used by any candidate in his campaign. The Secretary of Labor may provide for an election to remove a candidate from office if the union constitution does not provide adequate procedures for removal of officers guilty of misconduct. A court may declare an election void if the preponderance of evidence shows a violation that may have affected it. The Act also recognizes the fiduciary responsibility of officers of unions. All exculpatory clauses in union constitutions are void as against public policy. A member of a union may sue for funds mishandled by union officers after he has exhausted union proceedings and he will be repaid the cost of bringing suit.

The Act makes embezzlement of union funds a Federal crime. The penalty is imprisonment for up to five years or a fine up to $10,000 or both. Every union employee who handles funds must be bonded. No union may lend more than $2,000 to a union employee or official. Any person who wilfully violates either of these two provisions is subject to imprisonment for one year or a fine of up to $10,000, or both. Unions are not permitted to pay the fines imposed on their officers or employees who are convicted of violating the Act. However, the propriety of payments to cover legal fees in lawsuits is judged on an individual basis.

Landrum-Griffin also makes it a Federal offense to engage in extortionate picketing. This is picketing for the purpose of forcing an employer to pay money to a union official or other individual for his own personal use rather than for the benefit of the union membership generally.

Finally, as has been previously noted, the Landrum-Griffin Act contains a number of amendments to the Taft-Hartley Act, although its provisions in the main deal with union reform.

12 CONTEMPORARY PROBLEMS

Disputes between management and labor of varying degrees of significance exist today and will continue to do so. Employers are generally portrayed as being conservative and unions liberal when it comes to questions of social change. However, when production is involved, business is the radical, seeking cost-saving methods, and unions exert conservative pressures for job certainty and security. The solutions proposed by each to existing economic and social problems are bound to reflect these divergent positions, with management continuing to press for its rights to manage, innovate, and meet competition, and employees and unions seeking to restrict such moves when they threaten security and thus seeking an ever-widening voice in business decision making. Some experts feel that eventually these two sides will arrive at a compromise by which the needs and rights of each will be recognized and preserved.

One economic problem that probably will always be present to some degree is unemployment. Labor and management offer different reasons for its existence as well as different solutions. Some businessmen may contend that the answer lies in larger profits for business, because increased profits mean more capital for investment and thus more jobs. Increased profits could result from changed fiscal policy as well as other factors.

Labor has offered a solution of shortening the work week from the present 40 hours to 35 hours (eventually to 32 hours), while keeping the weekly wage at its present level, thus increasing the hourly wage. This would be accompanied by a raise in pay for overtime from time and a half to double time. Labor argues that this action would encourage management to hire additional employees to keep production at its present level, instead of working present employees overtime and paying the wage premium.

Other solutions to the economic problems of the country offered by labor are reduction of individual income taxes (in the lower- and middle-income brackets); increases in spending by government on public works to create jobs; and the extension of certain extra benefits to the laboring man, such as unemployment compensation. In addition, the AFL-CIO is seeking less government control of labor's activity in labor-management relations, stating that unless the government actually has taken control of an industry it should have no power to prevent strikes. At the same time, unions are pressing for continued governmental protection of labor's bargaining position. Some unions are steadfastly opposed to any moves by business toward automation and the replacing of men with machines to cut production costs.

Many collective-bargaining disputes are centered on the effects of automation on the labor force, labor arguing that the use of such methods will put many more out of jobs and reduce the domestic market for goods. Business counters that technological development in the past has not only resulted in more skilled jobs, but also was one of the most significant factors in making this country and its citizens relatively more wealthy than all others in the world, because of our consequent ability to produce more goods more cheaply.

Business may suggest that unions be made subject to the antitrust laws, while unions request new laws to aid union growth.

Government policy seems to have been to attempt to balance the bargaining power of business and labor so they can settle their disputes themselves by mutual agreement. However, one of the most serious questions involved in labor-management relations today is whether the power to make economic decisions which so greatly affect the public interest can or should be left in the hands of these private parties. It is clear that with today's competitive threats from foreign industry, it is in the interests of employers and unions as well as the public as a whole that our economy remain viable. However, it is doubtful that we can compete effectively and still have the slowdowns, strikes, make-work rules, and restrictions on the use of labor-saving machinery which have been so common in the past. In order to effectively compete with foreign economies with their low wages and high degree of mechanization, we must increase production per man-hour by utilizing technology.

Because of the magnitude of the decisions made at the bargaining table, it is clear that government cannot be satisfied simply to try to equalize the bargaining position of powerful unions and large corporate employers and sit back neutrally while they make all the decisions. In fact the status of equality may make long work stoppages more likely, to the public detriment, where giant unions and corporations are in conflict. Each may have the endurance to withstand a long siege. Throughout our history as a country, the people have been wary of bigness and large concentrations of power, first in government, then in business, and finally in the unions which grew to great strength, particularly after the enactment of the Wagner Act. It is likely that the future will bring more government action curbing union power because of public reaction to the wielding of that power, unless restraint is exercised by unions. Many have called for government-imposed compulsory arbitration to take the place of crippling strikes.

Perhaps no strikes have affected the economy and the public as a whole more adversely than those in the transportation industry. Recent years have seen several instances of railroad employees, dock workers, and others engaged in transportation striking over new contract terms when a collective-bargaining agreement has expired. In the period from 1964 to 1971, Congress was required to take special action five times to end railroad walkouts. In 1970, President Nixon proposed the Emergency Public Interest Protection Act, the first *permanent* legislation requiring compulsory settlements of disputes over the provisions to be included in a new collective-bargaining contract when the parties have been unable to reach agreement by themselves. This statute would include all transportation industries: railroads, trucking, airlines, maritime, and longshore. First, it would put all transportation bargaining under Taft-Hartley rather than the Railway Labor Act. Second, it would give the government three *additional* courses of action to those provided by Taft-Hartley which would be available when transportation emergencies exist. Under these, the President would have the power to: (1) impose thirty more days to the eighty-day cooling-off period provided by Taft-Hartley; (2) partially seize a struck industry, requiring that portion to operate: or (3) order the dispute ended by a choice between "final offers" submitted by each party. The third option has caused the most controversy. It would require the parties to a dispute to submit final offers for settlement to the Secretary of Labor. Then management and labor would negotiate for five days on these offers. If the dispute still remained unsettled, the President would appoint a neutral three-man board, which would select one of the initial final offers as submitted without change. Other, similar plans have been offered. One would simply add the power to require compulsory arbitration to the President's options mentioned. The proposed Emergency Public Interest Protection Act has met strong opposition from both labor and industry. Labor especially would prefer to see each emergency dealt with on a case-by-case, ad hoc basis, rather than by permanent legislation which would make even further inroads on its power than Taft-Hartley and Landrum-Griffin already have. However, many persons feel that the monopoly power of unions in the essential transportation industries is so great that compulsory arbitration must come about in order to protect the public interest. As of this writing, none of the proposed legislation has been enacted.

Recently, labor leaders have begun to recognize that the negative results of a strike may outweigh the gains it may achieve. In 1972, George Meany, president of the AFL-CIO, saying that the strike was no longer an effective tool, appointed a committee to study other means to resolve labor disputes. He recognized the fact that there was growing worker resistance to strikes because strike benefit payments have not been high enough for them. And no doubt he was sensitive to the fact that strikes bring public resentment which adds to pressures on Congress to pass more legislation cutting back on union power, such as the proposed Emergency Public Interest Protection Act. In other statements, Mr. Meany suggested that binding *voluntary* arbitration may be the answer as the substitute for strikes in arriving at the terms of a collective-bargaining agreement when the parties reach an impasse at the negotiating table. However, compulsory arbitration imposed by government rule remains unacceptable to labor.

If a real change in the attitude of organized labor toward the use of the strike does occur, the near future should bring dramatic changes in labor-management relations. It may be that fear of additional antistrike legislation has created a more conciliatory attitude on the part of some segments of labor. In any case, it would seem that further government intervention, probably in the form of requiring some type of compulsory arbitration of labor disputes, is inevitable if crippling strikes in essential industries continue to jeopardize the interests of the public as a whole.

REVIEW QUESTIONS—CHAPTER 15

1 Define the following terms introduced in this chapter: yellow-dog contract; blacklist; unfair labor practice; union authorization card; eighty-day cooling-off period; union shop; closed shop; right-to-work law; hot-cargo contract; secondary boycott; jurisdictional strike; informational picketing; mandatory bargaining issue; voluntary-bargaining issue; collective-bargaining agreement; management-rights clause.
2 Comment on the tripartite nature of labor-management relations.
3 Discuss the effect of the Clayton Act on labor-management relations.
4 Outline the major provisions of the Railway Labor Act. Include the procedures followed under it when a labor dispute exists.

5 Briefly discuss the purpose and state the major provisions of the Norris-LaGuardia Act. Does it prohibit all injunctions in labor disputes? Explain.

6 Briefly state the reasons for passage of the Wagner Act, and list its major provisions.

7 List the five practices by employers which were declared unfair by the Wagner Act.

8 Briefly state the reasons for passage of the Taft-Hartley Act, and list its major provisions.

9 List the six practices by unions which were declared unfair by the Taft-Hartley Act.

10 Trace the procedures for obtaining an eighty-day cooling-off period in labor disputes.

11 Why was the position of General Counsel of the NLRB created, and what are his responsibilities?

12 Briefly trace the procedures followed by the NLRB in resolving charges of unfair labor practices filed with it.

13 Give examples of the methods used by the NLRB to remedy the commission of unfair labor practices.

14 Briefly state some of the major criticisms which have been leveled at the NLRB.

15 Explain how the conferring of benefits on employees by an employer can amount to an unfair labor practice.

16 Is ''featherbedding'' illegal? Explain.

17 Give four examples each of mandatory- and voluntary-bargaining issues.

18 How may the employer and the union who are parties to a collective-bargaining contract enforce a clause in it requiring arbitration of disputes over its application and meaning?

19 Briefly state the reasons for passage of the Landrum-Griffin Act, and indicate generally the nature of its major provisions.

20 To what extent can a court review or overturn disciplinary action taken by a union against one of its members in determining if Landrum-Griffin requirements have been met?

21 Briefly state the reasons for the administration's proposal of the Emergency Public Interest Protection Act, and outline the provisions which were recommended for inclusion in it.

22 Discuss current developments in the attitude of labor leaders toward the resolution of labor disputes.

Chapter Sixteen

Business Organizations

1 INTRODUCTION

Business organizations operate under a variety of legal forms including sole proprietorships, partnerships, limited partnerships, and corporations. There are also specialized organizations such as professional service corporations, joint-stock companies, business trusts, and joint ventures.

This chapter will examine the factors that influence the actual selection of a particular form of organization for a particular business. The relative importance of the factors involved varies greatly, depending on the size of the business. As a practical matter, the very large business is incorporated, because this is the only form of organization that can bring a large number of owners and investors together for an extended period of time. The difficulty of deciding which is the best form of organization to select is most often encountered in the closely held business. The decision involves a consideration of several factors, the most significant of which are (1) taxation, (2) liability, (3) control, (4) continuity, and (5) legal capacity. "Legal capacity" refers to the capability of the business to sue and be sued in its own name and to its power to own and dispose of property as well as to enter into contracts in its own name.

Persons desiring to form a new business weigh the factors and the costs involved and then select the form of organization most suitable to their needs. Any form has disadvantages, and the decision often is to choose the one which is least objectionable. Taxation is usually the dominant factor. Not only new businesses must weigh these problems but also ongoing businesses when there is a substantial change in circumstance, such as a change in tax rates, earnings, or scope of business activity. As a result, the matters discussed in this chapter must be constantly considered and reviewed by closely held businesses.

Before an examination of these factors, some preliminary observations relative to the different forms of business organization should be helpful.

2 MANNER OF CREATION

A corporation is created by the state's issuing a charter upon the application of individuals known as "incorporators." A "partnership," which is an association of two or more persons to carry on as co-owners a business for profit, is created by an agreement of the parties who are to be the owners and managers. This agreement, usually known as "Articles of Copartnership," creates the partnership as between the partners. A partnership may also arise by implication from the conduct of the parties. The sharing of the net profits of a business enterprise by two persons gives rise to a presumption that a partnership exists between them, except where the share of profits is received by one of them for some special reason such as wages of an employee or rent to a landlord, or as interest on a loan. A partnership may be held to exist as between the partners and third persons where a person, by his conduct, leads third persons to believe he is a partner and the third person acts in reliance on this conduct (partnership by estoppel).

A partnership is easily formed, since all that is required is an agreement between the partners. The cost of formation is minimal, and the business need not qualify to do business in foreign states. Just as the partnership is easily formed, it is also easily dissolved. Dissolution occurs whenever a partner ceases to be a partner either by death or withdrawal. The perpetual existence of corporations is frequently a distinct advantage over the transitory existence of most partnerships.

Corporations are more costly to form, and there are annual costs in continuing the corporation, such as franchise taxes, the cost of annual meetings of shareholders, and continuing legal expenses. It should be noted that an attorney must be retained by a corporation involved in litigation, whereas individuals and partners may, if they so choose, appear in litigation personally. Among the costs of incorporation are filing fees, license fees, franchise taxes, attorneys' fees, and the cost of supplies such as minute books, corporate seals, and stock certificates. A corporation which desires to conduct intrastate business in any state must qualify to do business in that state. This point is illustrated in the *Eli Lilly* case on page 558.

One problem which is frequently a major concern in the creation of a business entity is the name to be used. Since a partnership is created by an agreement, the parties select the name. This right of selection is subject to two limitations in many states. First, a partnership may not use any word in the name, such as company, that would imply the existence of a corporation. Second, if the name is other than that of the partners, they must give notice as to the actual identity of the partners. Failure to comply with a state's assumed-name statutes may result in the partnership's being denied access to courts, or it may result in criminal actions being brought against those operating under the assumed name.

The application for a corporate charter contains the proposed name of the corporation. In order that persons dealing with a business will know that it is a corporation, the law requires that the corporate name include one of the following words or end with an abbreviation of them: "corporation," "company," "incorporated," or "limited." In addition, a corporate name must not be the same as, or deceptively similar to, the name of any domestic corporation or that of a foreign corporation authorized to do business in the state to which the application is made. Courts of equity may enjoin the use of deceptively similar names, and charters will be refused if the state believes that the names are deceptively similar.

The corporate name is an asset and a part of goodwill. As such, it is legally protected.

3 SPECIAL FORMS OF ORGANIZATION

The law has developed hybrid types of partnerships and corporations. These are designed to accomplish special purposes. For example, the limited partnership is a hybrid insofar as liability of its investors is concerned. It is made up of general partners with unlimited liability and limited partners with limited liability. Thus it has the characteristics of both a partnership and a corporation.

The "Subchapter S corporation" is the hybrid for tax purposes. It is a corporation which is treated in the same manner as a partnership by the Federal tax laws.

Historically, professional services, such as those of a doctor, lawyer, or dentist, could only be performed by an individual and could not be performed by a corporation. The relationship of doctor and patient or attorney and client was considered highly personal. Today, most states allow professional persons to incorporate in order that they may have some of the benefits of incorporation. The sections which follow will discuss the major forms of organization and the advantages and disadvantages of each in more detail.

4 TAXATION

There are several aspects to the taxation factor of the decision to select one form of organization over another. First of all, a partnership is not subject to the Federal income tax, but a corporation does pay an income tax on its earnings. In addition, shareholders pay an income tax on dividends received so that it is usually stated that corporate earnings are subject to double taxation. The corporate tax rate varies from time to time and currently includes a surtax on earnings above $25,000. In recent years the normal tax rate on income up to $25,000 has varied from 22 to 30 percent, and the tax rate, including the surtax, on amounts over $25,000 has varied from 48 to 52 percent. Thus, corporate income of over $25,000 per year has been subject to roughly a 50 percent tax. The profits paid out as dividends have been taxable income to the individual shareholders at their individual rates, which vary from one person to another depending on the other income they receive.

The fact that a partnership pays no income tax of course does not mean that the profits of the partnership are free of income tax. A partnership files an information return which allocates to each individual partner his proportionate share of profits or losses from operation, dividend income, capital gains or losses, and other items which would affect the income tax owed by a partner. Each partner then reports his share of such items on his individual income tax return, irrespective of whether or not the items have been actually received by him. One of the disadvantages of this scheme of taxation is that partners may be required to pay individual income taxes on profits retained in the business for growth.

Before going further into the tax advantages of the different forms of organization, it is necessary to recognize that there are certain techniques for avoiding in part the double taxation of corporate income. First of all, reasonable salaries paid to corporate officials may be deducted in computing the taxable income of the business. Thus in a closely held corporation in which all or most shareholders are officers or employees, this technique may avoid double taxation of substantial portions of income. As might be suspected, the Internal Revenue Code disallows a deduction for excessive or unreasonable compensation and treats such payments as dividends. Therefore the determination of the reasonableness of corporate salaries is an ever-present tax problem in that form of organization.

Second, the capital structure of the corporation may include both common stock and interest-bearing loans from shareholders. For example, assume that a company needs $100,000 of cash to commence business. If $100,000 of stock is issued, there will be no expense to be deducted. However, assume that $50,000 worth of stock is purchased by the owners, and $50,000 is loaned to the company by them at 8 percent interest. In this case $4,000 of interest each year is deductible as an expense of the company and thus subject to only one tax as interest income to the owners. Just as in the case of salaries, the Internal Revenue Code has a counteracting rule relating to corporations that are undercapitalized. If the corporation is undercapitalized, interest payments will be treated as dividends, and disallowed as deductible expenses.

The third technique for avoiding double taxation at least in part, is simply not to pay dividends and to accumulate the earnings. After the earnings have been accumulated, the shareholders can sell their stock or have the company dissolved. In either case the difference between the original investment and the amount received is given capital gains treatment. Here again, there are tax laws designed to counteract the above technique. There is a special provision for an income tax imposed on "excessive accumulated earnings" in addition to the normal tax. Each year, on the first $100,000 of excessive accumulated earnings, the additional tax is 27½ percent and on all amounts over $100,000 it is 38½ percent.

Finally, there is the aforementioned special provision in the Internal Revenue Code which allows small closely held business corporations to be treated as partnerships for income tax purposes and thereby to avoid having a tax assessed on the corporate income itself. These Subchapter S corporations cannot have over ten shareholders each of whom must elect to be taxed as a partnership, i.e., to have the corporate income allocated to the shareholders annually in computing their income for tax purposes, whether actually paid out or not. Corporations with more than 20 percent of their income from rents, interest, dividends, or royalties do not qualify. There are many technical rules of tax law involved in Subchapter S corporations, but as a rule of thumb, this method of taxation has distinct advantages for a business operating at a loss because the loss is shared and immediately deductible on the returns of the shareholders. It is also advantageous for businesses capable of paying out net profits as earned. In the latter case, the corporate tax is avioded. If net profits must be retained in the business, Subchapter S tax treatment is disadvantageous because income tax is paid on earnings not received, and there is a danger of double taxation to the individual because undistributed earnings which have been taxed once are taxed again in the event of the death of a shareholder. Thus it is evident that the theoretical advantage of using the Subchapter S corporation to avoid double taxation of corporate income must be heavily qualified.

The corporate form of organization has two important tax advantages which have greatly encouraged incorporation by small businesses. First of all, they may establish qualified pension and profit-sharing plans for their employees including the shareholder employees. Under a qualified plan, the company is entitled to deduct as expenses all payments made to the plan, but the amounts allocated to each employee are not taxable income to the employee at that time. All earnings of the plan are income tax–free until paid out; on retirement the benefits due an employee are received at a time when he has the advantage of increased exemptions and deductions as well as a lower tax rate. Moreover, there are Federal estate tax and income tax savings in the event of the death of the employee. Corporations can also adopt deferred compensation plans for their employees and are allowed to deduct the cost of health and accident insurance on employees. All of these special tax advantages are closely regulated to avoid discrimination between owner-employees and other employees.

In evaluating the impact of taxation on a business, an accountant or attorney will look at the projected earnings of the business, the policies to be followed in the distribution of those earnings, and the tax brackets of the individuals involved as owners. Then he will compute the estimated total tax burden under the various forms of organization. This will be considered along with the other factors in making the decision on which form of business organization to use.

5 LIABILITY

Traditionally, it has been said that the investors in a corporation have limited liability but those in a partnership have unlimited liability. As in the case of the usual statements made concerning taxation, this generalization is too broad and needs qualification. To be sure, if one invests in a company listed on the New York Stock Exchange, he will incur no risk greater than his investment and the concept of limited liability certainly applies. However, if the company is a small closely held corporation with limited assets and capital, it will be difficult for the corporation to obtain credit on the strength of its own credit standing alone, and as a practical matter, the shareholders will usually be required to add their own individual liability as security for the debts. For example, if the XYZ Company seeks a loan at a local bank, the bank often will require the owners X, Y, and Z to personally guarantee repayment of the loan. This is not to say that closely held corporations do not have some degree of limited liability. The investors in those types of businesses are protected with limited liability for contract-like obligations (such as taxes) which are imposed as a matter of law and for debts resulting from torts which are committed by company employees while they are about company business.

The limited partnership as a hybrid for liability has been previously mentioned. The Uniform Limited Partnership Act, which has been adopted by most states, requires that such a partnership have one or more general partners and one or more limited partners. The limited partners are not bound by the obligation of the partnership. They have liability limited to their contribution. A limited partner is, in effect loaning money to the business activity for a percentage of the profits rather than a fixed return such as interest. Since creditors ordinarily do not participate in management, neither do limited partners. Participation in management carries with it the liability of a general partner.

Just as the liability aspect of a limited partnership is a cross between a partnership and corporation, so also is the method of creating this type of business organization. A limited partnership, like a general partnership, is created by agreement. But, as in the case of a corporation, the statute prescribes the contents of a certificate similar to a corporate charter which must be recorded in order that the public be fully advised as to the details of the organization.

There are several restrictions on the rights and activities of a limited partner. His contribution to the firm may be cash or property but not services. His surname may not be used, unless there is a general partner with the same name, or he will incur unlimited liability to unsuspecting general creditors. Finally, as previously noted, he may not participate in management without incurring unlimited liability. The following case concerns some of the usual types of questions raised in litigation involving limited partnerships.

Filesi v. United States
352 F.2d 339 (1965)

BOREMAN, JUDGE: The Commissioner of Internal Revenue, asserting that the Jolly Tavern had been operated as a cabaret because dancing had been permitted to the music of a juke box, assessed deficiencies in cabaret excise taxes, penalties and interest in the amount of $46,567.28 against the taxpayer, Alfred Filesi, based on the receipts from the operation of the tavern. . . . Filesi paid $1,000 . . . and brought this action in the District Court to recover that sum. The Government filed a counter claim for the unpaid balance of $45,567.28. . . .

Filesi . . . contended that he was not liable for excise tax for the period from the first quarter of 1954 through the first quarter of 1956 as he was a "limited partner" during this period and did not become a general partner until a written partnership agreement was executed on April 4, 1956. . . .

At the close of all the evidence, the District Court ruled as a matter of law that Filesi was a general partner for the period in dispute. . . . The jury found that there was dancing at the tavern and that the total tax liability for the entire period from 1954 through the third quarter 1958 should have been $28,854.95 rather than the $46,567.28 assessed by the Commissioner. Judgment was accordingly entered.

The principal errors assigned on appeal relate to rulings of the court: first, that the court erred in ruling as a matter of law and instructing the jury that Filesi was a general partner for the period from the first quarter of 1954 through the first quarter of 1956. . . .

In his testimony Filesi admitted he and Muller were partners but contended he was a "limited partner" and not liable for the tax for the periods before the second quarter of 1956. The facts upon which this contention is based are these. From 1949 when Filesi first became associated with the management of the Jolly Tavern until April 14, 1951, Filesi along with Muller and John Marshall were the only shareholders of a corporation organized to operate the tavern. Marshall wanted out of the business and on April 14, 1951, the corporation was dissolved and Muller assumed to purchase Marshall's interest but to do so Muller borrowed money from an outside source and the loan was subsequently repaid from the profits of the Jolly Tavern before Filesi and Muller received their shares as partners. The effect of this transaction was that Filesi became the purchaser of one half of Marshall's interest. According to Filesi, Muller did not have funds to buy Filesi's interest also so Muller persuaded him to leave his investment in the tavern. In return, Filesi testified, it was orally agreed that he was to manage the business at a stipulated salary and receive fifty percent of all profits but was not to be liable for any losses. The liquor license was transferred to Muller's name and the business was operated under this arrangement until April 4, 1956. On that date Muller and Filesi executed a written partnership agreement under which both were to share gains and losses equally. From April 4, 1956, to April 5, 1957, the tavern was operated under this written agreement. On the latter date the partnership was dissolved and Muller sold his interest to Filesi who has since owned and operated the tavern.

Filesi argues that he was a limited partner from April 14, 1951, to April 4, 1956, and as such he was not liable for any losses of the partnership during this period; that, as the excise tax from the first quarter of 1954 through the first quarter of 1956 would constitute a loss he should not be held accountable for the tax. We cannot agree. It is well settled that to obtain the protections and privileges of limited liability a person must comply with the statutory requirements regulating the formation of limited partnerships or otherwise be held liable as a general partner. . . . [T]he Annotated Code of Maryland specified the acts which must be performed by a person desiring to become a limited partner in the operation of a business within that State. It was clearly shown that Filesi did not comply with these provisions and therefore, he cannot now claim the protection of a limitation of liability. It is clear from the evidence generally and from Filesi's own testimony that he openly and publicly took an active part in the management and control of the business. We think the District Court was correct in holding as a matter of law that Filesi was liable as a general partner for any excise tax properly assessed for the period in dispute.

Even assuming that Filesi was a limited partner his argument is unsound. According to applicable law a limited partner is liable for any losses of the partnership to the extent of his investment in the assets of the business. On this point, however, no evidence was produced to show what Filesi's investment was for the period, although in 1951 it was slightly in excess of $10,000. . . . [DECISION REVERSED FOR OTHER REASONS.]

Issues of liability are not restricted to that of the investors in the business or to financial liability alone. Corporation law has developed several instances in which the directors and officers of the corporation will have liability to shareholders or to the corporation for acts or omissions by such directors or officers in their official capacity. Directors are liable to the corporation for losses as a result of fraud or gross negligence in the performance of their duties. However, directors are not liable for losses caused by poor judgment if they acted honestly and within their powers. Statutes frequently impose liability in certain cases on directors. For example, directors who declare a dividend when there is no earned surplus have personal liability for the dividend to the corporation.

The case below is another example of the kind of liability which may be imposed on a director.

Precision Extrusions, Inc. v. Stewart
183 N.E.2d 547 (Ill. 1962)

Suit was brought against certain directors of a corporation for allegedly voting to purchase some of the corporation's shares while its assets were less than the sum of its stated capital and surplus accounts, and for voting to purchase the shares while the corporation was insolvent, contrary to the provisions of the Business Corporation Act. The defendants contended that the complaint failed to state a cause of action. The trial court held for plaintiff.

MCCORMICK, JUDGE: There are numerous cases in Illinois and elsewhere discussing the responsibility and liability of the directors of a business corporation. It is generally held that a director of a corporation, though not responsible for errors of judgment, is a fiduciary charged with the duty of caring for the property of the corporation and of managing its affairs honestly and in good faith. If this duty has been so violated as to result in an impairment of its assets or loss of its property he can, without the aid of statute, be compelled to make restitution. Directors are liable for misappropriation of funds where they act ultra vires in authorizing the corporation to purchase its own stock. . . . In *Lyons v. Corder,* 253 Mo. 539, it was held that where a loss results to the corporation because of the disregard of the duties of the directors as prescribed by statute the directors are liable. Ordinarily an action can be brought by the corporation against the directors, or in case of the insolvency of the corporation, by its receiver or assignee. . . .

In *Aiken v. Peabody,* 168 F.2d 615 (7th Cir.), the court held the directors of the corporation would be liable under Illinois law when they authorized a declaration of dividends the payment of which would reduce the "capital stock" of the corporation, providing that they acted in bad faith or were guilty of gross negligence or inattention, and the court further held that, while the case was based upon a statutory violation, the principle was one which had existed at common law. In the present case had the directors authorized the repurchase by the corporation of its own stock under the same circumstance, they could have been held liable at common law. Section 6 of the statute formulates rules with regard to an authorization of the repurchase of its own stock by a corporation, which places a definite duty on the directors. When the directors violate that duty it is not necessary that the statute specifically provide that they can be held responsible. At common law an action against them by the corporation or creditors would lie, since the result of such repurchase would be to illegally withdraw and pay to a stockholder a part of the assets of the corporation. When liability is imposed upon a director of a corporation by statute, his common law liability for misfeasance and negligence in the performance of his duty is not thereby excluded. . . .

The plaintiff further alleges in its complaint that the act of the directors was a violation of section 42 of the Act. Under that section it seems clear that a repurchase by a corporation of shares of its stock at a time when the corporation is insolvent or its net assets are less than its stated capital is a distribution of its assets in part. In *Pace v. Pace Bros. Co.*, 91 Utah 132, 59 P.2d 1 (1936), the court construes a statute which made it a misdemeanor for any director "to divide, withdraw or in any manner, except as provided by law, pay to the stockholders, or any of them, any part of the capital of the corporation." It was held that the statute was violated when the directors authorized the corporation to repurchase its own stock. The court says: "We see no reason why the prohibition against 'paying' to a stockholder a part of the capital does not include buying his stock. . . . Moreover, the phrase 'or any of them' is convincing that it does not contemplate purely a division pro rata, but the prohibition goes to paying any of the capital to any stockholder or stockholders, whether one or more." The court discusses at considerable length similar statutes in other states where the courts have reached the same conclusion. . . . In our opinion the complaint, defective in form as it is, does sufficiently state causes of action. . . .

The orders of the trial court . . . overruling defendant's motion to dismiss plaintiff's . . . complaint, . . . are affirmed. [CASE REMANDED FOR FURTHER PROCEEDINGS]

The Federal Securities Act of 1933 and the Securities Exchange Act of 1934 impose personal liability on directors and others for giving false information in a prospectus and for other acts. Likewise, the antitrust laws impose penalties on individuals who participate in violating them. Thus, directors and officers must be careful to comply with all the laws which govern the corporation or they may incur personal financial or even criminal liability.

Corporations may have criminal liability in addition to civil liability in tort or for breach of contract. However, the fiction of the corporate entity creates some difficult problems insofar as the criminal law is concerned. A corporation cannot be imprisoned, although in theory a death penalty of sorts could be imposed simply by the domiciliary state's dissolving it. Corporations act only through agents, and while it is possible to imprison the agents in many instances, this would not be satisfactory punishment for the corporate entity. It is, of course, possible to punish a corporation by imposing a fine. As was earlier discussed, such action is one of the enforcement sanctions of the antitrust laws.

Proving the commission of a crime by a corporation is often as difficult as imposing a meaningful penalty. "Crime" is usually defined in terms of intentional commission of some prohibited act, often with the *specific* intent to do so. How can an artificial being with no mind have criminal intent? The law has generally resolved this problem by imputing to the corporation the guilty intent of an agent, if the agent was authorized and acting within the scope of his employment at the time he committed the crime. Many cases have equated "acquiescence" by the company in the wrongful conduct with authority to commit the illegal act.

Modern criminal statutes recognize that a corporation may indeed commit a crime and provide fines in lieu of incarceration for crimes that usually are punished by incarceration. These criminal codes specify those classes of crimes for which the legislature intended corporate liability to exist and call for it only where an agent is acting within the scope of his employment or where the activity is authorized, requested, or performed by the board of directors. It is often a defense to a criminal charge against a corporation that a high managerial agent having supervisory responsibility over the conduct which is the subject matter of the offense exercised due diligence to prevent the commission of the crime.

6   CONTROL

In every business organization, some individual or some group of people will have the power to make decisions or will possess "control" of the business. In a partnership, unless the agreement provides to the contrary, each partner has an equal voice in the firm affairs and has an equal right to possess partnership property for business purposes. Partners are liable for all transactions entered into by any partner in the scope of the partnership business and are similarly liable for any partner's torts committed while he is acting in the course of the firm business. Each partner is in effect both an agent of the partnership and a principal, being capable of creating both contract and tort liability of the firm and his co-partners and being likewise responsible for their acts. There are many technical rules concerning what acts of a partner are within the scope or course of the partnership business. While knowing these is not essential to a general understanding of the concept of control of a partnership, one special rule is worthy of mention. A partner in a trading partnership, i.e., one engaged in the business of buying and selling commodities, has the implied authority to borrow money in the usual course of business and to pledge the credit of the firm; but a partner in a nontrading partnership, such as an accounting firm, has no implied power to borrow money. In the latter case, such authority must be actual before the firm will be bound.

In the corporate form of organization, legal problems created by persons in "control" and by those seeking "control" are quite numerous. In the very large corporations, control by management is maintained with a very small percentage of ownership of the stock through the utilization of corporate records and funds to solicit proxies. Management can at corporate expense solicit the right to vote the stock of shareholders who are unable to attend the meetings at which the directors of the company are elected. An outsider must either own sufficient stock to elect the directors or he must solicit proxies at his own expense. Although there are a few proxy fights, the management of the large United States corporation is usually able to maintain control with only a small minority of the actual stock ownership.

In closely held corporations or in corporations with only several hundred shareholders or fewer, a number of techniques are used to gain control without having a majority of the total investment. One technique is to issue classes of stock. In some states there can be nonvoting stock; the group seeking to keep control will buy voting stock while selling nonvoting stock to others. Preferred stock may be used to increase capital without losing control. For example, a group may invest $100,000 in common stock of $1 par value each. Then they will sell another $100,000 of the same common stock with the requirement that for each share of common stock purchased, a $5 share of nonvoting preferred stock must be purchased. Thus, the corporation would raise $700,000 and the $100,000 original investment made by the organizing individuals would have 50 percent of the voting power. There are other schemes which can be used such as selling some stock to the organizers for 10 cents per share and selling later shares for $1 to outsiders. Another method of gaining and keeping control is to pool the stock of several shareholders into a voting trust so that one person gains the power, by contract, to vote all the shares in the trust. It should be kept in mind that many issues of stocks and bonds are subject to regulation under state securities laws, usually called "blue-sky laws," which govern the issue and sale of securities. These laws are discussed in section 8 of this chapter.

A major subject of litigation concerns the rights of those who do not possess control in a closely held corporation—the so-called "minority interest." To a very large degree, the owners of the minority interest are subject to the whim or caprice of the majority. The majority may pay themselves high salaries to use up the profits and may never declare a dividend. However, the minority interest is not without some rights, because the directors and officers stand in a fiduciary relation to the corporation. This relation imposes a duty on directors to act for the best interests of the corporation rather than for themselves individually.

As a result of his fiduciary relationship, contracts made with the corporation by a dominant director or officer may be challenged. The burden is on the director or majority shareholder to prove good faith and inherent fairness in such transactions when suit is brought. Such suits are known as shareholder's derivative suits and are brought by a shareholder on behalf of the corporation. They generally cannot be commenced until all possible means to solve the problem within the corporate organization have been exhausted.

The basic difficulty of owning a minority interest in a closely held corporation arises from the fact that there is no ready market for the stock in the event the shareholder desires to dispose of it. While the shareholder has the right to attend meetings and vote for directors, he may be constantly outvoted. He has a right to any dividends that are declared but no right to have them declared. He also has a preemptive right, which is to purchase his proportionate share of any new stock issue, but he may not be interested in investing more money when no dividends are being paid. Therefore, as a practical matter, the majority may be able to reduce his percentage of ownership further.

The minority shareholder has a right to inspect the books and records of the company, but at a proper time and place; and the books may not have much meaning to him without having the entries and account balances analyzed by an expert.

Finally, a minority shareholder has the right to his proportionate share of assets on dissolution but he has no right to dissolution, except that he may seek it in a court of equity under circumstances that will cause a court to step in to protect creditors and the corporation.

All corporations are theoretically controlled by the majority of the shareholders who elect the board of directors. (While in small, closely held businesses this theory may be a fact, we have seen that in large corporations management's power to solicit and vote proxies has reduced the theory to a mere technicality. In the latter type of business, almost all shareholders except those who are the management team are in reality "minority" shareholders as far as actual control or rights are concerned.) The board of directors elects the officers and makes policy such as declaring dividends and amending the bylaws. Courts may occasionally step in to find a violation of the fiduciary relationship by directors or officers, but such cases are rare and as a practical matter the minority are at the mercy of the majority. The case which follows illustrates some of the problems of a minority shareholder.

Polikoff v. Dole & Clark Building Corp.
184 N.E.2d 792 (Ill. 1962)

ENGLISH, JUDGE: The complaint seeks to set forth a cause of action, on behalf of a minority shareholder, for the liquidation of an Illinois corporation in the exercise by the court of either statutory or inherent equity authority. . . .

The complaint fills fifty pages of the record. In brief, it alleges:

Defendant corporation was organized in 1933 under a plan of reorganization for a defaulted real estate bond issue. The real estate, which is the principal asset of the corporation, consists of a building containing a theater, nine stores, and a 65-room hotel, located at Clark Street and Drummond Place in Chicago.

The stock consists of 942.5 shares of Class A (ineligible for dividends, and having a value on liquidation of $100 per share), and 1015.2 shares of Class B (ineligible for dividends while any Class A shares are outstanding).

Members of defendant Grundman's family own 517.5 shares of Class A (approximately 55%), and 767.7 shares of Class B (approximately 76%).

Plaintiff owns 15 shares of Class A (approximately 1.6%), and 6 shares of Class B (approximately .6%). Her shares represent an investment of $1200 in 1951.

During the years in question (1952–1958), defendant Grundman was president, a director and manager of the property; his son-in-law was secretary and a director; and, since 1958, his daughter has held the third directorship.

During the years 1952 through 1957 the corporation sustained losses averaging $4,935 after making allowances for depreciation. During those years receipts exceeded expenditures by an average of approximately $4250. For the year 1958 the corporation showed a profit of $1740 after depreciation.

The net worth increased some $16,500 during 1958 to approximately $123,000.

The theater has been closed since April 3, 1958 and has produced no income. For several years prior to that time, the motion picture business in Chicago had been poor and many theaters had closed. There are at least two other motion picture theaters in the vicinity of the corporation's theater.

In 1953 Grundman's wife made a loan of $60,000 to the corporation and was given a mortgage on the real estate. The interest rate is 5% and all payments of interest have been made as they matured. No payment has been made on principal, which was due in 1958 but has been extended to 1963. The mortgage contains a waiver of the right of redemption.

Directors' fees of $300 per year were paid until 1958, when they were eliminated.

Grundman was paid $6000 per year for his services as president of the corporation, manager of the real estate and operating manager of the hotel. It is claimed that this compensation was grossly excessive in view of the financial condition of the corporation. Grundman also took a three-month vacation in 1957 without diminution in compensation.

The corporation spent $60,000 on rehabilitation of the building when it was uncertain whether or not the payments on Mrs. Grundman's mortgage could be maintained. Thus, a foreclosure would inure to the benefit of the Grundman family.

Only about half of the hotel rooms were rented; too little was spent on advertising the hotel; no new tenant was obtained for the theater; Grundman refused to have the corporation operate the theater itself, and failed to communicate with plaintiff concerning a lead to a possible tenant.

Contrary to plaintiff's advice, Grundman has refused to let the corporation sell the real estate. Because of Mrs. Grundman's mortgage, her husband is not in a position to exercise his fiduciary obligations impartially and in the best interest of the corporation.

The corporation's surplus was not used to retire Class A shares during the years in question.

The Grundman family have been buying shares at depressed prices.

Grundman refused to follow suggestions made by plaintiff for the management of the corporation's affairs and he caused the corporation to expend money for attorneys' fees in opposing plaintiff's suit. He and Mrs. Grundman also refused to accept other suggestions of plaintiff calculated to weaken the corporation's mortgage commitment to Mrs. Grundman.

The corporation is in danger of losing its principal asset to Mrs. Grundman through a foreclosure which could be manipulated by those in control of the corporation for their own benefit.

Because of the condition of the corporation there is no reasonable prospect of profitable operation and, therefore, no reasonable prospect of its achieving the principal object for which it was formed—the retirement of its Class A shares.

The prayer of the complaint is primarily for liquidation of the corporation. All its other prayers relate to the details of such a liquidation and are dependent upon it.

The gist of defendants' motion to strike is that the complaint does not allege facts constituting illegal, oppressive, or fraudulent acts on the part of those in control of the corporation, or facts constituting waste or misapplication of corporate assets. . . .

The burden of plaintiff's brief is that Grundman's acts, as outlined, were oppressive and constituted misapplication or waste of corporate assets. The background against which these charges are to be considered is of extreme importance. That background is the routine organization of all corporate entities. As stated by our Supreme Court in words fully as cogent today as when written sixty years ago:

It is, however, fundamental in the law of corporations that the majority of its stockholders shall control the policy of the corporation, and regulate and govern the lawful exercise of its franchise and business. . . . Every one purchasing or subscribing for stock in a corporation impliedly agrees that he will be bound by the acts and proceedings done or sanctioned by a majority of the shareholders, or by the agents of the corporation duly chosen by such majority, within the scope of the powers conferred by the charter. And courts of equity will not undertake to control the policy or business methods of a corporation, although it may be seen that a wiser policy might be adopted, and the business more successful if other methods were pursued. The majority of shares of its stock, or the agents by the holders thereof lawfully chosen, must be permitted to control the business of the corporation in their discretion, when not in violation of its charter, or some public law, or corruptly and fraudulently subversive of the rights and interests of the corporation or of a shareholder. . . .

The Business Corporation Act has given to the courts the power to relieve minority shareholders from oppressive acts of the majority, but the remedy of liquidation is so drastic that it must be invoked with extreme caution. The ends of justice would not be served by too broad an application of the statute, for that would merely eliminate one evil by substituting a greater one—oppression of the majority by the minority. . . .

Almost all aspects of plaintiff's charges relate solely to business decision-making which by our statute is made the responsibility of the board of directors and the officers of a corporation. Whether Grundman spent too much or too little for advertising, or for salaries, or for rehabilitation of the premises, are matters with which the court will not concern itself—at least not in so far as they bear on the question of liquidation. We do not find in the allegations of the complaint sufficient facts to establish oppressive conduct by the management. Nor do we find misapplication or waste of corporate assets.

Along a somewhat similar line, plaintiff argues for liquidation because there is no reasonable expectation of profitable operation. From the facts submitted, we cannot agree. We do not, of course, predict that this will be a profitable enterprise, but, as said in *Central Standard Inc. Co. v. Davis,* 10 Ill. 2d 566, 577, 141 N.E.2d 45, 51: "Time may show that there is no reasonable prospect of profitable operation. The present record does not."

As to the mortgage, the complaint does not allege any facts indicating impropriety in the corporation's borrowing from Mrs. Grundman the money which it needed for rehabilitation of its property. The fact, if it be a fact, that Mr. and Mrs. Grundman have thereby placed themselves in such a position that Grundman might violate his fiduciary obligations to the corporation—that is not enough to justify the relief sought in this complaint. Every corporate director or officer is in a position to betray his position of trust from the moment of his election.

The complaint was properly stricken, and, plaintiff having stood on her pleading, the action was properly dismissed. The order of the Circuit Court is, therefore, affirmed. [AFFIRMED]

7 CONTINUITY AND LEGAL CAPACITY

The legal fiction that creates a corporation brings into life an artificial being separate and apart from the shareholders who own it. It may have perpetual existence and will not be affected by death of a shareholder. Of course, the laws regulating corporations contain provisions concerning their dissolution, merger and consolidation—any of which will end corporate existence—but essentially, perpetual life is provided for.

On the other hand, a partnership may be dissolved at any time. It may occur by reason of the death of one of the partners. Even if the partnership agreement provides that the partnership will continue for a certain number of years, any partner has the *power* but not the *right* to dissolve the partnership. In other words, liability may attach for wrongful dissolution but dissolution will nevertheless take place if one partner withdraws in violation of his contract. Dissolution is not the equivalent of termination. The latter involves the winding up of the business, while dissolution involves a change in relationship among the partners.

Modern partnership law allows the entry of new partners by agreement among the old partners and contracts among the partners by which the business may continue even though a partner dies or withdraws. These contracts, usually known as "buy and sell agreements," are frequently a part of the articles of co-partnership and provide for payment to a withdrawing partner or to the estate or spouse of a deceased partner for his interest in the business. Formulas are frequently used to compute the value of assets other than cash and goodwill, these forming a part of the agreement. In the case of the death of a partner, the liquidity needed is often provided by the cash proceeds from life insurance which was taken out on the life of the deceased and made payable to the firm. Upon payment of the amount required by the buy and sell agreement to the estate of the deceased, all rights of the deceased end and the surviving partners continue the business. Actually, a new partnership now exists but as a practical matter, business continues as usual at the same place and under the same name. Partnerships of lawyers, doctors, or accountants may thus obtain almost perpetual existence.

In the early law, a corporation was considered a legal entity but a partnership was not. By being a legal entity, it was usually meant that capacity was present to sue and be sued and to hold title to and convey real and personal property in the name of the business instead of the names of the individual owners. Modern statutes on procedure allow suits by and against a partnership in the firm name. They also allow a partnership to own and dispose of real estate and personal property in the firm name. To this extent a partnership is a legal entity.

Actually, a corporation today although a legal entity has more difficulty in gaining access to the courts than does a partnership. Most states by statute require corporations doing business in a state other than that of incorporation to qualify under the local corporation laws. Qualification involves the furnishing of certain information in an initial registration and an annual report as well as the payment of such taxes as franchise taxes and annual license fees. One result of the failure to meet this requirement imposed by states on foreign corporations is illustrated by the following case.

Eli Lilly and Company v. Sav-On-Drugs, Inc.
366 U.S. 276 (1961)

BLACK, JUSTICE: The appellant Eli Lilly and Company, an Indiana corporation dealing in pharmaceutical products, brought this action in a New Jersey state court to enjoin the appellee Sav-On-Drugs, Inc. a New Jersey corporation, from selling Lilly's products in New Jersey at prices lower than those fixed in minimum retail price contracts into which Lilly had entered with a number of New Jersey drug retailers. Sav-On had itself signed no such contract but, under the New Jersey Fair Trade Act, prices so established become obligatory upon nonsigning retailers who have notice that the manufacturer has made these contracts with other retailers. Sav-On moved to dismiss this complaint under a New Jersey statute that denies a foreign corporation transacting business in the State the right to bring any action in New Jersey upon any contract made there unless and until it files with the New Jersey Secretary of State a copy of its charter together with a limited amount of information about its operations and obtains from him a certificate authorizing it to do business in the State.

Lilly opposed the motion to dismiss, urging that its business in New Jersey was entirely in interstate commerce and arguing, upon that ground, that the attempt to require it to file the necessary information and obtain a certificate for its New Jersey business was forbidden by the Commerce Clause of the Federal Constitution. Both parties offered evidence to the Court in the nature of affidavits as to the extent and kind of business done by Lilly with New Jersey companies and people. On this evidence, the trial court made findings of fact and granted Sav-On's motion to dismiss, stating as its ground that "the conclusion is inescapable that the plaintiff [Lilly] was in fact doing business in this State at the time of the acts complained of and was required to, but did not, comply with the provisions of the Corporation Act." On appeal to the Supreme Court of New Jersey, this constitutional attack was renewed and the State Attorney General was permitted to intervene as a party-defendant to defend the validity of the statute. The State Supreme Court then affirmed the judgment upholding the statute, relying entirely upon the opinion of the trial court. We noted probable jurisdiction to consider Lilly's contention that the constitutional question was improperly decided by the state courts.

The record shows that the New Jersey trade in Lilly's pharmaceutical products is carried on through both interstate and intrastate channels. Lilly manufactures these products and sells them in interstate commerce to certain selected New Jersey wholesalers. These wholesalers then sell the products in intrastate commerce to New Jersey hospitals, physicians and retail drugstores, and these retail stores in turn sell them, again in intrastate commerce, to the general public. It is well established that New Jersey cannot require Lilly to get a certificate of authority to do business in the State if its participation in this trade is limited to its wholly interstate sales to New Jersey wholesalers. Under the authority of the so-called "drummer" cases, such as *Robbins v. Shelby County Taxing District,* Lilly is free to send salesmen into New Jersey to promote this interstate trade without interference from regulations imposed by the State. On the other hand, it is equally well settled that if Lilly is engaged in intrastate as well as interstate aspects of the New Jersey drug business, the State can require it to get a certificate of authority to do business. In such a situation, Lilly could not escape state regulation merely because it is also engaged in interstate commerce. We must then look to the record to determine whether Lilly is engaged in intrastate commerce in New Jersey.

The findings of the trial court, based as they are upon uncontroverted evidence presented to it, show clearly that Lilly is conducting an intrastate as well as an interstate business in New Jersey. . . .

We agree with the trial court that "[t]o hold under the facts above recited that plaintiff [Lilly] is not doing business in New Jersey is to completely ignore reality." Eighteen "detailmen," working out of a big office in Newark, New Jersey, with Lilly's name on the door and in the lobby of the building, and with Lilly's district manager and secretary in charge, have been regularly engaged in work for Lilly which relates directly to the intrastate aspects of the sale of Lilly's products.

These eighteen "detailmen" have been traveling throughout the State of New Jersey promoting the sales of Lilly's products, not to the wholesalers, Lilly's interstate customers, but to the physicians, hospitals and retailers who buy those products in intrastate commerce from the wholesalers. To this end, they have provided these hospitals, physicians and retailers with up-to-date knowledge of Lilly's products and with free advertising and promotional material designed to encourage the general public to make more intrastate purchases of Lilly's products. And they sometimes even directly participate in the intrastate sales themselves by transmitting orders from the hospitals, physicians and drugstores they service to the New Jersey wholesalers. . . .

Lilly also contends that even if it is engaged in intrastate commerce in New Jersey and can by virtue of that fact be required to get a license to do business in that State, New Jersey cannot properly deny it access to the courts in this case because the suit is one arising out of the interstate aspects of its business. In this regard, Lilly relies upon such cases as *International Textbook Co. v. Pigg*, holding that a State cannot condition the right of a foreign corporation to sue upon a contract for the interstate sale of goods. We do not think that those cases are applicable here, however, for the present suit is not of that kind. Here, Lilly is suing upon a contract entirely separable from any particular interstate sale and the power of the State is consequently not limited by cases involving such contracts. [AFFIRMED]

As was indicated in Chapter 2, a business may be sued in a state with which it has certain minimal contracts under the so-called "long-arm statutes." We therefore have the unique situation that a company may be a defendant but not a plaintiff in a state in which it is a foreign corporation if it has failed "to qualify" when required to do so.

8 BLUE-SKY LAWS

The Federal government and most states have adopted laws which regulate the sale of securities. These laws, usually referred to as "blue-sky laws" because of their goal of preventing the sale of "blue sky" to the public, are paternalistic in character. Their purpose is to modify the common-law rule of "caveat emptor" and replace it with "caveat venditor," in order to protect people from their desire to "get rich quick," a desire which often supersedes and overrides judgment, wisdom, and common sense.

Blue-sky laws generally require full disclosure of all facts about the business selling the security. The facts about the business and the people involved are usually contained in a prospectus which must be furnished to each potential investor. The prospectus, in addition to financial data, usually includes most of the other facts which would be pertinent to an investment decision. In some cases, the regulatory body has authority to prohibit the sale of the security if minimum standards of fairness are not met, by refusing to register the security on request.

The blue-sky laws also provide the foundation for regulation of the sale of listed securities. Such matters as insider transactions are regulated by the Securities and Exchange Commission under the authority of the Securities Act of 1933 and the Securities Exchange Act of 1934.

State securities statutes are applicable to sales made within a particular state. The Federal statute is applicable to sales of securities in interstate commerce and to sales in which the United States mails are used in any part of the transaction.

The securities laws contain both civil and criminal sanctions. The usual approach is to provide that some violations are misdemeanors and others are felonies. Both imprisonment and fines are ordinarily authorized as punishment.

The civil remedies include suits for damages, rescission, and injunctions. The latter remedy is usually sought by a public official rather than by a purchaser of the security. The injunction is issued by a court of equity to prevent further illegal sales. In addition, cease and desist orders may be issued by an administrative agency with jurisdiction over securities transactions.

The most significant of the sanctions are those that allow a purchaser of (1) an unregistered security or (2) a security that has been misrepresented to rescind the purchase and to obtain a refund of the purchase price. Some statutes also provide for recovery of interest and attorney's fees. Misrepresentation is not required in cases involving unregistered securities. Statutory liability for the purchase price of an unregistered security is imposed as a matter of public policy.

The sanctions are not limited in their application to persons who receive the proceeds from the sale of securities. They may also be imposed against persons who assist in the sale. This latter group may include, in addition to the actual seller, issuers, controlling persons, underwriters, dealers, or other persons who shall have participated or aided in any way in making such sale. In case an issuer, controlling person, underwriter, or dealer is a corporation or unincorporated association, then the officers and directors of such organization are personally liable.

Recognizing that everyone connected with either an unregistered or fraudulent sale of a security, except those exempted, has civil liability and may be criminally prosecuted, it becomes essential to ascertain the meaning of the word "security." Most statutes attempt to define "security" and do so in a rather broad term. The Federal Statute definition which many states have followed provides:

"Security" means any note, stock, treasury stock, bond, debenture, evidence of indebtedness, certificate of interest or participation in any profit-sharing agreement, collateral-trust certificate, preorganization certificate or subscription transferable share, investment contract, investment fund share, face-amount certificate, voting-trust certificate, fractional undivided interest in oil, gas, or other mineral lease, right or royalty, or, in general, any interest or instrument commonly known as a security, or any certificate of deposit for, certificate of

interest or participation in, temporary or interim certificate for receipt for, guarantee of, or warrant or right to subscribe to or purchase, any of the foregoing.[1]

A key portion of this definition which has been used to apply the securities laws to a broad variety of investments is the term *"investment contract."* The Supreme Court of the United States in discussing the meaning of investment contract stated:

The term "investment contract" is undefined by the Securities Act or by relevant legislative reports. But the term was common in many state "blue sky" laws in existence prior to the adoption of the federal statute and, although the term was also undefined by the state laws, it had been broadly construed by state courts so as to afford the investing public a full measure of protection. Form was disregarded for substance and emphasis was placed upon economic reality. An investment contract thus came to mean a contract or scheme for "the placing of capital or laying out of money in a way intended to secure income or profit from its employment."... This definition was uniformly applied by state courts to a variety of situations where individuals were led to invest money in a common enterprise with the expectations that they would earn a profit solely through the efforts of the promoter or of some one other than themselves.[2]

This concept of a security being any investment in which the return is based on the efforts of others, has become increasingly important in the law. The typical investment in common or preferred stock of a corporation undeniably involves a security because the corporation is going to earn the profits and hopefully the return will be a dividend. A partnership on the other hand by the nature of its creation and operation is a joint effort for profit in which the partners share in management and control. Thus, an investment in a general partnership form of organization is not a security. However, it has been held that the interest of a limited partner in a limited partnership is a security because limited partners do not participate in management.

The resolution of doubts about whether an investment is a security is usually in favor of the purchaser. For example, it has been held that the sale of nominal units of ownership in an apartment building to "tenants in common" is the sale of a security.[3] In another case, a note secured by a deed of trust delivered in connection with a "Secured 10% Earnings Program"[4] was found to be a security. Interests in oil wells are usually held to be securities. It has even been held that a warranty deed to an orange tree or trees is a security.[5] In that case, a Florida promoter-owner of the orange grove sold his grove tree by tree to northern

[1] 15 U.S.C. Sec. 77b.
[2] *Securities & Exchange Com. v. W. J. Howey Co.,* 328 U.S. 293 (1964).
[3] *Sire Plan Portfolios, Inc. v. Carpentier,* 8 Ill.App. 2d 354 (1956).
[4] *Securities & Exchange Commission v. Los Angeles Trust D & M Exchange,* 186 F. Supp. 830 (1960).
[5] *S.E.C. v. W. J. Howey,* 328 U.S. 293 (1946).

tourists and leased them back under an arrangement by which he raised and picked the fruit and either sold it or shipped it to the owners. He was paid for his farming services and costs. Since the purchasers did not participate in management, the sale was one of a security.

It is apparent that real estate ventures comprise a major area in which promoters seek investors. The blue-sky laws can be used to control such investment activities, but victimized investors often use them improperly. This is due in part to a lack of understanding, not only by the investors but also by their attorneys. It also is apparent that part of the failure to utilize the remedies available arises from the unwillingness of the investor to publicly admit his stupidity by bringing suit. Many victims, when apprised of their legal rights, would rather suffer a financial loss than personal embarrassment.

Because of the large number of questionable investments involving real estate, many states have enacted additional laws regulating the sale of interests in land, especially when the sales are of undeveloped land or are in states with large numbers of retired persons or large tourist industries.

It must be kept in mind that if a worthless investment is sold in a transaction that complies with all the applicable laws, losses on such an investment cannot be recovered by using the remedies granted buyers by the securities laws. A seller of a security that has been duly registered and qualified in accordance with the applicable statutes has no liability, civil or criminal, in the absence of fraud or misrepresentation. The methodology of the securities laws is to make the *facts* available so that an investor can make a decision based on facts instead of sales talk, puffing, and the like. Where there is compliance, "caveat emptor" is still the law. Knowledge, wisdom, and business judgment must be present if the blue-sky laws are to accomplish their objectives.

REVIEW QUESTIONS—CHAPTER 16

1 Define the following terms introduced in this chapter: professional service corporation; Subchapter S corporation; limited partnership; blue-sky laws.
2 List the factors to be considered in selecting the form of organization for a new, closely held business.
3 How is a partnership created?
4 How is a corporation created?
5 What are the advantages and disadvantages of the partnership as a form of business organization?
6 What are the advantages and disadvantages of the corporation as a form of business organization?
7 Why have many professional persons formed corporation-like associations?
8 List the tax advantages of a qualified pension or profit-sharing plan.
9 List some techniques commonly used to avoid double taxation of corporate income.

10 What is the legal effect of a limited partner's participation in the management of an enterprise?

11 List methods by which a minority of the investors may control a corporation.

12 What are the shortcomings in owning a minority interest in a closely held corporation?

13 To what extent is a partnership a legal entity?

14 What is one penalty imposed on a foreign corporation which fails to qualify to do business in a state in which it is engaging in intrastate activities?

15 What remedies are available to investors who purchase securities that are not issued in compliance with the applicable blue-sky laws?

16 What penalties are imposed on persons who participate in the selling of securities in violation of the blue-sky laws?

Chapter Seventeen

Property

1 THE NATURE OF PROPERTY

Perhaps no legal concept has been as important in American history and to our cultural and economic development as that of property. As one might expect, the vast majority of statutes and decisions rendered by both the courts and administrative agencies deal in some way with issues involving the utimate determination of property rights. The term "property" is difficult to define. Its meaning is often indistinguishably tied to other terms such as government, contract, tort, right, or value.

The concept of property is frequently described in terms of ownership, title to and possession of corporeal objects. Ownership has to do with the extent of a person's rights in property and is usually synonymous with title. Title itself is a confusing term because it is frequently associated with a document of title such as that to an automobile. Because of this, people frequently think of title in terms of a document labeled "title." Yet a person usually has "title" to the clothes he wears and to his other property without a document of title. Possession is a term often indicative of physical control or dominion. However, in legal contemplation, possession must be defined in terms of the assistance that the law affords a person in controlling property. For example, it is easy to physically possess a book, but impossible to physically possess a 1,000-acre tract of land. However, one may be in legal possession of a 1,000-acre tract because of sanctions provided by law to keep others out.

A portion of a discussion concerned with the nature of property by Dean Roscoe Pound, one of this country's most eminent legal philosophers, is presented here.[1]

If we examine the law of property analytically we may see three grades or stages in the power or capacity which men have of influencing the acts of others with respect to corporeal objects. One is a mere condition of fact, a mere physical holding of or physical control over the thing without any other element whatever. The Roman jurists called this natural possession. We call it custody. Writers on analytical jurisprudence regard it as an element of possession. But

---

[1] Pound, *An Introduction to the Philosophy of Law* 124 (1922). Used by permission from the Yale University Press.

this natural possession is something that may exist independently of law or of the state, as in the so-called pedis possessio *of American mining law, where, before law or state authority had been extended to the public domain in the mining country, the miners recognized the claim of one who was actually digging to dig without molestation at that spot. The mere having of an object in one's actual grasp gives an advantage. But it may be only an advantage depending on one's strength or on recognition of and respect for his personality by his fellow men. It is not a legal advantage except as the law protects personality. It is the physical person of the one in natural possession which is secured, not his relation to the thing held. Analytically the next grade or stage is what the Romanist calls juristic possession as distinguished from natural possession. This is a legal development of the extra-legal idea of custody. Where custody or the ability to reproduce a condition of custody is coupled with the mental element of intention to hold for one's own purposes, the legal order confers on one who so holds a capacity protected and maintained by law so to hold, and a claim to have the thing restored to his immediate physical control should he be deprived of it. As the Romanist puts it, in the case of natural possession the law secures the relation of the physical person to the object; in juristic possession the law secures the relation of the will to the object. In the highest grade of proprietary relation, ownership, the law goes much further and secures to men the exclusive or ultimate enjoyment or control of objects far beyond their capacity either to hold in custody or to possess—that is, beyond what they could hold by physical force and beyond what they could actually hold even by the help of the state. Natural possession is a conception of pure fact in no degree dependent upon law. The legally significant thing is the interest of the natural possessor in his personality. Possession or juristic possession is a conception of fact and law, existing as a pure relation of fact, independent of legal origin but protected and maintained by law without regard to interference with personality. Ownership is a purely legal conception having its origin in and depending on the law.*

In general the historical development of the law of property follows the line thus indicated by analysis. In the most primitive social control only natural possession is recognized, and interference with natural possession is not distinguished from interference with the person or injury to the honor of the one whose physical contact with the physical object is meddled with. In the earlier legal social control the all-important thing is seisin, or possession. This is a juristic possession, a conception both of fact and of law. Such institutions as tortious conveyance by the person seised in the common law are numerous in an early stage of legal development. They show that primarily the law protected the relation to an object of one who had possession of it. Indeed the idea of dominium, *or ownership as we now understand it, was first worked out thoroughly in Roman law, and other systems got their idea of it, as distin-guished from seisin, from the Roman books. . . .*

Ownership, the third grade of power decribed by Pound, encompasses, besides the right to possess corporeal objects, the right to dispose of them in various ways, the right to use and enjoy them, the right to change their nature, and probably the right to destroy them. Pound makes it clear that these rights are creatures of the law which are backed by legal sanctions. Thus, without law, property is nonexistent. While the tendency of most people is to think of property as the thing owned itself, this approach is inaccurate. More correctly, it consists of a bundle of legal rights, such as those listed above, with respect to a thing. This concept of property views it as a series of legal relationships between the owner and all other persons, in which the owner has many rights, and the others, each individually, owe him many duties which are often negative in character. Ownership is further defined by a series of limitations imposed by law on the owner and often carries with it duties owed by the owner to other persons who enjoy the correlative rights. The nature of some of these restrictions and duties is discussed in section 7. Viewed in this manner, technically all property is intangible, consisting of specific legal rights and duties, but may exist *with regard to* a physical, tangible object. Nevertheless, it is generally accepted in legal terminology to refer to the property rights associated with corporeal things as being tangible property.

The reader is familiar with some of the more common rights which are attendant with ownership. Clearly, the owner of farm land generally has the right to sow crops on it, harvest them, sell them and keep the proceeds for his own use. (Unless, of course, he has contracted that right away by leasing the land to a tenant.) Also, the owner of a farm has the right, as a rule, to sell it and then use the proceeds of sale as he sees fit. And, by a properly executed will, he can, subject to some limitations, dispose of the farm on his death as he wishes. Fundamental to the concept of property are the rights to exclude others from its possession and use. Besides the foregoing, ownership may carry with it other rights which are not nearly so obvious. The cases which follow in this section are merely illustrative of the complex nature of the "bundle of rights" which is property. They indicate some of the meanings of ownership, and its significance and extent.

In re Forsstrom
38 P.2d 878 (Ariz. 1934)

LOCKWOOD, JUSTICE: . . . The question is solely one of law, and the facts may be briefly stated as follows: The main tracks of the Southern Pacific Railroad cross North Stone Avenue near an intersection of Sixth Street at the present grade of said Avenue. The authorities of the City of Tucson, believing that such grade crossing is a menace and hazard to public travel on the street determined to abolish it by the construction of an underpass or subway below the tracks. . . . [If this is done] ingress and egress to the premises of the abutting property owners will be made more difficult. . . .

We come then to the question as to whether the proposed action of the City of Tucson, in so far as it affects petitioners at all, is a "taking" [of property]. . . .

In order that we may understand the better what is meant by a "taking" of property, we should have a clear knowledge of what property really is. The word is used at different times to express many varying ideas. Sometimes it is taken in common parlance to denote a physical object, as where one says an automobile or a horse is his property. On careful consideration, however, it is plain that "property" in the true and legal sense does not mean a physical object itself, but certain rights over the object. A piece of land in an unexplored and uninhabited region which belongs to no one does not necessarily undergo any physical change merely by reason of its later becoming the property of any person. A wild animal may be exactly the same physically before and after it is captured, but, when it is running free in the forest, no one would speak of it as property. We must therefore look beyond the physical object itself for the true definition of property. Many courts and writers have attempted to define it, using different words, but meaning in essence the same thing. One of the great writers on jurisprudence says:

Property is entirely the creature of the law. . . . There is no form, or color, or visible trace, by which it is possible to express the relation which constitutes property. It belongs not to physics, but to metaphysics; it is altogether a creature of the mind. Bentham: Works (Ed. 1843) Vol. 1, p. 308.

[Others have said:]

. . . Property itself, in a legal sense, is nothing more than the "exclusive right of possession, enjoying and disposing of a thing." . . .

Property, in its broader and more appropriate sense, is not alone the chattel or the land itself, but the right to freely possess, use, and alienate the same; and many things are considered property which have no tangible existence, but which are necessary to the satisfactory use and enjoyment of that which is tangible. . . .

It is used in the constitution in a comprehensive and unlimited sense, and so it must be construed. . . . It need not be any physical or tangible property which is subject to a tangible invasion. . . . The right to light and air, and access is equally property. . . .

It would follow from these definitions and explanations of the meaning of the term "property" that since it consists, not in tangible things themselves, but in certain rights in and appurtenant to them, it would logically follow that, when a person is deprived of any of these rights, he is to that extent deprived of his property, and that it is taken in the true sense, although his title and possession of the physical object remains undisturbed. Any substantial interference, there-fore, with rights over a physical object which destroys or lessens its value, or by which the use and enjoyment thereof by its owner is in any substantial degree abridged or destroyed, is both in law and in fact a "taking" of property. It is apparently only of recent years that the meaning of the word "taking" when used in regard to eminent domain has been properly understood by the majority of the courts, although it would seem obvious that a careful analysis of the true nature of "property" would have shown it long since. . . .

[In one of the leading cases it was said:]

From the very nature of these rights of user and of exclusion, it is evident that they cannot be materially abridged without, ipso facto, taking the owner's property. If the right of indefinite user is an essential element of absolute property or complete ownership, whatever physical interference annuls this right takes "property"—although the owner may still have left to him valuable rights (in the article) of a more limited and circumscribed nature. He has not the same property that he formerly had. Then, he had an unlimited right; now, he has only a limited right. His absolute ownership has been reduced to a qualified ownership. Restricting A's unlimited right of using one hundred acres of land to a limited right of using the same land, may work a far greater injury to A than to take from him the title in fee simple to one acre, leaving him the unrestricted right of using the remaining ninety-nine acres. Nobody doubts that the latter transaction would constitute a "taking" of property. Why not the former? . . .

[In another case, the court stated:]

Property in land must be considered, for many purposes, not as an absolute, unrestricted dominion, but as an aggregation of qualified privileges, the limits of which are prescribed by the equality of rights, and the correlation of rights and obligations necessary for the highest enjoyment of land by the entire community of proprietors. . . .

. . . [T]he changing of the street grade which lessens the enjoyment of the easement of ingress and egress is within the true meaning of the constitutional provision a taking of property. . . .

Southwest Weather Research v. Rounsaville
320 S.W.2d 211 (Tex. Civ. App 1958) [2]

PER CURIAM: This is an appeal from an injunction issued by the Eighty-third District Court, Jeff Davis County, Texas, which said injunction commands the appellants "to refrain from seeding the clouds by artificial nucleation or otherwise and from in any other manner or way interfering with the clouds and the natural conditions of the air, sky, atmosphere and air space over plaintiff's lands and in the area of plaintiffs' lands to in any manner, degree or way affect, control or modify the weather conditions on or about said lands. . . ."

Appellees are ranchmen residing in West Texas counties, and appellants are owners and operators of certain airplanes, and equipment generally used in what they call a "weather modification program" and those who contracted and arranged for their services.

[2] Affirmed, 327 S.W.2d 417 (1959).

It is not disputed that appellants did operate their airplanes at various times over portions of lands belonging to the appellees, for the purpose of and while engaged in what is commonly called "cloud seeding." Appellants do not deny having done this, and testified through the president of the company that the operation would continue unless restrained. He stated, "We seeded the clouds to attempt to suppress the hail." The controversy is really over appellants' right to seed clouds or otherwise modify weather conditions over appellees' property. . . .

We have carefully considered the voluminous record and exhibits that were admitted in evidence, and have concluded that the trial court had ample evidence on which to base his findings and with which to justify the issuance of the injunction. . . .

Appellants maintain that appellees have no right to prevent them from flying over appellees' lands; that no one owns the clouds unless it be the state, and that the trial court was without legal right to restrain appellants from pursuing a lawful occupation; also that the injunction is too broad in its terms. . . .

Appellees urge here that the owner of land also owns in connection therewith certain so-called "natural rights," and cites us the following quotation in which Chief Justice Nelson Phillips states:

Property in a thing consists not merely in its ownership and possession, but in the unrestricted right of use, enjoyment and disposal. Anything which destroys any of these elements of property, to that extent destroys the property itself. The substantial value of property lies in its use. If the right of use be denied, the value of the property is annihilated and ownership is rendered a barren right. . . .

The very essence of American constitutions is that the material rights of no man shall be subject to the mere will of another.

In Volume 34, *Marquette Law Review,* at page 275, this is said:

Considering the property right of every man to the use and enjoyment of his land, and considering the profound effect which natural rainfall has upon the realization of this right, it would appear that the benefits of natural rainfall should come within the scope of judicial protection, and a duty should be imposed on adjoining landowners not to interfere therewith.

In the *Stanford Law Review,* November 1948, Volume 1, in an article entitled, "Who Owns the Clouds?", the following statements occur:

The landowner does have rights in the water in clouds, however, the basis of these rights is the common law doctrine of natural rights. Literally, the term "natural rights" is well chosen; these rights protect the landowner's use of his land in its natural condition. . . .

All forms of natural precipitation should be elements of the natural condition of the land. Precipitation, like air, oxygen, sunlight, and the soil itself, is an essential to many reasonable uses of the land. The plant and animal life on the land are both ultimately dependent upon rainfall. To the extent that rain is important to the use of land, the landowner should be entitled to the natural rainfall.

In *California Law Review*, December 1957, Volume 45, No. 5, in an article, "Weather Modification," are found the following statements:

What are the rights of the landowner or public today to natural rainfall? It has been suggested that the right to receive rainfall is one of those "natural rights" which is inherent in the full use of land from the fact of its natural contact with moisture in the air. . . .

Any use of such air or space by others which is injurious to his land, or which constitutes an actual interference with his possession or his beneficial use thereof would be a tresspass for which he would have remedy.

Appellees call our attention to various authorities that hold that although the old *ad coelum* doctrine has given way to the reality of present day conditions, an unreasonable and improper use of the air space over the owner's land can constitute a trespass. Other cases . . . apparently hold that the landowner, while not owning or controlling the entire air space over his property, is entitled to protection against improper or unreasonable use thereof or entrance thereon. . . .

We believe that under our system of government the landowner is entitled to such precipitation as nature deigns to bestow. We believe that the landowner is entitled, therefore and thereby, to such rainfall as may come from clouds over his own property that nature in her caprice may provide. It follows, therefore, that this enjoyment of or entitlement to the benefits of nature should be protected by the courts if interfered with improperly and unlawfully. [ORDER GRANTING INJUNCTION AFFIRMED]

State Highway Dep't v. Branch
152 S.E.2d 372 (Ga. 1966)

This case is an equitable action brought by a property owner and a lessee of his property to enjoin the State Highway Department from removing certain outdoor signs on petitioner's property adjoining an interstate highway. The defendants have threatened to do so under the authority of the Georgia Outdoor Advertising Control Act. The petitioners allege that the law under which the state officials intend to act is unconstitutional and in violation of the state constitution and the Fifth and Fourteenth Amendments of the United States Constitution in attempting to exercise the power of eminent domain without provision for the payment of just and adequate compensation. General and special demurrers were filed, and after a hearing certain of the general demurrers were overruled. The appeal is from that ruling.

DUCKWORTH, JUSTICE: The enactment of the so-called Outdoor Advertising Control Act was purely a legislative exercise in futility. Its sole purpose is to dictate, control and limit uses of private property for public purpose, without a semblance of provision for first paying for such taking or damaging. Anyone able and willing to read the Fifth Amendment, which provides "nor shall private property be taken for public use, without just compensation," the Fourteenth Amendment, which provides, "nor shall any State deprive any person of life, liberty, or property, without due process," and our own State Constitution, Art. I, Sec. III, Par. I, which provides that "[p]rivate property shall not be taken, or damaged, for public purposes, without just and adequate compensation being first paid," would know beyond possible doubt that the 1964 Act is a bold and brazen violation of each of these constitutional clauses.

Decisions of this court leave no room for reasonable doubt that the Constitutions stand as a bar to any invasion of those constitutional rights. It is inexcusable in light of these constitutional protections of private property and decisions of this court showing that legislation seeking to do so would be stricken down, to enact the 1964 Act which is thus foredoomed.

As pointed out in the brief of appellees, the Congress, which is not noted for observing constitutional safeguards of private property, amended the federal statute—in conformity to which the Georgia act was enacted—so as to cause it to provide that "just compensation" be paid for the removal of advertisements forbidden by the Act, and provides for the federal government to pay 75% of such costs. 23 U.S.C.A. § 131(g). By the 1964 Act, the Georgia legislature attempted to destroy private property, although as amended, the federal law requires the federal government to pay three-fourths of the damage suffered by the property owners. Georgia courts, to their eternal credit, have never allowed taking or damaging private property without first paying therefor, and this court stands ready to strike down this legislative attempt to do so.

We believe this matter is important enough to justify the following observations. Private property is the antithesis of Socialism or Communism. Indeed, it is an insuperable barrier to the establishment of either collective system of government. Too often, as in this case, the desire of the average citizen to secure the blessings of a good thing like beautification of our highways, and their safety, blinds them to a consideration of the property owner's right to be saved from harm by even the government. The thoughtless, the irresponsible, and the misguided will likely say that this court has blocked the effort to beautify and render our highways safer. But the actual truth is that we have only protected constitutional rights by condemning the unconstitutional method to attain such desirable ends, and to emphasize that there is a perfect constitutional way which must be employed for that purpose. Those whose ox is not being gored by this Act might be impatient and complain of this decision, but if this court yielded to them and sanctioned this violation of the Constitution we would thereby set a precedent whereby tomorrow when the critics are having their own ox gored, we would be bound to refuse them any protection. Our decisions are not just good for today but they are equally valid tomorrow.

We have gone to the heart of this case and decided the constitutional issue without being side-tracked by trivial incidental issues, thus putting an end to this case. For the reasons above stated, the 1964 Act is unconstitutional, and the judgment below is affirmed. [AFFIRMED]

Property is usually classified, according to the nature of the subject matter which is owned, as real or personal property and as tangible or intangible property. Real property is land or any interest in land and includes things permanently attached thereto, such as timber and buildings, which are called fixtures. Personal property encompasses chattels or things such as livestock, an automobile, clothing, or a television set. These and real property are referred to as tangible property because the subject matter of the ownership has physical existence (even though as noted above the bundle of rights which is in reality the "property" is intangible). Personal property also includes intangible property such as stocks, bonds, accounts receivable, and patent rights. Frequently intangible property is associated with a document such as a stock certificate. The document itself is not the property interest, or rights owned, but merely evidence of them. Even if the document is destroyed the property may still exist.

The terms "real" and "personal" in describing property originated because of early English common law procedures in which certain suits were described as "real" because they were brought to recover possession of the *res* or thing itself. Other suits were designated "personal" because they could be brought against the person of the defendant only for the remedy of money damages, rather than possession of the property. Thus, one can personally own both land and chattels. Likewise, some items of personal property are just as real in the sense of having tangible existence as real property is. Some people argue that a third category may exist called mixed property, or a chattel-real, because of the nature of the suit which is brought to enforce the rights involved. This distinction would appear to have decreasing significance today, and, for all practical purposes, all property rights not involving real estate can be classified generally as personal property. As a matter of fact, the reasons for distinguishing between these two classes of property are gradually disappearing. For example, the rights of relatives or a surviving spouse to property on the death of the owner often have differed depending on whether the property was real or personal. However, movements have been under way to abolish this distinction and some states have done so in their statutes governing the descent and distribution of property.

2 IMPORTANCE OF THE LEGAL CONCEPT OF PROPERTY

The entire social, political, and economic structure of a nation or state to a large degree both depends upon and is reflected in its laws governing ownership of property. The nature of the recognized rights of private individuals in property and the extent to which they are given sanction by the appropriate agencies of the government determine such things as: the nature of the social order, which may range from one in which the rights of the individual are highly valued and held supreme, to one in which these are always sacrificed for the benefit of the state or group; the form of the economic system, which may range all the way from laissez faire to some form of socialist-communistic; and, as shaped by the foregoing, the freedom of individuals in the society generally to act as they please without interference from the state. Clearly the ability to obtain and wield economic power is closely intertwined with political control. As society's attitudes and needs change, so to some degree does the law of property. Dean Roscoe Pound illustrates the spirit of "recent ethics, recent philosophy and recent political thought," by discussing several "noteworthy changes in the law." [3] Quoted here is one of Pound's illustrations dealing with changes in the law of property:

First among these we may note limitations on the use of property, attempts to prevent anti-social exercise of the incidents of ownership. At this point judicial decision has been the agency of progress. This is no time or place for details. I need only refer to the gradual but steady change of front in our case law with respect to the so-called spite fence, and to the establishment in American case law of doctrines with respect to percolating water and to surface water, in which a principle of reasonable use has superseded the old and narrow idea that the owner of the surface might do as he pleased. In this growing tendency of the law to impose limitations on the use of property, especially limitations designed to prevent what the French call "abusive exercise of rights," there is a suggestive parallel between the period of legal development on which we have entered and the earlier period of liberalization which I have called the stage of equity or natural law. Equity sought to prevent the unconscientious exercise of legal rights; today we seek to prevent the anti-social exercise of them. Equity imposed moral limitations; the law of today is imposing social limitations. It is endeavoring to delimit the individual interest better with respect to social interests and to confine the legal right to the bounds of the interest so delimited. More and more the tendency is to hold that what the law should secure is satisfaction of the owner's reasonable wants with respect to the property—that is those which consist with the like wants of his neighbors and the interests of society.

Changes in American law such as the one above indicate that, in the twentieth century, it has entered into a new stage of development which Pound calls "a stage of socialization of law." Explaining his meaning for this term, Pound continues:[4]

For in contrast with the nineteenth century it [law] appears to put the emphasis upon social interests; upon the demands or claims or desires involved in social life rather than upon the qualities of the abstract man in vacuo *or upon the freedom of will of the isolated individual. . . . Let us put the new point of view*

---

[3] Pound, *The Spirit of the Common Law* 185, 186 (1921), Beacon Press paperback edition. Used by permission from Marshall Jones Co.
[4] *Id.* at 195, 196.

in terms of engineering; let us speak of a change from a political or ethical idealistic interpretation to an engineering interpretation. Let us think of the problem of the end of law in terms of a great task or great series of tasks of social engineering. Let us say that the change consists in thinking not of an abstract harmonizing of human wills but of a concrete securing or realizing of human interests. From an earthly standpoint the central tragedy of existence is that there are not enough of the material goods of existence, as it were, to go round; that while individual claims and wants and desires are infinite, the material means of satisfying them are finite; that while, in common phrase, we all want the earth, there are many of us but there is only one earth. Thus we may think of the task of the legal order as one of precluding friction and eliminating waste; as one of conserving the goods of existence in order to make them go as far as possible, and of precluding friction and eliminating waste in the human use and enjoyment of them, so that where each may not have all that he claims, he may at least have all that is possible. Put in this way, we are seeking to secure as much of human claims and desires—that is as much of the whole scheme of interests—as possible, with the least sacrifice of such interests."

In applying his "engineering interpretation" to the change in law concerning the growth of limitations on the use of property, Pound states:[5]

. . . To the nineteenth-century way of thinking the question was simply one of the right of the owner and of the right of his neighbor. Within his physical boundaries the dominion of each was complete. So long as he kept within them and what he did within them was consistent with an equally absolute dominion of the neighbor within his boundaries, the law was to keep its hands off. For the end of law was taken to be a maximum of self-assertion by each, limited only by the possibility of a like self-assertion by all. If, therefore, he built a fence eight feet high cutting off light and air from his neighbor and painted the fence on the side toward his neighbor in stripes of hideous colors, this was consistent with his neighbor's doing the same; it was an exercise of his incidental jus utendi, and the mere circumstance that he did it out of unmixed malice was quite immaterial since it in no way infringed the liberty or invaded the property of the neighbor. But suppose we think of law not negatively as a system of hands off while individuals assert themselves freely, but positively as a social institution existing for social ends. Thinking thus, what claims or demands or wants of society are involved in such a controversy? There is an individual interest of substance on the part of each. Each asserts a claim to use, enjoy and get the benefit of the land of which the law recognizes him as the owner. Also the one asserts an individual interest of personality, a claim to exert his will and exercise his faculties freely and hence to employ them in such building operations upon his land as he thinks proper. What shall society say to these claims? If we think in terms of social interests and of giving effect to individual

[5] *Id.* at 196–198.

claims to the extent that they coincide with or may be identified with a social interest, we shall say that there is a social interest in the security of acquisitions, on which our economic order rests, and a social interest in the individual life. But that security of acquisitions is satisfied by use of property for the satisfaction of wants of the owner which are consistent with social life; or at least it is not seriously impaired by so limiting it in order to give effect to other wants which are consistent with social life. And the individual life, in which there is a social interest, is a moral and social life. Hence the social interest does not extend to exercise of individual faculties for anti-social purposes of gratifying malice. The moment we put the matter in terms of social life rather than of abstract individual will, we come to the result to which the law has been coming more and more of late throughout the world.

3 METHODS OF ACQUIRING PROPERTY

Both real and personal property can be acquired by transfer from the former owner to a new owner. This may be accomplished during the lifetime of the transferor by a sale, lease, or gift. A transfer may also be effected upon the death of the transferor, by reason of a properly executed and attested will. In the event an owner of property dies intestate, that is, without having a valid will which disposes of the property in question, the property is transferred to his heirs or next of kin according to the statute of descent and distribution of the appropriate state or states. Joint tenancy is sometimes used as a substitute for a will. Real property and, in many states, personal property which is co-owned by two or more persons in joint tenancy becomes the absolute property of the survivor of the owners. The foregoing methods will be discussed further in the three sections which follow.

Transfer of real and personal property can come about in a number of other ways. Judgment creditors may avail themselves of various procedures to obtain payment, such as garnishing the wages of the debtor, attaching his bank account, or levying execution on the nonexempt property of the debtor and having the sheriff sell it at a judicial sale and use the proceeds to pay the judgment debt. Similarly, the sheriff may sell real property for back taxes, the buyer getting a tax deed. Also, in the event of bankruptcy, the trustee in bankruptcy takes title to all of the nonexempt property in the bankrupt's estate for the purpose of using it to pay the expenses of bankruptcy and the creditors with provable claims, to the extent possible, in accordance with the Federal bankruptcy law.

One may involuntarily transfer property to another simply by failing to bring suit within the maximum time period allowed by the statute of limitations, thereby losing his right to recover possession of the property he claims as his. In such a case, the transferee is said to have acquired title by adverse possession. The possession must have been exclusive, open and notorious, adverse to the rights of the true owner, under claim of right or color of title, and continuous for the statutory period. The amount of time required varies somewhat from state to state, but in the case of land it is frequently twenty years. One may not obtain title by adverse possession of public lands owned by the state or the United States government.

In addition to the above, title to personal property may be acquired in a number of other ways. First, one may become the owner of personal property by original possession. For example, fish or wild animals belong to the one who captures them and reduces them to his possession and control. Property which was formerly owned by someone, but has been abandoned by him belongs to the first person to take possession of it again. By contrast, property which is misplaced or lost by its owner still belongs to him. However, as against everyone but him, the owner of the realty where the property was *misplaced* has the right to its possession as a general rule. And, ordinarily, the finder of *lost* property has the right to its possession against all but the true owner. These common-law principles can be and in some cases have been modified by statute. Whether any personal property one discovers has been abandoned, lost, or misplaced is a question of fact to be determined from all the circumstances, including exactly where it was found. It would be significant to know whether the property had been in a trash can, on a bench, or on the ground in reaching a conclusion. Of course, once this has been done, the rights of the finder in the property are determined.

One may add to personal property by his labor or by attaching other materials to it, or both. In such a case, it is generally held that the owner of the raw material or the larger unit of property becomes the owner of the whole by *accession*. "Fungible goods" are goods which are accounted for by weight or measure, such as grain or beer, rather than by individual unit, such as furniture or automobiles. The same kind of fungible goods of two or more persons may be mixed together for purposes such as storage. Then, by confusion, each of the former owners becomes a co-owner of an undivided fractional share in the whole mass, proportionate to the amount he contributed. When one wrongfully causes confusion of his property with that of another, the latter becomes the owner of the whole mass, unless the wrongdoer can clearly establish the amount which he added. Finally, title to personal property may be transferred to the owner of real estate to which it is permanently attached with the intent that it be so. The personal property by such attachment becomes a fixture and a part of the realty. Personal property may be physically attached to land and not become an actual part of it, however. The question of whether an attached item is a fixture or not is largely a question of intention of the one attaching it. The degree of physical attachment and whether the personal property is capable of being removed without substantial damage to the realty are factors which are considered in determining this intention. For example, when a contractor pours a concrete foundation for a building, it generally would become a part of the land and the property of the owner thereof. Machinery brought onto land for temporary use by one other than the owner of the land and attached merely by the force of gravity would most likely not become a fixture and would not be the property of the owner of the realty. Similarly, "trade fixtures," such as a soda fountain in a drugstore, usually do not become part of the land.

Because of the distinctive nature of real property, title to it can be acquired in several other ways than those previously mentioned. Many of the titles to land in this country were first obtained by *original entry* and patent from the United States government. Homesteaders acquired title in this fashion to a limited amount of acreage by complying with the requirements of the law. Also, when a river or stream by the slow and gradual process of cutting and filling adds deposits to land whose border is the river or stream, the owner generally obtains title to the land added by *accretion*. Finally, because the growth and development of society at large may vitally depend upon the right of government to obtain real property for public purposes such as highways, electric plants, schools, and the like, the state and Federal governments have the power to acquire land by condemnation, called the power of *eminent domain*. Whenever there is a taking by government of private property, both state and Federal constitutions require that fair and just compensation be given the former owner. This point was illustrated in *State Highway Department v. Branch* on page 571. The propriety of the condemnation of certain land may be challenged by the private owner of it on the ground that the intended purpose for the use of the land is not a public one.

4 THE CONTRACT AS A METHOD OF TRANSFERRING OR CREATING PROPERTY

As was indicated before, one of the methods of transferring both personal and real property is by a sale, which is the result of a contract between the buyer and the seller. Also, instead of transferring the ownership of property, the right to possession and use and enjoyment of it in a certain manner and for a certain time period may be created by a contract called a lease. Enforceable contractual promises may constitute property themselves. For example, in a contract of sale, the buyer's promise to pay is an account receivable of the seller, which is intangible personal property. Generally, such property may be sold and assigned by the creditor to a third party, who then obtains the right to payment of the debt.

The purpose of contract law is to provide the machinery whereby persons can create legal rights and impose legal duties on themselves by their own agreement. The whole force of organized society, exerted by the courts and the appropriate executive agencies, stands behind a valid contract, just as it does behind criminal and tort duties which are imposed on individuals by the law itself. Whenever a contract is breached, the injured party can obtain money damages equivalent to the economic loss which he can prove he suffered because of the breach. If the breach is serious enough, he may be permitted to rescind or cancel the contract. It would be grossly unjust to enforce the promise of the injured party in favor of the one guilty of the breach if the injured party did not obtain substantially what he had bargained for. In some circumstances, the remedy of an injured party may be a decree of specific performance, or order of a court of equity commanding the defendant actually to perform the bargain as he agreed. In this connection, see section 7, Chapter 2. It should be emphasized that one is not entitled to specific performance as a right but that the decision to grant this remedy lies within the discretion of the court of equity. Contracts for the sale of land, however, are usually specifically enforceable because each parcel of real estate is unique. Failure of a defendant to obey a decree of specific performance may result in his being held in contempt of court and fined or imprisoned or both.

A   OFFER AND ACCEPTANCE

The law prescribes certain requirements for a valid contract. First, there must be an agreement between the parties which is manifested by their words or conduct or a combination of both. In arriving at their mutual understanding, the parties may engage in bickering and in making preliminary suggestions or invitations to the other party to make an offer. When one of them makes a firm proposal which includes the major terms, that is, a promise of what he will do and what he demands from the other party in return, he is said to have made an offer, and is called the "offeror." The one to whom an offer is made is the "offeree," who acquires the legal power of acceptance. In other words, as long as the offer is open, the offeree can by his own act alone comply with the demands of the offeror and accept the offer in the manner requested, thereby creating a contract. If the offeror requests that the offeree actually perform in a certain manner in order to accept, the offer is said to be unilateral, and no contract results until the offeree has substantially performed. For example, a promise to pay $10 if the offeree mows the offeror's lawn would be unilateral. Neither the offeror nor the offeree in such a case is assured of the existence of a contract until the offeree has mowed substantially all of the lawn. Since the offer may be terminated before that happens, the disadvantages to unilateral offers are obvious. Frequently, the offeror would prefer to have the binding *agreement* of the other party to perform in a certain manner, and will request in his offer that the offeree simply promise to perform in a given manner. This is known as a bilateral offer, and requires that the offeree indicate his assent to its terms to create a contract. After he has accepted, the offeree is legally bound to perform as he has promised and the offeror is legally bound to perform as he has promised. In this case, there is an exchange of a promise for a promise.

Note, then, that it is not necessary for either of the parties to have actually performed in order to have a binding contract, but just that each undertakes to perform in a given manner in the future. The whole purpose of contract law is to make promises enforceable.

Besides stating the important terms and identifying the parties, a proposition must unequivocally indicate the intent to be contractually bound to those terms, if they are accepted, in order to be an offer. Clearly, any communication which falls short of these requirements creates no power of acceptance, and any attempted acceptance may in fact be an offer.

An offer cannot be accepted until the offeree obtains knowledge of it in the manner intended by the offeror. Even if a valid offer was created, it may terminate in a number of ways before an acceptance can become effective, which results in no contract. An offer will terminate upon the death or the insanity of either the offeror or offeree. Also, if the offer indicates the time period it is to remain open, it will automatically expire at the end of the time stated. Even if no period is mentioned, all offers terminate by lapse after a reasonable time has expired. It is a question of fact dependent upon all the circumstances as to what period of time is reasonable in each individual case. None of the foregoing methods of termination of an offer requires that any notice be given to the offeror.

An offer also expires if the offeree turns it down, by what is called rejection. A counteroffer amounts to a rejection by implication. If the offeree expressly indicates that he is still contemplating the offer, there is no implication of rejection by a counteroffer, however.

When the offeree repeats the terms in an attempted acceptance and changes one of them, either intentionally or by mistake, he makes a counteroffer and rejects the offer. An exception to this rule exists in the case of an offer to sell goods, wares, or merchandise. The Uniform Commercial Code provides that any attempted acceptance is an acceptance, even if it does appear to change the offer. The contract thereby formed is on the terms expressed in the original offer, except where the contract is between merchants and the change is a minor one. In this case, the change is incorporated into the contract, unless the offeror objects to it within a reasonable time after receiving the acceptance. A rejection is effective when the offeror learns of it.

Finally, an offer may be revoked by the offeror as long as he takes the necessary steps before an acceptance has become effective. This is true even if the offeror has previously indicated that the offer will be open longer. Such a promise is merely gratuitous and is not binding. Of course, an offeror can contract to keep the offer open for a given period in exchange for some consideration from the offeree. This is an option contract, and makes the offer irrevocable. Usually the consideration given is a sum of money. Here, too, the Code makes an exception if the offer involves a sale of goods, wares, or merchandise and is being made by a merchant. The merchant's written promise to keep his offer open is binding on him, without consideration being given to support it, for any period up to a maximum of three months. A revocation becomes effective as soon as the offeree learns of it, or learns of facts which imply it. It is also effective if written and placed where it would usually be available to the offeree, such as delivered to his residence, whether he reads it or not. Of course, offers, rejections, and revocations may all be communicated through the medium of the mails, by telegrams, by special messenger, or the like.

Like an offer, an acceptance must be unequivocal. It must show an intent to be bound by the terms stated in the offer. If there is more than one offer open, it must be clear which one is being accepted. Many of the legal problems involved in resolving the issue of whether there is an agreement between the parties or not boil down to determining *what various communications are* (that is, are they worded so as to be offers, rejections, or what?) and *when they become effective.* If an offer is in existence and it is accepted before it is terminated by one of the methods described above, there is a contract. Otherwise there is none. The case which follows concerns the time an acceptance becomes effective when the parties are communicating by mail.

Morrison v. Thoelke
155 So. 2d 889 (Fla. 1963)

The plaintiffs (appellees) owned certain land. On November 26, 1957, the defendants (appellants) mailed to the plaintiffs an executed contract for the purchase of the land. On November 27, 1957, the plaintiffs executed the contract also and mailed it to the defendants' attorney. After the contract was mailed, but before it was received, the plaintiffs called the defendants' attorney and repudiated the execution and the contract. However, the defendants caused the contract to be recorded. The plaintiffs then brought suit to quiet title, requesting that defendants be enjoined from making any claim for the sale of the land under the contract, arguing that their acceptance had been withdrawn before it had become legally effective. The defendants counterclaimed, seeking specific performance of the contract. The lower court entered summary judgment for the plaintiffs, and the defendants appealed.

ALLEN, ACTING CHIEF JUDGE: . . . Turning to the principal point raised in this appeal, we are confronted with a question apparently of first impression in this jurisdiction. The question is whether a contract is complete and binding when a letter of acceptance is mailed, thus barring repudiation prior to receipt. Appellants, of course, argue that posting the acceptance creates the contract; appellees contend that only receipt of the acceptance bars repudiation. . . .

As is abundantly clear from the quoted material excerpted from appellees' cases, the decision in each is predicated on an assumption, correct or incorrect, that the basis of the rule they reject was invalidated by changed postal regulations. The opinions cited by appellees each proceed on the theory that the "deposited acceptance" rule was based on a theory that the depositor lost control of his acceptance when it was deposited and that this fact rendered the acceptance complete upon deposit. To the extent that "loss of control" was the significant element in the "deposited acceptance" rule, the logic of appellees' cases is impeccable. On the other hand, if the rule is, in fact, not based on the "loss of control" element, the fact that this element has been altered may in no way affect the validity of the rule. Determination of the question presented in this appeal cannot then be had merely by adoption or rejection of the logic of appellees' cases. Rather, the source and justification of the "deposited acceptance" rule must be found and appellees' argument considered in light of this finding. Should the proffered justification for the rule be other than the "loss of control" theory, adoption or rejection of the rule must be based on considerations other than those relied upon in appellees' cases. . . .

The "meeting of the minds" justification advanced in *Adams v. Lindsell* is repeated in the first of two leading American cases on point. In *Mactier's Adm'rs v. Frith,* New York, 1830, 6 Wendell 103, 21 Am. Dec. 262, the offeree died while an acceptance was in the post. Since, if a "meeting of the minds" was essential to the contract, the contract could have been completed only during the offeree's lifetime, the court found it necessary to determine the effective date of acceptance. They deemed the posting of the assent sufficient and wrote:

All the authorities state a contract or an agreement (which is the same thing) to be aggregatio mentium. Why should not this meeting of the minds, which makes the contract, also indicate the moment when it becomes obligatory? I might rather ask, is it not and must it not be the moment when it does become obligatory? If the party making the offer is not bound until he knows of this meeting of minds, for the same reason the party accepting the offer ought not to be bound when his acceptance is received, because he does not know of the meeting of the minds, for the offer may have been withdrawn before his acceptance was received. If more than a concurrence of minds upon a distinct proposition is required to make an obligatory contract, the definition of what constitutes a contract is not correct. Instead of being the meeting of the minds of the contracting parties, it should be a knowledge of this meeting. It was said of the argument that if concurrence of minds alone would make a valid contract, one might be constructed out of mere volitions and uncommunicated wishes, I think such a result would not follow. The law does not regard bare volitions and pure mental abstractions. When it speaks of the operations of the mind, it means such as have been made manifest by overt acts; when it speaks of the meeting of minds, it refers to such a meeting as has been made known by proper acts, and when thus made known it is effective, although the parties who may claim the benefit of, or be bound by a contract thus made, may for a season remain ignorant of its being made.

However, the court went beyond this justification and proceeded to consider what facts constituted acceptance.

What shall constitute an acceptance will depend, in a great measure, upon circumstances. The mere determination of the mind, unacted on, can never be an acceptance. Where the offer is by letter, the usual mode of acceptance is the sending of a letter announcing a consent to accept; where it is made by messenger, a determination to accept returned through him, or sent by another, would seem to be all the law requires, if the contract may be consummated without writing. There are other modes which are equally conclusive upon the parties; keeping silence, under certain circumstances, is an assent to a proposition; anything that shall amount to a manifestation of a formed determination to accept, communicated or put in the proper way to be communicated to the party making the offer, would doubtless complete the contract; but a letter written would not be an acceptance so long as it remained in the possession of and under the control of the writer. *An acceptance is the distinct act of one party to the contract as much as the offer is of the other; the knowledge by the party making the offer, of the determination of the party receiving it, is not an ingredient of an acceptance. It is not compounded of an assent by one party to the terms offered, and a knowledge of that assent by the other.* [EMPHASIS ADDED]

Thus, the element of loss of control was introduced, not as a primary legal requisite to the existence of a contract but as a factual matter affecting the sufficiency of the manifestation of assent. . . .

The unjustified significance placed on the "loss of control" in the cases relied upon by appellee follows from two errors. The first error is failure to distinguish between relinquishment of control as a factual element of manifest intent, which it is, and as *the* legal predicate for completion of contract, which it is not. The second error lies in confusing the "right" to recall mail with the "power" to recall mail. Under current postal regulations, the sender has the "power" to regain a letter, but this does not necessarily give him the "right" to repudiate acceptance. The existence of the latter right is a matter of contract law and is determinable by reference to factors which include, but are not limited to, the existence of the power to recall mail. In short, the power to recall mail is a factor, among many others, which may be significant in determining when an acceptance is effective, but the right to effectively withdraw and repudiate an acceptance must be dependent upon the initial determination of when that acceptance is effective and irrevocable. . . .

The justification for the "deposited acceptance" rule proceeds from the uncontested premise of *Adams v. Lindsell* that there must be, both in practical and conceptual terms, a point in time when a contract is complete. In the formulation of contracts *inter praesentes* this point is readily reached upon expressions of assent instantaneously communicated. In the formation of contracts *inter absentes* by post, however, delay in communication prevents concurrent knowledge of assents and some point must be chosen as legally significant. . . .

In support of the rule proponents urge its sanction in tradition and practice. They argue that in the average case the offeree receives an offer and depositing an acceptance in the post, begins and should be allowed to begin reliance on the contract. They point out that the offeror has, after all, communicated his assent to the terms by extending the offer and has himself chosen the medium of communication. Depreciating the alleged risk to the offeror, proponents argue that having made an offer by post the offeror is seldom injured by a slight delay in knowing it was accepted, whereas the offeree, under any other rule, would have to await both the transmission of the acceptance and notification of its receipt before being able to rely on the contract he unequivocally accepted. Finally, proponents point out that the offeror can always expressly condition the contract on his receipt of an acceptance and, should he fail to do so, the law should not afford him this advantage.

Opponents of the rule argue as forcefully that all of the disadvantages of delay or loss in communication which would potentially harm the offeree are equally harmful to the offeror. Why, they ask, should the offeror be bound by an acceptance of which he has no knowledge? Arguing specific cases, opponents of the rule point to the inequity of forbidding the offeror to withdraw his offer after the acceptance was posted but before he had any knowledge that the offer was accepted; they argue that to forbid the offeree to withdraw his acceptance, as in the instant case, scant hours after it was posted but days before the offeror knew of it, is unjust and indefensible. Too, the opponents argue, the offeree can always prevent the revocation of an offer by providing consideration, by buying an option.

In short, both advocates and critics muster persuasive argument. As Corbin indicated, there must be a choice made, and such choice may, by the nature of things, seem unjust in some cases. Weighing the arguments with reference not to specific cases but toward a rule of general application and recognizing the general and traditional acceptance of the rule as well as the modern changes in effective long-distance communication, it would seem that the balance tips, whether heavily or near imperceptively, to continue adherence to the "Rule in *Adams v. Lindsell.*" This rule, although not entirely compatible with ordered, consistent and sometimes artificial principles of contract advanced by some theorists, is, in our view, in accord with the practical considerations and essential concepts of contract law. Outmoded precedents may, on occasion, be discarded and the function of justice should not be the perpetuation of error, but, by the same token, traditional rules and concepts should not be abandoned save on compelling ground. . . .

In the instant case, an unqualified offer was accepted and the acceptance made manifest. Later the offerees sought to repudiate their initial assent. Had there been a delay in their determination to repudiate permitting the letter to be delivered to appellant, no question as to the invalidity of the repudiation would have been entertained. As it were, the repudiation antedated receipt of the letter. However, adopting the view that the acceptance was effective when the letter of acceptance was deposited in the mails, the repudiation was equally invalid and cannot alone, support the summary decree for appellees.

The summary decree is reversed and the case remanded for further proceedings. [REVERSED AND REMANDED]

B   CONSIDERATION

Another prerequisite to the formation of a contract besides the agreement is that of consideration. Actually, consideration is not a separate element, but rather a minimum standard which the terms of the offer and acceptance must meet. From the terms it must appear that each party has incurred a detriment in exchange for the other party's doing so also. Thus, there are three aspects to the standard. The first is the concept of a *detriment.* A detriment consists of giving up a legal right *or* of promising to give up a legal right—of doing or promising to do something the promisor is not legally bound to do. Frequently the detriment to one of the parties benefits the other, but a third party who is not one of those entering into the contract may benefit from it, as in the case where a man takes out life insurance payable to his wife. Second is the requirement that the detriments incurred are exchanged for each other. This goes to the motivation of the parties. The reason that each has for giving up or promising to give up a part of his legal rights is to *bargain* for the other's detriment. This necessitates that there be a present exchange. The third aspect of consideration is sometimes called the requirement of *mutuality*. *Each* party, not just one of them, incurs a detriment or the terms of the agreement do not meet the minimum standard and are unenforceable. If both of the parties are not bound, then neither is. Thus, if one of the parties can cancel a purported contract at his unrestricted option, the other can ignore the agreement if he chooses.

After reaching an agreement, the parties sometimes decide to modify it later. Generally each must furnish new consideration for the modification to be binding. Otherwise there is no present exchange of detriments. The one who does increase his duties cannot be bargaining for the detriment of the other, since it has already been incurred. The Code, however, removes agreements to modify existing contracts for the sale of goods from the rule and makes them binding without the necessity of having new consideration. In cases other than a sale of goods, if each party gives up just *some* new legal right, no matter how insignificant, the modification is binding, since the value of consideration is not regarded as being important. This latter rule preserves freedom of contract by permitting the parties to weigh values themselves and preventing the courts from interfering and substituting their judgment for that of those entering into the contract. It makes the existence of contract duties much more predictable. In one situation, however, value does become important. To discharge a liquidated money debt by paying money, a debtor must pay in full. This is called the "lesser sum rule." Of course, the creditor can make a gift of the debt or its balance to the debtor, but a donative rather than a bargaining intent on his part must be demonstrated, and there must be constructive or symbolic delivery to the debtor. In settling an unliquidated claim, that is, one which is uncertain in amount, consideration is present even if the amount agreed upon by the parties later appears to be greater or lesser than the actual amount of the claim. A good example of an unliquidated debt is a claim which arises out of the commission of a tort. If the parties agree on a settlement out of court, consideration is present. Each is in reality giving up the right to sue and have the amount established by a judicial proceeding. In the following case, the offer was made by a check and the acceptance was the act of having it certified. The main issue concerns the application of the lesser-sum rule.

Nardine v. Kraft Cheese Co.
52 N.E.2d 634 (Ind. App. 1944)

FLANAGAN, JUDGE: For several years prior to August 24, 1941, the appellant, Lattie Nardine, a resident of Vincennes, Indiana, had operated a grocery in Lexington, Kentucky, under the name of Standard Market. During that time she had been an open account customer of appellee. In July 1941 she purchased from appellee 515¾ pounds of longhorn cheese. After a short time a dispute developed as to this cheese. Appellant said it was spoiled when received and that appellee should take it back. Appellee said that appellant spoiled it trying to force cure it and therefore it could not be returned. This dispute continued until after appellant closed her business on August 24, 1941.

Thereafter letters were exchanged between the parties concerning settlement of appellant's account, whereby it developed that there were other differences as to items in the account. About October 1, 1941, appellee's Lexington manager went to Vincennes to discuss the account with appellant but they were unable to agree as to the amount appellant owed. The dispute concerning the shipment of longhorn cheese above referred to was continued at that conference.

On October 30, 1941, appellant wrote appellee the following letter:

Enclosed please find check in the amount of One Hundred Forty Six Dollars and one cent ($146.01) which according to our records pays my account in full.

You will notice that I have taken a 10¢ per lb. deduction on the 515¾ lb. bad longhorn cheese, that I received from you. We are still at quite a loss on this cheese, as we really had to sacrifice it to get rid of it.

In regard to the balance on your statement of overcharges and deductions, I wish to advise that I find it impossible to check upon this as they are so old. I feel that if the deductions were not in order, that I should have been notified at the time they were taken from the checks. As you told me, these were left over from before the time you took over this account.

We are sorry to have had to make the above deductions, but I really feel that it is a just one. It has been a pleasure to do business with the Kraft Cheese Company at Lexington, and I want to thank you for all past favors.

With best regards to you, I remain.

Enclosed with the letter was a check for $146.01, marked, "This pays my account in full to date." After receiving the letter and check appellee mailed the check to the Vincennes bank on which it was drawn for certification. The bank certified the check and returned it to appellee who still retains it.

Thereafter appellee brought this action against appellant seeking to recover an account for the balance it claimed due after deducting the sum of $146.01. Appellant answered among other things that there had been an accord and satisfaction. Trial resulted in judgment for appellee to the sum of $87.88 and this appeal followed. The sufficiency of the evidence is properly challenged.

When the holder of a check has it certified by the bank on which it is drawn, the drawer is discharged and the debt becomes that of the bank. . . . If it was tendered in full payment of a claim which was unliquidated or concerning which a bona fide dispute existed, the acceptance of the check discharged the debt. . . .

Appellee says that there was no dispute because the trial court found that the longhorn cheese which appellant claims was spoiled when it arrived was in fact spoiled by appellant in trying to force cure it. The trial court could, and undoubtedly did, find that appellant spoiled the cheese. But in determining whether there was an accord and satisfaction we are not concerned with the question as to who was right and who was wrong in an existing dispute. We are concerned only with the question as to whether a good faith dispute existed at the time the check was tendered in full payment. The evidence on this question by both parties was all to the effect that such a dispute did exist.

It is true as appellee contends that the question of accord and satisfaction is ordinarily a question of fact, but where the controlling facts requisite to show accord and satisfaction are undisputed the question becomes one of law. . . .

Our conclusion is that the facts in this case show an accord and satisfaction of the claim sued upon. [JUDGMENT FOR APPELLANT (NARDINE)]

C VOIDABLE CONTRACTS

Even though the parties to a contract have arrived at an agreement and adequate consideration is present in the terms, one of them may be able to escape the duties he has undertaken because of special circumstances. Such a contract is called voidable because that party is given the right to rescind or disaffirm it. The party with this right can, if he chooses, enforce the contract. Among such contracts are those made by a minor. A minor lacks contractual capacity and can avoid by giving back what he has remaining of the consideration he received under the contract, if anything. The adult who contracts with a minor is bound, however. The minor must exercise his option to avoid within a reasonable time after he reaches the age of majority. In addition, one who is induced to contract by fraudulent misrepresentations of material fact made by another with the intent to deceive (or recklessly) is given a right to rescind provided he suffered damage as a result of relying on the misrepresentations. Fraud is also a tort, so the injured party may affirm the contract and recover money damages if he chooses. In the event he elects rescission, he must return everything he received or its equivalent (not just what he has left) as is the case with most types of voidable contracts other than minors' contracts. Unintentional misrepresentation has the same elements as fraud, except that the injured party does not have to establish that the misstatements involved were intentionally made. It also makes voidable a contract entered into with the guilty party in reliance on the misrepresentation. Duress, which involves the use of physical force or threats that reasonably cause fear to the injured party in order to obtain a contractual promise, is another ground for rescission. Duress, like fraud, is a tort. Generally if one of the parties enters into a contract under a misapprehension of material fact not due to misrepresentations by the other, he is bound anyway. In other words, normally unilateral mistake is no basis for disaffirming. However, bilateral or mutual mistake of material fact, where both of the parties to a contract have entered into it under a mistaken assumption, makes it voidable at the option of the one who is injured by the mistake.

D ILLEGAL CONTRACTS

An agreement which is illegal is void. Generally, the court will not enforce such an agreement for either of the parties. A contract may be illegal because its object is prohibited by statute, or is against the public policy of a statute or a public policy determined by judicial decision. Contracts in restraint of trade are, as a rule, illegal. However, under some circumstances, certain types of restraints are enforceable. The following case involves a restraint in a contract of employment under which the employer sought injunctive relief, arguing that the agreement in issue fell under the exception to the general rule. (Illegal contracts are discussed further in Chapter 19, section 3.)

Beltone Electronics Corp. v. Smith
194 N.E.2d 21 (Ill. App. 1963)

BURKE, PRESIDING JUSTICE: Victor G. Smith appeals from the order for a temporary injunction restraining him, a former employee, from disclosing or using at any time, any secret or confidential information or knowledge attained or acquired by him while employed by Beltone Electronics Corporation and from directly or indirectly performing at any time on or before February 1, 1964, any services for or continuing or accepting employment by or association in any capacity with Zenith Radio Corporation. The Chancellor rejected the recommendations of a Master in Chancery that the application for preliminary injunction be denied.

On May 13, 1957, defendant was hired by Beltone as chief industrial engineer. His initial task was to set up an industrial engineering department and assume responsibility for production control. At the time defendant ceased employment with Beltone he was manager of manufacturing. Smith's duties were largely administrative. He was not an inventor, designer or chemist. When Smith joined Beltone he signed an employment agreement with his employer which states that Smith, "shall not disclose or use at any time, either during or subsequent to his employment by Employer, any secret or confidential information or knowledge obtained or acquired by Employee while in Employer's employment; . . . that he will not, at any time within one (1) year subsequent to the termination of his employment with Employer, however occurring, directly or indirectly perform any service or be employed by, or become associated in any capacity with, any person, firm or corporation engaged in the manufacture or sale of hearing aids or hearing aid accessories or audiometers or be engaged on his own behalf in the manufacture or sale of any such products; . . . that for a violation by Employee of any of the covenants of this Agreement, Employer may have an injunction restraining Employee therefrom." The agreement was not limited as to its geographic scope.

The defendant, in the fall of 1961, began putting out "feelers," answering advertisements and mailing out resumes. He had interviews with Zenith Corporation in December 1962 and was employed by it on January 8, 1963. His position with Zenith Corporation was that of director of hearing aid production. Defendant left Beltone on February 1, 1963. Prior to his termination of employment with Beltone he was warned against taking employment with a competitor. He commenced to work for Zenith on February 18, 1963. An announcement of his retention by Zenith appeared in the Chicago press on February 26, 1963 and shortly thereafter the instant complaint was filed.

The 1931 case of *Parish v. Schwartz*, 344 Ill. 563, has spelled out the general Illinois rule with respect to enforcement of restrictive covenants in employment contracts. Where a covenant places restrictions upon a party not to engage in subsequent competitive employment or in a competitive line of trade, these restrictions must be reasonably related to safeguarding the employer without putting unreasonable restraints upon trade. An employee, after severing connections with his employer may compete with the former employer in his new position unless restricted by contract. While limitations may be placed upon an employee's freedom of action these limitations must conform to a test of reasonableness which will be stricter in the case of employment contracts.

The Restatement of Contracts, Secs. 313 to 315, 1932, states a test for the validity of post-employment restraints. Such restraining covenants are reasonable if (1) the restraint is no greater than that required for the protection of the employer, (2) they do not impose undue hardship on the employee, and (3) these are not injurious to the public. . . . It does not appear that the activities of the defendant while performing his duties for the plaintiff were such as to require a covenant which would prevent him from obtaining subsequent employment with a competitor for a period of 1 year. From the nature of Smith's work at Beltone and his non-technical position, the restraint upon his engaging in any other employment within 1 year would not be likely to produce corresponding benefits for the plaintiff. The covenant in prohibiting defendant's employment by anyone engaged in the manufacture or sale of hearing aids by anyone in any place goes farther than necessary to protect the plaintiff. Defendant by the covenant cannot be employed in a non-hearing aid capacity by firms employed in the manufacture or sale of other products as well as hearing aids. . . .

The case of *World Wide Pharmacal Dist. Co. v. Kolkey*, 5 Ill. App. 2d 201, relied upon by plaintiff, is not applicable to the facts at hand. The defendant there acquired an intimate knowledge of the methods and procedures used in the plaintiff's business, including the formula in the manufacture of a product. He also secretly organized a corporation and began distribution of the product. In the *Kolkey* case the former employee was engaged in unfair competition. The defendant in the case at bar had no such secret information nor was his conduct reprehensible. He was not using knowledge of any trade secret to benefit his new employer.

The business of plaintiff is highly competitive. The burden of business risks, inherent in its operation, however, cannot be allocated to the employee by placing such wide restrictions upon his right to future employment. . . . [ORDER REVERSED]

E THE STATUTE OF FRAUDS AND EXCUSES FOR BREACH OF CONTRACT

Although generally oral contracts are enforceable, the Statute of Frauds makes certain types of oral contracts unenforceable by either party unless and until sufficient written evidence of them is presented. No matter how many witnesses can be produced and no matter how convincing their testimony might be concerning the existence of these kinds of contracts, the court will not enforce them. The minimum evidence required by the law is a writing which sets forth the important terms of the agreement, identifies the parties to it, and is signed by the party whom one seeks to enforce the contract against. Although the types of contracts which must be evidenced by a writing differ from state to state, the various statutes almost universally include these four types: first, any contract to sell real estate or any interest in land; second, contracts by which one guarantees the payment of another person's debt and the guarantor does not stand to materially benefit from doing so (this provision does not include primary promises to pay money, but only secondary ones to pay if the principal debtor does not); third, contracts which cannot possibly be performed in accordance with their terms within a period of one year from the time they are made, except that if one of the parties has performed his part of the bargain fully, he can enforce the agreement against the other without written proof of it; and fourth, certain contracts for the sale of personal property which the Uniform Commercial Code controls. The Code provides for three different categories of sales of personal property which must be evidenced by a writing: contracts to sell tangible personal property (goods, wares and merchandise) where the value is $500 or over; contracts to sell investment securities (stocks and bonds) of any value; and contracts to sell intangible personal property other than investment securities (accounts receivable, notes, checks, patent rights, good will, and the like) where the value is $5,000 or over. The Code also provides certain exceptions to contracts which fall into the first two categories. First, if either the seller or buyer performs partially, he can enforce the agreement to the extent of his part performance. Also, if one of the parties admits the oral contract in his pleadings or testimony when being sued, he cannot use the Statute of Frauds as a defense. In addition, if the contract is between merchants, one of them can create enough evidence to enforce it by sending a written confirmation to the other, if the latter does not deny the oral agreement within ten days after he receives the confirmation. And finally, contracts to sell specially manufactured goods, which are not readily marketable in the ordinary course of the business of the seller, may be enforceable even if oral and for $500 or over.

If a party does not perform his contract he still may not have liability for a breach. While changing circumstances which merely result in additional hardship to one of the parties do not excuse him, those which make performance impossible do provide an excuse for not performing his contract obligations. For example, if a person who is contractually bound to perform personal services dies, his estate as well as the surviving contracting party are excused. Note here, however, that death does not have this effect in other types of contracts. The law may change and render an agreement impossible to enforce because its object has become illegal. Also, destruction of some subject matter without which the agreement cannot be performed furnishes an excuse. If a painter has contracted a paint a certain house, and that house burns down before he can perform, obviously impossibility exists. Some cases have excused a party from his contract where extreme hardship existed, but technically no true impossibility did. Such decisions probably provide an equitable result, but lend unpredictability to the law. For examples of two cases in which impossibility was an issue, see Section 5A, Chapter 6 starting on page 156. As is also noted there, the Uniform Commercial Code liberalizes the law in this area by excusing a seller of goods from his contract, if it has become "impracticable" to perform. He is required, however, to allocate existing supplies or production among his regular customers pro rata. The customers are not bound to accept only part of the goods their contract calls for, but are entitled to their share, if they want it.

F QUASI-CONTRACT

In some instances, the court will impose a duty on one party to pay for the reasonable value of a benefit he has received from another, in order to achieve justice, even though the parties do not have a contract. The duty imposed is very much like a contract debt and is said to arise out of quasi-contract. The case which follows discusses this remedy.

Anderson v. Copeland
378 P.2d 1007 (Okla. 1963)

PER CURIAM: This is an appeal from the District Court of Cotton County. The parties will be referred to in this Court as they appeared in the court below.

Plaintiff, Jack Copeland, doing business as Copeland Equipment Company, brought this action against defendant, Walter Anderson, to recover for the rental value of a tractor owned by plaintiff which was in defendant's possession for approximately two weeks.

The facts giving rise to this claim were for the most part undisputed. Defendant orally agreed to purchase a used tractor from plaintiff for the sum of $475.00. For eleven days thereafter defendant attempted to borrow money to cover the purchase price but was unable to, and so advised plaintiff. Plaintiff asked defendant to return the tractor, which was done within a few days. The only dispute appears to be in that defendant says the sale was conditioned on defendant's ability to borrow money to pay for it, while plaintiff says the sale was final and without conditions. In any event, both parties agree that the sale contract was rescinded when plaintiff asked that the tractor be returned.

The case was tried to a jury which returned a verdict for plaintiff in the amount of $50.00. Defendant's motion for new trial was overruled and he appeals.

It appears from the facts that the parties instead of attempting to enforce such rights as they may have had under the sale contract, rescinded it. The parties were then in the same position as before the agreement was made, except that defendant had had the use of plaintiff's tractor without paying for it. Under those circumstances the law would imply a contract for defendant would be unjustly enriched.

In the first paragraph of the syllabus in *Pigee v. Mercy Hosp.*, 199 Okla. 411, 186 P.2d 817, we held:

Contracts implied by law, or more properly quasi or constructive contracts, are a class of obligations which are imposed or created by law without regard to the assent of the party bound, on the ground that they are dictated by reason and justice, and may be enforced by an action ex contractu.

Defendant contends that there cannot exist at the same time an express contract and an implied contract between the same parties covering the same subject matter. This statement of law is not applicable in the instant case for the reason that the subject matter of the express contract was a sale, whereas the subject matter of the contract implied in law was a rental. The case of *Berry v. Barbour*, 279 P.2d 355 (Okla.), is somewhat similar. In that case a contractor was employed to make improvements and repairs of the owner's building. During the owner's absence in Europe, the roof of the building was partially destroyed by fire without the fault of the contractor who made necessary repairs of the fire damage, without knowledge of the owner. We held that a quasi contract arose obligating the owner to reimburse the contractor for the reasonable cost of material and labor furnished.

Defendant further contends that the trial court's instructions to the jury were erroneous. The instruction requested by defendant, however, covered contracts implied in fact. Such instruction was not applicable. In *First Nat'l Bank v. Matlock*, 99 Okl. 150, 226 P.328, 36 A.L.R. 1088, we distinguished between contracts implied in fact and contracts implied in law. In the former the intention of the parties is ascertained and enforced. We believe that the instruction to the jury in the instant case sufficiently covered the law to be applied to the facts. There was ample evidence in the case to support the verdict of the jury and the trial court's judgment rendered thereon. [AFFIRMED]

G THIRD PARTIES

When a person transfers property to another by a contract, the seller can only convey such title as he himself has, as a general rule. Thus, even a good-faith purchaser of goods from a thief obtains no title as against the true owner. Of course, if the owner reclaims such goods, the buyer has a remedy against the seller for breach of the seller's warranty that he had title. Also, one who buys real estate which has been mortgaged takes subject to the equity of the mortgagee, if the mortgage has been properly recorded at the office of the county recorder of deeds. In a similar way, the purchaser of goods or other items of personal property which are the collateral for a debt secured by a properly perfected security device may be subject to the lien of the secured party. But a good-faith purchaser of goods from one who has voidable title to them obtains good title. Suppose S is induced to sell goods on credit by B's fraudulent misrepresentations concerning B's ability to pay for them. S can rescind as against B and recover the goods. But, if B sells the goods to G, a good-faith purchaser, G can keep them free and clear of any claims of S.

Just as land and tangible personal property can be sold, so can intangible personal property, including contract rights themselves. When contract rights are transferred, the transferor is called an assignor and the transferee is called an assignee.

Generally even if the obligor objects, the assignment can be made anyway, and the obligor then becomes legally bound to perform for the assignee. Personal contract rights, however, such as those to the services of the obligor, cannot be assigned without his consent. Clearly, money debts are not personal and are usually assignable. The rights the assignee gets are those of the assignor—no better, no worse. In other words, if the obligor has any defense or right of set off which he can use against the assignor, he can also use it to escape or diminish liability to the assignee. For example, suppose D owes C $50 for goods which C delivered to D. If C assigns the right to payment to X, D must now pay X, unless he pays C in good faith before learning of the assignment. If the goods C delivered contained hidden defects and C breached his implied warranty that the goods were merchantable, D can rescind against C upon discovering the defects and will not have to pay C. Therefore, in this case X will not be able to collect from D either, even if X purchased the contract rights in good faith and had nothing whatever to do with the defects.

A different rule applies where the contract right transferred is commercial paper, or a negotiable instrument such as a promissory note, check or other draft, which meets the requirements of Article 3 of the Uniform Commercial Code. A holder in due course of such an instrument is not subject to the personal defenses the obligor may have against the original payee, and therefore actually may get better rights than his transferor had. A holder in due course, briefly, is one to whom the instrument has been properly negotiated (by delivery if bearer paper or by indorsement and delivery if order paper) and who has paid value for it in good faith before it has become overdue. Personal defenses frequently are those which are related to the consideration underlying a contract and would include such things as breach of contract, fraud in the inducement, and lack of consideration (as when a negotiable instrument is given as a gift). Assume that in the hypothetical given above D had given his $50 *check* to C, instead of just a simple contractual promise to pay in exchange for the goods, and C negotiated the check to X. If X qualifies as a holder in due course, he will have a legal right to recover the full amount of the check from D, free of D's defense, even if D stops payment on the check before it is cashed. D's defense is a personal one, and he is left with recourse against C only. Note that even a holder in due course of a draft or note cannot recover from the obligor who has a real defense, such as the fact that his signature was forged. The main object of these rules is to provide a special type of contract which can take the place of money, and will be, as nearly as possible, as acceptable to creditors as cash. Clearly, the ability of a contract to act as a medium of exchange like money depends upon its acceptability in commerce as such, and equally as clearly, the simple contract which carries with it all defenses would not be satisfactory to most creditors. A negotiable contract which is used in lieu of cash is needed for such purposes as convenience, safety, and to obtain credit. However, as was noted in Chapter 13, the Federal Trade Commission may abolish the holder-in-due-course concept insofar as it adversely affects consumers.

5 TRANSFER OF PROPERTY BY GIFT

One method of transferring property is by making a gift of it to another, which is a voluntary transfer without any consideration or compensation therefor. It should be noted that a *promise* to make a gift is not enforceable, since it lacks the necessary consideration. However, once a gift has been executed, it is final and cannot be revoked by the donor. In order to have a valid gift, three elements are essential. First, there must be an intention to give on the part of the donor (as contrasted with an intention to bargain, to lend or the like). Second, there must be an acceptance of the gift on the part of the donee. And, finally, there must be a delivery of the subject matter of the gift. Delivery may be conditional on the happening of an event, in which case, if the event does not occur, the gift is incomplete and the subject matter can be reclaimed by the donor. An engagement ring, for example, is given on the condition of marriage, and if the nuptials do not take place, the donor is entitled to recover the ring, perhaps to use it again later with better success. However, if the donor prevents the condition from occurring, as by standing up the bride at the church, he cannot reclaim the diamond (it being something in the nature of a consolation prize, in this instance). A gift of personal property causa mortis, or in anticipation of death where the apprehension of such is reasonably present, vests title in the donee immediately, subject to the condition subsequent that failure of the donor to die revokes the gift. Gifts without this condition are termed gifts "inter vivos."

Sometimes it is troublesome to find the requisite intent to give, since an alleged donor may have intended only to constitute the person to whom property was delivered as his agent or bailee. In resolving this issue, the court considers such things as the relationship between the parties, the value of the alleged gift in comparison with the donor's remaining property, the actions of the donor concerning the property after the gift is alleged to have been made, and the like. The weight of authority holds that if a gift is beneficial, acceptance of the gift will be presumed. If the gift is being made of goods which are capable of manual delivery, such as a book or watch, then manual delivery generally should take place. However, symbolic or constructive delivery may be made where the subject matter of the gift is incapable of manual delivery. It is generally held that a symbolic delivery is one where something is handed over in place of the actual thing itself, while a constructive delivery is the handing over of the means to gain possession or control of the thing, such as a key or a passbook. In order to be effective, delivery must completely divest the donor of dominion and control over the thing given. In one unusual case, it was held that a father effectively delivered a gift of buried treasure to his daughter, by taking her into the garden and pointing out the various places where it had been buried. In that case, the donor was extremely ill, and barely physically capable of even going into the garden and revealing the locations of the property being given.

6   TRANSFER OF PROPERTY UPON DEATH

One method of transferring property is by a validly executed will which takes effect at the death of the testator. Wills may include, besides a disposition of property, the naming of a personal representative to handle the estate, the designation of a guardian for minor children, or a revocation of former wills. A gift by will of personal property is called a bequest or legacy; a gift of realty is a devise.

Generally, a will is ambulatory during the lifetime of the testator and therefore can be revoked until he dies. A will usually must be in writing and signed by the testator or by some person in his presence and at his direction. In addition, it must be attested by two or more credible witnesses, who subscribe their names to the will. The testator must either sign or acknowledge the instrument as being his in the presence of the witnesses. Some states require that there be a minimum of three witnesses, although most states require only two.

Every person of the requisite age who is of sound mind and memory has the power to pass property by will. In most states the minimum age to execute a valid will is eighteen. This was true prior to the lowering of the age of majority for purposes of entering into binding contracts to eighteen. To have testamentary capacity, one does not have to be absolutely of sound mind and memory in every respect, but must at the time of executing the will have had sufficient mental capacity to comprehend and remember who are the natural objects of his bounty, to comprehend the kind and character of his property and the particular business in which he is engaged, and to make a disposition of his property according to some plan formed in his mind. He must have capacity, not actual knowledge of these matters. Old age, feeble health, or both, though combined with a defective memory, will not constitute lack of the testamentary capacity required to make a valid will. Mere eccentricity does not constitute unsoundness of mind.

When one dies without leaving a will, or intestate, in effect the state makes one for him. Every state has a statute of descent and distribution which provides rules for determining the manner in which a deceased person's property is to be distributed if he has not validly disposed of it himself by his will. In one state, for example, if a person dies with a surviving spouse and children, the spouse inherits one-third of both his real and personal property and the children inherit two-thirds. If he leaves just children surviving, they take all, and likewise if he is survived just by his spouse and no children, she takes all. In the latter eventuality, some states provide that the decedent's parents and brothers and sisters share with the spouse in some of his property. Statutes of descent and distribution provide further for a proper distribution under various fact situations, such as when a person dies without spouse, children or other decendants, brothers, sisters, parents, and so on. Finally, if no relatives qualify as heirs, the property escheats to the state.

Land or personal property held in the joint tenancy form of co-ownership passes to the surviving owner or owners upon the death of other joint tenants, and not to the deceased person's heirs. In contrast, property held by two or more persons in co-ownership as tenants in common passes upon the death of a co-owner according to either his will or to his heirs according to the statute of descent and distribution where he has no applicable will. In both of these forms of tenancy, each owner has an undivided interest in the whole. Many states by statute do not favor joint tenancies, and hold that they, with their attribute of right of survivorship, can be created only by language very clearly negating a tenancy in common. In such states, it is desirable to use the exact wording prescribed by the applicable statute if a joint tenancy is intended.

7 THE EXTENT OF RIGHTS OF OWNERSHIP

In the early common law, it was often indicated that the owner of land had rights that extended from the bowels of the earth up to the heavens. In this view, one who owned a square lot really had space in the form of an inverted pyramid with its tip at the center of the earth, and its base of infinite area somewhere beyond the galaxies. Of course, giving an owner absolute dominion of the air space, in theory, presented no particular practical problems in a time when airplane travel, let alone interplanetary space travel, was both impossible and unheard of. As technology has made air travel possible and even an economic necessity, the law has changed the property rights of the owner of land to the air space above it, cutting them back from the previous theoretical absolute rights to permit the ordinary and reasonable use of the air which does not unduly interfere with the use of his land by the owner.

As Dean Pound indicated on page 574, the twentieth century has brought about changes in the philosophy of the law of property from a viewpoint which seemed to protect the owner of property in doing whatever he pleased with it, regardless of the effect on others, to one limiting the rights of ownership where necessary to protect overriding social interests. The rights of owners are restricted in many instances, and similarly limited is the freedom of contract. As we have seen previously, the antitrust laws significantly limit what one may do with his property. So do tax laws and many labor laws. In addition, one's rights in his own property are limited by the rights others, who are not owners, may have in it. Sometimes these rights are created by statute, such as zoning ordinances which restrict the use of land. They may exist because of court decisions declaring certain uses of land to be private nuisances which unduly interfere with the use and enjoyment of neighboring lands by their owners. Rights of way across land may exist in favor of other persons. These are called easements. For example, a neighbor may have the right to use a private road across your land to get to his own. The telephone company may have an easement which permits it to string wires across land, in the air space of the owner, without being guilty of trespass. Similarly, sewer lines or pipe lines underneath land may be permissible because the owners thereof have an easement. Such rights may be conveyed by the grant of the owner of the land in which the easement exists. They may be taken from him involuntarily by exercise of the power of eminent domain. Easements may also be created by prescription, which is similar to obtaining title to property by adverse possession, simply by use of another's land in the required manner for the necessary statutory time period, which varies from state to state.

Besides being restricted in how his property can be used, an owner is in some instances limited as to how he can dispose of it. A classic example of this is the right which most states give a surviving spouse to renounce a will of his or her deceased spouse and take a certain minimum amount of the decedent's property. In one state, for example, a spouse is entitled to at least one-third of all property if there are also children surviving the decedent, or to one-half of all property if there are no children, regardless of the provisions in the decedent's will. There is no similar rule for the benefit of children or parents of a decedent. If they are "cut out" of his estate, their only hope is to contest the validity of the will and have a share of the property pass to them intestate under the statute of descent and distribution.

REVIEW QUESTIONS—CHAPTER 17

1 Define the following terms introduced in this chapter: bundle of rights; title; property; eminent domain; testate and intestate; offer and acceptance; consideration; joint tenancy; accession; rescission; statute of frauds; quasi-contract; holder in due course; easement.
2 Explain the difference between ownership of property and the mere right to possess it, and note the role that law plays in this distinction.
3 Give some examples of intangible property.
4 Under what circumstances does the government have the right to take private property?
5 List five methods of acquiring personal property and four methods of acquiring real property, and give an example of each.
6 What are the elements of a valid, enforceable contract?
7 What is the deposited acceptance rule, and what is its significance to the law of contracts?
8 Define consideration, and give three examples of situations in which consideration issues might be raised.
9 List four situations in which one party or the other may avoid a contract.
10 Under what circumstances are agreements not to compete legal?
11 Discuss the enforceability of oral contracts. Your discussion should include at least four examples of oral contracts which are unenforceable.
12 Compare the effect of a transfer of a simple contract and a transfer of a negotiable instrument insofar as defenses which may be used by obligors against transferees are concerned.
13 What are the elements of a valid gift?
14 What are the requirements for a valid will?

Chapter Eighteen

The Law of Torts

1 THE NATURE AND EXTENT OF TORT LITIGATION

A tort is a wrong other than a breach of contract committed against a person or his property for which the law gives a right to recover damages. It differs from a crime, which is a wrong against society, although the same act may be both a wrong against a person and against society, as for example, an assault.

Tort liability is predicated on the premises that in a civilized society one person will not intentionally injure another or his property, and that all persons will exercise reasonable care and caution in their activities. The first premise has resulted in a group of torts usually labeled intentional torts. These would include assault and battery, false imprisonment, libel, slander, trespass to real property, and conversion of personal property. The second premise has established the general field of tort liability known as negligence. The field of negligence is frequently further broken into degrees depending on the extent of carelessness involved and the extent of the duty owed. Each of these premises creates liability for wrongful conduct because of fault. Our legal system in effect says: "If you are at *fault* and cause injury to another or his property, you shall compensate him for his loss or damages with money."

Tort liability is imposed on masters for the torts of their agents or servants acting within the scope of their employment. This includes both intentional and unintentional torts but does not include torts committed by an agent or servant on a frolic of his own or while detoured from the scope of his employment. Employers are held liable for the torts of their employees primarily because of the "deep pocket" theory or simply because of the likelihood that the employer has more ability to pay for the wrong. Society therefore imposes tort liability on employers as a cost of doing business.

For many years tort claims have been the single largest source of civil litigation in this country. Most of these controversies have resulted from automobile collisions. In addition to automobile accident and other negligence cases, business is often a party to tort actions arising out of the sale of a product which has caused harm. Product liability suits involve injuries such as those resulting from deleterious food or defective drugs. While they have contractual aspects, such suits usually seek damages for injuries caused by the product. Therefore, product liability is discussed here as a part of the law of torts.

2   NEGLIGENCE SUITS

A person seeking damages for tort liability based upon negligence is usually required to establish that he was injured (1) without fault of his own (2) by conduct of the defendant which was the proximate cause of his injuries and (3) which was contrary to a duty owed to the injured party. This duty is usually expressed in terms of the degree of care and caution which the wrongdoer was bound to exercise for the other party by reason of the situation and their relationship. For example, an owner of property would owe a higher standard of care and caution to a business visitor than to a trespasser. Therefore, conduct which might be considered negligent to a business visitor might not be so to a trespasser. Negligence, then, is based on a violation of a duty owed which is the proximate cause of an injury to another.

The various degrees of negligence and the duties owed may be summarized and compared with other tort theories and duties as follows:

Theory of Fault	*Duty*	*Degree of Fault for Liability*
1. Slight negligence	To use extreme or high degree of care	Failure to use extreme or high degree of care
2. Ordinary negligence	To use ordinary care	Failure to use ordinary care
3. Willful and wanton misconduct	To use slight care	Actions with a conscious disregard for the safety of others (gross recklessness)
4. Intentional tort	Not to intentionally injure another	Actions with intent to harm
5. Strict liability	Not to injure	None

The following case has attracted nationwide attention as being at the extreme in imposing liability on a theory of fault. Note the remoteness of connection between the conduct and the injury, and the questionable foreseeability of risk on the part of the defendant. Could the defendant have reasonably been expected to prevent this injury?

Gallick v. Baltimore & Ohio R.R. Co.
372 U.S. 108 (1963)

Plaintiff sued his employer railroad under the Federal Employer's Liability Act alleging that the railroad was negligent in allowing a stagnant pool of water that attracted vermin and insects to remain on its property. Plaintiff was bitten by an insect. The bite became infected and plaintiff ultimately lost both of his legs. The jury found that the railroad was negligent and awarded plaintiff damages. The state appellate court reversed, holding that there was no liability as a matter of law and that there was insufficient evidence of negligence to submit the issue to the jury. The state Supreme Court declined to review the case, but the Supreme Court of the United States granted certiorari.

WHITE, JUSTICE: . . . The Court of Appeals . . . emphasized . . . that there was no "direct evidence that the existence of the unidentified bug at the time and place had any connection with the stagnant and infested pool," or had become infected by the pool with the substance that caused petitioner's infection, evidence which would negative the alternative possibility that the insect had emanated from "the nearly putrid mouth of the Cuyahoga River, or from weeds, or unsanitary places situated on property not owned or controlled by the railroad." The Court of Appeals therefore deemed the evidence merely "a series of guesses and speculations . . . too tenuous . . . a chain of causation . . . to support a conclusion of liability." "[W]e have a chain of possibilities that the negligence of the defendant might have shared in subjecting the plaintiff to damage and injury, but proof of a legal causal connection between the negligence and the damage falls short of that required for the consideration of a jury." Accordingly, it reversed the judgment of the Court of Common Pleas and entered final judgment for respondent.

I

We think that the Court of Appeals improperly invaded the function and province of the jury in this Federal Employers' Liability Act case. According to the Court of Appeals, the break in the causal chain that turned it into a mere "series of guesses and speculations" was the want of evidence from which the jury could properly conclude that respondent's fetid pool had had something to do with the insect that bit petitioner. The only question was whether or not the insect was from or had been attracted by the pool. We hold that the record shows sufficient evidence to warrant the jury's conclusion that petitioner's injuries were caused by the acts or omissions of respondent.

As the Court of Appeals stated, "insects were seen on, over and about this stagnant pool." According to petitioner's undisputed testimony, he stood near the pool for about a half a minute; then he started to walk away and was bitten on the leg after he took a few steps, perhaps one or two seconds later. Petitioner also testified, on cross-examination, that he had at times seen insects of about the same size as that which bit him crawling over the dead rats and pigeons in the stagnant pool. And on cross-examination by respondent two medical witnesses testified that stagnant, rat-infested pools breed and attract insects. Moreover, the jury specifically found that the pool accumulated and attracted bugs and vermin.

The Court of Appeals erred in demanding either "direct evidence that the existence of the unidentified bug at the time and place had any connection with the stagnant and infested pool" or else more substantial circumstantial evidence than that adduced here "that the pool created conditions and influences which helped to incubate or furnish an environment for the bug . . . or that the insect, having traveled from other areas, became contaminated or infected by the pool."

Under the ruling cases in this Court the evidence present was sufficient to raise an issue for the jury's determination as to whether the insect emanated from the pool. . . .

It is not the function of a court to search the record for conflicting circumstantial evidence in order to take the case away from the jury on a theory that the proof gives equal support in inconsistent and uncertain inferences. The focal point of judicial review is the reasonableness of the particular inference or conclusion drawn by the jury. It is the jury, not the court, which is the fact-finding body. It weighs the contradictory evidence and inferences, judges the credibility of witnesses, receives expert instructions and draws the ultimate conclusion as to the facts. The very essence of its function is to select from among conflicting inferences and conclusions that which it considers most reasonable. That conclusion, whether it relates to negligence, causation or any other factual matter, cannot be ignored. Courts are not free to reweigh the evidence and set aside the jury verdict merely because the jury could have drawn different inferences or conclusions or because judges feel that other results are more reasonable. . . .

Under this statute the test of a jury case is simply whether the proofs justify with reason the conclusion that employer negligence played any part . . . in producing the injury. . . . It does not matter that, from the evidence, the jury may also with reason, on grounds of probability, attribute the result to other causes. . . . Judicial appraisal of the proofs to determine whether a jury question is presented is narrowly limited to the single inquiry whether, with reason, the conclusion may be drawn that negligence of the employer played any part at all in the injury or death. Judges are to fix their sights primarily to make that appraisal and, if that test is met, are bound to find that a case for the jury is made out whether or not the evidence allows the jury a choice of other probabilities.

The facts before the jury fall within this standard and the Court of Appeals therefore erred in refusing to accept the jury's verdict.

II

Although we have concluded that the jury could properly find that there was a causal relationship between the railroad's negligence and petitioner's injuries, that does not end the case. Respondent makes the further argument that the judgment under review may be sustained on the alternative ground, not accepted by the Court of Appeals, that the injury was not reasonably foreseeable, and that therefore there was no negligence.

We agree with respondent that reasonable foreseeability of harm is an essential ingredient of Federal Employers' Liability Act negligence, but this requirement has been satisfied in the present case by the jury's findings . . . of negligence in maintaining the filthy pool of water. The jury had been instructed that negligence is the failure to observe that degree of care which people of ordinary prudence and sagacity would use under same or similar circumstances; and that defendant's duty was measured by what a reasonably prudent person would anticipate as resulting from a particular condition—"defendant's duties are measured by what is reasonably foreseeable under the circumstances"—by what "in the light of the facts then known, should or could reasonably have been anticipated." Thus when the jury found these facts: petitioner was bitten by an insect; the insect bite caused illness or disease and led to petitioner's present physical condition; the stagnant pool attracted bugs and vermin and was responsible for the insect bite and the injuries to petitioner; and respondent knew that the accumulation of the pool of water would attract bugs and vermin to the area—it is clear that the jury concluded that respondent should have realized the increased likelihood of an insect's biting petitioner while he was working in the vicinity of the pool. . . .

The Court of Appeals erred in depriving petitioner of the judgment entered upon the special verdict of the jury. The judgment of the Ohio Court of Appeals is reversed and the case is remanded for further proceedings not inconsistent with this opinion. [REVERSED]

HARLAN, JUSTICE, dissenting: Heartrending as the petitioner's accident has turned out to be, I think this case should not have been brought here. It involves no unsettled questions of federal law calling for decision by this Court, nor, in any acceptable sense, a departure by the state courts from legal principles already decided requiring this Court's intervention. The case thus does not qualify by review. . . . The case has necessarily required an inordinate amount of time, which the Court can ill afford in the present state of its docket.

Reaching the merits, however, I would affirm the judgment below. I cannot say that the view of the record taken by the state courts, in holding that the evidence on the issue of causation was insufficient to make a case for the jury, was an arbitrary or unreasonable one. The opinion of the Ohio Court of Appeals evinces a conscientious effort to follow this Court's decisions under the Federal Employers' Liability Act. . . . On this score the Court's reversal seems to me no more than an exercise in second-guessing the state court's estimate of the record.

From another standpoint this case does have significance. It affords a particularly dramatic example of the inadequacy of ordinary negligence law to meet the social obligations of modern industrial society. The cure for that, however, lies with the legislature and not with the courts.

3 PROBLEMS OF TORT LITIGATION

There are many problems inherent in our system of tort litigation and liability based on fault. First of all, the sheer number of automobiles and auto accidents has created congestion in the courts so that the trial may be several years after the occurrence. Witnessess die or move away or their memories lapse so that the testimony at the trial can hardly be described as accurate. Plaintiffs may tire of waiting because of the need for funds and may be forced to settle a case for less than their actual damages. For many other reasons, delayed justice is no justice at all. Justice requires easy and prompt access to courts which the congestion due to the large number of cases makes impossible.

Second, the nature of tort litigation has resulted in a contingent fee system for compensating attorneys. The contingent fee system means that the attorney is paid a percentage of the recovery or settlement. Usual contingent fees are 25 percent if the case is settled before trial, 33⅓ percent if a trial is held, and 40 to 50 percent if the case is appealed. Contingent fees eliminate the risk of high attorney's fees if the case is lost, but may create some undesirable side effects in many cases. For example, if the injuries are very substantial and liability is easily established, the fees of the attorney may be unfair and unreasonable. Assume a $240,000 verdict is given for the loss of two legs by a plaintiff. It is difficult to see how the $80,000 fee could have been earned. In addition, the chance of earning large fees has encouraged "ambulance chasing" of potentially big cases, especially in large cities. Referrals by doctors, ambulance drivers, undertakers, special investigators, and others who have direct contact with victims are not uncommon, although the organized bar has attempted to prevent these practices. As a direct result of contingent fees and congested courts, some lawyers have been advancing money to clients for current expenses. Such practices have tended to concentrate personal injury litigation in a relatively few lawyers or law firms. This has further added to court congestion and encouraged the lawyer to settle cases below the actual damage in order to get the client "off the payroll."

Another problem for society inherent in tort litigation is the cost of liability insurance. Personal injury verdicts have gone up substantially in recent years so that the cost of liability insurance has risen considerably and many insurance companies have become insolvent due to the number and extent of recoveries against their insureds. The cost of liability insurance has risen to the extent that many auto owners cannot realistically afford to pay the premiums.

The foregoing problems and others have resulted in proposals and suggestions to change many aspects of tort litigation. Some of these matters and proposed changes are discussed in the following article. Since its publication, the issues have become more acute and some states have taken remedial action, as will be discussed in the next section.

The Unreality of Accident Litigation: A Plea for a New Approach[1]
James Marshall

Recently the judges of the New York Supreme Court appeared before the City Planning Commission to appeal for more courthouse space because there were judges without chambers, special referees without hearing rooms and a library

---

[1] 50 *A.B.A.J.* 713 (Aug. 1964). Used by permission from the American Bar Association and the *American Bar Association Journal.*

spread into the corridors. What they failed to say was that a large part of the cases brought to trial and an even larger proportion of the cases on the docket are motor vehicle accident cases, which in this day and age should rarely be litigated. They are based on inaccurate testimony, antiquated concepts of liability and the distortion necessarily incident to the combat of litigation. If such cases were removed from the courts there would be smaller dockets, fewer cases tried, a need for fewer court clerks, judges and courthouse space. . . .

If a case comes to trial—and only a small proportion does—he [the injured victim] must "show either that the intention was unlawful or that the defendent was at fault; for if the injury was unavoidable and the conduct of the defendent was free from blame, he will not be liable." This judicial opinion written in 1850 defines the essence of the "fault liability" principle that still governs most personal injury litigation in today's courts. One further condition is that the plaintiff himself must be blameless. The question of fault is generally decided by a jury after several witnesses testify. Out of the conflicting stories they are to determine what did happen.

Are the trial procedures and theory of fault liability derived from pre-automotive centuries appropriate to our age and culture?

A recent report on automobile accidents compiled for the World Health Organization suggests that it may not be humanly possible to determine what happened, for the average "development time" of an automobile accident is estimated at "probably less than ten seconds." Furthermore, as this report (J. D. Norman, *Road Traffic Accidents*) says, "Road accidents do not usually have a single 'cause'," and "each individual accident is likely to have several causative factors. . . . The search for single causes of accidents is therefore likely to prove unproductive." Who can fairly say, then, that the preponderance of evidence supports a finding that one person or one factor caused the accident? Yet the search continues in our courts to find who was at fault during those crucial ten seconds. . . .

[S]cience has been able to show us . . . that the observations which are the essence of eye-witness and earwitness testimony are so conditioned by the witness himself as to have little probative value. . . . Variations in the accuracy of residual observations such as those of distance and motion we know to be great. Yet these are precisely the observations for which we generally rely upon eyewitness testimony in an automobile accident case.

[A] motor vehicle accident . . . is . . . in the course of litigation refracted indefinitely through the lenses of experience by the witness, by his hearers—judge and jury—and by the jurors deliberating among themselves. We may never know what happened during those ten seconds in which the accident occurred, and we may from his testimony learn more about the witness than about what he witnessed. Litigation, despite the proclaimed purpose of the law, is not a quest for truth, but rather a bitter contest in which winner takes all, and this very process further distorts the report of an objective situation such as an accident.

These refractions continue during the later stages of recollection and articulation, as well as during the initial perception and interpretation. In the course of recollection, inevitable distortions occur and the great lapse of time in many jurisdictions between the incident and the trial tends to increase this. The selectivity of recall becomes more pronounced with time and with "taking sides." We know that there is a "curve of forgetting" that is scoop-shaped, like the track of a ski jump. Both the rapidity of the initial drop and the rate of the subsequent gradual decline depend upon the conditions under which the observation was made, the intensity with which it was "learned," and the emotional context. Most observations that make no new demands on the observer will be readily forgotten. More of what is "overlearned," that is, learned with intensity, will be retained for a short while, but after that the curve of forgetting becomes almost a vertical line as the "overlearned" is almost entirely forgotten. This is exemplified by the efforts of a student cramming for examinations. The next morning he may remember enought to pass the course, but a week later he remembers little or nothing of what he overlearned.

Experiments have also shown that shock, fright or pain may enhance the vividness of recollection and its duration, but will reduce its accuracy. These emotional effects are usually in play during a traumatic experience like an automobile accident.

Acknowledging that memory may be imperfect, the law permits "refreshment" of the witness's recollection. . . .

We refer here to the refreshment that takes place inside the courtroom, although we cannot ignore the likelihood that at least as much refreshing goes on outside it. One report noted that "The distinction between coaching witnesses and preparing a case for trial is unfortunately too fine to be universally observed." But our concern, and the problem for the jury, is how to test "the vagaries of sound and honest minds." In the words of a veteran courtroom observer, "The great body of testimony is subjectively accurate, but objectively false."

When a witness is on the stand he inevitably tends to identify his interest with that of the party for whom he is testifying. Adversary proceedings intensify this identification. If the witness's side wins, he shares in society's endorsement; if his side loses, he too is rejected. When "his side" wins, the witness gets a sense of satisfaction, he feels rewarded, it was worth while for him to have testified. As Dr. William A. White observed long ago, "An unprejudiced individual does not exist."

This identification will work hand in glove with past experience to suggest to the witness ways in which to fill the gaps in his recollection. If a witness is not certain whether or not he heard the siren as he saw the fire engine racing down the street, he may "bet" on the basis of what he has learned through experience with sirens and engines that he did in fact hear it. He will not necessarily do this consciously, with intention to deceive. He simply may not want to appear to be a liar or be made to seem foolish on cross-examination. But it is precisely these departures from the norm, such as failure to sound a siren or horn, that may connote legal fault and are at the heart of a negligence case.

The vagaries of recollection are further modified by those of articulation. The use of words creates ambiguities. It creates a compulsion for the narrator to fill in gaps and obscures the varying degrees of certainty with which facts are recalled.

As Hutchins and Slesinger pointed out, when a witness reports that "It was raining and I wore my rubbers," we do not know whether he recalls both of these facts or infers one from the other or has inferred both from a third recollection such as the fact that he was carrying his umbrella. Language has been described as a rigidifying process creating "slippage between the abstraction as it functions in behavior and the abstraction as it is named."

"There is a basic tendency to treat whatever is perceived as both concrete and absolute despite its abstract and nonabsolute nature." Not only does the use of language obscure gradations of clarity, but the continued retelling will eliminate any uncertainty the narrator may have had. When he has repeated his story a number of times, as witnesses do before and during a trial, he becomes increasingly committed to it, more certain of its correctness and, perhaps, more anxious that he may contradict himself.

Beyond the unreliability of evidence and the unsuitability of the fault principle in accident cases, a further defect in the present system is lack of speed and consistency in the results, attributed by many to our reliance on the jury. As former Presiding Justice David W. Peck of New York wrote, "Jury trials in civil cases are only a matter of habit and history—ours is the only country in the world which any longer attempts to handle civil litigation within the jury frame, and coincidentally it is the only country which has court delay. . . ."

In Western Europe trial by jury is provided only in criminal cases, and in Great Britain it is specified in civil cases only when fraud, defamation or other nonphysical injury is alleged. The high esteem for trial by jury in our country again stems from the fact that our Constitution was framed at precisely that point in the development of English law when reliance on the jury was at its apex. Blackstone, the basic text of American law students for more than a century, praised the right to a jury trial as "the most transcendent privilege which any subject can enjoy" and viewed such a trial as "the best criterion for investigating the truth of facts that was ever established in any country."

At that time the jury in England was being strengthened as a bar to the corruption of judges and, even more so, to the subversion of the law by the monarchy. That was just one step in the evolution of the English legal tradition, one point in time out of a thousand years. Because it also happened to be the point at which we grafted onto our form of government many of the devices that symbolized anti-authoritarianism in England, these devices have become ends in themselves and are often viewed as above criticism. Thus while in England, from which it came, the civil jury trial has been greatly modified, we have continued to regard it as essential, as an essential right which may be waived by both litigants but which they cannot be forced to forgo.

From the mangled and contradictory accounts of witnesses the jury must make two decisions: (1) Was the defendant liable? and (2) If so, what damages should the plaintiff get? The first question is defined in terms of fault, as it was defined in England in the eighteenth century. This element of our Puritan heritage was intended to have a punitive effect on the wrongdoer and thus a deterrent effect on others. Its punitive function is illuminated by the rule of contributory negligence that excuses the defendant from liability if the plaintiff too was at fault to any extent. There is evidence, however, that in many cases contributory negligence is not viewed by the jury as a bar to recovery but as an element to be balanced in determining the amount of damages.

Although the liability issue is punitive, the damages to be awarded are compensatory, scaled to the plaintiff's injuries rather than to the degree of wrong done by the defendant. "The rule of damages is a practical instrumentality for the administration of justice," a Massachusetts court wrote in 1908 in deciding a suit brought against the Old Colony Street Railway Company. "The principle on which it is founded is compensation. Its object is to afford the equivalent in money for the actual loss caused by the wrong of another."

Yet in 1958 it could be said that "As recently as a decade ago there was no well-developed law of damages for personal injuries." Appellate courts are reluctant to overturn jury verdicts unless the award, according to the rule stated by Chancellor Kent in 1812 and still applied today, "be so excessive as to strike mankind, at first blush, as being beyond all measure unreasonable and outrageous, and as such, manifestly show the jury to have been actuated by passion, partiality, prejudice, or corruption." Beyond this, the jury has free rein.

Damages for the same injury will vary greatly. They will vary according to the person injured, as is appropriate in terms of his income, lost earning power and life expectancy. But they will also vary with the personality and skill of his attorney, with the size and wealth of the community in which the suit is brought and even sometimes with the season of the year.

Juries are asked to calculate awards in terms of such tangibles as lost wages, loss of anticipated earning power and the cost of medical services. They are also allowed to place a price tag on the plaintiff's pain and suffering caused by the injury so that he may be "made whole again," fully compensated in dollars for the financial and other impacts of the injury. In general, the larger the total award, the larger will be the percentage awarded for pain and suffering. Such factors give considerable rein to the attitudes of jurors and, by the very variances in the awards they make possible for similar injuries, necessarily result in injustice. We also know that juries, although they are not supposed to, often include in their award the fees for the attorney and taxes on the award—even though such awards are not taxable. There is no way to assure observance of the law by juries, or even consistent evasion of the legal principles. . . .

The likelihood that the defendant is insured also helps to increase the sum awarded. Jurors will be freer with the funds of an insurance company than with those of an individual, even though they will eventually pay in higher premiums for their generosity. There is no safeguard against this assumption and its impact for it has been found that telling the jury not to consider insurance serves only to emphasize that consideration.

In a few states automobile liability insurance is compulsory; in many others it is voluntary but extremely widespread. Most states have other mechanisms to maximize the likelihood that the motor vehicle owner will be a solvent defendant, so it is not unreasonable for juries to assume that the damages will be paid. In many states evidence is not permitted as to whether the defendant is insured—although it is permissible to question prospective jurors about whether they or members of their families are employed by an insurance company—and with the increasing incidence of insurance, juries have felt free to return substantial awards against defendants of modest income.

The prevalence of insurance has also affected the punitive function of liability, bringing us one step farther from the punitive concept and closer to the compensatory. Not only does the plaintiff often benefit from the jury's sympathy regardless of fault, but the defendant is scarcely punished when the judgment awarded against him is paid out of the pocket of his insurance company. He may ultimately have to pay a higher premium, but by then the chastisement has been greatly mitigated.

Studies have shown that juries may proportion their award to the degree of defendant's negligence as well as to the extent of plaintiff's injuries. Even if the jury disobeys instructions and does increase the damages to penalize a flagrantly negligent defendant, the insured defendant rarely feels the lash. On the other hand, if defendant's negligence is slight and it appears that the plaintiff too has contributed to causing the injury, the jury will still find the defendant at fault if the plaintiff has been injured seriously and they feel he should be compensated. So insurance has minimized the effectiveness of the theory of fault liability. . . .

Since we know that the rules of evidence with regard to eyewitness testimony are based on psychologically false assumptions, that the legal process is abused through the hostile adversary proceedings of the trial in which victory rather than discovering the truth is the object, that such abuses cannot fail to diminish general respect for the law and that damages rarely punish the wrongdoer or adequately compensate the victim, we may conclude that the courtroom is not the proper place for providing "justice" for the victims of millions of automobile accidents each year.

Even now, only a fraction of all personal injury suits are actually disposed of in the courtroom. It has been extrapolated from recent court records that in New York City only 77,000 of the 193,000 claims even reached the courts. The rest were either abandoned or settled during preliminary negotiations. Of the 77,000 only 7,000 went to trial and only 2,500 all the way to verdict. Thus jury awards were made in 3.4 per cent of all those personal injury cases, usually many years after the accident.

Perhaps we are not at a level of political sophistication that will permit us to question whether a civil jury trial, especially one that is conducted according to defective rules of evidence and liability, and ineffective rules of damages, is in fact serving the social goal that we call "justice." In recent years some judges have begun this scrutiny. The late Judge Jerome Frank of the Court of Appeals for the Second Circuit was one of the most outspoken critics of this system, and Judge Charles Clark of the same bench observed more recently that "The jury is too fine, as well as too clumsy and expensive an instrument . . .. it just isn't the correct way to achieve sound policy for the victims of this industrial age and our modern civilization."

The pressures against change are considerable. Beyond the sheer weight of tradition there would also be opposition from attorneys, insurance companies, political appointees to the courts, and those who appoint them and other beneficiaries of the present system. But in recognition of the defects of this system, its delays, inequities and costliness, some enlightened legislatures have begun to explore alternatives.

Foremost among these is the possibility of a compensation plan analogous to some of those already in effect elsewhere and to the workmen's compensation programs now in effect in every state of the Union. Such a plan would eliminate the requirement that the victim prove fault, it would eliminate belated trials to hear unreliable evidence and it would more explicitly and consistently reflect the consensus of the community that the victim of an automobile accident should be compensated to the extent of his injuries. . . .

The virtues of a compensation plan for automobile accident injuries should encourage us to try to work out some financial guidelines. Such accidents, like the motor vehicle itself, have become part of everyday life. . . . Whether we be drivers, riders in automobiles or buses, or pedestrians, there is not one of us in the United States today who is not a possible victim of an automotive accident. It is a more universal risk than an industrial accident or an impecunious old age. It is a risk that concerns us all throughout our lives.

Several halfway measures have also been suggested, such as enacting compulsory accident and liability insurance, abandoning the doctrine of contributory negligence as a bar to recovery, eliminating the jury from such cases or having automobile accident cases argued before an administrative board rather than in the courtroom. But these do not go to the heart of the matter, which is that the automobile is a necessity and the automobile accident an inevitability, that such accidents cannot be accurately witnessed and testified to and often that they are not the "fault" of anyone. Furthermore, this contentious litigation based on necessarily inaccurate, though not necessarily perjured, evidence demeans the judicial process. Few of those injured are promptly and adequately compensated; and finally, the more circuitous the devices for transferring payment to the injured, the higher the total cost to the entire public will be. A plan addressed to these considerations would not necessarily reduce the number of automobile accidents, but it would unburden the courts, elevate the law and do greater "justice" for the thousands of victims of our machine age. . . .

4   THE TREND TOWARD NO-FAULT

The 1970s saw the beginning of a trend toward "no-fault" systems for handling automobile accident cases. The first no-fault law was enacted in Massachusetts, and it became effective January 1, 1971. At least four other states also enacted no-fault in 1971, and Congress as of this writing is also considering Federal legislation in this area. While each of the state laws differs substantially from the others, they have similar approaches to correct the injustices and inadequacies of the fault system in auto accident cases.

No-fault systems, as the descriptive term implies, provide for the compensation of accident victims irrespective of fault. Under them, the victim is compensated for his damages as a result of his *contract* with his insurance company rather than on a tort theory. Auto accident insurance for cases covered by no-fault laws operates in a manner similar to medical insurance. Just as one's hospitalization plan pays hospital expenses irrespective of the cause of the illness or injury, so also does the auto insurance policy pay its benefits, irrespective of cause or responsibility.

While there are numerous approaches to no-fault, most of those plans enacted or suggested to date provide for:

1 Recovery for out-of-pocket medical expenses and lost earnings up to a stated maximum.
2 Little or no payments for pain and suffering.
3 The retention of common-law negligence actions in serious cases such as death, serious disfigurement, and permanent disability.
4 Periodic payments for out-of-pocket costs rather than lump-sum payments.
5 Payments only to the extent that other insurance does not cover the loss.

A primary goal of no-fault laws is to reduce the cost of automobile insurance. Cost savings are present because of the elimination or reduction of investigative costs and attorney's fees. Many lawyers have been and are opposed to these systems. Their opposition in part is probably based on their economic effect on trial lawyers. Savings will also come from the reduced payments for pain and suffering under most plans and from the elimination of duplicate payments for medical expenses. Under most plans, if the medical bills were paid by some other insurance, the auto insurer would not be required to pay.

The Supreme Court of Massachusetts has had occasion to review the constitutionality of its no-fault law. In the test case, portions of which are presented below, the American Trial Lawyers Association and the Massachusetts Bar Association filed amicus curiae (friend of the court) briefs challenging the constitutionality of the law. The case illustrates much of the background and the typical approach to no-fault laws.

Pinnick v. Cleary
271 N.E.2d 592 (Mass. 1971)

The plaintiff was injured in an auto accident. He had coverage under the Massachusetts no-fault plan called c. 670 in this opinion. The auto accident was exclusively the fault of the defendant. Plaintiff was covered by another hospitalization policy and was paid sick leave by his employer. At common law, plaintiff would have recovered $1,565, including $800 for pain and suffering, $650 for lost wages, and $115 medical expense. The defendant denied liability, contending that the plaintiff was required to collect his damages up to $2,000 from his own insurance company under the Massachusetts statute. If he had done so, he would have recovered only $100 because of his sick leave pay and recovery under the hospitalization policy. Plaintiff argued that the Massachusetts no-fault insurance law was unconstitutional.

REARDON, JUSTICE: . . .

Summary of Chapter 670

. . . [W]e believe it advisable to summarize the basic structure of the statute. . . . We wish . . . at this juncture to draw attention first to the difference in the legal position of the injured party under c. 670 from his position at common law, and, secondly, to the practical consequences of the statute on him, taking into consideration the interaction of various forms of compulsory and optional insurance with c. 670.

Those who challenge c. 670 have attributed to it not only a drastic stripping of legal rights but also, in its practical effect, a substantial diminution of the damages which the average non-negligent accident victim may reasonably expect. Analysis demonstrates, on the contrary, that the Legislature has acted with extreme caution in altering prior legal rights, changing in only one respect the elements of damage which are recoverable by the victim. As to the practical effect of c. 670, it appears that the statute affords the citizen the security of prompt and certain recovery to a fixed amount of the most salient elements of his out-of-pocket expenses and an increased flexibility in avoiding duplicate coverage, at double premiums, for the same expenses. In return for this he surrenders the possibly minimal damages for pain and suffering recoverable in cases not marked by serious economic loss or objective indicia of grave injury and the outside chance that through a generous settlement or a liberal award by a judge or jury in such a case he may be able to reap a monetary windfall out of his misfortune.

The key concept embodied in c. 670 is that of personal injury protection insurance, which is required of all owners of motor vehicles registered in Massachusetts. Under this coverage, personal injury protection benefits are paid by the insurer, as the expenses they cover accrue, to the insured, members of his household, authorized operators or passengers of his motor vehicle including guest occupants, and any pedestrians struck by him, regardless of fault in the causation of the accident. Limited in amount to $2,000, the benefits cover largely the same items of medical expense covered before by optional medical payments insurance. . . . Personal injury protection covers in addition . . . seventy-five percent of the actual lost wages of the injured party, calculated on the basis of his average weekly wage during the year preceding the accident. If the victim was unemployed, he is entitled to the same percentage of wages he can prove he would have received from work he would have had had he not been injured.

Benefits allocable to medical expenses are paid regardless of any other insurance covering the same costs. However, to avoid duplicate recovery and reduce the expense of insurance, c. 670 provides the option to elect a deductible, binding on the insured or on the members of the insured's household. These policies, for a reduced premium, provide that an amount from the first $250 up to the entire $2,000 otherwise recoverable as personal injury protection benefits shall not be paid by the insurer.

Benefits allocable to lost wages, on the other hand, are reduced by any amounts received under a wage continuation plan or its equivalent. . . .

Thus under c. 670 the accident victim, with a few minor exceptions, is entitled to immediate payment of his most pressing items of cost: medical expenses. In addition, he receives the major portion of his lost wages not covered by a wage continuation plan, and certain consequential expenses. These amounts, to a total of $2,000, are due from his own insurer, not from an adversary insurance company, and without the necessity for assignment of fault or the temptation on either side to bargain in the light of considerations which are often extraneous to the amount of expense incurred.

In exchange for the protection extended by c. 670, the accident victim loses his right to recover in tort to the extent he is eligible for personal injury protection benefits. Because the exemption of the tortfeasor is exactly matched to the availability of personal injury protection benefits to the plaintiff, the plaintiff loses nothing by it. With one restriction to be discussed below, the potential plaintiff retains in addition his common law action against the tortfeasor for any elements of damage not recovered as personal injury protection benefits. These would include any expenses in excess of $2,000 which would otherwise have been covered by personal injury protection and the difference between his diminished earning capacity, as measured at common law, and the substitute percentage of actual lost wages reduced by amounts received under any wage continuation plan recoverable under c. 670. Since the new law has retained the previous requirements of compulsory liability insurance under G.L. c. 90, § 34A, the victim who chooses to sue has the same assurance of at least limited recovery if he can prove negligence as he had before the passage of c. 670.

The plaintiff stresses that the residual tort action left after the payment of personal injury protection benefits is reduced in value inasmuch as the potential plaintiff must consider the extent to which legal fees will reduce his net recovery. However, legal fees are not a new burden imposed by c. 670; they have long been a factor to be considered in prosecuting any claim, including a tort action for personal injury instituted before the passage of c. 670.

The only limitation imposed by c. 670 on the potential plaintiff's prior right of recovery at common law is the elimination of damages for "pain and suffering, including mental suffering associated with . . . injury" except in certain specified categories of cases. Section 5 of c. 670 provides generally that the reasonable and necessary medical expenses incurred by a plaintiff in the treatment of his injuries must be over $500 to permit recovery for pain and suffering. However, recognizing that certain types of injuries could entail considerable pain and suffering which would warrant monetary compensation regardless of medical expense incurred, the Legislature provided by way of exception to the general rule that damages for pain and suffering could be sought in all cases involving five designated types of injuries. These are a fracture, injury causing death, injury consisting in whole or in part of loss of a body member, permanent and serious disfigurement, and injury resulting in loss of sight or hearing as elsewhere defind in the General Laws. The victim whose injury falls outside these categories and whose medical expenses are less than $500 cannot recover at all for pain and suffering. However, it is still possible for the person who desires to assure for himself recovery in excess of his out-of-pocket costs to do so. Just as he may elect a deductible if he has medical payments insurance to avoid duplicate recovery for medical expenses, so he may choose to keep both forms of insurance in full precisely to allow himself double recovery of these expenses. Other forms of duplicate coverage are equally possible. It is true that the amount of excess he will receive thereby will bear no necessary relation to the value of his pain and suffering as arbitrarily set by a jury but, on the other hand, he is assured of some profit over out-of-pocket expenses in every motor vehicle accident. This certainty he was never afforded by his prior "right" to recovery for pain and suffering in a suitable case, which in order to be realized even in such a case had to be actively pursued at considerable expense. . . .

Due Process Issues

A. Applicable Principles   We will deal first with the propriety of c. 670 under the due process clause. The overall test under this clause is whether the statute bears a reasonable relation to a permissible legislative objective. . . .

In the instant case, . . . , the Legislature has not attempted to abolish the preexisting right of tort recovery and leave the automobile accident victim without redress. On the contrary, . . . , the statute has affected his substantive rights of recovery only in one respect and has simply altered his method of enforcing them in all others.

. . . We will, therefore, consider c. 670 in the light of a twofold test: the general test required by the due process clause of whether it bears a rational relation to a legitimate legislative objective, and the more particularized test for which the plaintiff argues—whether it provides a reasonable substitute for preexisting rights.

B. Does C. 670 Bear a Rational Relation to a Legitimate Legislative Objective?   The ills against which c. 670 is aimed are obvious. One of the most prominent of these will be found in a brief consideration of the impact of the automobile on the burden of litigation carried by courts in general and Massachusetts courts in particular. No one who has for any time been in charge of a trial court system . . . can be unfamiliar with the devastating effect upon the administration of justice which the automobile has produced. For years, in the face of countless experiments, the trial calendars of this country, particularly in metropolitan areas, have become increasingly clogged with motor vehicle tort litigation. No one as yet, notwithstanding heroic efforts in this regard, has found a satisfactory method of disentangling this morass. Indeed, the problem intensifies as American courts are increasingly called upon to deal with complexities of our society not evident when the motor vehicle first appeared on the national scene and to broaden the scope of their activities into areas not traditionally subject to judicial cognizance. The courts with their scarce resource of time simply cannot respond to new challenges or meet the new requirements imposed on them in criminal matters as long as their time continues to be consumed to the extent it has been by motor vehicle accident cases. The problems of society to which the courts have been called no longer permit the luxury of using them as a forum for resolving the ever increasing numbers of automobile accident claims to the extent that has obtained hitherto.

. . . The seriousness of the problem in so far as it relates to current Massachusetts civil trial dockets can be seen in the following figures related to the Superior Court.

Total Law Entries	of which there were	Total Motor Vehicle Entries
1967 34,730		23,279
1968 33,558		22,289
1969 34,381		22,598
1970 35,155		22,690

When it is recognized that many of these automobile entries represent multiple party suits, the weight which this type of litigation places on Massachusetts courts is evident.

Less obvious is the burden on the clerks' offices, lawyers and litigants which follows this proliferation of entries of motor cases, currently at the rate of almost 2,000 a month in the Superior Court and more than 3,200 a month in the District Courts. Every paper submitted must be filed and docketed, and each entry prompts an avalanche of them. In addition to the writ, declaration, answer and appearance slips; interrogatories by parties on both sides, applications to nonsuit or default for failure to answer interrogatories, motions to extend time for answering or to remove nonsuit or default for not answering interrogatories, motions to strike answers to interrogatories and to answer over or further, motions for specifications, and demands to admit facts are only a few of the papers that follow as of course in almost every motor tort case entered. Court personnel are additionally burdened by the need to give notice to counsel or parties of every order of the court entered during these lengthy pre-trial proceedings. The time of the court consumed in this preliminary war of nerves between counsel, or between claimant and insurer, is almost impossible to estimate, but probably far exceeds that spent in the trial of the small percentage of all entries which must be tried.

Both in the pre-trial and later stages, claims for small amounts possess, of course, the same capability of clogging the judicial system as their larger brothers. . . .

Other non-American court systems, heirs with ourselves of the common law, have managed to solve this problem of the superabundance of motor vehicle tort claims in one way or another. It remains, however, a cancer to be rooted out in

American courts. Presumably the Legislature had this in mind. Chapter 670, in providing for limited recovery without the necessity for adversary proceedings in automobile accident cases, was an appropriate step to alleviate this problem which defied more conservative solutions.

Nor was court congestion the only problem at which c. 670 might have been aimed. The high cost of automobile insurance in Massachusetts was a present fact of which the Legislature did not need to be reminded. It might have suspected that there was a correlation between this high cost and the inefficiencies and administrative expense involved in running the traditional system, contributed to heavily by the prevalence of . . . elaborate pre-trial proceedings. . . . That any such suspicion would have been well founded was confirmed by a report of the United States Department of Transportation released in March of this year entitled, "Motor Vehicle Crash Losses and their Compensation in the United States; a Report to the Congress and the President." The report concluded on this subject that "[t]he automobile accident tort liability insurance system would appear to possess the highly dubious distinction of having probably the highest cost/benefit ratio of any major compensation system currently in operation in this country. As has been shown, for every dollar of net benefits that it provides to victims, it consumes about a dollar." P. 95.

Finally, and not to be discounted among the evils associated with automobiles which c. 670 might have been designed to cure, are the inequities which have been visited upon claimants. In this regard the Legislature might have felt, as expressed in the Department of Transportation Report, that "[t]he present tort liability reparations system allocates benefits very unevenly among the limited number of victims that it purports to serve." P. 94. The Legislature was also presumably aware of the long delays in getting financial aid to the injured person, confronted with medical and subsistence bills during a period of no employment for him and want for his family. The time spent in investigation, the time required for proof of negligence, the exaggerated claims, the all too common suspicion of perjured testimony, the horse and buggy approach to a twentieth century dilemma—all of this might well have influenced the Legislature, recognizing the right and need of all accident victims to simple and speedy justice, toward reform.

It cannot be seriously argued that it was beyond legislative competence to assess this situation and to effect the necessary statutory repair. What we have discussed are evils which it was within the province of the Legislature to consider and which it endeavored to correct or eliminate. We do not intimate that the legislative determination which is c. 670 was the only answer or solution to the problem, but it cannot be successfully maintained that its salient provisions, as outlined above, are not a rational approach to the solution of these patent inefficiencies and inequities.

[The court then held that the law provided a reasonable substitution for prior rights, did not violate due process on any other ground, and did not violate the equal protection clause of the Constitution. In its discussion of these issues, it found that the criteria under which pain and suffering would be recoverable were not arbitrary and unreasonable. Minor claims for pain and suffering could be eliminated.]

So ordered. [THE STATUTE IS CONSTITUTIONAL]

Other states such as Illinois have attempted to eliminate fault as a basis of recovery with a variety of approaches. For example, some have higher thresholds before the traditional tort lawsuit may be brought, and others have different methods for computing the amount to be paid for pain and suffering. The Illinois Supreme Court held the first Illinois law to be unconstitutional as a denial of equal protection to poor people and the unemployed. The suit challenging the Illinois version was brought by lawyers who contended that the amounts paid to poor people under the Illinois plan would be substantially less because of its provisions for benefits based on the amount of actual expenses incurred by claimants and because payment was also based on lost earnings.

The decade of the seventies will see attempts to enact no-fault plans in most states and perhaps even at the Federal level. It can be expected that there will be a great deal of litigation on the constitutionality and legality of such laws. It will probably take many years before any uniformity develops in the new approaches to the compensation of automobile accident victims. Notwithstanding the Illinois decision, it seems apparent that the fault system is on the way out and that ultimately a new system for compensating auto accident victims will emerge. The basic weaknesses in the fault system are so substantial and so compelling of change that change is inevitable.

5 PRODUCT LIABILITY

There is a substantial body of rules of law concerning product liability. These rules of law vary a great deal from state to state. Liability for injury caused by a product may be based on a theory of negligence or it may be contractual in nature arising from : (1) a breach of an express warranty about the goods, (2) a breach of an implied warranty that the goods are of merchantable quality (reasonably fit for their ordinary and intended purpose), or (3) a breach of an implied warranty of fitness for a particular purpose. The theories predicated upon breach of warranty have a statutory basis in the Uniform Commercial Code. Such cases were originally tortious in nature but today are often considered to be based on breach of contract because the statutes authorizing the suits are a part of the contract law of sales.

Cases concerning product liability involve retailers as well as manufacturers, packers, or growers of products. Liability may be imposed without fault in the traditional tort sense because of the contract theories. For example, a grocer who sells a can of beans containing cockroaches is not negligent because he has no reasonable way of ascertaining the contents of the can which he sells. Yet he has liability for the defect because he breaches his implied warranty that the goods are of merchantable quality. This product liability arises from contract. Questions immediately arise as to whether or not a person other than the one purchasing the product can sue for injuries and whether or not suit can be brought against a party by one who has no contract with him. For example, is it legally permissible for a member of the purchaser's family to sue the retailer who sold the defective goods which caused him injury or for the purchaser at retail of such goods to sue the manufacturer? These problems involve "privity of contract" and whether or not "privity" is required.

The trend is toward strict liability for injuries caused by products which are sold by a businessman in the ordinary course of business, regardless of whether he was at fault or negligent, and regardless of whether the injured party who is suing was a party to the contract of sale. Privity of contract as a requirement has been largely eliminated not only in cases of injury but also in cases of mere economic loss. The decision which follows is typical of modern cases on liability of manufacturers and sellers for defects in their goods. Note that this court did not like the term "strict liability" because of its confusion with "absolute liability."

Cova v. Harley Davidson Motor Company
182 N.W.2d 800 (Mich. 1971)

Plaintiffs purchased golf carts, which had been manufactured by the defendant, from a dealer. Plaintiffs sued the defendant alleging that the carts were defective and that this constituted a breach of an implied warranty of quality. The lower court dismissed the complaint because of lack of privity of contract and plaintiffs appealed.

LEVIN, JUDGE: . . . Although the Michigan Supreme Court has not in so many words declared that a consumer may recover from a manufacturer for breach of implied warranty without proving negligence and without regard to privity even in a case where the product is not inherently dangerous and no personal injuries have been suffered, the loss being entirely economic, we are persuaded from our review of the . . . decisions of our Supreme Court and from the trend of authorities in other jurisdictions that a consumer can sue a manufacturer directly for economic loss resulting from a defect in a product attributable to the manufacturer without proving negligence. . . .

On principle the manufacturer should be required to stand behind his defectively-manufactured product and held to be accountable to the end user even though the product caused neither accident nor personal injury. The remote seller should not be insulated from direct liability where he has merely mulcted the consumer.

This does not mean that the liability of the manufacturer is a liability without fault. . . . [O]ne who sues a manufacturer "must prove a defect attributable to the manufacturer and causal connection between that defect and the injury or damage of which he complains."

It has been suggested that the time has come further to define the nature of the liability of the manufacturer, to decide whether it is a "strict liability," and to decide to what extent it arises under and is affected by the warranty provisions in the sale of goods section of the uniform commercial code. In the judicial development of the consumer's direct remedy against the manufacturer, several dozen legal theories were coalesced in justification and rationalization of the results which the courts reached. Some of these concepts have been enacted into statutes, such as . . . the uniform commercial code. But, as the UCC draftsmen acknowledged, the remedy is not statutory, but essentially one fashioned by the courts.

The American Law Institute's partial restatement of the consumer's tort remedy and the recodification of his warranty remedy in the uniform commercial code record salient features of the common law as it had evolved through the dates that the restatement and code drafters did their work. These formulations, however, no more mark the boundaries of the consumer's remedy than did the earlier effort at codification, the uniform sales act.

The suggestion that we now label the manufacturer's liability a "strict liability" does not strike us as particularly sound or useful. . . . This term . . . appears to have been used in . . . judicial opinions . . . to convey the following concepts:

1 The manufacturer's liability does not depend on proof of negligence; it is the same kind of liability as arises from a breach of warranty, express or implied, or a false representation, express or implied.
2 Although traceable conceptually to warranty as well as tort, this liability, imposed by law, is a tort liability, not dependent on the existence of a contract or contract principles and, thus, it arises independently of the uniform sales act and the uniform commercial code.
3 While it is not necessary to prove negligence, the manufacturer is not absolutely liable. He is liable only if the product is defective. And, even if it is defective, in some cases he still may not be liable, *e.g.*, experimental drugs and other unavoidably unsafe products, the marketing of which does not imply they are free of defect.

If that is what the term "strict liability" means then it would appear that under Michigan law, as laid down by our Supreme Court, the manufacturer's liability is a strict liability or something akin to it. . . . [T]he manufacturer's liability arises by implication of law and is not limited by the uniform commercial code, and negligence need not be proved, only a defect attributable to the manufacturer causally related to the plaintiff's damage.

While the Michigan development has paralleled, even preceded, the development in other jurisdictions, we see no need to join the parade of States which have adopted the new terminology of "strict liability." To the new generation of lawyers, trained in the new jargon, the meaning of the term "strict liability" may be clear: "a rose by any other name," etc. But for many of the rest of us the concept of a strict liability carries overtones of its former rubric, "absolute" liability.

The manufacturer's liability, although arising even if he has exercised due care, is not the same liability absolutely or strictly imposed on persons who keep dangerous animals or who engage in abnormally dangerous activity.

If we adopt the "strict liability" terminology, lawyers who find it to their clients' advantage can be expected to urge upon us the analogies of the absolute (strict) nonproduct liability cases as being necessarily more pertinent than alternative sources of precedent and reasoning. There is a significant risk that the relabeling of the manufacturer's liability as a "strict liability" may result in the casual adoption of the absolute (strict) liability precedents developed in cases dealing with dangerous animals and abnormally dangerous activities without careful analysis of whether they are truly apposite. Nothing but further confusion is achieved by using the same label to describe both the liability of a manufacturer to a consumer and of a person who harbors dangerous animals or engages in abnormally dangerous activity.

Moreover, it is apparent from *Seely v. White Motor Company* (1965), 63 Cal.2d 9, 45 Cal.Rptr. 17, 403 P.2d 145, that it was either oversimplification, exaggeration, or simply misleading to say, as had the same Court in *Greenman,* that the manufacturer's liability to the consumer is a strict liability.

The fact is that no term is likely to be devised that will accurately communicate all the relevant concepts. This entire field of law, which developed through adaptation and analogy to the law of torts and contracts, has been plagued by the labels of these analogies and their appurtenant historical impeditions. Indeed, it might be helpful if we abandoned the continued use in this context of our present and misleading terminology of warranty and representation, express and implied, and strict liability in tort, and simply refer to the manufacturer's liability by the neutral term "product liability." We would thereby acknowledge that the consumer's remedy is an amalgam of all those concepts and of others as well; but also that it is something sufficiently dissimilar to any of these concepts so that emphasis on either the tort or contract origin is misleading and confusing.

The "product liability" of the manufacturer, and the corresponding right of the consumer, is simply the liability which in this developing jurisprudence the law imposes on a manufacturer in favor of a consumer for loss suffered by reason of a defective product attributable to that manufacturer. Elimination of the old terminology would permit this field of law to develop sensibly without continuing allegiance to warranty or tort concepts, whether the question presented is one of pleading, procedure, products and defects covered, disclaimers, abnormal use or misuse by the consumer, other defenses, kinds and measure of damages or some other substantive issue.

The need to eliminate the old terminology becomes apparent upon examination of the cases, not only in Michigan, but in other jurisdictions as well. Recovery has been allowed on a number of different theories against manufacturers for economic loss caused by defective products. Many of these cases could be limited and distinguished if we look too closely at the legal theories advanced by the courts instead of at the facts and the results which were reached. When we look at the facts and the results we find that courts throughout the land have allowed recovery for economic loss, . . . in cases similar to the present case.

In some of these cases the defect caused an accident resulting in the economic loss. Manufacturers have also been held subject to liability in cases where there was no accident and the product was simply in disrepair, deteriorated, or aesthetically defective. [REVERSED AND REMANDED FOR TRIAL]

6 BUSINESS TORTS

In recent years, several torts have arisen or grown in importance which may be classified under the heading "business torts." Such wrongful conduct as interfering with a business relationship, invading one's right of privacy, or violating a statute such as the Sherman Antitrust Act comes under this general category. The right of a victim of a violation of the Antitrust laws to collect treble damages was discussed in Chapters 10 to 12. Similar statutes may create liability for wrongful business conduct in other areas. For example, tort liability may be imposed and damages awarded a person denied equal privileges in using public accommodations under the Civil Rights Act of 1964.

Cases involving other kinds of torts, such as trespass or conversion of property, are common, and the legal principles involved are usually not considered to be complex. However, cases concerned with the invasion of the right of privacy or interference with a contract present complex questions of policy which require a balancing of conflicting objectives. The case which follows is typical of those which arise in this area of business torts.

Herron v. State Farm Mut. Ins. Co.
363 P.2d 310 (Cal. 1961)

GIBSON, JUSTICE: Plaintiffs' attorneys at law brought this action against Mr. and Mrs. Donald Halverson for breach of contract and against State Farm Mutual Insurance Company and its agent, Anthony Caruso, for intentional interference with contractual relations. The Halversons were not served, and a demurrer of State Farm and Caruso (who will be referred to as defendants) was sustained without leave to amend. Plaintiffs have appealed from the ensuing judgment.

The following is a summary of plaintiffs' allegations: The Halversons entered into a contingent fee contract with plaintiffs concerning claims reasonably worth $60,000 for personal injuries sustained in an automobile accident caused by the negligence of a person insured by State Farm. Plaintiffs were to advance all expenses necessary for the preparation of the case and for court costs and were to receive one-third of the amount of the recovery remaining after deduction of the costs. No settlement was to be made without the consent of plaintiffs and the Halversons, and in the event there was no recovery plaintiffs were to receive nothing for their services or for costs advanced. Plaintiffs notified defendants of the agreement immediately after its execution, and they proceeded to hire private investigators, photographers, and a draftsman, make an investigation, and incur expenses in the amount of $1,250. Defendants, by telling the Halversons that they did not need an attorney and that a satisfactory settlement would be made, induced them to breach the contingent fee contract and to discharge plaintiffs and deprive them of the benefits of the contract and the expenses incurred for investigation and preparation. Defendants assisted the Halversons in preparing letters which informed plaintiffs of their dismissal. The conduct of defendants was maliciously designed to injure plaintiffs' rights and lawful business, and it violated the rules of the National Conference Committee on Adjusters of which State Farm or its agents are members. The rules provide, in part, that an insurance company will not deal directly with any claimant represented by an attorney without the consent of the attorney and will not advise the claimant to refrain from seeking legal advice or retaining counsel to protect his interest. As a result of the conduct of defendants, plaintiffs suffered the loss of the expenses incurred in investigation and preparation and did not receive their one-third contingent fee.

Plaintiffs prayed for judgment against defendants for $20,000 or one-third of the judgment or settlement recovered by the Halversons, whichever is the lesser, and, in addition, for $25,000 punitive damages.

An action will lie for the intentional interference by a third person with a contractual relationship either by unlawful means or by means otherwise lawful when there is a lack of sufficient justification. . . . There is no valid reason why this rule should not be applied to an attorney's contingent fee contract. Such an agreement is a legal and valid contract entitled to the protection of the law, and an attorney who is wrongfully discharged is generally entitled to the same amount of compensation as if he had completed the contemplated services. . . . While a client is permitted to discharge his attorney without cause, this is allowed not because the attorney's interest in performing his services and obtaining his fee is unworthy of protection but because of the importance of the client's interest in the successful prosecution of his cause of action. . . . An attorney's interest in his contingent fee agreement is greater than that of a party to a contract terminable at will, as to which it has been held that an intentional and unjustifiable interference is actionable. . . .

Whether an intentional interference by a third party is justifiable depends upon a balancing of the importance, social and private, of the objective advanced by the interference against the importance of the interest interfered with, considering all circumstances including the nature of the actor's conduct and the relationship between the parties. . . . Justification is an affirmative defense and may not be considered as supporting the trial court's action in sustaining a demurrer unless it appears on the face of the complaint. . . . The only allegation relied upon by defendants as showing justification is that State Farm had issued an automobile public liability insurance policy to the person whose negligence caused the injuries to the Halversons. In our opinion this allegation does not establish justification.

The conduct of an insurance company in inducing an injured person to repudiate his contract with an attorney may be detrimental not only to the interests of the attorney but also to the interests of the client since, as we have seen, the client, in addition to being deprived of the aid and advice of his attorney, may also be liable for the full contract fee. Defendants argue that the policy of the law is to encourage settlement, that an insurance company has a legal duty to effect a settlement of a claim against its insured in an appropriate case . . . and that furtherance of the actor's own economic interests will justify an intentional interference with a contractual relationship in some circumstances where his interests are threatened by the contract. However, these considerations standing alone cannot justify inducing the Halversons to repudiate the contract to deprive plaintiffs of its benefits. So far as appears from the complaint, no cause for the dismissal of plaintiffs existed, no efforts were made to negotiate with them, and there is no indication that State Farm could not have protected its interests and obtained a satisfactory settlement without interfering with the contract. [JUDGMENT REVERSED WITH DIRECTIONS TO OVERRULE THE DEMURRER]

REVIEW QUESTIONS—CHAPTER 18

1 Define the following terms introduced in this chapter: tort; product liability; willful and wanton misconduct; contingent fee; ambulance chasing; amicus curiae; privity of contract; breach of warranty; the warranty of merchantable quality; strict liability.

2 List five torts and give an example of each.

3 Define negligence, and discuss the various degrees of negligence which may be involved in given occurrences.

4 List five factors which have prompted many persons to advocate the elimination of the fault system in automobile accident cases. Give an example of each.

5 Discuss the correlation between personal injury litigation problems and insurance costs.

6 How are the damages which a plaintiff in a personal injury case is entitled to recover computed?

7 What reasons are given by those who object to any change in the fault system of automobile accident compensation?

8 What is the basic approach of most no-fault proposals?

9 List three theories under which a manufacturer or seller of personal property may have liability to one injured by the product.

10 To what extent has the privity-of-contract requirement been eliminated in product liability cases?

11 Give three examples of business torts.

Chapter Nineteen

Protection of Consumers and Debtors

1 THE LAW AND CONSUMERS: INTRODUCTION

"Consumerism," the term used to describe activities of government designed to protect consumers, is not a recent development. The increase in emphasis on consumerism in recent years has given the appearance that the philosophy of government protection of consumers from certain business practices is a modern development. But there are many examples of such governmental activity which have been a part of our law for many years, some of which have been previously discussed in this text. For example, the Federal Trade Commission Act of 1914 authorized the regulation of unfair and deceptive business practices. The Securities Acts of the 1930s were paternalistic in character and were designed to protect the investing public. The law relating to warranties in the sale of goods, which is a major aspect of consumerism, has developed over many years and was noted in Chapter 18.

There are several additional statutes and common-law principles which aid consumers and debtors in their business transactions. Among ones which date back to the early consumer law are those relating to bankruptcy, fraud, and usury. This chapter will further discuss some of these legal protections given debtors and consumers.

It must not be overlooked that the late 1960s and early 1970s have seen a substantial increase in consumer protection legislation.

During this period both the Federal and state governments have enacted several laws designed to protect the consumer, and especially the consumer on credit, from various business practices. For example, at the Federal level the National Traffic and Motor Vehicle Safety Act and the Highway Safety Act were passed to improve the safety of automobiles, roads, and tires. The Department of Transportation was delegated the responsibility for implementing the safety standards. Typical of the results of these laws are the current seat belt and head rest requirements for new automobiles. These laws have been responsible in part for higher prices of automobiles as well as improved safety standards.

Under the Federal Fair Packaging and Labeling Act, better known as the Truth-in-Packaging Act, the Federal Trade Commission and the Food and Drug Administration establish standards for packages and for the information and identification which they must contain. This law is designed to protect consumers from unknowingly paying more for a packaged product than it is worth or from buying something other than intended. It authorizes the FTC to regulate such items as "cents off" claims and to control "slack filled" packages. The Truth-in-Packaging law encourages industry-wide standards for packaging.

A similar law is the Wholesale Meat Act of 1967, which strengthened and modernized the Federal standards on meat inspection.

The Consumer Credit Protection Act contains one part popularly known as the Truth-in-Lending Act, which is discussed more fully in section 7. Another new important Federal law is the Fair Credit Reporting Act, which is discussed in section 8.

As was noted in Chapter 14, the President in 1971, for a variety of reasons including the desire to protect consumers, imposed wage and price controls as authorized by the Economic Stabilization Act of 1970. In particular, persons with fixed income, such as the aged and retired, had been adversely affected by runaway inflation. The Price Commission appointed by the President adopted policies designed to hold the nationwide average increases in the price of goods, services, and rent to a rate of no more than 2.5 percent per year. (Of course some could be above that rate and others below.) The base price to which this test was applied for any product or service was the higher of the prices permitted to be charged for the product or service during an initial period of freeze (August 16, 1971–November 13, 1971) or the freeze base price as adjusted under Price Commission regulations.

Exemptions from price controls provided by the Cost of Living Council have included raw agricultural and seafood products, damaged or used products, tuition charged by public and nonprofit schools, sales of securities, commercial paper and commodity futures, retailers with annual sales of less than $100,000, and life insurance.

Rules issued by the Cost of Living Council provided requirements that certain retailers post price information for the consuming public. Small retail stores (those with annual sales of under $100,000) were exempted. Retailers whose sales were between $100,000 and $200,000 per year were not required to post signs listing base prices but were ordered to announce that base price information was available on request. Those retailers with annual sales of $200,000 or more were directed to post base prices prominently at the place of sale on all items not specifically exempted and to make them readily accessible in the shopping area to any customer, without the necessity of obtaining the permission or assistance of an employee of the store. Records sufficient to establish the base prices for property or services offered for sale or lease were ordered to be kept by sellers and leasors who were subject to price stabilization requirements for a minimum of four years.

The Economic Stabilization Program has relied heavily on voluntary compliance and public participation in enforcement of its rules. As stated by the Price Commission, "Whenever any person has reason to believe that a violation . . . has taken place, he should contact the nearest office of the Internal Revenue Service.

Such cooperation on the part of every citizen will ensure that the price stabilization program achieves its maximum intended effect."

Violations such as failure to keep necessary records, their falsification, or instituting an unjustified price or pay increase may result in the imposition of certain penalties. The Cost of Living Council, Price Commission, and Pay Board were authorized to petition the Attorney General to bring either a criminal or civil action against an accused violator. If an intentional violation has occurred, the defendant may be fined as much as $5,000. Unintentional infractions render him subject to a civil penalty of $2,500. In addition, the Council, Board, and Commission were empowered to request the Attorney General to seek an injunction requiring violators to discontinue their wrongful acts or to return any money which was received in violation of any regulation or order. Also, private citizens victimized by an intentional transgression of price or rent regulations were authorized to recover triple damages plus attorney's fees and costs in the proper U.S. District Court, without regard to the amount in question. The award may be, in the discretion of the court, whichever of the following is greater: an amount not more than triple the overcharge, or an amount not less than $100 or more than $1,000. Damages for an unintentional overcharge are limited to its amount, and the customer or tenant must first have presented a claim for its refund and not have been repaid within ninety days, in order to qualify to sue. A customer or tenant is also permitted to seek an injunction. As of this writing, the future of wage and price controls remains uncertain. Administration spokesmen have indicated the hope that they will be ended sometime in 1973. Of course, if economic conditions so dictate, we may expect their indefinite retention or some other form of price control to combat inflation.

2 PROTECTION FROM FRAUD AND MISREPRESENTATION

In the discussion about contracts in Chapter 17, it was noted that there are several grounds which a party may use to rescind or to avoid the obligations of a contract. Among these are lack of capacity (infancy or insanity), fraud, misrepresentation, mutual mistake, and material breach of contract by the other party.

The law as it relates to fraud and misrepresentation is of especial importance in the protection of consumers. The presence of fraud gives the injured party the right to sue for dollar damages in addition to the remedy of rescission. The suit for dollar damages is a tort action known as deceit, and a successful party may collect punitive damages as well as the actual damages caused by the fraud. When the victim of fraud sues in deceit, he keeps what he received and sues for the damages sustained as a result of the fraudulent representation. If the action is for rescission, the victim simply seeks "his money back" and returns what he received.

A defrauded party who wishes to rescind must act with reasonable promptness after he learns of the fraud. Undue delay will result in a waiver of his right to rescind, thus limiting the defrauded party to an action for recovery of damages.

Fraud in the law of contracts requires that the party alleging it prove that:

1 A *misstatement* was made with the *intent* to deceive.
2 The misrepresentation was of a *material existing fact.*
3 The plaintiff was justified in *relying* on the statement.
4 The plaintiff was damaged (in the legal sense) by the false statement.

Fraud must be distinguished from innocent misrepresentation. In the latter case, there need be no intention to mislead, and the victim is limited to the remedy of rescission, not being allowed to bring the tort action of deceit. The intent to mislead is often referred to as *scienter,* "knowingly" making a false statement. *Scienter* exists where there has been a concealment of a material fact or a nondisclosure of such a fact. Moreover, a statement which is partially true is fraudulent if it was made in order to create a substantially false impression. Intention to mislead may be established by showing that a statement was made with such reckless disregard as to whether it is true or false that intention to mislead may be inferred.

A misstatement of a material *fact* is the gist of fraud. False statements of opinion or of conditions to exist in the future do not constitute fraud. A misstatement of fact is material if it has a moving influence upon the contracting party, but it need not be the sole inducing cause for entering into the contract.

A misrepresentation may be made by conduct as well as by language. Any physical act which has for its ultimate object the concealment of the true facts relating to the property involved in a contract is, in effect, a misstatement. For example, one who turns back the speedometer on a car is concealing an important fact and asserting an untruth as effectively as if he were speaking. Before a false statement of fact can be considered fraudulent, the party to whom it has been made must reasonably believe it to be true and must rely on the truth of the statement to his damage. If he investigates and the falsity is revealed, no fraud exists.

The case which follows is a typical one in which a buyer of property alleges fraud.

Walsh v. Edwards
197 A.2d 424 (Md. 1964)

Plaintiffs brought an action of deceit against the defendants who had sold them a home. During an inspection of the property and at the time of closing the contract, plaintiffs expressed concern about a creek at the rear of the property. The defendant stated, "It would come over its banks in heavy rain, but it never came near the house." Actually the creek had overflowed several times in the past, and each time water had entered the house. After the purchase the creek overflowed causing extensive damage to the house. The plaintiffs brought action to recover damages. The lower court gave judgment to the plaintiff, and the defendant appealed.

HORNEY, JUSTICE: . . . The purchaser testified that when he inquired, prior to signing the contract of purchase, as to the likelihood of the creek overflowing during a storm, the seller replied that "it would come over its banks in heavy rain, but it never came near the house." That there had been a discussion concerning the creek was corroborated by the saleswoman. But the seller testified that the purchaser had not mentioned the creek to her and denied that she had made any representation with regard to it. She contends that even if she had made the statement attributed to her by the purchaser, it was not such as to represent that the property as an entirety had never been flooded and damaged.

We think that when the statement attributed to the seller by the purchaser and other parts of the evidence produced at the trial are considered together, there was enough evidence of misrepresentation to justify submission of the case to the jury and, if believed, to warrant finding a verdict for the plaintiffs.

Ordinarily, of course, the seller of real property is not legally obliged to disclose to a prospective purchaser the objectionable or undesirable conditions or features of the property offered for sale, and mere silence or nondisclosure of material facts by the seller would not constitute actionable fraud. But where, as here, the seller, in addition to not disclosing the facts, made an active misstatement of fact, or only a partial or fragmentary statement of fact, which misled the purchaser to his injury, the legal situation of the seller was reversed and there was imposed on her a duty to disclose all that she knew as to the probability of the creek overflowing. . . . Under the circumstances in this case, the failure to disclose the facts constituted actionable fraud.

The appellant further contends that the purchasers failed to prove by admissible evidence that they had relied on the representation made by the seller, but such is not the case. During the course of the examination of Nathen Edwards, he was asked whether he relied on the representation made by the seller, and he replied that he did. When he was asked on the next question whether he would have purchased the property if the representation had not been made, the witness answered that "we would not have purchased the house."

In the instant case there was proof that the representation was false, that its falsity was known to the seller, that it was made for the purpose of deceiving the purchasers, that the purchasers relied on the misrepresentation and would not have purchased the property had the misrepresentation not been made, and that the purchasers actually suffered damage as a direct result of the fraudulent misrepresentation. That is all that was required in this case. [JUDGMENT AFFIRMED]

3 PROTECTION FROM ILLEGAL CONTRACTS

Today, the social implications of contracts are often significant in determining their legality. The law does not allow complete freedom of contract. If a contract is prohibited by statute, contravenes the common law, or is contrary to public policy, courts will declare it to be illegal. A contract contravenes public policy if it is injurious to some established interest of society, violates the policy of a statute, or tends to interfere with the public health, safety, morals, or general welfare.

Public policy is a vague concept. It is variable and subject to change as the social, political, and economic climate changes. Therefore, contracts that at one time in history were legal may become illegal. Today, more and more contractual provisions which were traditionally recognized as enforceable are being declared contrary to public policy as the law tends toward broader protection of consumers.

Typical of the situations where courts are expanding their protection for consumers are contracts entered into between parties with unequal bargaining power. In such cases, courts may step in and declare provisions to be illegal if a party who had equal bargaining power would not have agreed to them. Since equality of bargaining power is not present, neither is freedom of contract, and harsh terms to which a reasonable man would not agree are held to be illegal and unenforceable. The following case illustrates such a contract and such a result.

Hunter v. American Rentals, Inc.
371 P.2d 131 (Kans. 1962)

Everett L. Hunter, plaintiff (appellee), brought suit against American Rentals, Inc., defendant (appellant), for negligence. Plaintiff rented a trailer and hitch from defendant, which was attached to plaintiff's car by defendant's servants. While plaintiff was driving the car, the trailer hitch broke, leaving the trailer and automobile attached only by the safety chain. The trailer started to move from one side of the highway to the other, causing plaintiff's car to overturn. Plaintiff received personal injuries and damaged the automobile.

By its answer defendant sought to avoid liability, contending that the plaintiff entered into a written rental agreement which contained the following clause absolving the defendant of any liability:

The renter hereby absolves the AMERICAN RENTALS of any responsibility or obligation in the event of accident, regardless of causes or consequence, and that any costs, claims, court or attorney's fees, or liability resulting from the use of described equipment will be indemnified by the renter regardless against whom the claimant or claimants institute action. . . .

AMERICAN RENTALS makes no warranty of fitness or usage, express or implied. The undersigned received said property in its present condition and waives all claims present and future against AMERICAN RENTALS including those resulting from defects, latent or apparent.

Plaintiff contended that the above provisions were void as being contrary to public policy. The trial court held that the contract terms did not constitute a valid defense and held for the plaintiff. The defendant appealed.

WERTZ, JUSTICE: . . . Contracts for exemption for liability from negligence are not favored by the law. They are strictly construed against the party relying on them. The rule is unqualifiedly laid down by many decisions that one cannot avoid liability for negligence by contract. The rule against such contracts is frequently limited to the principle that parties cannot stipulate for the protection against liability for negligence in the performance of a legal duty or a duty of public service, or where the public interest is involved or a public duty owed, or when the duty owed is a private one where public interest requires the performance thereof. There is no doubt that the rule that forbids a person to protect himself by agreement against damages resulting from his own negligence applies where the agreement protects him against the consequences of a breach of some duty imposed by law. It is, of course, clear that a person cannot, by agreement, relieve himself from a duty which he owed to the public, independent of the agreement. An analysis of the decisions indicates that even under the view that a person may, under some circumstances, contract against the performance of such duties, he cannot do so where the interest of the public requires the performance thereof.

. . . The defendant, being engaged in the business of renting trailers to the general public, including trailer hitches and other attendant equipment necessary to connect the rented trailers to the automobiles, owed a duty, not only to the plaintiff but also to the general public, to see that the trailer hitch was properly installed and the trailer properly attached thereto in order that the same might be safely driven on the highway for the purpose and use for which it was intended; and defendant, by contract, could not relieve itself from its negligent acts of failing to make those safe connections and installations. The contract on the part of the defendant to relieve itself from such negligent liability is against the public policy of this state and void.

An agreement is against public policy if it is injurious to the interests of the public, contravenes some established interest of society, violates some public statute, or tends to interfere with the public welfare or safety.

For the reasons stated, this court is of the opinion that the contract pleaded, being in contravention of the statute and the public policy of this state, is void and unenforceable and constitutes no defense to plaintiff's cause of action. [AFFIRMED]

In many states, exculpatory clauses similar to the one set forth above are illegal if contained in leases of real estate.

In the previous chapter, attention was given both to the implied warranty that goods sold by a merchant must be of merchantable quality and to the general demise of the privity requirement. It was also noted that there had been a definite trend toward what some courts call "strict liability." As courts have tended to hold that privity of contract is not required and that a buyer can sue a manufacturer directly, many manufacturers have attempted to limit their liability by placing in the contract of sale a disclaimer of liability which attempts to either eliminate or reduce the liability of the manufacturer. In discussing the legality of such disclaimer, the court in *Henningsen v. Bloomfield Motor, Inc.*, 161 A.2d 69 (N.J. 1960), stated:

The terms of the warranty (disclaimer) are a sad commentary upon automobile manufacturers' marketing practices. Warranties developed in the law in the interest of and to protect the ordinary consumer who cannot be expected to have the knowledge or capacity or even the opportunity to make adequate inspection of mechanical instrumentalities like automobiles and to decide for himself whether they are reasonably fit for the designed purpose. . . . But the ingenuity of the Automobile Manufacturers Association by means of its standardized form has metamorphosed the warranty into a device to limit the maker's liability. . . .

Under modern conditions the ordinary layman on responding to the importuning of colorful advertising has neither the opportunity nor the capacity to inspect or to determine the fitness of an automobile for use; he must rely on the manufacturer who has control of its construction, and to some degree on the dealer who to a limited extent called for by the manufacturer's instructions, inspects and services it before delivery. In such marketing mileu his remedies and those of persons who properly claim through him should not depend upon the intricacies of the law of sales. The obligation should not be based alone on the privity of contract. It should rest . . . upon the demands of social justice. . . .

The traditional contract is the result of free bargaining of parties who are brought together by the play of the market, and who meet each other on the footing of approximate economic equality. In such a society there is no danger that freedom of contract will be a threat to the social order as a whole. But in the present day commercial life the standardized mass contract has appeared. It is used primarily by enterprises with strong bargaining power and position. "The weaker party in need of the goods or services is frequently not in position to shop around for better terms, either because the author of the standard contract has a monopoly (natural or artificial) or because all competitors use the same clauses. His contractual intention is but a subjection more or less voluntary to terms dictated by the stronger party terms whose consequences are often understood in a vague way, if at all." . . . Such standardized contracts have been described as those in which one predominant party will dictate its law to an undetermined multiple rather than to an individual. They are said to resemble a law rather than a meeting of the minds. . . . The gross inequality of bargaining position occupied by the consumer in the automobile industry is [thus] apparent. Such control and limitation of his remedies are inimical to public welfare and at the very least call for great care by the courts to avoid injustice through the application of strict common-law principles of freedom of contract.

Courts have thus been willing to declare contract terms limiting liability to be illegal where the parties do not have equal bargaining power. The law, in effect, joins the controversy on the side of the consumer and eliminates contract provisions which are unfair and which would not have been agreed to if the bargaining power had been equal.

4 PROTECTION FROM UNCONSCIONABLE BARGAINS

Historically, courts of equity have not enforced a contract if its provisions are so harsh, severe, and unfair that the party resisting performance would be unduly oppressed. An unconscionable bargain or contract has been defined as ". . . one which no man in his senses, not under delusion, would make, on the one hand, and which no fair and honest man would accept, on the other." The Uniform Commercial Code has a special provision in Article 2, "Sales," which provides:

1 *If the court as a matter of law finds the contract or any clause of the contract to have been unconscionable at the time it was made, the court may refuse to enforce the contract; or it may enforce the remainder of the contract without the unconscionable clause; or it may so limit the application of any unconscionable clause as to avoid any unconscionable result.*

2 *When it is claimed or appears to the court that the contract or any clause thereof may be unconscionable, the parties shall be afforded a reasonable opportunity to present evidence as to its commercial setting, purpose and effect to aid the court in making the determination.*

While the Code does not define the term "unconscionable," the Official Comments states:

The basic test is whether, in the light of the general commercial background and the commercial needs of the particular trade or case, the clauses involved are so one-sided as to be unconscionable under the circumstances existing at the time of the making of the contract. The principle is one of the prevention of oppression and unfair surprise . . . and not of disturbance of allocation of risks because of superior bargaining power.

The provision on unconscionability will influence transactions not covered by the Code. It is evident that the concept is in keeping with the tenor of the times— protection of consumers from overreaching sellers, as illustrated by the following case.

Williams v. Walker-Thomas Furniture Company
350 F.2d 445 (1965)

Plaintiff, Walker-Thomas Furniture Company operated a retail furniture store in the District of Columbia. During the period from 1957 to 1962 the defendant purchased a number of household items from plaintiff. Payment was to be made in installments. The terms of each purchase were contained in a printed form contract which purported to lease the item to defendant for a stipulated monthly rent payment. The title would remain in Walker-Thomas until the total of all the monthly payments made equaled the stated value of the item, at which time purchaser would receive title. In the event of a default in the payment of any monthly installment, plaintiff could repossess the item.

The contract further provided that

The amount of each periodical installment payment to be made by (purchaser) to the Company under this present lease shall be inclusive of and not in addition to the amount of each installment payment to be made by (purchaser) under such prior leases, bills or accounts; and all payments now and hereafter made by (purchaser) shall be credited pro rata on all outstanding leases, bills and accounts due the Company by (purchaser) at the time each such payment is made.

The effect of this provision was to keep a balance due on every item purchased until the balance due on all items, whenever purchased, was liquidated. As a result, the debt incurred at the time of purchase of each item was secured by the right to repossess all the items previously purchased by the same purchaser, and each new item purchased automatically became subject to a security interest arising out of the previous dealings.

On April 17, 1962, defendant bought a stereo set with a stated value of $514.95. She defaulted shortly thereafter, and plaintiff sought to replevy all the items purchased since December, 1957. At the time of this purchase her account showed a balance of $164 still owing from her prior purchases. The total of all the purchases made over the years in question came to $1,800.

WRIGHT, JUDGE: . . . . Appellant's principal contention, rejected by both the trial and the appellate courts below, is that these contracts, or at least some of them, are unconscionable and, hence, not enforceable. In its opinion . . . the District of Columbia Court of Appeals explained its rejection of this contention as follows:

Appellant's second argument presents a more serious question. The record reveals that prior to the last purchase appellant had reduced the balance in her account to $164. The last purchase, a stereo set, raised the balance due to $678. Significantly, at the time of this and the preceding purchases, appellee was aware of appellant's financial position. The reverse side of the stereo contract listed the name of appellant's social worker and her $218 monthly stipend from the government. Nevertheless, with full knowledge that appellant had to feed, clothe and support both herself and seven children on this amount, appellee sold her a $514 stereo set. We cannot condemn too strongly appellee's conduct. It raises serious questions of sharp practice and irresponsible business dealings. A review of the legislation in the District of Columbia affecting retail sales and the pertinent decisions of the highest court in this jurisdiction disclose, however, no ground upon which this court can declare the contracts in question contrary to public policy. . . .

We do not agree that the court lacked the power to refuse enforcement to contracts found to be unconscionable. In other jurisdictions, it has been held as a matter of common law that unconscionable contracts are not enforceable. While no decision of this court so holding has been found, the notion that an unconscionable bargain should not be given full enforcement is by no means novel. In *Scott v. United States* . . . the Supreme Court stated:

. . . If a contract be unreasonable and unconscionable, but not void for fraud, a court of law will give to the party who sues for its breach damages, not according to its letter, but only such as he is equitably entitled . . . .

Since we have never adopted or rejected such a rule, the question here presented is actually one of first impression.

Congress has recently enacted the Uniform Commercial Code, which specifically provides that the court may refuse to enforce a contract which it finds to be unconscionable at the time it was made. (28 D.C. Code 2-302). . . . The enactment of this section, which occurred subsequent to the contracts here in suit, does not mean that the common law of the District of Columbia was otherwise at the time of enactment, nor does it preclude the court from adopting a similar rule in the exercise of its powers to develop the common law for the District of Columbia. In fact, in view of the absence of prior authority on the point, we consider the congressional adoption of 2-302 persuasive authority for following the rationale of the cases from which the section is explicitly derived. (See Comment, 2-302, Uniform Commercial Code (1962). Compare Note, 45 Va.L.Rev. 583, 590 (1959), where it is predicted that the rule of 2-302 will be followed by analogy in cases which involve contracts not specifically covered by the section.) Accordingly; we hold that where the element of unconscionability is present at the time a contract is made, the contract should not be enforced.

Unconscionability has generally been recognized to include an absence of meaningful choice on the part of one of the parties together with contract terms which are unreasonably favorable to the other party. Whether a meaningful choice is present in a particular case can only be determined by consideration of all the circumstances surrounding the transaction. In many cases the meaningfulness of the choice is negated by a gross inequality of bargaining power. The manner in which the contract was entered is also relevant to this consideration. Did each party to the contract, considering his obvious education or lack of it, have a reasonable opportunity to understand the terms of the contract, or were the important terms hidden in a maze of fine print and minimized by deceptive sales practices? Ordinarily, one who signs an agreement without full knowledge of its terms might be held to assume the risk that he has entered a one sided bargain. But when a party of little bargaining power, and hence little real choice, signs a commercially unreasonable contract with little or no knowledge of its terms, it is hardly likely that his consent, or even an objective manifestation of his consent, was ever given to all the terms. In such a case the usual rule that the terms of the agreement are not to be questioned should be abandoned and the court should consider whether the terms of the contract are so unfair that enforcement should be withheld.

In determining reasonableness or fairness, the primary concern must be with the terms of the contract considered in light of the circumstances existing when the contract was made. The test is not simple, nor can it be mechanically applied. The terms are to be considered "in the light of the general commercial background and the commercial needs of the particular trade or case." (Comment, Uniform Commercial Code 2-307.) Corbin suggests the test as being whether the terms are "so extreme as to appear unconscionable according to the mores and business practices of the time and place. . . ." We think this formulation correctly states the test to be applied in those cases where no meaningful choice was exercised upon entering the contract.

Because the trial court and the appellate court did not feel that enforcement could be refused, no findings were made on the possible unconscionability of the contracts in these cases. Since the record is not sufficient for our deciding the issue as a matter of law, the cases must be remanded to the trial court for further proceedings. [SO ORDERED]

5   PROTECTION FROM ILLEGAL INTEREST CHARGES

The law has traditionally attempted to protect debtors by limiting the amount of interest that may be charged upon borrowed money or for the extension of the maturity of a debt. Contracts by which the lender is to receive more than the maximum legal rate of interest are said to be "usurious." Laws regulating interest rates usually provide for criminal penalties, and in addition the lender is usually denied the right to collect any interest where the interest rate provided for is usurious. However, a few states permit recovery of interest at the legal rate.

The usury laws of most states are better known for permitting exceptions to the general principles than for applying them. Debtors who need the protection of usury laws usually find that their creditors are legally entitled to charge far in excess of the stated legal maximum rate because of some statutory exception. For example, it is not usurious in most states to collect the legal maximum interest in advance or to add a service fee that is no larger than reasonably necessary to cover the incidental costs of making the loan—such as inspection, legal, and recording fees. Both of these practices have the net effect of increasing the actual rate of interest paid. It is also allowable for a seller of goods to add a finance or carrying charge on long-term credit transactions in addition to the maximum interest rate. Other statutes permit special lenders such as pawnshops, small loan companies, or credit unions to charge in excess of the otherwise legal limit.

Another means of avoiding usury is to have a different "credit" price than a "cash" price. Another is to charge extra interest for delinquent payments. The add-on interest technique and the collection of the obligation in installments have been approved as nonusurious in most states.

Interest rates have increased substantially over the past few years. The prime interest rate sometimes exceeds the maximum rate allowed by law. The net result of legislation in recent years has been to raise the maximum legal rate and to create additional exceptions to the general rules of usury. As a result, little if any protection is actually given those persons whom the usury laws were designed to protect. The person with substantial assets and a good credit rating is usually able to borrow at less than the maximum legal rate, while persons with little capital assets generally are required to pay interest and finance charges substantially in excess of the stated maximum. They are legally required to do so because there are more exceptions to the usury law than applications of it.

6 DEBTOR RELIEF: BANKRUPTCY

Bankruptcy laws provide various methods for relieving debtors of their obligations or for postponing the time of their payment. They also protect some of the rights of creditors.

Bankruptcy proceedings are conducted in the Federal courts and may be either voluntary or involuntary, the former being at the instigation of the debtor and the latter at the instigation of creditors.

Bankruptcy proceedings are designed to accomplish two general purposes. The first is to provide a method of dividing a debtor's assets equitably among his creditors. The law prevents a debtor from preferring one creditor over another and tends to minimize the losses of all creditors. A second purpose is to relieve honest debtors of the indebtedness so that they may start afresh, free of their former obligations.

Involuntary bankruptcy proceedings may be commenced by creditors only if the alleged bankrupt has committed an act of bankruptcy within four months of the filing of the petition by the creditors. Acts of bankruptcy include making a fraudulent transfer of property with the intent to hinder, delay, or defraud creditors; having a receiver appointed; and making a transfer of property which prefers one creditor over another. Acts of bankruptcy usually occur when the alleged bankrupt is insolvent, i.e., his assets are less than his liabilities.

While the major purpose of voluntary bankruptcy proceedings is to obtain the discharge of debts, it must be kept in mind that not all debts are discharged. Discharge may be denied either because of the nature of the claim or because of the conduct of the debtor. The debtor's conduct which may result in a denial of discharge may occur before the proceedings are commenced or during the proceedings. When a discharge is denied, the assets are distributed among the creditors, but the debtor remains liable for the unpaid portion of all claims. The law provides that discharge will be denied if the bankrupt has: (1) committed a "bankruptcy crime" (one that is created by the bankruptcy law itself rather than by the general criminal law) punishable by imprisonment; (2) destroyed, mutilated, falsified, concealed, or failed to keep or preserve books of account or records, from which his financial condition and business transactions might be ascertained, unless the court deems such acts or failure to have been justified under all the circumstances of the case; (3) while engaged in business as a sole proprietor, partnership, or as an executive of a corporation obtained for such business money or property or credit, or obtained an extension or renewal of credit, by making or publishing or causing to be made or published, in any manner whatsoever, a materially false statement in writing respecting his financial condition or the financial condition of such partnership or corporation; (4) at any time subsequent to the first day of the twelve months immediately preceding the filing of the petition in bankruptcy, transferred, removed, destroyed, or concealed or permitted to be removed, destroyed, or concealed, any of his property, with intent to hinder, delay, or defraud his creditors; (5) within six years prior to bankruptcy been granted a discharge; (6) in the course of a proceeding under the Act refused to obey any lawful order, or to answer any material question approved by the court; or (7) failed to explain satisfactorily any losses of assets or deficiency of assets to meet his liabilities. If any creditor can show reasonable cause for believing that the bankrupt has done any of the things mentioned, the burden is on the bankrupt to show that he has not committed an act that will bar discharge.

The third ground (above) for barring discharge is limited to businessmen. Those not in business who furnish false financial statements to obtain property or credit are nevertheless discharged. Such false statements do, however, prevent discharge of the debt which arose out of the transaction in which the fraudulent financial statement was submitted. The following case illustrates the application of the third ground for barring discharge.

Branch v. Mills & Lupton Supply Company
348 F.2d 901 (1965)

Branch had made false statements in writing for the purpose of obtaining a loan from a creditor. Thereafter he was involved in bankruptcy proceedings and a creditor objected to his receiving a discharge. The referee allowed the objection and his decision was upheld by the federal district court. Branch appealed.

PER CURIAM: The bankrupt, who was engaged in the business of building shell homes, admitted that he furnished false affidavits for the purpose of obtaining a loan. One of the creditors filed specifications of objections to his discharge.

The referee in bankruptcy sustained the objections to the discharge in a memorandum opinion containing findings of fact and conclusions of law, saying:

One of the objects of the Act is to release an honest and insolvent person from his debts. From this evidence it does not appear that this bankrupt was honest in his dealings with his creditors and the public. While he claims that it was a recognized practice of the trade and that he had made this same affidavit in many other cases, that does not cure the fact that he swore falsely to a material fact for the purpose of obtaining a loan. The giving of an oath, either written or oral, should be treated as sacred. This bankrupt's act of swearing falsely for the purpose of obtaining a loan is not indicative of such honesty as Congress intended to protect.

I find as a fact that the bankrupt swore falsely, or made a false statement in writing, to material fact for the purpose of obtaining credit or property from Family Pride Homes, Inc., in Atlanta, Georgia, and that they knew at the time these statements were made they were false. I further find that Family Pride Homes, Inc., to whom the statements were made, relied upon them in extending the credit.

We find that the pertinent facts and applicable law are correctly set forth in the opinion of the district court. [AFFIRMED]

Among provable claims that are not discharged in bankruptcy are: (1) claims for taxes due any governmental body; (2) debts created by fraud, embezzlement, misappropriation, or defalcation of a debtor acting in any fiduciary capacity; (3) alimony and child support, (4) liability resulting from willful or malicious torts; (5) wages earned within three months of filing the petition in bankruptcy; (6) liabilities for property or money obtained under false pretenses or by fraudulent representations; and (7) claims for money of an employee which had been retained by his employer to secure the faithful performance of the employment contract.

The debtor may claim property as exempt from his bankrupt estate if an exemption is provided by either the laws of the United States or the laws of the state of his domicile. State law usually exempts certain personal property not to exceed a specified value and, in addition, provides that a certain sum out of the value of the homestead shall be paid to the debtor free of the debts.

Exemptions are not allowed out of property which a bankrupt has transferred or concealed and which is recovered by the trustee for the estate. The debtor is required to prepare a list of property claimed to be exempt. Failure to claim the exemptions may result in the use of assets otherwise exempt to pay the creditors.

The Bankruptcy Act also contains provisions which are for the purpose of debtor relief rather than the liquidation of assets. The debtor relief provisions are designed to assist debtors by developing a plan to enable them to pay their debts and avoid the stigma of bankruptcy. Most plans involve an extension of time for payment, so that the pressure by creditors is alleviated. Under wage-earner plans, the debtor submits his future earnings to the supervision and control of the court for the purpose of carrying out the approved plan. If the plan is not carried out, the wage earner may be entitled to convert it to straight bankruptcy.

7 TRUTH-IN-LENDING

The Truth-in-Lending Act authorized the Federal Reserve Board to adopt regulations "to assure a meaningful disclosure of credit terms so that the consumer will be able to compare more readily the various credit terms available to him and avoid the uninformed use of credit."

The Truth-in-Lending Act covers all transactions where: (1) the lender is in the business of extending credit in connection with a loan of money, a sale of property, or the furnishing of services; (2) the debtor is a natural person as distinguished from a corporation or business entity; (3) a finance charge may be imposed; and (4) the credit is obtained primarily for personal, family, household, or agricultural purposes. It covers loans secured by real estate such as a mortgage as well as unsecured loans and loans secured by personal property.

Truth-in-Lending imposes a duty on all persons regularly extending credit to private individuals to fully inform them of the cost of the credit. It does not regulate the charges which are imposed.

The Truth-in-Lending philosophy of full disclosure is accomplished through two concepts, namely, the finance charge and the annual percentage rate (APR). The borrower uses these two concepts to ascertain the amount he must pay for credit and what the annual cost of borrowing will be in relation to the amount of credit received. Theoretically, a debtor armed with this information will be better able to bargain for credit and to choose one creditor over the other.

The finance charge is the sum of all charges payable directly or indirectly by the debtor or someone else to the creditor or to a third party as an incident to or as a condition of the extension of credit. Included in the finance charge are interest, service charges, loan fees, points, finder's fees, fees for appraisals, credit reports or investigations, and life and health insurance required as a condition of the loan. Among the costs frequently paid by debtors which are not included in the finance charge are recording fees and taxes, such as a sales tax, which are not usually included in the listed selling price. These are items of a fixed nature, the proceeds of which do not go to the creditor. Other items of cost not included are title insurance or abstract fees, notary fees, and attorney's fees for preparing deeds.

The law requires the lender to disclose the finance charge expressed as an annual percentage rate and specifies the methods for making this computation. The methods used treat each payment as being first applied to the finance charge and then to the principal. The annual percentage rate is the percentage required to yield the amount required to be paid each year expressed in terms of an annual rate. For example, if the cost per month is 1½ percent of the principal borrowed, the APR would be 18 percent per year. This is the amount charged by most creditors on open accounts.

Compliance with the APR rules will result in the disclosure of the actual cost of add-on interest or discount methods of extending credit. For example, assume that a debtor borrows $100 at 6 percent add-on interest which is repaid monthly over one year. Since the debtor would have the $100 for only one month and the amount borrowed the last month would be under $10, the APR is actually 11 percent, and this fact would have to be disclosed. Similarly, if the loan was $100 discounted at 6 percent and repayable monthly, the APR would be 11 percent, because the original loan was actually only $94.

The finance charge and annual percentage rate are made known to borrowers by use of a financing statement. This statement must be given to the borrower before credit is extended and must contain in addition to the finance charge and the annual percentage rate the following information:

1 Any default or delinquency charges that may result from a late payment.
2 Description of any property used as security.
3 The total amount to be financed, including a separation of the original debt from finance charges.

There are both civil and criminal penalties for violation of Truth-in-Lending. The civil liability provisions make creditors liable to debtors for an amount equal to twice the finance charge but not less than $100 nor more than $1,000 plus the costs and attorney's fees required to collect it. A creditor may avoid liability in the event he makes an error, providing that he notifies the debtor within fifteen days after discovering the error and providing also that he corrects the error. In this connection, the law only allows for corrections in favor of the debtor. Creditors cannot collect finance charges in excess of those actually disclosed.

The Truth-in-Lending Act also gives a debtor the right to rescind or cancel certain transactions for a period of three business days from the date of the transactions or from the date he is given the notice of his right to rescind, whichever is later. For example, a consumer may generally cancel a transaction in which he gives a security interest on his principal residence if he does so within the three-day period. If the transaction is rescinded, the borrower has no liability for any finance charge, and the security which he has given is void.

Truth-in-Lending also has helped consumers in other ways. Most notably, it has limited the liability of a holder of a lost or stolen credit card to $50 in the event of unauthorized use.

8 FAIR CREDIT REPORTING ACT

The Fair Credit Reporting Act is applicable to anyone who prepares or uses a credit report in connection with (1) the extending of credit, (2) the sale of insurance, or (3) the hiring or discharge of an employee. It covers credit reports on consumers but not those on businesses. The purpose of the law is to prevent unjust damage to an individual because of inaccurate or arbitrary information in a credit report. It is also designed to prevent the undue invasion of individual privacy in the collection and dissemination of information about a person's credit record.

The law gives an individual consumer certain rights whenever he is rejected for credit, insurance, or employment because of an adverse credit report. These rights include (1) the right to be told the name of the agency making the report, (2) the right to require the agency to inform him of the information given in the report, and (3) the right to correct the information or at least give his version of the facts in dispute.

This law does have one important limitation. It provides that a report containing information solely as to transactions or experiences between the consumer and the person making the report is not a "consumer report" covered by the Act. To illustrate this limitation, assume that a bank is asked for information about the credit experience of the bank and one of its customers. If it reports only as to its own experiences, the report is not covered by the Act. The Act is designed to cover credit reporting agencies which obtain information from several sources, compile it, and furnish it to potential creditors. If the bank in the foregoing example passed along any information it had received from an outside source, then its credit report would be subject to the provisions of the Act. Also, if the bank gave its opinion as to the credit worthiness of the customer in question, it would come under the Act. The limitation is restricted to information relative to transactions or experiences, and the information furnished must be of a factual nature if the exception in the law is to be applicable.

Many businesses can avoid the pitfalls of being a credit reporting agency, but most businesses will be subject to the "user" provisions of this law. The "user" provision requires that the consumer who is seeking credit for personal, family, or household purposes be informed if his application is denied because of an adverse credit report. He must also be informed of the source of the report and of the fact that he is entitled to make a written request within sixty days as to the nature of the information received. If he requests the information in the report, he is entitled to receive it so that he may challenge the accuracy of the negative aspects of its contents.

The Act also contains a provision on "investigative consumer reports." These are reports on a consumer's character, general reputation, mode of living, etc., obtained by personal interviews in the community in which the consumer works or lives. No one may obtain such a report unless at least three days' advance notice is given the consumer that such a report will be sought. The consumer has the right to be informed of the nature and scope of any such personal investigation. Reports which are intended to be covered by this Act are those usually conducted by insurance companies and employment agencies.

This Act contains civil and criminal penalties similar to those involved in Truth-in-Lending.

9 POSSIBLE FUTURE LEGISLATION

This has been described as the era of consumerism. There will probably be many additional laws designed to protect consumers, because of the political popularity of the issue and because business does not always meet its obligations to society. Among the laws or areas in which one might expect change or new legislation are (1) the holder-in-due-course concept, (2) the area of class action or suits by consumers, (3) the collection process, and (4) franchising.

The holder-in-due-course rule was previously discussed in Chapter 13, where it was noted that the FTC is seeking to abolish the concept as it relates to consumers. It was also discussed in Chapter 17 as a part of the law of contracts as it relates to third parties. Several states have recently enacted legislation limiting the use of the holder-in-due-course rule in consumer transactions but retaining it in commercial transactions (those between businessmen). Additional states are likely to follow suit in the next few years because it is now thought that the protection of consumers is more important than encouraging the free movement of commercial paper. It should be noted that some courts have achieved a similar result by holding that banks and lending agencies which buy the paper of consumers from retailers are not holders in due course because of their close involvement in the transaction.

Class action suits by consumers, if authorized by legislation, would permit consumers with common claims against a business to join their claims together in one collective suit. Consumers would be authorized to lump together small complaints, none of which would be worth taking to court separately. Such individual causes of action supported by class action legislation could total millions of dollars annually. For example, representative automobile purchasers could bring a class action lawsuit over alleged defects. If successful, all purchasers of the car with the defect would be able to collect damages, not just those who actually filed suit, and the cost of collection to each would be minimal.

Class action suits have been used many times to assert the rights of a large number of persons with similar interests. The usual requirements for the maintenance of class action litigation are that the persons constituting the class must be so numerous that it is not practicable to bring them all before the court and that the representatives be such that they will fairly represent all parties. A typical example of a class action suit is a shareholder's derivative action in which representative shareholders bring an action for the benefit of all shareholders and the corporation. School desegregation suits are an example of class action litigation for a social purpose.

Consumer class action suits have not been successful in Federal courts because of the jurisdictional dollar requirement of $10,000. It would be a rare case in which any one consumer's claim would meet the jurisdictional amount test. By Federal law to date, it is not possible to aggregate claims to meet the jurisdictional amount, but legislation to allow this is under consideration.

Problems inherent in individual suits by consumers have encouraged class action legislation. The right of an individual to sue in state courts has not been a realistic remedy for consumers because the cost of individual litigation usually exceeds the damages which would or could be recovered. Class action suits are one solution to this problem. Legislation authorizing consumers to collect court costs and attorney's fees in addition to damages is also under consideration in many states and in Congress.

The business community is generally opposed to class action suits for several reasons besides the possible cost of consumer recoveries. One major reason is the potential for abuse which is inherent in class action suits. A party with malice or vindictiveness as a motive has the capacity to impose substantial and irreversible damage on a business simply by filing a class action suit. The publicity of the suit could do irreparable damage even though the allegations were unfounded.

Another problem which will be given attention in several states is the conduct of collection agencies. Some states such as California already have enacted laws regulating the activities and business practices of collection agencies. Among the activities which must be controlled in the view of many are (1) contacting the debtor's employer to gain assistance in the collection of the debt, (2) informing the debtor's neighbors of the situation, (3) attempting to collect at times other than business hours, and (4) using threats and other forms of harassment. The collection process is a difficult one, and legislation which achieves the proper balance between the interests of the creditor and those of the debtor is difficult to develop and to enact.

Another area of great concern today is the business of franchising. While many retail outlets have operated very successfully under a franchise, thousands of people have lost millions of dollars in purchasing franchises which turned out to be something less than represented. Laws are being considered at both the Federal and state levels to protect franchise purchasers in much the same way that the blue-sky laws protect investors. Among the approaches which may be used in such legislation are the following:

1 All franchisors, franchise salesmen and sales agencies would be required to register with the state.
2 Franchisors would be required to register their sales presentation in much the same way as a stock prospectus is registered.
3 An administrative agency would be granted investigative, supervisory and injunctive-like power to ensure compliance.
4 Criminal and civil penalties would be provided for.
5 The state would require escrow accounts to be set up to hold franchise fees to guarantee that franchisors fulfill their agreements with franchisees. The escrow fund also would keep the franchise fee out of the franchisor's income account, preventing overstatement of his financial success.
6 Advertising would be regulated and prior approval of it by the supervising agency would be required.

The large number of bankrupt franchisees and even franchisors dictates that some regulatory legislation be enacted in the future.

The foregoing are only examples of some consumer problems which may receive the attention of legislators and the courts. Business can eliminate the need for many of these laws by following business practices that are fair to the consuming public. Government can also eliminate the need for consumer-oriented legislation by educating the buying public so that consumers, by their refusal to deal with unethical businesses, will force such businesses either to change their practices or go out of business due to financial failure. An educated and informed buying public needs less consumer protection than one that is not capable of making intelligent choices.

REVIEW QUESTIONS—CHAPTER 19

1 Define the following terms introduced in this chapter: scienter; unconscionable bargain; usury; voluntary bankruptcy; involuntary bankruptcy; wage-earner plan; annual percentage rate; class action suit.
2 Give four examples of Federal laws designed to protect consumers.
3 What remedies are available to a victim of fraud?
4 What are the elements of fraud?

5 Give an example of a contract that would be unenforceable under the Uniform Commercial Code provision on unconscionability.

6 What are the purposes or goals of the bankruptcy law?

7 List three acts of bankruptcy.

8 List five grounds for denying discharge to a bankrupt.

9 List five claims that are not discharged in bankruptcy.

10 What is the effect in the law of bankruptcy of furnishing a false financial statement when obtaining a loan?

11 Briefly discuss the methodology used by the Truth-in-Lending Act to accomplish its purposes.

12 What types of transactions are covered by the Truth-in-Lending Act?

13 What are the penalties for violating the Truth-in-Lending Act?

14 What are the purposes of the Fair Credit Reporting Act, and how does the Act seek to accomplish these purposes?

15 Discuss four possible laws which may be enacted in the near future to help consumers in their problems with the business community.

Index